Marketing
Communications Classics

D1326589

Marketing Communications Classics

an international collection of classic and
contemporary papers

Maureen FitzGerald and David Arnott

Australia • Canada • Denmark • Japan • Mexico • New Zealand • Philippines
Puerto Rico • Singapore • South Africa • Spain • United Kingdom • United States

Marketing Communications Classics

For more information, contact Business Press, Berkshire House, 168–173 High Holborn, London, WC1V 7 AA or visit us on the World Wide Web at: http://www.itbp.com.

British Library Cataloguing-in-Publication Data
A catalogue record for this book is available from the British Library

ISBN 1-86152-507-9

First edition published 2000 by Thomson Learning

Typeset by LaserScript Limited, Mitcham, Surrey
Printed in China by L Rex

To Nicky and Zoe
for patience and understanding.
P.S. Maureen says thanks for the loan
of your husband and dad.

Contents

List of Contributors

Note: The affiliations or positions of the authors in the following list, were correct at the time of original publication of the articles.

Magid M. Abraham, president of product development and marketing, Information Resources, Inc, Chicago, USA.

Joseph Alba, Holloway Professor of Entrepreneurship, University of Florida, FL, USA.

Ullrich Appelbaum, executive with McCann Erickson, New York.

David Arnott, Warwick Business School, University of Warwick, Coventry, UK.

Howard Barich, Program Manager of Market and Image Studies, IBM, White Plains, New York.

Thomas E. Barry, Edwin L. Cox School of Business, Southern Methodist University, Dallas, TX, USA.

Kapil Bawa, Assistant Professor of Marketing, New York University, USA.

Paul D. Berger, Boston University, Boston, MA, USA.

Robert C. Blattberg, the Polk Brothers Distinguished Professor in Retailing in the Marketing Department at the J.L. Kellogg Graduate School of Management at Northwestern University.

Jean J. Boddewyn, Baruch College, City University of New York, USA.

Richard Cardozo, Curtis L. Carlson chair in entrepreneurial studies and professor of marketing at the Carlson School of Management, University of Minnesota, MN, USA.

Harold Cataquet, lecturer in business studies at the University of Manchester Institute of Science and Technology (UMIST), Manchester, UK.

William A. Dempsey, Assistant Professor of Marketing at Temple University, Philadelphia, PA, USA.

Caroline Desai, ESRC teaching fellow and a PhD candidate, Strathclyde, Scotland, UK.

Sally Dibb, marketing and strategic management lecturer at Warwick Business School, University of Warwick, Coventry, UK.

Robert J. Donovan, associate professor of management at the University of Western Australia and president of Donovan Research.

Mike Duffy, Director of Modeling, Planning and Forecasting, Kraft General Foods, Inc.

Thomas R. Duncan, director of the integrated marketing communications program at the University of Colorado, Boulder, CA, USA.

Stephen E. Everett, assistant professor in the School of Journalism and Mass Communication at the University of Colorado, Boulder, CA, USA.

Maureen FitzGerald, Canterbury Business School, University of Kent, Canterbury, UK.

Keith Fletcher, professor of business administration at the Strathclyde Graduate Business School, Scotland, UK.

Gordon R. Foxall, University of Birmingham, Birmingham, UK.

Richard Gatarski, School of Business, Stockholm University, Sweden.

Gordon E. Greenley, professor at Aston Business School, Aston University, Birmingham, UK.

Stephen Hague, account planner at a UK advertising agency.

Chris Halliburton, Professor of Marketing and Dean of Research and Development, EAP, European School of Management, Paris–Oxford–Berlin–Madrid.

Donna L. Hoffman, Associate Professor, Owen Graduate School of Management, Vanderbilt University.

Daniel J. Howard, Edwin L. Cox School of Business, Southern Methodist University, Dallas, TX, USA.

Don Hutson, co-author of the management training book *Insights into Excellence*.

Thomas N. Ingram, Professor of Marketing at the Fogelman College of Business and Economics, Memphis State University, TN, USA.

Lynn J. Jaffe, School of Management, Boston University, Boston, MA, USA.

Chris Janiszewski, Associate Professor of Marketing, University of Florida, FL, USA.

John Philip Jones, chairman of the advertising department at the Newhouse School of Public Communications, Syracuse University.

Brian K. Jorgensen, University of California, Los Angeles, CA, USA.

Alexa Kierzkowski, consultant in McKinsey's New York office.

Philip J. Kitchen, senior lecturer in marketing and Director, Research Centre for Corporate and Marketing Communications, Department of Marketing, Strathclyde University, Glasgow, Scotland, UK.

Philip Kotler, the S.C. Johnson Distinguished Professor of International Marketing at the Kellogg Graduate School of Management, Northwestern University.

Robert J. Lavidge, President of Elrick and Lavidge, Inc., Chicago, IL, USA, and member of the faculty of the Northwestern University Evening Division.

Monica Leardi, Baruch College, City University of New York, USA.

Leonard M. Lodish, the Samuel R. Harrell Professor of Marketing at the Wharton School.

Anders Lundkvist, School of Business, Stockholm University, Sweden.

Richard Lutz, Professor of Marketing, University of Florida, FL, USA.

John Lynch, Hanes Corporation Foundation Professor of Business Administration, Duke University.

Roger Marshall, University of Auckland, New Zealand.

Shayne McQuade, consultant in McKinsey's New York office.

Tony Meenaghan, Department of Marketing, University College Dublin, Eire.

T.C. Melewar, Lecturer in Marketing and Strategic Management, Warwick Business School, University of Warwick, Coventry, UK.

Paul C.N. Michell, professor of advertising and marketing at Manchester Business School, Manchester, UK.

Woon Bong Na, University of Auckland, New Zealand.

Thoman P. Novak, Associate Professor, Owen Graduate School of Management, Vanderbilt University.

Ken Peattie, Lecturer in Strategic Management, Cardiff Business School, Cardiff, Wales, UK.

Sue Peattie, Senior Lecturer in Statistics, University of Glamorgan Business School, Wales, UK.

Larry Percy, senior vice president: director of strategic research at Lintas USA.

Linda Peters, Cardiff Business School, Cardiff, Wales, UK.

Lisa A. Petrison, doctoral student in marketing at the J.L. Kellogg Graduate School of Management at Northwestern University.

Richard E. Plank, Instructor in Marketing at Montclair State College, Upper Montclair, NJ, USA.

Thomas L. Powers, Associate Professor of Marketing, The University of Alabama at Birmingham, Birmingham, AL, USA.

John R. Rossiter, professor of management at the Australian Graduate School of Management.

John Saunders, Head of School, Aston Business School, Aston University, Birmingham, UK.

Alan Sawyer, professor of Marketing, University of Florida, FL, USA.

Don E. Schultz, professor of Integrated Marketing Communications (IMC) at the Medill School of Journalism, Northwestern University.

Charles H. Schwepker, Jr, doctoral candidate in marketing at the Fogelman College of Business and Economics, Memphis State University, TN, USA.

Shannon Shipp, doctoral candidate at the Carlson School of Management, University of Minnesota, MN, USA.

Robert W. Shoemaker, Associate Professor of Marketing, New York University, USA.

Lyndon Simkin, marketing and strategic management lecturer at Warwick Business School, University of Warwick, Coventry, UK.

Gary A. Steiner PhD, Associate Professor of Psychology in the Graduate School of Business, the University of Chicago, IL, USA.

Randy Stone, Senior Vice President, Media Marketing Assessment, Inc.

Adam Vancini works in the marketing media.

Richard Vaughn, senior president and researcher of Foote, Cone and Belding, Los Angeles, CA, USA.

Robert Waitman, consultant in McKinsey's New York office.

Paul Wang, assistant professor in Direct Marketing at the Medill School of Journalism, Northwestern University.

Barton Weitz, JCPenney Eminent Scholar of Marketing, University of Florida, FL, USA.

Colin Wheeler, University of Strathclyde, Scotland, UK.

Stacy Wood, doctoral candidate in Marketing, University of Florida, FL, USA.

Arch G. Woodside, the Malcolm S. Woldenberg Professor of Marketing at the A.B. Freeman School of Business, Tulane University, New Orleans, LA, USA.

George Wright, professor of business administration at Strathclyde, Scotland UK.

Julia Wright, management consultant.

Michael Zeisser, consultant in McKinsey's New York office.

Acknowledgements

The authors would like to acknowledge a sincere debt of gratitude to both Professor Terence Shimp and Professor Philip Kitchen for their encouragement, support and suggestions for inclusions during the compilation of this book, and to Professor Shimp for kindly agreeing to writing the Foreword.

Foreword

Marketing Communications is an incredibly variegated, challenging, exciting, and dynamic subject matter. The field constantly changes. New practices and new theoretical accounts surface continuously. Enthusiasm for marketing communications and its most recent incarnation – integrated marketing communications, or IMC – is palpable among practitioners and academics alike. IMC is widely accepted as a key mechanism by which brand equity is built and maintained. Indeed, it has been claimed that communications is marketing and marketing is communications; the two are inseparable.[1]

It is against this backdrop that Maureen FitzGerald and David Arnott have edited their anthology, *Marketing Communications Classics*. The prospective reader of this volume might ask: 'Why should I invest in this volume?' Why indeed should someone purchase an anthology (or 'reading book' in American vernacular) and this one in particular? In my mind, a meritorious anthology on the subject of marketing communications would minimally satisfy the following desiderata:

- It would provide balanced coverage of all aspects of marketing communications – advertising, promotions, marketing-oriented public relations, event and sponsorship marketing, and so on – rather than being dominated by any single subject such as advertising.
- It would include a collection of the best conceptual and empirical work around the world.
- It would emphasize more recent contributions to the literature but not exclude older work that remains unsurpassed in its insight and clarity of expression.
- It would be organized in a thematically meaningful manner rather than 'thrown together,' as some anthologies are, in a haphazard manner.
- And, finally, it would represent insight into marketing communications from both sides of the marketing 'coin,' the marketer's perspective and the consumer's vantage point. An ideal volume would, in other words, capture the entirety of the subject matter.

How well does the FitzGerald and Arnott volume fare against these stringent demands? In my opinion, it performs admirably. The collection consists of a large number of articles, 38 in total. Eighty percent of these are articles published in the 1990s, with the remaining 20 percent published mostly in the 1980s. The collection is dominated by more recent articles, as it should be, but a sprinkling of classic contributions round out the volume. In terms of 'country of origin,' approximately three-fourths of the papers were published in U.S. journals, but international journals are well represented and some of the articles published in U.S. journals were by non-American scholars. The articles also represent a good mixture of theoretical/conceptual, empirical, and even practical papers. It is a nicely integrated, eclectic mix. Although the perspective is predominantly managerially oriented, several of the articles explore the underlying psychology that determines how consumers process marketing communications and extract meaning from advertisements and other forms of messages.

In addition to having compiled an excellent collection of papers, Maureen FitzGerald and David Arnott introduce each of the eight major sections with pithy remarks that explain how the papers in each section fit together. These comments are insightful and of special value to newcomers to the subject matter who require more direction than does the seasoned scholar or practitioner. I expect that this collection will serve the needs of both practitioners of marketing communications as well as their counterparts in academe. I am enthusiastic about this anthology and applaud the authors for their considerable efforts in compiling, synthesizing, and introducing the wide assortment of articles that fall within the broad purview of integrated marketing communications.

Terence A. Shimp
University of South Carolina
Columbia, SC 29208
February 1999

NOTE

1 Don E. Schultz, Stanley, I. Tannenbaum, and Robert F. Lauterborn, *Integrated Marketing Communications* (Lincolnwood, IL: NTC Publishing Group, 1993), 46.

Introduction

There can be few topics in the realm of marketing that have created such a plethora of material, articles, books or interest (from academics, practitioners and consumers) as the area more traditionally referred to in marketing texts as 'promotion' but more accurately labelled marketing communications. For many companies, even in today's more enlightened business environment, the communication function is erroneously the sole reason for having a marketing department. From the one-man-band or the corner store, to the largest international corporation or government department, there can be little doubt of the importance of communicating the existence and benefits of products and services to potential and actual customers – be it through word of mouth, public relations, publicity, sponsorship, exhibitions, sales promotions, advertising, direct mail, electronic media, motivated employees or a direct sales force (to name a few). From the consumers' perspective it is a bombardment of information (and not just product information) from multifarious sources and they find it impossible to escape this bombardment. From the communication practitioners' perspective, the main task is how to break through the clutter and make their communications more effective.

Despite the clearly central role of marketing communications in the minds of business managers the world over, the short list of tools in the above paragraph highlights one of the problems in dealing with the subject matter – the range of techniques at the communicator's disposal. In the past, for both the practitioner and the academic, these tools have tended to be viewed as independent with companies using individual, specialist agencies to deal with their PR, their advertising, their direct mail campaigns, etc., and academics focusing on one or two elements of the potential mix (and the majority – as evidenced by the titling of marketing communications textbooks of the past – focusing on 'advertising'). The result has been the development of individual periodicals, journals and texts to deal with each aspect of the communications mix. Invariably this creates both benefits and drawbacks. One benefit is the sheer volume of material about almost any aspect of communicating to customers and potential customers (and 'to', rather than the more useful and accurate 'with', has been the most operative word in the past). But it is that volume that creates the drawback. For the researcher, the student or the practitioner, finding the location of any particular article of interest, and especially articles that might be considered seminal, is a nightmare. It is hoped that collecting 38 of these works together in a single volume offers each of these parties access to key works, both classic and contemporary.

A great deal of thought and effort has gone into the selection of works included. As with any area of social science, readers may differ on whether a particular article deserves inclusion within the collection but the editors were seeking a balance between three powerful forces. First, the readings had to recognize the work of researchers and authors the world over and so the collection includes work from publications of American, Australasian and European origin. Given its consumer-oriented society, it is natural for most articles in the field to have been selected from researchers and practitioners based in the USA. But human communication is often reported as having a cultural dimension (e.g. in the use of humour in advertising) and so research from other parts of the world have been included. Secondly, it had to address the natural, historical bias towards 'advertising' for, while still forming the keystone of many communications campaigns, it is by no means the only or necessarily the most important element of the mix. Some forms of communication (e.g. publicity and PR) have only come under serious scrutiny within the past couple of decades and some, such as electronic media and direct mail, have only emerged or grown with the evolution of technology in the past few years. If we superimpose the drive towards the 'integrated' management of the marketing communications mix (as evidenced in the titles of many texts in the field and the subject of the first section of this collection), the need for balanced coverage of a wide range of tools and techniques is self-evident. Thirdly, the needs of the user were considered. The need for such a collection was recognized while researching in the field and while trying to develop a suitable reading list for a marketing communications course. The scope and number of journals and periodicals in the field means that few (if any) repositories and libraries offered access to the spectrum of material presented here. Even finding a suitable text proved difficult for while there are a number of excellent texts in print, most were dominated by advertising. One key concern of students (especially MBA students) was the need for access to the 'classic' articles in the field but also a need for currency, coverage and practicality. The editors think that they have managed to balance all these concerns within the scope of material presented.

The work includes many seminal articles (where time has allowed such works to emerge) but also includes works of more recent origin (and possibly the seminal works of the future, e.g. in Electronic Media). It also includes a few of the more conceptual and empirical works from researchers in the field but balances them with occasional commentary or articles from practitioners. It is the editors' sincerest wish that you not only enjoy reading this selection but that you also find it of use, whether a student, a researcher, or a practitioner in the field of marketing communications.

Each section has its own introduction and we will leave covering the content of each to the appropriate section. Suffice it to say that works included cover a spectrum of key issues in the areas of Integrated Marketing Communications, Advertising (from both a creative and channel management perspective), Direct Marketing, Electronic Media, Public Relations and Publicity, Sales Promotion, and Personal Selling.

One final point before leaving you to browse the collection. In such a vast field of research it is impossible to include everything the editors would have liked and so they apologize to any authors and researchers who feel that their seminal article has been excluded, and to teachers and students who feel their favourite article has been overlooked. Like any dynamic field of study some of these articles may change in future editions (especially the more contemporary ones) and feedback and suggestions for future editions of this work are most eagerly sought and welcome. Suggestions should be sent to Maureen FitzGerald at Canterbury Business School, University of Kent, Canterbury, Kent, CT2 7PE, UK.

Maureen FitzGerald and David C. Arnott, Editors.
September 1999

Section 1
Towards Integrated Marketing Communications

One of the more recent developments in the marketing communications field is the rise of the Integrated Marketing Communications concept. This may be defined as the planned combination of various communication tools and techniques to produce clear, consistent and high impact marketing messages.[1] The purpose of this first section is to explore the idea of IMC and its value to the organization. Given each element has resourcing implications, it also looks at some of the conflicts between various elements of the communications mix. As a recent area of research, there has been little time for the various papers to attain true 'classic' status but we present a few articles that have been or are likely to become influential in the field.

The first paper (Duncan and Everett, 1993) reviews and investigates the concept of integrated marketing communications from the marketing manager's perspective. It does not attempt to prescribe how it could (or should) be done but looks at the role and acceptance of the concept by marketing managers. They investigated the extent to which companies adopted the idea in the late 1980s/early 1990s. The surprise was that despite its general intuitive appeal, an extremely high level of belief that various tools should be used in unison, and a general acceptance of the IMC concept in the marketing industry, only about one-third of companies had heard of, or attempted to implement, IMC. The second paper (Schultz and Kitchen, 1997) continues the IMC theme from an advertising agency viewpoint. While it has a US bias, it is a logical place for the study given the state of development of the concept. As well as looking at the development and adoption of the IMC concept, the key added value of this paper lies in its exploration of the role and future of the traditional agency in the IMC marketplace.

FitzGerald and Arnott (1996) investigated 'integration' from a consumers' point of view by exploring how various promotional messages were perceived by airline consumers. Looking at a range of communication tools (advertising, service packaging, sales promotions, etc.) the one clear result was the different ways in which simple things like gender, age and income, as well as more complex variables such as flying experience, affected perceptions of the same message and so reinforces the need to evaluate the joint impact of communication tools, rather than treat them in isolation.

The fourth paper (Barich and Kotler, 1991) proposes a framework for managing and integrating the various communications elements of the corporate image. Conceptual rather than empirical in nature, it does offer an interesting view of how the various elements might be combined to present a clear consistent image (one key goal of IMC). This is followed by a very recent paper from Melewar and Saunders (1998), in which they look at one specific aspect of corporate image – corporate identity – and explore its use and benefits in one of the key contextual variables of modern marketing, globalization. As one of the very few papers in this field, this is very likely to become a future classic given the role a consistent corporate identity plays in the IMC context.

Taken as a whole this section illustrates the development and value of the Integrated Marketing Communication concept. The papers in it, although, like the subject, quite recent in origin, offer a balanced perspective of issues relating to coordination of the more traditional elements of the communications mix.

NOTE

1 Adapted from: Schultz, D.E. (1993) Integrated Marketing Communications: Maybe definition is in the point of view, *Marketing News*, 18 January.

Client perceptions of integrated marketing communications

1.1

Thomas R. Duncan and Stephen E. Everett

'New advertising', 'orchestration', 'whole egg', 'seamless communication', 'integrated marketing communications' – a number of terms are being used in the industry to talk about a new concept in marketing communications – the integration of specialized communications functions that previously have operated with various degrees of autonomy.

These functions include some that historically have been more closely related, such as advertising and sales promotion, than others such as advertising and public relations, which often have existed at arms length. At the same time, a growth in direct-response marketing has meant direct-response communications (i.e., direct mail advertising, telemarketing) are now being used by advertisers to a much greater extent than ever before. Packaging is also becoming recognized as an important marketing communications function. It's the last ad a consumer sees before buying a product, not to mention all those brand impressions it makes as consumers walk through store aisles.

This article will review the evolving concept of integrated marketing communications (IMC) and then report on the findings of a study undertaken to determine attitudes toward, and usage of, IMC by client organizations.

The pressure to integrate marketing communications is a result of numerous factors. Key among these are communications agency mergers and acquisitions, increasing sophistication of clients and retailers, increasing cost of traditional advertising media, increasing global competition, increasing pressure on organizations' bottom lines, decreasing effectiveness of traditional media, the decreasing cost of database usage, and other trends such as zapping, media fragmentation, and loss of message credibility (Dilenschneider, 1991). According to Tortorici (1991), IMC is one of the easiest ways an organization can maximize its return on investment.

One example of how a particular communications function has been brought into the marketing communications mix is the use of marketing public relations. This public relations tool – publicity – is being used more and more to increase message credibility and save media costs (Nakra, 1991). Duncan (1986) found in a national study of client marketing and communications managers that 95 percent thought marketing public relations (MPR) and advertising should work together; however, only 32 percent said they thought this was happening. The study also found that 69 percent thought the use of MPR would increase within the next five years. According to Tom Harris, former president of Golin-Harris Communications and author of the first book on MPR, it has now become, by far, the fastest growth area in public relations firms, generating 70 percent of their total revenue (Harris, 1991).

Some people feel IMC is not a new issue in that smaller communications agencies have been doing coordinated planning for their clients for years. Furthermore, on the client side, small marketing departments also have had a quasi-integrated approach by the mere fact that everyone in the department knew what was going on because all of them were involved with all major communications programs. Major textbooks with 'marketing communications' emphasis have also been around several years, starting with Michael Ray's *Advertising & Communication Management*, which was published in 1982.

Although marketing communications has been used for several years as an umbrella term to refer to the various communications functions used by marketing, the *strategic integration* of these functional areas is what makes IMC a new approach to reaching consumers and other stakeholders. The theory of an IMC program is that it has one basic communications strategy for each major target audience. This one strategy is then used as the basis for executing each communications function (advertising, PR, sales promotion, etc.) throughout a variety of communication channels.

DEFINITIONS

Integrated marketing communications has a variety of definitions. One-stop shopping, for example, suggests an offering of a variety of marketing communications functions with little emphasis on 'integration' of the functions or on the end result of the communication. The 'new advertising' phrase seems to be more self-serving for ad agencies (in their attempt to reposition themselves as offering something broader than just advertising expertise). According to Keith Reinhard (1990), CEO of DDB Needham Worldwide and former chairman of the American Association of Advertising Agencies, 'The new advertising must encompass all the voices directed towards consumers in a brand's behalf'. 'Orchestration', the title of Ogilvy and Mather's original push for IMC, and, 'seamless communication' seem to be more accurate labels of Reinhard's definition as these terms focus more on the process and results of integrated communications.

The definition of IMC used by the American Association of Advertising Agencies is a 'concept of marketing communications planning that recognizes the added value of a comprehensive plan that evaluates the strategic roles of a variety of communications disciplines, e.g., general advertising, direct response, sales promotion and public relations – and combines these disciplines to provide clarity, consistency and maximum communications impact'.

When a sample of executives from major U.S. corporations were given the AAAA definition of IMC and asked if their companies were integrated, 67 percent said 'yes'. Of these, nearly half said they had been integrated for more than three years, and a little over a third said they had become integrated within the last three years (Caywood, Schultz, and Wang, 1991).

Arriving at a definition is difficult, however, because IMC is both a concept and a process and the degree of integration within each dimension can greatly vary. An organization that has an IMC philosophy may or may not physically integrate into one department the people responsible for the various marketing communications functions, although the trend is to do so (Eisenhart, 1989). At General Motors, which received a lot of publicity four years ago when it combined a portion of its PR with marketing at the corporate level, a two-tiered organizational structure was set up to direct IMC. A Communication Council, made up of 41 communicators and directors from throughout the corporation, meets once a month and prioritizes IMC tasks. Once a task is agreed upon, the process for its execution is to appoint a Stakeholder Communication Team composed of a 'champion', a 'lead coordinator', and appropriate GM departmental representatives (Prescott, 1991).

Six years ago at Nestlé a position was created to coordinate advertising, packaging, and all the other marketing communications services used by the company. Nestlé is now putting pressure on its communications agencies to be 'totally integrated centralized communications consultants' (Wentz, 1988). In other words, Nestlé's corporate IMC philosophy is impacting how its global marketing communications programs are being executed. According to Stanley Tannenbaum (a member of Northwestern University's IMC faculty), 'It (IMC) also has to mean integrating communications with the mind of the consumer, and that puts the focus back on basic selling' (Hume, 1991).

An organization that subscribes to the IMC philosophy and also uses it as a process is IBM. Tom Reilly, head of marketing services and communications at IBM, says his company has adopted IMC at all levels to help ensure that the IBM 'brand' is properly maintained in the course of introducing, each year, more than 1,000 new products ranging from floppy disks to mainframe computers (Reilly, 1991).

The basic concept of IMC is synergism, meaning the individual efforts are mutually reinforcing with the resulting effect being greater than if each functional area had selected its own targets, chosen its own message strategy, and set its own media schedule and timing (Novelli, 1989–1990). Sometimes functional autonomy can even be counterproductive. For example, when a brand is new or has a major new improvement that has legitimate news value (and therefore can make good use of the marketing public relations function), PR releases must be sent out before the advertising begins or else the news value will be lost and the PR stories will be rejected by the editorial gatekeepers. In such situations, coordinated timing is essential.

Responsibility issues

Although there have been a lot of positive things written and said about IMC, getting the functional areas strategically focused and organized to work together has been difficult. Although most of the major advertising agencies have acquired agencies in the other communications areas, there are still very few clients that have been convinced to place all their communications business under one agency's communications umbrella. Some public relations people even consider the use of publicity, when directed by marketing people to be 'imperialism' (Lauzen, 1991). Another reason many communications agency mergers and acquisitions have not worked as well as anticipated is because everyone (in each of the 'family' agencies) wants to retain his or her authority, budget, and turf. Referring to the need for cooperation, Al Rosenshine, CEO of WPP, said, 'Until you overcome the ego and turf issues, you will never have truly integrated marketing communications' (*Advertising Age*, 1991).

Coordinating a corporation's marketing communications strategy and policy internally suggests that someone or some department must be in charge. Most communications professionals are specialists trained in their functional areas which may not be broad enough for the specialist to relate to, or direct, all of the other communications areas. If, however, a person from sales or legal takes charge, then there may be someone directing the IMC program who isn't trained in any area of communications.

Because IMC is evolving so fast and either causing, or resulting from, many changes in the marketing communications industry, the study of IMC responsibilities and attitudes was done. The body of literature on IMC is thin and what is available mostly deals with superficial case histories and anecdotes.

RESEARCH QUESTIONS

The overall purpose of this study was to investigate the organization and perceptions of integrated marketing communications among a cross section of client organizations in order to better understand what is driving the attention that IMC is receiving in both industry and the academy.

Because so little research has been conducted in this area, there was little material available to support the framing of hypotheses. Therefore, this study was designed to address several research questions:

1. To what extent are responsibilities for the major marketing communications functions (advertising, product publicity, packaging, sales promotion, and direct marketing) consolidated externally and internally? Is there more multiple-communication-function responsibility internally at the strategic or administrative level?
2. To what extent are clients aware of the term 'integrated marketing communications'? What does this mean to them from an organizational and responsibility standpoint.
3. When IMC is defined as 'the strategic coordination of all messages and media used by an organization to influence its perceived brand value', how valuable is/could IMC be to an organization?
4. What are the important elements of IMC?
5. What are potential barriers to using IMC?
6. How is a firm's level of sales related to the use and perception of IMC?

METHODOLOGY

A sample of 500 persons was selected from *Advertising Age*'s subscriber sublist identified as communications or marketing managers who worked for a 'client' as opposed to a communications agency or educational institution. A questionnaire was developed and pretested among a small sample of Colorado client marketing and communications managers. An initial mailing and one follow-up mailing generated 216 usable questionnaires, for a response rate of 43 percent.

If one makes the common assumption of randomly distributed response bias in this survey, the findings are generalizable to the population of marketing and communications managers in client firms that subscribe to *Advertising Age*.

The measurement of perceptions and attitudes about IMC posed some problems because IMC is not a concisely defined concept or a process that is practiced uniformly. It was realized, therefore, that if respondents were directly asked questions like 'Does your company use integrated marketing communications'? the findings would have little validity since each person would be responding from his or her own definition of IMC. To address these difficulties, the first battery of questions in the survey elicited a functional definition of IMC. This was done by asking respondents to indicate to what extent responsibilities for five major communications functions (advertising, product publicity, packaging, sales promotion, and direct response) were assigned to the same external communications agency and which were assigned to the same internal job position.

Respondents were then asked if they were familiar with the term 'integrated marketing communications'. Next, respondents were given four alternative relationships between a client and its communications agencies and asked which came the closest to describing the relationship that would exist with IMC:

1. The client and its agencies collectively set strategies, then each communications function is executed by a different agency of the firm.
2. The client and 'one-stop shopping' agency collectively set strategies, then the agency administers executions of all, or most, of the communications functions.
3. The client alone determines strategies and assigns individual functions to individual agencies, but all these communications suppliers stay in touch with each other.
4. The client alone determines overall strategies, then each communications function is executed by a different agency of the firm.

Finally respondents were given a definition of IMC as 'the strategic coordination of all messages and media used by an organization to influence its perceived brand value' and asked more direct questions, some using Likert scales, to appraise respondents' reactions to this operational definition.

To determine to what extent respondents' companies combined marketing communications responsibilities *internally*, respondents were asked about marketing communications responsibility on two levels, (a) objective and strategy setting and (b) administering day-to-day communications operations. Respondents were given a list of five functions (advertising, product publicity, packaging, sales promotion, and direct marketing) and were asked to indicate who had primary *internal* responsibility for each function. The choices were: brand/product manager (B/P manager); VP marketing; marketing communications (MC) manager; director of advertising (AD manager); or 'other'. A summed indicator was then created for each of these positions, based upon the number of functions for which each position was reported responsible. As an example, if a respondent reported that the VP marketing was primarily responsible for three functions, while the B/P manager handled two, the 'VP marketing' variable would take the value of 3 while the 'B/P manager' variable would be 2. These variables were then used as an implied measure of integration.

RESULTS

Degree of integration differs by agency and position

Looking first at coordination of functions by *external* communications agencies, it was found that advertising agencies, as shown in Table 1, are significantly more likely to be assigned multiple communications functions than are the other four types of

Table 1 Number of marketing communications functions for which external firms used are responsible

Position*	Number of functions					
	5	4	3	2	1	Total (%)
Advertising agency (177)	5.1	9.0	16.4	22.0	47.5	100
Sales promotion firm (94)	0	1.1	9.6	21.3	68.1	100
Direct response firm (60)	0	0	6.7	25.0	68.3	100
PR firm (85)	0	1.2	7.1	14.1	77.7	100
Packaging firm (95)	0	0	0	3.2	96.8	100

*Respondents reporting *no* assignment of MC functions to a given class of external firms are omitted from this analysis. For example, the percentages for 'advertising agency' refer to the 177 respondents who reported using external ad agencies for one or more MC functions.

communications agencies listed. More than 50 percent of the advertising agencies were responsible for two functions, and 30 percent were responsible for three or more. As would be expected, packaging firms were the least likely to have multiple function responsibility. Less than 25 percent of respondents reported that their public relations agencies were responsible for more than one function.

Internally it was found that the B/P manager position was operationally the most integrated, having the most multiple responsibilities at both the objective/strategy and the day-to-day administrative levels. Table 2 shows the number of objective/strategy functions held by each management position and the proportion of respondents reporting that number. (The zero column is the percent of respondent organizations in which positions did not have any responsibility for any of the five communications functions listed.)

More than 20 percent of the respondents indicated that the B/P manager, followed closely by the VP marketing position was responsible for three or more communications areas when it comes to setting communications objectives and strategies. No other positions came close. It's also interesting to note that the MC manager, unlike the position the title implies, clearly was *not* a highly integrated position at the objective/strategy level, with barely more than 16 percent reporting that position responsible for more than one function.

By adding the percentages indicated in Table 2 for managing three, four, and five functions, it can be determined that 70 percent of the respondents said three or more of the five communications functions were assigned to one of the five positions, indicating

Table 2 Percent within each position who set objectives and strategies for various numbers of communications functions (*N* = 216)

Position	Number of functions						
	5 (%)	4 (%)	3 (%)	2 (%)	1 (%)	0 (%)	Total (%)
Brand/product manager	7.9	7.4	8.8	8.3	19.0	48.6	100
VP/director of marketing	9.3	2.8	9.3	10.2	18.1	50.5	100
Marketing communications manager	0.0	4.2	4.2	7.9	27.3	56.5	100
Director of advertising	1.9	3.7	6.9	2.3	9.7	75.5	100
Other	1.9	0.5	1.9	4.6	10.6	80.6	100

a higher level of integration internally than externally. (Table 1 shows that 55 percent of the communications agencies used had responsibility for three or more functions.)

In terms of day-to-day administrative functions for which each position listed is responsible, as might be expected, the VP marketing position has little responsibility at this level (see Table 3). However, the B/P manager has nearly the same level of multiple communications responsibilities at this level (29 percent had three or more functions) as was reported for the objective/strategy level (25 percent). Although the MC manager was shown as having one or more day-to-day communications responsibilities by 54 percent of the respondents, compared to 32 percent for AD directors, the AD directors had nearly as many *multiple* function responsibilities (about 17 percent) as did the marketing communications manager (about 20 percent).

When these positions were reported to be responsible for at least one of the marketing communications functions listed, in every case but one, on both the objective/strategic and administrative levels, the modal response was that the position was responsible for only a single function. The exception is the B/P manager who, at the day-to-day level, is equally likely to hold responsibility for all five functions as she or he is for just one.

Taken together, these data suggest that the integration of marketing communications functions at this time is slightly more developed at the administrative level than at the objective/strategy level. However, they also indicate that the practitioners of IMC, as reflected in the present pattern of integration of responsibilities, comprise a minority of firms.

Low awareness of IMC term

Of the 216 responses, 59 percent reported being familiar with the term 'integrated marketing communications'. With a margin of error of 6.7 percent, this proportion suggests that more than half the population of client managers is familiar with the IMC term.

Clients want agencies involved in IMC

Although respondents familiar with IMC hold a wide range of views regarding the best client/agency relationship concerning how IMC functions, the majority indicated one or more outside agencies should be involved. The largest proportion (34.6 percent) believed IMC means the client *and* its agencies collectively set strategies,

Table 3 Percent within each position who administer various numbers of communications functions on a day-to-day basis ($N = 216$)

Position	Number of functions						
	5 (%)	*4 (%)*	*3 (%)*	*2 (%)*	*1 (%)*	*0 (%)*	*Total (%)*
Brand/product manager	15.3	7.9	5.6	7.9	15.3	48.1	100
VP/director of marketing	1.4	0.9	0.9	2.8	10.2	83.8	100
Marketing communications manager	0.0	8.3	11.6	6.5	27.8	45.8	100
Director of advertising	4.6	4.6	7.9	5.1	10.2	67.6	100
Other	2.8	2.3	4.2	5.6	16.2	69.0	100

then each communications function is executed by a different agency or firm. A somewhat similar relationship was endorsed by 21.3 percent of the respondents who reported IMC means the client *and one agency* collectively set strategies, then a 'one-stop shopping' agency administers executions for all, or most, of the communications functions. Less than a fourth (23.5 percent) believed that IMC means the client *alone* determines strategies and assigns individual functions to individual agencies/firms, but all these communications suppliers *stay in touch with each other*. Finally, only 7.4 percent believed IMC means the client *alone* determines overall strategies, then each communications function is executed by a different agency or firm. The remaining 13 percent of respondents provided a broad range of their own definitions of IMC.

When asked who should take the initiative to make IMC successful – an outside agency, client, or both simultaneously –56 percent said 'both simultaneously' and 42 percent said the client alone.

IMC perceived as valuable concept

After respondents were given the definition of IMC ('the strategic coordination of all messages and media used by an organization to influence its perceived brand value'), they were asked to indicate how valuable they thought this concept is/could be to their organization. The 5-point bipolar scale had 'very valuable' (1) and 'not at all valuable' (5) as anchors. The mean rating of 1.76 was decidedly on the 'valuable' side of the continuum. There's little doubt that these marketing and communications managers see IMC, as defined in this study, as being beneficial.

To determine how respondents perceived the effects of using IMC, they were asked to respond to a list of Likert items shown in Table 4. Of the items listed, 'reduces media waste' and 'gives a company a competitive edge' were the two with which respondents agreed most. A majority of respondents also agreed that their organizations would make more use of IMC within the next five years.

Respondents were virtually neutral (mean = 2.99) on whether or not an agency's IMC orientation would make their firm more likely to hire that agency. This was somewhat of an inconsistency compared to how valuable respondents perceived IMC to be.

The lowest rated item – 'IMC has influenced our hiring criteria' – was possibly low because most companies have either not yet made a commitment to using IMC or are still searching to determine the most effective way to organize and operate using this concept.

Table 4 Likert measures of perceived value of IMC* (*N*= 216)

Item	Mean
IMC reduces media waste.	1.98
Using IMC gives a company a competitive edge.	2.08
IMC will be used more in my organization within the next five years.	2.33
We are more inclined to hire communications agencies/firms who understand IMC.	2.99
The 'new advertising' is a good name for IMC.	3.64
The IMC concept has influenced our hiring criteria.	3.83

*Ratings are on 5-point scale with 'strongly agree' and 'strongly disagree' as anchors with values 1 and 5, respectively.

Egos and turf battles impede IMC

The most serious perceived barrier to integration was internal turf battles, as shown in Table 5 (mean = 2.02). Next in order was an external barrier, 'agency egos' (mean = 2.17). It is interesting that both of these are psychological or political attitudes. Internal and external budget reductions also comprise a set of barriers, though respondents saw them as less of a threat than the turf and ego problems.

Sales not a major integration variable

The last research question dealt with the relationship between an organization's size and the degree to which it has assigned multiple communications responsibilities. This question was analyzed through a series of univariate analyses of variance (ANOVAs). The dependent variables were those constructed for the original measure of integration, as shown in Tables 2 and 3. In the ANOVAs, however, mean differences in degree of multiple responsibility, i.e., integration, were tested for two independent variables, annual sales and annual spending.

The first variable, the firms' annual sales, was operationalized as a three-level ordinal variable: low – 'less than $25 million annual sales'; medium – '$26 million to $500 million annual sales'; and high – 'over $500 million annual sales'. These categories comprised 13.0 percent, 41.4 percent, and 45.7 percent of the sample, respectively. (Note: Respondents who reported no functions for a given management position were assigned a 'missing value' for that position, for the purpose of the ANOVA.)

In testing the relation between annual sales level of the firm and the degree of combined *strategic* MC functions (see Table 6) it was found that the degree of integration decreases for MC managers as annual sales levels increase, although this effect is marginal. Directors of advertising in medium-sized firms were the only other group for which a difference was found, with the data showing they are responsible for significantly more functions than their counterparts in larger and smaller firms.

Looking at the relation between sales and the *administration* of marketing communications responsibilities (see Table 7), the MC manager shows a marginally

Table 5 Likert measures of perceived barriers to integrating marketing communications functions* (N = 216)

Item	Mean	Standard error
Internally		
Turf battles	2.02	.073
Fear of department budget reductions	2.58	.077
Fear of losing expertise in each communications area	2.94	.080
Externally		
Agency egos	2.17	.073
Fear of budget reductions	2.41	.073
Lack of knowledge about more than one communications area	2.44	.079
Loss of motivation	2.92	.071

*Ratings are on 5-point scale with 'strongly agree' and 'strongly disagree' as anchors with values 1 and 5, respectively.

Table 6 Relation between degree of strategic integration for various managerial positions and firms' annual sales level

| Dependent variable | F | p > F | Mean functions by annual sales level | | | Category size |
			High	Medium	Low	
Brand/product manager	1.59	.2092	2.78	2.29	2.22	110
VP/director of marketing	0.99	.3746	2.25	2.49	2.83	103
Marketing communications manager	2.67	.0746	1.42	1.83	2.00	92
Director of advertising	3.98	.0252	2.00	2.95	1.95	51
Other	0.92	.4077	1.25	1.67	2.05	39

Table 7 Relation between degree of administrative integration for various managerial positions and firms' annual sales level

| Dependent variable | F | p > F | Mean functions by annual sales level | | | Category size |
			High	Medium	Low	
Brand/product manager	0.74	.4799	3.23	2.85	2.82	107
VP/director of marketing	2.81	.0753	1.31	1.79	2.63	35
Marketing communications manager	2.41	.0950	1.76	2.10	2.39	112
Director of advertising	8.21	.0007	1.97	3.34	2.71	67
Other	2.25	.1145	2.20	2.05	1.00	63

significant effect of sales level, in the same inverse manner as that found for handling *strategic* marketing communications functions. Also, as noted above, the director of advertising position in medium-sized firms shows responsibility for more functions than does the same position in larger and smaller organizations, although small firms differ by a much greater extent from their large counterparts in terms of mean administrative functions for this position. One additional effect emerged from this analysis. The VP marketing position shows a marginally significant trend toward being responsible for a reduced number of communications functions as sales levels increase, similar to that for MC managers.

CONCLUSIONS AND IMPLICATIONS

The findings indicate that IMC is perceived as a valuable concept and that a substantial number of clients are assigning, both internally and externally, multiple responsibility for communications functions to a single agency and a single position. With this recognition of IMC's value and the organization in place to do the necessary coordinating and focusing, it seems the use of IMC will continue to spread.

Although IMC seems to be established within the marketing industry, how fast its use spreads will depend on how fast the barriers of turf battles and egos can be resolved. It would seem that these barriers could be reduced through training (or retraining) and the realization of those involved that there is going to be some rebalancing of communications budgets. It would seem that those individuals and agencies who are best prepared to work within an IMC atmosphere are the most likely to survive and prosper.

The overall mean score for 'more likely to hire agencies with an IMC understanding' was neutral; however, it should not be overlooked that 40 percent of the respondents either agreed or strongly agreed with this statement. This would seem to indicate there is a sizable group of clients who are, or will be, looking for this attribute in their agencies. Also, the finding that the majority of respondents (59 percent top two boxes) indicated their organizations will make more use of IMC within the next five years would underscore that agencies that have an understanding of IMC will have a competitive edge in attracting clients.

Based on the amount of discussion in the trade press about integrated marketing communications over the last three years, it was surprising that less than two-thirds (59 percent) were familiar with the term. It is possible that IMC has been discussed under so many different labels that many of those who said they were *not* familiar with the IMC term knew it by one of its other labels, such as 'new advertising' or 'orchestration'.

The finding that the VP marketing and B/P manager positions were the most integrated at the strategy level (based on the number of communications functions for which each position was responsible) compared to the MC manager would seem to indicate that the MC manager position is a lower level one. This may reflect the fact that in a number of companies the MC manager is the title given to the person who is primarily responsible for marketing publicity.

Although the MC managers are responsible for fewer communications functions in the larger companies, the findings show that this position exists in nearly the same number of companies as does the B/P manager position, indicating that a substantial number of companies are either moving away from functional assignments and/or are making more use of publicity, e.g., integrating that function of public relations that deals with media tours, press releases, and event sponsorships into the total marketing communications mix.

One of the biggest industry questions regarding IMC concerns whether an outside agency or the client should be responsible for directing the IMC program. The finding that 57 percent indicated that an outside agency should share the responsibility with the client is considerably different from what was found by Caywood *et al.* (1991). More than three-fourths of the respondents in that study said the client alone should direct IMC activities. This difference might be an artifact of Caywood *et al.* studying primarily large corporations (mean sales of $9.6 billion).

The finding that slightly over half of the advertising agencies have responsibility for more than one communications function, compared to only a third of the direct-response and sales promotion agencies, suggests that advertising agencies have a distinct advantage over the other communications agencies in taking the leadership of IMC.

The finding that advertising, sales promotion, and direct-response agencies had more multiple communications assignments than did packaging and PR agencies suggests that clients are more likely to assign multiple communication functions to the more marketing-oriented agencies. This is particularly interesting in light of the idea held by some people, mostly from the PR arena, that a PR person is conceptually the most logical one to manage integrated marketing communications activities for companies (Dilenschneider, 1991).

Intuitively, multiple communications assignments to a single agency or company position seem to be an indication of integration; however, this issue may be more complex. Just as responsibility for multiple functions might reflect integration, the lack of multiple responsibility of assignments does not necessarily mean that an organization's communications do not have a single focus, i.e., are integrated.

Future studies of IMC should focus on actual planning and executional activities in order to obtain a more complete reading of the degree of integration that is actually taking place, both internally and externally. This will require developing a set of 'integration' measurements and more specific operational questions in order to measure the extent of communications integration. Also, more work needs to be done on identifying and defining the various dimensions of integration. It is also possible for an organization to back into IMC through economic pressures resulting in staff consolidations and budget reductions. To what extent this is happening would be worth examining, especially during recessionary periods.

Another issue that was not addressed in our questionnaire but is central to the use of IMC is: To what extent can, and should, communications programs be integrated? The industry is still suffering from a lack of empirical data which proves that using IMC is more efficient and effective in achieving marketing communications objectives.

REFERENCES

Advertising Age. 'Most of the Vision Died in Issues of Ego, Turf'. *Advertising Age*, September 30, 1991.
Caywood Clarke, Don Schultz and Paul Wang. 'Integrated Marketing Communications: A Survey of National Consumer Goods Advertisers'. Northwestern University report, June 1991.
——, and Raymond Ewing. 'Integrated Marketing Communications: A New Master's Degree Concept'. *Public Relations Journal* 17, 3 (1991): 237–44.
Dilenschneider, Robert L. 'Marketing Communications in the Post-Advertising Era'. *Public Relations Journal* 17, 3 (1991): 228.
Duncan, Thomas R. 'A Study of How Manufacturers and Service Organizations Perceive and Use Marketing Public Relations'. Ball State University, unpublished report, 1986.
Eisenhart, Tom. 'Playing Together: Marketing and Communications Catch the Team Spirit'. *Business Marketing*, July 1989.
Harris Tom. *The Marketer's Guide to Public Relations*. New York: John Wiley & Sons, 1991.
Hume, Scott. 'Campus Adopts "New Advertising"'. *Advertising Age*, September 23, 1991.
Lauzen, Martha M. 'Imperialism and Encroachment in Public Relations', *Public Relations Review* 17, 3 (1991): 245–56.
Nakra, Prema. 'The Changing Role of Public Relations in Marketing Communications'. *Public Relations Quarterly* 36, 1 (1991): 42–45.
Novelli, William D. 'One-Stop Shopping: Some Thoughts on Integrated Marketing Communications'. *Public Relations Quarterly* 34, 4 (1989–90): 7–9.
Prescott, Dan. 'Public Relations at General Motors: An Integrated Marketing Communications Approach'. Master's thesis, University of Colorado School of Journalism and Mass Communication, 1991.
Ray, Michael L. *Advertising & Communication Management*. Englewood Cliffs, NJ: Prentice-Hall, 1982.
Reilly, James. 'The Role of Integrated Marketing Communications in Brand Management'. *The Advertiser*, Fall 1991.
Reinhard, Keith. Speech to the Advertising Federation of Australia, Sydney, Australia, April 5, 1990.
Rothschild, Michael L. *Marketing Communications*. Lexington, MA: D. C. Heath, 1986.
Schultz, Donald. 'New Directions for 1992'. *Marketing & Media Decisions*, September 1989.
Tortorici, Anthony J. 'Maximizing Marketing Communications Through Horizontal and Vertical Orchestration'. *Public Relations Quarterly* 36, 1 (1991): 20–22.
Wentz, Laurel. 'Reinard Orchestrates Nestlé Ad Instrument'. *Advertising Age*, May 23, 1988.

Duncan, T. R. and Everrett, S. E. (1993) 'Client perceptions of integrated communications'. *Journal of Advertising Research*, May/June: 30–39. Reproduced with permission.

Integrated marketing communications in U.S. advertising agencies: an exploratory study

Don E. Schultz and Philip J. Kitchen

This paper is one of a series relating to a continuing, now becoming worldwide, investigation of the emergent concept and field of Integrated Marketing Communications (IMC). The original research in this field began in 1991 by faculty at the Medill School of Journalism, Northwestern University, in the United States (Caywood *et al.*, 1991). This paper extends knowledge on how the concept of IMC is diffusing by providing an initial analysis of data on how senior advertising agency executives perceive IMC use and development in the United States. It provides a perspective on the current state of IMC and levels of implementation and usage in an important segment of the marketing communications landscape. Additional studies will follow with advertising agencies in India, Australia, New Zealand, and Norway. A similar study has already been conducted in the United Kingdom. Results of that study are not included here.

The paper represents an interactive effort among three groups: the IMC faculty, Medill School of Journalism, Northwestern University, Evanston, Illinois, U.S.; the Research Centre for Corporate and Marketing Communications, Strathclyde University, Glasgow, Scotland, U.K.; and the American Association of Advertising Agencies (AAAA), New York, NY, U.S. The second group was responsible for adapting and extending the original research study conducted by Northwestern University in 1991 (Caywood *et al.*, 1991). The study was furthered by the support of the 4A's which provided not only a membership list of active agencies for questionnaire distribution but a cover letter of support as well. The research explored three related objectives:

1. To deepen understanding of how and in what areas the IMC concept is developing in the United States.
2. To examine the extent to which a group of major U.S. advertising agency executives are developing, practicing, or utilizing IMC on behalf of their clients.
3. To understand the importance and value of traditional advertising agencies in a marketplace where IMC is apparently becoming more important.

The research is predicated on the dynamic that there may well be wide variation and differing views concerning what IMC conceptually represents and how it might be practiced. Thus, the implementation of an integrated approach by advertising agencies for their clients may well differ not only in thought but in practice. Thus the paper is not necessarily concerned with either a consensual or conclusive mission. Its overall aim is to explore the multiple dimensions of the IMC concept, thus helping underpin future research.

LITERATURE REVIEW

Prior to the study conducted by Caywood *et al.* (1991) there appears to be little or no formal discussion or even description of what is now called Integrated Marketing Communications. While doubtless there had been practitioner discussions and trade press articles, the Northwestern study, funded by the 4A's and the Association of National Advertisers (ANA) appears to be the first formal, well-defined attempt to bring some understanding of the concept to the literature. Thus, most of the history of IMC thinking and discussion is generally less than seven years old. While there has been considerable debate and discussion of the subject, i.e., who does it, how it is done, etc., the formal presentation of research, theory development, and other materials by either practitioners or academics has been slow in coming.

Given its history, much of the IMC literature and learning has focused on the explanation of IMC in the marketplace, i.e., what it is, how it operates in the communications arena, etc., rather than on theory building or understanding of the basic principles. These points must be kept in mind, for while the literature is sparse at this point, it is apparently growing rather rapidly.

Schultz (1991) formalized the IMC discussion in the United States by arguing that nothing [in the United States] had received as much publicity and discussion at learned meetings, while seeing little real activity, as had the concept of IMC in 1990. At that time most manufacturers and marketing organizations in the United States were still trying to sort out the need for and value of IMC. What is evident now, some six years later, is that the concept is still undergoing development.

A special issue of the *Journal of Marketing Communications* (1996) devoted to IMC found virtually all the papers dealt with theory building and/or identification of key issues – in other words IMC still appeared to be in a pre-paradigm as opposed to a post-paradigm state. This is as expected for integration is not the norm in Western cultures despite papers to the contrary (Kotler, 1972, 1986, 1997; Kitchen and Proctor, 1991; Kitchen, 1993, 1994, 1996; Kitchen and Moss, 1995; Duncan, 1993, 1995; Duncan and Everett, 1993, Novelli, 1989–1990; Waterschoot and van Bulte, 1992). However, most mainstream marketing texts and more specialized books on marketing communications have practically *all* adopted some type of integrated communication approach or perspective (Kotler, 1997, Zikmund and D'Amico, 1996; Shimp, 1993; Belch and Belch, 1995; Krugman *et al.*, 1994), a sure sign that IMC is progressing into acceptability and is becoming entrenched as perceived 'academic wisdom' in general marketing.

While various authors and researchers have developed some type of IMC approach or concept for their teaching and research, each appears to have done so independent of the others, or at least each has developed the concept from his or her own view. There does not, at this time, appear to be any consistent or mutually agreed upon definition, description, or process to identify what is IMC and what it is not. Thus, while the subject is generally accepted in the marketing literature, at this point there are still many grey areas which are in need of clarification.

Against this groundswell of academic opinion, ably supported by case study material (mainly U.S. in origin), discordant voices can be heard asking 'what's new'? (Hutton, 1995; Wolter, 1993; Griffin, 1997); or 'what does IMC actually mean'? (Phelps *et al.*, 1994; Nowak and Phelps, 1994). The real issue expressed by many academics and practitioners (Kitchen, 1996) is that IMC may be no more than another management 'fad', no different from Total Quality Management (TQM) or reengineering or Efficient Customer Response (ECR). Indeed, these experts argue that IMC is simply another term used, perhaps to embrace many already well-known notions, or a minority concern voiced by those anxious to differentiate themselves in some way from the mainstream, perhaps 'much ado about nothing'.

It could be argued that these latter arguments are missing the point. Insofar as marketing communications is concerned, most activities in the past have focused on breaking down concepts and activities into ever more finite specializations. Few marketing or communications approaches have involved integration or holistic thinking. It appears that much marketing thought is driven by the basics of segments and segmentation. So, despite the development of integrative or systems thinking, particularly in the area of marketing and marketing communications, this may not be reflected in companies practicing communications or in advertising agencies servicing their needs. Indeed, generally, the decomposition of existing systems and processes underpins the nature of social science investigation, that is, to separate, reduce, or individualize activities and events, the assumption apparently being that if the parts of the subject can be understood, the whole can be understood as well. So, the concept of integration, while conceptually sound, may be met with skepticism, challenge, even rejection by both academicians and practitioners alike. Certainly specialists, say in advertising or direct marketing or sales promotion, may not want to see the whole, only their part of it.

Recent studies have tended to show that while IMC is welcomed, accepted, and attempted elsewhere, its prevalence may not be as strong as in the United States (Rose, 1996). Its practice is still indeterminate in global communication strategies (Grein and Gould, 1996) despite the overarching integration of advertising and only advertising in global promotional campaigns (Keegan, 1995). Further, evidence (Duncan and Caywood, 1996) tends to support the view that IMC is contingent on the extensive use of behavioral (preferably individualized) databases (Jackson and Wang, 1994; Junu, 1993) which underpin the process of active organizational learning in order to develop increasingly sophisticated integrated marketing communication techniques and activities.

Since databases are often considered to be so critical to the development and practice of IMC, it is worth considering how these are evolving on a global scale. To alleviate the concerns that a behavioral database is required for the practice of integrated marketing communications, an emerging concept of what a database is and what data is or may be needed to practice IMC in a less research-developed economy should be considered. Increasingly, the concept of a database is taken to include all the information which an organization can gather on both customers and consumers (Schultz, 1996). While there is often a critical lack of consumer or end-user data in channel-delivered systems, business-to-business and service organizations have considerable internal data. This allows them to develop the required behavioral databases. Indeed, even within fast-moving consumer goods organizations, there is substantial customer (channel) data which could provide the basis for the development of a consumer (end-user) database. Unfortunately, it is the lack of connection or cooperation between marketing, sales, and research which prevents the use of this systemwide data. So, it may be that the lack of actual data is more a function of the lack of internal ability to gather existing data than it is one of lack of actual marketplace information (Schultz, 1996).

From this scenario two arguments arise: The first, in favor of integration, centers on rapidly diffusing information technologies which are impacting the marketplace, consumers, media, and distribution of products and services (Shocker *et al.*, 1994). This argument has been particularly well advanced by Rayport and Sviokla (1994) whose approach to retailing as 'marketspace' rather than 'marketplace' leads to a wide variety of supporting arguments for new forms of electronic communication which impact not only existing systems but evolve into new forms such as the World Wide Web and the nebulous Internet (Kitchen and Wheeler, 1997). These arguments, though led by U.S. academics and practitioners, are finding some correspondence in the literature, albeit embryonic and emergent, drawn from the international market. The second argument against IMC challenges the approaches as being nothing more than traditional marketing and advertising dressed up in new clothes and given a new title. Such an argument suggests that integration is nothing new, that it revolves around an academic argument, and has few real managerial implications (Sloan, 1994; Griffin, 1997). The latter would appear to be an argument that would find some correspondence in many practitioner groups. Therefore the time is ripe for an exploratory academic study, tackling not companies, but advertising agencies in the United States. Results of this initial study follow.

METHODOLOGY

The study was based upon the 'construct explication' approach. IMC was defined, both conceptually and operationally, and 'real world' measurements were then developed through a series of scaled questions. The conceptual definition of IMC used in this research was:

> IMC is a concept of marketing communications planning that recognizes the added value of a comprehensive plan that evaluates the strategic roles of a variety of communications disciplines (for example, general advertising, direct response, sales promotion, and public relations) ... and combines these disciplines to provide clarity, consistency, and maximum communications impact (Schultz, 1993).

Operational exploration focused on areas related to this definition. The original research instrument was developed to quantify perceived conceptual and operational aspects of IMC and was adapted from the original Northwestern University study (Caywood *et al.*, 1991). Thus, some comparisons of the U.S. adoption and development in 1990 and the diffusion of the concept in 1997 are possible.

The research instrument was an 89-item, self-administered questionnaire (estimated completion time – 30 minutes). Questions were organized into three major topic areas, each related to the three objectives: (1) reaction to the definition; (2) personal and organizational demographics; (3) agreement or otherwise with contingent statements using a 10-point Likert scale (1 – strongly disagree to 10 – strongly agree). The remainder of the questions were categorical, descriptive, or open-ended. The questionnaire, originally developed by the faculty at Northwestern University, was adapted and extended. It was then pretested by submission to experts at the 4A's and via screening by 10 industry practitioners.

Questionnaires were sent to a selected list of members of the 4A's in the United States which was provided by that organization. Each questionnaire was accompanied by a cover letter from the researchers along with a letter of support from the CEO of the 4A's encouraging participation. A postage-paid envelope was enclosed. Respondents could request a summary of the research findings. The questionnaire was sent via first-class mail to 4A members in fall 1996. A follow-up mailing was made in early 1997. By the cut-off date 126 usable responses had been received, a response rate of 28 percent. Thus perceptions of IMC as given relate purely to a judgment sample of advertising agency executives who were members of the 4A's.

RESEARCH FINDINGS

Who responded

Responses were received from agency executives with titles ranging from president, CEO/chairman to chief integration officer, director of integrated marketing, account supervisor, research director, and even creative director. Respondents have spent an average of 13.4 years with their current firm. Of the respondents, the majority (65) possessed a bachelor's degree, 36 possessed a graduate degree, and 22 possessed a post-graduate degree. Only 3 of the total of 126 respondents had an educational level lower than a bachelor's degree.

Executives from agencies of all sizes responded to the survey. The mean annual gross billings were $161.98 million (range from $18 thousand to $6 billion). Gross billings were used to stratify the size of agency to enhance the analysis for specific questions. Agencies were arbitrarily divided into three categories: small (billings less than $50 million), medium (billings from $50 to $100 million), and large (billings greater than $100 million). Table 1 shows the number of responses from agencies in the three groups. As can be seen, responses were skewed toward smaller agencies, i.e., $50 million or less in billings.

Amount of time devoted to client IMC programs

Table 2 indicates the amount of time agency executives estimated they devoted to IMC programs on behalf of client firms. Most agencies are spending a substantial portion of their time assisting clients with Integrated Marketing Communications

Table 1 Respondent by billings

Agency billing (last reported annual figure)	Number of agencies	% of total respondents
Small	69	54.76
Medium	24	19.04
Large	28	22.22
Missing Data	5	3.96
Total	**126**	**100.00**

Table 2 Amount of time devoted to IMC programs for client firms

Amount of time (%)	Percentage distribution for all agencies
10% or less	9.68
10 to 24%	15.32
25 to 49%	25.00
50 to 74%	25.00
75% or more	25.00

programs. Table 2 shows that 75 percent of all agencies responding devote at least 25 percent of their client time to IMC programs. And, a full 25 percent report spending 75 percent + of their client time on IMC programs.

To develop further understanding of how much time is being devoted to client IMC programs, the data from the table above was cross-tabulated with agency-size information. The results are shown in Table 3. One hazard of separating the agencies by size is that the number of respondents in each cell becomes quite small. But, to fully understand the size of agency involved in IMC programs, this was necessary.

It is interesting to note that almost 60 percent of small agencies devote over 50 percent of their time to IMC programs for clients. Only 46 percent of medium and 36 percent of large agencies responding devote over 50 percent to client IMC programs. Also of interest is the high percentage of medium-size agencies reporting over 75 percent of their time devoted to IMC and a much lower percentage for large agencies at about 17 percent. Almost 40 percent of large agencies reported spending less than 25 percent of their time developing client IMC programs while small and medium were both about half that. This data appears to confirm the industry perception that small agencies spend more time devoted to client IMC programs than do large or larger agencies.

Table 3 Amount of time devoted to IMC by agency size

Agency size	Amount of time devoted	Total number	% of that agency size
Small	under 10%	8	11.59
	10% to 24%	5	7.25
	25% to 49%	15	21.74
	50% to 74%	24	34.78
	over 75%	17	24.64
Total of Small		**69**	**100.00**
Medium	under 10%	1	4.17
	10% to 24%	4	16.67
	25% to 49%	8	33.33
	50% to 74%	2	8.33
	over 75%	9	37.50
Total of Medium		**24**	**100.00**
Large	under 10%	4	14.29
	10% to 24%	7	25.00
	25% to 49%	7	25.00
	50% to 74%	5	17.86
	over 75%	5	17.86
Total of Large		**28**	**100.00**

IMC impact on budgets

Agency executives believe client budgets will be positively affected by Integrated Marketing Communications activities. Two-thirds of respondent agencies feel that Integrated Marketing Communications will have a positive effect on client budgets. There has often been concern that the adoption or use of IMC approaches will result in lower or decreased client spending. Such is not the case based on the response from agencies in the survey. Table 4 shows the responses for agencies who work with clients who practice IMC and those who do not.

The discussion of budgets and budgeting now leads to where and how client moneys are being spent. Table 5 shows the client budget breakdown for 1996.

Advertising, for clients who in the opinion of U.S. advertising agencies are not considered integrated, accounts for almost 60 percent of client communication budgets. The Standard Deviation column is a measure of the dispersion around the mean. Thus, the budget allocation for Advertising could have been as high as 77 percent or as low as 41 percent depending on the respondent. In comparison, Direct Marketing could be as low as 3 percent or as high as 21 percent, a substantially lower variability around the mean.

How agencies are compensated for IMC

IMC has also raised questions about agency compensation. Table 6 shows a summary of agency compensation methods.

Of the 126 total agencies who responded to the question regarding mode of compensation 82 had some part of their compensation received as a 'fee'. The traditional mode of compensation based on commissions is very low compared to the other forms, with the 'mix of commission and fee' being the second highest.

When asked to respond to the statement, 'Clients will compensate agencies for additional responsibilities of developing integrated programs', there was a mean response score of 5.82, meaning only a few more agency executives agree with the statement than those who do not. Thus, it does not appear agencies believe they will be paid more for developing IMC programs.

Table 4 Client budget changes in 1996

Client budget will:	No. for all clients	% of total agencies	No. for the integrated clients	% of total agencies
Increase	92	73.0	84	66.6
Remain the same	25	19.8	32	25.4
Decrease	4	3.1	5	4.0

Table 5 Nonintegrated clients' budget allocations for 1996

Function	Mean	Standard deviation	Count
Advertising	59	18	81
Sales Promotion	18	13	75
Marketing–PR	9	8	70
Direct Marketing	12	9	73

Table 6 Compensation system

Mode of compensation	Number of agencies
Full commission	47
Reduced commission	32
Fee	82
Project basis	51
Mix of commission and fee	77

WHAT IS IMC?

A definition for IMC was proposed. It was:

> IMC is a concept of marketing communications planning that recognizes the added value of a comprehensive plan that evaluates the strategic roles of a variety of communications disciplines (for example, general advertising, direct response, sales promotion, and public relations) ... and combines these disciplines to provide clarity, consistency, and maximum communications impact (Schultz, 1993).

Respondents were asked if this particular definition captures the meaning of IMC. Table 7 shows the response to that question and includes respondent comments about the definition.

The scale for the question went from (1) Strongly Disagree to (10) Strongly Agree. The mean response value of 6.31 shows there is some agreement but no real conviction. From the comments, it appears that, while conceptually most respondents agreed with the definition, they seemed to be looking for an additional input about the measurability and execution: needing ways to operationalize the concept. Some comments implied that the strength of IMC lay in focusing on specific target markets and in its execution, not just planning.

Are there barriers to IMC implementation?

Agency executives were asked about barriers involved in effectively implementing IMC for clients. Their responses are summarized in Table 8. It is apparent that agencies are quite confident IMC can be implemented in client organizations. It is

Table 7 Reactions of IMC definition

Statement	Mean	Standard deviation
Definition captures IMC meaning	6.31	2.26

Comments:
Integration is about letting an idea drive how and when media is used.
The starting point is consumer and the product message.
Need to add an element of measurement/quantification analysis.
It is more than planning – it is results oriented.
It is influencing the client's decision process from awareness to point-of-sale.
It starts with an integrated strategy which all disciplines can work against.
Add that it starts with the consumer's needs.

Table 8 Perceived barriers to IMC programs

Abbreviated statement	Mean	Standard deviation
IMC programs at one agency help bring client SBUs together.	7.04	2.19
Requires client staff to be more generalist.	6.31	2.26
Integrated agencies do not have talent in all marcom areas.	5.99	2.61
IMC means client staff have to develop new skills.	5.68	2.42
IMC gives a few individuals too much control.	5.54	2.46
Clients decide the 'what' and 'how' of IMC programs.	5.17	2.37
Client staff lack expertise to undertake IMC programs.	5.17	2.32
Client centralization difficulties.	4.78	2.35
Client organizational structures constrain IMC development.	4.73	2.62
Goes against client's corporate culture.	4.15	2.21
Over-dependence on single suppliers.	4.12	2.42
IMC implies additional staff to manage programs.	3.69	2.02
IMC programs modification difficulties.	3.27	2.09
Provides advertising agencies too much control.	3.23	1.84
Increased cost.	2.89	1.81

also apparent that agencies feel they are qualified to work across SBUs at a client company and believed they could do a better job if one agency handled more of the client business.

Of interest in the agency responses is the strong disagreement that IMC programs will increase costs or that extra staff will be required to manage an IMC program. Thus, even with the perhaps increased efforts needed to integrate, agency executives apparently believe cost is not an IMC problem.

CONTINGENT ISSUES

We now explore some more specific areas of agency views of IMC. The first of these relates to internal beliefs and considerations about IMC. Major aspects are summarized in Table 9.

The strong agreement that IMC would 'increase impact', make 'creative ideas more effective ...', and provide 'greater communication consistency' all support the agency view that IMC could and would improve client returns from their marketing communication investments. However, it is not clear whether agency executives feel clients will achieve a greater control over their budget or responsibilities. Agency executives also do not agree they can provide faster solutions, or more effective measurement if they apply IMC, perhaps indicating that while agencies recognize the potential value of IMC, they are not certain about its time and cost efficiencies.

Table 10 shows how agency executives perceive their client organizations and their drive toward integration. Respondents believe the drive for Integrated Marketing Communications is coming mostly from marketing personnel (mean 7.44), then advertising (mean 7.02), followed by other corporate functions (mean 6.63), and less likely from sales (mean 5.57). One of the challenges to further adoption of IMC will be the degree to which various groups across organizations grasp the concepts and implement the process of IMC.

Table 9 Internal beliefs and considerations about IMC

Abbreviated statement	Mean	Standard deviation
Increased impact	9.41	1.43
Creative ideas more effective when IMC used	9.41	1.43
Greater communications consistency	9.31	1.16
Increases impact of marcom programs	9.24	1.11
Increases importance of one brand personality, one voice	8.53	1.76
Enables greater client control over marketing communication	8.47	1.42
Helps eliminate miscommunications that can occur when several agencies are used	8.26	2.05
Greater client control over their communication budget	7.89	3.63
Provides client with greater professional expertise	7.49	2.19
IMC necessitates fewer meetings	7.01	2.51
Enables client consolidation of responsibilities	6.94	2.12
Agency can provide faster solutions	6.91	2.39
Provides method for effect measurements	6.87	2.43
Reduces cost of marcom programs	6.82	2.41

Table 10 Drive for IMC

The drive for IMC comes from:	Mean
Marketing personnel	7.44
Advertising personnel	7.02
Other corporate functions	6.63
Sales group	5.57
Other	3.33

Can one agency do IMC?

Respondents to the survey did not agree that clients will work with a variety of unaffiliated agencies. Respondents do agree, however, that agencies will have to offer a broader spectrum of services in an IMC environment. Table 11 shows how respondents agreed or disagreed with various statements.

Agency executives do not strongly expect clients to work with large numbers of unaffiliated agencies to provide marketing communication solutions. The broader range of services may be related to a 'one stop' shopping mentality for all marketing

Table 11 Perceived interaction among different communication agencies

Abbreviated statement	Mean	Standard deviation
Agency will offer a broader range of services	9.09	1.48
Clients expect closer interaction between advertising agencies	7.42	2.73
Client firms' reliance on external marcom personnel	7.25	2.01
Clients expect closer interaction between PR and ad agency	6.55	2.76
Clients expect closer interaction between direct marketing and ad agency	6.51	2.98
Clients expect closer interaction between sales promotion and ad agency	6.21	3.28
Clients to work with variety of unaffiliated agencies	5.54	2.63

communications tactical needs. but it also may be more than that. Clients may be expecting more involvement in strategic development, customer information gathering, or a whole spectrum of services along the value chain.

Agency executives also seem to guardedly agree that clients will continue to utilize external marcom people and facilities. They don't agree with any certainty that advertising agencies will work more closely with public relations, direct marketing, or sales promotion agencies. This leaves the responsibility for integration, in the opinion of the agency, squarely on the shoulders of the marketer and not the agency.

IMC AND MEASUREMENT

Clients and agencies developing and executing IMC programs do not perceive IMC as avoiding the issue of measurement. Table 12 shows responses to questions specifically dealing with the issue of measuring the effects, value, or return on marketing spending.

There is, however, no strong agreement on whether the measurements currently used can be effective in measuring IMC programs. How to measure IMC programs seems to be an issue that most executives are not able to clearly answer, though it is a criteria which is very important to them. Some of the suggestions for measurement were:

- Each element needs to be measured individually.
- The total program should be evaluated against its objectives and goals.
- The objectives should be measurable.
- Results should be measured.

From the responses to these questions it is clear that no satisfactory methodology is currently known to agency executives or their clients to measure marketing communications effectiveness. Or, if there is such a methodology available, it has not been sufficiently disseminated among IMC practitioners, especially agency executives.

Is IMC a fad?

IMC does not appear to be a fad. It is being driven into client organizations due to real business needs and is not the 'philosophy of the day'. Agency executives note a number of reasons for the adoption of IMC by many clients. Table 13 shows responses to questions regarding where IMC is coming from and why it is moving ahead.

The first three statements from Table 13, which have the highest means, are the factors that express the *'concept'* (synergy among promotional tools), *'belief'*

Table 12 IMC measurement issues

Abbreviated statement	Mean	Standard deviation
IMC evaluation relies on measurements similar to those used.	5.56	2.53
IMC makes evaluation of Marcoms' effectiveness more difficult.	3.29	2.37
IMC neatly sidesteps the issue of measuring program.	2.61	1.96

Table 13 Marketing communication criteria

Abbreviated statement	Mean	Standard deviation
Call for synergy among promotional tools	8.04	1.65
Rapid growth and development of database marketing	7.55	2.11
Recognizing that future success depends on helping clients	7.46	2.15
Emergence of a variety of compensation methods	7.39	2.25
Rapid growth of IMC importance	7.34	2.05
Fragmentation of media markets	6.92	2.31
Ongoing revolution changing rules of marketing	6.88	2.36
Changing role of advertising agencies	6.84	2.61
Changes in media buying practices	6.34	2.25
Shift in marketplace power from manufacturers to retailers	5.86	2.34
Shift in advertising dollars to sales promotion	5.53	2.31
Escalating price competition	5.21	2.06
Lack of the 'rules of marketing'	5.12	3.07
Recognizing that traditional advertising is too expensive	4.94	2.29

(recognizing that future success depends on helping clients), and *'tool'* (rapid growth and development of database marketing) of IMC. Because of the acceptance of these concepts, it is logical that the response to 'rapid growth of IMC importance' has a high degree of agreement.

Also in Table 13, there are sets of queries that explore the changes occurring in the marketplace. From the above responses we see that agency executives acknowledge that some of the traditional rules of communication and marketing are changing, which require substantial change in communication objectives and attitudes.

DISCUSSION

With this survey, we have attempted to develop and provide a baseline of how IMC is considered, developing, and what agency executives in the United States believe will result from this new concept. It does appear from the survey that agency leaders believe IMC is an important concept and approach and believe that their clients feel the same. There are, however, questions and concerns, chief of which seems to be how IMC programs should or could be evaluated. Intellectually, most agency executives seem to agree that 'integration' and 'IMC' are good ideas. They seem to have less evidence of why this is so or how the increased value of an integrated approach over more traditional discipline-related campaigns might be measured.

As was apparent in the initial study by Caywood *et al.*, agency executives agreed that integration must come from the client. Agencies, no matter how skilled or capable, simply can't integrate a client's marketing communication programs unless the client leads the way. Agency executives do appear to believe that, given client support, they can create effective marketing communication programs across business units and divisions, but they are reliant on the client organization to commit to the process.

From this study, it does appear that IMC has moved from the 'what is it'? to the 'how can we do it'? stage of development in the United States. Agency executives appear to believe that IMC is important, that it is good for their clients, and are ready to 'get on with it'. Some nagging concerns still appear to be evident. The compensation issue appears to be one. Measurement, as mentioned earlier, is another. And, the issue of how the agency can become skilled and capable in all areas of communication is another. These are not easy issues to address nor does there appear to be much agreement among agency leaders how this might be done.

As noted in the tables, many of the questions asked had mean values in the 5 to 6 range. This meant that as many disagreed as agreed and that, perhaps more important, the agency executives neither agreed nor disagreed with many of the questions asked. They either had no strong feelings one way or the other or did not known how to respond to the challenges which IMC presents. This seems to open the door for all types of research to help build a solid theoretical and practical approach to IMC.

DIRECTIONS FOR FUTURE RESEARCH

From this study, it is clear that compensation, measurement, and IMC development in terms of execution and implementation of integrated programs appear to be the key areas for future research. This is to be expected in any emerging field and IMC certainly appears to be that in the United States. The measurement issue seems to be particularly important. While agency executives believe IMC has value, measurement, which would justify these 'gut feelings', appears to be critical to the development of the area. If there is no evidence that an IMC approach is better than or more effective than the traditional approaches agencies have been using, it is likely clients and agencies both will and should challenge the need for such IMC programs. Thus, measurement would appear to be a key element for future research.

The second major area for additional research is that of how clients and agencies can or should work together to develop and implement an IMC program. Clients apparently believe and agencies agree, that the client must drive the integration process. Yet, having one group drive the process creates major issues for the agency. How do and how should clients and agencies work together in this new communication arena? That appears to be a critical question.

Finally, in theory building, an agreed-upon and agreeable definition of the subject is critical. Given the responses to the agree/disagree question on the IMC definition we supplied, it does not appear there is widespread agreement on the Schultz definition. A mean score of 6.31 does not give that definition resounding support. Thus, one of the major issues for the academic community, if IMC is to develop a theory base, is to develop a more acceptable or relevant definition. Until that is done, we will likely find ourselves continuing to disagree on what IMC is and how we might practice it.

REFERENCES

Belch, G. E., and Belch, M. A. *Introduction to Advertising and Promotion: An Integrated Marketing Communication Perspective*, 3rd ed. Chicago, IL: Irwin, 1995.

Caywood, C., Schultz, D. and Wang, P. 'Integrated Marketing Communications: A Survey of National Goods Advertisers'. Unpublished report, Medill School of Journalism, Northwestern University, June 1991.

Duncan, T. 'Integrated Marketing? It's Synergy.' *Advertising Age*, March 8, 1993.

——. 'The Concept and Process of Integrated Marketing Communication'. *Integrated Marketing Communications Research Journal* 1, (1995): 3–10.

——, and Everett, S. E. 'Client Perceptions of Integrated Marketing Communications'. *Journal of Advertising Research* 33, 3 (1993): 30–39.

——, and Caywood, C. 'The Concept, Process, and Evolution of Integrated Marketing Communications'. In *Integrated Communications: Synergy of Persuasive Voices*, Thorson, E. and Moore, J. eds. Hillsdale, NJ: Earlbaum, 1996.

Grein, A. F., and Gould, S. J. 'Globally Integrated Marketing Communications'. *Journal of Marketing Communications* 2, 3 (1996): 141–58.

Griffin, T. 'Integrated Marketing Communications So What's New?' In *Proceedings of the Second International Research Seminar on Marketing Communications and Consumer Behavior*, 1997.

Hutton, J. 'Integrated Marketing Communications and the Evolution of Marketing Thought', Paper presented at the American Academy of Advertising Annual Conference, March 1995, and forthcoming in the *Journal of Business Research*.

Jackson, R., and Wang, P. *Strategic Database Marketing*, Lincolnwood, IL: NTC Publishing, 1994.

Journal of Marketing Communications (special edition devoted to Integrated Marketing Communications) 2, 3 (1996), guest edited by Don Schultz.

Junu, B. K. 'Databases Open Doors for Retailers'. *Advertising Age*, February 15, 1993.

Keegan, W. J. *Global Marketing Management*. 5th ed. Englewood Cliffs, New Jersey: Prentice Hall International, 1995.

Kitchen, P. J., and Proctor, R. A. 'The Increasing Importance of Public Relations in U.K. FMCG Firms'. *Journal of Marketing Management* 7 (1991): 357–91.

——. 'Marketing Communications Renaissance'. *International Journal of Advertising* 12, 4 (1993): 367–86.

——. 'The Marketing Communications Revolution: A Leviathan Unveiled', *Marketing Intelligence and Planning* 12, 2 (1994): 19–25.

——. Quotes from unpublished letters from leading U.K. academics and CEOs in U.K. Public Limited Companies.

——, and Moss, D. A. 'Marketing and Public Relations: The Relationship Revisited'. *Journal of Marketing Communications* 1, 2 (1995): 105–19.

——, and Wheeler, C. 'Global Developments in Marketing Communications: A Time of Renaissance or Reflection'? Under review by the *Journal of Marketing Research*.

Kotler, P. 'A Generic Concept of Marketing'. *Journal of Marketing* 36 2 (1972): 46–50.

——. 'Megamarketing'. *Harvard Business Review* 64, 2 (1986): 117–24.

——. Marketing Management, 9th ed. Englewood Cliffs, New Jersey: Prentice Hall International, 1997.

Krugman, D. M., *et al. Advertising: Its Role in Modern Marketing*, 8th ed. New York: Dryden Press, 1994.

Nowak, G., and Phelps J. 'The Integrated Marketing Communications Phenomenon: An Examination of Its Impact on Advertising Practices and Its Implications for Advertising Research'. *Journal of Current Issues and Research in Advertising* 16, 1 (1994): 49–66.

Novelli, W. D. 'One-Stop Shopping: Some Thoughts on Integrated Marketing Communications'. *Public Relations Quarterly* Winter (1989–90): 7–8.

Phelps, J., Plumley, J., and Johnson E. 'Integrated Marketing Communications: Who Is Doing What?' In *Proceedings of the 1994 Conference of the American Academy of Advertising*, King, K. W. ed. Athens, GA: University of Georgia, 1994.

Rose, P. B. 'Practitioner Opinions and Interests Regarding IMC in Selected Latin American Countries'. *Journal of Marketing Communications* 2, 3 (1996): 125–39.

Shocker, A. D., Srivastava, R. K., and Ruekert, R. W. 'Challenges and Opportunities Facing Brand Management: An Introduction'. *Journal of Marketing Research* 31, 2 (1994): 149–57.

Schultz, D. E. 'Integrated Marketing Communications: The Status of Integrated Marketing Communications Programs in the U.S. Today'. *Journal of Promotion Management* 1, 1 (1991): 37–41.

——, Tannenbaum, S. I., and Lauterborn, R. F. *Integrated Marketing Communications: Pulling It Together and Making It Work*. Lincolnwood, IL: NTC Business Books, 1992.

——. 'Integrated Marketing Communications: Maybe Definition is in the Point of View'. *Marketing News*, January 18, 1993.

——. 'Is IMC Finally Becoming Mainstream?' *Marketing News*, July 1, 1996.

Shimp, T. A. *Promotion Management and Marketing Communications*. 3rd ed. Harcourt, Brace, Jovanovich International Edition, 1993. (N.B. fourth edition is far more integrated in its approach.)

Sloan, J. R. 'Ad Agencies Should Learn the Facts of Life'. *Marketing News*, February 28, 1994.

Wolter, L. 'Superficiality, Ambiguity Threatens IMC's Implementation and Future'. *Marketing News*, September 13, 1993.

Waterschoot W., and Bulte, C. 'The Four P Classification of the Marketing Mix Revisited'. *Journal of Marketing* 56, 4 (1992): 83–93.

Zikmund, W. G., and D'Amico, M. *Marketing*, 5th ed. New York: West Publishing Company, 1996.

Schultz, D. and Kitchen, P. J. (1997) 'Integrated marketing communications in US advertising agencies: an exploratory study'. *Journal of Advertising Research*, 37(5), September/October: 7–18. Reproduced with permission.

Understanding demographic effects on marketing communications in services

1.3

Maureen FitzGerald and David Arnott

INTRODUCTION

Demographics and product attributes were identified as the variables most frequently used to segment the market as far back as 1976, with demographic categories used to match segments with media profiles, mainly because most media described their audiences by demographics (Assael and Roscoe, 1976). Although subsequent research has identified new bases for segmentation, including lifestyle, benefits, etc., profiling of target audiences by media has changed very little. Media reach and pricing continue to be based on the demographic characteristics of the targets, and thus demographics continue to play an influential role. However, although the demographic profile of consumers in many markets has changed considerably over time, research into demographic factors appears to have waned in favour of more 'exotic' variables.

The market for passenger air travel in the UK has grown steadily for several decades (*Transport Statistics Great Britain, 1977–1987, 1992, 1993*), segmented at the highest level into two broad user categories – leisure and business (Civil Aviation Authority, 1993). The latter – deemed more important because it is more profitable – is characterized by frequent, repeat purchases at premium prices (Fisk *et al.*, 1984). Other segmentation opportunities exist, however, not the least of which are those based on simple demographics, but recent changes due to economic and social trends do not appear to be reflected in published segmentation research, although links have been demonstrated between several demographics and service expectations (Webster, 1989). It is known, for example, that the percentage of female business travellers is increasing (Civil Aviation Authority, 1993), and there is evidence to suggest that this segment receives poorer service than their male counterparts (FitzGerald, 1994).

Consumers develop internal 'scripts' of their service transactions which they recall for future purchases of that service (Beaven and Scotti, 1990), and thus personal experience is a key driver in the repeat purchase of service products. One might hypothesize that the more frequently a service is experienced, the more rigid that script (or service expectation) becomes, and so the influence of deliberate marketing communications, such as advertising, should decline. When frequent flyers are exposed to airlines' communications or other related messages (e.g. editorials), they are likely to interpret them using their prior experiences both of life and of product usage. Thus, there should be some discernible relationships between customer demographics, product usage rates, and perceptions of communication content, and this paper investigates such relationships and their effects on interpretation of marketing communications.

DEMOGRAPHICS AND THE COMMUNICATIONS MIX

Investigation of the literature identified some interesting imbalances. The majority of papers investigating demographic influences in marketing communications were found to focus on advertising and gender, and only a few considered either other demographic variables, or other communications mix tools. No work was identified which investigated any relationship with more than one demographic factor, or their effects on interpretation of one or more communications mix tools.

Advertising

Marketing communications literature is replete with analyses of advertising content from a range of perspectives, such as the portrayal of minorities, environmental claims, services versus products, etc., yet few articles on advertising consider whether a relationship exists between membership of a demographic category and the demographic profile of that segment. Men, for example, do nearly 30 percent of the USA's laundry and yet advertisements retain a strongly female orientation (Sandor, 1994). By contrast, airlines' communications aimed at the frequent business traveller are seen to be male-oriented even though the demography of frequent flyers is highly diverse, and the female business traveller now makes up nearly 24 percent of that segment. Gender is thus one area that has received some attention, but that attention is heavily focused on advertising and content analysis.

Studies of gender response and communication tools have been confined traditionally to certain key areas – gendered advertising content (Alreck et al., 1982; Belkaoui and Belkaoui, 1976; Bellizzi and Milner, 1991; Courtney and Lockeretz, 1971; Courtney and Whipple, 1974; Zotos and Lysonski, 1994), responses of men and/or women to advertising content (Alreck, 1994; Debevec and Iyer, 1986; Duker and Tucker, 1977; Kanugo and Pang, 1973; LaTour and Henthorne, 1994; Leigh et al., 1987; Schmitt et al., 1988; Seonsu and Barnes, 1989; Widgery and McGaugh, 1993; Wortzel and Frisbee, 1974), and responses of consumers to advertising where gendered response differences are identified (Kellaris and Rice, 1993).

More recently, a study by Darley and Smith (1995) identified that men and women process advertising messages differently, with females being found to be more sensitive to the level of product risk than males. Other studies have identified a relationship between the gender orientation of advertisements and the responses of males and females and – building on the work of Leigh et al. (1987), Jaffe and Berger (1988), and Jaffe (1989) – Jaffe (1991) confirms that women respond more positively to a contemporary representation of female roles in advertising – as opposed to traditional role depiction. Jaffe and Berger (1994) further identified that the most effective portrayal of gender roles in advertising for household goods aimed at the female purchaser were those using an 'egalitarian image' depicting a husband and wife sharing household chores, concluding that firms will be 'rewarded for their astuteness to women's changing needs'. But creating advertisements oriented to one gender or the other may have pitfalls. Bellizzi and Milner (1991) examined the responses of men and women to advertisements which were purposefully designed to be male and female-oriented and identified that the use of female-oriented advertisements can create a positive effect among women, without creating a male backlash. However, Alreck (1994) conversely found that, while women will accept advertisements for masculine-gendered brands, men will reject feminine-gendered brands.

Other demographics, other communications tools

Gender, however, is not the only important demographic factor, and advertising is not the only marketing communications tool, yet other demographic categories appear to receive scant attention in the marketing communications literature. Harrison-Walker (1995) reports that negative interaction between a consumer of one culture and a service provider of another can be overcome by increasing the information content in advertising to meet the specific information needs of the target culture. Research into sales promotion and demographic segmentation centres largely on purchases of domestic and personal goods. Age segmentation is relatively crude (children, senior citizens, baby boomers, etc.). Warner (1994) reports the link between concise demographic targeting and the growth of free-standing inserts. Certain cultural groups in the USA were found to respond well to frequent-purchaser promotions for overseas telephone calls (Cacas, 1995), and Reda (1994) noted the success of an in-store promotion resulting from the use of discounts plus competition where the choice of competition prize was linked to the demographics of the target customer group. Peattie and Peattie (1995) report the rapid growth of sales promotion during the 1980s, noting its usefulness as an effective strategic communications tool for services.

What becomes clear from the literature is that marketing communications research has focused mainly on advertising of consumer goods, with gender as the dominant demographic grouping. This has identified that products positioned to target audiences which include women need to give careful consideration to the perceptions that they have of their changing role as women, and their relationships with men. The literature fails to come to a firm conclusion, however, for product positioning where the target audience is composed of both sexes. The research seems to indicate that firms are paying inadequate attention to the whole *marketing mix* needs of their consumers. While men and women may consume the same product for the same reasons – and so be part of the same need-based segment – it may be that their marketing communications needs are different. These implications appear to be confirmed further by the lack of investigation into understanding responses of different demographic categories to the different marketing communications tools. This paper attempt to redress this imbalance.

THE DEMOGRAPHY OF FREQUENT FLYERS

Data analysed in this paper are taken from a research instrument investigating gendered perceptions of airlines' marketing mix using a stratified random sample of frequent flyers. The method chosen was that of a mailed, self-administered questionnaire given out to a large, stratified, random sample of business flyers geographically dispersed throughout the UK. Mail administration was chosen because it allowed a large sample to be reached over a wide area at reasonable cost (Zikmund, 1991), while minimizing any bias which might occur through personal interaction between respondents and researchers (Benny *et al.*, 1956; Groves and Fultz, 1985; Nealon, 1983; Pol and Ponzurick, 1989; Tucker, 1983). A large, stratified, random sample was deemed desirable to maximize the accuracy of the research and to allow generalizability of the results to the population (Sudman, 1976; Zikmund, 1991).

A population frame was established using a database of 24,207 business travellers resident in the UK, being the active members of a major airline's Frequent Flyer Club. The population was composed of 21,219 males and 2,988 females. This population was stratified by occupation, using the nine categories of the CASOC scheme (Thomas and Elias, 1989; HMSO, 1990) and by gender, forming 18 strata. Sample sizes for each strata were determined using the Krejcie and Morgan (1970) model to minimize researcher bias, and random samples were drawn providing 3,254 potential respondents.

The research instrument was designed to investigate the influence of the marketing mix elements on airline selection among frequent flyers. The structure of the questionnaire was based on a series of qualitative interviews with frequent business flyers. The demographic and product usage variables (see Table 1) were measured at a nominal or ordinal level, using dichotomous or multichotomous response structures, as appropriate.

Three areas of the marketing communications mix – advertising, sales promotions and publicity – were included. Personal selling was excluded as this tool is directed primarily at members of the distribution channel (e.g. intermediaries, travel agents), as opposed to the consumer in whom we are interested. Eighteen variables relating to these areas were derived from the interviews. Perceptions were measured using three- and five-point Likert-type scales to identify respondent level of agreement/ disagreement with given statements. In addition, respondents were asked to indicate which of 20 factors they felt influenced their choice of an airline.

Cases for analysis were selected based on two variables: 'gender' (as one of the key demographic variables) and 'favourite airline' (a surrogate for a level of satisfaction with at least one carrier), and only cases where responses to both were complete were included, resulting in 1,129 (34.7 percent) usable responses (see Table 2).

Appropriate tests for validity (pilot tests, early vs. later response comparisons, within-strata response rates, etc.) were conducted and found to be acceptable. Relationships within the data were analysed using a series of cross-tabulations with the level of significance of association being indicated with the Pearson chi-square statistic (Fienberg, 1977). Although significant differences between a number of demographic, product usage, and communications elements were demonstrated, it is

Table 1 Demographic and product usage variables investigated

Demographics	Product usage
Sex	Number of business flights per year
Income	Recency of last business flight
Age	Class usually flown
Cultural origins	Has favourite airline
Industry sector	Avoids certain airlines
Family structure	

Table 2 Cross-tabulated sample structure of 'gender' by favourite airline

Favourite airline	Male (%)	Female (%)	Totals
Yes	493 (69)	224 (31)	717
No	284 (69)	128 (31)	412
	777	352	1,129

Notes:
$p = 0.900$
Figures in parentheses are percentages

noteworthy that secondary analysis proved not to increase the parsimony of the analysis. For example, a factor analysis of the 18 marketing communications variables produced five clearly defined factors (explaining 65 percent of the variance). However, interpretation of the data was not enhanced and so the intended pursuit of such analysis was curtailed.

DEMOGRAPHICS AND PRODUCT USAGE

From the demographic data, the expected significant relationships ($p = 0.000$) were found to exist between gender, age and income (see Table 3). The data can be interpreted to suggest that: the female frequent flyer is generally younger (59.3 percent < 35, 11.7 percent > 45 years old) than her male counterpart (30.5 percent < 35, 32.9 percent > 45 years old); the female frequent flyer earns less (65.2 percent < £30,000, 11.6 percent > £40,000) than her male counterpart (45.4 percent < £30,000, 28.9 percent > £40,000); no female flyers reported salaries in the very high range (i.e. > £100,000); and younger flyers were found to be lower paid.

Two other interesting significant variables were those of family structure and industry sector. There was a clear gender distinction in terms of family structure. The male sample was found to be dominated by those who lived 'with partner and dependants' (57 percent), whereas females were either single and/or living with a partner without dependants (86 percent).

The industry sector in which respondents worked was also highly significantly related to gender ($p = 0.000$) with a considerably higher percentage of females and/or younger respondents being employed in the service sector. Given the growth in

Table 3 Tests of significance for demographic versus product usage

	Gender	Age	Income	Culture	Flights per year	Last flight	Class	Favourite airline	Family structure
Age	0.000								
Income	0.000	0.000							
Culture	0.015	0.207	0.953						
Flights per year	0.002	0.101	0.000	0.912					
Last flight	0.649	0.912	0.000	0.329	0.000				
Class	0.627	0.101	0.343	0.144	0.145	0.407			
Favourite airline	0.896	0.148	0.045	0.022	0.003	0.784	0.632		
Avoid airlines	0.119	0.286	0.000	0.852	0.060	0.075	0.030	0.000	
Family structure	0.000	0.000	0.000	0.022	0.031	0.075	0.958	0.388	
Industry sector	0.000	0.079	0.001	0.596	0.612	0.591	0.629	0.944	0.053

services in recent decades (*Employment Gazette*, 1990), this is also an unsurprising relationship, but one which is hypothesized as contributing to the apparently harsher evaluation of services delivered by airlines exhibited by those groups (FitzGerald, 1994). Industry sector was also related to family structure (although at a lower level of significance: $p = 0.053$) with a clear bias among the 'with partner and dependant' towards employment in the traditional primary and secondary sectors (i.e. agriculture, mining, construction, manufacturing, etc.).

Another factor appearing to influence repeat purchase behaviour is the national origin of the frequent flyer. Although the sample was dominated by Anglo-Irish travellers, reflecting the dominant racial category in the UK (Church, 1995), there was a significant difference ($p = 0.022$) between males and females in terms of their national origin. The percentage of males exceeded that of females in the Anglo-Irish group but females, while not in the majority, were more common in other nationalities.

Analysis of product usage offers insights into the phrase 'frequent flyer'. Some 65 percent of respondents flew at least once per month and 76 percent had flown within the last month. Of greater interest are the highly significant relationships between flights per year and both gender ($p = 0.002$) and income ($p = 0.000$). It is clear that females make fewer flights (43 percent < 12 flights p.a., 20.4 percent > 30 flights p.a.) than males (32.2 percent < 12 flights p.a., 28.9 percent > 30 flights p.a.) and that a high percentage of flyers are found in the lower usage-lower income bracket (35.7 percent < 12 flights p.a., 51.2 percent < £30,000). The consequent expectation that age and produce usage would also be related proved marginally false ($p = 0.101$) under normally accepted confidence levels. Three other product usage variables (class normally flown, airline preference, and avoids certain airlines) were also tested, but proved effectively independent of both gender and age, although they did show expected correlations with other product usage variables.

DEMOGRAPHICS AND MARKETING COMMUNICATIONS

Respondents were presented with a list of 20 factors that might affect their choice of airline, and asked to indicate those most influential on their choice. Ranked on the percentage of respondents indicating a factor as a primary influence (Table 4) 'previous experience' is clearly the key driver (> 73 percent) providing strong support

Table 4 Ranking of top ten factors affecting choice of airline

Rank overall	Variable	Male n = 717		Female n = 412		Total n = 1,129
1	Previous experience	73.7	(1)	72.2	(1)	827
2	Frequent flyer programmes	64.0	(2)	61.6	(4)	714
3	Schedule	60.2	(3)	61.9	(3)	686
4	Connections	56.1	(4)	66.5	(2)	670
5	No-smoking policies	55.3	(5)	58.0	(5)	634
6	Advertising influence	47.6	(6)	44.0	(6)	525
7	Advance seat reservations	32.0	(7)	27.0	(7)	344
8	Routes	31.1	(8)	28.7	(8)	343
9	Airport location	20.8	(9)	27.6	(9)	259
10	Recent press articles	14.8	(10)	19.6	(10)	184

for Beaven and Scotti (1990). Thus, after attracting a customer, the airline must make sure that the experience is a positive one if repeat purchases are to be achieved.

Overall, the rankings were nearly identical for males and females, although an exception was females' ranking of connections and schedules ahead of frequent flyer programmes (ranked second by male respondents). A further difference was the generally higher percentage of females that ranked any particular category, indicating support for Webster's (1989) findings with respect to women having higher expectations of service. A chi-square test of the number of items ticked versus other variables revealed some interesting associations – for example, a highly significant relationship existed between this variable and both gender and age. Females ticked a greater number than their male counterparts. The number ticked reduced considerably as the traveller gained experience, with that experience – coupled with the need to fly more often – becoming the primary motivator to fly with a particular airline again.

The survey requested opinions on several aspects of airline marketing communications, particularly about elements of advertising content, press coverage and sales promotions, and on how influential the various channels were perceived to be in airline selection. The analysis revealed interesting differences in the demographic and product usage categories. The following analysis is divided into the three communications elements tested, and relationships are presented in Table 5.

Advertising

Less than 9 percent of respondents agreed that passengers were portrayed adequately and accurately in airline advertisements. Less than 25 percent agreed that the portrayal of cabin crews and service levels was accurate, and less than 9 percent admitted to being influenced positively by 'sexist' and/or 'sexual' imagery in advertising. Less than 1 percent agreed that advertising had a strong influence on their choice of airline. These perceptions held true across all demographic groupings which suggests that advertising to frequent flyers may be an inefficient way of using limited communications resources, or it may be that advertising is not sending the right signals. The latter of these explanations is certainly part of the problem. For example, a significant relationship ($P = 0.003$) was identified between the high service levels promised by airlines in their advertisements and respondents specifying a favourite airline, with a large percentage (41 percent) rejecting such promises as unrealistic.

Significant within-group differences were also identified in all demographic and product-use segments on at least two of the ten advertising-related questions, but the strongest and perhaps most important differences were those between the genders. More females offered opinions than males (again supporting Webster, 1989) with a greater percentage of women falling at both or either ends of the scales (e.g. a significantly ($p = 0.007$) greater percentage of women (29 percent vs 22 percent) agreed that cabin crew were portrayed accurately by actors). This is not necessarily a positive outcome, since women feel that the service they receive is poor (FitzGerald, 1994), and it suggests that women interpret the advertisements as reinforcing that poorer level of service and so the communication objective is not achieved.

The tendency of women to express opinions in relation to purchase choice was noteworthy with respect to sex-related imagery in airline advertisements. Airline

Table 5 $\chi 2$ tests of significance for demographics versus communications

Demographic variables[a]	Gender	Age	Income	Culture	Flights per year	Favourite airline
Factors ticked	0.008	0.008	0.723	0.611	0.225	0.135
Advertising						
The actors/actresses used to represent passengers in airline advertisements adequately reflect me as a passenger	0.199	0.078	0.173	0.508	0.084	0.523
The actors/actresses used in airline advertisements are realistic portrayals of the average passenger	0.006	0.285	0.015	0.057	0.000	0.053
The actors/actresses used in airline advertisements are realistic portrayals of cabin crew	0.009	0.359	0.125	0.795	0.554	0.863
The attitude of cabin crew in airline advertisements is a realistic portrayal of the attitude of real-life cabin crews	0.488	0.622	0.373	0.513	0.245	0.996
The high levels of service promised by airline advertisements are realistic portrayals of real-life service levels when flying	0.090	0.749	0.105	0.449	0.225	0.003
Airline advertisements are a true reflection of the diversity of airline passengers	0.011	0.017	0.094	0.518	0.128	0.131
Advertisements show businessmen being cared for by stewardesses ... more likely to choose airline	0.000	0.001	0.064	0.919	0.003	0.248
Airline which promotes the beauty of its stewardesses ... more likely to choose airline	0.000	0.000	0.019	0.749	0.054	0.876
Airline advertisements are interesting and thought-provoking	0.010	0.031	0.989	0.004	0.068	0439
Highly influenced by airline advertisements when choosing an airline	0.026	0.006	0.414	0.849	0.436	0.441
Publicity						
Press article indicates that an airline gives poor service ... less likely to choose airline	0.189	0.013	0.045	0.108	0.749	0.190
Press article indicates that an airline gives good service ... more likely to choose airline	0.059	0.094	0.028	0.082	0.427	0.027
Press article is negative about an airline ... less likely to choose airline	0.093	0.333	0.485	0.048	0.657	0.266
Press article is positive about an airline ... more likely to choose airline	0.320	0.029	0.025	0.083	0.684	0.405
Highly influenced by press articles when choosing an airline	0.026	0.014	0.011	0.252	0.682	0.759
Promotions						
Special lounges offered by airlines ... influence on flight selection	0.000	0.123	0.002	0.071	0.000	0.000
Frequent flyer programme gifts ... influence on flight selection	0.184	0.209	0.273	0.377	0.068	0.274
Appropriateness of gifts to respondent personally	0.156	0.433	0.211	0.692	0.000	0.000

Notes:
[a]Demographic variable categories used are:
Gender = male, female
Age (years) = < 24, 25–34, 35–44, 45–54, 55+
Income (£) = < £20,000, £20–30,000, £30–40,000, > £40,000

Culture = Anglo-Irish, European, Other
Flights per year = < 12, 13–20, 21–30, > 30
Favourite airline = yes, no

advertisements foolish enough to promote the beauty of female cabin crew were dismissed by 89 percent of women and 61 percent of men ($p = 0.000$). Advertisements depicting traditional gender roles (women serving men) were rejected by 78 percent of women – confirming Jaffe (1991) – and a surprising 52 percent of men ($p = 0.000$). One interpretation is that the use of egalitarian gender roles in advertisements reflects gender roles in the 1990s and is consequently effective for both male and female purchasers – supporting the work of Jaffe and Berger (1994).

Publicity

Here the foci were press reports on service levels, on the airline in general, and on their influence on respondents' purchase choice. Several significant relationships were identified but only at the $p = 0.050$ level (Table 5). Nevertheless, some interesting observations arise. For example, the effect of negative reports was linked with respondent age, with purchase intentions of younger flyers being less affected than older flyers. Conversely, positive service reports had a beneficial effect on respondents with a favourite airline, indicating that such reports may reinforce their judgement – with consequent positive effects on repeat purchase of that airline. Positive press reports also appeared to affect equally all demographic categories positively, with the exception of cultural origin – the non-Anglo-Irish being less impressed. While the reason for this is not known, the hypothesis that the use of single-cultural norms in communications to multicultural audiences is ineffective is worthy of investigation. Some clues may be derived from Harrison-Walker (1995) who argues that information content specific to the target nationality may help to increase purchase yield among minorities.

In terms of the overall influence of press reports, not only do some 63 percent agree that such communications affect their choice of airline, there are also significant differences by gender, by age, and by income (although the extent to which this is because of collinearity among these variables is not known).

Sales promotions

Perhaps the most frequently used promotional tools of airlines are Frequent Flyer Programmes (FFPs), special lounges, and 'two-for-one' type discounts. For business travellers, only the first two are generally pertinent as incentives (the second often being linked to the first), and so these were used as a surrogate for sales promotions in general (Table 5). Clear, if narrow, majorities in all demographic categories agreed that they were influenced by such promotions, suggesting that they have become integrated into the expected product. As such, their value as a differentiating promotional tool appears to have passed the 'use-by' date. This hypothesis is reinforced by the highly significant relationships ($p = 0.000$) identified between respondents having a favourite airline and the positive influence on them of FFP gifts and special lounges.

Respondents were a little more ambivalent about the type of FFP gifts available to them. In terms of demographic-related differences, however, the main conclusions are that special lounges are more important to men, to the middle-income bracket (£20–40,000) and to middle-to-upper frequency flyers (> 12 flights per year). Perhaps not surprisingly, there are highly significant differences between the flight frequency groupings on the appropriateness of gifts offered, with the more frequent flyer being more generally satisfied. Thus it would seem that airlines have a slight imbalance in their promotional offers. For example, the less frequent business flyer with one particular airline may well be spreading flights across several airlines owing to lack of routes covered by the preferred carriers, or simply because of the number of required business trips. This means that accumulation of points will be necessarily slower. However, the sample structure suggests that there is some scope and likelihood for these flyers to increase their usage rate over time. Combine this with the findings on the importance of previous experience and the opportunity to become the specified airline of these future more-frequent travellers becomes clear. There is thus an argument to suggest that FFP gifts that are more appropriate to the less frequent traveller might pay dividends, in the context of customer lifetime values.

DISCUSSION AND IMPLICATIONS

So what does this tell us about business travellers and airlines' marketing communications? Clearly, the demographic make-up of frequent flyers is diverse and, as hypothesized, this diversity affects interpretations of marketing communications. Such travellers are more likely to take note of – and be influenced by – press reports than advertisements, and are influenced by both negative and (perhaps more importantly) positive reports. The influence of promotions such as FFPs and special lounges remains strong, but acting as a defection deterrent rather than a strategic marketing communications tool.

The findings from this research identify that gender is a major demographic influence in interpretation of marketing communications. The findings also reflect two key social trends. First, the rising percentage of women in the workforce – from 37 percent in 1971 to 44 percent in 1993 and projected to rise still further over the next decade and characterized by the notable rise in young, single, economically-active women (Griffin, 1991; Church, 1995) – is reflected in the rise in young, single, female frequent flyers. Second, the gender distribution of income in the UK – where men continue to earn around 25 percent more per annum that women (Church, 1995) – is also reflected in the lower earnings of female respondents. Clearly, any marketing communication which does not take into consideration the totally atypical profile of these travellers is certain to fail in efficient targeting. Furthermore, any communications placed in a medium seen by both genders is likely to alienate the female target consumers if traditional role depictions are used (Jaffe 1991; Jaffe and Berger, 1994).

The increase in female business travellers (currently 24 percent) suggests that serious thought should be given to the communications mix used by airlines. The incentive value of special lounges is less effective for women than men. Private lounges are designed and managed for mainly male clientele and purposely offer a 'clubby' atmosphere as an attraction, and it is unlikely that businesswomen will feel as 'at home' here as their male colleagues. Faced with ranks of chairs filled with besuited men, absorbed in television showing rugby, cricket or football – or hiding behind the financial pages – women are likely to feel tolerated rather than welcome. While grateful for a comfortable chair away from the tourist hordes, in their present form such lounges are unlikely to appeal to the businesswoman as the gratifying retreat they represent to her fellow male travellers.

The use of advertising also appears to be ripe for a strategic review. While advertising itself is shown to be one of several factors which influence purchase choice, the images themselves appear to be counter-productive. The use of 'sexist' and/or 'sexual' imagery in communications is ineffective, supporting Jaffe (1991) and Zotos and Lysonski (1994), and the negative responses of both males and females to such images confirms the work of LaTour and Henthorne (1994). It is therefore surprising, given the research on the use of gendered images in advertisements and contemporary studies on the changing roles of men and women, that airlines should fail either to note the gender changes in their passenger profile or to identify the need to reposition themselves towards passengers of *both* sexes.

This research also indicates that the main sales promotional activities of airlines are failing in their primary function. At best, they are now a purchase prerequisite for repeat users. At worst, they have ceased to generate new sales and so confer no competitive advantage. While it is recognized that the FFP generates a level of loyalty among regular flyers, a clear imperative exists for airline marketers to revisit urgently their present use of FFPs, and to look for alternative, differentiating sales promotions. Further exploration of how frequent flyer lounges may be made more attractive to women would also be gainful.

It appears that airlines are serving their female customers despite their best efforts to rebuff them. It seems indisputable that airlines must reorientate their communications mix, and one cannot help but wonder what consequence effectively-targeted communications might have on the re-buy rate of female business passengers! Nevertheless, the scope for more research into understanding the complex relationships between customer gender, reaction to the communications mix, and purchase behaviour is considerable.

Specific areas worthy of further work include investigation into the relationship between advertisement content, consumer responses and purchase behaviour for services, where men and women are present in a single *need-based* segment. Other research into the relationship between customer demographics and the effect of sales promotions on new-buy and re-buy behaviour in services would also be beneficial, as would investigation of the relationship between consumer age and purchase risk behaviour derived from negative service reports. Exploration into alternative sales promotions which might prove attractive to the various demographic groups is also indicated.

The importance of the business segment to airline success, and the size and clear demographic differences demonstrated, suggests that ensuring that communications are well targeted is essential. When coupled with the varying levels of satisfaction with service delivery, the message is even more clear. For example, all aspects of communication, from staff interaction with passengers, through to advertising and publicity, need to consider the gender of the audience. This research goes part way to filling the gap, but a great deal more work needs to be done.

It is thus clear that a simple division of the air passenger market into business and leisure travel is insufficient for effective marketing communications and that, despite the advent of more sophisticated means of segmenting markets, demographics can still provide some useful and cost-effective insights. It is unlikely that these results are specific to the air-travel market alone, and thus there is considerable scope for investigation into demographic segmentation and marketing communications – both for services, and other industries.

REFERENCES

Alreck, P.L. (1994), 'A new formula for gendering products and brands', *Journal of Product and Brand Management*, Vol. 3 No. 1, pp. 6–18.

Alreck, P.L., Settle, R.B. and Belch, M.A. (1982), 'Who responds to gendered ads?', *Journal of Advertising Research*, Vol. 22 No. 2, pp. 25–31.

Assael, H. and Roscoe, A.M. (1976), 'Approaches to market segmentation', *Journal of Marketing*, October, pp. 67–76.

Beaven, M.H. and Scotti, D.J. (1990), 'Service-oriented thinking and its implications for the marketing mix', *Journal of Services Marketing*, Vol. 4 No. 4, pp. 5–19.

Belkaoui, A. and Belkaoui, J.M. (1976), 'A comparative analysis of the roles portrayed by women in print advertisements: 1958, 1970, 1972', *Journal of Marketing Research*, Vol. 13 No. 2, pp. 168–72.

Bellizzi, J.A. and Milner, L. (1991), 'Gender positioning of a traditionally male-dominant product', *Journal of Advertising Research*, Vol. 31, June/July, pp. 72–9.

Benny, N., Reisman, D. and Star, A.S. (1956), 'Age and sex in the interview', *American Journal of Sociology*, Vol. 62, pp. 143–52.

Cacas, S.R. (1995), 'Marketing the mainline to Manila', *American Demographics*, Vol. 17 No. 7, July, pp. 15–16.

Church, J. (Ed.) (1995), *Social Trends 25*, HMSO, London.

Civil Aviation Authority (1993), 'Passengers at the London area airports in 1991', *CAP 610*, January, London.

Courtney, A.E. and Lockeretz, S.W. (1971), 'A woman's place: an analysis of the roles portrayed by women in magazine ads'. *Journal of Marketing Research*, Vol. 8 No. 1, pp. 92–5.

Courtney, A.E. and Whipple, T.W. (1974), 'Women in TV commercials', *Journal of Communication*, Vol. 24 No 2, pp. 110–18.

Darley, W.K. and Smith R.E. (1995), 'Gender differences in information processing strategies: an empirical test of the selectivity model in advertising response', *Journal of Advertising*, Vol. XXIV No. 1, Spring, pp. 41–56.

Debevec, K. and Iyer, E. (1986), 'Sex-roles and consumer perceptions of promotions, products and self: what do we know and where should we be headed?', in Lutz, R.J. (Ed.), *Advances in Consumer Research*, Vol. 13, Association for Consumer Research, Provo, UT.

Duker, J.M. and Tucker, L.R. Jr (1977), '"Women's lib-ers" versus independent women: a study of preferences for women's roles in advertisements', *Journal of Marketing Research*, Vol. 14 No. 4, pp. 469–75.

Employment Gazette (1990), Department of Employment, London, December 1990.

Fienberg, S.S. (1977), *The Analysis of Cross Classified Data*, The MIT Press, Cambridge, MA, p. 9.

Fisk, R.C., Grove, S.J. and Ramachandran, V. (1984), 'Consumer satisfaction with airline services in a deregulated environment', in Belk, R.W. *et al.* (Eds), *American Marketing Association Educators Conferences Proceedings Series*, No. 50, American Marketing Association, Chicago, IL.

FitzGerald, M. (1994), 'Are male and female airline passengers equally well served? Satisfaction levels in male and female customers', *British Academy of Management Conference Proceedings*, September 1994, pp. 206–7.

Griffin, T. (Ed.) (1991), *Social Trends 21*, HMSO, London.

Groves, R.M. and Fultz, N.H. (1985), 'Gender effects among telephone interviewers in a survey of economic attitudes', *Sociological Methods and Research*, Vol. 14 No. 1, August, pp. 31–52.

Harrison-Walker, L.J. (1995), 'The relative effects of national stereotype and advertising information on the selection of a service provider: an empirical study', *Journal of Services Marketing*, Vol. 9. No. 1, pp. 47–59.

HMSO (1990), *Standard Occupational Classification, Volume 1: Structure of the Classification*, Office of Population Censuses and Surveys, and Employment Department Group, London.

Jaffe, L.J. (1989), 'The effect of positioning on the purchase probability of financial services among women with varying sex-role identities', in Goldberg, M.E., Gorn, G. and Pollay, R.W. (Eds), *Advances in Consumer Research*, Vol. 17, Association for Consumer Research, Provo, UT.

Jaffe, L.J. (1991), 'Impact of positioning and sex-role identity on women's responses to advertising', *Journal of Advertising Research*, Vol. 31, June/July, pp. 57–64.

Jaffe, L.J. and Berger, P.D. (1988), 'Impact on purchase intent of sex-role identity and product positioning', *Psychology and Marketing*, Vol. 5 No 3, pp. 259–71.

Jaffe, L.J. and Berger, P.D. (1994), 'The effect of modern female sex role portrayal on advertising effectiveness', *Journal of Advertising Research*, Vol. 34 No. 4, July/August, pp. 32ff.

Kellaris, J.J. and Rice, R.C. (1993), 'The influence of tempo, loudness and gender of listener in response to music', *Psychology and Marketing*, Vol. 10 No. 1, January/February, pp. 15–29.

Kanugo, R.N. and Pang, S. (1973), 'Effects of human models on perceived product quality', *Journal of Applied Psychology*, Vol. 57 No 2, pp. 172–8.

Krejcie, R.V. and Morgan, D.W. (1970), 'Determining sample sizes for research activities', *Education and Psychological Activities*, Vol. 30, pp. 607–10.

LaTour, M.S. and Henthorne, T.L. (1994), 'Ethical judgements of sexual appeals in print advertising', *Journal of Advertising*, Vol. 23 No. 3, September, pp. 81–90.

Leigh, T.W., Rethans, A.J. and Whitney, T.R. (1987), 'Role portrayals of women in advertising: cognitive responses and advertising effectiveness', *Journal of Advertising Research*, Vol. 27 No.5, pp. 54–62.

Nealon, J. (1983), 'The effects of male vs. female telephone interviewers', *Proceedings of the Section on Survey Research Methods*, American Statistical Association, pp. 139–41.

Peattie, K. and Peattie, S. (1995), 'Sales promotion – a missed opportunity for services marketers?', *International Journal of Service Industry Management*, Vol. 6 No. 1, pp. 22–39.

Pol L.G. and Ponzurick, T.G. (1989), 'Gender of interviewer/gender of respondent bias in telephone surveys', *Applied Marketing Research*, Vol. 29 No. 2, Spring, pp. 9–13.

Reda, S. (1994), 'Loehmann's scores with wild card sweepstake', *Stores*, Vol. 76 No. 7, July, pp. 33–4.

Sandor, G. (1994), 'Attention advertisers: real men do laundry', *American Demographics*, March, pp. 13–14.

Schmitt, B.H., LeClerc, F. and Dube-Rioux, L. (1988), 'Sex typing and consumer behaviour: a test of gender schema theory', *Journal of Consumer Research*, Vol. 15 No. 1, June, pp. 122–8.

Seonsu, L. and Barnes, J.H. (1989), 'Using color preferences in magazine advertising', *Journal of Advertising Research*, Vol. 29 No. 6, December/January, pp. 25–30.

Sudman, S. (1976), *Applied Sampling*, Academic Press, New York, NY.

Thomas, R. and Elias, P. (1989), 'Development of the standard occupation classification', *Population Trends*, No. 55.

Transport Statistics Great Britain 1977–1987 (1988), HMSO, London.

Transport Statistics Great Britain 1992 (1992), HMSO, London.

Transport Statistics Great Britain 1993 (1993), HMSO, London.

Tucker, C. (1983), 'Interviewer effects in telephone surveys', *Public Opinion Quarterly*, Vol. 47, pp. 84–95.

Warner, F. (1994), 'Hold the comics, sports, and give them that FSI', *Brandweek*, Vol. 35 No. 12, 21 March, pp. 40–2.

Webster, C. (1989), 'Can consumers be segmented on the basis of the service quality expectations?', *The Journal of Services Marketing*, Vol. 3 No. 1, Spring, pp. 35–53.

Widgery, R. and McGaugh, J. (1993), 'Vehicle message appeals and the new generation woman', *Journal of Advertising Research*, Vol. 33 No. 5, pp. 36–42.

Wortzel, L.H. and Frisbee, J.M. (1974), 'Women's role portrayal preferences in advertisements: an empirical study', *Journal of Marketing*, Vol. 38 No. 4, pp. 41-6.

Zikmund, W.G. (1991), *Exploring Market Research*, Dryden Press, London.

Zotos, Y.C. and Lysonski, S. (1994), 'Gender representations: the case of Greek magazine advertisements', *Journal of Euromarketing*, Vol. 3 No. 2, pp. 27–47.

FitzGerald, M. and Arnott, D. C. (1996) 'Understanding demographic effects on marketing communications in services'. *International Journal of Service Industry Management*, 7(3), July: 31–45. Reproduced with permission.

1.4 A framework for marketing image management

Howard Barich and Philip Kotler

As markets grow more competitive, companies need to improve their understanding of their target customers' needs, attitudes, and buying behavior. They must design their offers and their images to be competitively attractive. The target customers carry images in their heads about each supplier's product quality, service quality, prices, and so on. The images are not always accurate, but nevertheless they influence supplier selection.

Suppliers sometimes attempt to measure their image among target customers. A manufacturer of stereo components, for instance, found its share slipping. The president commissioned an image study to learn how his company was perceived relative to its two main competitors. The president thought that the company would rate higher than its two competitors on product quality and customer service. In fact, his company ran a weak third. His first reaction was to attack the image study as flawed. But when he looked at several of the transcribed statements from customers, he began to realize that he was not seeing his own company the way the customers were seeing it.

Although many companies commission an occasional image study, few do it systematically and on a regular basis. We would argue that companies should design and operate an image tracking and management system, which we define as follows: a system of periodically collecting, analyzing, and acting on information that describes how different publics view key attributes of the company's performance.

The main advantages of an image tracking and management system are that (1) the company can detect unfavorable image shifts early and act before they hurt the company; (2) the company can identify key areas where its performance lags behind its competitors and work to strengthen those areas; (3) the company can identify key areas where it outshines its competitors and can capitalize on those strengths; and (4) the company can learn whether its corrective actions have improved its image.

While numerous articles describe the nature and importance of images and image measurement, the literature gives little guidance on designing and developing an image tracking and management system. Some Fortune 500 corporations have designed such systems but their features differ and they are not widely known. Since these systems are costly, they need to be designed correctly, if their value is to exceed their costs.

This article describes a method for designing and operating an image tracking and management system, and addresses, in particular, two critical concerns of the company – identifying its image and its competitive standing.

THE NATURE AND IMPORTANCE OF IMAGE ANALYSIS

We use the term 'image' to represent the sum of beliefs, attitudes, and impressions that a person or group has of an object. The object may be a company, product, brand, place, or person. The impressions may be true or false, real or imagined. Right or wrong, images guide and shape behavior. Companies need to identify their image strengths and weaknesses and take action to improve their images.

Figure 1 suggests a starting point for image analysis. It shows the relationship between a company's reputation and level of public awareness. Suppose the residents of an area are asked to rate four local hospitals; A, B, C, and D. Their responses are averaged and displayed on two perpendicular axes. The horizontal axis shows awareness of the organization and the vertical axis shows attitude toward the organization. Hospital A has the strongest image; most people know it and like it. People are less familiar with Hospital B but those who know it like it. Those who know Hospital C view it negatively; fortunately for Hospital C, not many people know it. Hospital D is the weakest position; everyone knows it and thinks it is a poor hospital.

Each hospital faces a different task. Hospital A must work at maintaining its good reputation and high community awareness. Hospital B is doing a good job but must bring itself to the attention of more people. Hospital C needs to find out why people dislike it and take steps to improve its service, while keeping a low profile. Hospital D would be well advised to lower its profile (avoid news), mend its ways, and wait to attract public attention until it is a better hospital. In general, sometimes the company needs to improve its performance and sometimes it needs to communicate its actual performance level more effectively.

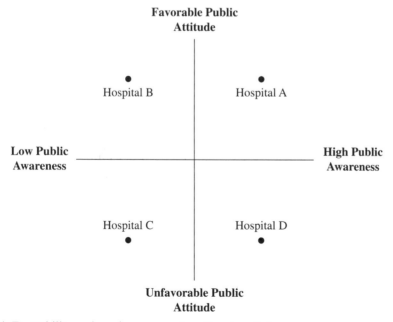

Figure 1 Favorability and awareness mapping: Four hospitals.

The above assumes that negative reputation correlates with negative performance. In fact, a perceived weakness may not be real. In that case, the company needs to direct communications to correct this misperception.

MARKETING IMAGE FRAMEWORK

A company has not one, but many images, depending upon the specific object being studied, the public whose view is being assessed, and other conditions. Figure 2 lists the components that make up a company's image: factors – the company's controllable image mix elements; offerings – the particular objects being measured, such as brands, products, or services; and publics – the various constituencies whose perceptions the company would like to measure. Clearly, a company's image depends on the particular offering and the particular public. For example, a local hospital's image will vary with the offering (emergency room, birthing center, surgery, etc.) and the public (local residents, physicians, nurses, etc.). Its image may vary even within a public, as when affiliated physicians see the hospital differently than unaffiliated physicians.

Sidney Levy of Northwestern University introduced the concept of 'image' in 1955, and it has been applied since to various objects. First, there is the *corporate image*, the way people view the whole corporation. Second, there is the *product image*, the way people view a particular product category. Third, there is the *brand image*, the way people view a particular brand that is in competition with other brands.

We would like to introduce a fourth type of image, a company's *marketing image*: the way people view the quality of the company's overall marketing offer and marketing mix. The shaded box in Figure 2 highlights the components that make up a company's marketing image. The company's corporate image and its marketing image play different roles. The corporate image describes how the public views the company's goodwill toward society, employees, customers, and other stakeholders. A company may have a very strong corporate image because it is a good citizen and invests heavily in communicating its good deeds. However, good corporate image may not contribute much to its bottom line, especially if the company suffers from a poor marketing image. Thus, the fact that the firm gives money to charities and civic organizations will not convince buyers to overlook product and marketing weaknesses.

A company's marketing image consists of how customers and other publics rate the 'exchange value' of the company's offering compared to that of competitors. A company has a strong marketing image if customers believe that they get high value when they buy from it. The high value comes from such factors as good products and services, reasonable prices, and so on.

Both marketing image and corporate image management aim to influence behavior in various publics. Marketing image management seeks to encourage customers to purchase the company's products and services and to recommend its products and services to others. Corporate image management, in contrast, seeks to inspire improved attitudes toward the company's stock, desire to join and work hard for the company, and support of legislation favorable for the company.

Each image factor is made up of a number of attributes, as shown in Figure 3. Consider communications, for example. The image of a company's communications

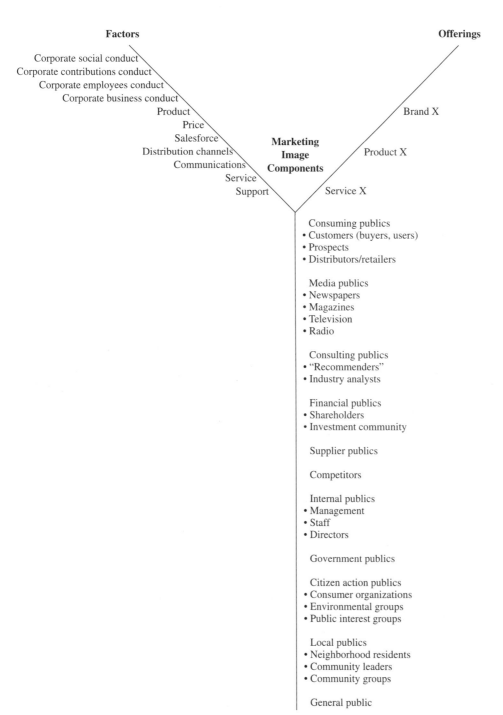

Figure 2 Company image components.

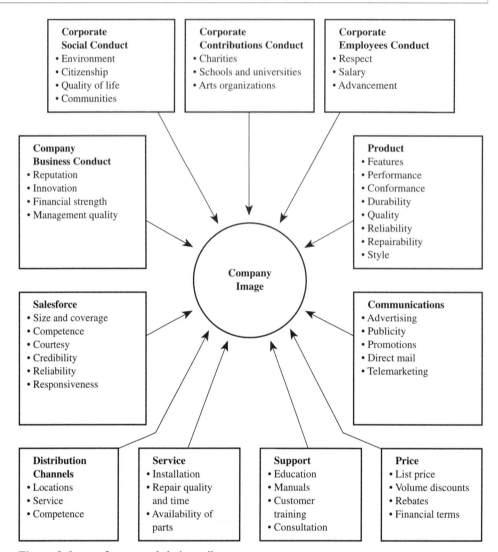

Figure 3 Image factors and their attributes.

is made up of the public's perception of its advertising, publicity, promotions, direct mail, and telemarketing. By measuring these attributes separately, we might detect a particularly weak attribute within the communications mix.

In this paper we focus on tracking the company's marketing image, not its corporate image. Consequently, certain factors, offerings, and publics are more important in our discussion.

THE IMAGE MANAGEMENT PROCESS

A company attempting to measure and manage its marketing image must make sure the process is feasible, affordable, and repeatable, and that the attributes are actionable. The process involves four phases:

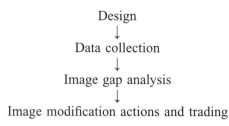

Design
↓
Data collection
↓
Image gap analysis
↓
Image modification actions and trading

Design phase

Let us assume that a company wishes to set up an image tracking and management system. Clearly, this company cannot hope to track the image of every one of its products and brands in every location and in the minds of every significant public. Since reliably sampling any single public costs thousands of dollars, the company must decide which image factors, for which products, among which publics, in which locations, it needs to track.

The company's headquarters may want to track the corporate image. The general manager of a particular division may want to track the division's overall image and the images of some specific products and brands within the division. The general manager of another division may not want to spend money to measure any of its images with any of its publics.

We believe that the task of measuring and tracking image should be assigned to the corporate marketing research department. Specialized talent can be developed in this department to hire research agencies, collect data, analyze results, and make recommendations. A centralized image measurement department can capitalize on economies of scale for data collection. Each division can then pay a general tax for measuring the corporate image and a separate fee for the specific image measurement projects that it requests.

During the design phase, the company determines the factors, offerings, publics, and appropriate competitors to track over time. Focus groups and one-on-one interviews are useful mechanisms for determining these. The following types of questions must be considered:

- **What factors will be tracked?** Is the company most interested in the image of the product, price, salesforce, distribution channels, communications, service, or support? This decision should be based on the attributes that most influence the purchase decision. To identify these, the company must first determine the various actors in the buying decision and the roles they play as gatekeepers, influencers, decision makers, purchasing agents, and end users. In group buying, each participant focuses on a different set of attributes. The researchers must avoid assuming that only one buying participant matters as they arrive at the right set of attributes to measure.
- **Which offerings should be studied?** The company must decide which offerings are most important to study, since image research funds may be limited. The offerings may be ordered by revenue contribution or market share or both. A company may want to emphasize those offerings with low market share, while others will study the key offerings with large revenue contributions.

Table 1 Relative importance of publics for consumer goods and services*

Buying decisions	Consuming publics			
	Customers	Distributors/ Retailers	Media publics	Consulting publics
Routine • Low-cost goods and services • Frequently purchased goods and services	Primary	Primary	Secondary	Secondary
Moderately complex • Familiar offerings • Unfamiliar suppliers	Primary	Secondary	Secondary	Primary
Highly complex • Unfamiliar offerings • Unfamiliar suppliers • High-cost goods and services • Infrequently purchased goods and services	Primary	Secondary	Primary	Primary

*See also J.A. Howard and J.N. Sheth, *The Theory of Buyer Behavior* (New York: John Wiley & Sons, 1969).

- **Which publics should be included in the study?** This decision will vary with the particular offering. Table 1 shows the relative importance of different publics for three types of consumer buying decisions. The customer is always a key public. When a product is expensive, infrequently purchased, and unfamiliar to the buyer, the customer needs to gather information about the product. In that case, the consulting and media publics play a key role in the decision process and become primary publics for image studies. For consumer goods that are inexpensive and frequently purchased and where shelf space is a key consideration, retailers and distributors are a primary audience. A similar approach may be taken for industrial goods and services.
- **How many members and which members of each specified public should be sampled each period?** How should they be distributed by type, geographical location, and other factors? For example, a company might need to choose between large corporate buyers on the East Coast and all buyers. In the case of computers, one might need to decide whom to interview among data processing managers, department heads, end users, and so on.
- **Who are the relevant competitors?** The company's management should not unilaterally decide who the relevant competitors are. The customers and distributors should be surveyed to discover who they think are the major competitors. A facsimile machine vendor may feel that other 'fax' vendors are its competitors. But customers may consider 'express mail' or 'electronic mail' as competitive alternatives.
- **How often should the specified images be tracked?** Here, a company must strike a compromise between the high cost of frequent image measurement and the benefit of detecting attitude shifts as early as possible. Suppose, as an example, the image is tracked two times a year. If the image were tracked more often, it might

show some shifts that were not meaningful. If the image were tracked less often, the company might miss some basic shifts. Since image tracking is costly, the division has to decide on a time interval that gives useful information while not costing too much. Generally speaking, the following circumstances dictate more frequent tracking: rapid technological change, changing competitors' strategies, active government regulation, and other signs of market environment turbulence. Major events such as new product announcements or new communications campaigns may require additional tracking measurements.

Due to budgeting constraints and potential respondent fatigue, the company may want to perform a cost–benefit analysis to limit the number of attributes, competitors, and publics examined in the quantitative phase. The information for this analysis is obtained from the design phase (focus groups and in-depth interviews).

First, the company needs a qualitative measure of the importance of the attributes in the buying decision. Participants in focus groups can be asked to sort the generated list of attributes into categories of 'most important', 'important', and 'least important'. The researchers can then focus on the 'most important' attributes in their image study.

Second, the company needs a qualitative measure of the key competitors. Participants can be asked to list and rank the key competitors.

Third, the company needs a qualitative measure of the salient publics. Participants can be asked to list and rank the most important publics.

It is important to include qualitative research for each of the salient publics, including purchasers and users, especially if they are not the same. This avoids the possibility of a misdirected image measurement.

In summary, the design phase should accomplish the following objectives;

- identify the major factors and attributes involved in the buying decision;
- explore the salient issues;
- explore the relevant publics;
- explore the language of the publics;
- identify the key competitors; and
- develop hypotheses to be tested in the quantitative phase.

Data collection phase

After the design phase is finished, a company can proceed to collect data. Typically, the data will be collected by telephone surveys. The telephone offers several advantages over mailed questionnaires: the information can be obtained faster, a higher response rate can be obtained, and the interviewer can clarify questions that arise. In some situations, if the questionnaire is long or complex, for example, personal interviews may be preferred.

Image gap analysis phase

In the next phase of the process, the marketing research department summarizes and analyzes the collected data, and graphically portrays the results. Typically, the image is portrayed on a set of bipolar scales. Figure 4 shows a bipolar mapping with five

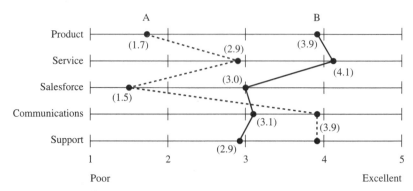

Figure 4 Bipolar mapping: Two images.

scales. Each scale runs from one (poor) to five (excellent). The two profiles plotted over the scales can represent many different comparisons:

- **Two publics' views**. Profile A may represent how small buyers see the company and profile B may represent how large buyers see the company. Alternatively, profiles A and B may represent how buyers in two different geographical locations view the company.
- **Two time periods**. Profile A may represent the particular public's view of the company last year and profile B may represent that public's view of the company this year.
- **The company and its major competitor**. Profile A may represent the company and profile B may represent a major competitor.
- **Two products**. Profile B may represent the company's major new product and profile A may represent the company's current product.
- **Actual image and desired image**. Here management would like to improve its image from A to B. B may not represent the public's desired (ideal) image of an excellent company. But it may cost company A too much to achieve the public's ideal image. B represent a feasible image for management to pursue given the public's desired image, the major competitor's image, and the company's resources and objectives.

Clearly, profiling the company's marketing image on a carefully selected set of bipolar scales can yield rich insights. The one limitation is that the importance that the public attaches to each factor is missing, since people will assign different weights to different attributes. When collecting image data, the researcher must ask respondents to indicate the relative importance of each attribute. There are different ways to gather importance ratings. The direct method ('stated' importance) includes asking the respondents to simply rank the attributes by distributing a constant sum of points over the attributes, or using a rating scale (see Table 2). The indirect method ('derived' importance) can be obtained from the data using a regression or conjoint methodology.

The underlying theory is that to be effective, a company strives to achieve a high image rating on each attribute that is highly important to its target public. If a company cannot perform well on a highly important attribute, it will lose sales to its competitors. At the same time, a company may overspend on an attribute of low importance to the customer. It should consider shifting resources away from

Table 2 Direct rating scale: Two images and perceived importance

Factor	Perceived importance	Image A	Image B
Product	3.5	1.7	3.9
Service	4.3	2.9	4.1
Salesforce	3.2	1.5	3.0
Communications	2.0	3.9	3.1
Support	4.1	3.9	2.9

This direct rating scale compares the two images mapped in Figure 4 with the public's perceived importance of the factors. The factors are rated on a scale of 1 to 5, where 5 is extremely important. The images are rated on a scale of 1 to 5 where 5 is excellent. The scores are then averaged.

overperforming on less important attributes and towards improving its performance on more important attributes. Generally, one should devote resources to the various attributes according to their importance to the target market.

The importance of the attributes or factors will usually vary with the publics and the offerings. A customer who is a member of the consuming public may highly value good fuel efficiency when purchasing an automobile for commuting purposes. However, when that customer purchases a family car, the most important feature may be its roominess. The same individual, as a stockholder of an automobile company, may value its record for innovativeness.

The findings in Table 2 can be usefully graphed on an importance and image rating map. For this exercise, we will assume that A and B are companies. Figure 5 shows such a map of company A's perceived image. Each quadrant of the map carries a different implication for management. Quadrant 1 indicates important attributes in which the company is performing well, in this case, support quality. Management's task is to continue to maintain high-quality customer support. Quadrant 2 shows important attributes in which the company is not performing well and where action is required. In this case, the company is lagging in service quality, product quality, and salesforce quality. Here, early and substantial marketing improvement is needed. Quadrant 3 represents attributes of low importance in which the company is not performing well. In this case, the company has none. Since these attributes are less important to customers, the company need not bother to improve its performance unless it can gain a competitive advantage with some market segments that value these otherwise unimportant attributes. Finally, quadrant 4 represents attributes of low importance in which the company is performing well; for this company, such an attribute is communications quality. Unless the company has a specific reason for performing well on communications quality, it should think seriously about shifting resources away from communications and toward improving its standing on more important attributes or factors.

In Figure 5, the sampled respondents' perceptions of performance and importance were averaged. Since each plotted point is an average, it is important to understand how specific or diffuse the image is. This can be accomplished by calculating the variance on each measure. In addition, one may segment the respondents on their importance ratings (benefits sought) or on their image ratings (attitudes). Each segment or cluster can be mapped on its own importance and image rating map. After segmenting and profiling the respondent set, the company can then select the target markets and position their products and services by adopting the proper marketing mix to meet the needs of the chosen segments. Service can be very important to one

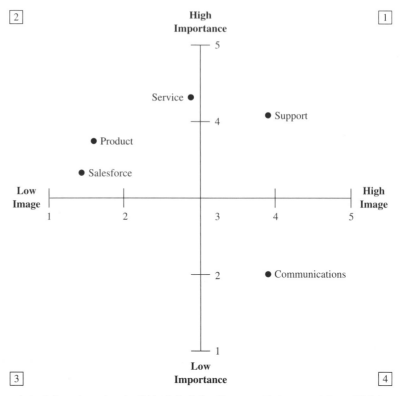

This mapping, derived from the ratings in Table 2, includes Company A's image and the public's perceived importance of the factors.

Figure 5 Importance and image mapping: Company A.

segment, while another segment is more interested in product quality. The company needs to prepare action plans for the target segments.

Image modification actions and tracking phase

The analysis thus far has yielded a picture of the company's major strengths and weaknesses as perceived by respondents. However, before the company develops plans to modify any of its attribute standings, it needs to extend the analysis to include a picture of its competitors' standings on these same attributes. For example, if the company's chief competitor (company B) is also deficient in an important attribute, then the company may be less pressed to improve its standing. Or it may see this as an opportunity to 'get a jump on' the competitor. Figure 6 compares company A with company B. A 'plus' indicates that the company is performing significantly better than the competitor, an 'equal' that it is performing similarly, and a 'minus' that it is performing worse than the competitor. Company A is performing better in support than company B, but worse than company B in product quality, service quality, and salesforce quality. It is also performing better than company B in communications quality, but this factor is of low importance in customer decision making.

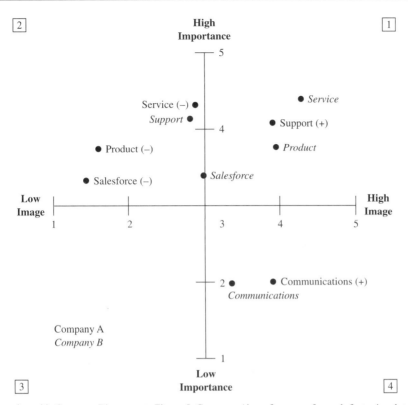

This mapping adds Company B's scores to Figure 5. Company A's performance for each factor is related either '+' (better than that of Company B), or '−' (worse than that of Company B).

Figure 6 Importance and imaging mapping: Company A relative to Company B.

The firm's standing in each quadrant has different ramifications for management action (see Figure 7). The plus attributes in the upper right hand quadrant are company strengths that can be highlighted in communication messages. The minus attributes in this quadrant are important items warranting improvements.

If a company is viewed as a 'plus' on an attribute that falls in the lower two quadrants, then the company should try to raise the respondents' perceptions of how important the attribute is. At the same time, if the company is perceived as a 'minus' in the upper quadrants, then the company should try to reduce the respondents' importance rating.

Yet it should be acknowledged that changing the perceived attribute importance is usually more difficult than changing the perceived attribute rating. Suppose a car buyer is looking for a car with high acceleration. He enters a dealer showroom and likes the looks of a particular car. But he is disappointed to hear that it has a four cylinder engine. The salesperson can try three strategies to increase the buyer's interest in the car:

- Decrease the perceived importance of 'acceleration'. Tell the buyer that cars with high acceleration accelerate too fast for safety, that fuel costs will be high, and so on.

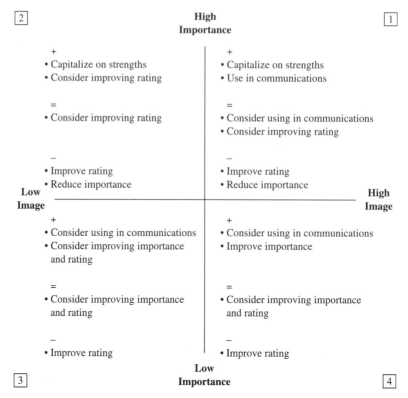

Figure 7 Prescriptions for management action.

- Increase the perceived importance of other attributes that the buyer likes in this car, such as the car's looks.
- Increase the perceived rating of an important attribute that the buyer had incorrectly assessed.

In the last case, suppose the buyer also values a car's reliability (i.e., repair-free record). Suppose the buyer will perceive the car to have either average or high reliability. Furthermore, suppose the car's actual reliability will be average or high. This leads to the four possibilities shown in Figure 8.

In cell 1 the buyer thinks the car has high reliability and he is correct. If the car's reliability is even higher than the competitor's reliability, the salesperson may mention this.

In cell 2 the buyer thinks that the car has high reliability but in fact it only has average reliability. If he buys the car and subsequently experiences only average reliability, he will be disappointed and will likely bad-mouth the car. Therefore, cell 2 portends a future problem for the company.

In cell 3 the buyer thinks that the car only has average reliability but in fact it is highly reliable. Here the salesperson needs to correct the buyer's misperception; this will increase the customer's likelihood of buying the car. She can quote consumer reports, cite authorities, display service records, and so on.

Actual Reliability

	High	Average
High	1 Perception: True. Action: Compare with competitor.	2 Perception: False. Action: Improve reliability.
Average	3 Perception: False. Action: Demonstrate reliability.	4 Perception: True. Action: Improve reliability.

Perceived Reliability (row label)

Figure 8 Actual and perceived reliability.

In cell 4 the car has only average reliability, which matches the customer's perception. Here the company needs to consider building more reliable cars in the future.

Or, suppose a retail department store conducts an image study and discovers that its customers view the store as weak relative to its chief competitor in three areas: knowledgeable sales reps, modern facilities, and service. When management identifies more than one image gap, whether they are real gaps or perception gaps, they need to be prioritized. Management needs to consider the following five questions:

- **How significantly does the gap influence buyer behavior?** Here a company must ascertain the magnitude of each gap and how much it affects buyer behavior.
- **What is the best strategy to close the gap?** Suppose the department store management ascertains that the gap in modern facilities is the most serious. But is it a real or perceived gap? If it is a real gap, then management needs to renovate. If it is a perceived gap, then the department store needs to more effectively communicate the high quality of its facilities.
- **What are the costs and benefits of closing the gap?** Reducing an image gap involves a cost that depends on the strategy for reducing the gap and the amount of reduction sought. For example, the cost of improving sales reps' knowledge will depend on the instruction method and the target level of improvement. This cost must be viewed against the expected benefit of increased sales due to more knowledgeable sales reps. The estimated costs and benefits must be further modified if the competitor is likely to retaliate.
- **How much time is needed to close the gap?** Here a company must decide how swiftly it can implement the image improvement plan, as well as how fast respondents' perception will improve. Images tend to change slowly.
- **Is it better to change importance ratings or attribute ratings?** Here a company must conduct a cost–benefit analysis to decide the relative merits of reducing a

particular gap or altering its perceived importance. If the department store is viewed less favorably on service, it may want to emphasize low prices and downplay the importance of service as a buying criterion.

In all cases of specifying strategies to close image gaps, a thorough cost–benefit analysis must include potential competitor responses. It makes little sense to invest resources and time in improving either the importance or image perception of a particular factor or attribute if competitors can close the image gap rapidly and at low cost. If a competitor bases differentiation on a particular attribute, then retaliatory moves may be more probable. In such a case, closing a different image gap may reduce the possibility of competitive countermoves and result in advantageous niche positioning.

By answering the questions above, management will be in a good position to prepare a sound image modification strategy. After the action plans are implemented, management can track whether the marketing image has improved in the desired direction.

CONCLUSION

An image tracking system permits management to measure and manage important components of the company's marketing image. Management is able to determine where it can capitalize on its strengths, and where it must improve its image or its product. The system allows management to set priorities for addressing its image gaps. By periodic monitoring, a company can verify whether it has succeeded in improving its image standing on important attributes. The image tracking system may also be used as an early-warning system to identify present or future shifts in the company's competitive performance.

Barich, H. and Kotler, P. (1991) 'A framework for marketing image management'. *Sloan Management Review*, Winter: 94–104. Reproduced with permission.

Global corporate visual identity systems: standardization, control and benefits

1.5

T.C. Melewar and John Saunders

INTRODUCTION

A multinational company's personality and identity will become the biggest factor in consumer choice between its products and those of another (Eales, 1990). The pressures of a free, competitive marketplace coupled with extremely rapid technological development have generated a situation where customers 'buy' the company that makes the product: its character, its size, its identity and the confidence it inspires. At the centre of a business's projected image is its corporate visual identity system (CVIS) with its five elements: name, symbol and/or logotype, typography, colour and slogan (Dowling, 1994; Olins, 1986).

CVISs are promoted as an aid to selling companies to their customers and other stakeholders globally. Despite being championed by designers and adopted by many leading businesses, there is little evidence to back the proposed benefits of CVIS globalization and its implementation requirements. Globalization is one of the key catalysts of corporate identity programmes (Ind, 1992). Changing businesses, geographical emphasis and marketplaces all have become incentives for companies to change their corporate identities. As companies begin to operate on an international basis, the image that they acquired as national producers often becomes inappropriate (Mills, 1988).

Some companies opt for a unified global brand in spite of the negative reactions of governments or consumers. The degree of adaptation of the identity to the host country's culture depends upon the strength of that culture and whether competitive advantage is derived primarily from co-ordinating activities centrally or by devolving activities to operational markets. However, if the company has a true global orientation it will generally need to convey consistent values wherever it competes. Thus, the worldwide image that emerges is more likely to be notable for its homogeneity than not. While there are reasons for closer integration of the visible manifestations of a multinational, they need relating to the market and product range (Pilditch, 1970). International organizations face the incessant conflict between the local area and the international headquarters in attempting to arrive at a consistent impression.

A key component of a corporate identity is the corporate structure (Chajet, 1989; Olins, 1986; Strong, 1990). In reality there are two structures (Ind, 1992). There is the organizational structure with its lines of communication and reporting responsibilities. Then there is the visual structure, which concerns itself with the branding of the products, business units and the corporate umbrella and how they appear to an organization's audience (Gray and Smeltzer, 1985). The fundamental concern with the organizational structure is the degree of centralization and decentralization. A decentralized structure creates companies in each country with their own distinctive identities. The pull towards the centre comes primarily from financial accountability. As a demonstration of this there is no central control over the use of logos in any markets. In direct contrast to this type of highly decentralized structure, there are companies who operate highly centralized structures which deny local autonomy and control all key functions at the centre. The identity in this instance will be strongly similar in both the parent and the subsidiary.

The paper empirically examines the implementation and control of global CVIS. In particular, we investigate the benefits sought from global CVIS standardization, senior management involvement, the degree of headquarters' control of CVIS, and how headquarters' and subsidiaries' views of CVIS standardization differ.

CVIS STANDARDIZATION

The wider literature on globalization partly compensates for the lack of theoretical work on CVIS standardization. Literature on corporate strategy, multinational strategic planning and the international marketing mix element was reviewed. These sources provided some important guidelines, although the majority of the work in the area is anecdotal rather than empirical.

Benefits of CVIS standardization

Buzzell (1968) and Hovell and Walters (1972) argue that standardization of international marketing helps companies achieve a consistent image that is a powerful means of increasing sales. Others take a less ambitious view. Peebles *et al.* (1977), on advertising, and Sorenson and Wiechmann (1975), on marketing practices, concluded that standardization makes consumers familiar with the company and its products and services, and helps establish a uniform corporate image. Through its corporate identity, of which CVIS is a core component, customers and prospects recognize the company (Smith, 1990) and become aware of the organization's business capabilities, management strengths, product and service diversity and competitive distinction (Downey, 1986).

This moderate expectation is close to what most marketers would claim for a corporate image in isolation of broader marketing activities. The global corporate identity programme of TRW doubled the awareness and recognition of TRW among the target audience (Hartigan, 1987). With this recognition came the customer's perception of TRW as a high quality manufacturer, a good investment, a good corporate citizen, a reliable supplier and increased receptivity of the local inhabitants toward the company's facilities. However, TRW did not anticipate their global corporate identity programme having a direct influence on sales.

In contrast, Lippincott and Margulies' (1988) survey suggests that some managers do have high expectations of corporate identity programmes. They found that a favourable effect on familiarity was most expected – by 50 percent of their respondents – though nearly as many expected sales, advertising awareness, general consumer goodwill and market share returns. A few managers even expected the impact of corporate image filtering through to investment ratings and the value of the company stock. Olins (1990) suggests that corporate identity programmes help the recruitment of high calibre staff and raises morale generally; a view supported empirically by Belt and Paolillo (1982). Gray and Smeltzer (1987) link both the personnel and marketing benefits of corporate image to financial performance. They argue that corporate identity programmes make recruiting easier, enhancing morale and lower labour turnover, correlate with strong sales and can be instrumental in achieving a high price/earnings ratio.

Measuring communications effects is one of the least tractable problems facing management. Advertisers rarely have the courage to predict market share gains or improved financial performance from campaigns. Yet in the more diffuse domain of corporate image, of which the CVIS is a part, claims extend well beyond the directly measurable effects on awareness and attitude. Are these ambitious claims shared by managers or are they the exaggerations made by those with wares to sell?

Headquarters control and CVIS standardization

Whether they are excessive or not, the benefits claimed for the global standardization and corporate image are based on their favourable influence on customers, employees and the money market. However, much of the literature on the global standardization of CVIS and other elements of the communications mix relate them to corporate structure not external returns. Do CVIS standardization and centralization go hand in hand?

Wiechmann's (1974) study of the integration of multinational marketing activities found that for 17 out of 20 firms sampled, standardization did mean centralization. These firms saw globally standardized international brand names as an important source of competitive strength and tried to integrate marketing worldwide to the creation of a uniform company and product image. For advertising in Western Europe, Roostal (1963) hypothesized that an international marketer with a centralized organization can more easily carry through standardization than an international marketer with a decentralized organization. The greater the centralization of authority for setting policies and allocating resources, the more effective the implementation of a standardized strategy (Jain, 1989). These studies suggest that global standardization and centralization are related but that the centralization flows from the needs of globalization.

Other evidence suggests that globalization flows from standardization. Companies with centralized operations tended to agree more on the applicability of standardized advertising (Onkvisit and Shaw, 1985) and the higher the headquarters' control, the greater the likelihood of standardization (Kirpalani et al., 1988). Standardized marketing communication programmes complemented the procedures adopted by headquarters to maintain a tight rein over subsidiary decisions (Brandt and Hulbert, 1977). Standardized strategy tends to facilitate or result in centralization in the planning and organization of international activities whereas emphasis on local management autonomy stems from the advantages traditionally associated with decentralization and a concern with encouraging local entrepreneurship (Douglas and Wind, 1987).

Independent of global standardization, the serious consideration of CVIS itself leads to centralization. According to Pilditch (1970), corporate identity programmes cannot be handled in a fully delegated and democratic way. Someone must decide an approach and then impose strict central control. Furthermore, corporate identity is a means of establishing the unity and standardized approach. Subsidiaries in highly decentralized structures are likely to have identities of their own (Ind, 1992). On the other hand, in the companies which operate with a highly centralized structure, which deny local autonomy and control all key functions at the centre, the identity will be strongly similar in both the parent and the subsidiary.

Standardization of corporate identity does not necessarily mean rigid control of overseas subsidiaries. Gorb (1980) argues that in striving for maximum flexibility and creativity, corporate identity guidelines should be centrally administered. This occurs because corporate identity is an important asset that needs running by an authoritarian force within the company. The degree of centralization of control influences the degree of standardization of corporate visual identity of a multinational corporation (Topalian, 1984). One of the organizational factors in globalization as explained by Yip (1988) is centralization of global authority.

Whether the flow is from centralization to global standardization or vice versa, observers suggest they are linked. Since the consideration of corporate image itself leads to tight control, CVIS standardization and centralized control are likely to be even more closely allied. Is this the case? Does a globally standardized CVIS reflect centralization generally?

Chief executive involvement

Not only does the adoption of CVIS lead to centralization but, according to Baker and Balmer (1997), it is the prime responsibility of the chief executive officer to define and communicate the company's identity. Devising a well-managed corporate identity programme requires the involvement and support of the company's chief executive officer (Margulies, 1977) and its success depends upon the supervision of a staff officer or a specially appointed corporate identity manager.

Lippincott and Margulies (1988) found that more than half of the companies interviewed said that the chief executive officer was greatly involved in the implementation of their corporate identity programmes. The research added that senior managers are generally important participants in the development and implementation of corporate identity programmes but the chief executive officers often play key roles.

Implementing corporate image programmes should not be left to chance, given the importance of corporate image to competitive success (Gray and Smeltzer, 1987). The chief executive officer and senior executives need to know how to plan for and communicate an effective corporate image programme. According to Olins (1990), the two natural points of contact between the client organization and its corporate identity consultants are the chief executive officer and a senior manager with the chief executive officer as the final arbiter and the ultimate owner of the identity.

The implementation of many business activities are said to depend upon the support of the chief executive so it is to be expected that the intrinsically conspicuous CVIS is no different. However, consistency of this call for chief executive involvement and the scope of implementing a globally standardized CVIS suggest that the chief executive will be involved. Chief executive involvement in CVIS decisions will also encourage standardization since it is unlikely that any one person would have the time or inclination to orchestrate anything other than a global CVIS. Does this convergence exist? Does the globalization of CVIS depend upon chief executive involvement?

Subsidiary views of CVIS standardization

The benefits of CVIS standardization and the pressures towards its centralized control suggest that local needs will be ignored. Themes imposed by corporate headquarters leave management thinking local issues have been neglected with the resultant lack of autonomy having a deleterious effect on their morale and motivation. Overseas executives believed that key promotional programmes should be developed locally because 'standardized strategy won't work here – things are different' (Douglas and Wind, 1987). Such concerns are shared by many. Organization conflicts may arise between headquarters and subsidiaries because of their different points of view (Das, 1981; Nowakowski, 1982; Reynolds, 1987).

The position of the CVIS within the communications mix makes it a component of marketing, a poly-centric function that is deeply affected by local factors (Jain, 1989) that is often delegated to foreign subsidiaries (D'Antin, 1971; Doz, 1988). Since marketing decisions are often decentralized in favour of host country managers (Aylmer, 1970), there is a likelihood of conflict between the globalization of CVIS and perceived local market needs.

In their survey of headquarters control of advertising, Kirpalani *et al.* (1988) found that over 35 percent of the firms allow their subsidiaries and affiliates flexibility in adapting the campaign to local conditions, while 21 percent allow for translation and idiomatic changes only, and 25 percent allow local development of their own advertising. Headquarters management has a significantly higher level of participation in establishing objectives and establishing the budget for international advertising than in home markets (Wills and Ryans, 1977). However, headquarters management tends to be less involved in the creative strategy and media decisions. Most of these decisions relied on local management and agency people.

Multinational managers must realize that local managers are likely to resist any precipitate move toward increased headquarters direction (Quelch and Hoff, 1986). Brandt and Hulbert (1977) concluded that control and integration of subsidiary activities present formidable problems for multinational firms. In many firms the marketing decisions rest with the subsidiary managers with little or no help from the head office. Other companies maintain a tight rein on overseas marketing by developing controls and standardized programmes which are implemented around the world (Harris, 1984).

Although headquarters expect benefits to flow from CVIS standardization, its implementation is intrinsically headquarters and chief executive oriented, so neglectful of local needs. It is therefore likely that local managers do not see the same benefits of CVIS standardization as do headquarters. This disquiet among locals is often suggested, but does it exist? Are the benefits from global CVIS standardization so strong that local managers agree with their headquarters on its value?

HYPOTHESIS

The dilemma facing MNCs over the standardization or local adaptation of their CVIS is between one set of centripetal forces for control, centralization, and simplicity that favour the standardization of CVIS. In the opposite direction are centrifugal forces of local culture, markets and languages that favour CVIS varying from country to country (see Figure 1).

All aspects of international marketing face the counteracting centripetal and centrifugal forces. However, there are moderating forces that vary across product-markets and the marketing mix. These constitute the benefits sought from a strategy. A MNC may prefer standardization of the communications mix but its implementation is moderated by the achievable returns. For instance, although multinational sales promotions are potentially inexpensive to produce, the moderating influence of consumer responses and legislation limits the benefits from such programmes. In contrast, for CVIS, the literature suggests that standardization will beneficially influence several groups of stakeholders, so encouraging the centripetal forces for standardization. Hypotheses 1 to 9 express this centripetal bias.

H1: CVIS standardization has a favourable impact on sales.
H2: CVIS standardization has a favourable impact on consumer goodwill.
H3: CVIS standardization has a favourable impact on consumer's familiarity with the company and its products/services.
H4: CVIS standardization has a favourable impact on consumer's advertising awareness.
H5: CVIS standardization has a favourable impact on market share.
H6: CVIS standardization has a favourable impact on executive recruitment.
H7: CVIS standardization has a favourable impact on the receptivity of the local inhabitants toward the company's facilities in the area.
H8: CVIS standardization has a favourable impact on value of shares.
H9: CVIS standardization has a favourable impact on investment rating.

Headquarters control and implementation are major centripetal forces associated with CVIS standardization. Centralization and global standardization are generally related but the nature of CVIS suggests a particularly strong link between the two. The mere consideration of corporate image itself leads to tight control, so CVIS standardization

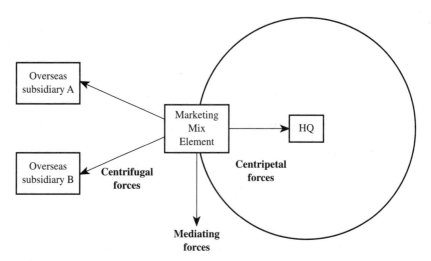

Figure 1 Centripetal, centrifugal and mediating forces.

and centralized control are likely to be particularly closely allied. In addition, the consistent call for chief executive involvement in implementing globally standardized CVIS suggests strong chief executive input where standardized CVIS exist. Hypotheses 10 to 12 examine these centripetal forces.

H10: The higher the degree of headquarters control, the greater the degree of CVIS standardization: name (*H10a*), symbol and/or logotype (*H10b*), typography (*H10c*), colour (*H10d*) and slogan (*H10e*).

H11: The chief executive is the key internal driving force in initiating a high degree of global CVIS standardization.

H12: High chief executive involvement in the CVIS development is more likely where there is a high degree of global CVIS standardization.

Although chief executive involvement, headquarters control and the benefits expected from global CVIS standardization reinforce a centripetal tendency, local managers will be concerned about the centrifugal force of local market needs. For this reason headquarters and local managers will view global CVIS standardization differently. Hypothesis 13 examines this tension.

H13: There is a significant difference in the opinions given by the headquarters and the subsidiary executives concerning the degree of importance to standardize CVIS: company name (*H13a*), symbol and/or logotype (*H13b*), typography (*H13c*), colour (*H13d*) and slogan (*H13e*).

METHODOLOGY

The hypotheses were tested by interviewing a sample of British MNCs with Malaysian subsidiaries. Malaysia was chosen because of the large number of British companies with subsidiaries there and the cultural diversity of the country: about 50 percent Muslim Malays, 40 percent Chinese of various dialects and religions, a well-established Indian community, and a small number of indigenous people such as the Dayaks and Kadazan. The national language is Malay. Since Malaysia is part of the British Commonwealth, many British companies have been there for decades although the economy's rapid growth has attracted many new ones. Malaysia is also particularly interesting because it is one of the Asian tigers with an economy growing at 8 percent per annum.

A sample frame of 111 British MNCs operating in Malaysia came from Dun and Bradstreet's *Who Owns Whom 1991*. The 111 companies were grouped according to their primary business and a proportionate stratified sample of 40 randomly selected: 19 industrial, nine consumer goods, and 12 service companies (see Table 1). Sampling this way is more efficient than simple random sampling where among-strata differences are greater than within-stratum differences (Green *et al.*, 1988). Where among-strata differences are small the efficiencies of stratified and simple random sampling converge (Cochran, 1965). Although their familiarity and their size suggested that the sample were MNCs, telephone contact with the firms confirmed that they were multinationals with more than ten major overseas subsidiaries, including Malaysia.

The interviewees were the senior persons responsible for CVIS at the headquarters and subsidiary (Table 2). The importance given to CVIS is reflected in the seniority of the respondents in the HQ sample where 80 percent were main board members. In the subsidiaries the CVIS was usually the responsibility of the national and regional chief

Table 1 Companies participating in the survey

Industrial	BICC, Blue Circle Industries, British Aerospace, British Petroleum, BTR, General Electric, GKN, Hickson International, High Point, Imperial Chemical Industries, Laing, Laporte, Lucas Industries, Redland, Renold, Tarmac, Taylor Woodrow, Tilbury Douglas, Wimpey
Services	Barclays Bank, British Airways, British Gas, British Telecommunications, Forte, Guardian Royal Exchange, PA Consulting Group, Royal Insurance, Standard Chartered, Sun Alliance Group, Willis Corroon, WPP
Consumer goods	BAT, Courts (Furnishers), Glaxo Holdings, Gestetner, London International Group, Pearson, Shell, SmithKline Beecham, Wellcome

Table 2 Executives participating in the survey

Position	HQ	Subsidiary
Chief executive/president	3	12
Regional director/vice president	0	2
Other executive director/vice president	29	0
Senior manager	4	14
Corporate identity manager/co-ordinator	4	2
Total	40	30

executive or their immediate subordinate. Both groups stated that the attention given to CVIS has increased over the past five years.

The sample is small but consistent with similar semi-structured studies of companies (Baker *et al.*, 1988; Buckely *et al.*, 1998; Doyle *et al.*, 1986; Johne and Snelson, 1989). In these cases the large sample obtainable by mail survey is traded for the quality of personal interviews where more information can be gathered, the quality of respondents controlled and non-response bias minimized. These small samples have some drawbacks. Lack of degrees of freedom prevents the valid use of some multivariate techniques and sample differences have to be large to be statistically significant. However, the hypotheses' tests use simple cross tabulations that have been successful in recovering meaningful results in similar studies. Moreover, small numbers do not make a sample non-representative, particularly when they represent much of the population (Saunders, 1994).

The questionnaire was mainly structured but had some open-ended questions at the end. The questionnaire was self-administered by headquarters' respondents with the researcher present and the results cross checked using a questionnaire mailed to Malaysian subsidiaries. The open questions allowed respondents to further explain their answers. The closed questions used multi-item, 11-point rating scales. The 11-point rating scale use was consistent with measuring the percentage change in CVIS: 0 corresponding to completely different, and 10 corresponding to exactly the same. The dependent construct, the degree of standardization of CVIS, was measured by averaging the scores of each element of CVIS; name, symbol and/or logotype, typography, colour and slogan.

The process of measurement or operationalization involves 'rules for assigning numbers to objects to represent quantities of attributes' (Nunnally, 1967). The validity and reliability of measures used to do this are critical (Bearden *et al*., 1989; Lichtenstein *et al*., 1990; Samiee and Roth, 1992). In this case we used the scale development procedure recommended by Churchill (1979). We refined the scales using a three stage process with Business Schools with operations in Malaysia, local businesses with overseas operations, and finally the stratified sample. The measures used appear in Table 3 which shows all the Cronbach's alpha for multiple-item measures to be within acceptable limits.

FINDINGS

Benefits of CVIS standardization

The firms with highly standardized global CVIS saw themselves reaping more, but not uniformly more, reward from their CVIS than did those with low CVIS standardization. All customer based measures are significantly higher with highly standardized CVIS than those without: favourable impact on sales (86 percent for those with highly standardized CVIS versus 43 percent for those without), favourable impact on consumers (92 percent versus 43 percent), advertising awareness (89 percent versus 50 percent) and market share (73 percent versus 52 percent). These results lend support to hypotheses *H1*, *H2*, *H3*, *H4* and *H5* respectively. The firms with high CVIS standardization also see a significant impact upon executive recruitment (*H6*: 79 percent versus 50 percent) and the local community (*H7*: 86 percent versus 50 percent) (see Table 4).

The corporate communications executive of a consumer non-durable goods company emphasized:

> ... again one of the things I've said specifically in Malaysia, the Kulim and Penang area of Malaysia, I think our corporate identity has had a strong impact

Table 3 Multi-item measures

Variables	Measure	Cronbach alpha
Perceived impact of CVIS	A 27-item measure	0.9217
Headquarters control	A 15-item measure	0.7134
Management involvement	A 12-item measure	0.9655

Table 4 Benefits of CVIS standardization

Hypotheses	Variables	Significance level	Result
H1	Sales	$\chi^2 = 5.33$, p = 0.01	Supported
H2	Consumer goodwill	$\chi^2 = 2.51$, p = 0.05	Supported
H3	Consumer's familiarity	$\chi^2 = 4.72$, p = 0.02	Supported
H4	Advertising awareness	$\chi^2 = 4.17$, p = 0.02	Supported
H5	Market share	$\chi^2 = 1.99$, p = 0.07	Supported
H6	Executive recruitment	$\chi^2 = 2.26$, p = 0.06	Supported
H7	Receptivity of locals	$\chi^2 = 3.97$, p = 0.02	Supported
H8	Value of shares	$\chi^2 = 0.00$, p = 0.95	Not supported
H9	Investment rating	$\chi^2 = 0.00$, p = 1.00	Not supported

Note: Yates' correction is used to adjust for small sample cell size.

in the region. I've been here for over 10 years, I understand we do have a good working relationship with the local community and the local and central Malaysian government. Our corporate identity has also helped us in attracting and recruiting brighter and better candidates for our executive positions. We have obtained positive feedback, acceptance and recognition amongst our shareholders, suppliers, employees and the market.

In contrast, companies do not see the favourable impact of standardized CVIS on these stakeholders feeding through to financial markets (*H8* or *H9*). However one corporate marketing executive of a consultancy-based company did see some financial return:

> We have experienced a fairly strong (favourable) visual impact. Being a public company, the shareholders, city analysts, bankers, employees and the customers have conveyed to us that our new CVIS have put us in the forefront in our industry.

Headquarters control and CVIS standardization

Each of the hypotheses linking CVIS standardization with headquarters control is supported. All the companies that adopt a high degree of corporate name also have a high degree of control from head office in the UK. One communication executive of a leading industrial-based company stated:

> ... in all of these, I think very strict views that corporate identity should be tightly controlled centrally. I think you need an international culture in multinational companies now, therefore you need an internationally recognised identity. It (corporate visual identity) is controlled by our internal corporate communications department which I manage. Most of what goes out in terms of literature and so on is approved by either me or by one of my colleagues.

In contrast, among the companies that implement a low degree of name standardization between the UK and Malaysia, only 47 percent had a high degree of control (*H10a*). Similarly, the hypotheses associating headquarters control to the standardization of symbol and/or logotype (*H10b*), typography (*H10c*), colour (*H10d*) and slogan (*H10e*) are supported. A total of 100 percent of companies with a high degree of symbol and/or logotype standardization had a high degree of control from head office with the corresponding figures for typography, colour and slogan being 96, 93 and 86 percent respectively. The corresponding figures for companies with low CVIS standardization are all significantly lower: 36 percent of those with low standardization symbol and/or logotype had a high degree of control from head office, 23 percent for typology, 36 percent for colour and 17 percent for slogan.

Chief executive involvement

In 62 percent of the companies that implement a high degree of CVIS standardization the chairman and/or the chief executive officer is the key internal driving force behind the development of the CVIS. 38 percent of these companies state that 'others', namely, the senior management, and marketing sales or communication executives are the key internal driving forces behind the development of CVIS. In contrast, among the companies with a low degree of CVIS standardization, 86 percent state that 'others' are the key internal driving force behind the development of CVIS. This supports *H11*: the chief executive is the key internal driving force in initiating a high degree of global CVIS standardization (see Table 5).

Hypothesis *H11*, linking high chief executive involvement with a high degree of global CVIS standardization, is similarly well supported. In 81 percent of the companies that adopt a high degree of CVIS standardization, the chief executive officer has been highly involved in CVIS development. The advertising executive of a petroleum company emphasizes that the chairman is the force in their CVIS decisions:

> The key internal driving force and the ultimate control of our CVIS decisions is our chairman. There is a specific message from the chairman explaining why he regards a standardized CVIS as very important.

For the multinational corporations that implement a low degree of CVIS standardization, 64 percent state that the chief executive officer has a low degree of involvement and 36 percent state that the chief executive officer has a high degree of involvement in the development of CVIS.

Subsidiary view of CVIS standardization

Unexpectedly, managers in the Malaysian subsidiaries had similar views on the importance of CVIS standardization, to their counterparts at headquarters. In the headquarters 72 percent felt it important to standardize name, 75 percent symbol/logo, 63 percent typeface, 70 percent colour and 70 percent slogan. The corresponding figures for Malaysian subsidiaries being 80, 81, 63, 75 and 63 percent respectively. The differences between these percentages are not significant so none of hypotheses *H13a* to *H13e* are supported but it is noticeable that for name, symbol and typeface, the Malaysians are more in favour of standards being imposed on them than the headquarters are on imposing them (see Table 6).

DISCUSSION

The perceived benefits of global CVIS standardization are wide: the perceived impact on sales, ability to recruit executives, general consumer goodwill towards the

Table 5 Control and chief executive involvement in CVIS

Hypotheses	Variables	Significance level	Result
Headquarters control			
H10a	Corporate name	$\chi^2 = 13.50$, p = 0.00	Supported
H10b	Symbol/logotype	$\chi^2 = 17.61$, p = 0.00	Supported
H10c	Typography	$\chi^2 = 19.39$, p = 0.00	Supported
H10d	Colour	$\chi^2 = 11.19$, p = 0.00	Supported
H10e	Slogan	$\chi^2 = 6.05$, p = 0.01	Supported
Management involvement			
H11	Chief executive driving force	$\chi^2 = 6.41$, p = 0.01	Supported
H12	Chief executive involvement	$\chi^2 = 6.26$, p = 0.01	Supported

Note: Yates' correction is used to adjust for small sample cell size.

Table 6 Headquarters and local's views compared

Hypotheses	Variables	Significance level	Result
H13a	Corporate name	$\chi^2 = 0.10$, p = 0.75	Not supported
H13b	Symbol/logotype	$\chi^2 = 0.30$, p = 0.51	Not supported
H13c	Typography	$\chi^2 = 0.00$, p = 1.00	Not supported
H13d	Colour	$\chi^2 = 0.01$, p = 0.91	Not supported
H13e	Slogan	$\chi^2 = 0.00$, p = 1.00	Not supported

Note: Yates' correction is used to adjust for small sample cell size.

company, consumers' familiarity with the company and products, consumers' advertising awareness, receptivity of the local inhabitants towards the company's facilities and market share. However, there was no perceived benefit to value of shares or investment rating.

Companies that implement a high degree of CVIS standardization benefit in several ways. Buzzell (1968) and Hovell and Walters (1972) stated that the standardization of marketing presentations is a powerful means of increasing sales. The study suggests that this is also true of CVIS. The findings also supported the proposals by Sorenson and Wiechmann (1975), Pebbles *et al.* (1977) and Lippincott and Margulies (1988) of CVIS standardization enhancing consumers' goodwill and familiarity towards the company, consumers' awareness of the company's advertising and consumers' receptivity towards the company and its products.

Belt and Paolillo (1982), Gray and Smeltzer (1985, 1987) and Olins (1990) suggested that corporate identity can help companies recruit high calibre executives. This study supports that view and extends the findings suggesting that benefits flow to the MNCs who standardize their CVIS. In contrast the results show no relationship between CVIS standardization and financial measures. This suggests that while consumers and potential employees are influenced by the strong and consistent visual presentation of a company, financial institutions personnel are not that well-trained to link CVIS to marketing and business performance.

The global CVIS standardization is not an independent decision but reflects the centralized control of the businesses and top management involvement in CVIS. The relationship between the chief executive and/or chairman and standardization of CVIS reveals two outcomes. First, the chief executive is normally the key internal driving force in initiating a high degree of CVIS standardization. Second, the chief executive who is highly involved in the CVIS development is more likely to be associated with a high degree of CVIS standardization. This suggests that many chief executives who initiate and who are active in the development and implementation of the CVIS perceive that the high standardization strategy exhibits the size, power and strength of the corporation in the light of the global competitive arena.

Surprisingly, headquarters and subsidiary executives had similar views on CVIS standardization. Although the differences between the sample of headquarters and subsidiary executives are not statistically significant, in most cases the subsidiary's managers favour having to follow a standardized CVIS more than the headquarters like imposing one! This enthusiastic acquiescence to headquarters control could be a manifestation of what Singapore's Lee Kuan Yew and Malaysia's Mahathir Mohammed call the 'eastern way' where people happily forego independence to follow the guidance of successful leaders. Maybe the previous literature in this area reflects how Americans or Europeans think they would feel about outsiders imposing standards upon them. Would the results be different if the sample was of American subsidiaries of European companies?

Another explanation of subsidiary executive acceptance of CVIS standardization could be the indoctrination of the multinationals' overseas staff after decades of contact. An international culture permeates multinational corporations where importance is attached to what the head office thinks. Alternatively Anglicization could have occurred after years of colonial and commercial occupation by Britain. The one exception to locals' willingness to conform is the slogan which, because of language, is less easily transferred than a colour or logo. Nevertheless, these findings suggest that subsidiaries are more willing to accept standardized communication than expected.

Implications

These results have several implications for managers. They provide evidence that MNCs that have implemented expensive global CVIS can expect direct returns from the response of customers, employees and the general population. This is particularly important since the rate of technological change means that consumers are increasingly relying upon the reputation, communicated by a firm's CVIS, to guide their purchase decisions. The globalization of all parts of the communications mix faces the tension between the centrifugal forces for localization and the centripetal for standardization. For many marketing communications, legal and consumer differences limit the opportunity to benefit from global standardization. The CVIS is an exception. Its standardization produces benefits, local managers favour its application and its nature lends itself to centralization and control. This has implications for the whole communications mix since it suggests an advantage of global campaigns based on corporate reputations over local product based promotions.

There are subsidiary benefits of these findings. The cost of launching and maintaining brands is now prohibitive even to the largest of companies. When the support has to be stretched across many countries with different advertising needs and regulations, the situation becomes even less tractable. Campaigns aimed at promoting the company, using its CVIS, help stretch budgets across both products and countries. The approach can also help promote products to wealthy and internationally mobile customers who regularly cross boundaries where the rest of the marketing mix has to change.

For managers, the benefits from CVIS standardization are fortunate since it appears that global CVIS standardization is almost an inevitable result of top managers taking an interest in the issue. The link between CVIS standardization is not one of just correlation but is a consequence of CVIS needing to be centrally controlled. The very complexity of MNCs means that if control is to be exerted that will very likely lead to a simple, standardized CVIS. The need to involve the chief executive leads to the same result.

CONCLUSIONS

The degree of control of CVIS decisions in headquarters is related to the degree of CVIS standardization. The higher the degree of control of the CVIS, the higher the degree of standardization. Furthermore, the high CVIS standardization strategy is associated with the centralization of the CVIS decisions. The headquarters controls the decision regarding how the corporate name is presented, how the symbol is designed, how the typography is styled, what colours and slogan to use. Top management, especially the chief executive, are the key figures in the development of the highly standardized strategy. However, CVIS lends itself so strongly to centralization that the mere act of the chief executive and headquarters considering their CVIS could lead to it being standardization globally.

The results here show local managers more in favour of using a standardized CVIS than the headquarters enforcing it. Does this finding just apply to CVIS or even more narrowly to the CVIS of UK MNCs in Malaysia? Have ICI, Shell and Glaxo names that transcend cultural heritage?

Limitations

The pioneering nature of this research leaves it with several limitations and opportunities for further research. Two of the major limitations are to do with scope. Although the headquarters questions were asked in a global context, they were only cross validated in one country: Malaysia. Would the results hold true in other countries without such long lasting relationships with Britain? Particularly the willingness of local managers to accept standardized CVIS imposed from the centre. Is acquiescence of these locals typical of other choices between localization and globalization? Has our concern for local sensitivities resulted in our forgetting the cross-cultural strengths of global brands?

The study is also limited to UK MNCs. Do the results hold for MNCs from other countries? The prominence of brands, such as Mercedes, Kodak and Sony, that use their CVIS to globally promote their products suggests so.

Like previous studies of global standardization, this paper lacks a strong theoretical framework and looks at one element of the corporate context in isolation. The model representing the interplay between centripetal, centrifugal and mediating forces helped in this study and its subjective application to other marketing mix elements suggests it could have broader implications. In it the tension between the headquarters and each local subsidiary are fixed across all activities while the mediating forces determine the level of adaptation to local needs. At one extreme, 'selling' adjusts to each customer in local markets while CVIS exists at the other extreme where the mediating forces encourage global standardization. A further study could determine if the mediating forces vary in unison or independently.

REFERENCES

Aylmer, R.J. (1970), 'Who makes marketing decisions in the multinational firm', *Journal of Marketing*, Vol. 34, October, pp. 25–30.

Baker, M.J., Black, C.D. and Hart, S.J. (1988), 'The competitiveness of British industry: what really makes the difference', *European Journal of Marketing*, Vol. 22 No. 2, pp. 70–85.

Baker, M.J. and Balmer, J.M.T. (1997), 'Visual identity: trappings or substance?', *European Journal of Marketing*, Vol. 31 No. 5/6, pp. 366–82.

Bearden, W.O., Netemeyer, R.G. and Teel. J.E. (1989), 'Measurement of consumer susceptibility to interpersonal influence', *Journal of Consumer Research*, Vol. 15, pp. 473–81.

Belt, J.A. and Paolillo, J.G.P. (1982), 'The influence of corporate image and specificity of candidate qualifications on response to recruitment advertisements', *Journal of Management*, Vol. 8, pp. 105–12.

Brandt, W.K. and Hulbert, J.M. (1977), 'Headquarters guidance in marketing strategy in the multinational subsidiary ', *Columbia Journal of World Business*, Winter, pp. 7–14.

Buckley, P.J., Pass, C.L. and Bruce, K. (1988), 'Measures of international competitiveness: a critical survey', *Journal of Marketing Management*, Vol. 4 No. 2, pp. 175–200.

Buzzell, R.D. (1968), 'Can you standardize multinational marketing?', *Harvard Business Review*, December, pp. 102–13.

Chajet, C. (1989), 'The making of a new corporate image', *Journal of Business Strategy*, May–June, pp. 18–20.

Churchill, G.A. (1979), 'A paradigm for developing better measures of marketing constructs', *Journal of Marketing Research*, February, pp. 64–73.

Cochran, W.G. (1965), *Sampling Techniques*, John Wiley, New York, NY.

D'Antin, P. (1971), 'The Nestlé product manager as demigod', *European Business*, Vol. 6, Spring, pp. 41 and 49.

Das, R. (1981), 'Impact of host government regulations on MNC operations: learning from third world countries', *Columbia Journal of World Business*, Vol. 16, Spring, pp. 85–90.

Douglas, S.P. and Wind, Y. (1987), 'The myth of globalization', *Columbia Journal of World Business*, Vol. 22 No. 4, pp. 19–29.

Downey, S.M. (1986), 'The relationship between corporate culture and corporate identity', *Public Relations Quarterly*, Vol. 31 No. 4, pp. 7–12.

Dowling, G. (1994), *Corporate Reputations: Strategies for Developing the Corporate Brand*, Kogan Page, London.

Doyle, P., Saunders, J. and Wong, V. (1986), 'A comparative investigation of Japanese marketing strategies in the British market', *Journal of International Business Studies* Spring, pp. 27–46.

Doz, Y.L. (1988), 'Strategic management in multinational companies', *Sloan Management Review*, Winter, pp. 27–46.

Eales, R. (1990), 'Multinational report: multinational corporate communications, a growth sector', *Multinational Business*, Vol. 4, pp. 28–31.

Gorb, P. (1980), *Design Talk*, The Design Council, London.

Gray, E.R. and Smeltzer, L.R. (1987), 'Planning a facelift: implementing a corporate image program', *The Journal of Business Strategy*, Vol. 8 No. 1, pp. 4–10.

Gray, E.R. and Smeltzer, L.R. (1985), 'SMR Forum – corporate image – an integral part of strategy', *Sloan Management Review*, Summer pp. 73–8.

Green, P., Tull, D.S. and Albaum, G. (1988), *Research for Marketing Decisions*, Prentice-Hall, Hemel Hempstead.

Harris, G. (1984), 'The globalization of advertising', *International Journal of Advertising*, Vol. 3, pp. 223–34.

Hartigan, M.F. (1987), 'A company study organizing for global identity', *Journal of Business and Industrial Marketing*, Vol. 2 No. 3, Summer, pp. 65–73.

Hovell, P.J. and Walters, P.G.P. (1972), 'International marketing presentations: some options', *European Journal of Marketing*, Vol. 6 No. 2, pp. 67–79.

Ind, N. (1992), *The Corporate Image: Strategies for Effective Identity Programs*, Kogan Page, London.

Jain, S.C. (1989), 'Standardization of international marketing strategy: some research hypotheses', *Journal of Marketing*, Vol. 53, January, pp. 70–9.

Johne, F.A. and Snelson, P. (1989), 'Product development approaches in established firms', *Industrial Marketing Management*, Vol. 18 No. 2, pp. 113–24.

Kirpalani, V.H., Laroche, M. and Darmon, R.Y. (1988), 'Role of headquarters control by multinationals in international advertising decisions', *International Journal of Advertising*, Vol. 7, pp. 323–33.

Lichtenstein, D.R. Netemeyer, R.G. and Burton, S. (1990), 'Distinguishing coupon proneness from value consciousness: an acquisition-transaction utility theory perspective', *Journal of Marketing*, Vol. 54, pp. 54–67.

Lippincott, A. and Margulies, W. (1988), *America's Global Identity Crisis 2: Japan and Europe Move Ahead*, Lippincott and Margulies Inc., New York, NY.

Margulies W.P. (1977), 'Make the most of your corporate identity', *Harvard Business Review*, July–August, pp. 66–74.

Mills, J.T. (1988), 'Why this Report', in Simpson, M. (Ed.), *Corporate Identity: Name, Image and Perception*, The Conference Board, 898, USA.

Nowakowski, C.A. (1982), 'International performance measurements', *Columbia Journal of World Business*, Vol. 17, Summer, pp. 53–7.

Nunnally, J.C. (1967), *Psychometric Theory*, McGraw-Hill, New York, NY.

Olins, W. (1986), *Corporate Identity: Making Business Strategy Visible Through Design*, Thames and Hudson, London.

Olins, W. (1990), *The Wolf Olins Guide to Corporate Identity*, Design Council, London.

Onkvisit, S. and Shaw, J.J. (1985), 'A view of marketing and advertising practices in Asia and its meaning for marketing managers', *Journal of Consumer Marketing*, Vol. 2, pp. 5–17.

Peebles, D.M., Ryans, K. and Vernon, I.R. (1977), 'A new perspective on advertising standardization', *European Journal of Marketing*, Vol. 11, pp. 569–76.

Pilditch, J. (1970), *Communication By Design: A Study in Corporate Identity*, McGraw-Hill, New York, NY.

Quelch, J.A. and Hoff, E.J. (1986), 'Customising global marketing', *Harvard Business Review*, Vol. 64, May–June, pp. 59–68.

Reynolds, J. (1987), 'Developing policy responses to cultural differences', *Business Horizons*, Vol. 21, August, pp. 30–4.

Roostal, I. (1963), 'Standardization of advertising for Western Europe', *Journal of Marketing*, Vol. 3, pp. 15–20.

Samiee, S. and Roth, K. (1992), 'The influence of global marketing standardization on performance', *Journal of Marketing*, Vol. 56, pp. 1–7.

Saunders, J. (1994), *The Marketing Initiative: Economic and Social Research Council Studies into British Marketing*, Prentice-Hall, Hemel Hempstead, UK.

Smith, P.J. (1990), 'How to present your firm to the world', *The Journal of Business Strategy*, January–February, pp. 32–6.

Sorenson, R.Z. and Wiechmann, U.E. (1975), 'How multinationals view marketing standardization', *Harvard Business Review*, Vol. 53, May–June, pp. 38–54 and pp. 166–67.

Strong, F.P. (1990), 'A company study: Kodak beyond 1990', *Journal of Business and Industrial Marketing*, Vol. 2 No. 4, pp. 29–36.

Topalian, A. (1984), 'Corporate identity: beyond the visual overstatements', *International Journal of Advertising*, Vol. 3, pp. 55-62.

Wiechmann, U. (1974), 'Integrating multinational marketing activities', *Columbia Journal of World Business*, Winter, pp. 7–16.

Wills, J.R. and Ryans, J.K. Jr (1977), 'An analysis of headquarters executive involvement in international advertising', *European Journal of Marketing*, Vol. 11 No. 8, pp. 577–84.

Yip, G.S. (1988), 'Global strategy . . . in world of nations?', *Sloan Management Review*, Vol. 4, pp. 29–41.

Melewar, T. C. and Saunders, J. (1998) 'Global corporate visual identity systems: standardization, control and benefits'. *International Marketing Review*, 15(4): 291–308. Reproduced with permission.

Section 2
Advertising – Creativity and Effectiveness

Despite the drive for integrated communication and the rise in importance of other communication tools, 'advertising' is still at the heart of many marketing communication programmes and advertising expenditure world-wide is still rising in real terms. It is the 'sexy' end of marketing and is certainly the most visible and memorable. For individual companies, especially in the consumer goods field, advertising still absorbs the greatest individual share of the communications budget (about 25–30 per cent). Also, it forms the core offering of most large communication agencies and (in terms of texts and writings) is probably the largest single area of marketing. As a subject in marketing communications it simply cannot be ignored. Thus, the rationale for the inclusion of a section or two on advertising is self-evident. The papers are divided into two key aspects of advertising: what works and how it works are covered in Section 2 and the comparison of various media and the client–agency relationship are covered in Section 3 (q.v.).

Vaughn (1986) is probably the best known and most quoted work in its field. Using a model from the Foote Cone Belding agency, Vaughn suggests that the type of advertising that works can be determined by consideration of where a product is positioned on two key dimensions – level of product involvement and level of emotional commitment. In this paper Vaughn updates his 1980[1] conceptual paper with the addition of some empirical findings. While grounded in the psychological, consumer behaviour and hierarchy of effects literature, the resultant model still has a great deal of intuitive appeal. Rossiter, Percy and Donovan (1991), in an equally well known (although essentially conceptual) article, extend the Vaughn work, suggesting that the FCG grid only addresses brand attitude and that brand awareness is a necessary element to effectively define the appropriate type of advertising vehicle. One of the underpinnings of the Vaughn paper – the hierarchy of effects model – is discussed fully in the Barry and Howard (1990) paper. Starting with a review ranging from the AIDA model of the early 1900s to the ACALTA model of the 1970s, these authors offer criticisms of the model, the most damning of which is lack of empirical verification. However, they conclude that, even without this validation, the model may be used as an heuristic for planning and guidance of advertising (and other marketing communications).

We open the discussion of advertising effectiveness with another true classic, Lavidge and Steiner (1961). Linking the various advertising media and sales promotional tools to the various stages in a hierarchy of effects model, the authors suggest appropriate measures to evaluate the effectiveness of those tools. Although conceptual in nature this article makes a great deal of intuitive sense and, based on citations, has certainly been an influential article. In another frequently quoted article, Abraham & Lodish (1990) attempt to add an empirical dimension to the argument by using a longitudinal study to 'examine the productivity of the marketing dollar . . .'. In doing so they offer insights into that most difficult of tasks – measurement of communications effectiveness. Stone and Duffy (1993) is written from a practitioner's (rather than academic's) viewpoint and explores how and why Kraft use advertising, how much they spend and how they measure the effectiveness of that spend. As a single case it offers good insights, not only into that one approach, but also into the problems of measuring advertising effectiveness in general.

Factors that are traditionally argued as being related to effectiveness (i.e. reaching the intended target with the intended message) are things like style, content, format, etc. There are, especially in today's business environment, other issues to consider. For example, one key environmental issue affecting advertising is that of globalization of industries and companies and the standardization versus localization arguments. Applebaum and Halliburton (1993) address this issue in the European food and beverage sector. Testing such factors as positioning, advertising appeal, tone and format and the use of music, they move the argument from one of opinion to one based on empirical evidence. We will not steal their thunder by too detailed a summary here. Following on, consumer responses to advertisements are identified, by Jaffe and Berger (1988), to vary by respondent gender and the gender orientation of the advertisement. This paper directly addresses an issue often missed in advertising literature, but which is of increasing importance in a world where women's spending power is equal to men's.

This collection of papers pulls together some key issues in advertising. The first three papers address the conceptual underpinnings of effective advertising and are followed by articles looking at effectiveness from a more empirical perspective. The section concludes with two papers looking at specific factors – globalisation and gender – and how they impact on consumers' interpretations of advertising.

NOTES

1   Vaughn, R., 1980, 'How Advertising Works: A Planning Model', *Journal of Advertising Research*, 20(5): 27–33.

How advertising works: a planning model revisited 2.1

Richard Vaughn

In response to a need for strategic discipline and creative stimulation during advertising planning, Foote, Cone & Belding explored and developed a comprehensive communication model (Vaughn, 1980). Building upon traditional consumer response theories (Kotler, 1965) and the hierarchy-of-effects model and its variants (Lavidge and Steiner, 1961; Robertson, 1970), this new model combined high–low involvement and left–right brain specialization. The result was a visually coherent and intriguing matrix (see Figure 1)

The advertising planning propositions inherent in the quadrants in Figure 1 suggested that communication response would certainly be different for high versus low involvement products/services and those which required predominantly thinking (left brain) or feeling (right brain) information processing. This map was not only

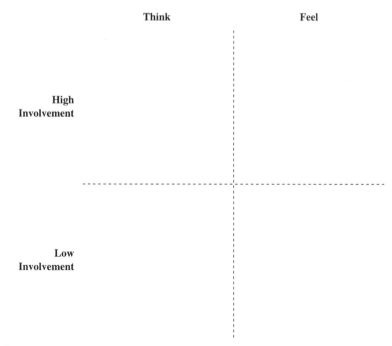

Figure 1

intuitively appealing; it conveniently helped place Kotler's consumer response theories in useful perspective and also provided niches for several low involvement models (Ray, 1973; Robertson, 1976) developed to explain consumer behavior which did not follow the learn–feel–do sequence of the basic hierarchy-of-effects.

Now identified simply as the FCB Grid (Berger, 1985), this planning model delineates four primary advertising planning strategies – 'informative,' 'affective,' 'habitual,' and 'satisfaction,' with their most appropriate traditional and variant hierarchy-of-effects models (see Figure 2).

Quadrant 1. The *informative* strategy is for highly involving products/services where thinking and economic considerations prevail. The classical hierarchy-of-effects sequence – awareness → knowledge → liking → preference → conviction → purchase – abbreviated to 'learn → feel → do' – is the designated model for such big-ticket items as cars, appliances, and insurance.

Quadrant 2. The *affective* strategy is for highly involving and feeling purchases, those more psychological products fulfilling self-esteem, subconscious, and ego-related impulses requiring perhaps more emotional communication. A variant hierarchy putting 'feel' before 'learn' and 'do' is the priority for such products as cosmetics, jewelry, and fashion clothing.

Quadrant 3. The *habitual* strategy is for those low involvement and thinking products with such routinized consumer behavior that learning occurs most often after exploratory trial buying. This implies a responsive, behavioral learning-by-doing. Although some minimal level of awareness may precede purchase, deeper learning is not necessary for such commodity decisions as paper products, household cleaners or gasoline.

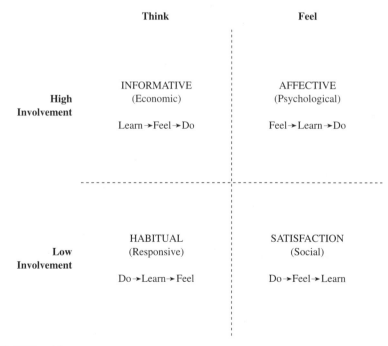

Figure 2 FCB grid.

Quadrant 4. The *satisfaction* strategy is for low involvement/feeling products, items of personal taste, 'life's little pleasures' such as beer, cigarettes, and candy. A social model is useful for many of these peer-oriented items, and the hierarchy places 'do' before 'feel' and 'learn' because product experience is so necessary a part of the communication process.

Reaction to the grid was positive and enthusiastic. Despite, or perhaps because of, its simplicity many advertisers accepted it as a practical, creative way around the overutilization of the classical learn → feel → do hierarchy model in *all* advertising strategy planning. Even in its earliest applications, the grid:

- helped organize available research and management opinions about category and brand placement in consumer involvement and think–feel terms;
- stimulated insightful questions and hypotheses about a product's advertising options in the context of the competitive situation;
- and brought previously unconsidered emotional, nonverbal, and sensory strategic possibilities into legitimate contention with rational, verbal, and semantically more powerful suggestions.

Because the grid managed to condense almost three decades of consumer behavior theory into a practical format, it worked surprisingly well in a variety of problem-solving situations. It was even pointed out that the grid itself exemplified the unity of left–right brain complementarity in being both verbal and visual, thereby virtually compelling a new way of approaching strategic planning for even a long-established product.

It was also apparent, however, that some preliminary implications of the grid in several areas were premature if not unrealistic. For example, specific creative, media, and copy-test activities were proposed for each strategic quadrant before it was sensibly realized just how category or brand-specific such issues were. Also, think and feel were mistakenly viewed as independent rather than complementary and interrelated. One particularly flamboyant bit of generalization suggested that high involvement or think-oriented products would naturally decay over time to low involvement or feel.

These impractical hypotheses were abandoned during early, judgmental applications of the grid, but two questions did emerge which could not be ignored with grid experience:

1. Did the grid accurately depict real consumer involvement and think–feel dimensions?
2. Where were major product categories actually located in grid space?

The value of the grid in providing workable strategic solutions had been demonstrated in several advertising success stories, but FCB nevertheless undertook an extensive research and development program (Ratchford, 1985). A considerable effort went into operationalizing involvement and think–feel, and eventually eight scales were accepted:

Involvement
- Very important/unimportant decision
- Lot/little to lose if you choose the wrong brand
- Decision requires lot/little thought

Think
- Decision is/is not mainly logical or objective
- Decision is/is not based mainly on functional facts

Feel
- Decision is/is not based on a lot of feeling
- Decision does/does not express one's personality
- Decision is/is not based on looks, taste, touch, smell, or sound (sensory effects)

The primary grid validation study was conducted in the United States among 1,800 consumers across some 250 product categories. Respondents rated recently purchased products/services using the eight scales, which permitted grid mapping on the basis of involvement and think–feel dimensionality. Ten representative categories are illustrated in Figure 3.

Products and services plotted where reasonably expected; analysis of individual scale scores helped profile which construct had contributed most to category location. And, as a quality control check on the test instrument, the scales were correlated by factor (see Table 1). Some think and feel items correlated with involvement, which confirmed that it was possible to have varying amounts of think and feel – high or low – depending on involvement. The involvement and think–feel factors, however, worked very well in discriminating consumers' product-decision space.

To date, over 20,000 consumer interviews have been completed in 23 countries. Correlations of common products were computed between pairs of countries and were

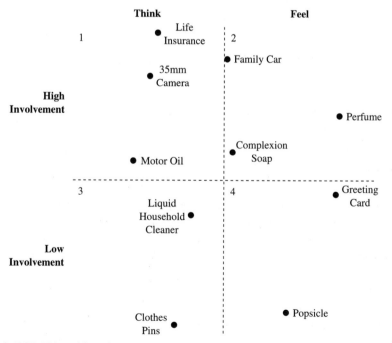

Figure 3 FCB U.S. grid study.

Table 1 FCB U.S. grid study – factor correlations

	Involvement	Think/Feel
Important	.96	.03
Lose	.90	− .03
Thought	.97	.12
Logical/objective	.93	− .28
Functional facts	.75	− .50
Feeling	.70	.66
Personality	.47	.80
Sensory effects	− .47	.65

quite high, which told us that consumer mental processes were similar over the marketing world despite necessary concessions to communication distinctions in advertising.

Previous judgmental use of the grid had included not only category plotting but exploratory placement of brands as well. Major grid studies provided large sample sizes for brand plotting, as shown in Figure 4 for aspirin brands.

It was also practical and stimulating to cluster consumers around a category plot. Obviously not everyone placed each category at the mean. A typical three-cluster solution produced dispersions much like the example shown in Figure 5. Examining different involvement and think/feel scores for these clusters, and their brand preferences, helped isolate new strategic advertising options.

And, in a follow-up to the U.S. grid study, it was also possible to plot characteristics for selected categories. Derived from prior research and brainstorming,

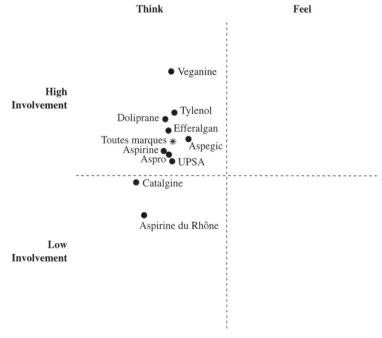

Figure 4 Headache remedy – France.

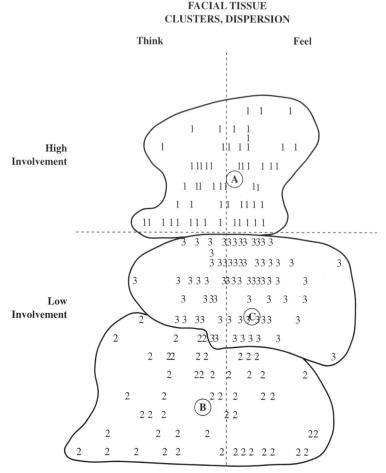

Figure 5 Headache remedy clusters, dispersion.

category and brand attributes were scaled for involvement and think-feel. As shown in Figure 6, the wine attributes that were most involving and feeling-oriented (upper right skew) were the most useful in differentiating consumer brand preferences.

While brand and attribute mapping are far from unique, having such analysis anchored to a strategic planning model is extremely useful in advertising development. The linkage to consumer decision processes reassures that the executional options are being created in a relevant context and that final advertising is more likely to be motivating.

Despite the successful application of the grid in planning advertising, we have nonetheless continued to speculate about the involvement and think-feel dimensions. Fortunately, many others are doing so as well. For example, while the FCB grid defines involvement in the context of a consumer's purchase decision, it is clear that it could also be defined in the purchase situation or in product consumption (Kassarjian, 1981).

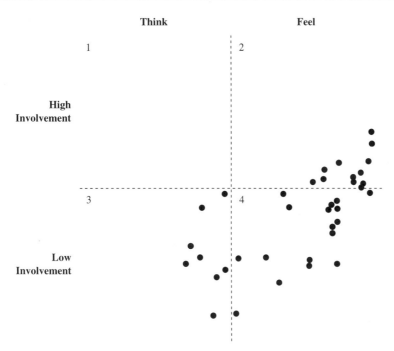

Figure 6 Wine for dinner parties – attributes.

Since the grid is often used to reflect on previous consumer research as well as current marketing judgments about a product's positioning and advertising opportunities, it is important to be flexible and insightful about consumer involvement. The real question often is not how much involvement but what kind and what it means. Recent projects by Laurent and Kapferer (1985) and Slama and Tashchian (1985) are promising in their exploration of an array of involvement elements.

The think–feel dimension is more problematic. While split-brain research supports specialized cognitive and affective mental styles, it is also recognized that the brain is actually a unified system (Levy, 1981) that integrates complex stimuli and adroitly manages both information and emotion. But most discussion of this topic in the marketing literature has been metaphorical rather than empirical.

Some advertising applications (Hansen, 1978; Appel, 1979; Krugman, 1980; Weinstein, 1982) suggest that what we may be contending with, in its simplest communication form, is a verbal/nonverbal and semantic/sensory continuum that allows people to integrate information and emotion as necessary.

Perhaps the best that can be said at this time is that emotion has at least become a legitimate topic for discussion in making effective advertisements (Zajonc, 1982; Holbrook and O'Shaughnessy, 1984; Stout and Leckenby, 1984), and there is also renewed interest in nonverbal elements in advertising (Watson, 1979; Childers, 1984; Haley, 1984).

While there is still much to be learned about thinking and feeling in advertising, the distinction made by Holbrook (1978) between 'logical, objectively verifiable descriptions of tangible product features' and 'emotional, subjective impressions of intangible aspects of the product' are fundamentally important for anyone confronting the uncertainties of advertising strategy and the perplexities of creative executions.

Other work continues on the hierarchy-of-effects model (Preston and Thorson, 1984), behavior-oriented consumer learning models (Nord, 1980; Rothschild, 1981), and attitude-dominant (Mitchell, 1981; Shimp, 1981) consumer models to further our understanding of how advertising works. Moran (1985) has put forth a computer microchip analogy with various consumer processing paths activated toward purchases much the way energy flows through a microcircuit, clearing gates and following channels set by consumer needs and advertising response.

Regardless of how these further explorations come out, thus far the FCB Grid has helped to break through a previously rigid strategic barrier and become more expansive and creative in developing advertising. It has made strategic creative planning more relevant in terms of potential consumer response and stimulated more exciting executions. It has done so largely by opening up the advertising planning discussion to how advertising works. Strategists have isolated rational versus emotional appeals, suggested involvement-raising options, and considered moving a brand in consumer perception – all within the context of a unified model of advertising effectiveness.

We may not now, or ever, know definitely how advertising works. But we do know it works in some definable ways well enough to make more effective advertising. The FCB grid has proved useful in that effort and continues to grow in the hands of diligent and inspired advertising people.

REFERENCES

Appel, Valentine; Sidney Weinstein; and Curt Weinstein. 'Brain Activity and Recall of TV Advertising.' *Journal of Advertising Research* 19, 4 (1979): 7–15.

Berger, David, 'The FCB Grid.' In *Proceedings of the Advertising Research Foundation 31st Annual Conference*, March 1985.

Childers, Terry L., and Michael J. Houston. 'Conditions for Picture-Superiority Effect on Consumer Memory.' *Journal of Consumer Research* 11 (September 1984): 643–653.

Haley, Russell I.; Jack Richardson; and Beth M. Baldwin. 'The Effects of Non-Verbal Communications in Television Advertising.' *Journal of Advertising Research* 24, 4 (1984): 11–18.

Hansen, Fleming. 'Hemispheral Lateralization: Implications for Understanding Consumer Behavior.' *Journal of Consumer Research* 8 (June 1981): 23–36.

Holbrook, Morris, B. 'Beyond Attitude Structure Toward the Informational Determinants of Attitude.' *Journal of Marketing Research* 15 (1978): 545–556.

Holbrook, Morris B., and John O'Shaughnessy. 'The Role of Emotion in Advertising.' *Psychology & Marketing* 1, 2 (Summer 1984): 45–64.

Kassarjian, H. H. 'Low Involvement – A Second Look.' In *Advances in Consumer Research*, Vol. 8, K. B. Monroe, ed. Ann Arbor, MI: Association for Consumer Research, 1981.

Kotler, Philip. 'Behavioral Models for Analyzing Buyers.' *Journal of Marketing* 29 (1965): 37–45.

Krugman, Herbert E. 'Point of View: Sustained Viewing of Television.' *Journal of Advertising Research* 20, 3 (1980): 65–68.

Laurent, Gilles, and Jean-Noel Kapferer. 'Measuring Consumer Involvement Profiles,' *Journal of Marketing Research* 22, 1 (1985): 41–53.

Lavidge, R., and G. A. Steiner. 'A Model For Predictive Measurements of Advertising Effectiveness.' *Journal of Marketing* 25 (1961): 59–62.

Levy, Jerre. 'Children Think With Whole Brains: The Myth and Reality of Hemisphere Difference and Inter-hemispheric Integration.' Paper presented at the conference of *The National Association of Secondary School Principles*, November 1981.

Mitchell, Andrew A., and Jerry C. Olson. 'Are Product Attribute Beliefs the Only Mediator of Advertising Effects of Brand Attitude?' *Journal of Marketing Research* 18 (1981): 318–332.

Moran, William T. 'The Circuit of Effects in Tracking Advertising Profitability.' *Journal of Advertising Research* 25, 1 (1985): 25–29.

Nord, Walter R., and J. Paul Peter. 'A Behavior Modification Perspective on Marketing.' *Journal of Marketing* 44 (1980): 36–47.

Preston, Ivan L., and Esther Thorson. 'The Expanded Association Model: Keeping the Hierarchy Concept Alive.' *Journal of Advertising Research* 24, 1 (1984): 59–65.

Ray, Michael L. 'Marketing Communication and the Hierarchy-of-Effects.' *Sage Annual Review of Communication Research*, F. Kline, ed, 1973.

Ratchford, Brian S. 'Operationalizing Involvement and Thinking/Feeling Dimensionality in the FCB Grid.' Working Paper, 1985.

Robertson, T. S. 'Low Commitment Consumer Behavior.' *Journal of Advertising Research* 16, 2 (1976): 19–24.

——. *Consumer Behavior*. Scott, Foresman & Co., 1970.

Rothschild, Michael L., and William C. Gaidis. 'Behavioral Learning Theory: Its Relevance to Marketing and Promotions.' *Journal of Marketing* 45 (1981): 70–78.

Shimp, T. A. 'Attitude Toward the Ad as a Mediator of Consumer Brand Choice.' *Journal of Advertising* 10, 2 (1981): 9–15.

Slama, Mark E., and Armen Taschian. 'Selected Socio-economic and Demographic Characteristics Associated with Purchasing Involvement.' *Journal of Marketing* 49 (1985): 72–82.

Stout, Patricia, and John D. Leckenby. 'The Rediscovery of Emotional Response in Copy Research.' In *Proceedings: American Academy of Advertising*, 1984.

Vaughn, Richard. 'How Advertising Works: A Planning Model.' *Journal of Advertising Research* 20, 5 (1980): 27–33.

Watson, P. J., and R. J. Gatchel. 'Autonomic Measures of Advertising.' *Journal of Advertising Research* 19, 3 (1979): 15–26.

Weinstein, Sidney. 'A Review of Brain Hemisphere Research.' *Journal of Advertising Research* 22, 3 (1982): 59–63.

Zajonc, R. B., and H. Markus. 'Affective and Cognitive Factors in Preferences.' *Journal of Consumer Research* 9 (1982): 123–131.

Vaughn, R. (1986) 'How advertising works: a planning model revisited'. *Journal of Advertising Research*, February/March: 57–66. Reproduced with permission.

2.2 A better advertising planning grid

John R. Rossiter, Larry Percy and Robert J. Donovan

There is much debate and conflicting evidence about 'how ads work.' What is clear is that there is no *one* way in which ads work. Rather, it depends on the advertising situation: the type of product, the nature of the target audience, and the purchase motivation for buying the brand are some of the major factors that determine what type of ad will work best. For certain products, a single-fact 'USP' ad may be most effective (e.g., Crest toothpaste), whereas for others an 'image' ad with no explicit copy claims may be most effective (e.g., Coca-Cola). Moreover, situations where the target audience is highly involved with the purchase decision may require ads with multiple, convincing claims (e.g., first purchase of a personal computer), whereas situations of low purchase involvement (e.g., repeat purchase of bathroom tissues) may most effectively use ads with rather 'peripheral' content (Petty and Cacioppo, 1986), such as a celebrity presenter or an exaggerated humorous approach as in the Mr Whipple ads for Charmin tissues. Gone are the days when a single model, such as ACCA or AIDA or Ehrenberg's (1974) ATR model, to name just a few, would suffice for the advertising manager. Rather, the manager now needs a more comprehensive model which accounts for the major *differences* in how ads work depending on the advertising situation.

In particular, models expressed in the relatively simple descriptive 'grid' format are very likely to be used by managers; witness the persistent popularity in marketing texts and executive seminars of the Boston Consulting Group's 'growth-share' grid ('Stars,' 'Problem Children,' 'Cash Cows,' and 'Dogs') which the originators, incidentally, have considerably updated. Despite the risk of oversimplification, the grid format is easily grasped and will stimulate the manager – in the case of advertising, the product manager, advertising planner, or creative director – to think about major options that might otherwise be ignored in an intuitive planning process. The well-known FCB advertising planning grid (Vaughn, 1980, 1986; Ratchford, 1987; Ratchford and Vaughn, 1989) has played this valuable role over the past decade.

Our purpose in this article is to present and discuss a newer and improved alternative advertising planning grid based on the work of Rossiter and Percy (1987), which we call the Rossiter-Percy Grid. The paper is divided into five sections which discuss the advantages of the Rossiter-Percy Grid while at the same time pointing out the limitations of the FCB Grid. These sections discuss: (1) brand awareness as a necessary precursor to brand attitude; (2) the involvement dimension of brand attitude; (3) the motivational dimension of brand attitude; (4) advertising tactics based on the grids; and (5) theoretical extensions of the Rossiter-Percy Grid.

BRAND AWARENESS AS A NECESSARY PRECURSOR TO BRAND ATTITUDE

The FCB Grid (see Figure 1) and the main part of the Rossiter-Percy Grid (see Figure 2) are essentially models of attitude (representing how consumers evaluate products or brands). The FCB Grid dimensionalizes consumers' attitudes (toward products) in terms of two dimensions, 'involvement' and 'think–feel,' and the Rossiter-Percy Grid dimensionalizes consumers' attitudes (toward products and brands) in terms of two dimensions, 'involvement' and 'type of motivation.' These attitude dimensions are discussed later since our first point is more fundamental.

The Rossiter-Percy Grid posits *brand awareness* as a necessary communication objective for advertising, *prior* to brand attitude (whereas the FCB Grid is an attitude-only model). Especially in today's commercially cluttered environment, with so many brands to choose between, it is no use advertising to develop a favorable consumer

Figure 1 The FCB Grid.
Note that *higher* involvement is toward the *top* of the vertical axis and both dimensions are continua. The Rossiter-Percy Grid has the high-involvement quadrants at the bottom. (*Source*: Ratchford, 1987, p. 31.)

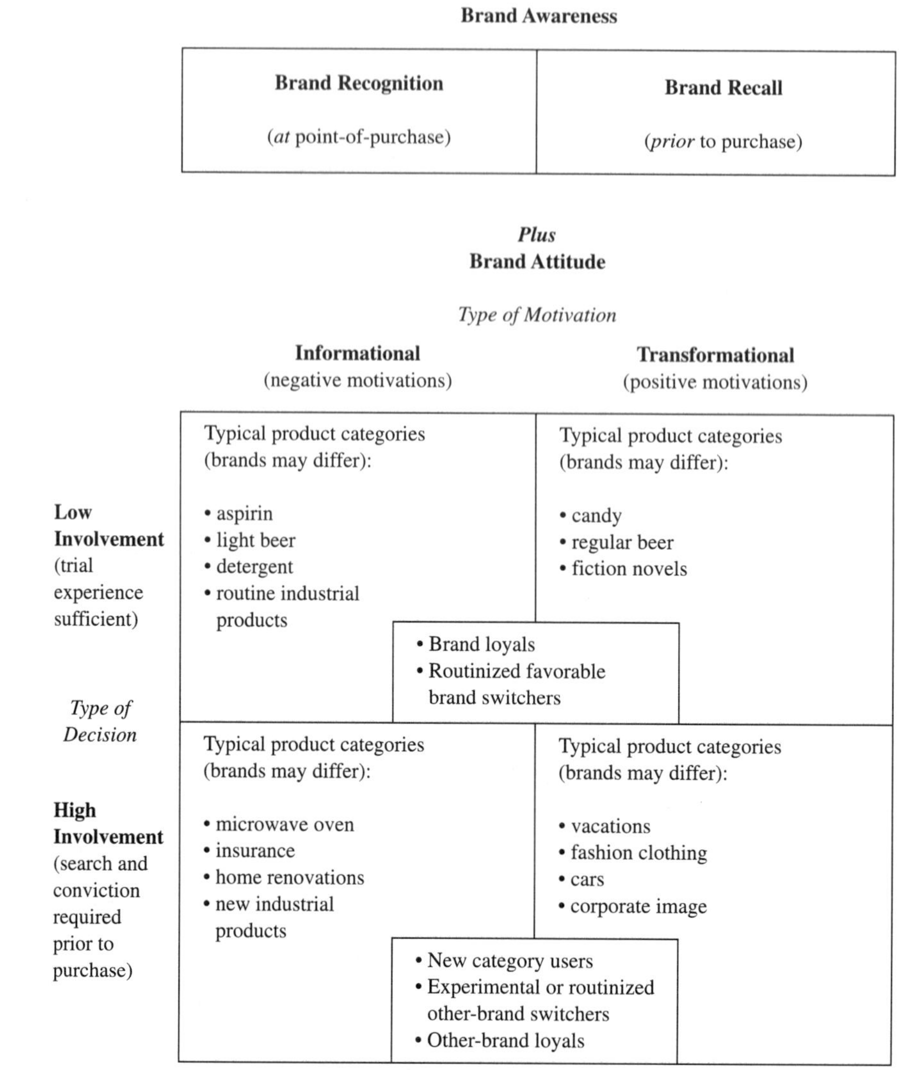

Brand Awareness
Brand Recognition
(*at* point-of-purchase)
Brand Recall
(*prior* to purchase)
Plus
Brand Attitude
Type of Motivation
Informational
(negative motivations)
Transformational
(positive motivations)
Low Involvement (trial experience sufficient)
Type of Decision
High Involvement (search and conviction required prior to purchase)
Typical product categories (brands may differ):
• aspirin
• light beer
• detergent
• routine industrial products
Typical product categories (brands may differ):
• candy
• regular beer
• fiction novels
• Brand loyals
• Routinized favorable brand switchers
Typical product categories (brands may differ):
• microwave oven
• insurance
• home renovations
• new industrial products
Typical product categories (brands may differ):
• vacations
• fashion clothing
• cars
• corporate image
• New category users
• Experimental or routinized other-brand switchers
• Other-brand loyals

Figure 2 The Rossiter-Percy Grid.

attitude toward a product or brand unless the advertising first makes the consumer reliably aware of the brand either before or when in the choice situation. Brand attitude without prior brand awareness is an insufficient advertising communication objective. The fundamental advertising communication objectives are to maximize brand attitude *given* brand awareness (that is, to maximize brand attitude *conditional on* the prior establishment of brand awareness). It may also be noted that the most successful new-product market share or sales-prediction models, such as ASSESSOR (Urban and Katz, 1983) and NEWS (Wilson, Pringle, and Brody, 1982), begin with brand awareness as the initial communication objective of advertising.

As shown in Figure 2, the Rossiter-Percy approach distinguishes brand awareness in terms of brand recognition, where the brand is chosen *at* the point of purchase, and brand recall, where the brand, in order to be chosen, must be remembered *before* the point of purchase. Table 1 shows the advertising creative tactics recommended for the two types of brand awareness in the Rossiter-Percy Grid. When the brand awareness communication objective depends on *brand recognition*, the creative executions should show the package or the visually recognizable brand name; moreover, for a new brand, the package or name should be shown in (associated with) the category-need context. On the other hand, when the brand awareness communication objective depends on *brand recall*, the advertising executions must encourage associative learning (Allen and Janiszewski, 1989) between the category need and the brand name, since our brand's name is but one brand name that will be trying to 'attach itself' to the category need in the consumer's memory. Various other devices, such as bizarre executions and jingles, are also recommended for specific types of advertising where they may be appropriate to increase brand recall.

The first way in which the Rossiter-Percy Grid is an improved planning model, therefore, is that it incorporates the prior step of brand awareness. Without brand awareness, the management and creative effort put into generating brand attitude is in vain because the attitude can never be operational.

THE INVOLVEMENT DIMENSION OF ATTITUDE

It is now widely accepted that purchase decisions differ according to the consumer's level of *involvement* in making the product or brand choice and that involvement is most evidently manifest in the complexity or simplicity of attitudes formed and held toward the product or brand.

The FCB Grid implies a somewhat mixed conceptualization of 'involvement.' Its measure of involvement (Ratchford, 1987) asks consumers to 'Please rate the process of choosing a brand of (product) on each of the following scales. Please base your rating on your most recent choice of a brand of (product).' The three scales defining involvement encompass decision importance, degree of thought required (note the

Table 1 Brand awareness tactics with specific tactics for brand recognition and brand recall

Brand awareness: general tactics
1. Determine the predominant type of brand awareness for the target audience.
2. Match the ad's brand awareness stimuli with buyer response.
3. Seek a unique advertising execution.
4. Maximize brand awareness contact time.

Brand recognition tactics	*Brand recall tactics*
a. Ensure sufficient exposure of the brand package and the name in the ad.	a. Associate the category need and the brand in the main copy line.
b. The category need should be mentioned or portrayed (unless immediately obvious).	b. Keep the main copy line short.
c. After the initial burst, less media frequency is needed for brand recognition (though check brand attitude strategy first).	c. Use repetition of the main copy line for brand recall.
	d. Include a personal reference (unless it is already strongly implied).
	e. Use a bizarre execution (as long as it is appropriate to brand attitude).
	f. (For broadcast ads) a jingle may increase brand recall.
	g. Requires high media frequency relative to competitors.

possible confounding here with the 'think–feel' dimension), and perceived risk of choosing the wrong brand. The respondent sample is confined to those who have bought the product category at least once in the past, and the involvement ratings are averaged across all respondents.

This approach confuses product-category involvement, brand-choice involvement, and the differential perceived risk experienced by target audiences who differ in their experience or familiarity with the product category and brand. The Rossiter-Percy Grid, in contrast, defines involvement purely in terms of perceived risk (Nelson, 1970). Specifically, involvement is defined as the risk perceived by the typical *target audience* member – who could range from a completely naive noncategory user to a very experienced loyal buyer of the brand – in choosing *this* brand on *this* (the next) purchase occasion.

The FCB conceptualization of involvement is inadequate on at least three counts. Firstly, a consumer could be quite an experienced buyer of the product category such that it has become low involvement, yet become highly involved when a new brand enters the category (see also Howard's 1977 model of Limited Problem Solving). Therefore, the first factor in which involvement with the brand purchase decision must vary is target-audience familiarity, which translates into knowledge or 'ability to choose.' As Gensch and Javalgi (1987) have shown, experienced consumers and inexperienced consumers have quite different choice processes, and, from an advertising communications standpoint, it seems obvious that a consumer who has never heard of the brand must acquire more communication effects and become more involved in the choice than a consumer who is a regular buyer of that brand. The FCB Grid makes no such distinction between target-audience types. Rather, Ratchford (1987) offers only the general caveat that 'readers should be aware that there is considerable dispersion of individual responses around the means for some products.' The FCB Grid proposes no conceptual basis for consumer differences.

The second problem with the FCB conceptualization of involvement is that it confuses product-category involvement with various brands' involvement. By the argument above, if consumers differ in their involvement in choosing a given brand, then brands too must differ in their 'involvement rating' depending on the target audience in question. The FCB Grid plots gross product-category involvement across all users of the category (conceptually) and employs 'last brand bought' to measure this (operationally). This approach provides inadequate and probably erroneous information to the advertiser, who must specifically consider how the *advertised* brand is perceived by a *particular* target audience – as represented in the Rossiter-Percy approach.

A third problem with the FCB conceptualization of involvement is that involvement is seen as a continuum, despite the dichotomous-looking diagram they use to portray their grid. In the FCB Grid, the division between low and high involvement is made arbitrarily. And, along the involvement dimension within low and high, some products are more involving than others.

MacInnis and Jaworski (1988) have criticized involvement continuum models for their failure to specify when consumer decision-making changes from being low involvement to high involvement or vice versa. For example, the well-known Elaboration Likelihood Model proposed by Petty and Cacioppo (1986) is a unidimensional involvement model that fails to specify the situations in which consumers will follow the 'peripheral' (low involvement) route versus the 'central' (high involvement) route in processing advertising messages.

The Rossiter-Percy approach, on the other hand, makes a purely empirical and simply dichotomous distinction between low and high involvement. The particular target audience consumer, in choosing this brand on this occasion, either regards the choice as being sufficiently low in perceived risk to simply 'try the brand and see,' representing low involvement; or else regards the brand-choice decision as being risky enough to be worth processing advertising information at a more detailed level, representing high involvement. Numerous qualitative interviews with consumers, commissioned or conducted by the authors over an extensive range of product categories (commercial and government studies conducted by IMI, Inc. in the United States and by Donovan Research Pty. Ltd. in Australia), have convinced us that virtually all consumers regard brand-choice decisions in this dichotomous low- or high-involvement manner rather than operating as if involvement were a continuum.

The second way in which ours is an improved advertising planning model, therefore, is that, in the Rossiter-Percy Grid, involvement is clearly defined (in terms of perceived risk in the target audience's choice of this brand on this occasion); involvement is more precisely conceptualized as being dependent on both the brand and the target audience's familiarity with it within the product category; and an operational dichotomy for assigning brands and target audiences to either low- or high-involvement quadrants is provided.

THE MOTIVATIONAL DIMENSION OF ATTITUDE

Product or brand attitudes are distinguished not only by the level of involvement in making the choice but also by the purchase *motive* which caused the attitude to be formed initially.

Motives play the important function of energizing consumer purchase action; a product and brand usually are bought to satisfy a motive or occasionally multiple motives. Through purchase and subsequent usage, the attitude based on each motive is thus consummated. Qualitative researchers spend a good deal of their time trying to identify purchase motives, and advertising agencies, too, are always seeking these 'triggers to action.'

As noted, the FCB Grid does not distinguish product-category choice from brand choices. This poses a problem for the FCB Grid's motivational 'think–feel' dimension when it is realized that product-category purchase motives are often different from brand-choice motives. For instance, in the Rossiter-Percy terminology (1987), purchase of an automobile, the product category, is generally due to the straightforward informationally-based problem-removal motive (convenience of transport), whereas choice of particular brands or models of automobiles is likely to depend in a more complex way on transformationally-based sensory gratification or social-approval motives (manifest in benefits such as attractive appearance, exciting power, admiration by others, and so forth). The FCB Grid's classification of 'think–feel' does not allow for differences between product-category and brand-purchase motivations.

The FCB 'think–feel' dimension is rather superficially conceptualized. As the various spokespersons for the FCB Grid have intimated, 'think' and 'feel' are cute summary labels that do not in any way do justice to the complexity of consumer purchase motivations. Yet, the FCB authors have done little to expand on this weak conceptualization of motivation. In Ratchford's paper, the 'think' category is translated into one single motive, 'utilitarian.' This hardly does justice to all the types of motives that may cause consumers to 'think' about their decision.

In the Rossiter-Percy approach, which was suggested by Katz's functional approach (1960) and Fennell's original application of multiple motives to advertising (1978), there are five motives that would correspond approximately with the 'think' side of the FCB Grid. In our approach, these are defined as *informational* motives which are (negatively reinforcing) purchase motivations that can be satisfied by providing information about the product or brand. These negatively-originated motives are: problem removal, problem avoidance, incomplete satisfaction, mixed approach-avoidance, and normal depletion. Each of these motives is operatively distinct and has different implications for advertising message strategy (Rossiter and Percy, 1987).

The 'feel' class of purchase motives has been somewhat more elaborated by the FCB researchers, which is surprising in that the 'think' motives undoubtedly are more prevalent and diverse. In the most recent FCB paper, by Ratchford and Vaughn (1989), the 'feel' classification is separated into three motives: ego gratification (although this is mistakenly given also a negative, ego defensive, conceptualization); sensory; and social acceptance.

In the Rossiter-Percy approach, the approximate analogy to the 'feel' motives are our *transformational* motives, a term borrowed from Wells (1981), which are (positively reinforcing) purchase motives that promise to enhance the brand user by effecting a transformation in the brand user's sensory, mental, or social state. Our system distinguishes three such positive transformational motives: sensory gratification, intellectual stimulation (achievement, mastery), and social approval. Whereas two of our motives, sensory gratification and social approval, are similar to FCB's, Rossiter and Percy (1987) give these motives much clearer definitions and theoretical support.

A further difficulty with the FCB approach, and with that of many other writers who have focused on 'emotions' and 'feelings,' is that the writers tend almost always to be referring to positive emotions or feelings when they use these terms. It should be evident that *negative* feelings are also necessary for effective advertising when the product or brand purchase decision is negatively motivated (see also Bagozzi and

Table 2 Typical emotions that might be used to portray each motivation

Motives	*Typical emotional states*
Informational motives	
1. Problem removal	Anger → relief
2. Problem avoidance	Fear → relaxation
3. Incomplete satisfaction	Disappointment → optimism
4. Mixed approach-avoidance	Guilt → peace of mind
5. Normal depletion	Mild annoyance → convenience
Transformational motives	
6. Sensory gratification	Dull* → elated
7. Intellectual stimulation	Bored* → excited
8. Social approval	Apprehensive* → flattered

*Optional prior negative emotions for transformational motives. Positive emotions can arise from a *neutral* prior state and do not require negative emotions beforehand.

Moore, 1989, and Yalch, 1990). Table 2 shows how negative motives (informational in our attitude grid) and positive motives (transformational in our attitude grid) both incorporate 'feelings.' Negative motives generate negative feelings but may also induce positive feelings subsequently; positive motives need to generate only positive feelings.

The negative-motivation versus positive-motivation distinction is crucial to advertising tactics (see later) and is not represented in the FCB Grid. Negative feeling or affect is caused by an aversive event such as a consumer problem occurring. Although negative, this causes motivational drive to *increase*, which energizes the consumer to remove the aversion by solving the problem through acquiring information about product or brand choice and then buying and using the chosen item. Drive or motivation level is thus reduced, and the consumer returns to the equilibrium state and action ceases.

Positive feeling or affect is caused by appetitive or intrinsically rewarding events such as sensory, intellectual, or social stimulation. Presentation of these positive stimuli through anticipated and then actual consumption also causes drive or motivation to increase. Although the drive increase in this case is accompanied by enhanced positive affect, the action doesn't continue indefinitely, because of biological cessation mechanisms. For example, you can only eat a limited number of candy bars in succession! Thus, in the positive motivation cases as well, the consumer seeks eventually to return to an equilibrium.

Yet another difficulty with the motivational dimension in the FCB Grid concerns measurement. Ratchford (1987) is of the opinion that motivational classifications can be measured quantitatively. We differ and believe that motivational assessment is essentially a *qualitative* skill which gave rise to the original name for 'motivation' research. This is not to say that all consumer purchase motives are hidden or psychoanalytic or otherwise unmeasurable so much as that consumers frequently do not have accurate insight into what motivated them to purchase a particular brand. Anyone who has worked closely in designing advertising creative strategy will be familiar with the extreme subtlety in motivational differences (see also Fennell, 1989).

It is our belief, based on numerous case histories we have observed, that qualitative researchers are in the best position to make motivational classifications of product and brand choices for particular target audiences. A good example of the failure of the quantitative approach is in Ratchford (1987) where the investigator gave up trying to measure the social-approval motive, and thus dropped this quantitative measurement scale, because 'respondents tended to say that the decision was not based on what others think.' So many brand choices are patently based on social approval that to omit this motive because of the inability of quantitative measures to measure it is testimony to the sterility of the overly quantitative approach. Motivational classification requires qualitative inference from what consumers say and do and can rarely be validly achieved by asking consumers themselves to make the classification.

A final criticism of the FCB Grid's conceptualization of the 'think–feel' dimension is that it correlates highly positively with the 'involvement' dimension. In the Ratchford (1987) series of studies, the correlation between the 'involvement' scale and the 'think–feel' scale was .63. This is not too surprising at a superficial level when one realizes that consumers generally think carefully about things that are highly involving and do less thinking about things that they buy based on feelings alone. However, such a conceptualization omits the whole class of high involvement-transformational products, such as new cars, houses, or luxury vacations, that are certainly 'thought' about but are primarily motivated by expected positive affect or positive 'feelings.'

The Rossiter-Percy conceptualization of motivation is more comprehensive and sounder than the overly simplistic 'think–feel' conceptualization. It is based on motivational mechanisms taken from learning theory: it looks at negative and positive motives, and their associated negative and positive feelings, but does not invoke the notion of 'thinking' in what is essentially a motivational rather than a cognitive dimension.

To summarize, the third way in which the Rossiter-Percy Grid is an improvement upon the FCB Grid is in the respective models' conceptualization of consumer motivations. The Rossiter-Percy model allows product-category purchase motives and brand purchase motives to differ, whereas the FCB approach does not. Rossiter and Percy's model identifies eight operatively distinct purchase motives, in comparison with the FCB model which distinguishes only one 'think' motive and several 'feel' motives and cannot measure the obviously important motive of social approval. Furthermore, the FCB model concentrates solely on positive 'feelings' despite the fact that negative 'feelings' motivate consumers at least equally as often, as reflected in the Rossiter-Percy distinction between 'informational' and 'transformational' motives. Finally, FCB's admittedly vague conceptualization of 'think–feel' is reflected in quantitative results where this dimension is shown to be highly correlated with the 'involvement' dimension. The Rossiter-Percy model eschews the quantitative approach in favor of the fundamentally qualitative identification of motives. These motives operate independently of the degree of involvement in purchasing the product category or the brand.

GRIDS AND ADVERTISING TACTICS

The Rossiter-Percy Grid is much richer than the FCB Grid in terms of specifying advertising tactics. Writing about the FCB Grid, Ratchford (1987) makes the comment that 'The advertising implications of positioning in a particular quadrant . . . should be fairly obvious . . .' Oh that it were this easy! An attempt to relate the FCB Grid to stimuli that might be used in ads is the subject of the Ratchford and Vaughn (1989) paper. They attempt to relate the FCB Grid to two proprietary FCB techniques, VIP, or Visual Image Profile, which consists of 100 photos of faces representing different personalities and lifestyles, and ICON, or Image Configurations, which consists of 60 photos of situations of differing emotional content. An irony with pictorial rating-scale methodology is that, whereas it was developed to escape the 'confines' of purely verbal techniques, it is ultimately validated against verbal rating-scale methodology (e.g., Ruge, 1988). Ratchford and Vaughn go along with this fallacy in claiming validity for their pictorial rating by comparing them with verbal ratings. (The analogy is: if English is okay, why worsen things by translating the English into Japanese and then back again?) But the more serious criticism is that, in their study, neither the personality-lifestyle photos nor the emotional photos are related to the various motives nor even to the general distinction between 'think' and 'feel.' For instance, the authors state that the 'emotional associations uncovered through ICON might be related to any one of the three categories of feeling . . .' (1988). This is hardly very helpful tactically for advertising planners or creative people. Similarly, the authors make the concluding comment that: 'While there doesn't seem to be an elaborate body of theory linking the emotions revealed by ICON to brand choice, this probably is not needed.' This lack of theory means that, when using the FCB Grid, it is by no means clear which advertising tactics to employ.

Contrast the theoretical development of tactics in the Rossiter-Percy Grid as shown in Tables 3 to 6. It may be seen that there are cognitive and affective tactics (considerations B and A, respectively), or in FCB's parlance 'thinking' and 'feeling' tactics, in every quadrant of the Rossiter-Percy Grid. This reflects the fact that all

Table 3 Advertising tactics for the low involvement/informational brand attitude strategy*

Consideration A (emotional portrayal of the motivation):
1. Use a simple problem-solution format.
2. It is not necessary for people to like the ad.

Consideration B (benefit-claim support for perceived brand delivery):
3. Include only one or two benefits or a single group of benefits.
4. Benefit claims should be stated extremely.
5. The benefits should be easily learned in one or two exposures (repetition serves mainly as a reminder function).

*In each brand attitude quadrant of the Rossiter-Percy Grid, Consideration A tactics relate to the Motivation dimension and Consideration B tactics relate to the Involvement dimension (see Figure 2).

Table 4 Advertising tactics for the low involvement/transformational brand attitude strategy*

Consideration A (emotional portrayal of the motivation):
1. Emotional authenticity is the key element and is the single benefit.
2. The execution of the emotion must be unique to the brand.
3. The target audience must like the ad.

Consideration B (benefit-claim support for perceived brand delivery):
4. Brand delivery is by association and is often implicit.
5. Repetition serves as a build-up function and a reinforcement function.

*See note, Table 3.

Table 5 Advertising tactics for the high involvement/informational brand attitude strategy*

Consideration A (emotional portrayal of the motivation):
1. Correct emotional portrayal is very important early in the product life cycle but becomes less important as the product category reaches maturity.
2. The target audience has to accept the ad's main points but does not have to like the ad itself.

Consideration B (benefit-claim support for perceived brand delivery):
3. The target audience's 'initial attitude' toward the brand is the overriding consideration that must be taken into account.
4. Benefit claims must be pitched at an acceptable upper level of brand attitude (don't overclaim).
5. Benefit claims must be convincing (don't inadvertently underclaim).
6. For target audiences who have objections to the brand, consider a *refutational* approach.
7. If there is a well-entrenched competitor and your brand has equivalence or advantages on important benefits, consider a *comparative* approach.

*See note, Table 3.

Table 6 Advertising tactics for the high involvement/transformational brand attitude strategy*

Consideration A (emotional portrayal of the motivation):
1. Emotional authenticity is paramount and should be tailored to lifestyle groups within the target audience.
2. People must identify personally with the product as portrayed in the ad and not merely like the ad.

Consideration B (benefit-claim support for perceived brand delivery):
3. Many high involvement/transformational advertisements also have to provide information.
4. Overclaiming is recommended but don't underclaim.
5. Repetition serves as a build-up function (often for subsequent informational ads) and a reinforcement function.

*See note. Table 3.

advertisements represent a balance between so-called 'rational' and 'emotional' stimuli in ads (and once more we emphasize that emotions can be negative as well as positive). As can be seen from the tables, the low-involvement tactics tend to focus on just one or two benefits as in the typical consumer packaged-goods ('USP') type of approach. On the other hand, the high-involvement tactics tend to focus on the multiple-benefits type of approach which characterizes the carefully considered comparative decisions made when consumers perceive considerable risk in choosing the right brand from the product category. Elaborate discussion of these tactics can be found in Rossiter and Percy (1987). Thus, in terms of advertising tactics, the Rossiter-Percy approach is more fully specified than the FCB approach. This is the fourth and probably most important way in which ours is an improved planning model.

RELATIONSHIP TO OTHER THEORETICAL CONSTRUCTS

Constructs developed in one area that can accommodate constructs and data in other areas are clearly of greater theoretical and practical value than are constructs that are limited to relatively narrow domains. Unlike the FCB Grid, the Rossiter-Percy Grid accommodates a number of other theoretical constructs in consumer decision-making and advertising. By way of illustration, the relation of the Rossiter-Percy Grid to three contemporary areas of consumer behavior and advertising theory is described below.

Holbrook and Hirschman (1982) contend that the traditional information-processing 'problem-solving' approach to consumer behavior ignores experiential aspects of consumer behavior. They propose an alternative processing model, the 'experiential' view, to account for hedonistic and aesthetic consumption behavior. Holbrook and Hirschman's experiential view appears to describe consumer decision-making processing for Rossiter and Percy's positively originating motives. Their information-processing approach describes consumer decision-making processing for negatively originating motives.

A second area that can be related to the Rossiter-Percy Grid is the relationship between attitude toward the ad (A_{ad}) and attitude toward the brand (A_B), and their relative contributions to ad impact, as measured by attitude change, purchase intention, or purchase brhavior (e.g. Lutz, MacKenzie, and Belch, 1983; Gardner, 1985; Batra and Ray, 1986; Machleit and Wilson, 1988). The major issue in much of this research is whether or not A_{ad} is a necessary precursor to A_B. The Rossiter-Percy model predicts that A_{ad} would be a major mediator of A_B for transformational advertising and especially low-involvement transformational advertising, but not for informational advertising. Support for this prediction is given in Rossiter and Percy (1987).

A third area to which the Rossiter-Percy Grid can be linked, though somewhat more tenuously than in the above two cases, is the distinction between 'lecture' and 'drama' styles of advertising (Wells, 1988; Deighton, Romer, and McQueen, 1989). Lecture is persuasion via 'reasoned argument,' whereas drama is an attempt to persuade more by 'expressions of feeling and judgments of verisimilitude' (Deighton et al., 1989). In Rossiter and Percy's theory, lecture executions should be more effective than drama for low- and high-involvement informational advertising; drama should be more effective than lecture for low-involvement transformational advertising; and a combination of lecture and drama should be more effective (than either alone) for high-involvement transformational advertising, such as by using drama ads on TV followed by lecture ads in print.

Overall, therefore, a further advantage of the Rossiter-Percy Grid is that it can accommodate other theoretical constructs in consumer decision-making and advertising. Therefore, the Rossiter-Percy Grid should be of broad and lasting use. The grid itself is a necessary simplification of the detailed theory to be found in Rossiter and Percy (1987). However, as noted at the outset, the grid format makes the theory more likely to be referred to and used by advertising managers.

SUMMARY

Our purpose in this paper has been to propose a 'grid' approach to advertising planning that is better than the widely known FCB Grid. The improved approach, developed by Rossiter and Percy (1987), has numerous theoretical and practical advantages over the FCB approach. The advantages of the Rossiter-Percy Grid include:

- Advertising communication objectives that include brand awareness as a necessary precursor to brand attitude (thereby constituting a six-cell grid). Brand awareness is classified as either brand recognition or brand recall.
- Definition of the involvement dimension of attitude in terms of perceived risk for a particular product type, target audience, and brand choice. Involvement with the purchase decision is functionally dichotomized into low versus high involvement.
- Definition of the motivational dimension of attitude in terms of eight specific motives that can be qualitatively distinguished. The eight motives are categorized as negatively reinforcing, informational motives versus positively reinforcing, transformational motives.
- Identification of advertising creative tactics that fit the two brand-awareness cells and that fit the four brand-attitude cells – to provide guidance to managers in planning advertising campaigns and to agencies in creating ads.
- Accommodation of constructs from other contemporary theories of consumer behavior and advertising.

The FCB Grid, in contrast, omits brand awareness and focuses only on attitude; it does not distinguish product-category choice and brand choices; it does not allow for target-audience familiarity with the advertised brand in measuring involvement with the purchase decision; it makes too simple a distinction between motives in terms of thinking and feeling such that thinking is confounded with involvement and feeling fails to distinguish positive and negative emotions; it is basically unspecified overall in terms of theory and cannot be readily related to other constructs in consumer behavior and advertising; and, finally, the FCB Grid falls short by not making recommendations for advertising tactics.

We offer these criticisms with full recognition and appreciation of the valuable pioneering contribution that the FCB Grid has made. Its many limitations, however, should suggest to managers that it is time to move onto a better advertising planning grid. We are flattered that the Rossiter-Percy Grid has recently been put to practical use as the major input for a new expert system for advertising developed by Wharton marketing professors (Burke, Rangaswamy, Wind, and Eliashberg, 1990) in conjunction with Young & Rubicam. We propose the Rossiter-Percy Grid as a planning approach for advertising creative strategy that overcomes the FCB Grid's limitations while still retaining the simplicity of the grid format that makes such models easy to understand in theory and likely to be used in practice.

REFERENCES

Allen, C. T., and C. A. Janiszewski. 'Assessing the Role of Contingency Awareness in Attitudinal Conditioning with Implications for Advertising Research.' *Journal of Marketing Research* 26, 1 (1989): 30–43.

Bagozzi, R. P., and D. J. Moore. 'Intense Negative Emotions as Positive Mediators of Behavioral Intentions.' Paper presented at the Annual Conference, Association for Consumer Research, New Orleans, October 1989.

Batra, R., and M. L. Ray. 'Affective Responses Meditating Acceptance of Advertising.' *Journal of Consumer Research* 13, 2 (1986): 234–49.

Burke, R. R.; A. Rangaswamy; J. Wind; and J. Eliashberg. 'ADCAD: A Knowledge-Based System for Advertising Design.' *Marketing Science* 9, 3 (1990): 212–29.

Deighton, J.; D. Romer; and J. McQueen. 'Using Drama to Persuade.' *Journal of Consumer Research* 16, 3 (1989): 335–43.

Ehrenberg, A. S. C. 'Repetitive Advertising and the Consumer.' *Journal of Advertising Research* 14, 2 (1974): 25–34.

Fennell, G. 'Consumers' Perceptions of the Product-Use Situation.' *Journal of Marketing* 42, 2 (1978): 38–47.

——. 'Action vs. Attitude: Motivation Makes the Difference.' In *Proceedings of the Society for Consumer Psychology, American Psychological Association.* D. W. Schumann, ed. Washington, DC: American Psychological Association, 1989.

Gardner, M. P. 'Does Attitude Toward the Ad Affect Brand Attitude Under a Brand Evaluation Set?' *Journal of Marketing Research* 22, 2 (1985): 192–98.

Gensch, D. H., and R. G. Javalgi. 'The Influence of Involvement on Disaggregate Attribute Choice Models.' *Journal of Consumer Research* 14, 1 (1987): 71–82.

Holbrook, M. B., and E. C. Hirschman. 'The Experiential Aspects of Consumption: Consumer Fantasies, Feelings, and Fun.' *Journal of Consumer Research* 9, 2 (1982): 132–40.

Howard, J. A. *Consumer Behavior: Theory and Applications.* New York: McGraw-Hill, 1977.

Katz, D. 'The Functional Approach to the Study of Attitudes.' *Public Opinion Quarterly* 24, 2 (1960): 163–204.

Lutz, R. J.; S. B. MacKenzie; and G. E. Belch. 'Attitude Toward the Ad as a Mediator of Advertising Effectiveness: Determinants and Consequences.' In *Advances in Consumer Research*, Vol. 10, R. P. Bagozzi and A. M. Tybout, eds. Ann Arbor, MI: Association for Consumer Research, 1983.

Machleit, K. A., and R. D. Wilson. 'Emotional Feelings and Attitude Toward the Advertisement: The Roles of Brand Familiarity and Repetition.' *Journal of Advertising* 17, 3 (1988): 27–35.

MacInnis, D. J., and B. J. Jaworski. 'Two-Routes to Persuasion Models in Advertising.' Working paper, Department of Marketing, Graduate School of Management, University of Arizona, Tucson, 1988.

Nelson, P. E. 'Information and Consumer Behavior.' *Journal of Political Economy* 78, 2 (1970); 311–29.

Petty, R. E., and J. T. Cacioppo. *Communication and Persuasion: Central and Peripheral Routes to Attitude Change.* New York: Springer-Verlag, 1986.

Pringle, L. G.; R. D. Wilson; and E. I. Brody. 'NEWS: A Decision-Oriented Model for New Product Analysis and Forecasting.' *Marketing Science* 1, 1 (1982): 588–98.

Ratchford, B. T. 'New Insights about the FCB Grid.' *Journal of Advertising Research* 27, 4 (1987): 24–38.

——, and R. Vaughn. 'On the Relationships Between Motives and Purchase Decisions: Some Empirical Approaches.' In *Advances in Consumer Research*, Vol. 16, T. K. Srull, ed. Provo, UT: Association for Consumer Research, 1989.

Rossiter, J. R., and L. Percy. *Advertising and Promotion Management*. New York: McGraw-Hill, 1987.

Ruge, H. D. 'The Imagery Differential.' Working paper, Institute for Consumer and Behavioral Research, University of the Saarland, West Germany, 1988.

Urban, G. L., and G. M. Katz. 'Pretest-Market Models: Validation and Managerial Implications.' *Journal of Marketing Research* 20, 3 (1983): 221–34.

Vaughn, R. 'How Advertising Works: A Planning Model.' *Journal of Advertising Research* 20, 5 (1980): 27–33.

——, 'How Advertising Works: A Planning Model Revisited.' *Journal of Advertising Research* 26, 1 (1986): 57–66.

Wells, W. D. 'How Advertising Works.' Video presentation, Needham, Harper & Steers (now DDB Needham), Chicago, 1981.

——. 'Lectures and Dramas and Measurement Challenges.' Paper presented at the Marketing Science Institute Conference, Wellesley, MA, June 1988.

Yalch, R. F. 'Review of *Cognitive and Affective Responses to Advertising*, P. Cafferata and A. Tybout, eds. Lexington, MA: Lexington Books, 1989.' *Journal of Marketing Research* 27, 2 (1990): 238–40.

Rossiter, J. R., Percy, L. and Donovan, R. J. (1991) 'A better advertising planning grid'. *Journal of Advertising Research*, October/November: 11–21. Reproduced with permission.

2.3 A review and critique of the hierarchy of effects in advertising

Thomas E. Barry and Daniel J. Howard

INTRODUCTION

For close to a century, advertising and marketing researchers and practitioners the world over have diligently sought to understand just how advertising influences buyers' purchase decisions. At stake is the effectiveness of strategies developed in this multi-billion dollar industry. At the core of current understanding is the body of literature referred to as the hierarchy of effects. This literature deals with the way in which target audiences process and ultimately use advertising information to influence product and brand choices and is considered a top priority research area for contemporary marketing and advertising researchers (Schmalensee, 1983).

One testimonial to the importance of the hierarchy of effects is the number of diverse communities interested in the topic. Among those interested are advertising and marketing researchers and practitioners, sociologists, communication theorists, cognitive psychologists, social psychologists and others who have debated the realities of advertising effects on consumption behaviour. A second testimonial to the importance of the hierarchy literature is its longevity. The first published suggestion that a hierarchy of effects was operative in marketing communications appeared in 1898 and researchers and practitioners continue to contest the hierarchy notion today. Scores of hierarchy-of-effects models have been proposed. The vast majority of them merely offer changes in nomenclature to the traditional hierarchy-of-effects model which hypothesizes that audiences respond to messages in a cognitive, affective, and conative (behavioural) sequence. More recently, however, researchers have begun to debate the existence of a single hierarchy sequence and have proposed alternative-order hierarchy models.

The purpose of this article is to review the large body of hierarchy literature that has accumulated over nine decades. The review first describes the traditional hierarchy models and is followed by a discussion of alternative-order hierarchy models. A critique of the evidence supporting the hierarchy proposition as a model of advertising effectiveness is then presented.

THE TRADITIONAL HIERARCHY OF EFFECTS: COGNITION–AFFECT–CONATION

Proponents of the traditional hierarchy framework claim that audiences of advertising and other marketing communications respond to those messages in a very ordered way: cognitively first ('thinking'), affectively second ('feeling'), and conatively third ('doing').

The most often cited hierarchy model was posited by Lavidge and Steiner (1961) and is presented in Table 1. These writers believed that advertising was an investment in a long-term process that moved consumers over time through a variety of stair-step stages, beginning with product 'unawareness' and moving ultimately to actual purchase. Their view of the stages of the advertising hierarchy is implicitly a causal one. However, by recognizing that advertising is essentially a 'long-term' process, it suggests that a causal influence between stages must occur only in the long-run, although it may not be found in the short-run. The argument that a favourable response at one step is a necessary, but not sufficient condition for a favourable response at the next step is central to the idea of advertising hierarchy of response models to this day (Preston and Thorson, 1983).

Predecessors to the Lavidge–Steiner model

Prior to the development of the Lavidge–Steiner model, there were many proponents of the cognition-affect-conation sequence. These proponents and their models appear in Table 2. The most well-known is AIDA (attention-interest-desire-action), generally attributed in the marketing and advertising literature to Strong (1925b). Actually, this model originated with E. St Elmo Lewis in the late 1800s and early 1900s (Strong, 1925a). Lewis theorized that sales people, in order to be successful, had to attract attention (cognition), maintain interest and create desire (affect), and then 'get action' (conation). Sheldon (1911) included 'permanent satisfaction' as a fifth step (AIDAS). This step was an early treatment of the now recognized importance of post-purchase

Table 1 The Lavidge–Steiner traditional order hierarchy of effects

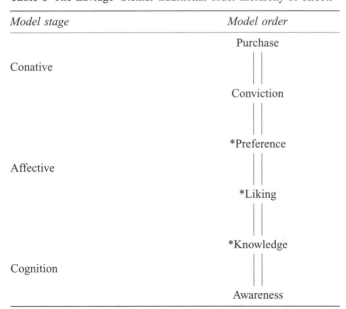

Model stage	Model order
	Purchase
Conative	
	Conviction
	*Preference
Affective	
	*Liking
	*Knowledge
Cognition	
	Awareness

*Indicates a stage not presented in predecessor models.

Table 2 A summary of popular hierarchy models preceding the Lavidge–Steiner model

Year	Model		Developer	Comment
1898	AID	Attention, Interest, Desire	E. St Elmo Lewis	Developed as a sales guide for salesmen to be successful in moving a prospect to buy.
Circa 1900	AIDA	Attention, Interest, Desire, *Action**	E. St Elmo Lewis	Added the action stage as necessary to convince salesmen to move buyer prospects through complete selling process.
1910	AICA	Attention, Interest, *Conviction*, Action	*Printer's Ink* Editorial	The first mention of the hierarchy model for advertising use; a complete advertisement must follow this model of persuasion.
1911	AIDAS	Attention, Interest, Desire, Action, *Satisfaction*	Arthur F. Sheldon	Added 'Permanent satisfaction' as a necessary part of the persuasive and long-run selling process: this final stage not carried through to contemporary literature.
1915	AICCA	Attention, Interest, *Confidence*, Conviction, Action	Samuel R. Hall	The necessary steps in writing a good, persuasive advertisement.
1921	AIDCA	Attention, Interest, Desire, *Caution*, Action	Robert E. Ramsay	Mentioned this model at the beginning of his book on how to write effective direct advertising although the model is not developed in the book.
1921	AIDCA	Attention, Interest, Desire, Conviction, Action	Harry D. Kitson	Used this model in writing about how the mind of the buyer works.
1922	AIJA	Attention, Interest, *Judgement*, Action	Alexander Osborn	Writing about the creative/persuasive process in advertising.
1940	AIDCA	Attention, Interest, Desire, Conviction, Action	Clyde Bedell	For advertising to sell it, it must follow these 'proved selling stratagems' as formulated by Kitson in 1921.
1956	AIDMA	Attention, Interest, Desire, *Memory*, Action	Merrill Devoe	Referred to the importance of different psychological sequences in constructing advertisements (AIDCA and AIDMA) but does not develop these in his book.

*Italics indicate change in stage/nomenclature from previous model(s).

reactions. In the selling process, an ordered process of getting the sale was critical to Sheldon:

> The great problem of salesmanship is so to master this fact that the customer, realizing his best interests are being served, is persuaded to make a purchase because you follow the right method. You do not try to make him take action before you have stimulated his desire: and you do not try to create desire until you have secured his interest. (p. 31).

The basic stages of the AIDA model were adhered to by the vast majority of advertising writers for 60 years after its publication. The banner of the traditional hierarchy was directly or indirectly supported by Scott (1903, 1908), *Printer's Ink* (1910), International Correspondence Schools (1911), Hall (1915), Adams (1916),

Eastman (1916), West Coast Life Insurance Company (1920), Ramsay (1921), Kitson (1921), Osborn (1922), Starch (1923), Jenkins (1935), Hawkins (Strong, 1938), Bedell (1940), and Devoe (1956). So important was the AIDA formulation at the turn of the century that Strong (1925b) estimated that 90 per cent of persons engaged in selling and the vast majority of advertising and selling textbooks fully endorsed the Lewis–Sheldon hierarchical framework.

These early writers played a key role in shaping the minds of advertising and selling practitioners and researchers. While the authors of many of these early 'models' merely changed the nomenclature of their predecessors or added or deleted stages, and while there was no empirical validation of any kind, the way to development of effective marketing communications was clearly thought to be the route of cognition, affect and conation and only in that order.

Recent traditional hierarchy support

While the Lavidge–Steiner model appeared to be developed independently of its 'predecessors', it clearly advocated the traditional ordering notion. However, its authors went further than earlier writers in holding that the hierarchy steps were not necessarily equidistant from each other. Furthermore, consumers could move 'up' several steps simultaneously. Lavidge and Steiner (1961) were also really the first to refer to the concept of respondent 'involvement'. According to the authors, the consumer's psychological or economic commitment would have an important bearing on his or her succession to the conation stage of the hierarchy with the more committed purchasers taking longer to go through the process. Nevertheless, the more committed or 'involved' consumers would go through the same ordered procedure as less committed or 'involved' consumers. Only the speed of the progression might differ.

Several more recent publications also advocate the traditional hierarchy framework. The most important are illustrated in Table 3. Among those is the work of Colley (1961) who in his well-known DAGMAR (Defining Advertising Goals for Measured Advertising Results) suggested that a hierarchy of advertising objectives should be used by managers to measure advertising effects rather than focusing on sales alone. At the same time, the Advertising Research Foundation (1961) developed a separate, but similar hierarchy model suggesting the stages of exposure, perception, communication (knowledge), communication (attitude), and action.

Further evidence that the cognition-affect-conation ordering process was popular came in the form of Rogers' (1962) adoption model. Rogers proposed that consumers followed a hierarchical process of awareness, interest, evaluation, trial, and adoption in the new product-adoption process. This model was expanded upon by Robertson (1971) when he proposed an awareness, comprehension, attitude, legitimization, trial, and adoption hierarchy.

The first to attach probabilities to the traditional sequence was McGuire (1969; 1978). According to McGuire, the probability that one would engage in the purchase of a brand as a result of advertising was conditional upon one's retention of a message, which was conditional upon yielding to the message, which was conditional upon comprehension, which, itself, was conditional upon attention to a presented message. Ultimately, purchase of a brand as a result of advertising had a very low probability because of multiplicative conditional probabilities.

Table 3 A summary of recent hierarchy models supporting the traditional cognitive-affective-conative ordering

Year	Model		Developer	Comment
1961	ACCA	Awareness, *Comprehension**, Conviction, Action	Russell H. Colley	Proposed this model as important to the development of specified advertising goals and measuring advertising effectiveness.
1961	EPCCA	*Exposure, Perception, Communication (Knowledge)*, Communication (Attitude), Action	Advertising Research Foundation	The model supported by the foundation of advertising practitioners and researchers to be used for developing more effective advertising campaigns.
1962	AAPIS	Awareness, *Acceptance*, Preference, *Intention, Sale, Provocation*	Harry D. Wolfe, James K. Brown, C. Clark Thompson	Illustrated how business used the hierarchy concept as a guideline to develop advertising strategy.
1962	AIETA	Awareness, Interest, *Evaluation, Trial, Adoption*	Everett M. Rogers	Proposed the first application of a hierarchy-type model to the process of new product adoption.
1969	PACYRB	*Presentation*, Attention, Comprehension, *Yielding, Retention*, Behaviour	William J. McGuire	The first to suggest that probabilities could be associated with the stages of the hierarchy models to show ultimate behavioural impact of advertising.
1971	ACALTA	Awareness, Comprehension, Attitude, *Legitimation*, Trial, Adoption	Thomas S. Robertson	Expanded on the adoption hierarchy of Rogers, this model more based on Howard and Sheth buyer behaviour model (attention, comprehension, attitude, intention, purchase).
1982 1983 1984	The Association model and the expanded Association model		Ivan L. Preston Esther Thorson	Proposed more comprehensive hierarchy model that preserved the traditional order: *distribution*, vehicle exposure, advertising exposure, advertising awareness, *advertising elements awareness, association evaluation, product perception, integrated perception, products evaluation, prior evaluation, integrated evaluation, product stimulation, prior stimulation, integrated stimulation, search, search perception, search evaluation, search stimulation*, trial, *trial perception, trial stimulation*, adoption, *adoption perception, adoption evaluation, adoption stimulation.*

*Italics indicate change in stage/nomenclature from previous model(s).

The most recent conceptualization which supports the traditional hierarchy-of-effects framework comes form the work of Preston and Thorson (Preston, 1982; Preston and Thorson, 1983, 1984) and their 'association model'. This model focuses on a comprehensive advertising process that takes into account advertising research techniques (e.g., syndicated data, surveys, experimentation) and concepts consistent with behavioural intentions models (Fishbein and Ajzen, 1975).

ALTERNATIVE-ORDER HIERARCHIES OF EFFECTS

While there is little disagreement among researchers regarding the importance of the three stages of the hierarchy, there has been significant disagreement regarding the order of the three stages. This has been the area of the most intense criticism and debate concerning the hierarchy of effects.

The first alternative model, formally recognized as such, followed the suggestions of Krugman (1965, 1966) and was labelled a 'low involvement' hierarchy. In this perspective, consumers are seen to be passive and disinterested recipients of many advertising messages. With little motivation to filter those messages, massive repetition of advertisements eventually leads to a modified cognitive structure in those consumers, who may purchase a product on that basis alone, and decide afterwards whether they like it. Thus, Krugman appears to suggest a cognition-conation-affect sequence.

Zajonc (1980a, 1980b, 1984, 1986) and Zajonc and Markus (1982), on the other hand, suggest that preferences do not require a cognitive basis, but instead are primarily affectively based. The position that preferences can be decided on the basis of affect alone presents the potential for an affect-behaviour path. If an individual later saw a need to justify or further reflect on a preferred choice (c.f., Mayer *et al.*, 1980), an affect-conation-cognition sequence could arise.

Citing Bem (1972) and Kelly (1973), Ray *et al.* (1973) suggested another alternative sequence that would have relevance to marketing communications. In this situation, a person first behaves, attitudes are then formed to bolster choice, and selective learning follows to further support that action. Thus, a conation-affect-cognition sequence was indicated. However, a conation-cognition-affect sequence also appears plausible. Kiesler (1971) states that a behaviour often wields a power of commitment which results in the reorganization of cognitions to be consistent with that commitment. Affective formation or change may then follow commitment with both behaviours and cognitions. In a marketing context, for example, purchase of a product may cause one to think about it in a manner that supports the action and then feelings are developed consistent with those thoughts and the behaviour.

The work of Vaughn (1980, 1986) of Foote, Cone and Belding presents an applied interpretation of the conation-affect-cognition and conation-cognition-affect orderings noted above. However, this author offers another possibility: affect-cognition-conation. This sequence is thought to typify the responses of 'feeling' consumers who respond more to emotion than information in making purchase decisions resulting from advertising messages. Vaughn posits that this hierarchy is applicable to consumers when buying 'emotional products' such as fashions, jewelry, and cosmetics. The possibility of an affect-cognition-conation sequence has also been suggested by Zajonc (1980a, b), and is consistent with his position that affect usually, if not always, temporally precedes cognition.

In summary, theoreticians and researchers appear to have provided a foundation for at least six different hierarchical models with the potential for explaining consumption-related activities, in general, and responses to advertising specifically. The models that have been presented are:

1. cognition-affect-conation
2. cognition-conation-affect

3. affect-conation-cognition
4. conation-affect-cognition
5. conation-cognition-affect
6. affect-cognition-conation

These various models have been presented here for the sake of completeness (i.e., they represent all possible combinations). The relevance of these different models with respect to understanding how advertising works is a separate issue that needs to be considered.

A CRITIQUE OF THE HIERARCHY OF EFFECTS

What can be made of these proposals with respect to understanding how advertising works? For guidance, a review of the empirical literature was conducted. One immediate problem encountered is that there does not appear to be an accepted means of distinguishing between cognition and affect which is devoid of criticism by workers in the hierarchy area. This seems attributable to two related concerns: 1. uncertainty over how to define cognition and affect precisely (which, in turn, may determine one's conclusions concerning temporal or causal relationships between them); and 2. the difficulty in using measures which fully incorporate all possible dimensions of the constructs (which, again, may determine one's conclusion concerning temporal or causal relationships between them). Nevertheless, cognition is typically defined as 'mental activity' as reflected in knowledge, beliefs or thoughts that someone has about some aspect of their world. For the present purposes, measures of cognition will be distinguished by their non-valenced nature. For example, advertisers have historically relied on measures of memory, such as various recall, recognition and key comprehension scores, to operationalize cognition.

Peterson *et al.* (1986) note that affect is typically treated as feelings and emotions which are physiologically based or have some physiological component. However, advertisers often use affect synonymously with the concept of 'attitude'. One possible difficulty here, as alluded to by Lazarus (1984), is that someone's self-reported attitude may simply be an intellectual choice (cognition) and not solely a feeling-based preference. Nevertheless, for the present purposes, any measure distinguished by its valenced nature, or feeling and emotional measurements in a more general sense, is included in the affective component of the hierarchy.

For the sake of simplicity, workers in the hierarchy area have used the term 'conation' to refer to either intentions to perform a behaviour or performance of the behaviour *per se*, and this definition was likewise used for the present purposes. The type of behaviour most commonly discussed in the hierarchy literature is product purchase, although other consumption-related behaviours might include recommending a product, initiating information search, facilitating product usage, and so forth.

Using the above guidelines, the literature was reviewed for empirical evidence supporting the different models. Several criteria were used for study selection. First, the study had to directly examine the effects of advertising. Second, measures of all three constructs had to be present. Third, each construct had to be modelled as a separate and distinct component with definitions corresponding to those presented above. Fourth, either temporal precedence or causal relationships among the three constructs had to be examined, but not necessarily found.

Use of these criteria seemed reasonable. The first corresponds to the historical premiss of the hierarchy of effects, that is, that it describes the process by which advertisements come to influence recipients of those advertisements. The extent to which the hierarchical process associated with advertising differs from the process associated with non-commercial messages, or consumer decision-making in general, is questionable, but that issue is incidental to the objectives here. This critique focused on investigations using advertising messages to assess the degree to which some hierarchical process involving cognitive, affective, and conative measures has been demonstrated in the advertising area.

The second criterion seemed necessary since bivariate relationships may provide misleading indications of trivariate relationships. The third and fourth criteria simply correspond to a key premiss underlying the hierarchy of effects: each stage is causally related (or at least temporally prior) to the next. Using these criteria, two studies were found (Zinkhan and Fornell, 1988; Batra and Vanhonacker, 1986). Zinkhan and Fornell (1988) provided some causal evidence consistent with the traditional hierarchy. Batra and Vanhonacker's (1986) time-series investigation provided a complex set of results difficult to reconcile with any given model. On the basis of the evidence presented to date, it is difficult to make a clear statement concerning any of the hierarchy-of-effects models in advertising. This conclusion remains even given other studies that have been frequently cited in the advertising hierarchy literature (e.g. Ray *et al.*, 1973; Palda, 1966; Assael and Day, 1968; O'Brien, 1971) which did not fit the criteria utilized here.

For obvious reasons, the results of our empirical review led us to conclude that something was amiss in the hierarchy debate. Part of the problem may lie in the inherent difficulty in being able to make firm conclusions concerning the situations in which different models do and do not operate. A second aspect of the problem may relate to uncertainty over why it is important to address the hierarchy problem. These issues, and their related implications, are addressed in the following sections.

The hierarchy sequence debate

One issue that needs to be mentioned is whether each of the six models reviewed above is equally relevant to understanding the effects of advertising. Two of the models, conation-cognition-affect and conation-affect-cognition, appear less relevant than the others. Strictly speaking, these models suggest that the advertising influence process begins with purchase-related behaviour with *no prior cognition or affect*. On that basis alone, we feel their utility is questionable, although it would be difficult to support that contention in an absolute sense.

One potential value of the above two models is the recognition that behaviour can influence both cognitive and affective processing. It is clear that the use of a product in itself can have strong influence on what one thinks and how one feels about the product. However, in order for the influence of a behaviour on cognition and/or affect to be relevant to the advertising hierarchy of effects, that influence must be shown to be different for consumers exposed to advertising than for those not exposed. The same point might be argued for other relationships in the hierarchy as well. The demonstration of the influence of advertising on any process requires appropriate and controlled comparison points.

The remaining four models reviewed were: cognition-conation-affect, affect-conation-cognition; cognition-affect-conation; affect-cognition-conation. In one sense, the hierarchy sequence debate is easy to summarize with respect to these models since so little is known with any certainty. However, the principle issue that is central to the controversy surrounding these models is concerned with the independence and sequential ordering of cognition and affect. This debate, in various forms, has already been heatedly contested for years and shows little promise of being quickly resolved. Much of the debate is currently motivated by the replicable and seminal work of Zajonc. Zajonc has demonstrated (e.g., Moreland and Zajonc, 1977, 1979; Kunst-Wilson and Zajonc, 1980) that increased liking of a stimulus can occur without recognition memory for that stimulus and argues for the partial independence of cognitive and affective systems in the human species. Zajonc, (1980a, b) also contends that affective reactions usually, if not always, precede cognitive processing. Others persuasively argue that affect is post-cognitive (Mandler, 1982; Lazarus, 1981, 1982, 1984; Tsal, 1985). For example, Tsal (1985) points out that recognition failure does not necessarily indicate the absence of prior cognitive mediation of affect given the fallibility of memory processes. Measures of either recognition or recall can only serve as indirect indicators of what was learned.

On a theoretical (or empirical) level it appears that there are no clear grounds to dismiss any of the four models noted above. On a practical level, the value of the debate is unclear. This is discussed next.

Perspectives on the hierarchy sequence debate

The cognitive and affective systems in the human species are closely interwoven. The question of whether (or when) a cognitive or affective response 'comes first' is not easily answered. As summarized by Peterson *et al.* (1986), 'from a practical perspective this distinction is probably arbitrary and partially depends 'on how cognition and affect are defined' (p. 158). Debates on this issue (e.g., Zajonc, 1980a, 1984; Lazarus, 1982, 1984; Watts, 1983) appear to ultimately regress to differentiations between neural and physiological processes separated by milliseconds. However, it seems unlikely that millisecond level differentiations will play a dominant role in eventual consumer decision-making. It is even more unlikely that the most commonly employed advertising research tools are capable of distinguishing such effects. Yet, once cognitive and affective processing begin to interact, even at the millisecond level of initial stages of information processing, the quest for clearly defining a hierarchy based on the idea of sequential ordering of effects loses meaning. If it is contended that we can only be concerned with the ordering of cognitive and affective processes that we are able to 'reliably determine', then the notion of a sequential hierarchy becomes a contingent one that will vary as a function of the sophistication of the research tools employed and the sensitivity of the chosen measurements. If it is argued that the 'cognition' and 'affect' of interest to practitioners are different, in some way, from the meaning of those constructs when debated at the basic research level, then a sequential hierarchy in advertising will require a unique set of theoretical and measurement assumptions which has yet to be provided. If it is conceded that, on a managerial level, the real issue is one of degree of response and not absolute order of response, then the notion of a sequential hierarchy of effects becomes vague and undefined. However, by embracing the idea of 'degree of response', the question concerning 'which comes first' is replaced by a question concerning how the two operations can together be most usefully considered in their influence on some criterion. This issue is discussed next.

An integrated perspective

Fishbein and Ajzen (1975) view beliefs as a measure of cognition in which the evaluative implications of those beliefs are immediately assessed by an individual when the beliefs are formed such that 'as a person forms beliefs about an object, he automatically and simultaneously acquires an attitude towards an object' (p. 216). This expectancy-value formulation is conceptually based on the premiss that cognition determines affect (i.e., beliefs determine attitude), although the sequential ordering and causal relationship between the two is considered a secondary issue: 'although we have argued that a person's salient beliefs determine his attitude, the model itself is not predicated on an assumption of causality but merely deals with ... the way in which different beliefs (and the evaluations of the associated attributes) are combined or integrated to arrive at an evaluation of the object' (Fishbein and Ajzen 1975, pp. 222–223). It is the explicit *integration* of non-valenced (beliefs) and valenced (evaluative implications of those beliefs) information which distinguishes the Fishbein-Ajzen behavioural intention model from most discussions of hierarchy-of-effects models in advertising. This expectancy-value is often called 'cognitive attitude'.

In the advertising area, Smith and Swinyard (1982, 1988) argue for the benefits of expectancy-value formulations (along with the concept of 'trial' versus 'commitment' behaviour) in helping to resolve sequence controversies in the hierarchy of effects. Preston's (1982) 'association model' includes as its final steps 'integrated evaluation' (where recipients of advertising are thought to engage in expectancy-value type processing) which is postulated to lead to 'integrated stimulation' (purchase intentions) which leads to 'action' (typically, purchase behaviour). The incorporation of an expectancy-value framework in advertising hierarchy-of-effects models amounts to a recognition that the *joint* consideration of cognitive and affective processing has particular utility with respect to understanding preferences.

The need to know?

From a practical perspective, why do we need to know about the sequential hierarchy of effects in advertising?

One reason is that determining hierarchical processes allows us to predict behaviour (Preston and Thorson, 1983). Yet, the easiest way to predict what someone will do is simply to ask them what they intend to do (i.e., the intention-behaviour relationship). Determining temporal precedence or a causal relationship between cognition and affect is not necessary if one's interest is simply the prediction of behaviour. The most immediate determinant of behaviour is behavioural intentions.

A second reason is that understanding the hierarchy of effects provides information on what advertising strategy to emphasize. The notion of different hierarchical sequences appears to have influenced management by the assumption that if a given component comes first, it dominates what follows and thus can have important implications for advertising strategies (Vaughn, 1986). The problem is that such an event has yet to be empirically demonstrated. It is unclear whether primacy of an initial cognitive or affective response has a significant influence on the processing of advertising-related information. Most importantly, even if such an influence could be demonstrated, its magnitude is likely to be relatively minor and 'washed out' prior to behaviour. No evidence currently exists supporting the contention that the sequential ordering of cognitive versus affective responses to advertising communications 'ultimately matters' in terms of what people purchase or consume.

A third reason is that the hierarchy of effects has proven valuable for helping to organize planning, training, and conceptual tasks within a firm. This appears valid. As previously reviewed, the advertising literature has historically utilized the idea of a hierarchy of effects for identifying important concepts which need to be addressed. As a heuristic tool, the hierarchy concept has survived because it has an intuitive appeal. The fact that there is a difference between the use of a model as a heuristic tool and its empirical realization may not be a critical issue in the minds of many practitioners.

From an empirical perspective, however, the primary difficulty appears to lie in defining when one stage ends and another begins, or when one stage starts, but another does not. This issue is frustratingly complicated by the fact that any such sequential determinations will be very sensitive to how the hierarchical components are operationalized and the research methods employed. Add to this the uncertain relevance of results to management. Concerning the cognition-affect controversy, Peterson *et al.* (1986) suggest:

> The question 'did the person think first or feel first' is not very meaningful. Individuals are always in a stream of thinking or feeling; therefore, it is irrelevant to say 'Are there any thoughts preceding an affect' or 'is there affect preceding cognition.' Both of these activities are continually occurring … Mental activities are dynamic, not static. The important issue to be addressed is how affect and cognition interact to influence behaviour.

To this date in the advertising hierarchy literature, the views of Smith and Swinyard (1982) come closest to addressing this issue.

Hierarchical prospects

The empirical evidence one can offer to support the hierarchy of effects depends, of course, on how one wishes to define the various components and other characteristics of a study one considers desirable. Nevertheless, using the criteria selected here, little evidence was found to support the existence of an advertising hierarchy. However, the conclusion that a hierarchy does not exist would be contrary to the principal point we wish to raise. We believe the lack of published research may reflect the opinion of many researchers that there is uncertain value in undertaking such research. Two possible reasons for this could be offered: one is the question of whether (or when) cognition precedes affect, or *vice versa*. This shows little promise of being resolved in the immediate future and may vary as a function of how the constructs are arbitrarily defined. Lazarus (1984) argues that this 'primacy' issue is fundamentally indeterminant. If he is wrong, this sensitive question probably shows the least promise of being conclusively resolved using a complex stimulus such as an advertisement, especially since for most products consumers *already possess* product-related cognitions and affect in memory, further complicating the search for a sequential order of response. Secondly, even if the first issue were resolved, researchers would still be faced with the difficulty of demonstrating that the information provided by conducting a hierarchical investigation was not only valuable to management, but could not be obtained more easily in other ways.

The onus is on future research in the hierarchy area to address the above two concerns before other issues are considered. First, efforts must be made to assure that the various hierarchies can be confirmed or disproved, even if this involves limiting the meaning of the terms 'cognition' and 'affect'. The framework required will include a set of *well-defined* theoretical and measurement assumptions and an acceptable (as well as unacceptable) means of testing those assumptions. For example, are advertisers content with assuming that if a consumer is unable to recall or recognize an advertisement then 'cognition' did not occur? If that assumption is unacceptable (e.g., the information was learned, but was lost in the period between acquisition and attempted retrieval) then a precise means of resolving the issue must be delineated. Simply suggesting that a given assumption is unacceptable is of little benefit unless one can provide an assumption that *is* acceptable. Are advertisers content with assuming that if attitude change is not found after exposure to advertising then 'affect' did not occur? If that assumption is unacceptable (e.g., affective processing did occur, the end-product of which happened to be 'no change' in the criterion score) then a means of resolving the issue must be presented. Since the effects of advertising are often 'long-term' (Lavidge and Steiner, 1961), can it be assumed that investigations of 'short-term', especially single-advertisement exposures, provide insufficient evidence concerning the hierarchy? Consider, for example, a finding of cognition-affect-conation causal linkages, which would be *consistent* with the traditional hierarchy of effects. However, without defining what is meant by 'long-term' effects of advertising, there is no requirement that a lack of causality obtained at any given point in time be considered *inconsistent* with that hierarchy. The problem is that a theory in which causality is consistent, but a lack of causality is not inconsistent, with its underlying assumptions is potentially non-falsifiable.

Assuming that the first concern is addressed, the contributions of results stemming from hierarchy investigations must be vigorously compared to other means of obtaining the same information. A choice can then be made about which method is most practical. For example, Vaughn's (1986) extensive study arrived at conclusions thought to be consistent with different hierarchies, but were not obtained by empirically examining those different hierarchies.

Accomplishing the first two steps should then allow workers in the area to distinguish, if necessary, between the hierarchy of effects as a heuristic model which provides guidance to management in a general sense, as opposed to an empirical model which can be relied upon to provide consistent and interpretable results which deserve to be specifically addressed.

CONCLUSION

The concept of an advertising hierarchy of effects has been advocated for at least 80 years. The major challenge for those researching the possibility of such a hierarchy in the future is the conceptualization of a framework which, when tested, allows clear and unambiguous inferences to be made concerning competing sequences. This must be followed by coming to grips with whether the information is both valuable to management and cannot be more easily obtained in other ways. If success with both of these tasks cannot be attained, viewing the hierarchy of effects simply as a heuristic model which may have utility for general planning and guidance purposes may be most appropriate.

ACKNOWLEDGEMENTS

The authors appreciate the financial support of the Research and Development Council and the Center for Marketing Management Studies as well as comments of Professor John Slocum, Cox School of Business at SMU.

REFERENCES

Adams, H. F. (1916) *Advertising and its Mental Laws*. New York: The Macmillan Company.

Advertising Research Foundation (1961) Audience Concepts Committee. *Toward Better Media Comparisons*. New York.

Assael, H. and Day, G. S. (1968) Attitudes and awareness as predictors of market share. *Journal of Advertising Research*, 8, 3–10.

Batra, R. and Vanhonacker, W. R. (1986) The hierarchy of advertising effects: an aggregate field test of temporal precedence. New York: Columbia Business School. (Avis Rent a Car System Working Paper Series in Marketing, March).

Bedell, C. (1940) *How to Write Advertising that Sells*. New York: McGraw-Hill.

Bem, D. J. (1972) Self-perception theory. *Advances in Experimental Social Psychology*. Berkowitz, L. (Ed.) New York: Academic Press.

Colley, R. H. (1961) *Defining Advertising Goals for Measured Advertising Results*. New York: Association of National Advertisers.

Devoe, M. (1956) *Effective Advertising Copy*. New York: The Macmillan Company.

Eastman, G. R. (1916) *Psychology of Salesmanship*. New York: A. F. Fenno and Dayton, OH: Service Publishing.

Fishbein, M. and Ajzen, I. (1975) *Belief, Attitude, Intention and Behavior*. Reading, Massachusetts: Addison-Wesley.

Hall, S. R. (1915) *Writing an Advertisement: Analysis of the Methods and Mental Processes that Play a Part in the Writing of Successful Advertising*. Boston: Houghton Mifflin Co.

International Correspondence Schools (1911) *The Conducting of Sales*.

Jenkins, J. G. (1935) *Psychology in Business and Industry*. New York: John Wiley & Sons, Inc.

Kelley, C. A. (1973) The processes of causal attribution. *American Psychologist*, 28, 107–128.

Kiesler, C. A. (1971) *The Psychology of Commitment: Experiments Linking Behavior to Belief*. New York: Academic Press.

Kitson, H. D. (1921) *The Mind of the Buyer: A Psychology of Selling*. New York: The Macmillan Company.

Krugman, H. E. (1965) The impact of television advertising: learning without involvement. *Public Opinion Quarterly*, 29, 349–356.

Krugman, H. E. (1966) Answering some unanswered questions in measuring advertising effectiveness. *Proceedings, 12th Annual Meeting, Advertising Research Foundation*, New York, 18–23.

Kunst-Wilson, W. R. and Zajonc, R. B. (1980) Affective discrimination of stimuli that cannot be recognized. *Science*, 207, 557–558.

Lavidge, R.C. and Steiner, G.A. (1961) A model for predictive measurements of advertising effectiveness, *Journal of Marketing*, 25, 59–62.

Lazarus, R. S. (1981) A cognitivist's reply to Zajonc on emotion and cognition. *American Psychologist*, 36, 222–223.

Lazarus, R. S. (1982) Thoughts on the relations between emotion and cognition. *American Psychologist*, 37, 1019–1024.

Lazarus, R. S. (1984) On the primacy of cognition. *American Psychologist*, 39, 124–129.

Mandler, G. (1982) The structure of value: Accounting for taste. In *Cognition and Affect*. (Ed.) Fiske, S. and Clarke, M. New York: Academic Press.

Mayer, F. S., Duval, S. and Duval, V. H. (1980) An attributional analysis of commitment. *Journal of Personality and Social Psychology*, 39, 1072–1080.

McGuire,W. J. (1969) An information-processing model of advertising effectiveness. Paper presented to Symposium on Behavioural and Management Science in Marketing, University of Chicago.

McGuire, W. J. (1978) An information-processing model of advertising effectiveness. In *Behavioral and Management Science in Marketing* (Ed.) Davis, H. L. and Silk, A. J., pp. 156–180. New York: Ronald Press.

Moreland, R. L. and Zajonc, R. B. (1977) Is stimulus recognition a necessary condition for the occurrence of exposure effects? *Journal of Personality and Social Psychology*, 35, 191–199.

Moreland, R. L. and Zajonc, R. B. (1979) Exposure effects may not depend on stimulus recognition. *Journal of Personality and Social Psychology*, 32, 1085–1089.

O'Brien, T. (1971) Stages of consumer decision making. *Journal of Marketing Research*, 8, 282–289.

Osborn, A. F. (1922) *A Short Course in Advertising*. New York: C. Scribner's Sons.

Palda, K. S. (1966) The hypothesis of a hierarchy of effects: a partial evaluation. *Journal of Marketing Research*, 3, 13–24.

Peterson, R. A., Hoyner, W. D. and Wilson, W. R. (1986) Reflections on the role of affect in consumer behavior. In *The Role of Affect in Consumer Behavior: Emerging Theories and Applications*. Lexington, Massachusetts: Lexington Books, pp. 141–159.

Preston, I. L. (1982) The association models of the advertising communication process. *Journal of Advertising*, 11, 3–15.

Preston, I. L. and Thorson, E. (1983) Challenges to the use of hierarchy models in predicting advertising effectiveness. *Proceedings of the Annual Convention of American Academy of Advertising*, 27–33.

Preston, I. L. and Thorson, E. (1984) The expanded association model: keeping the hierarchy concept alive. *Journal of Advertising Research*, 24, 59–65.

Printers' Ink (1910) December 1, 74.

Ramsay, R. E. (1921) *Effective Direct Advertising: The Principles and Practice of Producing Direct Advertising for Distribution by Mail or Otherwise*. New York: Appleton and Company.

Ray, M. L., Sawyer, A. G., Rothschild, M. L., Heeler, R. M. Strong, E. C. and Reed, J. B. (1973) Marketing communications and the hierarchy of effects. In *New Models for Mass Communication Research*, (Ed.) Clarke, P., pp. 147–176. Beverly Sage, CA: Publishing.

Robertson, T. S. (1971) *Innovative Behavior and Communication*. New York: Holt, Rinehart, Winston.

Rogers, E. M. (1962) *Diffusion of Innovation*. New York: Free Press.

Schmalensee, D. H. (1983) Today's top priority advertising research questions. *Journal of Advertising Research*, 23, 49–60.

Scott, W. D. (1903) *The Theory of Advertising: A Simple Exposition of the Principles of Psychology in Their Relation to Successful Advertising*. Boston: Small, Maynard and Company.

Scott, W. D. (1908) *The Psychology of Advertising: A Simple Exposition of the Principles of Psychology in Their Relation to Successful Advertising*. Boston: Small, Maynard and Company.

Sheldon, A. F. (1911) *The Art of Selling*. Chicago: The Sheldon School.

Smith, R. E. and Swinyard, W. R. (1982) Information response models: an integrated approach. *Journal of Marketing*, 46, 81–93.

Smith, R. E. and Swinyard, W. R. (1983) Attitude-behavior consistency: the impact of product trial versus advertising. *Journal of Marketing Research*, 20, 257–267.

Smith, R. E. and Swinyard, W. R. (1988) Cognitive response to advertising and trial: belief strength, belief confidence and product curiosity. *Journal of Advertising, 11, 3–14.*

Starch, D. (1923) *Principles of Advertising*. New York: McGraw-Hill Book Company.

Strong, Jr., E. K. (1925a) *The Psychology of Selling and Advertising*. New York: McGraw-Hill.

Strong, Jr., E. K. (1925b) Theories of selling. *The Journal of Applied Psychology*, 9, 75–86.

Strong, Jr., E. K. (1938) *Psychological Aspect of Business*. New York: McGraw-Hill.

Tsal, Y. (1985) On the relationship between cognitive and affective processes: a critique of Zajonc and Markus. *Journal of Consumer Research*, 12, 358–362.

Vaughn, R. (1980) How advertising works: a planning model. *Journal of Advertising Research*, 20, 27–33.

Vaughn, R. (1986) How advertising works: a planning model revisited. *Journal of Advertising Research*, 26, 57–66.

Watts, F. N. (1983) Affective cognition: a sequel to Zajonc and Rachman. *Behavioral Research and Theory*, 21, 89–90.

West Coast Life Insurance Company (1920) The five steps of a sale.

Wolfe, H. D., Brown, J. K. and Thompson, G. C. (1962) *Measuring Advertising Results*, p. 7. New York: National Industrial Conference Board.

Zajonc, R. B. (1980a) Feeling and thinking: preferences need no inferences. *American Psychologist*, 35, 151–175.

Zajonc, R. B. (1980b) Cognition and social cognition: a historical perspective. In *Four Decades of Social Psychology*. (Ed.) Festinger, L., pp. 1–42. Oxford: Oxford University Press.

Zajonc, R. B. and Markus, H. (1982) Affective and cognitive factors in preferences. *Journal of Consumer Research*, 9, 123–131.

Zajonc, R. B. (1984) On the primacy of affect. *American Psychologist*, 39, 117–123.

Zajonc, R. B. (1986) Basic mechanisms of preference formation. In *The Role of Affect in Consumer Behavior: Emerging Theories and Applications*. (Ed.) Peterson, R. A., Hoyer, W. D. and Wilson, W. R., pp. 1–16. Lexington, Massachusetts: Lexington Books.

Zinkhan, G. M. and Fornell, C. (1989) A test of the learning hierarchy in high and low-involvement situations. *Association for Consumer Research*, 16, pp. 152–159.

Barry, T. E. and Howard, D. J. (1990) 'A review and critique of the hierarchy of effects in advertising'. *Internatioal Journal of Advertising*, 9: 121–135. Reproduced with permission.

2.4 A model for predictive measurements of advertising effectiveness

Robert J. Lavidge and Gary A. Steiner

What are the functions of advertising? Obviously the ultimate function is to help produce sales. But all advertising is not, should not, and cannot be designed to produce immediate purchases on the part of all who are exposed to it. *Immediate* sales results (even if measurable) are, at best, an incomplete criterion of advertising effectiveness.

In other words, the effects of much advertising are 'long-term.' This is sometimes taken to imply that all one can really do is wait and see – ultimately the campaign will or will not produce.

However, if something is to happen in the long run, *something* must be happening in the short run, something that will ultimately lead to eventual sales results. And this process must be measured in order to provide anything approaching a comprehensive evaluation of the effectiveness of the advertising.

Ultimate consumers normally do not switch from disinterested individuals to convinced purchasers in one instantaneous step. Rather, they approach the ultimate purchase through a process or series of steps in which the actual purchase is but the final threshold.

Seven steps

Advertising may be thought of as a force, which must move people up a series of steps:

1. Near the bottom of the steps stand potential purchasers who are completely *unaware of the existence* of the product or service in question.
2. Closer to purchasing, but still a long way from the cash register, are those who are merely *aware of its existence*.
3. Up a step are prospects who *know what the product has to offer*.
4. Still closer to purchasing are those who have favorable attitudes toward the product – those who *like the product*.
5. Those whose favorable attitudes have developed to the point of *preference* over all other possibilities are up still another step.
6. Even closer to purchasing are consumers who couple preference with a desire to buy and the *conviction* that the purchase would be wise.
7. Finally, of course, is the step which translates this attitude into actual *purchase*.

Research to evaluate the effectiveness of advertisements can be designed to provide measures of movement on such a flight of steps.

The various steps are not necessarily equidistant. In some instances the 'distance' from awareness to preference may be very slight, while the distance from preference to purchase is extremely large. In other cases, the reverse may be true. Furthermore, a potential purchaser sometimes may move up several steps simultaneously.

Consider the following hypotheses. The greater the psychological and/or economic commitment involved in the purchase of a particular product, the longer it will take to bring consumers up these steps, and the more important the individual steps will be. Contrariwise, the less serious the commitment, the more likely it is that some consumers will go almost 'immediately' to the top of the steps.

An impulse purchase might be consummated with no previous awareness, knowledge, liking, or conviction with respect to the product. On the other hand, an industrial good or an important consumer product ordinarily will not be purchased in such a manner.

Different objectives

Products differ markedly in terms of the role of advertising as related to the various positions on the steps. A great deal of advertising is designed to move people up the final steps toward purchase. At an extreme is the 'Buy Now' ad, designed to stimulate immediate overt action. Contrast this with industrial advertising, much of which is not intended to stimulate immediate purchase in and of itself. Instead, it is designed to help pave the way for the salesman by making the prospects aware of his company and products, thus giving them knowledge and favorable attitudes about the ways in which those products or services might be of value. This, of course, involves movement up the lower and intermediate steps.

Even within a particular product category, or with a specific product, different advertisements or campaigns may be aimed primarily at different steps in the purchase process – and rightly so. For example, advertising for new automobiles is likely to place considerable emphasis on the lower steps when new models are first brought out. The advertiser recognizes that his first job is to make the potential customer aware of the new product, and to give him knowledge and favorable attitudes about the product. As the year progresses, advertising emphasis tends to move up the steps. Finally, at the end of the 'model year' much emphasis is placed on the final step – the attempt to stimulate immediate purchase among prospects who are assumed, by then, to have information about the car.

The simple model assumes that potential purchasers all 'start from scratch.' However, some may have developed negative attitudes about the product, which place them even further from purchasing the product than those completely unaware of it. The first job, then, is to get them off the negative steps – before they can move up the additional steps which lead to purchase.

Three functions of advertising

The six steps outlined, beginning with 'aware,' indicate three major functions of advertising. (1) The first two, awareness and knowledge, relate to *information or ideas*. (2) The second two steps, liking and preference, have to do with favorable *attitudes or feelings* toward the product. (3) The final two steps, conviction and purchase, are to produce *action* – the acquisition of the product.

These three advertising functions are directly related to a classic psychological model which divides behavior into three components or dimensions:

1. The cognitive component – the intellectual, mental, or 'rational' states.
2. The affective component – the 'emotional' or 'feeling' states.
3. The conative or motivational component – the 'striving' states, relating to the tendency to treat objects as positive or negative goals.

This is more than a semantic issue, because the actions that need to be taken to stimulate or channel motivation may be quite different from those that produce knowledge. And these, in turn, may differ from actions designed to produce favorable *attitudes* toward something.

FUNCTIONS OF ADVERTISING RESEARCH

Among the first problems in any advertising evaluation program are to:

1. Determine what steps are most critical in a particular case, that is, what the steps leading to purchase are for most consumers.
2. Determine how many people are, at the moment, on which steps.
3. Determine which people on which steps it is most important to reach.

Advertising research can *then* be designed to evaluate the extent to which the advertising succeeds in moving the specified 'target' audience(s) up the critical purchase steps.

Table 1 summarizes the stair-step model, and illustrates how several common advertising and research approaches may be organized according to their various 'functions.'

Over-all and component measurements

With regard to most any product there are an infinite number of additional 'sub-flights' which can be helpful in moving a prospect up the main steps. For example, awareness, knowledge, and development of favorable attitudes toward a *specific product feature* may be helpful in building a preference for the *line* of products. This leads to the concept of other steps, subdividing or 'feeding' into the purchase steps, but concerned solely with more specific product features or attitudes.

Advertising effectiveness measurements may, then, be categorized into:

1. Over-all or 'global' measurements, concerned with measuring the results – the consumers' positions and movement on the purchase steps.
2. Segment or component measurements, concerned with measuring the relative effectiveness of various *means* of moving people up the purchase steps – the consumers' positions on ancillary flights of steps, and the relative importance of these flights.

Measuring movement on the steps

Many common measurements of advertising effectiveness have been concerned with movement up either the *first* steps or the *final* step on the primary purchase flight.

Table 1 Advertising and advertising research related to the model

Related behavioral dimensions	Movement toward purchase	Examples of types of promotion or advertising relevant to various steps	Examples of research approaches related to steps of greatest applicability
CONATIVE —the realm of motives. Ads stimulate or direct desires.	PURCHASE ↑ ↑ CONVICTION	Point-of-purchase Retail store ads Deals 'Last-chance' offers Price appeals Testimonials	Market or sales tests Split-run tests Intention to purchase Projective techniques
AFFECTIVE —the realm of emotions. Ads change attitudes and feelings.	PREFERENCE ↑ ↑ LIKING ↑	Competitive ads Argumentative copy 'Image' ads Status, glamor appeals	Rank order of preference for brands Rating scales Image measurements, including check lists and semantic differentials Projective techniques
COGNITIVE —the realm of thoughts. Ads provide information and facts.	KNOWLEDGE ↑ AWARENESS	Announcements Descriptive copy Classified ads Slogans Jingles Sky writing Teaser campaigns	Information questions Play-back analyses Brand awareness surveys Aided recall

Examples include surveys to determine the extent of brand awareness and information and measures of purchase and repeat purchase among 'exposed' versus 'unexposed' groups.

Self-administered instruments, such as adaptations of the 'semantic differential' and adjective check lists, are particularly helpful in providing the desired measurements of movement up or down the middle steps. The semantic differential provides a means of scaling attitudes with regard to a number of different issues in a manner which facilitates gathering the information on an efficient quantitative basis. Adjective lists, used in various ways, serve the same general purpose.

Such devices can provide relatively spontaneous, rather than 'considered,' responses. They are also quickly administered and can contain enough elements to make recall of specific responses by the test participant difficult, especially if the order of items is changed. This helps in minimizing 'consistency' biases in various comparative uses of such measurement tools.

Efficiency of these self-administered devices makes it practical to obtain responses to large numbers of items. This facilitates measurement of elements or components differing only slightly, though importantly, from each other.

Carefully constructed adjective check lists, for example, have shown remarkable discrimination between terms differing only in subtle shades of meaning. One product may be seen as 'rich,' 'plush,' and 'expensive,' while another one is 'plush,' 'gaudy,' and 'cheap.'

Such instruments make it possible to secure simultaneous measurements of both global attitudes and *specific* image components. These can be correlated with each other and directly related to the content of the advertising messages tested.

Does the advertising change the thinking of the respondents with regard to specific product attributes, characteristics or features, including not only physical characteristics but also various image elements such as 'status'? Are these changes commercially significant?

The measuring instruments mentioned are helpful in answering these questions. *They provide a means for correlating changes in specific attitudes concerning image components with changes in global attitudes or position on the primary purchase steps.*

Testing the model

When groups of consumers are studied over time, do those who show more movement on the measured steps eventually purchase the product in greater proportions or quantities? Accumulation of data utilizing the stair-step model provides an opportunity to test the assumptions underlying the model by answering this question.

THREE CONCEPTS

This approach to the measurement of advertising has evolved from three concepts:

1. Realistic measurements of advertising effectiveness must be related to an understanding of the functions of advertising. It is helpful to think in terms of a model where advertising is likened to a force which, if successful, moves people up a series of steps toward purchase.
2. Measurements of the effectiveness of the advertising should provide measurements of changes at *all* levels on these steps – not just at the levels of the development of product or feature awareness and the stimulation of actual purchase.
3. Changes in attitudes as to specific image components can be evaluated together with changes in over-all images, to determine the extent to which changes in the image components are related to movement on the primary purchase steps.

Lavidge, R. J. and Steiner, G. A. (1961) 'A model for predictive measurements of advertising effectiveness'. *Journal of Marketing*, October: 59–62. Reproduced with permission from *Journal of Marketing*, published by the American Marketing Association.

Getting the most out of advertising and promotion

2.5

Magid M. Abraham and Leonard M. Lodish

Until recently, believing in the effectiveness of advertising and promotion has largely been a matter of faith. Marketing departments might collect voluminous statistics on television program ratings and on coupon redemptions and carefully compare the cost of marketing with total sales. But none of this data measures what is really important: the *incremental* sales of a product over and above those that would have happened without the advertising or promotion.

Thanks to a new kind of marketing data, that situation is changing. The data correlate information on actual consumer purchases (available from universal-product-code scanners used in supermarkets and drugstores) with information on the kind of television advertising those consumers receive or the frequency and type of promotion events they see. Armed with this consumer products data from a 'single source', managers can measure the incremental impact of marketing-mix variables such as advertising, merchandising, and pricing.

Forward-looking senior managers are beginning to realize that single-source data provide an unparalleled opportunity to increase their company's marketing productivity – if they know how to take advantage of it. Doing so requires developing new marketing strategies and radically redefining the responsibilities of a company's sales force.

At the strategic level, managers must evaluate marketing data differently and put incremental sales and profits into management objectives. This means continually examining the appropriate balance between advertising and promotion, based on marginal-productivity analysis.

The search for fresh, innovative television advertising to boost sales of established products should be constant. Until such advertising is found, it may pay to cut back on advertising spending. Using single-source test markets as 'lead markets' for national advertising campaigns can substantially lower the risk of this approach.

Managers must also cut back on unproductive promotions in favor of hard-to-imitate promotion events that directly contribute to incremental profitability. And they must use the new data to shape distinctive promotional efforts for specific local markets and key accounts.

In this dynamic marketing environment, the sales force will have a different and extremely important job: to demonstrate to retailers the consumer pull of its company's advertising and promotion programs, as well as the effect these programs have on retailer profitability. New strategies that benefit *both* retailer and manufacturer must replace the traditional practice of using advertising and promotion as inducements to carry a product.

Above all, senior managers must throw out much of the conventional wisdom about advertising and promotion that has formed over the years. Replacing these widely held but unsupported beliefs with marketing strategies based on hard data is the key to attaining a new kind of market power.

WHAT'S WRONG WITH THE CONVENTIONAL WISDOM

Because they have been unable to measure the incremental sales of advertising and promotion before now, marketing managers have had to rely on a number of unexamined assumptions. For example, those who believe advertising works also tend to assume that in all cases, more of it is better than less. This assumption is frequently justified by another: that advertising takes a long time – many months or, sometimes, even years – to increase sales.

Another by-product of the traditional lack of data on incremental sales is the common belief that once advertising does start producing sales, its impact is short term. A popular rule of thumb is that if increased advertising spending does not generate enough sales to pay for the incremental expense within a year, then a company shouldn't implement the advertising.

Finally, many marketing managers will tell you that even if advertising is *not* directly boosting sales, it still serves an important function. When salespeople can point to a big ad budget, this convinces retailers that the manufacturer supports the product, thus assuring its distribution in the stores.

So too with promotions. Traditionally, the focus has been on gross rather than incremental sales. The conventional wisdom is that a successful promotion is one where a company sells a lot of goods to the trade and that a promotion for an established brand can be used to attract and retain new users of the brand. In fact, promotions have become so popular that they now account for more than 65% of typical marketing budgets.

Our research challenges all of these beliefs. Since 1982, we have been using single-source data to examine the productivity of the marketing dollar spend on advertising and promotions for consumer packaged goods. The results are striking:

- In 360 tests in which the only variable was advertising weight – the amount of television advertising to which consumers are exposed – increased advertising led to more sales only about half the time.
- Analyses of trade promotions for all brands in 65 different product categories suggest that the productivity of promotion spending is even worse. Only 16% of the trade promotion events we studied were profitable, based on incremental sales of brands distributed through retailer warehouses. For many promotions, the cost of selling an incremental dollar of sales was *greater* than one dollar.
- Judging from our aggregate statistics, managers have been spending too much of their marketing budgets on promotion (in lieu of advertising). Many companies could reduce their total advertising and promotion budgets *and* improve profitability.

To measure the productivity of television advertising, we use a technique known as a 'split cable' market test. About 3,000 households in test markets receive ID cards that household members show when they purchase goods at scanner-equipped supermarkets. These supermarkets typically account for more than 90% of the total volume of all products sold in the area.

The test markets are far enough away from television stations that residents' only choice for good reception is cable TV. By agreement with the cable company and the advertiser, we intercept the cable signal before it reaches each household and send different advertisements to different households. To test advertising copy, some households receive advertisement A, while others simultaneously receive advertisement B. To test advertising weight, households receive different amounts of advertising for the same brand.

Split-cable tests typically run for one year, and we have conducted them for both new and established products. We control for variables such as past brand and category purchases and statistically adjust the sales data to account for the impact of promotions for the test brand or for competing brands. This instrumented test environment provides the ultimate degree of experimental control and is well suited for isolating the sales effect of advertising.

Some of the findings from our 360 split-cable tests conducted over the past decade support traditional assumptions. For example, most people believe that advertising is more effective for new brands than for established brands, and this turns out to be the case. We found that 59% of new-product advertising tests showed a positive impact on sales, compared with only 46% of the tests for established brands. Furthermore, when advertising showed a significant effect on a new product, the increase in sales averaged 21% across all new-product tests.

But in most respects, our findings clearly contradict conventional wisdom. In more than half of the established-brand experiments, increased advertising did not result in more sales.

Nor does advertising take a long time to work. When a particular advertising weight or copy is effective, it works relatively rapidly. Incremental sales begin to occur within six months. The converse of this finding is even more important. If advertising changes do not show an effect in six months, then they will not have any impact, even if continued for a year.

When advertising does boost sales, the extra profits often do not cover the increased media costs – at least in the short term. Company payout analyses are highly sensitive, and we have only partial pay-out statistics on a subset of our test database. They show that only about 20% of advertising-weight tests pay out for established brands during the first year. For new products, profitable advertising ranges from 40% to 50%, reflecting the higher productivity of advertising spending on new products.

However, the long-term effect of advertising is at least as substantial as its short-term effect. This is the upside to the downside that advertising works only about half the time. Even if increased advertising returns only half the money spent over the course of one year, it will break even on average if the long-term effects are taken into account.

We have evaluated the sales effect of advertising over the long term by analysing 15 market tests up to two years after they ended. In these experiments, the test group viewed more advertisements than the control group during the test year. We then stopped the extra advertising and sent both groups the same amount. Across 15 cases, there was a demonstrable carryover effect. The sales increase for the groups receiving more advertising averaged 22% in the test year, 17% in the second year, and 6% in the third year. Although the carryover effect declined on average, in six cases it actually widened.

More important that the pattern is the magnitude of the carryover. On average, 76% of the difference observed in the test year persisted one year after the advertising increase was rolled back. Over a three-year period, the cumulative sales increase was at least twice the sales increase observed in the test year.

WHY MOST PROMOTIONS LOSE MONEY

To evaluate trade promotions, we have developed computer programs that measure the marginal productivity of promotional events.[1] Anywhere from 30% to 90% of the time, a consumer product is not on promotion in a particular store. Using sales data from individual stores, the programs compare sales from these non-promotion weeks with those from promotion weeks. Algorithms then project what the sales of the product would have been during the promotion week if the promotion had not taken place. This provides a baseline against which we can measure the incremental impact of the promotion. The only possible bias is that our programs may overestimate the incremental sales of a particular event since promotions tend to accelerate purchases by consumers. Thus we may mistakenly count purchases borrowed from a later period's normal sales as incremental sales caused by the promotion.

At first glance, our finding that only 16% of the promotions studied were profitable may seem surprising. But when you consider the economics underlying promotions, it is easy to see why. Consider the hypothetical example of a brand with very good support from retailers (see the exhibit 'The unprofitable economics of trade promotions'). The brand promotes to the trade at a 15% price discount over a four-week period. Assume that all the stores in the market feature the brand for one week in their weekly newspaper advertising supplement. What's more, half the stores support the brand with three weeks of in-store display and consumer price reductions, while the other half only reduce the price but for the full four weeks. These are excellent trade-support statistics that would be hard to achieve in reality.

Nevertheless, when we compute the incremental sales generated from this excellent trade activity (also assuming above-average consumer response), the promotion ends up costing 64 cents for each incremental dollar it generates. In other words, unless the product's gross margin is more than 64%, the promotion will lose money. The reason is that the manufacturer has to sell an extraordinarily high number of cases at the discounted price to cover the normal base sales that would have taken place without the promotion. What's more, the manufacturer must cover the practice of retailer 'forward buying' – accumulating discounted inventory in the warehouse during the time window of the promotion and selling it later at the regular price. In fact, only about 23% of the cases sold on promotion are incremental in this example.

Forward buying helps explain why promotions often have a dramatic – and highly misleading – impact on a manufacturer's shipments. Typically, a retailer will take in thousands of cases during a promotion. But after a promotion, shipments will halt for several weeks while the retailer depletes its forward-buying inventory. Normally, that inventory has no benefit to the manufacturer. On the contrary, it substantially raises the costs of promotions and makes them unprofitable.

Another disadvantage, of promotions is that unlike advertising, they almost never have a positive long-term effect on established brands. Promotions for new products

The unprofitable economics of trade promotions

	Cases	Gross dollars
Baseline* (Sales that would have occurred during the four-week promotion period even without the promotion)	400	$ 4,000
Incremental sales to consumer[†] Due to one week of feature	100	$ 1,000
Due to 50% of stores with three weeks of display and price reduction	250	$ 2,500
Due to 50% of stores with four weeks of price reduction only	80	$ 800
Total	430	$ 4,300
Ten weeks of forward buying by retailers[†]	1,000	$10,000
Total sales during promotion	1,830	$18,300
Cost of promotion ($18,300 × 15% Discount)		$ 2,745
Cost per incremental dollar of sales (Promotion costs divided by total incremental sales)		$ .64
Promotion efficiency (Incremental cases sold to consumer divided by total cases sold)		23.5%

*Assume weekly base sales of 100 cases and a list price of $10 per case.
[†]Based on our analysis of single-course data and retailer promotion purchases.

Despite the ideal conditions of this hypothetical example, the promotion ends up costing the manufacturer 64 cents for each incremental dollar it generates. Unless the product's gross margin is greater than 64%, the promotion will lose money.

may be quite productive because they encourage consumers to try an unfamiliar product. But the probability that consumers who buy an established brand on promotion will purchase it the next time is about the same as their likelihood of doing so even if no promotion had taken place. In fact, promotions for established brands usually attract either current users who would buy the product anyway or brand switchers who bounce between brands on deal.

Another hidden cost of promotions is competitive escalation. The advantage of running an extra promotion or offering higher incentives is usually short-lived. Competitors retaliate with promotions of their own, neutralizing whatever incremental volume is generated. The most insidious escalation is that of trade promotion discounts. When retailers are offered higher discounts once, they come to expect them regularly.

The flip side is de-escalation – a cycle where competitors refrain from undercutting each other's profits through promotions. Discontinuing a money-losing promotion not only stops a manufacturer's losses; it also sends a de-escalation signal, which if heeded by competitors (and chances are higher if the manufacturer's brand is a market leader), ends up improving profits even more. However, if de-escalation doesn't take place, then cutting promotions will cost sales and market share even as it increases profits. Only if de-escalation works can profits be enhanced without losing sales or share.

FACT-BASED STRATEGIES AND TACTICS

With single-source data, managers can balance investments in advertising and promotion to improve the contribution of each to long-term profit. Intelligent use of the data can help the ad manager determine not only when and where to increase spending but also when and where to decrease it.

The idea is to start with a zero budget and allocate money incrementally to various advertising and promotion options. The goal is to identify the option that marginally contributes most to the long-term profitability of the product. Allocations should continue on this incremental basis until all options that provide a suitable return on the incremental investment are found.

Since advertising doesn't always work, the first challenge is to maximize the chances of getting productive campaigns. Ad execs should increase spending as long as a particular campaign remains productive and cut back as soon as market tests show its productivity declining significantly. Meanwhile, they should constantly search for new, more compelling advertising and test it against the old.

For new products, advertising can provide significant help when it fulfills its primary role of communicating product news. Increasing weight behind effective new-product advertising is a productive strategy. Because new-product advertising primarily influences trial, which may lead to repeat purchases, its effectiveness is likely to be long term. The combination of a successful new product and successful advertising is rare. When this happens, it is no time for skimping.

To determine whether a particular new-product advertisement is working, test it at different weight levels in test markets before the national rollout. If the new product sells as well in those groups with low exposure as in those with high exposure, then heavy spending is not necessary. Conversely, if the higher weight groups try the product faster or more frequently, then higher levels of advertising make sense – if the company considers the long-term value of the new triers greater than the advertising cost. Thus testing 'How high is up?' is an important tactic for new products.

Once new-product advertising has generated trials and positioned the new product in the market, continuing with the same large advertising budgets may not be necessary. In fact, without compelling new copy, approximately one-half of established-brand advertising does not produce any incremental sales. On the other hand, fresh copy for established products can prove extremely productive. Positive advertising effects on sales will continue long after the advertising has stopped, generally for at least one year.

These findings imply a very different form of 'pulsing' for many established products. Current practice is to pulse in short bursts of two to four weeks, on and off, using the same advertising each time. We would recommend pulses of at least six months, carried out over several years and using different advertising campaigns.

When advertising cannot demonstrate that it is incrementally contributing to sales of an established product (as shown by tests comparing the current advertising level with lower budgets), cut it back to some lower maintenance level – perhaps even to zero. Do not increase spending until a new campaign has demonstrated greater productivity. It is possible to estimate the likely incremental effect of a new campaign by showing both the old campaign at the old weight and the new campaign at several different weights to matched groups in test markets.

Having identified an effective new campaign, a company should run it at a high level nationally until it no longer shows any incremental sales effect, measured by comparing it with no advertising in a test market. As soon as this new campaign's incremental sales effect stops, the advertising should cut it back until yet another effective campaign can be developed.

Because of the risk associated with radical decreases in advertising, an even safer approach is to use the single-source test markets as 'lead markets' for national advertising. For example, conduct a six- to nine-month test comparing a lower advertising weight with the current national weight. If the lower weight does not harm sales in the test markets, implement it nationally. In the test markets, however, continue sending the 'normal' weight advertising to the group that has been receiving it. That way, if sales to the test households exposed to the lower advertising weight begin to decline compared with sales to normal-weight households, the national advertising budget can be immediately returned to the higher levels.

This strategy gives the decision maker a cushion so that decreasing national advertising poses little risk. Should the original decision prove to be a mistake, the company can return the national campaign to normal levels some six to nine months before sales begin to decline. Of course, a continuous search for new and more effective campaigns should occur simultaneously with this lower advertising.

Companies can use similar techniques to identify productive promotions. In promotions as in advertising, there is a premium on ingenuity and creativity. An effective promotion idea can be three or four times as efficient as the typical prior promotion. A company should spend significant resources to develop creative, hard-to-imitate promotion events, then use single-source data to test the idea. Not all ideas will make it past the test, but those that do will enhance profits. And depending on diminishing returns and competitive response, a company may be able to use the new event or idea more than once, helping further to amortize the investment in promotion development.

Finally, marketing managers can also apply the same analytical concepts to promotion and advertising decisions for particular local areas and for a manufacturer's key accounts – if they use the single-source data carefully. For example, the data can provide market-by-market estimates of promotional response and retailer support that may offer insights for allocating promotion funds and making necessary tactical changes.

The exhibit 'Customizing promotions for local markets' divides geographic markets according to their levels of promotion response and trade-promotion support for a particular product, then summarizes suggested actions. We index each market to national averages for the number of weeks (weighted by store volume) that the brand was on some type of promotion, as well as by the markets' average response (incremental sales per week of feature or display activity) and the weeks the brand was on price reduction only and not supported by feature or display ('unsupported price reductions').

The decision rules that support the actions are only a somewhat crude way to point management in a generally more profitable direction. Those markets with above-average unsupported price reductions might need greater featuring and display support from the retailer. Those low in promotion response probably require higher quality promotions – larger newspaper features, say, or better display locations.

Customizing promotions for local markets

	Retailers support (Weighted weeks product is on promotion)	Consumer response (Incremental sales per week of features and displays)	Unsupported price reductions (Weeks of price reductions with no features or displays)
Local market			
Seattle	106	117	156
Recommended action			

Better support of price reductions should contribute to the higher-than-average consumer response.

Houston	120	115	85

High retailer support and customer response combined with low unsupported price reductions mean that the manufacturer should continue doing what it's doing.

Tampa	116	60	89

Retailers are supporting the product well, but consumers aren't responding. It's time to improve the quality of features and displays.

Boston	82	115	102

Retailer support is below average, but consumers are still responding well. More features and displays could build on an already good situation.

Philadelphia	99	156	132

Consumer response is very high, but so is the number of unsupported price reductions. Supporting reductions with features and displays should increase sales and profits.

Kansas City	79	72	72

Both retailer support and consumer response are below national levels. It's time for more frequent and higher quality features and displays.

The numbers index promotion activity and consumer response in local markets to the national average (= 100) and suggest ways to improve future promotions in each market.

Similarly, companies can use single-source data to target key accounts and isolate mutually beneficial situations for the retailer and the manufacturer. The exhibit 'Identifying mutually beneficial markets' shows how Jewel Food Stores could have almost doubled its profits from a particular promotion event (here called the XYZ event) by adding one more week of feature and display. The result would be good for the manufacturer as well because incremental cases sold would have increased from 933 to 1,633 without any additional investment.

A NEW ROLE FOR THE SALES FORCE

One final caveat about these new marketing strategies merits discussing. Single-source data measure the effect of advertising and promotions on consumers, *not* on the distribution of a given product by retailers. One of the traditional uses of both advertising and promotion has been to convince retailers that the manufacturer supports the product and that the brand will pull consumers into the stores. Thus if a company cuts back on unproductive advertising between pulses or discontinues ineffective promotions, it runs the risk that retailers will interpret the move as a lack of support and therefore cut back on distribution.

To avoid this predicament, the sales force has a new and extremely important job to do. It must communicate to retailers that unproductive advertising with no consumer pull has no value to the retailer or the manufacturer. Likewise, smart

Identifying mutually beneficial promotions

	Jewel XYZ promotion event	XYZ event plus one more week of feature and display
Incremental cases sold to consumer	933	1,633
Nonpromoted retail case price	$90	$90
Gross incremental dollars	$83,970	$149,670
Retailer price reduction	16%	16%
Cost of retailer price reduction	$13,435	$23,947
Promoted wholesale case price	$50	$50
Cost of goods to retailer	$46,650	$83,150
Retailer profit	$23,885	$42,573

By comparing the results of the XYZ event with single-source data from other promotions in the same market, we determined that with only one more week of feature and display, Jewel would have increased its profit by $18,688, and the manufacturer would have sold an extra 700 cases.

retailers will begin demanding hard evidence on the consumer pull of advertising instead of merely being impressed with large media budgets.

The role of the sales force in promotion also will change. Instead of viewing trade promotions as a competitive payment to make sure the brand has distribution, sales personnel have to demonstrate to retailers how specific promotions will increase their incremental profits.

Taking advantage of this opportunity will require salespeople to have greater analytical abilities than they have needed in the past. In effect, they will have to become marketers in partnership with retailers. The retailers, like the manufacturers, now know what items are moving because they are seeing the same single-source data. As more retailers become sophisticated users of this information, it will be more difficult for manufacturers to get them to execute promotion programs that are not in retailers' best interests. Over time, there will be a bigger and bigger productivity difference between simply giving a retailer a price discount and hoping for the best and giving a price discount to support a well-documented, mutually beneficial promotion program.

NOTE

1 For the technical details of these programs, see our 'Promoter: An Automated Promotion Evaluation System', *Marketing Science*, Spring 1987, p. 101; and 'Promotionscan: A System for Improving Promotion Productivity for Retailers and Manufacturers Using Scanner Store and Household Panel Data', Wharton School Marketing Department Working Paper (Philadelphia: University of Pennsylvania, February 1990).

2.6 Measuring the impact of advertising

Randy Stone and Mike Duffy

Measuring the impact of advertising ... that is what Randy Stone, from Media Marketing Assessment, and I, Mike Duffy, from Kraft USA, would like to discuss. We will also be discussing the concept of the advertising 'halo' effect, but that is only part of our story.

First I'll share a few thoughts on why we at Kraft care about measuring the impact of advertising. Randy will then show what he and his company, Media Marketing Assessment, are doing to measure the sales impact for Kraft and a number of other marketers. Then I will show you how Kraft is using these new findings, and finally, Randy will finish up with a few thoughts on how these quantitative techniques may affect the way we plan our advertising in the future.

Why should we care?

We're spending lots of money on advertising. We're not altruistic. We don't do this to make our agencies happy .. we want to make money. Advertising is an investment for us, and we need to know if it's a profitable investment.

Phillip Morris, which includes Kraft and General Foods, has been spending over 2 billion dollars per year on measured media according to *Advertising Age*. *Advertising Age* estimates the top 100 advertisers spent over 33.7 billion dollars on advertising in 1991.

In spite of all this ad spending, things may still be getting out of balance. Is the split between benefit communication through advertising and price manipulation through promotion in balance? Is the A&P mix optimized to create maximum brand value?

And what about some of our conventional beliefs ... like identifying the right spending level as some percentage of operating revenue. Is it time to rethink some of the traditional concepts?

These are some of the issues that occupy much of our time at Kraft, and probably at many other companies too.

We have been particularly worried about the shifting mix of trade promotion, consumer promotion, and advertising. Total marketing spending has been growing at about 8 per cent per year over the last seven years. Ad spending has not been keeping pace at 2 per cent per year. In 1985 ad spending accounted for 35 per cent of total marketing expenditures. This dropped to 25 per cent in 1991. This is certainly not new news but has a lot of us worried ... worried about the potential damage to the perceived value of our brands with the emphasis on price rather than benefits.

Some people have suggested that a product's value is a function of its benefits relative to its price.

We need to be able to demonstrate that it makes economic sense to add value through communicating product benefits. We need to quantify the investment potential of advertising, just as the research suppliers of scanner data have shown the profitability of investing trade dollars in communicating price messages through newspaper feature ads and in-store displays.

If 25 percent of marketing expenditures devoted to advertising isn't right, what is?

Should ad spending be based on a percent of operating revenue? Should it be based on share of voice measures? Should it be based on some ratio to previous spending?

We want to spend the right amount, but how do we determine what the right amount is?

How do we know how much to spend on advertising?

At Kraft we are taking three different approaches to answer the question, and we look for convergence of evidence before we become comfortable with any of the answers.

In-market tests, high spending tests: These are not always easy to read and historically are very expensive to execute. The availability of detailed marketing data, store sales, and enhanced local market household samples is making this approach more feasible.

Conceptual models: We are heavy users of this approach, but it can become labor-intensive when applied at the local level. Still, it is a cost-effective addition to our mix of research methodologies.

Empirical analyses: This is another product of the increased availability of comprehensive marketing information. This approach provides an exciting opportunity to quantify the relationship between sales and marketing activity at the market level. Randy and MMA have been a key asset to Kraft in executing this research option – as he'll now tell you a little bit about it.

Thanks Mike. On the empirical side, there's good news and better news for advertising. First, the good news is that in four years of analyzing many brands, MMA has seen a positive and measurable contribution from advertising in 98 out of 102 separate instances. The better news is that our clients are then able to learn from this and make advertising work even harder.

We're able to measure this by building empirical models that use up to four years of a brand's marketing and sales history. This information on sales and marketing is used by week, by market, and covers up to 23 major markets which typically account for about half of the brand's total U.S. volume.

Once all this data is assembled from other suppliers and internal client sources, (which is no small task), and after a lot of effort, we produce a model which says that sales is a function of a series of coefficients behind marketing efforts, competitive actions, and other exogenous factors like weather and commodity pricing.

What you see in Figure 1 is a half-year slice of time which shows:

- what actual weekly sales were in Boston for Brand A
- what the model estimated sales were
- and where the model missed

The closer the two lines are, and the less pattern to the miss, the better we feel about the model.

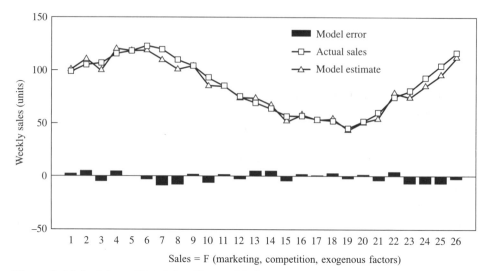

Sales = F (marketing, competition, exogenous factors)

Figure 1 Methodology: Brand A – Boston Market.

Once we get past the model parameters, what are we looking for? Well, we certainly want to quantify the sales effects of price, promotion, and distribution. We also want to know how competitive actions helped or hurt.

But, perhaps most important is quantifying the full effects of advertising on sales. This goes beyond the immediate effects to include the longer term and cross-brand 'halo' effects.

On the immediate side, it is essential that clients like Kraft be able to answer two key questions:

- Am I undersupporting my brand?
- And, how much is enough?

In order to do that, an advertising elasticity curve like the example shown in Figure 2 is developed for each market. It shows what the effect on total sales would be if advertising expenditures were raised or lowered by various levels.

However, while it is important for Kraft to know what the immediate effects of advertising are, advertising can be incredibly undervalued if the investigation stops here. Ignoring the long-term contribution of advertising would radically change the payout calculations Kraft conducts.

There's another important area which can't be ignored in advertising and that's the brand to brand 'halo' impact. In the case shown in Figure 3, there are two distinct forms the brand is available in, and each form is supported by its own copy.

As you can see, while Form 1's ads sell Form 1, they also help sell Form 2. The reverse is also true. This is a finding which, while I think we all intuitively knew, had never been quantified. We have seen it, in varying degrees, across every trademark analysis we've done. And once again, being unaware of the 'halo' effect can either mean missed opportunity, or a disaster waiting to happen.

Mike will now show you how this type of learning is put to practical use at Kraft.

What are we doing at Kraft? How are we using the results of this new advertising research to make better business decisions?

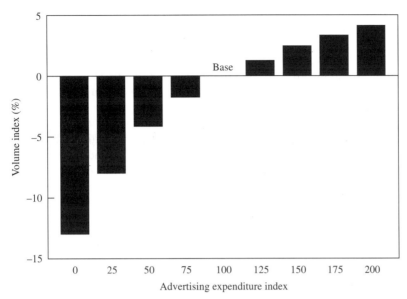

Figure 2 Advertising – immediate effect.

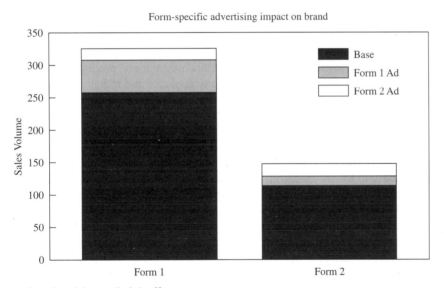

Figure 3 Advertising – 'halo' effect.

Calculating the bottom-line impact of our advertising investments . . . is the spending going to pay for itself? How long will it take to pay back our original investment?

Can we use this information to realign our marketing mix? Are the findings powerful enough to give us the confidence to reverse the escalation of our trade promotion budgets at the expense of our advertising funds?

And what products should we spend our money on? Can we focus our advertising messages on a trademark, or do the various trademark forms (regular versus fat free, swiss cheese versus cheddar) require their own support? Can we identify ad spending efficiencies by understanding the 'halo' effects of specific form advertising?

By quantifying the sales response to various levels of advertising spending, we can also calculate the profits, or the return on our marketing investment. With this information, we can identify the level of ad spending that maximizes profitability, the point at which the marginal return on the next dollar's worth of advertising results in less than a dollar's worth of profit.

We can also understand the opportunity to invest in the growth of the product. We can determine just what the profit trade-off is to support additional brand growth.

At Kraft, we also have a few beliefs relating to total brand value. Our business objectives include not only profitable volume growth but also the maintenance or even the increase of 'brand value.' We believe that the best way to have a lasting and positive effect on brand value is through benefit communication (advertising) rather than price manipulation (promotion).

We equate the concept of 'brand value' with trademark equity. Our research efforts in defining behavioral market structures have shown the importance of trademarks in many of the categories that Kraft competes in. By bundling the right products within a trademark umbrella, we can often reach a critical sales mass that can profitably support meaningful levels of ad spending.

But what should be included in a trademark definition?

In the Parkay line there are nine separate and distinct margarine and spread products. They all have the same Parkay trademark and package style, but can they be bundled together for purposes of advertising? Is there a risk in blurring the distinction between tubs and sticks, or margarine versus spreads?

Is the Parkay Light line the same trademark? Can these products be advertised with the Parkay line? Or, do these items require separate and independent advertising support?

We are using market structure concepts to help us understand how consumers view and use a category. The structure concepts define the specific marketable groupings and explain the 'halo' effects that we are quantifying with the empirical analyses that Randy has taken you through.

Kraft makes a lot of macaroni and cheese products. We support this growing category with a large number of unique product offerings under a variety of brand names. How should we group, or bundle, these items into meaningful advertising units?

With the Kraft and Velveeta lines should we have three trademarks, Kraft, Velveeta, and Deluxe? Or only two ... Kraft and Velveeta? The structure research, integrated with advertising 'halo' findings, have led us to some very specific and actionable conclusions.

And does the trademark 'halo' effect extend to other categories? When advertising Kraft Macaroni and Cheese, does Kraft cheese benefit? Is there an opportunity to advertise the Kraft trademark across a variety of categories? Would it be cost effective? These are the types of questions we find ourselves asking now ... and with the help of the new marketing data bases that include elements from the full marketing mix, and the use of increasingly sophisticated models, we are comfortable with many of the answers that we're getting.

And finally, we believe that we can assess the productivity of the various elements of the marketing mix at our disposal and make reasoned decisions on where to spend our next marketing dollar.

Not surprisingly, we are finding that advertising is our most profitable investment. The return on our ad dollars far exceeds that of either trade or consumer promotion spending. This is true, however, only when we take into account all three components of advertising's impact ... immediate effects, long-term effects, and the 'halo' effect.

Our industry is changing the way we view things. These days, precision is becoming outweighed by accountability. We are all in an environment where everything must be accountable.

So the question is: Where does this go?

It leads to a new level of accountability in three critical areas:

- Local planning
- Spending optimization
- Media scheduling

First, in local planning, if I know my advertising elasticity by market, I know what will happen if I change my ad spending in that market. The strategy becomes tactical. Looking at the example shown in Figure 4, if the strategy is to increase spending, I'd start in Albany. If the strategy is to reduce spending, I'd start in Philadelphia.

I also have this type of information on other elements of the marketing mix, and for all the brands in my portfolio.

This is now the state of the art. It's not just maximizing return; it's meeting objectives by brand and by market. Now that media spending is more fully accounted for, it can compete for its fair share of the marketing-mix budget.

This brings us to a new area which is now the focal point of a lot of our development efforts at MMA: media scheduling and planning.

Our goal is to bring new tools and learning to media scheduling, whose accountability is also being demanded. The first two points, local market efficiencies and timing, are basic and essential. Yet there's a new wrinkle ...

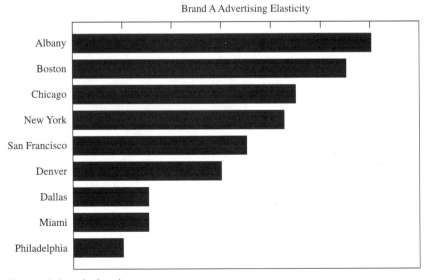

Figure 4 Local planning.

The fact that brands interact with each other is known. We've quantified it. When one applies this information in the planning process we see that you can't plan an individual brand in a vacuum. It must be in the context of the related brand plans as well. This argues for the need for a Planning Agency of Record.

So, what's the payoff? The payoff is that advertising has been losing ground to the other elements of the marketing mix. Yet once one recognizes that advertising has a long-term impact, and a 'halo' effect, the share-of-budget fight becomes a lot fairer.

Stone, R. and Duffy, M. (1993) 'Measuring the impact of advertising'. *Journal of Advertising Research*, 33(6): RC9–RC12. Reproduced with permission.

International advertising campaigns: the example of the European food and beverage sector

2.7

Ullrich Appelbaum and Chris Halliburton

1 EUROPE 1993

With the Single European Market about to be achieved, most manufacturers in Europe are trying to evaluate the exact challenges this immense market of 343 million consumers will represent. Most manufacturers are also trying to evaluate what business approach will best serve their purposes. How to rationalize their production? How to rationalize their marketing efforts? Part of this questioning concerns cross-cultural advertising, its opportunities, and its constraints.

This question becomes particularly relevant in the context of 1993 because of the increasing importance of international advertising as a way to build and maintain a competitive advantage in tomorrow's European market-place.

This is especially true, but also especially difficult, in the European food and beverage sector. The abolition of trade barriers between member states will induce potential gains estimated to range between 500 and 1000 million ECUs (Cecchini, 1989), placing it in the third place in terms of expected benefits, after the telecommunications and automotive industries. It is therefore not surprising that the European companies operating in this sector are eager to gain a major share of this 'Euro-cake'.

But developing cross-cultural advertising campaigns for the food and beverage sector is particularly difficult. Food is an expression of culture. Cultural differences in eating and drinking habits are often used as an argument against standardized marketing and advertising in this sector. Therefore, the opportunity to develop international advertising campaigns for such products has either to appeal to cultural trends that are similar in the different countries, or at least not to be in contradiction with existing local values about the usage of food and drink.

2 THE INCREASING IMPORTANCE OF ADVERTISING

As a result of the forces currently shaping Europe, which will be reinforced by the advent of the Single European Market, international advertising is becoming an even more important weapon in the European marketing battle. Three of the most important forces influencing the role of advertising are briefly discussed below.

2.1 The European retailing sector

'In no industrial sector is the value-added shift towards distribution more dramatic than in the food industry' (Gogel and Larréché, 1989). The concentration phenomenon currently taking place in the European retail sector, as well as the increasing importance of retailer brands, already estimated at 20–30% of the retailers' turnover (Mermet, 1991), gives the retailers more weight in deciding which brands will appear on the shelves. Manufacturer brands therefore become increasingly important, as 'Brands which are not in the top three positions in terms of market share in particular markets will find it increasingly difficult to secure shelf space at the retail level' (Ryan and Rau, 1990). This factor will be reinforced by the surge in European retailer cooperation, alliance and market entry.

2.2 Increased competition

The abolition of the non-tariff trade barriers, currently estimated at 218 for the food sector (Cecchini, 1989), is expected to boost the general level of competition. Not only will European companies become more competitive through advantages, such as economies of scale, that the Single Market will represent, but also the abolition of trade barriers between member states will increase the number of competitors operating in any specific market. As a consequence, gaining and maintaining a competitive advantage solely based on technology and product attributes will become increasingly difficult. Competition is able to duplicate and even improve a product very quickly. Even though superior product quality still remains a prerequisite to successful marketing, the marketing battle will increasingly be won on the communication level.

2.3 Internationalization

With the abolition of trade barriers, the internationalization of competition, and the emergence of transnational markets, companies must reappraise their European strategies. Their survival may depend upon it.

These three forces make it increasingly important for manufacturers to develop and continually invest in strong Euro-brands, which are trusted by the consumers. Their presence in distribution outlets, taking into account the level of competition, depends upon it.

Many manufacturers are already aware of these factors. Research shows that most manufacturers are aware of the need for international communication. From a survey of 350 top European companies on communications needs and expectations for 1993, the Ballester Independent Marketing and Management Study Group found that, even though only 10% of the respondents have already established a truly pan-European communication approach, most companies are currently asking their advertising agencies to prepare and coordinate European communication strategies (source: *Advertising Age*, 7 October 1991, p. 35).

3 BRANDS

International advertising, and advertising in this sector in general, increases in importance through its ability to create brands, and manufacturers' need to survive in the market place. Research carried out by the Nielsen company in 1989 found that advertising was considered as the second most important element of a brand after quality (Brummer, 1989). Brands are critical for three main reasons.

3.1 Brands as economic factors

Brands enable a company willing to continually invest in them, to create and maintain a competitive advantage that is difficult to match by competition. Do people buy Coca-Cola rather than Pepsi-Cola because Coke contains 50% more cola berries, or because of the cumulative power of the imagery created through advertising? Furthermore, research has shown that the ROI is directly linked to the position of the brand. The higher the brand's market share and the higher the ratio of advertising to sales promotion, the higher the return (Light, 1989). Companies, much too eager to achieve short-term profits – for example, through sales promotion, have ignored this principle at their peril.

3.2 Brands as short-cuts

Brands also 'offer the consumer a means of minimizing information search and evaluation. Through seeing a brand name which has been supported by continual marketing activity, the consumer can use this as a rapid means of interrogating memory and if sufficient relevant information can be recalled, only minimal effort is needed to make a purchasing decision' (De Chernatony, 1991). Brands increase consumer loyalty. The purchasing risk any consumer faces is reduced by the amount of trust the consumer has in every brand.

3.3 Brands as means of communication

Last but not least, brands enable consumers to communicate something about themselves. The motivation to buy a Mercedes has less to do (outside Germany) with the reliability of the car than with the image the buyer wants to convey. Because of the current European consumer trend toward individualism, brands become excellent means for the consumer to express his/her individuality.

Therefore, the ultimate objective of an advertising strategy should be to achieve dominance of the target consumer's shortlist of considered brands.

4 INTERNATIONAL ADVERTISING IS REALITY

These considerations lead to the interpretation not only that international advertising is feasible, but that it can also be desirable in the food and beverage sector. The relevant question in international advertising therefore seems less to be 'is international advertising possible or not?' The evidence suggests that it often is so. The relevant question rather seems to be 'how is it possible?'

Most advertising agencies are able to develop international advertising themes, either as a value-added service to, or upon request from, their clients. The decision to standardize has therefore been, as stated by Kenneth Robbins, Chairman of Lintas Worldwide '... far more to do with corporate culture than with the cultures of markets and nations' (Robbins, 1987).

The first research question that this paper will try to answer is:

RQ1: What are the similarities that can be identified in the creative execution of international versus national television advertising campaigns?

5 NEED FOR MORE CREATIVITY

There are two elements which are keys to success in marketing a product: (1) the product has to be noticed, and (2) it has to be trusted by the consumer. To market brands that will be noticed and trusted by the consumer, the advertising will first have to stand out from the crowd.

The challenge facing advertising reflects the problem that, according to one study, as much as 98% of the information provided to the consumer is ignored (Kroeber-Riel, 1990). Advertising therefore will have to catch the consumer's attention, and deliver the message in an original way that will enable the consumer to remember and identify with the message and the brand.

Furthermore, consumer expectations and attitudes towards advertising are also changing. Research carried out by the BBDO advertising agency showed that people's attitude toward advertising is much more positive than it was five years ago (source: *Advertising Age*, 25 November 1991, p. 28). Last but not least, in addition to its key function to inform, advertising is increasingly expected to entertain.

As a consequence, advertising will tend to rely more heavily on emotions and images to attract the consumer's attention and interest. Images have this ability to provide much more information, more accurately and faster than words can. As such, they can be absorbed and remembered with much less effort by the viewer. Finally, images also have a much higher entertainment power, that satisfies more easily the consumer's need for immediate pleasure and entertainment.

Advertising will also have to become more emotional. As it becomes increasingly difficult to base a competitive advantage on the functional attributes of a brand, emotional brand attributes become key to differentiation.

To conclude, one could say that advertising in general, and international advertising in particular, will enable European manufacturers to 'outsmart rather than outspend competition'. This point increases in importance as the trade barriers between member states are about to come down. In fact, as most manufacturers competing in specific markets have at their disposal the same financial and human resources, and similar marketing and production know-how, one of the few options they have at their disposal is to outsmart competition by building distinctive brands and images that are salient to the consumer's needs. Furthermore these brands will have to be communicated through strong images, in an original and creative way, thus enabling them to stand out from the crowd.

In one word, advertising will have to become more creative. Creativity is a very subjective concept that is notoriously hard to define. For the purpose of this research, creative advertising will be defined as advertising that is original (that 'stands out from the crowd'), in that it relies on strong visuals and/or emotions.

The second research question will therefore address:

RQ2: What are the characteristics of creative television advertising?

As international advertising becomes increasingly important, it would also be interesting to see if there is a fit or a distortion between these two trends. The third research question will therefore be:

RQ3: Are international and creative television advertising compatible?

6 DEVELOPING INTERNATIONAL ADVERTISING STRATEGIES

To answer these research questions it was decided to carry out a content analysis which analyses and compares international versus national television advertisements from the food and beverage sector, that were considered to be of an above-average creative execution by competent authorities across the countries concerned.

6.1 The data base

To answer the research questions, 28 international commercials have been analysed and compared to 185 commercials from France, Germany, England and the United States, all from the food and beverage sector. The detailed breakdown by country is listed in Table 1.

As the national commercials had to be 'above average' in creative execution, it was decided to use a selection from the German Lürzer Archiv. The Lürzer Archiv has set itself the objective to issue quarterly a selection of 'the best advertisements' in the world.

As the number of German commercials featured in the Lürzer Archiv was not sufficient to be compared to the commercials from the other countries covered in this research, it was decided to complement the German commercials with a selection of the most creative examples from the 'New Comer Rollen', a monthly service available to advertising agencies, summarizing all the commercials that went 'on air' in Germany.

The international commercials were obtained from the CTC Communications Trading Company in Hamburg, a company specializing in the provision of commercials. The basis for the international commercials has been commercials that were used in at least two countries, including at least either France, Germany or England. Table 2 summarizes the origin of the data base, as well as the period covered by the commercials that were analysed.

The next section will describe a development model of an advertising strategy that was used to structure the research.

Table 1 Breakdown by country

Country	Number of commercials	% of total
Germany	41	19.2
France	47	22.1
England	54	25.4
United States	43	20.2
International	28	13.1
Total	213	100

Table 2 Origin of the data base

Origin	Period	% of total
Lürzer Rollen	Jan 1987–Jan 1991	71.4
New Comer Rollen	Jan–June 1991	15.5
CTC	1991	13.1
Total		100.0

7 A DEVELOPMENT MODEL OF AN ADVERTISING STRATEGY

Creative strategy can be divided into 'what is said', and 'how it is said'. This is also true for the development of international advertising campaigns.

7.1 The positioning

Positioning is the very difficult answer to the very simple question: 'What does the product do, for whom, and in place of what'? In this sense, it can be defined as what the product stands for in the consumer's mind in reference to competition.

Kroeber-Riel (1990) has classified positioning according to two main elements: a functional element (what the product does), and an emotional element. According to Kroeber-Riel, the functional and emotional elements of the position will depend on two main elements:

1. the consumer's awareness of a need (the need is 'obvious' or it is not), and
2. the consumer's knowledge about the available products (the information about the products is obvious or it is not).

The positioning strategy can therefore be:

1. informative and emotional (need and information are not obvious)
2. informative only (only the need is obvious)
3. emotional only (only the information is obvious) '
4. 'updating' (both need and information are obvious).

As the product moves along its product life cycle towards the decline stage, the consumer's need and information requirements become trivial (the consumer is aware of the need and knows all about the products that can satisfy his need). As a consequence, the positioning will tend to be informative in the introduction stage and become increasingly emotional in the growth stage. In the maturity stage it will become mainly emotional. Finally the 'updating' positioning may be used in the decline phase.

For the purpose of the research, Kroeber-Riel's four positioning strategies have been adapted, resulting in the five positioning alternatives defined below:

1. The 100% informative positioning (100 info): the advertisement includes only information about the product or its use. To classify the content of information, the model developed by Stern, Krugman, and Resnik (Johnstone, Kaynack and Sparman, 1987) identifying 14 of these criteria was adopted.
2. The 100% emotional positioning (100 emo): The advertisement includes only emotions. The purpose of the advertiser is to associate emotions with the product.

Emotions are difficult to define. As outlined by Ray (1982), emotions have to do with feelings that are not normally under our physical control. It has therefore been decided to consider as emotion everything that does not include any kind of information.

3. The informative and emotional positioning (50/50): This kind of advertisement includes information as well as emotions. A commercial has been classified as 50/50 when it was not possible to clearly identify if the informative content or the emotional content was dominant.

Finally as a subdivision of the 50/50 positioning:

4. Mainly informative positioning (75/25 info): the advertisement provides mainly information, but is supported by strong emotions. The purpose of the advertiser seems to be the provision of information, 'wrapped up' in an emotional context.
5. Mainly emotional positioning (75/25 emo): the advertisement is used to convey mainly emotions, but some information is included. The purpose of the advertiser seems to be to link emotions to the product.

7.2 The appeals

An advertising appeal is defined here as any message designed to motivate the consumer to purchase: the reason why.

A condition for international advertising is that the same appeal will motivate the consumer in the different countries to buy the product. It would make no sense to use the 'social reward' appeal, for example, for a food product in a country where individuality is a highly cherished cultural value.

Based upon the work of Fieldhouse (1986) and a classification developed by the Lintas: Worldwide advertising agency, we have identified 24 appeals that are usually used to advertise food and beverage products (Table 3)

7.3 The tone

To communicate the product's positioning, the advertiser has to decide about the tone and the format of the advertisement: the 'How it is said?'

Table 3 Appeals used to advertise food and beverages

1. Loving care	13. Snob appeal
2. Relief from stress	14. Social reward/punishment
3. Nostalgia and security	15. Newness
4. Personal gratification	16. 'It's good'
5. Health appeal	17. Natural
6. Friendship and togetherness	18. Traditional
7. Romance and sex	19. Convenience
8. Fashionability	20. Costs
9. Express individuality	21. Value for money
10. Demonstrate belongingness to a group	22. 'Specials'
11. Proclaim a separateness of a group	23. 'Economy packs'
12. Signify social status	24. Country of origin

The tone and format, which are sometimes referred to as the 'advertising concept', are an integral part of the advertising strategy. In fact, these two elements are important in attaining credibility and in creating the image around the product. Whether the advertiser uses the 'testimonial format' to directly address the viewer (using an argumentative tone) to gain credibility, or 'a slice of life' format (for example, in a 'life-style' commercial), trying to build a relationship between the consumer and the viewer (using a narrative tone) has important implications on the way the product is perceived by the consumer.

For the purpose of this research, five dimensions have been identified according to which the tone of a commercial can be analysed. These five dimensions have been chosen for their relevance, but with no claim to be exhaustive, and are discussed below.

7.3.1 The use of humour
Humour is a delicate subject in international advertising. According to Ray (1982), humour is only effective when the communication objective is to attract attention and create awareness. If on the other hand, the communication objective is to achieve comprehension, humour can be a distraction. It has therefore been analysed if the commercials in the data base made use of humour or not.

7.3.2 Argumentative versus narrative
This dimension has been researched in more detail by Olson (1989), who defines an argumentative advertisement as a commercial in which the viewer is directly talked to. The viewer is a passive recipient of the message that he/she is expected to process. This approach is trying to address the viewers at the rational level.

In the narrative advertisement, on the contrary, the viewer is not directly talked to. He is more of a witness. The advertisement is like a story, with no explicit statement made to the viewer. The viewer is more involved, and interprets and processes the content of the advertisement. The purpose of such an approach is to build a relationship between the consumer and the product. This approach is more emotional.

7.3.3 Competitive versus non-competitive
This dimension refers to the comparison of the product to competition. Competitive advertising has a different meaning in Europe than in the United States. In the latter country comparative advertising is much tougher than in Europe. Any reference to competition or any superiority claim has therefore been considered as competitive.

7.3.4 Hard-sell versus soft-sell
The definitions are provided by Barbara Mueller (1987). By soft-sell appeal is meant that mood and atmosphere are conveyed through a beautiful scene or the development of an emotional story or verse. Human emotional sentiments are emphasized over clear-cut product related appeals.

By hard-sell appeal is meant that sales orientation is emphasized, stressing brand name and product recommendations. Explicit mention may be made of competitive products, sometimes by name (this is not the case in Europe), and the product's advantage depends on performance.

7.3.5 *Direct versus indirect*

In the direct approach, information about the product is conveyed through words, whereas in the indirect approach, they are conveyed through images. Providing the information through image carries a risk, however, that the message can be misunderstood by the consumer.

7.4 The international format

The second element of the advertising concept is the format of the commercial. The formats shown in Table 4 have been identified.

The advertising format is the way an advertisement is presented, structured, and delivered. As such it helps to build the brand, but also tries to solve the credibility problem the advertiser has to face.

7.5 The use of music

Music has been analysed because of its importance in advertising, and because of the opportunities it represents for international advertising. Music often transmits emotions better than words do. We only have to switch off the sound while watching a horror movie to understand the importance of music in conveying emotions.

Music also represents opportunities for international advertising. Much of today's music is international in character, be it classical music or the Top 50 hits broadcast on MTV. Using music therefore enables the advertiser to avoid language problems which are sometimes used as an argument against international advertising.

It was therefore felt to be important to analyse the exact use of music in international and national advertising. The elements that have been analysed were:

1. Music versus no music at all
2. Music alone versus music and words
3. Music in the background versus music in the foreground
4. Use of jingle or not.

The first two elements are self-explanatory.

The classification foreground/background has been made according to the balance of words or music. Commercials were coded as 'foreground' if music dominated over words. It was coded as 'background' when the importance was given to the words.

Table 4 The formats used

---

 1. Slice of life
 2. Little story around the product
 3. Testimonials (by experts, stars, or 'typical' persons)
 4. Talking heads
 5. Characters associated with the products
 6. Demonstration
 7. Product in action
 8. Cartoon
 9. International versus national
10. Others: every other format not classified above

Regarding the jingles, which can be described as a short piece of music associated with the brand (including words or not), opinions are divergent. David Ogilvy, for example, represents the point of view that 'When you have nothing to say, sing it' (Ogilvy, 1983). This statement devalues the role of jingles. A jingle can enable the consumer to memorize information more easily, and can increase recall.

The different steps in the development of an advertising strategy are summarized in Table 5. This model has been used to analyse and compare the international and national commercials described earlier in this article. The intention in setting up this model was not to be exhaustive. Its intention was rather to analyse elements felt to be particularly relevant for the development of international advertising strategies, as well as to propose a new way of looking at the issue of international advertising. The remaining part of this article will now concentrate on the results and implications of the findings.

8 SUMMARY OF THE FINDINGS

8.1 The positioning strategies

It is interesting to notice the very high level of emotional positionings (Table 6). The emotional positioning is dominant in the international examples *and* in all countries apart from Germany. The level of information provided in the international commercials is nevertheless higher than in the national commercials.

These results seem to indicate that emotions travel better across frontiers than information. It does not mean, however, that information cannot be provided

Table 5 Developing advertising strategies

1. Definition of a clear positioning (informative/emotional; appeals used)
2. The advertising concept
   (a) The tone – Humour
                 – Argumentative versus narrative
                 – Competitive versus non-competitive
                 – Hard-sell versus soft-sell
                 – Direct versus indirect.
   (b) The format
3. The use of music

Table 6 Classification of the positioning strategies (in %)

	Int	F	Ger	UK	USA	Average
100 emo	50.0	51.0	36.6	48.2	48.8	46.9
75/25 emo	10.7	29.8	41.5	35.2	34.9	31.9
50/50	21.4	19.2	17.1	9.3	11.6	15.0
75/25 info	10.7	0.0	2.4	7.4	4.7	4.7
100 info	7.2	0.0	2.4	0.0	0.0	1.4

Note:
The percentages indicated in this table are calculated in relation to the total number of advertisements from that country. For example in Germany, 2.4% of the German commercials used a 100 informative positioning.

internationally. In fact, the level of information provided in the international commercials is higher than in the national commercials. The use of information nevertheless implies as a condition that this information has the same salience and relevance in all the targeted countries.

The lower level of emotional positioning in Germany is not surprising. In fact, German advertising has the reputation of being much more informative than French or English advertising. This point is also confirmed by the smaller number of German advertisements in the Lürzer Archiv. This may be partly due to the German consumer, but mainly to the clients who have a more conservative attitude than their French, English or American counterparts. Someone following the evolution of German advertising will nevertheless have noticed a trend towards more emotional advertising.

The high level of emotional positioning in the national advertisements can be explained by the fact that most of the products whose advertisements have been analysed are in their maturity stage. It has been argued earlier in this article that in this stage of the product life cycle, emotions become a key element for differentiation, as the consumer is relatively familiar with the offer.

8.2 The advertising appeals

Two appeals were used with similar, higher, intensity both internationally *and* in the four countries: the 'it's good' appeal (24%), and the evergreen 'romance and sex' (10%) appeal (Table 7).

International advertising seems to favour appeals reinforcing the consumption trends currently shaping Europe. In fact, three out of the five top appeals used in international advertising express these new trends: the 'personal gratification' and the 'it's good' appeal (trend towards a more hedonistic consumption), and the 'health' appeal (trend towards healthy eating).

The high percentage of 'it's good' appeals on the national level can be explained by two factors. It can be seen as the exploitation of the hedonistic trend shaping Europe. It can also be explained by the fact that in mature markets, where the 'what is said' loses some relevance, the 'how is it said?' plays the key role, as in this stage the advertiser's objective would be to create a positive, differentiated image for the consumer.

Table 7 Main appeals used (in % of country total)

	Int	F	Ger	UK	USA	Average
Loving care	2.8	2.7	8.1	0.0	1.5	3.0
Personal gratification	8.7	2.7	6.7	6.7	1.5	5.1
Health appeal	10.9	6.8	4.0	4.0	4.5	5.7
Romance and sex	8.7	9.6	9.5	8.0	15.0	10.2
Express individuality	6.5	11.0	6.7	6.7	4.5	7.2
Demonstrate belongingness	8.7	0.0	0.0	8.0	6.0	4.4
Newness	10.9	2.7	2.7	0.0	0.0	2.7
'It's good'	17.4	28.8	27.0	18.7	24.2	23.7
Natural	0.0	9.6	4.0	10.7	7.5	6.9
Traditional	4.4	2.7	5.4	9.4	9.0	6.3
Country of origin	6.5	4.1	9.5	6.7	7.5	6.9

The appeals used in the different countries obviously vary. 'Tradition' scores more highly in the UK and in the USA, 'country of origin' in Germany and 'express individuality' in France. On the international level it is interesting to notice that most of the appeals have been used. This is important, as it shows that the consumers in the different markets can be sensitive to the same appeals. The argument that consumers are not sensitive to the same appeals because of cultural differences, which is often used against global advertising, seems to be contradicted here.

Economic appeals, such as 'cost', 'value for money', 'specials' and 'economic packs' have almost never been used. Economic appeals are the expression of either a sales promotion action or a pricing strategy, and therefore less implementable internationally. However, in the national cases, the results were also strikingly low. Only the 'special' appeal was used in 1.4% of the German and 3% of the American commercials. Does this suggest that creativity and economic appeals are incompatible?

The percentage of the remaining appeals ranged from only 2.7% to 6.7%.

8.3 The advertising tone

A striking difference that can be observed in the tone of the commercials is the very low level of international advertisements using humour compared to the national advertisements. Humour is dominant in all the countries, while only one third of the international commercials make use of it (Table 8).

On the national level, the results seem to confirm Ray's comments. Humour seems to be used to create awareness.

The low level of humour used in international advertising should nevertheless not lead advertisers to the rapid conclusion that humour should systematically be avoided in international advertising. Rather, the question that should be asked at this point, and that would merit further research, is 'what kind of humour is implementable internationally?' The Kit-Kat campaign 'Take a break, take a Kit-Kat', for instance, is a very good example of a humorous international advertising campaign which appears to work across a number of countries.

The narrative tone is dominant in the international and English commercials. French, German and American advertising, on the other hand, prefer addressing the consumer directly.

Table 8 The tone

	Int	F	Ger	UK	USA
Serious	67.8	25.5	39.0	11.2	23.3
Humour	32.2	74.5	61.0	88.8	76.7
Argumentative	39.3	55.3	53.6	42.6	58.1
Narrative	60.7	44.7	46.4	57.4	41.9
Competitive	21.4	12.8	17.0	24.0	27.9
Non-competitive	78.6	87.2	83.0	76.0	72.1
Hard-sell	28.6	4.3	2.5	0.0	2.3
Soft-sell	71.4	95.7	97.5	100.0	97.7
Direct	53.6	80.9	83.0	68.5	90.7
Indirect	46.4	19.1	17.0	31.5	9.3

The level of non-competitive advertisements is low internationally as it is in the various countries. In fact, using a competitive tone internationally would presume an identical competitive environment in the different countries. Besides the soft-drinks market, where Coca-Cola and Pepsi-Cola are engaged in an international marketing battle, this situation occurs only in very few cases.

International advertising is significantly more hard-sell than the national advertising. Almost 30% of the international commercials use this tone, compared to an average of 3% nationally.

International and British advertising also rely more heavily on images to provide information. These results therefore confirm the expected higher use of visual images internationally.

8.4 The advertising format

Three main formats are mainly used, with little difference internationally and nationally: the 'slice of life', 'the little story around the product', and the 'character' format. Table 9.

For international advertising, these results are rather surprising. In fact, the execution of international advertising strategies often faces the problem of small differences between the countries. This would suggest that it is more difficult to feature 'slice of life' and 'little stories around the product' formats. It does not seem to be the case here, however.

Two formats seem to be under-used in the international advertisements analysed in this sample: the 'product in action' and the 'international' format.

For food products the typical 'product in action' format would be food in motion. A commercial featuring a product in action has two main advantages. Firstly, it increases the appeal to the consumer. According to David Ogilvy, 'the more appetizing you make it look, the more you sell. It has been found that food in motion looks more appetizing' (Ogilvy, 1983). The second reason is that if the advertisement only features the product, the risk of cultural inadequacies is avoided (assuming that the food in itself is not too culturally bound). Food in motion should therefore be a potential execution strategy for international advertising.

The 'international' format, which typically features actors from different racial origins, avoids the risk of cultural or morphological inadequacy the actors may

Table 9 The advertising format

	Int	F	Ger	UK	USA	Average
Slice of life	35.1	33.4	24.5	35.8	17.5	28.8
Little story around the product	24.3	31.3	20.8	23.9	22.2	24.2
Testimonial	5.4	4.2	8.2	0.0	7.9	4.9
Talking head	0.0	4.2	2.0	7.5	3.2	3.8
Character	16.2	10.4	32.7	16.4	31.7	22.0
Demonstration	0.0	0.0	0.0	1.5	1.6	0.7
Product in action	8.1	10.4	10.2	6.0	7.9	8.3
Cartoon	5.4	2.0	2.0	6.0	7.9	4.9
International	3.0	0.0	0.0	0.0	0.0	0.4
Other	3.0	4.3	0.0	3.0	0.0	1.9

represent. This format has, for example, been implemented by Coca-Cola and Heineken ('Multi-racial bar'), and by Bennetton in the textile sector ('United Colors'). This technique is often used in the United States to appeal to (or not to exclude) the variety of minorities living in this country. For the same reason, it could also represent good opportunities for international advertising.

8.5 The use of music

Not surprisingly, music was given an important role in the majority of commercials that have been analysed. This is true for the national commercials as well as for the international commercials (Table 10).

Only a small proportion of the commercials featured solely music. Surprisingly enough, the percentage was the highest in the United States rather than for the international commercials. It may therefore be the case that the anticipated language problems, used as an argument against international advertising, have been exaggerated.

In the commercials in which music was used, the place given to music is more important that the place given to words. Typically the advertisement uses music to attract attention and convey emotions. Words are then used either because the story in the commercial required it (in a 'slice of life' format, the dialogue of the actors, for example), or because the advertiser provides some information about the product.

Except for the USA, music was usually featured in the foreground.

Finally, the results of the analysis indicate that jingles are used in a minority of cases, except in England where almost all of the musical commercials used a jingle.

We can conclude by observing that although music is given an important role in advertising (especially in international advertising), words are nevertheless still necessary to convey the advertising message.

9 DISCUSSION

The results of the content analysis have enabled the identification of a number of possible guidelines for international advertising in the food and beverage sector. They thus provide an answer to the first research question.

The evidence from this sample also suggests the following *criteria for international television advertising campaigns*, as it relates to food and beverages:

Table 10 The use of music

	Int	F	Ger	UK	USA
Music	89.3	83.0	87.8	77.8	76.7
No music	10.7	17.0	12.2	22.2	23.3
Only music	16.0	12.8	16.6	26.2	27.3
Music/words	84.0	87.2	83.4	73.8	72.7
Foreground	64.0	61.5	66.7	57.1	48.5
Background	36.0	38.5	33.3	42.9	51.5
Jingle	28.0	12.8	36.1	15.2	42.9
No jingle	72.0	87.2	63.9	84.8	57.1

1. The positioning should be more emotional than informative. Products which, because of their very nature, do not need any explanation, or products which are in their maturity stage in the targeted countries, are therefore more likely to be advertised internationally. An obvious prerequisite is that the product has similar positioning in all the countries.
2. Information is not a factor of exclusion for international advertising. The information has nevertheless to have the same salience in the countries in which the international campaign is implemented, and the product should be in a similar stage of the international product life cycle.
3. An advertising message based either on evergreen appeals such as 'it's good' and 'romance and sex', or on appeals reinforcing the new European consumption trends, may stand more chance of success in international implementation.
4. Humour should only be used with great care. However, it should not automatically be excluded, because of its potential for attracting the viewers' attention and creating awareness, when carefully researched and found to transfer across borders.
5. Advertisements that place the viewer in the role of witness (narrative tone) are also more likely to work internationally. Furthermore, in the case where information is provided, this information should be reinforced by appropriate visual images (the indirect approach).
6. If it is not in contradiction with existing practices in the targeted countries, then a hard-sell tone can be used for international advertising.
7. Music should definitely play a major role in international advertising through its ability to convey emotions and to reinforce atmospheres. Whether or not jingles are used does not seem to be relevant, and will probably depend on the advertiser's attitude towards this practice.

Not only has the content analysis enabled the identification of some guidelines for international advertising, it has also resulted in some conclusions concerning creative advertising, based upon the national 'creative' samples. It thus also enables us to respond to the second research question.

In fact *creative advertising* seems to share the following characteristics:

1. It is mainly emotional, as classified earlier in this paper.
2. The 'How is it said?' seems to be more important than the 'What is said?' – the objective of the advertiser being to create a differentiation through the way the message is conveyed rather than its content. In this sense, the appeals used seem to be a 'hygiene factor'; the appeal isn't playing the key role, as long as it is salient and relevant.
3. Humour definitely plays a key role.
4. Furthermore, the tone is soft-sell and non-competitive. Whether or not it is argumentative and direct does not seem to be so relevant.
5. The format used in creative advertising is an expression of the soft and non-competitive tone. It is more important to create a favourable impression, a positive image, rather than 'assaulting' the viewer.
6. Music also plays an important role and has a dominant position in creative advertising, without necessarily relying only on music. Whether or not jingles are used does not seem to be determinant either, as for the international commercials.

The answer to the first two research questions also enables us to address the third research question, the *compatibility* issue of creative versus international advertising.

The strong similarities between the international and the creative, national advertising are striking. The type of positioning, the appeals that are used, some elements of the tone, the format, and the importance given to music are very similar. This finding therefore *contradicts* the prevalent industry view that 'international' implies bland, uncreative or even 'lowest common denominator', standardized advertising.

However, these similarities conceal some interesting differences, mainly focusing on the tone of the commercials. *International* advertising is narrative, 'harder-sell', and relies much more on images to reinforce the message, than national creative advertising. It also uses much less humour.

The results suggest a further conclusion: that international advertising is more orientated towards building the brand, whereas creative advertising is more orientated to image creation. This difference is subtle but important. International advertising focuses upon building brand equity. The findings show that international advertising is narrative and indirect in tone. The viewer, having the role of a witness, is more involved, and processes the content of the advertisement. Using this tone reflects the advertiser's intention to build a relationship between the product and the consumer. In other words to build brand equity.

The formats used reinforce this point. The results show that the main formats were 'slice of life', and 'little story around the product'. The purpose of this type of format is to place the viewer in the role of a witness. The third format that was most often used was the 'character' format. Typically the objective of the advertiser is to associate a character with the brand: Captain Igloo for Findus, Fido for Sprite, the Jolly Green Giant for Pillsbury, and the numerous cartoon animals associated with the Kellogg's cereals brands are such characters.

Finally, the importance given to music is also contributing to the brand equity, as it reinforces and dramatizes the tone of the commercials. As such it can be seen as an 'amplifier'.

Creative advertising, as expressed in the national creative examples, showed many similarities with the international counterparts of format, tone and the use of music. There were some important differences, however. The first difference concerns the tone, which as we have seen is more argumentative and direct (providing information through words). The major difference is in the appeals used. In describing the characteristics of creative advertising, it has been argued that the way the message is conveyed is more important than the message itself, as the very high level of 'it's good' appeals seem to indicate. The percentage of this appeal is much higher in creative advertising than in international advertising. Creative advertising therefore seems to be more oriented towards building an image, rather than to the 'content' element of the brand, as compared to the international examples.

This important difference does not fully enable us to answer positively the third research question: international and creative advertising are not totally compatible. A more appropriate answer would be that they are more closely related than would perhaps have been expected, and the differences are more of degree than of substance.

10 CONCLUSION

The advertising challenge for European marketing managers faced with the advent of the Single European Market demands new ways of looking at the issue of international advertising. More important than arguing about the feasibility of international advertising, which often degenerates into an opinion debate, it would be more productive to consider international advertising as one possible advertising alternative, whose importance is growing. As stated by Bill Young, Head of Marketing at Unilever, 'it avoids fruitless discussions about whether to do it or not, and allows you to concentrate your efforts on better creative proposition' (*Campaign*, 1992).

The analysis of 218 commercials from France, Germany, England and the United States, including 28 international examples, has led to some interesting conclusions. It has enabled us to identify guidelines which seem to increase the chances of success in the execution of international television advertising campaigns as evidenced in the food and beverage sector. It has also enabled us to identify some of the characteristics of advertising that are considered to be very creative. Last but not least, it has enabled us to highlight the role of branding in international advertising.

As well as trying to provide a constructive contribution to the debate concerning international advertising, the purpose of this article is to provide an original, proactive and content-based approach to cross-cultural advertising in Europe.

REFERENCES

Brummer, B. (1989). Wie reagieren handelserfolgsfaktoren der marken-differenzierung, in Nielsen basis studie: marktwirksame differenzierung. *Sondernummer*, 10, 56–69.

Cecchini, P. (1989). *1992: The Benefits of a Single Market*. Wildwood House: London.

De Chernatony, L. (1991). Formulating brand strategies. *European Management Journal*, 9 (2), 194–200.

Fieldhouse, P. (1986). *Food and Nutrition, Customs and Culture*. Chapman and Hall: London.

Gogel, R. and Larréché, J. C. (1989). The battlefield for 1992: product strength and geographic coverage. *European Management Journal*, 7 (2), 132–140.

Johnstone, H., Kaynack, E. and Sparman, R. (1987). A cross-cultural/cross-national study of the information contents in television advertising. *International Journal of Advertising*, June/July, 223–235.

Kroeber-Riel, W. (1990). *Strategie und Technik der Werbung: Verhaltenswissenschaftliche Ansatze*. Kohlhammer, Edition Marketing, 2, Auflage: Stuttgart.

Light, L. (1989). The power of market rank, *Werbeforschung und Praxis*, 2, 41–49.

Mermet, G. (1991). *Euroscopie: Les Européens: Qui sont-ils? Comment vivent-ils?* Larousse: Paris.

Mueller, B. (1987). Reflections of culture: an analysis of Japanese and American advertising appeals. *Journal of Advertising Research*, June/July, 51–59.

Ogilvy, D. (1983). *Ogilvy on Advertising*. Pan Books: London.

Olson, B. (1989). Wie werbung wirkt: narrative und argumentative werbung im vergleich. *Werbeforschung und Praxis*, 4, 135–136.

Ray, M. (1982). *Advertising and Communication Management*. Prentice-Hall: New York.

Robbins, K. (1987). Does standardisation work in international advertising? *European Management Journal*, 5 (4), 253–256.

Ryan, J. and Rau, P. (1990). *Marketing Strategies for the New Europe: a North American Perspective on 1992*. Dow Jones Irwin: USA.

Campaign, anon. (1992). The Unilever client who risks a rare spirit of adventure. *Campaign*, 28 February, 18–19.

Appelbaum, U. and Halliburton, C. (1993) 'International advertising campaigns: the example of the European food and beverage sector'. *International Journal of Advertising*, 12(3), September: 223–241. Reproduced with permission.

Impact on purchase intent of sex-role identity and product positioning

2.8

Lynn J. Jaffe and Paul D. Berger

No one can deny the changes women have undergone in the past several decades. The growing number of women entering the workforce has triggered a change in sex-roles that many feel will continue for some time and have an impact on all our lives. In a report prepared for the President's Advisory Committee, (Yankelovich & Barron, 1980), men and women were asked to share their feelings about American women today. Respondents indicated that women haven't really changed, but the idea of femininity and appropriate sex-role behavior has. Furthermore, 73 per cent of the sample indicated that they expect these changes to continue. Understanding women's changing sex-role identity has important implications for effective marketing strategies, particularly, promotional and positioning strategies (Debevec & Iyer, 1986).

Early research focused on the fact that while women were changing, advertisers were still depicting them in stereotyped roles (Belkaoui & Belkaoui, 1976; Courtney & Lockeretz, 1971; Courtney & Whipple, 1974; Wagner & Banos, 1973). Researchers next began to show that role portrayals of women presented a problem for marketers because many women objected to ads showing them in well-worn stereotypes (Lundstrom & Sciglimpaglia, 1977). Furthermore, these researchers found that progressive sex-role portrayals were preferred over traditional ones.

However, this early wave of research neglected the crucial issue as to the effectiveness of the advertisements. The Equal Opportunities Commission supported an independent study by The Sherman Group (1982) to determine whether print advertisements depicting women in less rigid roles would sell products better than those showing women in well-worn stereotypes. Researchers conducted personal interviews with a representative sample of 622 women. Products were positioned in traditional and modern ways in several product categories. To test the effectiveness of the positionings, the researchers used both recall and persuasion, two popular advertising effectiveness measures (Ostlund & Clancy, 1982). Not surprisingly, the modern positioning enhanced the advertising effectiveness in all product categories among all segments of women. The researchers concluded that the modern positionings were more effective because they portrayed women as attractive, independent, capable people in and out of the home.

Studies examining the effects of modern versus traditional positionings are generally lacking in the marketing literature. Future studies need to examine the advertising effectiveness of the positioning, and in particular, its persuasiveness in getting the consumer to purchase the product (Debevec & Allen, 1984). Our research in this pilot study presents a clear methodology for examining this issue.

Furthermore, while most research suggests that sex-roles are changing and therefore positionings must also change, our research incorporates a measure of sex-role identity to measure its impact on positioning preference. Before discussing the methodology, the construct of sex-role identity and its measurement are examined.

SEX-ROLE IDENTITY AND ITS MEASUREMENT

Masculinity and femininity have long been conceptualized at opposite ends of a continuum. Consequently, society has assigned unique roles to both men and women. In the matter of sexual polarization we have accepted, for a long time, that the psychological qualities considered virtuous in men are often offensive in women (Heilbrun, 1982). The result has been a strict divison of gender norms; sex-role identity manifests itself in the degree to which one adheres to these norms.

Recently, we have observed a new individual, the androgynous person. The androgynous individual has joined the 'masculine' and 'feminine' psychological aspects of personage into a single unified whole. The androgynous person has the capacity to show both the masculine and feminine personality characteristics as the situation demands (Bem, 1974, 1979; Locksley & Colten 1979; Mowen, 1987; Singer, 1977; Spence & Helmreich, 1979; Spence, 1983).

In 1974, Bem developed a sex-role inventory to test her hypothesis that many individuals are psychologically androgynous. The results of her study, conducted on 300 university women, confirmed her hypothesis: roughly 27 per cent of her sample were scored androgynous, while 54 per cent were feminine, and 19 per cent were masculine.

Typical masculine characteristics of the inventory are: 'aggressive,' 'analytical,' and 'leadership ability.' Feminine traits include: 'yielding,' 'compassionate' and 'passive.' Respondents rate themselves as to how well each of the traits describes himself. The Bem Sex-Role Inventory (BSRI) now has a short form, consisting of 10 masculine and 10 feminine items, items with low item-to-total correlations having been dropped from the original pool of 60 items (Bem, 1981).

Lubinski, Tellegen, and Butcher (1983) assessed the reliability and validity of the BSRI and a second inventory, the Personality Attributes Questionnaire (Spence, Helmreich, & Stapp, 1974). Both inventories showed a high degree of reliability and also a high degree of convergent and discriminant validity. The authors concluded that the two inventories could be used interchangeably. We chose the BSRI because it showed a slightly higher degree of reliability. It should be noted, however, that Kelly, Furman & Young (1978) found that subjects may be classified differently depending on which inventory is employed.

HYPOTHESES

We hypothesize that women in different sex-role identity groups will show significantly different degrees of preference for modern versus traditional (female portrayal) positionings. Masculine women will prefer the modern positioning over the traditional one to the greatest extent. Feminine women will have the least preference for the modern positioning; (and in fact, in absolute terms, may prefer the traditional positioning). Androgynous women will fall in between these two groups with respect to their preference for the modern positioning.

METHODOLOGY

Dependent variables

There were three dependent variables used to capture the advertisements' persuasive ability. Respondents indicated their purchase intent on a seven-point scale anchored by the phrases 'product I would definitely not buy' (1) and 'product I would definitely buy' (7). They also indicated on an identical scale whether they would use the product and whether or not they would recommend it to a friend. Since the three measures were clearly intercorrelated (Cronbach's Alpha = 0.68), they were averaged to form an overall measure of persuasion which was labeled 'purchase intent.'

Independent variables

Positioning

Modern and traditional positionings were selected in the following manner: a portfolio of seventy print advertisements was developed depicting both types of positionings. Marketing professors, and doctoral students in both marketing and psychology rated the ads on the extent to which they portrayed a woman's sex-role as either modern or traditional. The scale used was a five-point semantic differential, the purportedly modern ads anchored by the phrases 'woman appears modern' and 'woman appears not modern,' the purportedly traditional ads anchored by the phrases 'woman appears traditional' and 'woman appears not traditional.' Advertisements were selected based on the ratings of the ad's ability to capture these dimensions.

In general the modern positioning showed women in multi-dimensional roles, at work and at home; the traditional positioning portrayed women as uni-dimensional, whose major role centered around her family. Specifically, in the food category the modern positioning portrayed a woman as successful both at home and at work. She was shown in her office and in her home, cooking. The headline read, 'The Taste of Success.' The traditional one showed a woman cooking for her husband. She was wearing an apron with the words, 'Nobody Cooks Like Me,' printed on it. In the cleaner category, the modern positioning showed men and women sharing in household tasks, implying that both partners have responsibility for cleaning chores. The traditional positioning showed a woman making sure her home was clean for her children. The headline read, 'For my family, I know it's clean.'

We assumed that, in general, the modern positioning would be favored or have an 'advantage' over the traditional one with respect to purchase intent. We based this on the Equal Opportunities Commission Study (1981), which found that the modern positioning enhanced the advertising effectiveness among all groups of women in all product categories. We computed the magnitude of this advantage by subtracting the purchase intent when viewing the traditional positioning from the purchase intent when viewing the modern positioning, to obtain a measure of the 'modern positioning advantage.' However, our interest was not in the main effect of positioning per se, but with the degree to which it varied across the sex-role identity levels (i.e., the interaction of positioning and sex-role identity). In addition, it was of interest whether this interaction varied across product categories (i.e., the three-way interaction among positioning, sex-role identity and product category).

Product category

The product categories were frequently purchased, low-involvement products: food and cleaners. The food category was represented by tomato paste and the cleaner was represented by a bathroom cleaner. We chose low-involvement categories because purchase decisions for them are rarely based on tangible attributes and are thus ripe for more emotional decisions based on imagery (Petty & Cacioppo, 1981; Tyebjee, 1979).

Sex-role identity

Sex-role identity (SRI) was determined using the short Bem Sex-Role Inventory (Bem, 1981). After rating themselves on the masculine and feminine traits, the respondents were classified into four groups: masculine, feminine, androgynous, and undifferentiated. Group classification was based on the normative data for females in Bem's 1978 study at Stanford University cited in Bem (1981). Those classified as masculine score high on masculine attributes and low on feminine ones, while the converse is true of the feminine classification. The androgynous women score high on both masculine and feminine characteristics, while the undifferentiated rate low on the two dimensions.

Design

The experimental design is a three-factor complete factorial, with two within-subject variables (positioning and product), and one between subject variable (sex-role identity). Sex-role identity scores were categorized into four mutually exclusive, collectively exhaustive sets; thus, each respondent was placed into one specific SRI category, and was 'repeated' for the four product category/positioning combinations. As the reader knows, a repeated measure design has two advantages: it reduces the sample size and, hence, costs and reduces overall variability by using a common subject pool for all treatments (Howell, 1982). Order effects were dealt with by balancing the sequences in which product categories and positionings were viewed by respondents.

Sample

The sample consisted of 100 women from a large metropolitan university in the Northeast. A quota sample of subjects between the ages of 19 and 50 was obtained. It consisted of approximately equal numbers of graduates and undergraduates with a diversity of majors. Additionally, both working and nonworking women were represented in roughly equal proportions.

At an early stage in our research, we had considered including age and working status as independent variables. However, two factors suggested we not do this. Spence & Helmreich (1979), in their study of data from over 1300 adults, found a striking resemblance to the data obtained from college students with respect to the percent classified in each SRI group, and mean and variance of SRI scores within groups. Secondly, statistical tests confirmed that for our data there was no difference in mean age and variance of age among SRI groups. Furthermore, there was no difference in the proportion of working/nonworking women among the groups. (For the tests alluded to in this paragraph, the one 50-year-old student was considered an outlier and not included).

Procedure

The subjects viewed one product category at a time, positioned in both the modern and traditional manner. Thus, each person saw a total of four print advertisements. They first indicated the main message of each ad to ensure that the treatment was taking effect. For example, in response to the modern positioning in the food category, a respondent remarked, 'She looks confident, successful, and involved with her career,' in response to the traditional positioning in the cleaner category, a respondent said, 'She appears to be very content as a homemaker.' Their responses assured us that they were aware of the main positioning theme. Furthermore, virtually all product information was removed from the copy, forcing subjects to focus on the positioning and to respond solely to it.

For each of the two positionings within the two product categories, they related their purchase intent. Next, they filled out the short Bem Sex-Role Inventory and were classified into the four groups. The undifferentiated were dropped from the subject pool because they numbered only four. The masculine, androgynous and feminine categories were represented by the following numbers, 30, 36, 30, respectively. For the sake of clarity, six respondents were randomly chosen and eliminated from the group of 36, resulting in three equal cell sizes of 30.

RESULTS

The data was analyzed using a standard ANOVA software package. The dependent variable is 'purchase intent,' the independent variables are SRI, product category, and positioning. The resulting ANOVA is shown in Table 1.

Of primary interest are (1) the two-way interaction effect between SRI and positioning and (2) the three-way interaction effect among SRI, product category and

Table 1 Purchase intent ANOVA results

Source of variation	DF	MSQ	F
Between Subjects	89		
Sex Role (SRI)	2	1.940	1.41
Subjects within SRI	87	1.380	
Within Subjects	270		
Product	1	5.720	2.82
SRI × Product	2	3.540	1.75
Subject × Product within SRI	87	2.029	
Positioning	1	44.180	22.61[a]
SRI × Positioning	2	12.410	6.35[b]
Subject × Positioning within SRI	87	1.954	
Product × Positioning	1	18.200	18.06[a]
SRI × Product × Positioning	2	18.980	18.83[a]
Subject × Product × Positioning within SRI	87	1.008	
Total	359		

[a] $p < 0.001$.
[b] $p < 0.01$.

positioning. The two-way interaction addresses whether the impact of positioning on purchase intent is different for different SRI levels. The three-way interaction relates to whether the two-way interaction is constant across product categories.

The basic results are:

1. The two-way interaction effect between SRI and positioning is significant at $p < 0.01$. In other words, the impact of positioning on purchase intent is different for different SRI groups. Since this two-factor interaction does not include 'product category' as one of the factors, it is automatically an average across product categories. (See third row of means in Table 2).
2. The three-way interaction effect among SRI, product category and positioning is significant at $p < 0.001$. In other words, the two-way interaction between SRI and positioning is different for different product categories. This suggests we consider the SRI/positioning interaction *separately for each product category*.
3. (a) For the product category, food, the two-way interaction effect between positioning and SRI is significant at $p < 0.001$. (See first row of means in Table 2).
   (b) For the product category, household cleaner, the two-way interaction effect between positioning and SRI is not significant, $(p > 0.25)$. (See second row of means in Table 2).

Recall that the 'modern positioning advantage' is the difference between purchase intent when presented with the modern positioning and purchase intent when presented with the traditional positioning. Thus, the higher the value, the greater the preference for the modern positioning.

In the food category, for women with a masculine SRI score, the mean purchase intent when presented with the modern positioning was 1.65 (on the seven-point scale noted earlier) above the mean purchase intent of *these same women* when presented with the traditional positioning. For women with an androgynous SRI score, the modern positioning advantage was still positive, but not so large. For the women with a feminine SRI score, the advantage was negative, i.e., slightly in favor of the traditional positioning. As previously mentioned, the difference among these three means is significant at $p < 0.001$. A Newman-Keuls Test indicated at $p < 0.05$ that all three means are different from one another. In the household cleaner category, the three means are not significantly different $(p > 0.25)$.

Table 2 Mean modern positioning advantage

Product category	SRI		
	Masculine	Androgynous	Feminine
Food Mean	1.65	0.56	− 0.14
Cleaner Mean	0.23	−0.05	−0.36
Combined Mean	0.94	0.26	−0.25

DISCUSSION AND IMPLICATIONS

What is apparent is that not all women prefer the same positioning in the food category. The significant two-way interaction between sex-role identity and positioning supports the hypothesis that women who ascribe to a masculine sex-role identity prefer the modern positioning above the traditional one. Androgynous women also prefer the modern positioning, but to a lesser degree. Women who adhere to a feminine sex-role identity prefer a traditional positioning. As was determined by the Newman-Keuls Test, all three groups are significantly different from one another.

Many of the psychological studies that have attempted to explore the relationship between sex-role identity and measures of well-being have found that androgynous women do not differ from masculine ones. Therefore, it is indicated that masculinity is the driving force in predicting well-being (Adams & Sherer, 1982; Anhill & Cunningham, 1979; Lubinski, Tellegen, & Butcher, 1983).

In marketing studies, the results are somewhat mixed. Stern (1987), after reviewing the marketing literature, concluded that masculinity, not femininity, is more relevant to consumer behavior because of the high variance explained in areas of family decision-making and reactions to women's roles in advertising. Coughlin & O'Conner (1985), on the other hand, found that each of three different SRI groups did differ from the other two when measuring purchase intent with ads portraying different positionings of women.

Our results are more in line with the Coughlin & O'Connor (1985) study in the sense that each of the three SRI groups was significantly different from the other two. As to why the androgynous women are different from the masculine women, perhaps when purchase intent is the dependent variable, masculinity is not the sole force determining consumer behavior. We think it's a case of 'the jury is still out' when dealing with purchase behavior.

A limitation of this study is the possibility of a 'Northeastern bias,' Northeasterners are thought to be more liberal. This potential bias may have caused the masculine women to have a stronger negative reaction to the traditional positioning (relative to the country as a whole). This could have resulted in this group's having an extra large 'modern positioning advantage,' thus further distancing this group from the adrogynous group.

The significant three-way interaction speaks to the fact that this preference is *not* consistent across product categories. Women who ascribed to a masculine sex-role identity could not be said to prefer the modern positioning over the traditional one in the cleaner category.

In order to determine what accounted for the different results with respect to product category, in-depth interviews were conducted with twenty respondents. What emerged was the sense that while men are apt to share in certain household chores, such as cooking or grocery shopping, they are reluctant to clean. The modern positioning showing men sharing in cleaning chores was unrealistic for many women.

This finding is supported by a study prepared for the President's Advisory Committee for Women (Yankelovich & Barron, 1980). A universal sample of married people were asked to indicate in which chores the husband actively participates. While 68 per cent of married men are likely to shop for groceries and help with the dishes, only 23 per cent are likely to clean bathrooms.

Our positioning in the cleaner category (which showed men cleaning) was 'too' modern to be believable. Perhaps a modern positioning which portrays a less extreme scenario would have gotten similar results as the food category. More research is needed to determine exactly what type of modern positionings are appropriate for specific product categories.

The value of product positioning analysis is best realized when coupled with segmentation analysis, because the effect of positioning on purchase intent often differs by segment. In this study, it is indicated that the impact of positioning on purchase (i.e., which positionings engender more or fewer purchases by which groups of people for which products), is different for segments of women with different sex-role identities. Moreover, these differences by sex-role identity are product dependent. The potential exists for marketers to gain increased efficiency (and, thereby, profits) by including the interrelations among positioning, product, *and sex-role identity*.

It might be noted that the Equal Opportunity Commission (EOC) study discussed in the literature review found that a modern positioning was favored by all segments of women considered. Our study in no way contradicts this result. In fact, if we average over both product categories and the three SRI levels, thus getting the main effect of positioning, we also find a significant preference for the modern positioning. However, when segmenting by sex-role identity, which was not done in the EOC study, we found a significant difference in positioning preference.

Future research will include a variety of product categories such as financial and health-care services, to determine for which categories sex-role identity plays a key role. To capture advertising effectiveness, a hierarchy of measures including recall, like/dislike and credibility will be used in conjunction with persuasion. Finally, future research will include both men and women because surely both genders have been affected by women's changing sex-role.

REFERENCES

Adams, C. H., and Sherer, M. (1982). Sex-role orientation and psychological adjustment: Comparison of MMPI profiles among college women and housewives. *Journal of Personality Assessment*, 46, 607–613.

Anhill, J. K., and Cunningham, J. D. (1979). Self-esteem as a function of masculinity in both sexes. *Journal of Consulting and Clinical Psychology*, 47, 783–785.

Belkaoui, A., and Belkaoui, J. M. (1976). Comparative analysis of the roles portrayed by women in print advertisements: 1958, 1970, 1972. *Journal of Marketing Research*, 13, 168–172.

Bem, S. L. (1974). The measurement of psychological androgyny. *The Journal of Consulting and Clinical Psychology*, 42, 155–162.

Bem, S. L. (1979). Theory of measurement of androgyny: A reply to the Pedhazur-Tetenbaum & Locksley-Colten critiques. *Journal of Personality and Social Psychology*, 37, 1047–1054.

Bem, S. L. (1981). Bem sex-role inventory. *Consulting Psychological Press*.

Coughlin, M., and O'Connor, P. J. (1985). Gender role portrayals in advertising: An individual difference analysis. In E. C. Hirshman and M. B. Holbrook (Eds.), *Advances in Consumer Research*, Vol. 12 (pp. 238–241). Ann Arbor, MI: Association for Consumer Research.

Courtney, A. E., and Lockeretz, S. W. (1971). A woman's place: An analysis of the roles portrayed by women in magazine ads. *Journal of Marketing Research*, 8, 92–95.

Courtney, A. E., and Whipple, T. W. (1974). Women in TV commercials. *Journal of Communication*, 24, 110–118.

Debevec, K., and Allen, C. T. (1984). Theoretical frameworks for examining the effectiveness of stereotyping in persuasive communications. In P. Anderson and M. Ryan (Eds.), *Winter Educators' Conference Proceeding*. Chicago, IL: American Marketing Association.

Debevec, K., and Iyer, E. (1986). Sex roles and consumer perception of promotions, products, and self: What do we know and where should we be headed? In R. J. Lutz (Ed.), *Advances in Consumer Research*, Vol. 13 (pp. 210–214). Provo, UT: Association for Consumer Research.

Heilbrun, G. (1982). *Toward a recognition of androgyny*. New York: W. W. Norton.

Howell, D. C. (1982). *Statistical methods for psychology*. Boston, MA: PWS Publishers.

Kelly, J., Furman, W., and Young, V. (1978). Problems associated with the typological measurement of sex roles and androgyny. *Journal of Consulting and Clinical Psychology*, 46, 1574–1576.

Locksley, A., and Colten, E. (1979). Psychological androgyny: A case of mistaken identity. *Journal of Personality and Social Psychology*; 37, 1017–1031.

Lubinski, D., Tellegen, A., and Butcher, J. N. (1983). Masculinity, femininity, and androgyny viewed and assessed as distinct concepts. *Journal of Personality and Social Psychology*, 44, 428–439.

Lundstrom, W., and Sciglimpaglia, D. (1977). Sex portrayals in advertising. *Journal of Marketing*, 41, 72–79.

Mowen, J. C. (1987). *Consumer behavior*. New York: Macmillan, pp. 103–104.

Ostlund, L. E., and Clancy, K. J. (1982). Copy testing methods and measures favored by top ad agency and advertising executives. *Journal of the Academy of Marketing Science*, 10, 72–89.

Petty, R., and Cacioppo, J. (1981). Issue involvement as a moderator of the effects on attitude of advertising content and context. In R. J. Lutz (Ed.) *Advances in Consumer Research*, Vol. 8 (pp. 20–24). Provo, UT: Association for Consumer Research.

Singer, J. (1977). *Androgyny*. New York: Doubleday, pp. 1–24.

The Sherman Group. (1982). Adam & Eve. (Unpublished study carried out for the Equal Opportunity Commission).

Spence, J. T. (1983). Comment on Lubinski, Tellegen & Butcher's masculinity, femininity, and androgyny viewed and assessed as distinct concepts. *Journal of Personality and Social Psychology*, 44, 440–446.

Spence, J. T., and Helmreich, A. L. (1979). The many faces of androgyny: A reply to Locksley and Colten. *Journal of Personality and Social Psychology*, 37, 1032–1046.

Spence, J. T., Helmreich, R., and Stapp, J. (1974). The personality attributes questionnaire: A measure of sex-role stereotypes and masculinity-femininity. *JSAs Catalogue of Selected Documents in Psychology*, 4, (MS. NO. 617).

Stern, B. B. (1987). Gender research and the services consumer: New insights and new directions. In M. Waldendorf and P. Anderson (Eds.) *Advances in Consumer Research*, Vol. 14 (pp. 514–519). Provo, UT: Association for Consumer Research.

Tyebjee, T. T. (1979). Refinement of the involvement concept: An advertising planning point of view. In J. C. Maloney and B. Silverman, *Attitude research plays for high stakes*. Chicago: American Marketing Association, p. 106.

Wagner, L. C., and Banos, J. B. (1973). A woman's place: A follow-up analysis of the roles portrayed by women in magazine advertisements. *Journal of Marketing Research*, 10, 213–214.

Yankelovich, D., and Barron, D. (1980). Today's American woman: How the public sees her. Washington, DC: Public Agency Foundation.

Jaffe, L. J. and Berger, P. D. (1988) 'Impact on purchase intent of sex-role identity and product positioning'. *Psychology and Marketing*, 5(3): 259–327. Reproduced with permission.

Section 3
Advertising – Media Channel Management

Unlike many areas of marketing communications, the complexity of and creativity in the development of an advertisement requires the use of an agency. While a company may have its own PR people, negotiate their own sponsorships, develop their own exhibition material, etc., when it comes to advertising, almost without exception, the company will turn to an agency. This section covers some of the issues of selecting and using agencies.

An offering from New Zealand (Marshall and Na, 1994) opens the discussion by looking at the formation and behaviour of the team created to make the complex decision over which advertising agency to use. This article also has uses in fields outside of advertising (e.g. in the use of teams) but its focus on agency selection makes it a valuable contribution to the literature. Mitchell, Cataquet and Hague (1992) look at the problem from the other end of the agency-relationship, i.e. having already selected and used your agency, what are the primary causes of dissatisfaction with the agency's service? Again with implications beyond its primary focus (e.g. it contributes to the literature in the service quality field) the main conclusion from the study was the identification of a set of factors that appeared to be consistent across both time and country boundaries. While the advice offered may be most useful for agencies, it also offers marketing managers a series of warning signals to help nip an impending crisis in the bud (important because of the cost, both real and in terms of disruption, created by a need to switch agencies).

The last paper in this section offers the perfect link between the IMC and advertising sections, and Section 4 (on direct marketing). Woodside (1994) develops a '20 step, customer–marketer, database advertising framework' in which he attempts to integrate (there is that word again) the information search strategies of both customer and marketer with the use of databases for building relationships and more accurate targeting of the advertising message. He concludes by offering implications of his model in the 'designing and implementing of effective IMC programmes'.

The advertising agency selection process 3.1

Roger Marshall and Woon Bong Na

INTRODUCTION

There is a plethora of marketing literature about industrial buying centres; there is little doubt that the composition of buying centres does vary in relationship to a number of variables such as the size of the organization and the importance of the product being purchased (Lynn, 1987). Furthermore, it is generally acknowledged that the influence of various functional role-players waxes and wanes over different types of decisions and at different stages of the decision process (Naumann *et al.*, 1984). There is, however, a lacuna in the reported research concerning the purchase of services (Parasuraman and Zeithaml, 1983). In particular, there is a real dearth of information about the nature of the buying centres formed to purchase the services of an advertising agency. It is somewhat surprising that this is the case, in view of the ubiquity, high risk and relative importance of this type of decision (Cagley, 1986; Harvey and Rupert, 1988).

There is also a notable lack of empirically-based information on the evaluative criteria used by different functional role-players in the advertising agency selection team. Both Hannan (1970) and Cagley and Roberts (1984) have focused on the advertising agency selection process and the evaluative criteria used; but neither study is founded in empiricism or placed within an organizational (buying centre) framework.

Hence the objectives of this article: first, to investigate the composition of buying centres formed to select an advertising agency; second, to ascertain the relative importance of different functional role-players over the process; finally, to determine the evaluative criteria held by these role-players within this organizational context.

HYPOTHESES DEVELOPMENT

The composition of advertising agency selection teams

The buying centre is rarely a formal sub-unit of an organization; rather, it is a somewhat nebulous group of executives drawn from several functional departments and hierarchical levels, whose lines of communication are typically neither strictly prescribed nor officially documented. The structure of the group may therefore evolve as expertise is required or pressure felt. This creates difficult research conditions, but attempts to untangle the complex influence structures of buying centres (in areas other than advertising agency selection) are widely reported. Sheth (1973), in his pioneering work in the area, suggested that buying centre structure would vary according to company-specific factors. What those factors actually are has been researched in more detail since that time. The size of buying centres has variously been reported to relate to the size of the organization (Bellizzi, 1981; Crow and Lindquist, 1985; Spekman and Stern, 1979); the value or importance of the purchase being made (Johnston and Bonoma, 1981); the length of time a buying relationship has existed (Lynn, 1987); and the type of industry in which the purchasing firm operates (Crow and Linquist, 1985). There seems no obvious reason why the size of the advertising agency selection team should vary in response to different factors than any other buying centre. Hence:

> *H1*:   There are significant differences in the size of advertising agency selection teams, dependent upon:
>
> 1. the size of the business firm (measured in terms of sales revenue);
> 2. the dollar value of the purchasing firm's annual advertising billings;
> 3. the purchasing firm's industry type;
> 4. the length of purchase association.

The second aspect concerning the structure of the selection team relates to the variation in the influence of functional role-players throughout the purchase process. Again, there is plenty of evidence that variation does exist in buying centres other than for advertising agency selection, and that it may well vary in response to the same variables that affect the size of the selection team (Choffray and Lilien, 1980; Lynn, 1987; Naumann *et al.*, 1982; Robles, 1984). This provides a framework for a further two hypotheses:

> *H2*:   The influence of functional role-players in the selection team will vary over the decision process.

> *H3*:   The influence of functional role-players in the selection team will vary in response to:
>
> 1. the size of the business firm (measured in terms of sales revenue);
> 2. the dollar value of the purchasing firm's annual advertising billings;
> 3. the purchasing firm's industry type:
> 4. the length of purchase association.

DETECTION OF EVALUATIVE CRITERIA

Some empirical work has been undertaken in recent times to unearth the criteria that business organizations use in evaluating and selecting their advertising agent; in particular Cagley and Roberts (1984) and Harvey and Rupert (1988) have produced large lists of evaluative criteria. If, however, the functional structure of the selection team does vary in accordance with the company-specific variables discussed above, then it is not unreasonable to suggest that the dominant evaluative criteria of the group could also change in response to the same stimuli. Hence:

> *H4*:   There are significant differences between the evaluative criteria used by companies categorized on the basis of:

1. the size of the business firm (measured in terms of sales revenue);
2. the dollar value of the purchasing firm's annual advertising billings;
3. the purchasing firm's industry type;
4. the length of purchase association.

RESEARCH METHOD

Procedure

A mail survey of companies in the Auckland region was conducted. The initial contact was the Marketing Manager (or General Manager if the company did not have a marketing manager). This person was asked to identify the participants in the selection process, and permission was sought to direct mail personally to each of those executives identified. A stamped, addressed return envelope and a covering letter on university letterhead was delivered with each questionnaire. No attempt was made to promise total confidentiality, simply an assurance that we were only interested in aggregate answers. Companies' and individuals' names were printed on the questionnaire, thus follow-up letters and telephone calls were possible.

Questionnaire design

The questionnaire comprised four sections: the first to identify team members; the second to assess their influence; the third to establish the relevant evaluative criteria; and the fourth to ascertain the company-specific factors to allow cross-tabulation.

Identification of participants was by free elicitation, which is claimed to minimize the bias imposed by forced choice scales, and to allow the flexibility to cope with the complex structures involved (Robles, 1984). Assessment of the relative influence of selection team members was undertaken through application of a modified version of March's measure of attribute influence (Crow and Lindquist, 1985). Key respondents were asked to allocate one hundred points among identified members of the group in order to reflect their perception of those members' influence. This type of measure has in the past provided satisfactory results in this situation (Choffray and Lilien, 1978; Naumann et al., 1984). The measure of influence was taken for four stages of the decision process in order to compare members' influence over that process. There is little doubt that measuring influence at separate stages offers superior discriminatory power to a global measure (Robles, 1984; Silk and Kalwani, 1982); but the choice of four stages is somewhat arbitrary. There is a balance to be achieved between increasing discriminatory power through including more stages, and the practical realities of relieving the boredom and fatigue of respondents. There is a precedent for choosing four stages; among others, Naumann et al. (1984) found this number very satisfactory. The four stages selected were:

1. Initiating the selection or change of an agency.
2. Establishment of objectives and needs configuration.
3. Identification and evaluation of possible agencies.
4. Final selection.

Cagley and Roberts (1984) and Cagley (1986) point to a number of sources for the establishment of evaluative criteria. These include case history investigations of factors leading to current relationships; descriptions of the process of selection (Hannan, 1970); presentation of so-called ideal criteria (Campbell, 1970); and various checklists (Anderson and Thomas, 1979). For the purposes of this study, a list of possible evaluative criteria was gleaned in the first place from the relevant empirical work of Cagley and Roberts (1984) and Parasuraman and Zeithaml (1983). Several other items were added to the list after consultation with a number of local experts and scrutiny of the previously mentioned sources. The importance of each of these items, listed in Table 1, was rated by respondents on a seven-point forced choice scale, with the end points anchored by 'extremely important' and 'extremely unimportant'. Cronbach's α for the scale was 0.84, suggesting that the instrument is reliable.

Sample selection

A stratified quota sample of 101 firms was selected from a list of advertisers published in *Ad Media* magazine (March, 1989), the official publication of the Association of New Zealand Advertisers. Quotas were based on type of industry, size of company, advertising expenditures and an estimate of the length of time a company has used an advertising agency. Eight international companies were removed from the frame because their advertising was dictated by head offices along a global alignment. Usable responses were received from forty-one companies. Profiles of the companies, and the operational categorization of them, are listed in Table 2.

Table 1 List of potential evaluative criteria

1. Quality of personnel on account.
2. Complete agreement between agency/client about goals/objectives.
3. Agency's willingness to learn client's business.
4. Reputation for integrity.
5. Interaction with client while developing creative strategy.
6. Compatibility of agency and client personnel.
7. Willingness of agency to make recommendations and object to advertiser's decisions.
8. Creativity of agency media plans.
9. Cost-consciousness of agency.
10. Tailoring of cooperative plan to fit advertiser's needs/desires.
11. Management chemistry/synergy.
12. Business management of the agency.
13. Extent of management participation in client services.
14. Marketing analysis and consultation.
15. Full range of agency services.
16. Sales promotion ideas and capability.
17. Assistance with development of marketing plans.
18. Experience with advertisers that produce similar products.
19. Referral by satisfied clients.
20. Personal solicitation.
21. Personnel qualifications.
22. Agency's self-advertising.
23. Price of services.

Table 2 Operationalization of firm-specific characteristics

a) Annual sales revenue			Operational category	b) Percentage advertising spend		
Category (In $NZm)	n	%		Category (% of sales)	n	%
>5	2	4.9		⩾1	8	19.6
6–10	5	12.2	Treated as	2	10	23.4
11–50	6	14.7	Group 1	3	5	12.2
51–100	5	12.2				
101–250	15	36.6		4	1	2.4
251–500	1	2.4	Treated as	5	7	17.0
>500	7	17.0	Group 2	6	3	7.3
				7	2	4.9
				<7	5	12.2

c) Length of time with agencies			Operational category	d) Type of product		
Category (years)	n	%		Category	n	%
5	9	21.9	Treated as	Consumer	20	48.8
6–10	9	21.9	Group 1	Pkg. goods		
11–20	15	36.6	Treated as	Others	21	51.2
>20	8	19.6	Group 2			

The re-categorization of companies by characteristic for operational purposes was arbitrary; but it was felt by the researchers that this sort of comparative approach was meaningful within the context of the requirements of the research.

In order to investigate the non-response bias, non-respondents were contacted and asked to provide approximations of the stratifying variables for their organization. The results of a comparison of the characteristics of respondents and non-respondents in Table 3 suggest that the sample was reasonably representative.

RESULTS

Size of the selection team

The overall mean size of the identified selection teams was 2.98 persons. This compares to the mean size of 6.20 for North American industrial buying centres

Table 3 Comparison of company-specific characteristics of respondent and non-respondent firms

	Company characteristics							
	Industry type		Sales ad spend		Agencies used		Time with agency	
Group	1	2	1	2	1	2	1	2
Respondents	49	51	44	56	55	45	44	56
Non-respondents	50	50	50	50	46	53	38	62

Note: Figures represent percentage of relevant sample.

identified by Spekman and Stern (1979); and of 3.53 for selection teams buying CPA services identified by Lynn (1987). While it is possible that the smaller number in the team could reflect a cultural bias stemming from the overall small size of New Zealand companies, it seems to the authors that a more likely explanation relates to the need for very specific expertise or experience of participants in the decision process for this type of service.

This interpretation of the data is supported by further analysis of the participation pattern over the four stages of the decision process. Ten functional roles were identified, and Table 4 shows that the marketing and advertising specialists are heavily involved over the early stages, but that the final decision seems to rest mainly with the Marketing Manager and the Managing Director.

Unlike Johnston and Bonoma (1981), who found no clear differences between the average number of participants at various stages in the purchase process, the results of the present study indicate that there are more players involved at the later, rather than earlier, stages. A possible explanation is that financial managers or directors are already part of a CPA selection centre in the early part of the selection process, whereas the selection team for an advertising agency is unlikely to include these functional role-players until the closing stages when the decision hinges less on expertise in promotion and more in financial management.

The main point of interest here, however, revolves around Hypothesis 1; does the size of the selection team vary by the four company-specific factors of size, percentage advertising spend, type of industry and the length of time the company has used an agency? Analysis by t-test reveals a significant difference only in the case of sales revenue, which was the proxy chosen to represent organization size. The mean number in the team for companies with sales of more than $100 million was 2.29, while larger companies had a mean number of 3.46 ($t = 4.72$ p $<.01$). Sheth also noted the commonsense fact that larger companies are more likely to have the resources to devote to the selection process (1973).

Table 4 Mean influence of functional role-players, and number of participants through the stages of the decision process

Function	Stage of decision process								Mean
	Initiate		Configure		Evaluate		Final		
Marketing manager/director	41.6[1]	(26)[2]	37.9	(27)	41.0	(28)	36.0	(29)	39.0
Advertising manager	16.5	(9)	17.0	(11)	17.0	(10)	9.4	(10)	15.0
Production manager	6.8	(7)	11.2	(11)	10.0	(8)	8.1	(9)	9.0
Managing director	26.4	(20)	23.0	(20)	22.3	(21)	32.0	(26)	26.0
Sales manager/director	1.3	(2)	2.4	(3)	2.0	(2)	2.9	(4)	2.2
Divisional manager	2.7	(4)	3.5	(5)	4.3	(5)	2.7	(4)	3.3
Chief executive	1.9	(3)	1.6	(3)	1.0	(2)	5.4	(4)	2.5
Consultant	1.3	(2)	1.6	(2)	1.4	(2)	2.2	(4)	1.6
Finance manager	0.8	(1)	1.1	(1)	1.0	(1)	0.9	(1)	1.0
Planning manager	0.7	(1)	0.7	(1)	0.0	(–)	0.4	(1)	0.4

[1] Columns total 100; a higher number indicates more influence
[2] Frequency of functional participation in parentheses

Variation in the influence of role-players

The overall pattern of influence has already been demonstrated in Table 4 above, where the Marketing Manager and Advertising Director exercise a major influence early in the process and less later, and the Managing Director demonstrates increasing influence over all four stages. To determine if this pattern differs according to the four defined company-specific factors, analysis of variance was conducted for influence patterns between role functions and stages of decision. Although there was a significant main effect found for role function ($F_{(Function)} = 6.25$, $p = <.001$), the F statistic was significant for neither stage nor the interaction between the two variables ($F_{(Stage)} = 1.701$, $p = .167$; $F_{(Function \times stage)} = .790$, $p = .759$). Thus although influence does seem to change over the process, Hypothesis 3 (i.e. that the change is dependent on company-specific factors) must be rejected.

Evaluative criteria

The potential evaluative criteria are listed in Table 1. The principal purpose of asking respondents to rank the importance of these criteria was to find out if there is variation in the importance of these criteria between firms grouped by the four company-specific factors as defined in this article. Table 5 lists the same factors, but in rank order of importance for the sample as a whole. The test of Hypothesis 4 is contained within the table, which shows little significant difference between the importance of

Table 5 Evaluative criteria ranked in order of importance; differences by company-specific factors

Criterion	Mean	Difference[1]
1. Quality of personnel on account	6.68	Sales volume
2. Interaction with client while developing creative strategy	6.31	No
3. Cost-consciousness of agency	6.24	No
4. Complete agreement about goals/objectives	6.09	No
5. Agency's willingness to learn client's business	6.09	No
6. Reputation for integrity	6.09	No
7. Creativity of agency media plans	6.09	No
8. Compatibility of agency and client personnel	6.04	No
9. Management chemistry/synergy	5.90	No
10. Willingness of agency to make recommendations and object to advertiser's decisions	5.68	Product type
11. Tailoring of cooperative plan to fit advertiser's needs/desires	5.65	No
12. Price of services	5.53	No
13. Business management of the agency	5.41	No
14. Extent of management participation in client services	5.36	No
15. Marketing analysis and consultation	5.36	No
16. Full range of agency services	5.19	No
17. Sales promotion ideas and capability	4.97	Product type
18. Assistance with development of marketing plans	4.46	No
19. Personnel qualifications	4.31	No
20. Experience with advertisers that produce similar products	3.95	No
21. Referral by satisfied clients	3.53	Sales volume
22. Agency's self-advertising	3.09	No
23. Personal solicitation	2.78	Sales volume

[1] Difference significant to <0.01.

criteria between companies along the hypothesized lines. The differences that did emerge fitted no particular pattern; in no instance was the difference large enough to change the rank order.

To make sure that there were no concealed differences, a factor analysis of the list was carried out. Seven factors emerged on the varimax rotation, and are shown in Table 6. For the sake of clarity, items with loadings of less than five are omitted from the table.

The factor analysis does assist to shorten the list of criteria (by combining those items that clustered together into one evaluative criterion), and makes it easier to understand. Although an arbitrary division, it seems reasonable and convenient to discuss the new, shorter list of evaluative criteria in three groups. The first are those held by the sample to be the most important, shown in Table 7 (note that the scale had seven points, with point 7 being extremely important). These results follow those of Cagley and Roberts (1984) quite closely, particularly in respect to the concern that the people working on the account are thoroughly compatible in personal terms with the advertiser's personnel.

The second group of criteria (shown in Table 8) still has marginal importance. Although there is no statistical basis for saying so, it is possible that these are seen as 'trade-off' items that could give agencies a competitive edge, rather than those of the first group which are more likely to represent the basic requirements for staying in contention. The most noteworthy item here is that price features in this second echelon of factors rather than the primary role it is sometimes assumed to adopt.

The final three criteria were considered to be relatively unimportant. The ability of agencies to help with marketing plans (mean = 4.46) is one of the items that one

Table 6 Factor analysis of evaluative criteria

Attributes	Factors						
	1	2	3	4	5	6	7
Personal solicitation	.83						
Referral by clients	.76						
Agency self-advertisements	.64						
Sales promotion ideas		.81					
Marketing analysis		.65					
Full range of services		.60					
Agreement on goals			.84				
Reputation for integrity			.77				
Willingness to object				.81			
Quality of a/c personnel				.54			
Personnel qualifications					.76		
Business management					.72		
Learn client's business						.78	
Creativity of media plan						.56	
Fitting client's plan							.59
Interaction with client							.58
Eigenvalues	5.7	2.5	2.1	1.9	1.5	1.3	1.1
Variance explained (%)	25	36	45	54	60	66	70

(Cronbach's Alpha = 0.845)

Table 7 Most important evaluative criteria

Criterion	Mean
1 Cost-consciousness	6.24
2. Interpersonal factors	6.18
3. Professional integrity	6.09
4. Empathy	6.09
5. Managerial skills	6.05
6. Compatibility	6.04

Table 8 Moderately important evaluative criteria

Criterion	Mean
7. Cooperation	5.98
8. Management chemistry	5.90
9. Price	5.53
10. Management participation	5.36
11. Marketing capability	5.17

would have thought smaller companies would appreciate – but there is no evidence of that here. Experience with similar products or companies is likewise seen as relatively unimportant at 3.95 (every company thinks that they are unique, in any case); and the self-promotion efforts of agencies does not go a long way to influence potential clients (mean = 3.13).

This latter point is an interesting one, in the light of the prevalence of self-advertising by many agencies. It could well be claimed that the influence of such advertising may not be assessed well on an instrument such as that used in the present research. Although this activity does not seem to provide an important guide in a logical search for an agency, much advertising works at a different level to this; the importance of the advertising may better be measured by the building of awareness, or by the teaching of relevant cues.

CONCLUSION AND DISCUSSION

In spite of the limitations imposed by the use of a convenience sample, the major findings of the research have face validity and are in accord with other research in the area and therefore allow some conclusions to be drawn with reasonable confidence.

The selection of an agency to handle a company's advertising seems to involve a fairly complex decision process, but (probably due to the specialized nature of the product being purchased) fewer people are included in the buying centre than for other industrial product purchases, and at least some other services. The key personnel are the Marketing Manager and the General Manager; the former has greater importance in the earlier stages of the decision while the latter plays a more confirmatory role in the later stages. This pattern of influence seems unaffected by the company-specific factors of industry size and type, percentage of sales revenue spent on advertising, and company experience with advertising agencies.

It is of real interest that the evaluative criteria used by companies in their assessment of an agency also vary very little across these same company-specific factors. The criteria that emerged as most important were not of themselves surprising; other studies have pinpointed the importance of the interpersonal factors before. In the light of the fact that there are few tangible and objective factors that can be used in the evaluation process, it is not strange that relationships and trust come to the fore. Local advertisers with diverse client portfolios will be relieved that their marketing mix need not be adjusted too dramatically for the different sectors, and may benefit from the affirmation of international findings concerning key evaluative criteria in New Zealand.

REFERENCES

Anderson, R. L. and Thomas, E. B. (1979) *Advertising Management*. Columbus OH: Charles E. Merrill Publishing Co.

Bellizzi, P. (1981) Organizational size and buying influence. *Industrial Marketing Management*, 10, 17–21.

Cagley, J. W. (1986) A comparison of advertising agency selection factors: Advertiser and agency perceptions. *Journal of Advertising Research*, 28 (June), 39–44.

Cagley, J. W. and Roberts, C. R. (1984) Criteria for advertising agency selection: An objective appraisal. *Journal of Advertising Research*, 24, 27–31.

Campbell, R. P. (1970) Getting the most from your advertising agency. In V. P. Buell (ed.), *Handbook of Modern Marketing*. New York: McGraw-Hill.

Choffray, J. M. and Lilien, G. L. (1978) Assessing response to industrial marketing strategy. *Journal of Marketing*, 42, 20–31.

——(1980) Industrial market segmentation by the structure of the purchasing process. *Industrial Marketing Management*, 10, 17–21.

Churchill, G. A. Jnr (1979) Paradigm for developing better measures of marketing constructs. *Journal of Marketing Research*, 16, 64–73.

Crow, L. E. and Lindquist, J. D. (1985) Impact of organizational and buyer characteristics on the buying centre. *Industrial Marketing Management*, 14, 49–58.

Hannan, M. (1970) Criteria for advertising agency selection. In V. P. Buell (ed.), *Handbook of Modern Marketing*. New York: McGraw-Hill.

Harvey, M. G. and Rupert, J. P. (1988) Selecting an industrial advertising agency. *Industrial Marketing Management*, 17, 117–127.

Johnstone, W. J. and Bonoma, T. V. (1981) The buying centre: Structure and interaction pattern. *Journal of Marketing*, 45, 143–156.

Lilien, G. L. and Wong, M. A. (1984) Structure of the buying centre. *Journal of Marketing Research*, 21, 1–11.

Lynn, S. A. (1987) Identifying buying influences for a professional service: Implications for marketing efforts. *Industrial Marketing Management*, 16, 119–130.

Naumann, E., Lincoln, D. and McWilliams, R. D. (1984) The purchase of components: Functional areas of influence. *Industrial Marketing Management*, 13, 113–122.

Parasuraman, A. and Zeithaml, V. A. (1983) Differential perceptions of suppliers and clients of industrial services. In L. L. Berry, G. L. Shostack & G. Upah (eds), *Emerging Perspectives in Services Marketing* (pp. 35–39). Chicago, IL: American Marketing Association.

Robles, F. (1984) Buying in a matrix organization. *Industrial Marketing Management*, 13, 201–208.

Sheth, J. (1973) A model of industrial buying behavior. *Journal of Marketing*, 37, 50–56.

Silk, A. J. and Kalwani, M. U. (1982) Measuring influence in organizational purchase decisions. *Journal of Marketing Research*, 19, 165–181.

Spekman, R. E. and Stern, L. W. (1979) Environmental uncertainty and buying group structure: An empirical investigation. *Journal of Marketing*, 43, 54–64.

Marshall, R. and Na, W. B. (1994) 'The advertising agency selection process'. *International Journal of Advertising*, 13: 217–227. Reproduced with permission.

Establishing the causes of disaffection in agency–client relations

Paul C. N. Michell, Harold Cataquet and Stephen Hague

While there are major costs in both time and money involved in changing agencies (Newsome, 1980), there nevertheless seems to be no propensity among clients to reduce the rates at which they switch agencies. Michell (1988), for example, reports that 46 percent of accounts by billings switched agencies in the United Kingdom during 1981–85, exactly the same rate as during the previous five years. Doyle, Corstjens, and Michell (1980) have researched the main reasons for agency–client breakups, through qualitative questionnaires, using a base for U.K. switches for the period 1976–77. Michell (1987) has replicated the study, using U.S. breakups during 1983–84, and has recommended a performance audit to watch for signals of creeping disenchantment in the relationship. Martindale (1984) has, however, counselled that agencies do not appear to learn from their own or other agencies' losses and rarely monitor the service level offered to clients.

Since the above qualitative research was completed, the advertising industry has, of course, undergone major structural change – in particular, acquisition/merger activity and the emergence of 'mega agencies'. One client reaction to such events was reported by Wilson (1986): 'I'm the client, and I'm selfish. Show me how mergers will improve my service.' Given the changing context, it appeared worthwhile to replicate the research on U.K. breakups and thus show trends and consolidate knowledge on the subject.

As the original U.K. and U.S. studies had shown strikingly similar results, it was predicted, despite the industry's structural changes, that clients would continue to report a generally consistent set of reasons over time for changing their agencies. However, it was also anticipated that the increasing intensity of agency policy changes and frequency of agency management changes would translate into reduced levels of service as perceived by clients, thus detrimentally affecting agency–client relations. The results do indeed indicate a continuing theme in the relative importance of the broader factors responsible for switching agencies and also the emergence of a number of specific signs of increasing conflict. In particular, the customer orientation of agencies appears to have declined since the survey was last conducted.

STUDY DESIGN

The methodology used in this U.K. study fully replicated that used earlier by Doyle, Corstjens, and Michell (1980). The data were obtained from a seven-page questionnaire mailed to all U.K. advertisers identified in *Campaign*, the advertising trade journal, as having changed agencies during the 12 months preceding June 1989. One hundred and ten responses (representing a 44 percent response rate) were obtained, compared with eighty-four (51 percent response) in the earlier study. The questionnaire sought to identify the reasons for breakdown in the agency–client relationship. It postulated five broad reasons for the breakups: (1) 'changes in client marketing policies'; (2) 'changes in client management'; (3) 'changes in agency policies'; (4) 'changes in agency management'; and (5) 'dissatisfaction with agency performance.' Respondents were asked to rank these five broad causes in order of importance from 1: high to 5: low. The five broad reasons were further sub-divided into thirty-four variables which were rated from 1: crucial to 5: unimportant. These variables were originally developed from the literature and personal interviews with clients and agents. Respondents were also encouraged to add their comments. Lastly, the questionnaire inquired into the client decision-making process about who was responsible for the decision to end the relationship. The survey was directed to the chief executives of client organizations, and the covering letter requested them to forward the questionnaire to the executive most closely involved with the account at the time of the switch. The breakdown of respondents by job title and product group, respectively, are listed in Tables 1 and 2.

Thus, the same questionnaire was used for both time periods, with similar response rates, respondent profiles, and mix of product categories.

FINDINGS

Consistency in client perceptions of the broad factors responsible for account switches

The results, both across time and between countries, point to a consistent picture in the clients' perceived reasons for switching agencies, both in the rank order and the means of the five broad categories. Thus, Table 3 relates how the U.K. clients ranked the five hypothesized reasons for their switch of agencies in 1988–89 compared with 1976–77, with the U.S. findings for 1983–84 also given in brackets. 'Dissatisfaction with agency performance' is always ranked first in each of the studies, well ahead of the two client factors, 'policy' and 'management', and followed up by the 'agency management' and 'agency policy' factors.

Within the mainstream results, cluster analysis suggests that four subgroups exist with their own special reasons for ranking the five broad factors in differing order. Given the range of factors involved in agency–client relations, cluster analysis was

Table 1 Breakdown of respondents to questionnaire by job title

Job title	U.K. study 1988–89 (%)	U.K. study 1976–77 (%)
Chief executive/managing director	9	9
Marketing director	13	22
Marketing manager	27	25
Advertising manager	36	37
Marketing services manager	15	7
	100	100

Table 2 Breakdown of respondents to questionnaire by product group

Product group	U.K. 1988–89 (%)	U.K. 1976–77 (%)
Agriculture	1	2
Charity	3	2
Beverage	8	7
Entertainment	3	2
Financial	10	7
Food	10	11
Government	7	6
Travel	4	8
Household appliances	5	5
Household equipment	5	6
Household stores	3	2
Institutional	5	4
Leisure	4	7
Motors	6	5
Office equipment	5	4
Pharmaceuticals	5	2
Publishing	2	4
Retail	7	6
Tobacco	1	2
Toiletries	5	5
Apparel	1	3
	100	100

Table 3 Comparison of perceived reasons for account switch

Reasons for account switch	U.K. clients – 1988–89 Rank	U.K. clients – 1988–89 Mean	U.K. clients – 1976–77 Rank	U.K. clients – 1976–77 Mean	U.S. clients – 1983–84 Rank	U.S. clients – 1983–84 Mean
Dissatisfaction with agency performance	1	1.8	1	2.0	(1)	(2.1)
Changes in client policy	2	2.6	2	2.8	(2)	(3.0)
Changes in client management	3	3.2	3	3.4	(3)	(3.1)
Changes in agency management	4	3.4	4	3.6	(4)	(3.7)
Changes in agency policy	5	4.1	5	4.3	(5)	(4.3)

conducted on the sample to ascertain how many groupings of clients existed and the differences between the groups on their rank ordering of the five factors. Table 4 shows the four resulting groups. The main cluster, comprising 43 percent of the sample, ranked the factors in identical order to the overall result. The second largest group, at 28 percent, also placed 'dissatisfaction with agency performance' first but thereafter ranked 'agency management' and 'policy' ahead of 'client management' and 'policy.' In particular, the overall results obscured the views of two small clusters, one comprising 18 percent and the other 11 percent of the sample, which ranked, respectively, 'client policy' and 'agency policy' ahead of all other factors. These are clearly two segments with totally differing reasons for switching agencies compared with the majority of the sample. Detailed analysis of the responses identified no product group or respondent job title bias and simply confirmed that particular

Table 4 Cluster Analysis: subgroups and their rankings of factors

% Sample	Overall 100% Rank	Overall 100% Mean	Group 1 43% Rank	Group 1 43% Mean	Group 2 28% Rank	Group 2 28% Mean	Group 3 18% Rank	Group 3 18% Mean	Group 4 11% Rank	Group 4 11% Mean
Dissatisfaction with agency performance	1	1.8	1	1.3	1	1.3	3	3.3	2	2.1
Changes in client policy	2	2.6	2	2.1	5	4.3	1	1.5	3	2.6
Changes in client management	3	3.2	3	3.2	4	3.9	2	1.6	5	4.6
Changes in agency management	4	3.4	4	3.9	2	1.9	4	3.8	4	3.9
Changes in agency policy	5	4.1	5	4.6	3	3.7	5	4.8	1	1.8

situations influenced the order of ranks. The 'client policy' cluster may be summated by a verbatim quote from a respective questionnaire: 'We focused on direct marketing and went elsewhere for the expertise'; and the 'agency policy' cluster by the quote: 'The agency merged with another where a bigger account in our category existed.'

Moreover, interrelationships need to be emphasized, since a key variable from one broad factor may correlate strongly with a variable within another. For example, 'personality conflict,' a variable from 'changes in client management,' is strongly correlated with two 'changes in agency management' variables, 'agency top management changes' and 'agency organization structure changes.' Similarly, 'agency merger/acquisitions activity' was strongly correlated with 'disagreement over advertising objectives,' a 'dissatisfaction with agency performance' variable. Sometimes, there is one variable which is so crucial to the client, for example, 'conflicting accounts,' that it becomes the discriminating variable alongside which all other variables appear insignificant. In these cases, ranking of the remaining categories is very marginal and likely to be somewhat arbitrary. There were fortunately few instances in the sample.

Similarities and divergencies in the incidents leading to breakups

Overall, there was a strong statistical correlation between the results of the two studies. Table 5 indicates, for the two time periods, the percentages of U.K. advertisers noting a series of 34 variables as important or crucial in leading to the breakup. U.S. figures are given in brackets for comparison. Strong commonality is indicated by the high correlation coefficients printed at the bottom of the table. In particular, comparison of percentages shows a similar overall pattern, with high-score variables typically achieving similar scores in both U.K. studies and in the U.S. survey. Nevertheless, differences also need to be stressed. Eleven variables showed statistically significant differences across the two U.K. surveys. Of these, 10 increased in magnitude of importance as reasons for the breakup.

The 'dissatisfaction with agency performance' variables achieved the highest percentile scores, with 'standard of creative work' the most important variable of all (69 percent in each sample). Four of the eight variables in this broad category received significantly higher importance than in 1976–77. 'Disagreement over advertising objectives' moved from 19 to 41 percent ($p < .005$), the highest rate of increase. A related variable, 'standard of agency marketing advice,' also moved up

Table 5 Comparative importance of variables responsible for account switches

Variable	U.K. 1988–89 (%)	U.K. 1976–77 (%)	U.S. 1983–84 (%)
Disatisfaction with agency performance			
Standard of agency creative work	69	69	(62)
Agency 'not close enough' to client's business	59	45 $p < .05$	(55)
Relative image weakness of campaigns	53	41 $p < .10$	(43)
Standard of agency marketing advice	50	39 $p < .10$	(52)
Relative sales weakness of campaigns	41	37	(47)
Disagreement over advertising objectives	41	19 $p < .005$	(37)
Standard of agency media buying	33	24	(29)
Standard of agency sales promotions/PR	7	14	(21)
Changes in client policy			
Changes in marketing policies/strategies	51	46	(59)
'Time for a change' of agency	38	42	(29)
Routine reevaluation of 'short listed' agencies	22	18	(7)
Rationalization of agencies within client group	21	24	(17)
Need for 'full service' agency	14	27 $p < .05$	(34)
Need for services of 'specialist' agency	11	18	(26)
Transfer to below-the-line	11	8	(5)
Increase in advertising budget	11	16	(15)
Group or international group dictate	9	8	(6)
Changes in client management			
Client–agency personality conflict	40	24 $p < .01$	(35)
Changes in client top management	37	35	(38)
Changes in client marketing organization structure	36	32	(45)
Changes in client advertising management personnel	17	14	(27)
Changes in client product management personnel	12	11	(17)
Introduction/development of product management system	8	7	(14)
Changes in agency management			
Changes in agency account management personnel	36	35	(34)
Changes in agency top management personnel	30	17 $p < .05$	(12)
Changes in agency creative personnel	29	33	(37)
Changes in agency organization structure	29	16 $p < .05$	(29)
Changes in overall reputation of agency	24	12 $p < .10$	(16)
Changes in agency policy			
Agency involved in merger/acquisition	23	11 $p < .10$	(8)
Development of conflicting accounts in agency	17	4 $p < .05$	(7)
Attempt to change remuneration (fees)	13	8	(8)
Rationalization of account by agency	6	11	(11)

Correction matrix =	U.K. 1988–89	U.S. 1983–84
U.K. 1976–77	.89	.91
U.K. 1988–89	–	.86

significantly from 39 to 50 percent ($p < .10$). Agencies were also found to be 'not close enough to clients' business' in 59 percent of cases compared with 45 percent previously ($p < .05$). All three are damning reflections on agencies' lack of sensitivity in understanding their customers' needs. Lastly, the 'relative image weakness of campaigns' was mentioned by 53 percent of respondents compared with 41 percent previously, again an important criticism given the move toward more perceptual, longer-term creative executions in the United Kingdom during the 1980s. Verbatims from the interviews confirmed these findings:

> The agency was no longer producing the required standard of advertising (advertising manager, large glass manufacturer).

> Our new agency board director did not show a great depth of understanding about our business and creativity. The strategies were felt to be wrong (advertising manager, corporate institution).

> Despite the closeness of the relationship, the agency had a profound misunderstanding of our needs (promotions officer, charitable institute).

> The agency did not possess an understanding of our brand or market (managing director, pharmaceuticals).

'Changes in client policy' variables received similar scores to those in the previous survey, with only one significantly different result, namely 'need for a full service agency' down from 27 to 14 percent ($p < .05$). This suggests that clients are becoming less concerned with the breadth of services they receive as compared with their quality. 'Changes in marketing policies/strategies' remains one of the key variables at 51 percent (46 percent previously), as described by the following.

> Our company terminated the relationship because we were dissatisfied with the agency's attitude towards us (marketing services manager, oil company).

> Our company has grown very fast with a parallel increase in advertising expenditure and professionalism, coupled with a change in strategy. The agency could not keep up with the pace of change (advertising manager, multiple retailer).

'Changes in client management' variables received comparable importance ratings to the previous study, with only one variable, 'client–agency personality conflict,' receiving a higher percentage score: 40 percent as compared with 24 percent ($p < 0.01$) last time. This variable was strongly correlated with 'changes in agency management' variables, warning agencies against taking for granted a willingness by clients to accept replacement managers, particularly top agency management changes.

By contrast, 'agency management and policy factors' changed considerably, with five out of nine variables showing increases in relative importance. Within 'changes in agency management,' 'changes in agency top management' and 'changes in agency organization structure' moved from 17 to 30 percent and 16 to 29 percent, respectively (both $p < .05$). Of particular concern to agencies, 'changes in overall reputation of the agency' moved from 12 to 24 percent ($p < .10$), and this variable was strongly correlated with 'disagreement over objectives.'

While the overall regression coefficient between the two U.K. surveys was .89, for 'changes in agency policy' it was only .15. This is the one area where there has been indisputable change in client behavior, and much of the variation in the data between the samples may be ascribed to 'changes in agency policy.'

'Merger/acquisitions activity' and the 'development of conflicting accounts' increased in prominence as reasons for break-ups going from 11 to 23 percent ($p < .10$) and from 4 to 17 percent ($p < .05$), respectively. The mergers variable correlates with 'time for a change,' indicating that an agency merger focuses the client's mind on the idea of switching agencies. 'Conflicting accounts' correlated with no other variables and are thus independent and situationally specific.

> The change in agency was purely the result of acquisition leading to account conflict (marketing services manager, corporate industrial sector).

> Our ex-agency was acquired and the account withdrawn as a direct result of a major conflicting account in the new dominant agency (marketing manager, financial services).

The analysis appears to suggest that clients may be segmented into several levels of sensitivity regarding account conflicts (Alter, 1986): (1) highly sensitive clients who reject the concept of an agency-holding company carrying conflicting accounts in semiautonomous agencies; (2) highly tolerant clients who accept the parallel agencies concept entirely; and (3) pragmatic clients who assign accounts internationally market by market based on local agencies' strengths and conflict circumstances.

The underlying causes of account switches

Factor analysis was applied to the data base to discover how the 34 variables correlated, thereby seeking to determine the underlying dimensions causing disaffection in agency–client relations. In both studies, 'dissatisfaction with agency performance' was the main factor, accounting for 25.0 percent variance in the 1988–89 data but only 18.5 percent in 1976–77. Similarly, both studies had 'changes in advertising management' as the second factor, accounting for 10.2 percent of variance on both occasions. In the original analysis, eleven factors explaining 71.7 percent of total variance were produced, and in the present study nine factors explaining 67.1 percent were created. For brevity, only the results of the 1988–89 survey have been presented in Table 6. Only those factors with an eigen value greater than 1.00 have been retained, and only those variables achieving factor loadings of 0.45 and over have been used to interpret the factors.

'Dissatisfaction with agency performance' has strengthened as a factor in explaining even more of the variation in the data than it did for the 1976–77 study. Table 7 shows that 'client–agency personality conflict,' arbitrarily placed in the

Table 6 Factor analysis of U.K. results (1988–89)

Factor	Eigen value	% Variance	% Cumulative variance
1. Dissatisfaction with agency performance	8.51139	25.0	25.0
2. Changes in agency management	3.45954	10.2	35.2
3. Change/failure of client marketing strategies	2.76945	8.1	43.3
4. Changes in client personnel	1.73000	5.1	48.4
5. Changes in role of advertising	1.50304	4.5	52.9
6. Client profitability analysis of account	1.43055	4.2	57.1
7. Need for specialist advertising services	1.17727	3.5	60.6
8. Changes in agency policies	1.13149	3.3	63.9
9. Client need for wider agency involvement	1.09312	3.2	67.1

Table 7 Principal component analysis

Variable	Factor loadings
Factor 1: Dissatisfaction with agency performance	(25.0% variance)
Relative image weakness of campaigns	.77474
Disagreement over advertising objectives	.76520
Change in overall reputation of agency	.72215
Standard of agency marketing advice	.70364
Standard of agency sales promotion/PR work	.66359
Relative sales weakness of campaigns	.63748
Changes in client advertising management personnel	.60395
Standard of agency creative work	.32848
Factor 2: Changes in agency management	(10.2% variance)
Changes in agency organizational structure	.85467
Changes in agency top management personnel	.85396
Client–agency personality conflict	.80047
Changes in agency account management personnel	.79383
Changes in agency creative personnel	.62387
Standard of agency creative work	.31999
Factor 3: Changes/failure in client marketing policies	(8.1% variance)
Rationalization of agencies within client group	.81298
Need for 'full-service' agency	.72648
Changes in marketing policies/strategies	.63273
Changes in client marketing organization structure	.55141
Decrease in advertising budget	.46688
Group or international group dictate	.43089
Standard of agency creative work	.33546
Factor 4: Changes in client personnel	(5.1% variance)
Routine re-evaluation of 'short listed' agencies	.72042
Changes in client product management personnel	.60339
Changes in client top management	.57533
Factor 5: Changes in role of advertising	(4.5% variance)
Increase in advertising budget	.73671
Need for services of specialist agency	.55911
Transfer from above to below-the-line	.49091
Decrease in advertising budget	.46777
Factor 6: Client profitability analysis of account	(4.2% variance)
Attempt to change agency remuneration	.77483
Introduction of 'in-house' advertising	.66063
Factor 7: Need for specialist advertising services	(3.5% variance)
Standard of agency media buying	.65481
Introduction of 'in-house' advertising	.55192
Rationalization of account by agency	.51348
Standard of agency creative work	.34165
Factor 8: Changes in agency policies	(3.3% variance)
Agency involved in merger/acquisition	.85025
'Time for a change'	.84111
Development of conflicting accounts in agency	.41751
Factor 9: Client need for wider agency involvement	(3.2% variance)
Agency 'not close enough' to client's business	.81426
Need for services of specialist agency	.56091

questionnaire within the broad client management questions, has in fact been loaded with the 'agency management' variables. The two main factors are followed by 'changes in client marketing policies' (8.1 percent variance) and 'changes in client management' (5.1 percent), together with specific secondary client policy and personnel factors. The 'agency policy' variable is placed well down the list as factor eight (3.3 percent variance).

Client decision-making responsibilities for account changes

Decisions to switch agencies are usually taken at the highest client level, and the move is rarely made by the marketing manager or product manager most closely involved with the agency day-to-day, although they are important influencers. Thus, clients were asked who the key people were in the decision to switch the agency, and these responses are shown in Table 8 with comparative 1976–77 findings in brackets. Overall, there was a high degree of agreement, although there was a tendency for marketing directors and managers to become more involved while product managers and advertising managers appear to have been less influential. Decisions are usually made at the highest level, by the chief executive in 42 percent of cases and the marketing director in 33 percent. The fact that agency decisions are taken at this level in companies may well protect agencies from arbitrary decision making. In general, clients appear to evaluate agencies as a decision-making unit, suggesting that termination decisions can be justified on the basis of inadequate agency performance. Termination appears to be a process rather than a single decision. The formal break will therefore invariably be preceded by clear warning signals and a long period of relative disaffection.

CONCLUSION

The results of this survey suggest the existence of a prevailing set of variables which are responsible for agency–client breakups. They appear consistent over time and between countries. Agencies should be vigilant toward these signals of failure and undertake frequent performance audits to forestall the impending switch. Moreover, the findings also indicate a deepening intensity of client disaffection, with 10 of the

Table 8 Client decision-making responsibility for the agency switch

| Perceptions of advertisers in 1988–89 with 1976–77 in brackets | Degree of importance | | | | |
	Final decision-maker (%)	Very important influence (%)	Important influence (%)	Of some importance (%)	Little or no importance (%)
Chief executive	42 (45)	15 (9)	8 (8)	8 (8)	27 (30)
Marketing director	38 (27)	32 (23)	4 (8)	2 (5)	24 (37)
Marketing manager	14 (6)	30 (30)	20 (10)	8 (4)	28 (50)
Product manager	0 (1)	4 (11)	19 (10)	15 (8)	62 (70)
Advertising manager	5 (5)	15 (21)	12 (13)	7 (4)	61 (57)
Marketing services manager	3 (2)	9 (5)	5 (4)	4 (4)	79 (85)
Other	8 (7)	9 (13)	4 (2)	2 (3)	77 (75)

34 factors showing significant increases in their frequency of importance in explaining why clients make the final break. Measurement of service quality by agencies is therefore becoming an increasingly crucial activity.

REFERENCES

Alter, S. 'P and G, Mars Loosen Megashop Strictures.' *Advertising Age.* December 15, 1986.
Doyle, P., M. Corstjens; and P. C. N. Michell. 'Signals of Vulnerability in Agency–Client Relations.' *Journal of Marketing* 40, 4 (1980): 18–23.
Martindale, J. 'How to Spot the Danger Signals in a Relationship.' *Campaign*, October 19, 1984.
Michell, P. C. N. 'Auditing of Agency–Client Relations.' *Journal of Advertising Research* 26, 6 (1986): 29–41.
—— 'Advertising Account Loyalty – A Segmentation Approach.' *Journal of Advertising Research* 27, 6 (1987): 61–67.
Newsome, J. E. 'A Basis for Partnership: Choosing an Advertising Agency.' *Advertising 66* (1980): 26–28.
Wilson, J. T. 'RJR CEO: What's in Megamergers for Me?' *Adweek*, November 3, 1986.

Mitchell, P. C. N., Cataquet, H. and Hague, S. (1992) 'Establishing the causes of disaffection in agency–client relations'. *Journal of Advertising Research*, March–April: 41–48. Reproduced with permission.

Modeling linkage-advertising: going beyond better media comparisons

3.3

Arch G. Woodside

In a 1993 editorial in this journal, Cook reports that 'Gradually media researchers are moving, from documenting that advertising was placed and exposed as planned, to documenting that it had the desired impact.' What appears needed for picking up the pace (in linking media research with both sales and customer–marketer relationships) is a deep understanding of how to document media placements–exposures–impacts. A modeling approach is described in this article that emphasizes the need to document the *processes actually occurring and impacts of the multiple attempts both the marketer and customer make* to reach and impact each other.

The failure to capture process-data in building marketer–customer relationships is the big problem/opportunity in assessing message, media, and execution performances. Too often most of us still view advertising as a one-way path: from us-to-them. Measuring links among advertising placements (attempt-to-contact), the achievement of contact attempts, and outcomes of each contact made by *both parties through time* are the next steps to take for better media comparisons. Given the widespread availability of low cost, powerful, computer hardware and software (see Clarke, 1993), and the advances using marketing decision models by managers, now is the time for: (1) integrating media comparisons into models of customer–marketer relationships, and (2) embracing and implementing database marketing technologies and strategies.

The Media Vehicle Performance Grid model (see Woodside and Soni, 1990) demonstrates desired-impact, media-performance, spreadsheet comparisons emphasized by Cook (1993). This grid approach includes four quadrants to compare media vehicle performance on high and low sales revenues as well as high and low cost per inquiry (see Figure 1).

A 'best buy' is a media vehicle placement that results in quartile A performance: high revenue per inquiry (RPI) and low cost per inquiry (CPI). 'Worst buys' (low RPI and high CPI) usually, not necessarily always, are associated with negative net revenue returns for advertising investments. 'Upscale buys' are represented by quadrant B, that is, relatively expensive media placements that should result in relatively higher revenues; 'horizontal buys' are represented by quadrant C, that is, media vehicles with low advertising rates explained in part by broad demographic-lifestyle reader or viewer profiles. An empirical examination of this performance grid is described by Woodside and Soni (1990). Garrick (1984) and Wang and Schultz (1993) provide additional insights and empirical examples of evaluating media performance using both revenue-generation and costs measurements related to media

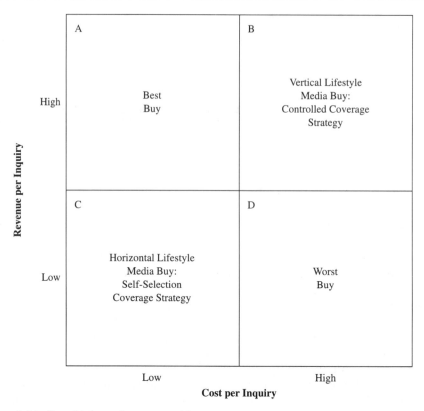

Figure 1 Media vehicle performance grid

placements of advertisements. The important point here is that advertising performance models represent tracking media performance beyond exposure measures.

In 1992 Joe Cappo, senior vice president and publishing director at *Advertising Age*, described the advertising revolution and advertising performance assessments occurring now in the following terms:

> If you are one of those advertising agency or media executives who have been quoted as saying that everything will be just peachy as soon as the recession is over, WAKE UP. This is no mere recession. What is happening in the advertising industry right now is a massive revolution that is changing the rules of marketing. If this kind of talk bothers you, then don't continue reading this article. It could be hazardous to your health. Those affected the most by the revolution will be traditional advertising agencies. They blossomed in the 1970's and 80's. They will become largely irrelevant before we leave the 1990's unless they change radically.

Cappo describes seven characteristics of the revolution including the following present reality: the rapid rise of database marketing, with its ability to collect dozens of data bits on hundreds of millions of consumers. This 'is a long-term trend that will profoundly change the way advertisers sell their products.'

Why have calls for the revolution finally resulted in action and the transformation of image advertising to advertising–customer–database relationships? Because user-friendly computer software programs are now available and being used *by advertising decision makers and not only by marketing scientists* for handling-analyzing prospect and customer data files. The technical expertise and capabilities of advertisers thus are increasing dramatically.

Bulkeley (1993), writing in *The Wall Street Journal*, offers the following description of the new database marketing.

> For years, marketing gurus have been preaching the merits of 'mining' corporate databases. But the databases used for billings, deposit records and instalment-plan payments usually have been inaccessible except to the programmers who maintain them. Marketers designing direct-mail campaigns have had to stand-in-line to ask programmers to search for particular types of customers. Now the marketing experts themselves [programmers not needed] can get at the data. High-end pc's with two-gigabit hard drives – 20 times faster than the 100 megabyte drives most home users buy now – can hold several million customer names on hardware that costs about $10,000 now. The software to manage such data starts as low as $15,000.

MODELLING MARKETER–CUSTOMER INFORMATION SEARCH AND RELATIONSHIP MARKETING

Figure 2 is an overview of two-way responses that may occur in advertising strategies and for starting an integrated marketing communications (IMC) program with customers (see also Duncan and Everett, 1993). An IMC program may be defined usefully as building and sustaining a marketer–customer relationship using: (1) multiple media (often including combinations of schedule media and direct, personal communications); (2) coordinated implementation of multiple messages (often including multiple image and linkage-advertising messages); and (3) continual assessment, using multiple measurement tools, of multiple process and outcome variables of the state-of-the-relationship (including the marketer's performances in responding to direct customer requests as well as customer reception and use of image and linkage-advertising, purchase of the brand/service, satisfaction with experiences when using the brand/service, and intentions to continue the relationship.

Figure 2 is intended to be a model of the sequence-of-steps that may occur following advertising placement and to describe the many possibilities for communication breakdowns failures. The model is relevant for both business and consumer marketing. The steps in the model and some research findings related to these steps are summarized in this section.

This advertiser–customer communications model begins with asking whether or not the customer is exposed to an advertisement that includes a direct-response offer. Prior media steps, such as vehicle distribution and customer exposures to the vehicle, are described in the Advertising Research Foundation's six-stage model for evaluating media (see ARF, 1961; Chook, 1989; Phelps, 1993). The six stages include: I. Vehicle Distribution; II. Vehicle Exposure; III. Advertising Exposure; IV. Advertising Perception; V. Advertising Communication; and VI. Sales Response.

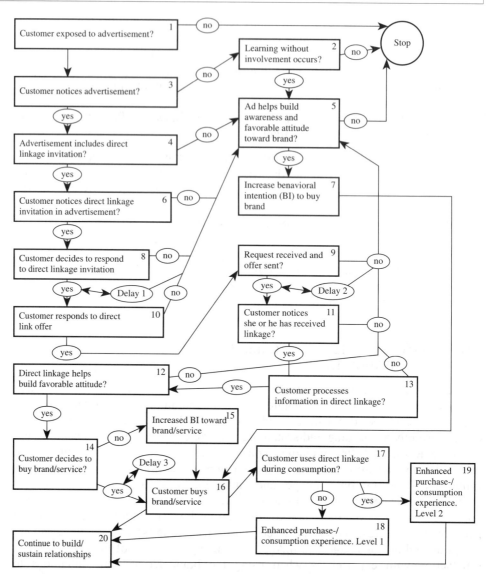

Figure 2 Model of Customer–marketing initial communications and relationships

The point should be emphasized here that the intention for developing an advertiser–customer communications model is to go beyond, not replace, the 1961 ARF model for evaluating media and work done in the late 1980s of the ARF New Model Committee. (Much of the recent work of the ARF New Model Committee is summarized in a special issue of the *Journal of Media Planning* – see Naples, 1989). The advertiser–customer communications model reflects a major theme expressed by Naples (1989) that 'the worlds of advertising, marketing and media research are coming together, that electronics is propelling that joining, that capturing data from consumers is going to be done in such a way that it is going to bring this together.'

In part, the advertiser-communications model summarized in Figure 2 is a response to the call by Seymour Banks (1989) for recognizing the need for a refocus:

> In calling for media models, I call for systems which work on a respondent-by-respondent basis, like the models currently being used for magazines, not the reach and frequency models offered by Telmar, IMS or MSA for television. In constructing, or using such [new] models, I recommend that you use them purely on an evaluative basis rather than seeking optimization. Years of experience have led me to believe that optimization techniques lead to increased costs and complications and, in addition, their results are often regarded with suspicion rather than with awe.

The proposed model is focused actually to include, and to go beyond, the individual respondent; the model is proposed to recommend focusing on the on-going *relationship* of the advertiser–customer. The model is a recommendation for timely tracking of the two-way contact-attempts, linkage-completions, and outcomes of the linkages between the advertiser and individual customers. Naples's (1989) point is that the power of electronics via computers is finally causing the design and use of such models.

The need for measuring on-going, advertiser–customer relationship processes is made clear by the widespread use of linkage-advertising. About two-thirds of all advertising in the United States, Canada, the United Kingdom, and other developed nations include one or more ways for viewers, listeners, or readers to respond directly to request additional information on the product/service being promoted. In the United States, this two-thirds amounts to $142 billion in 1992 (*Direct Marketing*, 1993). Linkage-advertising is the follow-up literature, and related communications, offered in media advertisements for viewers-readers to request; the offer of linkage-advertising is often made by coupons, telephone numbers, and references to a number appearing in magazine reader-service cards.

A major change in advertising philosophy occurs when an account manager in an advertising agency advocates 'linkage' advertising to a client, that is, a direct-response element that encourages a media target to become a prospect and possibly a customer. Including a linkage-advertising offer in advertising is a critical step to joining the revolution. Rapp and Collins (1994) emphasize this point again in their latest book: 'Too often, advertising leaves the prospect dangling, with no idea of what to do next, where to buy, or how to obtain more information. At the very least, the ideal advertising and marketing process should bridge this gap between advertising and sale by offering – and providing – additional information. We call this "linkage"; it involves reaching out in meaningful ways – far more than merely offering where-to-buy information.'

However, many advertisers and their agencies are unsuccessful in their initial linkage-advertising strategies. They fail to follow up with providing additional literature and sales offers that help build up the new one-to-one marketer prospect relationship. Some advertisers making linkage-advertising offers fail to respond to the prospects' requests to receive the offers; and, sometimes, many customers fail to remember asking for or receiving the linkage offer requested, sent, and delivered (see Woodside and Soni, 1991).

Mere exposure and peripheral persuasion effects of advertising

Given that customer exposure to an advertisement occurs (see Figure 2, box 1), the advertisement may have an influence even if the customer does not notice the ad (nodes 3 to 2), or she or he notices but processes the ad under low-involvement conditions. The link between nodes 3 and 2 is intended to represent Chook's (1989) principle that open eyes and ears should govern whether or not exposure occurs.

> In the case of a magazine, an advertising exposure occurs whenever a person opens to the page containing the ad. Nothing more and nothing less. If a person doesn't choose to look at or read the print ad, that does not invalidate the ad exposure.
>
> In the case of television, a commercial exposure occurs if a person with open eyes is in the room with a tuned-in set at the time the commercial comes on. Again, nothing more and nothing less. If a person doesn't choose to watch the commercial and leaves the room, that does not invalidate the commercial exposure.

Most, but not all, advertising included in the path from nodes 4 to 5 represent low-involvement conditions: during most customer exposures to advertising, customer elaboration (i.e., issue-relevant thinking during message processing) is low (cf. Deighton, 1983; Kassarjian, 1978; Olshavsky and Granbois, 1979). As elaboration declines, peripheral persuasion, that is, the influence stemming from stimuli perceived as irrelevant to making a reasoned evaluation or choice grows stronger in its effect on attitude-toward-the-ad and product advertised and on influence on choice; for example, Petty, Cacioppo, and Schumann (1983) found that celebrity status of the product endorser was unimportant under high-involvement ad-processing conditions but exerted a strong influence on product attitudes when ad-processing involvement was low.

Thus, including this relationship in the model is to include the hypothesis supported by empirical evidence that mere exposure can influence attitude and purchase choices (see Krugman, 1965; Zajonc and Markus, 1982; Fazio, Powell, and Williams, 1989; Petty, Unnava, and Strathman, 1991), and peripheral ad persuasion can affect attitude and brand choice. The possible impact of perception-without-awareness (see Bornstein and Pittman, 1992) is indicated by the sequence through nodes 1–3–2–5–7–16. The sequence of moving through nodes 1–3–4–2–5–7–16 includes the peripheral-route to persuasion described by Petty, Cacioppo, and Schumann (1983). The substantial possibilities of peripheral advertising cues affect customer product/brand attitudes (Miniard *et al.*, 1991; Mitchell, 1986; Petty, Cacioppo, and Schumann, 1983; Stuart, Shimp, and Engle, 1987) and choices (see Gorn, 1982; Miniard, Sirdeshmukh, and Innis, 1992).

In node 5, advertising may build positive attitude-toward-the-brand in two ways: (1) through cues relevant to making reasoned evaluation or choice or, as described, (2) peripheral persuasion. As discussed by Miniard, Sirdeshmukh, and Innis (1992), in examining peripheral persuasion effects of advertising it is important to assess whether or not cues intended to be peripheral might somehow convey product-relevant information. Stimuli presumed to represent peripheral cues have sometimes been reinterpreted as actually affecting issue-relevant thinking (e.g., Kahle and Homer, 1985; Petty *et al.*, 1983).

The central-route to persuasion

The central-route of persuasion described (see Petty and Cacioppo, 1986; Petty *et al.*, 1991), as applied to advertising-database-marketing, is reflected in the customer noticing and being motivated to elaborately process the contents of the ad and to request the linkage offer (linking of nodes 4–6–8), or increases in customer awareness of the advertising affecting favorable attitude-toward-the-brand (linking of nodes 4 and 5) under high-involvement conditions.

$TOMA_a$ and $TOMA_b$ linkage: to node 5 and beyond

Image advertising effects are accounted for in the model by the link between nodes 4 and 5, besides the image advertising effect that may occur without involvement (from node 3 to 2). $TOMA_a$ is the customer's top-of-mind-awareness for an ad in a product category. Shares of $TOMA_a$ for different brands in different product categories are reported in one issue each month in *Advertising Age* from monthly U.S. household surveys sponsored by Gallup and *Advertising Age*. Unaided $TOMA_a$ by brand is measured by asking sample members to name the advertising that first comes to mind from all they have seen, heard, or read in the previous 30 days. The hypotheses are supported empirically that: increasing $TOMA_a$ is associated with increasing $TOMA_b$, top-of-mind-awareness toward the brand; and, $TOMA_b$ is associated positively to building preference (node 5), intentions (node 7), and sales (node 15) (see Woodside and Wilson 1985).

The customer linkage-request route to persuasion

Rapp and Collins (1987, 1994) emphasize that advertisements can and should, 'do double-duty by inviting a [direct] response from your best prospects while increasing general awareness of your product or service.' Rapp and Collins (1987) then advocate that, 'Advertising a high-price, high-involvement product should focus first on getting a response from prime prospects rather than on creating an image. Then, convert that response to a sale by providing powerful linkage [the fulfillment literature].'

The active noticing of a direct-response offer is a central route to persuasion that may lead to deciding to request the offer in the ad, for example, request a free catalog or brochure offered in a television commercial or magazine or newspaper ad (linking nodes 4, 6, and 8). Note in Figure 2 that a delay is indicated between nodes 8 and 10: customers may decide to request the direct-response offer but never get around to doing so. Thus, one path out of this delay is toward node 5. Advertisers sometimes attempt to reduce the delay (the possible permanent delay) by reducing the effort and time necessary for the customer to respond; such attempts include placing a telephone number in the ad, sometimes toll-free, using free-standing-inserts (FSIs), and suggesting in a magazine ad that a number be circled on the reader-service card to respond.

Systematic differences occur in buying behavior according to the mode customers use to request information (see Manville, 1987; Woodside and Soni, 1988). For example, when advertising a high-involving service, vacation destination travel, the proportions buying the service (visiting the destination) varied from a low of .26 for reader-service card inquirers, to .36 for direct-response coupon inquiries, to .43 for toll-free telephone inquirers (Woodside and Soni, 1988).

Marketers' responses to customer inquiries

According to the Direct Marketing Association (DMA), direct marketing is 'an interactive system.' Thus, two-way marketer/customer communications are planned for implementation. However, substantial numbers of marketers do not fulfill requests made by customers to offers included in the marketers' ads. In one five-year study, Performark researchers, pretending to be potential customers, mailed in thousands of reader-response cards, the kind found in business and trade publications with offers of more information on goods and services. They responded to solicitations from hundreds of companies selling industrial products costing at least $5,000.

What happened? It took an average of 58 days for the requested pamphlets or brochures to arrive. Nearly one out of four inquiries went unanswered. Only one in eight generated a follow-up call by a sales representative, and those contacts came an average of 89 days after Performark's initial indication of interest (Gibson, 1993).

The President of Performark, Joseph Lethert, reports, 'The problem is sales and marketing aren't working together. No one has responsibility for making sure prospects are converted to customers.' Too often marketing people blame the sales force for not pursuing leads, while salespeople are loath to share information about their customers (Gibson, 1993).

Similar findings are reported in a second study of business-to-business and consumer marketers' responses to inquiries (Woodside, Brose, and Trappey, 1991). Acting as customers, inquiries were sent to 90 direct marketers (47 business and 43 consumer firms). After eight weeks, 25 percent of the business marketers and 28 percent of the consumer marketers had yet to respond in any manner. However, the proportion of responses did vary according to media used to make the inquiry: overall, 80 percent of the marketers responded to telephone inquiries; 80 percent to direct-mail inquiries; but only 60 percent responded to reader-response inquiries. Follow-up calls after responding to the inquiries were made by only 34 percent of the business marketers and 25 percent of the consumer marketers.

Thus, the marketing activity of getting back to the customer (nodes 10 to 9 to 11) is not a given; it has to be built-in and monitored actively as part of advertising and IMC programs. This first fulfillment step is often subcontracted out by the advertiser or the advertising agency to a 'fulfillment house.' Such a marketing strategy has the advantage of bringing in the expertise of fulfillment experts but also increases the need for careful coordination and attention to customer requests.

Customer use of fulfillment-materials

What happens after customers receive the fulfillment literature they request? Customers vary considerably in how they process fulfillment literature; some are not aware of receiving it; some do not report ever asking for it when later asked; and some do use the materials extensively for making buying decisions.

In one study, 45 percent of inquirers, who were sent the literature they requested, did not report either asking for nor receiving the literature when asked (see Woodside and Soni, 1991). Thus, customers may not process (notice, look at, or read thoroughly) information they request and receive: reaching node 13 in Figure 2 is not a certainty; monitoring this step in the direct-marketing process is necessary to ensure customer usage of fulfillment literature. 'Great advertising creative work that results in high inquiry rates is not good enough; the direct-response offer may have to be even better to get through the second level of clutter – all the competing advertising brochures and catalogs being received by the inquirer' (Woodside and Soni, 1991).

Customer information-processing of the linkage materials often may be helpful in building favorable brand attitude (node 12), in convincing the customer to buy (node 14), and in her or his purchase choices (node 15). Note that a delay is shown in Figure 2 between node 14 and 15 to indicate that the effects of linkage-advertising on buying behavior may be long-term and not immediately visible in one advertising campaign. Monitoring the impact of linkage-advertising on sales should include assessing the effects over several time periods beyond the immediate advertising-and-buying time frame.

The term 'enhanced purchase-consumption experience' is used in nodes 18 and 19 to express the proposition that the customers' experiences in buying-using the product or service is affected by processing the linkage literature versus not requesting, receiving, or processing such literature. In some industries, customers may refer to the linkage materials while using the product or service (node 19). For example, consumers buying seeds and plants using mail-order may refer to their catalogs for planting information and recipes for preparing vegetables grown; vacation travelers may refer to destination 'visitor guides' during traveling to learn about places to visit, things to do, and products to buy during their visit. In one tourism advertising study of visitors to Prince Edward Island in Canada (Woodside, MacDonald, and Trappey, 1993), total dollar purchases more than doubled among customers using linkage literature during their destination visit compared to customers using the literature only before, but not during, their PEI visits (comparing sales results between nodes 18 and 19).

The node in the model in Figure 2 (node 20) appears to emphasize the ongoing need for measuring the specific linkage attempts, contacts made, and outcomes in advertiser–customer relationships. The implication intended with node 20 is that lifetime and trans-generational relationships should be recognized and included in measurement systems. This is a big job, but the capability to do it is available now; and several 'frequency marketing' programs are in place now for this task. One example is airline frequent-flyer clubs; see Rapp and Collins (1994) for other examples.

Limitations

For many customer-marketing interactions, the model summarized in Figure 2 is a simplification of the first stages in an IMC program. The model describes the multiple two-way contacts that may occur between the customer and marketer before the first purchase-sale. In the U.S. office-furniture industry, for example, customer response to a direct mail or newspaper ad is often followed by several telephone conversations and perhaps 4 to 7 personal sales calls and customer visits to the marketer's showrooms – all before the first purchase! The recent and long-term history of interactions with many established customers may exist only in the long-term memories of one or two persons in the marketing firm; no computer database software has yet been developed for monitoring such relationships.

However, some firms (including some office-furniture marketers) and entire industries have accomplished IMC programs with long-term customers that meet the needs of monitoring linkage-advertising. Handling a database built on such long-term interactive systems, and estimating customer response functions to advertising and marketing actions in such systems, are more than a possibility. Such interactive systems and the use of decision models for sensitivity analysis is now more than the future promise of linkage-advertising. However, building and using computer databases for forecasting net contribution effects of marketing decisions is still time-consuming, not inexpensive, and requires management science expertise. The good news is that many useful high-performing, low-price, computer software and hardware tools, and modeling skill-training, have become available in the 1990s.

Another limitation of the model summarized in Figure 2 is that word-of-mouth effects of advertising and linkage-advertising is not included. As emphasized by Chook (1989), 'advertising in special interest publications affects not only the buying behavior of readers themselves, but also of some friends and colleagues who turn to these special interest mavens for buying advice.' Also, research results in one industry (mail-order seed and plant buying) supports the hypothesis that the recommendations by parents, who are in their 50s and 60s, on which linkage-advertising is most helpful, plays a dominant influence on what linkage-advertising their children use when buying (Woodside and Wilson, 1994). Such third-party, 'diagonal,' relationships need to be considered in further modeling work to remove the restriction suggested by a 'two-way' model.

ADVERTISING STRATEGY IMPLICATIONS FOR DESIGNING AND IMPLEMENTING EFFECTIVE IMC PROGRAMS

In 1986 Stan Rapp predicted, 'When the light of a new day dawns on January 1, 1990, I believe that all service companies and many product manufacturers will be spending as much time and money maximizing their relationships with known customers as they now do on their brand-image advertising to the world at large' (Rapp and Collins, 1990). The review here of some of the empirical studies in direct marketing indicates that this prediction has not come to pass. However, substantial strides have been made in achieving the opportunities and benefits of direct marketing by some marketers.

The transformation from the illusion of knowledge into marketing wisdom is now occurring in many linkage-advertising programs because of two reasons: (1) advances in computer software/hardware tools in creating and handling databases and (2) marketers' use of customer response functions in decision models for 'what if' analyses. The model described here of the initial stages in customer–marketer interactions indicates that the monitoring of each of multiple points-of-contact needs to occur for a linkage-advertising program to be accountable.

Transforming marketing from image-advertising to linkage-advertising and relationship marketing, that is, toward an effective, working IMC program, requires technical, computer software, skill-training by marketers, including the CEO and CMO, chief marketing officer. The tools and skill-learning materials are now available. Creating and using decision models in linkage-advertising will enable marketers to justify their advertising strategies with hard evidence. CEOs continue to demand nothing less.

The biggest problem in creating the linkage-advertising and customer database needed for relationship marketing may be that the firms' management information systems (MIS) are programmed only to meet the needs of the finance and accounting departments. For example, banks generally have customer account databases for each product: mortgages, car loans, savings and credit cards, and savings accounts. The databases may even identify the same customer differently – without a middle initial, for example, or last name first. Marketers want one customer database that includes all details of the firm's relationship with each customer.

The most workable solution to this problem is *not* in trying to transform a firm's existing MIS to a complete customer database. Given the substantial decreases in costs of customer database software programs and computer workstations, the faster and most workable solution is to create a customer database from scratch – by selecting from several high-quality, readily-available database and spreadsheet software programs and using a workstation or personal computer with the necessary hard-disk capacity. A critical point related to this approach: the time is now for the marketer to develop finger-tip computer capability to mine its customer database on its own personal computer (see Bulkeley, 1993).

Thus, given that the marketer is willing to invest some time, it is now able to personally have the technical capability and wisdom to create and handle a customer database to fulfill the two major benefits of linkage-advertising: (1) relationship marketing including forecasting net profit contributions of marketing tactics using customer response functions and financial data; and (2) hard-evidence measuring of how much advertising and marketing influences sales. Before the 1990s, low-cost approaches for high-quality relationship marketing (IMC) programs were not widely available. The situation has finally changed.

REFERENCES

Advertising Research Foundation. *Toward Better Media Comparisons*. New York, 1961.

Banks, Seymour. 'Considerations for a New ARF Media Evaluation Model.' *Journal of Media Planning* 4, 2 (1989): 8–10.

Bornstein, Robert F., and Thane S. Pittman, eds. *Perception Without Awareness*. New York: Guildford Press, 1992.

Bulkeley, William M. 'Marketers Mine Their Corporate Databases.' *The Wall Street Journal*, June 14, 1993.

Cappo, Joe. Editorial in *Advertising Age*, November 16, 1992.

Chook, Paul H. 'The Need for a New Model.' *Journal of Media Planning* 4, 2 (1989): 11–15.

Clarke, Darral G. *Marketing Analysis and Decision Making*. South San Francisco, CA: The Scientific Press, 1993.

Cook, Thomas D., and Donald T. Campbell. *Quasi-Experimentation*. Chicago: Rand McNally, 1979.

Cook, William. 'The Media Are the Messages.' *Journal of Advertising Research* 33, 1 (1993): 7–8.

Direct Marketing. 'Direct Marketing . . . An Aspect of Total Marketing.' *Direct Marketing Magazine*, April 1993.

Deighton, John. 'How to Solve Problems that Don't Matter: Some Heuristics for Uninvolved Thinking.' In *Advances in Consumer Research*, 10, Richard P. Bagozzi and Alice M. Tybout, ed. Provo, UT: Association for Consumer Research, 1983.

Duncan, Thomas T., and Stephen E. Everett. 'Client Peceptions of Integrated Marketing Communicating.' *Journal of Advertising Research* 33, 3 (1993): 30–37.

Fazio, R. H.; M. C. Powell; and C. J. Williams. 'The Role of Attitude Accessibility in the Attitude-to-Behavior Process.' *Journal of Consumer Research* 16, 3 (1989): 280–88.

Garrick, George. 'Optimizing Media Planning, Buying and Frequency through Electronic Single-Source Data.' In *Transcript Proceedings of the 30th Advertising Research Foundation Annual Conference*. New York: Advertising Research Foundation, 1984.

Gibson, Richard. 'Poor Handling Turns Leads into No-Sales.' *The Wall Street Journal*, March 31, 1993.

Gorn, Gerald J. 'The Effects of Music in Advertising on Choice Behavior: A Classical Conditioning Approach.' *Journal of Marketing* 46, 1 (1982): 94–101.

Kahle, Lynn R., and Pamela M. Homer. 'Physical Attractiveness of the Celebrity Endorser: A Social Adaptation Perspective.' *Journal of Consumer Research* 16, 4 (1985): 354–60.

Kassarjian, Harold H. 'Presidential Address, 1977: Anthropomorphism and Parsimony.' In *Advances in Consumer Research*, 5, H. Keith Hunt, ed. Ann Arbor, MI: Association for Consumer Research, 1978.

Krugman, Herbert. 'The Impact of Television Advertising: Learning without Involvement.' *Public Opinion Quarterly*, 29, 2 (1965): 349–56.

Manville, Richard. 'Does Advertising – or Product 'Publicity' – Pull More Inquiries? Which Ones Are More Valuable?' In *BPAA Communicator*. New York: Business and Professional Advertising Association, 1987.

Miniard, Paul W.; Sunil Bhatla; Kenneth R. Lord; Peter R. Dickson; and H. Rao Unnava. 'Picture-based Persuasion Processes and the Moderating Role of Involvement.' *Journal of Consumer Research* 18, 2 (1991): 92–107.

——; Deepak Sirdeshmukh; and Daniel E. Innis. 'Peripheral Persuasion and Brand Choice.' *Journal of Consumer Research* 19, 3 (1992): 226–39.

Mitchell, Andrew A. 'The Effect of Verbal and Visual Components of Advertisements on Brand Attitudes and Attitude toward the Advertisement.' *Journal of Consumer Research* 13, 2 (1986): 12–24.

Naples, Michael J. 'The Role of the Advertising Research Foundation in Solving the Media Model Problem.' *Journal of Media Planning* 4, 2 (1989): 4–7.

Olshavsky, Richard W., and Donald H. Granbois. 'Consumer Decision Making – Fact or Fiction?' *Journal of Consumer Research* 6, 3 (1979): 93–100.

Petty, Richard E.; John T. Cacioppo; and David Schumann. 'Central and Peripheral Routes to Advertising Effectiveness: The Moderating Role of Involvement.' *Journal of Consumer Research* 10, 3 (1983): 135–46.

——, and J. T. Cacioppo. *Communication and Persuasion: Central and Peripheral Routes to Attitude Change.* New York: Springer/Verlag, 1986.

——; Rao Unnava; and Alan J. Strathman. 'Theories of Attitude Change.' In *Handbook of Consumer Behavior*, Thomas S. Robertson and Harold H. Kassarjian, ed. Englewood Cliffs, NJ: Prentice-Hall, 1991.

Phelps, Stephen P. 'A Media Evaluation Model for the 21st Century.' In *Proceedings of the 1993 Conference of the American Academy of Advertising*, Esther Thorson, ed. Columbia, MO: School of Journalism, University of Missouri-Columbia, 1993.

Rapp, Stan, and Tom Collins. *Maxi-marketing.* New York: McGraw-Hill, 1988.

——, and ——. 'Special Report: The Great Marketing Turnaround." *Direct Marketing Magazine*, October 1990.

——, and ——, *Beyond Maximarketing.* New York: McGraw-Hill, 1994.

Stuart, Elnora W.; Terence A. Shimp; and Randall W. Engle. 'Classical Conditioning of Consumer Attitudes: Four Experiments in an Advertising Context.' *Journal of Consumer Research* 11, 2 (1987): 522–27.

Wang, Paul, and Don E. Schultz. 'Measuring the Return on Investment for Advertising and Other Forms of Marketing Communications Using an Integrated Marketing Communications Approach.' Unpublished paper. Evanston, IL: Medill School of Journalism, Northwestern University, 1993.

Woodside, Arch G.; Frederick C. Brose; and Randolph J. Trappey III. 'Assessing Performance of Business-to-Business and Consumer Direct Marketing Fulfillment Strategies.' Working paper. New Orleans: Freeman School of Business, Tulane University, 1991.

——; Roberta MacDonald; and Randolph J. Trappey III. 'Effects of Knowledge and Experience on Purchasing Behavior and Consumption Experiences.' Working paper. New Orleans: Freeman School of Business, Tulane University, 1993.

——, and Praveen K. Soni. 'Assessing the Quality of Advertising Inquiries by Mode of Response.' *Journal of Advertising Research* 28, 4 (1988): 31–37.

——, and ——. 'Performance Analysis of Advertising in Competing Media Vehicles.' *Journal of Advertising Research* 30, 1 (1990): 53–66.

——, and ——. 'Direct-Response Advertising Information: Profiling Heavy, Light, and Non-users.' *Journal of Advertising Research* 31, 6 (1991): 26–36.

——, and Elizabeth J. Wilson. 'Effects of Consumer Awareness of Brand Advertising on Preference.' *Journal of Advertising Research* 25, 4 (1985): 41–48.

——, and ——. 'Applying the Long Interview in Direct Marketing Research.' Unpublished working paper. New Orleans: Freeman School of Business, Tulane University, 1994.

Zajonc, Robert B., and Hazel Markus. 'Affective and Cognitive Factors in Preferences.' *Journal of Consumer Research* 9, 3 (1982): 123–31.

Woodside, A. G. (1994) 'Modeling linkage-advertising: going beyond better media comparisons'. *Journal of Advertising Research*, 34(1), July/August: 22–31. Reproduced with permission.

Section 4
Direct Marketing

The use of direct marketing has increased rapidly in recent years, and is now considered an essential tool in effective integrated marketing communications. The aim of this section is to describe and evaluate direct marketing communication, its use and management, and regulatory and customer-based issues.

The first paper from Petrison, Blattberg and Wang (1993) provides a sound foundation to the subject by examining the development of the discipline and identifying core concepts in direct marketing. Following on, Fletcher, Wheeler and Wright (1991) explore the role, participants and purpose of direct marketing, identifying structural changes and threats to traditional relationships between firms and advertising agencies. They explore integration of above- and below-the-line communications activities and identify a trend towards re-evaluation of traditional mass communications in favour of clearly identified target customers.

Ethics and issues of customer privacy are explored by Fletcher and Peters (1996), who investigate the relationship between the market research industry and direct marketing. The growth of customer information held in-house will both supplement and/or replace ad-hoc market research, they suggest, as well as impact on customer privacy.

The final article from Fletcher, Wright and Desai (1996) considers organizational factors affecting adoption of sophisticated strategic information systems for direct marketing, finding that cultural orientation emphasizing market and customers, decision-making style and availability of resources are influential organizational variables.

Database marketing: past, present, and future 4.1

Lisa A. Petrison, Robert C. Blattberg and Paul Wang

INTRODUCTION

Of the wide-ranging changes that have occurred in the field of marketing during the past century, few have been more dramatic than the ways that marketers have addressed and viewed their customers. Both direct and traditional marketers took a mass-market approach for several decades following the industrial revolution, targeting a broad range of consumers with advertising or direct mail with a generalized appeal. As time went on, however, marketers gradually began to segment their customers in a more sophisticated manner, and to strive to present messages and products that were relevant to specific groups of consumers rather than to a broad consumer aggregate.

The most recent step in the progression toward more targeted communication has been in the area of database marketing, which suggests that companies can become more effective if they are able to learn about and communicate with their customers based on individual characteristics rather than only as part of an overall group. The continuing trend toward increased targeting suggests that this type of individualized marketing should become more and more prevalent, and should eventually result in products and communications that are able to meet specific customers' needs and wants.

Before the field of database marketing moves forward, however, it is desirable for both academics and practitioners to take a focused look at related past events and experiences. Although the concept of database marketing has gained wide attention during the past several years, many of the underlying themes, such as individualized communication and the lifetime value of a customer, have in actuality been used for decades. In addition, many of these core concepts developed long ago in some industries are still not fully used or appreciated in others, thereby resulting in slow overall implementation of the practice of database marketing.

The following historical information is designed to allow practitioners and academics to understand more about how marketers have targeted their customers on an individual basis over time, thereby allowing them to better prepare for what is likely to occur in the future. In addition, it is hoped that it will inform companies just beginning database marketing efforts, or those who have utilized only some of the concepts discussed, of the activities that other companies have developed in the past, thereby allowing more cross-fertilization across industries.

The information that follows was collected from a number of sources, including articles published in *Direct Marketing* magazine (formerly *The Reporter of Direct*

Mail Advertising) and in other trade publications since the 1930s. In addition, in-depth interviews with more than 40 prominent practitioners and academics were also conducted.

DATABASE MARKETING: PRE-1950

Mass marketing through the mail

Prior to the 1950s, direct marketing – or what was then called 'mail order' – was assumed to be a mass-marketing business (123). In fact, the growth of direct marketing in those early years can be directly tied to technological innovations that allowed consumers to be addressed as a group, rather than on the one-on-one basis practiced by the craftsmen and storekeepers who produced and sold merchandise specifically for individual customers.

The development of the first trade catalogs, for instance, followed Gutenberg's invention of movable type in the late 1400s, an innovation that made it possible to print multiple copies of the same document (123). Catalogs of books and of nursery items were especially popular in those early days. Later, catalogs began to include such elite items as wine, furniture, and china, especially as settlers in the New World, such as Thomas Jefferson, an inveterate mail-order buyer, began to acquire money and to develop a taste for the refined goods of Europe (123).

Although the publishers of these early direct marketing efforts did not consciously see themselves as segmenting the marketplace, these catalogs were nevertheless targeted, since only a tiny percentage of the population was literate enough to read the catalogs and wealthy enough to buy from them. In addition, these early catalogers kept records of their buyers, to ensure that good customers like Jefferson received future mailings (123).

It wasn't until the late 1800s that the field of mail order really came into its own. New technology made the mass production of consumer goods possible, bringing down prices to the point where a majority of consumers were able to afford a variety of products manufactured outside the home. However, most people lived far away from major metropolitan centers where department stores stocking a variety of merchandise were located; in addition, travel was difficult and expensive. On the other hand, mail delivery was becoming increasingly reliable and affordable. As a response, catalogs like Montgomery Ward (1872) and Sears, Roebuck (1887) were developed to deliver the new mass-produced goods to rural and small-town residents throughout the United States (123).

Although catalog companies were at first fairly specialized and small-volume, they quickly blossomed into some of the biggest businesses in the United States. In 1927, for example, Sears sent out 75 million pieces of mail, including 10 million letters, 15 million general catalogs, 23 million sale catalogs, and a variety of special catalogs. The size of the catalogs also expanded rapidly – by 1897, for example, the Sears, Roebuck catalog had approximately 700 pages with 6,000 items (123).

During the early twentieth century, catalog companies began taking steps to evaluate the profitability of their buyers, and to focus more resources on those who were better customers. Although most catalog companies were quite profitable, it eventually became clear that some households accounted for a higher-than-average share of sales volume. Around 1910 catalog companies developed the '12-month prune rule,' whereby consumers who had not purchased anything for the past year were dropped (123).

This measure was soon followed by the development of more sophisticated analysis techniques, including the recency–frequency–monetary amount (RFM) model still used today (122). These techniques were developed because catalog companies had begun to realize that the '12-month prune rule' could be somewhat inefficient; for instance, many households who purchased one or a few small items each year were unprofitable, whereas a consumer who purchased a major item (such as an electric washing machine or refrigerator) every two years might be very profitable. The catalog company Alden's is generally credited with developing in the 1920s the RFM model, which took into consideration overall profitability of the account in deciding who was to receive the catalog (122).

Although the model was quickly adopted by other catalog companies, the use of RFM in those pre-computer days was a laborious process. Possible combinations of recency, frequency, and amount of consumer purchases were rated into discrete categories; these categories were then entered into a matrix to predict which were likely to be profitable in the future. Then, through an automated process sometimes called 'cell selection,' customers who fit into certain categories were removed from the list of those slotted to receive future mailings.

Cell selection was achieved using either cardboard stencils made by companies such as Elliott, or heavy metal plates made by Addressograph and its competitors. Punches were made in the consumer's card or plate for each purchase made; then, through a mechanical process, those consumers whose punches matched certain criteria were pulled from the rest for mailing. The stencil or plate was then used to impress the name and address on the envelope of the piece to be mailed.

Although many direct marketers kept detailed records of their interactions with current customers prior to and during World War II, prospecting for new customers was much more difficult. One way companies obtained names was through list bureaus, which haphazardly compiled lists of diverse kinds of prospects, such as 'professional people,' 'flora and fauna collectors,' 'music lovers,' 'harmonica buyers,' and 'career girls' – each available for a fixed price of about $15 per thousand. *The Reporter of Direct Mail Advertising* also suggested that companies could collect their own lists from sources such as club rosters, annual reports, magazines and newspapers, government lists, telephone directories, customer recommendations, and employee and stockholder referrals (9).

The specificity of bureau lists was useful in certain kinds of circumstances. In 1912, for example, L. L. Bean had good response when it mailed its new catalog of outdoor apparel and equipment to nonresidents of Maine who had applied for hunting licenses in the state. Nevertheless, many lists were composed of people who were not obvious targets for many products. That issue was compounded by the fact that most lists contained only a few thousand names, and many lists contained up to 10 percent duplicates of other names on the same list, as well as many out-of-date addresses that were up to 10 years old. (The problem of undeliverables was so widespread that more reputable list brokers in the late 1940s began offering a refund for every undeliverable 'nixie' letter that was returned to the company.) The inherent nature of these early lists meant that it was almost impossible to predict response rates, a problem that led most companies to do extensive testing before conducting full mailings of any list (11,39,40,65).

Despite the difficulty companies had in prospecting for customers, relatively little attention was addressed to this issue prior to the 1950s. The industry appeared to accept the problem of finding customers as a given, and directed much more attention to the issues of testing creative and integrating direct mail with other types of marketing communications (7,34,35,55,90,91).

DATABASE MARKETING: THE 1950S

The list decade

During the years following World War II, the issue of prospecting for customers, which had been practically ignored in previous years, became a major concern. During the 1950s direct mailers became more interested in the quality of the lists they were purchasing and the response rates likely to be achieved, and became more willing to pay a premium for lists that were likely to produce results (2,39,40,88,89,107,120,126,152).

During the late 1940s, R. L. Polk and Reuben H. Donnelley began to compile the first comprehensive prospect lists from external sources, including telephone directories, auto registrations, and driver license records. In addition, the U.S. Postal Service permitted Donnelley to compile the first 'Occupant' list, which enabled mail-order companies and packaged-goods manufacturers distributing samples to mail to all addresses in the United States or within a particular region without knowing who lived there (122).

The availability of compiled data helped to make the direct mail industry more sophisticated, as it allowed marketers to send out large mailings on a systematic basis. In addition, the compiled information sometimes allowed certain companies to conduct surprisingly targeted mailings. Auto registration data, for instance, often functioned as a surrogate for income, since less-affluent families were presumed to own no car or to drive a lower-end model. Old American Insurance was successful, starting in the late 1940s, at targeting older persons with direct mail solicitations for life insurance through driver license records, since these records listed age and since persons driving cars were assumed to be affluent and in reasonable good health (A).

The availability of comprehensive compiled lists and the growing demand for consumer products following World War II prompted a number of specialized companies to enter the direct marketing business. In turn, the successes of a wide variety of direct-mail businesses led to the increased availability of response lists, creating a need for more sophisticated list brokers. These list companies helped direct marketers by supplying them with names of other companies' customers, who were assumed to be direct-mail responsive, and who also sometimes proved to be good prospects for related products.

For the first time, lists were priced according to their apparent value, with some much more expensive than others (11, 13). Although direct-mail advertising was typically mailed to everyone on the purchased lists, 'hotline' data of the most recent buyers was sometimes appended to the names, allowing companies to eliminate prospects whose value was more uncertain.

DATABASE MARKETING: THE 1960S

The computer decade

The decade of the 1960s brought a revolution in how direct marketers were able to target and address current and potential customers, due primarily to the application of computer technology to customer files. Although the first computers had been developed two decades earlier and were a vast improvement over handling data manually, the early machines were too expensive and slow to be very useful in handling the millions of names managed by direct mailers. List compilers and brokerage firms began to apply computer technology to their customer lists in the late 1950s, but it was several more years before individual direct marketing firms began to use or purchase their own computer systems for this purpose (53,62,104,146).

The integration of computers into the direct marketing industry is a watershed moment because nearly all of the developments in the business since then have been based on computer technology. In addition to replacing the cumbersome address plates and stencils previously used to record customer information, computer technology also led to the development of statistical modeling, merge/purge, personalized communications, credit cards, scanner technology, and dozens of other innovations.

ZIP codes and the computer

One major problem that confronted the direct marketing community throughout the 1960s was the necessity of matching customer addresses with the correct ZIP codes and sorting the mail in ZIP-code order, a procedure that became mandatory in 1967 (104,122). The costs of matching addresses and sorting envelopes by hand were anticipated to be enormous, and many direct marketers feared that the new regulations would mean the end of their businesses. Ultimately, however, the ZIP code issue turned out to be beneficial to the industry, since it caused most direct marketers to transfer their customer lists to computer systems, which were able to match ZIP codes with addresses and to sort labels in ZIP-code order.

Although some direct marketers had owned computers since the late 1950s, prior to 1967 many used them only for inventory or accounts receivable, or as fast adding machines to calculate profitability or RFM. The ZIP code issue, however, caused direct marketers with computer systems to begin to use them for customer records, and prompted many other companies to invest in the new technology.

ZIP codes and segmentation

Long before the 1960s, marketers had tried to segment consumers according to the city and state in which they lived, since this information was readily available. Although this information could sometimes be helpful, such as in separating city and rural residents, it proved to be inadequate most of the time.

In the early 1960s, a number of marketers experimented with using census tract information to predict buying behavior. In 1960, the U.S. Census Bureau divided most metropolitan areas into groupings, and released basic demographic information on each, suggesting to marketers that there might be differing demand for products in different census tracts. For example, one thought was that people who lived in affluent areas with children were likely to be responsive to mailings promoting frozen juice. A test confirmed this theory, with 35 percent of consumers living in these kinds of neighborhoods redeeming a coupon for juice sent to them by mail, according to *The Reporter of Direct Mail Advertising* (98).

O. E. McIntyre, a list management company eventually acquired by Metromail, took the census tract concept a step further in 1964 in an ambitious effort that was creative, if a bit ahead of its time. First, the company developed its own 'census tract' system for the rural areas of the country ignored by the Census Bureau, arriving at a total of 30,000 geographical units described by demographics. Then, using a system dubbed Selection by Individual Families and Tracts (SIFT), they combined this geographical data with individual data, including telephone ownership, length of residence, sex of head of household, and type of dwelling. With the geographical information on the horizontal axis and the individual information on the vertical axis, McIntyre was able to divide its 40 million names into 1.8 million groupings, each containing 22 names and supposedly having different product needs and buying power (99).

The problem with SIFT, and with census tract information in general, was that it tended to be unwieldy and limited in its application. In order for companies to use the information, each name on a list had to be matched by hand with tract information. Even after this painstaking process occurred, the usefulness of census tract information was primarily limited to an estimation of wealth, family size, and type of occupation.

It wasn't until the late 1960s that marketers realized that ZIP codes might be of some use in geographical segmentation. In 1967, Martin Baier, vice president of marketing at Old American Insurance Company, wrote an article for the *Harvard Business Review* entitled 'ZIP Codes – New Tool for Marketers,' which outlined the potential ease of use and increased household coverage of ZIP codes compared to census tracts in conducting geographical segmentation (15,24). Although Baier recommended that each company develop its own ZIP-code classification system, based on demonstrated demand for its products in those areas, Baier's theory was nonetheless a precursor to general cluster systems such as Claritas' RESIDE and PRIZM, which were used extensively in the late 1970s and 1980s. (Unlike Baier's proposal, these general cluster systems divided ZIP codes into groupings, or 'clusters,' and drew generalized portraits of each.) (122)

In addition, ZIP code analysis proved to be useful for companies with field locations, such as automobile dealerships and fast-food restaurants. In 1968, for example, a company called Geodatic described in *The Reporter of Direct Mail Advertising* how one automobile manufacturer had used ZIP codes to find the dealership located closest to the home of prospects, and to send personalized mailings listing the name and address of the dealer (121).

Merge/Purge

Before the late 1960s, direct marketers found it almost impossible to avoid sending more than one solicitation to the same consumer, or to abstain from soliciting current customers. Most companies were not particularly troubled by this fact, however, since mailing costs were low and customers' annoyance at receiving multiple solicitations was not presumed to be an important factor.

Several list brokers, such as Names Unlimited and The Kleid Company, experimented with using computers to pull duplicates from their own lists during the 1960s, and a few individual companies such as Tandy Corporation also had their own programs (16,36). List consultant Alan Drey introduced in 1968 the first widely used, publicly available merge/purge program, which permitted a variety of companies to benefit from the new technology (17,31,103).

Merge/purge programs not only made it easier for companies to avoid sending out duplicates, they also changed the way that direct marketers were able to target and view their customers. For instance, prior to 1968, many large-scale direct marketers rented only large, broadly targeted mailing lists, because combining a number of small lists inevitably resulted in many duplicates and a large amount of waste. Merge/purge programs allowed these marketers to combine many small lists and weed out the duplicates, thereby prospecting in a more targeted and efficient manner.

Another early benefit was in using merge/purge to remove certain prospects that were unlikely to buy a product because of certain personal characteristics. For instance, Metromail purged apartment dwellers from a list of consumers scheduled to receive a catalog of outdoor plants, since these people were assumed to have no gardens (S).

In addition, merge/purge programs allowed marketers to estimate the expected pulling power of the prospect list without conducting a test. Lists with high duplication rates were assumed to be good ones, while those with low duplication were often found to be composed of the wrong target audience, provided that the market as a whole had not been saturated with the product (A).

Merge/purge programs also proved to be useful in appending information from other lists onto one's own customer file, for use in the future. This type of usage has often been limited by list-rental agreements that allow only one-time use of information, however.

Computer-generated letters

Marketers have long realized that personalization could bring increased response to direct mailings. During the 1940s, for instance, the American Automatic Typewriter Company sold a machine called the Auto-Typist, which was able to insert personalized salutations into up to 200 letters per day. During the same time period, *Time* magazine experimented with sending mass-produced letters that began 'Dear Mr Smith' to all persons with the surname of Smith on the company's mailing lists (118).

In the mid-1960s, however, direct marketers began using computer technology to target personalized letters to mass groups of consumers. Billy Graham's organization sent out one of the first computer-generated letters, a plea for funding written in all capital letters. Other types of companies followed a year or two later with other, often creative approaches. One publication queried, 'Your neighbor, Mr X, reads *National Geographic* – why don't you?' American Motors suggested to consumers that if they had been eyeing the Rambler owned by their neighbor, 'Mr X,' maybe it was time to get one of their own. Fingerhut targeted New York residents with personalized letters that began, 'Remember last January? When temperatures in the state of New York dropped to a chilly-32 degrees?' Reader's Digest, a frequent user of personalization, suggested in one sweepstakes offer that the recipient could win 'a new Corvette, to go with the Ford Station Wagon in your driveway' (71,122,141).

Personalization was used much less in the 1970s, however. While letters personalized only with a 'Dear Mr X' salutation pulled as much as six times as many responses as nonpersonalized responses in the mid-1960s, the increase in response became much less noticeable after the novelty wore off, and often didn't compensate for the increased cost of producing the letter. And while creative approaches to personalization continued to pull fairly well, complaints from a few consumers over what they perceived to be threats to their personal privacy discouraged most marketers from using personal information (such as the make of the family car) that had not been supplied by the consumer to the company (71).

The genesis of 'direct marketing'

Prior to the late 1960s, what is today called 'direct marketing' was known as 'mail order' or 'direct mail' or 'the catalog business.' Although 'direct marketing' has today become synonymous to some people with 'direct mail,' the term was actually developed in the late 1960s to encompass the newer concepts of targeting and long-term value. It also was designed to lend credibility to what had become a somewhat disreputable field (134).

The concept of 'direct marketing' did not receive immediate favor, however. Although in 1968 *The Reporter of Direct Mail Advertising* changed its name to *Direct Marketing*, protests from traditional mail-order firms prevented the Direct Mail Advertising Association from immediately changing its own name. In 1973, as a compromise, the Direct Mail/Marketing Association was reached. It was 1984 before the group became the Direct Marketing Association.

Targeting the affluent

Wealthy consumers have always been coveted by direct marketers, but during the 1960s many marketers became more serious about targeting them. The type of car owned had been used as a surrogate for income since the early days of the industry; this was supplemented during the 1960s with census tract and ZIP code information that identified the wealthiest neighborhoods. Conversely, many marketers routinely dropped inner-city households from their mailing lists, assuming that these people either wouldn't buy anything or would be poor credit risks.

Metromail took the affluence concept a step further in 1967 by compiling a list of 'elites' – male heads of households in the top 30 metropolitan areas with superior education, influence, and purchasing characteristics. To collect the information, Metromail sent out lengthy questionnaires asking for data on hobbies and ownership of homes, TVs, credit cards, pets, air conditioners, and cars. Clients could choose segments of the list, or could rent all 1 million names for $70,000 (14).

By the end of the 1960s, however, direct marketers began to look at more sophisticated measures that went beyond income, such as blue-collar versus white-collar mentality, psychographics, and lifestyles. Although some of these factors were difficult to ferret out through conventional techniques, they nevertheless allowed marketers to acquire a better understanding of their customers' needs and wants (25,26,27,42,52,59,72).

DATABASE MARKETING: THE 1970S

The analysis decade

A number of factors converged in the 1970s to make direct marketing more scientific and sophisticated than it had been in the past. Postage costs began increasing rapidly, making it uneconomical to continue sending out mailings on a mass basis. More 'niche' catalogs and mail-order companies went into business, making the identification of targeted prospects crucial. Computer technology improved and a number of mathematicians became involved in the field, meaning that sophisticated statistical and financial analysis could take place. In addition, scoring models put credit cards in the hands of more consumers, which, combined with new 800 numbers, increased the volume of orders through direct mail solicitations.

Lifetime value (LTV) models

During the early 1940s, a few companies began to attempt to estimate the value of their average customer. A 1941 survey by *The Reporter of Direct Mail Advertising* stated that about 29.5% of respondents were able to state the average value of their customers, with amounts ranging from $23.50 for a business calendar producer to $60 for a resort hotel to $6,000 for a manufacturer of heavy equipment (3). In a follow-up letter to the magazine, Jules Paglin of Porter's in New Orleans took the concept a step further, advising, 'Survey the actual customer records for worth. You will find so many worth $150 . . . so many worth $100 . . . so many worth $75 . . . and a whole lot worth $50 and under. When you have that, decide which ones you want to keep working on (or how intensively) and you have your problem solved' (4).

Another early recognizer of the importance of lifetime value was Chaman L. Jain, a professor at St. Johns University in New York City, who applied the concept of lifetime value to donors to the Epilepsy Foundation in Washington, D.C., helping the group to increase its donor base from an original 200,000 in 1958 to 1.5 million in 1964 (M).

Insurance companies, who already had actuarial information needed to calculate rates, began applying that information to their direct marketing efforts during the 1950s. For instance, Old American Insurance Company used a concept called 'par' to determine how much they could afford to spend to acquire each new customer (A).

At the end of the 1960s, with the availability of computer technology to aid in analysis, many other companies began experimenting with the concept that later became known as lifetime or long-term value. Chaman L. Jain introduced the concept in the trade press in 1969 with an article in *Direct Marketing* entitled, 'How much can you afford to get new customers?' (84). Doubleday (which called it 'Return on Promotion'), Columbia ('Allowables'), Kiplinger's *Changing Times* ('Allowable Order Costs'), Meredith, and Time-Life all had developed their own systems by the beginning of the 1970s (R). Epsilon, a consulting firm, introduced the concept to its several hundred not-for-profit clients with a booklet entitled 'Donors and Dollars' (N). By the late 1970s, the application of lifetime value had become commonplace among sophisticated direct marketers.

Statistical analysis

Prior to the 1970s, marketers' decisions concerning which prospects should be targeted with direct-mail solicitations were relatively haphazard. Often, such decisions were made on the basis of common sense; for example, teenagers were assumed more likely to want to join a record club than were senior citizens. A somewhat more refined method was list testing, whereby a small percentage of people on a particular list were sent solicitations. If the response was good, letters were then mailed to the rest of the names on the list.

Reader's Digest was the first direct marketer to use statistical analysis to make decisions concerning customer targeting. The company's experiments began in 1966, when circulation director Gordon Grossman noticed in *Variety* a prediction of the following month's Top 40 record hits. According to the magazine, the predictions were 97 percent accurate, and were based on such factors as current sales and movement up or down on the chart compared to the previous month.

Intrigued, Grossman contacted Jerry Greene of MarketMath, the company responsible for the hit record predictions, and suggested that he attempt to use similar methodology to predict the responsiveness of consumers to direct mailings. By 1967, Reader's Digest had begun using the technique, multiple regression analysis, on its prospect lists, lifting response rates significantly (H, J).

Usage of multiple regression contributed to the strong growth of the *Reader's Digest* magazine and related products during the late 1960s and 1970s. The company was successful at keeping the analysis technique under wraps until the early 1970s, when other firms began similar efforts.

Another early experimenter with statistical analysis was R. L. Polk, which applied the Automatic Interaction Detection (AID) system developed at the University of Michigan to direct marketing efforts in 1968. Polk client Meredith, publisher of *Better Homes and Gardens* magazine, agreed to pay for Polk to analyze one million names with the method, which used tree analysis to divide consumers into different segments. Polk's computer took two days and three nights to analyze a 400,000 'sample,' including auto registration and census tract information, and ultimately arrived at 14 meaningful segments out of the 30 billion possible combinations (U).

Although the AID technique was useful to Meredith and to other large companies such as Spiegel, it had a significant limitation in that it required very large sample sizes. However, AID eventually evolved into CHAID (Chi-Squared Automatic Interaction Detector), which was developed in 1980 and is still used by some companies to analyze interaction effects between different types of data (96).

By the mid 1970s, a wide variety of companies had begun to analyze their customers using statistical techniques (48,63,66,75). MarketMath's Jerry Greene described in 1971 in *Direct Marketing* the difference between multiple regression, discriminant analysis and AID (66); factor analysis and log linear analysis both began being used around 1974 (75). In addition, the introduction of prepackaged statistical programs such as SPSS and SAS (both released in the 1970s) helped those people who were less sophisticated about computers to begin working with data.

Most of the organizations that used statistical analysis during the early- to mid-1970s were in fields such as publishing or not-for-profit, where it was important to constantly find new prospects who were similar to current customers. *The Saturday Evening Post*, Time-Life, Rodale Press, Easter Seals, and some of the women's and shelter magazines were early adopters of this technology. Catalog companies and other direct-mail organizations, which typically relied on RFM analysis to generate more sales from current customers, did not on the whole make much investment in statistical analysis until the late 1970s.

Credit cards and 800 numbers

Two of the major factors accounting for the large growth in the field of direct marketing during the 1970s were the widespread acceptance of bank and travel cards, and the increasing popularity of 800 numbers. Together, credit cards and 800 numbers made it easier for customers to order direct, increasing consumer demand for products delivered through the mail (122).

Although credit had long been a part of the direct marketing industry, prior to the 1970s it was only offered by individual catalog companies. Spiegel, which built its business on the availability of credit, began offering it to consumers in 1905; Sears and other catalogers soon followed.

However, most direct marketers continued to offer merchandise on a prepaid cash (or sometimes COD) basis. Even after bank and travel cards (Diners Club in 1950, Bank Americard in 1956, American Express in 1958, and MasterCard in 1966) were launched, most direct marketers did not honor them, since consumer demand was light. Only affluent people possessed credit cards during the 1950s and 1960s, and those who did have cards did not feel entirely comfortable using them for transactions conducted through the mail (122).

All of this changed in the 1970s. By using credit scoring models, credit card companies were able to separate good risks from bad, and were therefore able to begin to offer credit cards to consumers with moderate incomes. In addition, credit card companies began to actively solicit good prospects with credit offers (56).

With more consumers possessing credit cards, and with the introduction of toll-free 800 numbers in 1967, mail order quickly became a credit-driven industry. Although many companies balked at accepting credit cards until the late 1970s, 80 percent of mail-order purchases were paid with credit cards in 1988 (122).

Direct marketing and 'consumerism'

As the size of the direct marketing industry expanded throughout the late 1960s and 1970s, it became the target of numerous attacks from government and consumer groups. Activists complained that direct marketers harassed prospects with unwanted junk mail, and irresponsibly mailed pornographic or otherwise offensive material to persons who had not requested it. As a result, the Nixon Administration Bill proposed that it become a criminal offense to send 'sexually offensive' material to homes containing minors, and several other bills proposed outlawing the exchange of consumer names by marketers without those consumers' explicit permission.

These issues were taken seriously at the time, but in reality were solved rather easily. Legitimate direct marketers were quick to condemn those who sent pornography through the mail and to cease sharing information with them. In 1971, the Direct Mail Advertising Association established the Mail Preference Service, which allowed consumers who did not want to receive unsolicited mailings to opt off all member companies' lists. Another similar name removal program, the Telephone Preference Service, was later created (33,122,127).

These self-regulation measures did a good job of stemming consumer protests over direct marketing for more than a decade. However, the privacy issue resurfaced in a more complicated way during the early 1990s, as consumers began to object not only to receiving mailings but also to the fact that direct marketers were storing and selling information about them.

Direct marketing: more segmented, more mainstream

The direct marketing industry grew rapidly during the 1970s, spurred on by factors such as availability of credit cards and toll-free telephone numbers, gas shortages, and newly working women's lack of shopping time. In addition, more information on consumers became easily accessible – for instance, the 1970 Census Report was available on tape, and included 25 times as much information (such as age, gender, race, income, housing costs, and capital goods ownership, all by small geographic units) as the 1960 Census (115,131). Standards for computerized customer information were released in 1970, making it easier for companies to share information with one another (18).

Other factors forced the direct marketing industry to begin to become more targeted. Research techniques made it easier to predict who would purchase a particular item, allowing specialty companies to profitably enter the market. In addition, postage costs began rising, with third-class per-ounce costs doubling between 1970 and 1980. As a result, many companies became more selective, mailing only to those customers who were relatively likely to respond (33).

General marketers also began experimenting with the field and many companies narrowed their focus to individual consumer segments, many of which had grown large enough to be profitable. Spiegel, a general catalog company, gradually changed its approach to appeal to higher-income working women. General Foods purchased Burpee Seeds, an established gardening cataloger, and launched Creative Village, an arts and crafts catalog. Campbell Soup launched a specialty catalog of Pepperidge Farm products.

Also in the 1970s, not-for-profit and political organizations began to use direct marketing as an effective way to target select groups of supporters. Not-for-profits were among the first to use lifetime value models and statistical analysis, and televangelists successfully integrated direct-response TV, inbound 800 numbers, and direct mail to solicit donations. Consultants at Epsilon recall developing up to 300 versions of personalized letters for organizations such as fraternities and alumni associations. Epsilon also helped Kevin White to become mayor of Boston in 1972 by mailing to 55,000 voters in certain neighborhoods computer-customized instructions on how to walk from their homes to the polling place (N).

DATABASE MARKETING: THE 1980S

The implementation decade

The 1960s and 1970s brought a revolution in the tools that direct marketers had available to target their customers. The sophistication of computers and computer software, credit cards, toll-free telephone numbers, ZIP codes, and census tract information, statistical and financial models, and a host of other innovations gave the industry the potential to become the fastest-growing and most scientific area of marketing (102).

However, most of the new technology was used during the 1960s and 1970s on an experimental, piecemeal basis. In the 1980s, further advances in technology and the sharing of information allowed companies to begin to implement more sophisticated and integrated programs. Just as important, during the 1980s many established, nondirect-mail companies began to apply industry concepts to their core businesses, finally moving the direct marketing industry beyond the concept of mail order.

Database technology

A major innovation in the field of database marketing was the development of the relational database, which made it easier to access and manipulate customer information and to share it with other companies. In the early 1980s, IBM released DB2, an SQL-based mainframe system. Other companies soon followed with similar programs for mainframes and later, personal computers.

The importance of the introduction of relational databases was primarily in the flexibility that the systems offered. Relational databases allowed records to be stored and analyzed more easily, as well as to be combined with external information. In addition, relational database managers were able to create menu-driven systems for marketing managers, thereby allowing them to make quicker and better use of information about their customers.

Increasing computer power

The development of computer technology progressed geometrically throughout the 1980s, permitting increasingly sophisticated manipulation and analysis of marketing data. The first personal computer was released in the late 1970s; although its capability was small, technology quickly advanced to the point where, by the mid-1980s, marketing managers could handle at their desks tasks that had required a mainframe only a few years earlier. Mainframe computers also became more powerful, making it possible to store and manipulate detailed information about millions of customers.

Increased computer capabilities allowed companies to keep comprehensive records of their own interactions with customers, and to append large amounts of external information or 'overlays' to their own data files. The improved ability of computers to handle such information prompted the growth of companies that collected consumer information, including National Demographics and Lifestyles (NDL), which surveyed individual consumers on hobbies and purchases through warranty cards (32), and ACORN, which analyzed households by geographical block group (49).

Database marketing

The advances in computer and database technology quickly led to a new age of what eventually became known as 'database marketing.' While expressing some of the same concepts that the term 'direct marketing' had been designed to address a decade earlier, the term 'database marketing' also suggested that the use of individualized consumer information did not have to be confined to the direct mail industry, but instead was also relevant to manufacturers of packaged and durable goods and to business-to-business companies (124).

As the field of database marketing became more scientific, and as its importance grew, it became the focus of more serious scholarship, encouraging further developments in the field. Old American Insurance Company's Martin Baier helped to establish the Center for Direct Marketing Education and Research at the University of Missouri – Kansas City. Northwestern University launched the *Journal of Direct Marketing* and its own graduate program in direct marketing, and a number of faculty members at other schools also began teaching courses and conducting research related to the field.

Beyond direct mail

The 1980s marked the first time that traditional mass marketers began to apply database marketing concepts to their core businesses. During the decade, companies not only learned their customer's names and addresses, they also began to collect detailed personal and purchasing information, thereby beginning to understand them as individuals rather than as part of a traditional mass audience (122).

Prior to the 1980s, some traditional direct marketers had experimented with using direct mail techniques, but in a less comprehensive way. In 1958, for example, Ford distributed information on its new models through the mail to 20 million potential customers (12). Companies like Procter & Gamble distributed coupons and samples through the mail prior to World War II, and several companies, including Quaker and General Foods, experimented with running direct-mail subsidiaries in the 1970s.

The airlines were the first nonmail-order companies to begin to establish major database marketing programs, although they backed into the area almost by accident. In the late 1970s, following deregulation, airlines began offering frequent flyer discounts in order to create consumer loyalty. Customers were at first rewarded with coupons, which could be combined and redeemed for free flights. However, the black market for these coupons that quickly arose caused the airlines to begin keeping records of their frequent flyer club members and purchase behaviors, and they eventually began to use this information for marketing purposes.

Another early user of database marketing technology was American Express, which used purchase behavior to target its cardmembers with information related to the card and peripheral products (76,82,137). Other credit-card companies, which had during the 1970s required applicants to supply detailed information about their finances, during the 1980s began using credit bureau information to offer pre-approved cards.

By the late 1980s, a number of other mass marketers had begun to collect information about their customers and to use it for marketing efforts. Following the lead of the airlines, other travel businesses such as hotels and car-rental agencies launched frequent-user programs. R. J. Reynolds and Philip Morris both established databases that eventually included the names of the majority of U.S. smokers. General Foods, Lipton, and Quaker Oats began to collect and use information about their customers, and were eventually followed by other packaged goods companies (130). Long-distance phone companies began using their transaction records to conduct targeted efforts to attract and keep good customers. Auto manufacturers also began using database marketing – for instance, Austin Rover introduced a consumer magazine using selective binding, which allowed articles to be targeted to consumers based on their individual interests.

DATABASE MARKETING: THE 1990S AND BEYOND

The future of the field of database marketing now appears to stand at a crossroads, with practitioners and academics holding a variety of opinions about the direction that they believe the field will take. One thought is that general marketers who have in the past relied on mass marketing will increasingly use more targeted and individualized means by which to communicate with their customers, and that database marketing will therefore become integrated into the overall marketing environment. Others believe that database marketing will remain a subsegment of the field of direct marketing, and will therefore be used in less broad and mainstream ways by most companies.

In addition, opinion is divided on the impact that current trends will have on the practice of database marketing. For example, some people are concerned about whether concerns over consumer privacy will severely limit the ability of marketers to communicate with their customers on an individualized basis; others believe that privacy issues are a relatively minor threat, or that the issue may cause marketers to improve their effectiveness by focusing their efforts on current, proven customers. Another thought is that the growth of database marketing may depend on whether companies can find new appropriate ways to reach their customers on a targeted and individualized basis, as well as ways for their customers to reach them.

Despite these uncertainties, there appear to be a number of trends that are likely to have an impact on the field of database marketing in coming years. Some of these trends include the following.

Relationship marketing

'Relationship marketing,' or the concept of developing individualized relationships with customers based on their specific needs and wants, became a popular theme for marketers during the 1990s. However, the concept of relationship marketing in fact dates back to the earliest days of direct marketing, when the industry was small enough to actually address its customers individually.

For example, during the 1870s, Montgomery Ward received the following letter from a customer: 'I suppose you wondered why we haven't ordered anything from you since the fall. Well, the cow kicked my arm and broke it, and besides my wife was sick, and there was that doctor bill. But now, thank God, that is paid, and we are all well again, and we have a fine new baby boy, so please send plush bonnet number 29d8077. . . . '

The customer immediately received a personal reply: regrets about the broken arm and the wife's illness, congratulations over the son, thanks for the order for the bonnet – and an inquiry as to whether the customer had noticed the anti-cow kicker shown in the catalog (123).

This type of personal marketing through the medium of direct mail was relatively short-lived; catalog companies soon began growing so fast that it became impossible to communicate with consumers on a one-on-one basis. However, the concept of listening and responding at an individual level resurfaced in the 1990s, under the guise of 'relationship marketing.' The concept, touted by many database marketers, suggested that by better understanding their customers on an individual level and by delivering to them information and products targeted to their specific needs, marketers can develop long-term customer bonds that will eventually translate into substantial profits.

According to many experts, the move toward using database marketing information to create long-term relationships with customers has been and will continue to be fueled by a number of factors: improved technology, the saturation of the marketplace with products, increased costs of targeting a mass audience, and consumer concerns over the environment and personal privacy (122).

Technology improvements

Computer technology, which grew rapidly during the 1970s and 1980s, is expected to continue to expand during the next few decades, allowing more information to be stored and quickly analyzed. In addition, new modeling techniques, such as neural networks ('artificial intelligence') and fractal geometry ('chaos theory') may eventually help researchers to better analyze the information being stored (44,89). The result of this is that companies should gain the potential of being able to better understand and target individual consumers in even the most frequently purchased categories.

Privacy and the environment

Consumer concerns over personal privacy and over the large amount of unwanted, unrecyclable 'junk mail' cluttering the environment are likely to change the way that marketers using database technology will address consumers in the future. Already, many European countries have passed restrictive laws that greatly limit the ability of traditional direct marketers to do business there. The U.S. has begun to follow suit with media coverage of the issue and with laws restricting the dissemination of credit, auto registration, and other consumer data.

How the privacy issue will be resolved is still an unanswered question. However, an immediate impact is likely to be that direct mailings will become more targeted, and that consumers may gain more control over the types of mailings that they do and do not wish to receive.

Relationships: fewer, but more meaningful

Until a few years ago, growth in the U.S. economy, population and demand for products caused marketers to target a mass audience and to constantly attempt to attract new customers. It has only been recently that many companies, affected by stagnating demand and decreasing brand loyalty, have begun to target their core customers in an active fashion.

The retention of customers has often been cited as the single biggest predictor of the future profitability of a company. Because of this, and because consumers are relatively unconcerned about privacy threats from companies with whom they already do business, database marketing efforts in the near future are likely to focus on servicing current customers in ways that go beyond direct mailings.

Niche marketing

Saturation of the mass market, and the increasing demands of consumers, have recently caused marketers to start thinking about developing niche products to target the consumers once missed. During the early 1990s, for instance, many niche products (such as Cheer Free, a hypo-allergenic laundry detergent; Benadryl, a medication for allergy sufferers; Rogaine, a hair-growth stimulant for balding men; and Amore, a premium food for 'pampered cats') asked appropriate consumers to 'stand up and identify themselves' through such means as inbound 800 numbers; these consumers were later approached repeatedly with targeted messages through direct marketing. These types of targeted database marketing activities are likely to increase markedly in the near future.

International markets

Prior to the 1990s, database marketing was much more prevalent in the United States (and, to a lesser extent, Canada) than in the rest of the world. Advances in technology and the growing globalization of marketing operations, however, are likely to cause database marketing techniques to be used more frequently in other parts of the world, such as Europe, Asia, and South America, during the next decade or so.

However, global database marketing may need to be implemented in a somewhat different way than it traditionally has been practiced in the United States. Europeans tend to be very fearful of organizations collecting and selling personal information about them, and have already passed numerous privacy laws. Asians, especially the Japanese, tend to be very conscious of the quality and reputations of the products they use; however, once they have tried a particular product and are satisfied with it, they are often very brand loyal. Both of these factors will increase the desirability of using database technology to improve relationships with existing customers, rather than to constantly prospect for new, one-time buyers.

SUMMARY

The last century or so has brought to marketers many advances in technology and in the way they look at their customers. The unifying factor of these changes is that each has allowed marketers to target their customers on a more personalized, segmented, and customized basis. Marketers began by addressing their customers as a mass; today, they use database marketing techniques to view them as individuals.

This trend, despite consumer privacy concerns, is likely to continue into the future. Whatever new developments occur in the field of database marketing, it is likely that they will be most successful if they enable marketers to target their consumers in ways that are relevant, inoffensive, and conducive to stronger relationships between the marketer and the customer – in short, that are meaningful to the *customer*, rather than simply convenient for the marketer.

Exhibit 1 Database marketing: major historical events

Pre-1950s
First Trade Catalogs Issued (1400s)
First Mass-Market Catalogs Issued (1880s)
'12-Month Prune Rule' Developed (1910)
RFM Model Developed (1920s)
R. L. Polk and R. H. Donnelley Prospect Lists Compiled (1940s)
Rudimentary Lifetime Value Models Developed (1940s)

1950s
Lists Priced According to Value
List Brokers Formed

1960s
Computer Systems Begin Being Used for Marketing
ZIP Code System Used for Segmentation (1967)
Merge/Purge Systems Developed (1968)
Personalized Computer-Generated Letters Used
Genesis of 'Direct Marketing'
Multiple Regression Analysis Used for Marketing (1967)
AID System Used for Marketing (1968)
800-Numbers Are Introduced (1967)

1970s
Lifetime Value Model Use Becomes Widespread
Credit Card Use Becomes Widespread
Mail Preference Service Established (1971)

1980s
Relational Databases Developed
Computers Become More Powerful
Genesis of 'Database Marketing'
Mass Marketers Begin Using Database Marketing

APPENDIX

Alphabetical References

The authors would like to thank the following persons for contributing to this project through in-depth interviews.

A)   Martin Baier, University of Missouri
B)   Jock Bickert, NDL
C)   Richard J. Courtheoux, Precision Marketing Corporation
D)   Bob DeLay, Direct Marketing Association (Retired)

E)   Alan Drey, Alan Drey Company
F)   John Flieder, Allstate Insurance
G)   Steve Gasner, North American Communications
H)   Jerome Greene, MarketMath
I)   John Groman, Epsilon
J)   Gordon Grossman, Gordon Grossman Consulting
K)   Rose Harper, The Kleid Company
L)   Henry 'Pete' Hoke, Direct Marketing Magazine
M)   Chaman Jain, St Johns University
N)   Thomas Jones, Epsilon
O)   Robert Kestnbaum, Kestnbaum Consulting
P)   Jim Kobs, Kobs, Gregory & Passavant
Q)   Herb Krug, Krug Consulting
R)   Joe Malone, Time-Life (Retired)
S)   Jim McQuaid, Metromail
T)   Pierre Passavant, Kobs, Gregory & Passavant
U)   Len Quenon, R. L. Polk (Retired)
V)   Tom Rocco, Rodale Press
W)   Don Schultz, Northwestern University
X)   David Shepard, David Shepard Associates
Y)   Bernie Silverman, The Signature Group
Z)   Edward Spiegel, Northwestern University
AA) Robert Shaw, Shaw Consulting
BB) John Stevenson, American Express
CC) Bob Stone, Stone & Adler
DD) Robert Weinberg, Kobs, Gregory & Passavant
EE) Joseph Weissman, DRC
FF) Lester Wunderman, Wunderman Associates

REFERENCES

1. —— (1939), 'Regaining Lost Customers!,' *The Reporter of Direct Mail Advertising*, (March).
2. —— (1939), 'What Are the Important Trends in Direct Mail?,' *The Reporter of Direct Mail Advertising*, (April).
3. —— (1941), 'How Is Direct Advertising Planned?' *The Reporter of Direct Mail Advertising*, (April).
4. —— (1941), 'How Much Is a Customer Worth?' *The Reporter of Direct Mail Advertising*, (March).
5. —— (1945), 'Public and Employee Relations,' *The Reporter of Direct Mail Advertising*, (November).
6. —— (1946), 'How Direct Mail Is Planned,' *The Reporter of Direct Mail Advertising*, (October).
7. —— (1946), 'A Testing Opportunity,' *The Reporter of Direct Mail Advertising*, (October).
8. —— (1948), 'Direct Mail Volume,' *The Reporter of Direct Mail Advertising*, (February).
9. —— (1949), 'About Mailing Lists,' *The Reporter of Direct Mail Advertising*, (October).
10. —— (1954), 'How to Think about Mail Order.' *The Reporter of Direct Mail Advertising*, (April).
11. —— (1954), 'Lists and Control,' *The Reporter of Direct Mail Advertising*, (September).
12. —— (1958), 'Ford's Booklet Offer to 20,000,000 Families Designed to Build Huge Dealer List,' (November).
13. —— (1964), 'The List – A Key Element,' *The Reporter of Direct Mail Advertising*, (May).
14. —— (1967), 'A Select List for Advertisers, *Business Week*, (May 27).
15. —— (1967), 'Zip Code: New Look in Mail Marketing,' *The Reporter of Direct Mail Advertising*, (September).
16. —— (1968), 'Brokers Offer Computer Service to Pull Duplicates from Lists.' *The Reporter of Direct Mail Advertising*, (June).
17. —— (1970), 'Duplicate Names on Lists Use Wasted Dollars,' *Direct Marketing*, (March).

18. —— (1970), 'Standards for Computerized Mailing Lists Released,' (November).
19. —— (1979), 'Profits Generated for Fingerhut through Computer Technology,' *Direct Marketing*, (February).
20. —— (1987), 'Guide to List Suppliers,' *Direct Marketing*, (August).
21. —— (1987), '1987 List Issues and Practices,' *Direct Marketing*, (August).
22. Adler, Max (1967), 'How Spencer Gifts Uses a Computer to Increase Profitability,' *The Journal of Direct Mail Advertising*, (June).
23. Anderson, A. M. (1949), 'What's Wrong with Direct Mail,' *The Reporter of Direct Mail Advertising*, (September).
24. Baier, Martin (1967), 'Zip Code – New Tool for Marketers,' *Harvard Business Review*, (January–February).
25. Baier, Martin (1969), 'Environment, Self-Perception Keys to ZIP-code Marketing,' *Direct Marketing*, (June).
26. Baier, Martin (1971), 'Psychographics: Newest Key to Segmenting Markets, Lists,' *Direct Marketing*, (February).
27. Baier, Martin (1975), 'How Lifestyle Segmentation Selects Prospects from Zips,' *Direct Marketing*, (March).
28. Baier, Martin (1976), 'Complex Marketing Activities Bring Need for Segmentation,' *Direct Marketing*, (January).
29. Baier, Martin (1982), 'Direct Marketing: Multifaceted Concept,' *Direct Marketing*, (April).
30. Baier, Martin (1983), 'Why Is the Press So Misinformed about Direct Marketing?,' *Direct Marketing*, (September).
31. Benson, George and Jain, Chaman L. (1971), 'Matching Direct Mail Lists for Duplicate Name Selection,' *Direct Marketing*, (March)
32. Bickert, Jock (1982), 'Lifestyle Selector Builds Data Base Through Inserts,' *Direct Marketing*, (May).
33. Blau, Barry (1973), 'Computers, List Segmentation, Consumerism in '70s Forecast,' *Direct Marketing*, (March).
34. Bolton, Paul H. (1945), 'Direct Mail Force and Velocity Should Be Important Factors in Your Public Relations Program,' *The Reporter of Direct Mail Advertising*, (July).
35. Brodie, Julian P. (1948), 'Direct Advertising Is the Agencies' Business,' *The Reporter of Direct Mail Advertising*, (April).
36. Buckellew, C. O. (1967), 'Computer Know-How Keeps Tandy Corporation's Lists Alive and Up-to-Date,' *The Reporter of Direct Mail Advertising*, (November).
37. Burnett, Ed (1983), 'Database: A Major Fact of Life in the List Business,' *Direct Marketing*, (April).
38. Burnett, Robert A. (1981), 'New Directions in Media: Revolution of Evolution?,' *Direct Marketing*, (May).
39. Chait, Lawrence G. (1952), 'Our Mailing List Thinking Needs Drastic Overhaul,' *The Reporter of Direct Mail Advertising*, (August).
40. Chait, Lawrence G. (1952), 'Mailing Lists . . . Danger Spot of Direct Mail,' *The Reporter of Direct Mail Advertising*, (February).
41. Chait, Lawrence G. (1967), 'The Experts Speak Up on the Ideas That are Changing the Face of Direct Mail,' *The Reporter of Direct Mail Advertising*, (June).
42. Chait, Lawrence G. (1979), 'Psychology of MO Promotion and Consumer Purchasing,' *Direct Marketing*, (February).
43. Chait, Lawrence G. (1982), 'Lists of the Future: Election DataBanks,' *Direct Marketing*, (April).
44. Chait, Lawrence G. (1985), 'Direct Marketing in the New Artificial Intelligence Age,' *Direct Marketing*, (January).
45. Cody, Don (1973), 'Shoe Firm Solves Mail Order Growing Pains with Computer,' *Direct Marketing*, (August).
46. Courtheoux, Richard J. (1984), 'The Practical Side of Database Theory: Everyday Applications,' Speech, 16th Annual Direct Marketing International Symposium, (April 30–May 4).
47. Courtheoux, Richard J. (1987), 'Database Modeling: Maximizing the Benefits,' *Direct Marketing*, (March).
48. Cremer, Richard E. (1974), 'How to Find Treasure in Your Customer File,' *Direct Marketing*, (July).
49. Davies, Paul (1983), 'ACORN/M.O.M.S. System May Increase Profitability of Lists,' *Direct Marketing*, (April).
50. DeLay, Robert (1957), 'Can an Advertising Agency Successfully Integrate Direct Mail into Your Advertising Program?,' *The Reporter of Direct Mail Advertising*, (August).
51. DeLay, Robert (1981), 'The 1980s: A Time for International Cooperation,' *Direct Marketing*, (May).
52. Demby, Emmanuel (1969), 'Consumer Life Style More Vital to Marketing than Income Level,' *Direct Marketing*, (June).
53. Dooley, James (1954), 'A Tell-All Report Details How an IBM Tab Card System Is Simplifying List Selection and Customer Control . . . How It Is Keeping Track of 7 Million Pieces Per Year,' *The Reporter of Direct Mail Advertising*, (August).
54. Doppler, William A. (1957), 'A Mail Order Test to End All Tests', *The Reporter of Direct Mail Advertising*, (September).
55. Drew, Alice Honore (1948), 'The Plain Jane of Direct Mail,' *The Reporter of Direct Mail Advertising*, (September, October, November).

56. Esti, Robert (1975), 'Tracking Debt Delinquents by Pre-screening Applicants,' *Direct Marketing*, (March).
57. Fields, Michael J. (1970), 'New Image for Computers in Direct Marketing,' *Direct Marketing* (June).
58. Fleischer, Richard L. (1988), 'Databases: Retail Style,' *Direct Marketing*, (March).
59. Forrest, Ed and Blumberg, Leo (1981), 'Mailing List Psychographics: An Inside Look at Prospects,' *Direct Marketing*, (September).
60. Frain, Jim (1985), 'Laura Ashley Breaks New Ground in Building Retail Customer Base,' *Direct Marketing*, (February).
61. Freel, Edward T. (1951), 'Protecting Direct Mail Records by Microfilming,' *The Reporter of Direct Mail Advertising*, (May).
62. Friedrich, Bede (1957), 'How a Mechanized Punch Card System Can Help Fund Raising by Mail,' *The Reporter of Direct Mail Advertising*, (May).
63. Gaeddert, Orian (1974), 'Using Statistical Approach in Direct Marketing Campaign,' *Direct Marketing*, (May).
64. Ginsburg, Dan (1985), 'Business-to-Business in 1990: How to Get Ready for Change,' *Direct Marketing*, (March).
65. Gould, Anthony R. (1938), 'Testing Accuracy of Tests,' *The Reporter of Direct Mail Advertising*, (June).
66. Greene, Jerome D. (1971), 'Gain-From-Selectivity Finds Special Lists within Master,' *Direct Marketing*, (June).
67. Grossman, Gordon (1976), 'Conceptions, Misconceptions about Direct Marketing Today,' *Direct Marketing*, (August).
68. Grossman, Gordon (1982), 'Your Customer Database: Foundation for Success,' *Direct Marketing*, (April).
69. Grossman, Gordon (1982), 'Circulation Management: An Art or a Science,' *Direct Marketing*, (September).
70. Grossman, Gordon (1982), 'Foreshadowing Response: The Muscle in Your Merge,' *Direct Marketing*, (December).
71. Hanau, Robert C. (1971), 'Development & Marketing of Computer Letters,' *Direct Marketing*, (March).
72. Harper, Rose (1974), 'Supplementing Demographics with Psychographic Profile,' *Direct Marketing*, (May).
73. Harper, Rose (1975), 'Changing Patterns of Lists and How They Affect Marketers,' *Direct Marketing*, (April).
74. Harper, Rose (1978), 'Correct Analysis of Mailing Lists Is Key to Successful Mail Order,' *Direct Marketing*, (February).
75. Harper, Rose C., Posgay, Anthony G., and Tyszler, Marcel (1975), 'Selection of Mailing Lists by Multivariate Analysis,' *Direct Marketing*, (February).
76. Hilleman, Jeri and Young, Ray (1985), 'American Express Finds Breakthrough Mail Response,' *Direct Marketing*, (January).
77. Hoke, Pete (1973), 'Pulse of List Business Quickened by List Managers,' *Direct Marketing*, (March).
78. Hotchkiss, H. Stuart (1987), 'Creating a Better Continuity Model,' *Direct Marketing*, (March).
79. Hubbell, William (1988), 'Fine Tune Your Mailing Campaign,' *Direct Marketing*, (October).
80. Hughes, Arthur M. (1991), *The Complete Database Marketer*, Probus Publishing Company: Chicago.
81. Hydendael, Arthur (1982), 'Two Golden Opportunities for Expanding into New Markets,' *Direct Marketing*, (December).
82. Jaffee, Larry (1984), 'AMEX Targets Mailings Precisely to List Segments,' *Direct Marketing*, (May).
83. Jain, C. L. and Migliaro, A. (1968), 'The Fundamentals of List Segmentation,' *The Reporter of Direct Mail Advertising*, (February).
84. Jain, C. L. (1969), 'How Much Can You Afford to Get New Customers?,' *Direct Marketing*, (June).
85. Johnson, Rob (1984), 'Databases: Great Opportunities but Beware of the Pitfalls,' *Direct Marketing*, (February).
86. Kestnbaum, Bob (1974), 'List Creation and Maintenance for Maximizing Your Investment,' *Direct Marketing*, (March).
87. Kirby, Fred P. (1956), 'Innoculating Direct Mail Prospects,' *The Reporter of Direct Mail Advertising*, (September).
88. Kleid, Lewis (1952), 'What's in a Name?,' *The Reporter of Direct Mail Advertising*, (November).
89. Kleid, Lewis (1953), 'How to Select and Use Mailing Lists Effectively,' *The Reporter of Direct Mail Advertising*, (December).
90. Konselman, Charles B. (1947), 'Advertising Coordination Requires Planning,' *The Reporter of Direct Mail Advertising*, (June).
91. Konselman, Charles B. (1947), 'Media Coordination – An Advertising Essential,' *The Reporter of Direct Mail Advertising*, (April).
92. Layer, Richard H. (1968), 'Statistics – The Necessary Evil in Mail Order Selling,' *The Reporter of Direct Mail Advertising*, (September).
93. Lewis, Herschell Gordon (1988), 'Database: Is It Your Creative Servant . . . or Your Creative Master?,' *Direct Marketing*, (June).
94. Li, Richard (1989), 'Preventing Model Muddle,' *Direct Marketing*, (August).
95. Liang, Yuan (1985), 'Direct Mail Applications of Small Area Demographics,' *Direct Marketing*, (December).

96. Magidson, Jay (1990), 'CHAID, LOGIT and Log-Linear Modeling,' *Datapro Reports on Marketing Information Systems*, NY: McGraw-Hill.
97. Mandel, Jack K. (1988), 'The Local Database: What's in Store,' *Direct Marketing*, (March).
98. McCollum, Giles B. (1964), 'All Those Coupons,' *The Reporter of Direct Mail Advertising*, (April).
99. McIntyre, Randall P. (1965), 'Mail Marketing in Three Dimensions,' *The Reporter of Direct Mail Advertising*, (October).
100. McKelvey, Tara (1991), 'Business Week to Offer Rich Readers Special Edition with Eight Pages of Ads,' *Magazine Week Advertising News*, (July 22).
101. Meyer, Otto F. (1959), 'How We Work with Mailing Lists at the *Wall Street Journal*,' *The Reporter of Direct Mail Advertising*, (June).
102. Meyer, Sandra (1981), 'Direct Marketing: A Concept Whose Time Has Arrived,' *Direct Marketing*, (March).
103. Migliaro, A. L. (1966), 'Putting a Name and Address on a Computer,' *The Reporter of Direct Mail Advertising*, (February).
104. Miller, Murray (1964), 'Mail Order and the Computer,' *The Reporter of Direct Mail Advertising*, (October).
105. Moore, Lorence E. (1963), 'How to Mail Effectively into Varying Markets,' *Direct Marketing*, (March).
106. Morgan, Boyce (1951), 'Public Relation and Direct Mail,' *The Reporter of Direct Mail Advertising*, (May).
107. Morgan, Boyce (1957), 'What's Wrong with List Testing?,' *The Reporter of Direct Mail Advertising*, (September).
108. Muchnick, Paul (1947), 'The A.B.C.'s of Mail Advertising,' *The Reporter of Direct Mail Advertising*, (August).
109. Murphy, Gerald (1967), 'How a Computer Can Work for You,' *The Reporter of Direct Mail Advertising*, (August).
110. Nebenzahl, Paul (1970), 'Computer Bright Picture for Retail Marketing Plans,' *Direct Marketing*, (December).
111. Ostrom, David M. (1965), 'Family Standards Define New Mail Markets,' *The Reporter of Direct Mail Advertising*, (March).
112. Passavant, Pierre (1974), 'New Economic Climate Demands Greater Marketing Selectivity,' *Direct Marketing*, (February).
113. Pelley, Donald G. (1983), 'Lists: The Shrinking Universe or Big Bang Segmentation?,' *Direct Marketing*, (April).
114. Pickholz, Jerome W. (1988), 'The End of the World (As We Know It),' *Direct Marketing*, (September).
115. Quenon, Len (1971), 'Extended Census Information to Yield Selection Formula,' *Direct Marketing*, (March).
116. Raphel, Murray (1984), 'Supermarkets Target Customers, Create Loyal, Steady Shoppers,' *Direct Marketing*, (September).
117. Randall, William A. (1987), 'The New Technologies – Can They Really Work?,' *Direct Marketing*, (July).
118. Reed, Orville (1949), 'Some Random Thoughts . . . On Personalizing,' *The Reporter of Direct Mail Advertising*, (April).
119. Reed, Orville E. (1949), 'Mailing Lists Can Be Too Good,' *The Reporter of Direct Mail Advertising*, (August).
120. Reed, Orville E. (1951), 'Postage Increase a Boon to Direct Mail,' *The Reporter of Direct Mail Advertising*, (November).
121. Riskin, Bernard (1968), 'Where Can I Buy Your Product? Computer Map Answers – Fast,' *The Reporter of Direct Mail Advertising*, (August).
122. Roel, Raymond (1988), 'Direct Marketing's 50 Big Ideas,' *Direct Marketing*, (May).
123. Ross, Nat (1992), 'A History of Direct Marketing,' Unpublished Paper, NY: Direct Marketing Association.
124. Savini, Gloria (1988), 'A Database Dozen,' *Direct Marketing*, (May).
125. Savini, Gloria (1988), 'Developing and Maintaining Business Lists,' *Direct Marketing*, (March).
126. Schulz, Peter (1957), 'A Four-Step Method for Obtaining a 100% Correct Mailing List.' *The Reporter of Direct Mail Advertising*, (February).
127. Schwartz, Marvin (1987), 'List Usage Ethics and Marketing Opportunity in Merge/Purge,' *Direct Marketing*, (August).
128. Schwedelson, Roy (1988), 'New Wave Database,' *Direct Marketing*, (March).
129. Shepard, David B. (1976), 'Direct Mail Order Economics and its Financial Planning,' *Direct Marketing*, (February).
130. Slade, Samuel B. (1983), 'Quaker Oats Expands Business through Direct Mail/Retail Mix,' *Direct Marketing*, (January).
131. Sprowls, Clay (1970), '1970 Summary Tape Census Data – Gold Mine for Mailers,' *Direct Marketing*, (May).
132. Stevens, Milton S. (1964), 'How Market Research Can Improve List Results,' *The Reporter of Direct Mail Advertising*, (January).
133. Stevens, Milton S. (1964), 'How Market Research Identifies Hidden Prospects,' *The Reporter of Direct Mail Advertising*, (August).

134. Stevens, Milton S. (1966), 'Direct Mail Marketing: What Is It?,' *The Reporter of Direct Mail Advertising*, (July).

135. Stevenson, John (1985), '98% Negative Database Holds Power of Expansion Benefits,' *Direct Marketing*, (March).

136. Stevenson, John (1987), 'The History and Family Tree of "Databased" Direct Marketing,' *Direct Marketing*, (December).

137. Stevenson, John (1988), 'What American Express Did When It Ran Out of Trees,' *Direct Marketing*, (November).

138. Stone, Bob (1973), 'Should Mass Marketers Go into Direct Marketing? Here Are Ways to Decide,' *Advertising Age*, July 16.

139. Stone, Bob (1988), 'Direct Marketing: Then and Now,' *Direct Marketing*, (May).

140. Straub, Daniel H. (1982), 'Target Your Markets with Computer Maps and Graphics,' *Direct Marketing*, (March).

141. Trenbath, Richard P. (1968), 'The Opportunities and Pitfalls of the Computer Letter,' *The Reporter of Direct Mail Advertising*, (June).

142. Weinberg, Robert E. (1985), 'Checklist Offers Approaches to Utilize Records for Growth,' *Direct Marketing*, (May).

143. Weissman, Joseph (1980), 'Using The Census, Zip Codes, and Maps to Target Markets,' *Direct Marketing*, (April).

144. Weissman, Joseph (1985), 'Geo-Select Confusion: Which G-Factor is Best?,' *Direct Marketing*, (June).

145. Welch, George D. (1959), 'How a Tab Card System Cut Direct Mail Costs,' *The Reporter of Direct Mail Advertising*, (September).

146. Wentzel, Nelson B. (1947), 'A Report from the United States Post Office Department,' *The Reporter of Direct Mail Advertising*, (September).

147. Wiersema, Fred D. (1987), 'Advanced Segmentation's Practical Parameters,' *Direct Marketing*, (March).

148. Wolf, Walter (1987), 'Net Name Arrangements Interact with Segmentation Techniques,' *Direct Marketing*, (October).

149. Wunderman, Lester (1981), 'Frontiers of Direct Marketing,' Company Booklet, Wunderman Associates: New York.

150. Wunderman, Lester (1967), 'Mail Order: The Coming Revolution in Marketing,' *The Reporter of Direct Mail Advertising*, (June).

151. Yeck, John D. (1952), 'Direct Mail's Golden Age,' *The Reporter of Direct Mail Advertising*, (January).

152. Yochim, Leo (1979), 'How to Make the Most of your Merge-Purge Program,' *Direct Marketing*, (April).

4.2 Database marketing: a channel, a medium, or a strategic approach?

Keith Fletcher, Colin Wheeler and Julia Wright

INTRODUCTION

The potential impact of new technology and new media on the way in which a company communicates with its target audience has been of interest to advertisers for a number of years. If advertising campaigns are to remain effective then the changing audiences must be monitored, their use of media studied, and the impact of changed market conditions considered (Fletcher, 1985).

In reality many of the changes have not been as predicted; the adoption of new media has been delayed through technical and financial problems and lack of consumer acceptance. During the last decade there has however been one major change to the communication process between companies and customers, and this has been the dramatic growth in direct marketing, stimulated by new technology and market conditions. This paper reviews this growth and its implications for the advertising industry and its practitioners.

THE GROWTH AND DEVELOPMENT OF DIRECT MARKETING

While the use of direct marketing varies by industry sector, one survey in 1988 found that over 90 per cent of companies used some form of direct marketing (Direct Response, June 1988). Figures from the British Direct Marketing Association (BDMA) showed that in 1987 direct marketing accounted for 27 per cent of total advertising spend in the UK, and this figure continues to grow.

Numerous definitions of direct marketing exist. In a general sense it can be seen as 'any activity which creates and exploits a direct relationship between company and customer' (Ogilvy and Mather Direct, 1985). More specifically, 'direct marketing is an interactive system of marketing which uses one or more advertising medium to effect a measurable response and/or transaction at any location' (Baier, 1985).

It is generally agreed that the recent developments in information technology have vastly improved the effectiveness of direct marketing. A computerized customer database allows for analysis and identification of individual customers, prospects or distributors. These 'targets' can then be reached through personalized direct marketing; for example, using mail or telephone contact. To many practitioners direct marketing has now become database-dependent. British Telecom and the Automobile Association are examples of companies – now with large sophisticated database systems – who initiated database developments in order to improve direct communications. Statements such as 'Direct marketing will evolve into database marketing,' and 'Database marketing is direct marketing done properly' are widely accepted.

It is suggested that direct marketing usage, (enhanced by computer technology), has gone through three phases:

1. The 'sales oriented' phase, in which direct marketing was seen as a *channel of distribution* to sell low-involvement, low-priced products very effectively.
2. The 'image building' phase in which direct marketing is, in a sense, 'a personalized image system': the customer receives regular mailings targeted according to his or her life-style or behaviour. A profile is thus built up and is used to motivate usage. Direct marketing, although still incomplete, is used as a *medium*.
3. The integrated system phase is that in which the uses of direct marketing as a channel of distribution and as a medium come together to be used for both tactical and strategic purposes. In this stage direct marketing (dm) is integrated into the marketing process and database marketing (dbm) ensures a long-term view of customer relationships.

Along with the transfer of advertising spend from above-the-line to below-the-line, has been a growth in specialist agencies. Ten years ago only three or four direct marketing agencies existed, but the BDMA now lists approximately 70 specialist agencies – although some would be better described as general agencies with experience in direct marketing, business-to-business agencies or consultancies (Keynote, 1988). Like conventional agencies they can be big, small, specialist or full-service, but most tend to focus on direct mail with a few selling media services as well. Some of the biggest are multinationals or subsidiaries of international agencies. Saatchi and Saatchi, for example, moved into direct marketing as Saatchi & Saatchi Direct in 1986; Ogilvy & Mather founded Ogilvy & Mather Direct in 1977.

As direct and database marketing increase in importance there may be two main challenges to direct marketing agencies (Tom Lester Marketing, January 19th 1989). Clients may see that direct marketing is too important to be left to the agencies and may set up their own direct marketing departments, and indeed this may be a key factor in long-term and dm and dbm success. A more immediate threat may come from sales promotion companies which are expanding into direct marketing by internal growth or acquisition, to improve the quality of direct marketing services offered.

In the past, one of the main criticisms levelled against direct marketing agencies was their failure to integrate direct marketing into the overall marketing strategy, using it for short-term tactical objectives. However, the majority of the agencies' clients came from backgrounds such as mail order and did not actually want strategic work, with agencies being employed on a project-only basis.

More recently the move of large 'mainstream' companies (such as RAC, Austin Rover, British Airways) into the dm and dbm arena has led to a demand for a different kind of service from agencies. Many clients now take a more sophisticated approach and no longer view direct marketing as a last minute add-on to a campaign. Indeed database marketing techniques are increasingly seen as essential to long-term marketing success.

REASONS FOR GROWTH OF DM AND DBM

The reasons for growth of dm and dbm can be classified under four main headings, the changing role of dm, the changing cost structures, changing technology, and changing market conditions.

Changing role of direct marketing

The special strengths of direct marketing, together with the increased sophistication of techniques available, give a partial explanation for the growth of dm and dbm. The tactical use of the discipline has already been touched upon. It can be used as a sales promotion tool to give a short-term sales boost, to target specific customers who cannot be reached by the usual media, to obtain leads for the sales force, or to sell directly, but it has frequently occupied a role inferior to above-the-line advertising.

At the Abbey National Building Society (according to Karen Pearce, head of direct marketing) it was initially used almost as a last resort, and was often considered only after above-the-line advertising had failed! Dbm techniques have helped to create a strategic role for direct marketing. Companies have recognized that 'building and maintaining customer relationships have significant long-term implications and therefore affect the strategic and long-range planning of the firm's marketing' (Gummesson, 1987).

Rapp and Collins (1987) list five ways in which dbm can maximize development of a company's overall sales and profits.

1. *Repeat Sales*: There seem to be three basic ways to accomplish repeat sales using the database: establish an ongoing rewards programme, give preferential treatment to the best customers, or custom-tailor special offers or benefits for special segments.
2. *Customer loyalty*: This can be encouraged, for example, by setting up a programme which will frequently re-promote a company's customer development process where a sale is not necessary. However, the non-responsive forms of direct marketing must ultimately be measured against increase in product sales and customer retention.
3. *Cross-promotion*: A company which offers a number of different products or services can use its combined database to introduce a customer who has bought one type of purchase to other opportunities. However, companies using the database to cross-sell need to have (i) a large number of customers (since many of the modelling and statistical techniques actually *require* large numbers) and (ii) a wide range of products. Cross-selling is a method particularly favoured by retail banks. The Automobile Association which offers a wide range of products and services also makes significant use of its database for this purpose.
4. *Line extension*: The customer database can be used in line extension by using mail shots to existing customers inviting them to try a new product.
5. *New ventures*: A further method of diversified growth is to use the database as a launching pad for new profit centres. Again a large database is needed, although existing customers can provide a core for making the initial sales until a unique database is built.

Database marketing can thus be used not only to maintain sales from existing customers and product lines, but also to develop new markets and products. To do this it moves away from the distribution and promotion role of direct marketing and adopts a strategic dimension.

Shaw and Stone (1988), for example, work from the five major competitive opportunity areas for IT identified by Michael Porter; arguing that dbm offers potential in *all* these areas:

1. Changing the basis of competition.
2. Strengthening customer relationships.
3. Overcoming supplier problems.
4. Building barriers against new entrants.
5. Generating new products.

An example of the strategic use of direct marketing is Direct Line Insurance, a subsidiary of the Royal Bank of Scotland, which was established in 1985 as a 'new way of marketing motor insurance'. By marketing the product direct, the company avoids paying brokers' commissions and so is able to offer the public a more personal service, a faster response, and a lower price. In 1988, Direct Line launched a second product (home insurance) and intends, according to marketing manager Steven Ashman, to concentrate more effort in future on *customer retention* and *service*, and on cross-selling. The concept of Direct Line, in a sense, changed the basis of competition in the motor insurance industry; since its inception a number of competitors have entered the field. Direct Line, however, sees its customer database (and its links with sister companies' databases) as a means of *defending* its business against new entrants.

A further example is Freemans which made its first significant move into selling catalogues direct to the public with the launch of 'Bigmail' (a joint venture with Jeff Banks). The move was partially fuelled by the identification of *long-term* trends in the agency market: the number of customers that each agent has now declining across the industry. According to the head of marketing, Andrew Collins, dbm techniques can principally be used for developing more targeted specialist catalogues where the primary focus is on the customer. Freemans' direct catalogues – for example, the recently launched *Complete Essentials* – can be targeted at new segments of the market, particularly at those people who are *not* used to buying mail order goods through the agency system.

In terms of direct marketing campaigns, most experts and users agree that a balance of *qualitative* and *quantitative* objectives needs to be set. For Rod Wright, the managing director of Ogilvy & Mather Direct, campaigns should be justified through research and response, although in certain key sectors, response is more important. In general terms, marketing departments have to justify communications (direct and indirect) in terms of commercial performance: a balance of short-term results and long-term consistency of brand or company image and overall strategy.

Changing cost structures

Eric Fiegenthaler, Secretary General of EDMA (the European Direct Marketing Association), emphasizes the changing cost structures when he attributes the growth of direct marketing in the past decade to two trends: 'In the early 1980s, two things began to happen simultaneously. Electronic data processing costs declined and marketing costs climbed, both dramatically'. These two curves crossed 'and this was the catalyst for European direct marketing's current growth'.

A brief examination of changing cost structures in the last five years appears to substantiate this view (Table 1).

The inflating cost of television and press advertising has been significant. Today, for example, an *average* television commercial costs around £150,000 to produce – a more 'glamorous' commercial may cost up to £500,000. In addition, airtime may cost around £1 million. As a result, marketers are being increasingly required to *measure* and *justify* their company's spends on advertising. Although it would be misleading to assume that direct marketing is *cheaper* than, for example, television advertising, direct marketing is inherently *measurable*. With the use of a customer database, it is always possible to trace back customers' responses to the original communication. Moreover, direct marketing may well require a similar amount of money to above-the-line advertising but, if the customer database is segmented effectively, the communications which result will be *targeted* to the right people at the right time. As people have become better at measuring the effects of advertising, they have become less impressed by the claims made by the vendors of the various media.

Cost justification was the primary reason behind the introduction of direct marketing to the Abbey National Building Society in 1985. The Abbey had a very large marketing budget which was mostly spent on above-the-line television and press advertising without any data about how the budget was actually performing. Since 1985, the direct marketing budget at least doubled every year until 1988. Although the overall budget has remained similar, more and more money has gone into direct marketing.

Rod Wright of Ogilvy & Mather Direct has pointed out that had there been an improvement in the productivity of conventional media, then nobody would have questioned the cost. Since these media have been 'increasing clutter (in terms of audience fragmentation) and no greater improvement in efficiencies – in terms of message and originality of usage', then major advertisers have started to ask whether a more *focused* audience cannot be reached in a more *efficient* way. As a result, 'people feel that they want to remove themselves from their dependency on above-the-line'.

The reality then is that there has been, in many companies, a re-evaluation of the role and efficiency of the various elements of the marketing mix, often resulting in increased importance being given to direct marketing.

Technological development

The third reason for dbm development relates to the changing technology. The combined forces of reduced computer costs and increased processing and storage capabilities mean that it has become increasingly feasible for a firm to harness the power of the computer to increase the effectiveness of its marketing communications. Increased amounts of data on individual customers can now be stored and

Table 1 Changes in cost structures

Percentage changes in cost		
	Office space costs	+300
	Sales call costs	+250
	TV advertising costs	+200
	Real computer time costs	−1400

(Source: Clark, 1989)

manipulated, thus increasing the targeting possibilities available to direct marketers. Moreover, the development of microcomputers has put the use of computers within the reach of small, as well as large, companies. Some typical prices serve to illustrate the range of technology available to all sizes of firm: the mainframe and mini-computers on the market today cost tens of thousands of pounds; while desktop microcomputers can be bought for less than £1000.

The range of computer software now available to direct marketers has increased the effectiveness of the process. Today a company can use internally produced or bought-in software packages to perform direct and database marketing functions. Database management systems have become increasingly flexible, and can allow non-programmers to access and manipulate data. Because of this, marketers can be closely involved in the direct marketing process which, in turn, may enhance marketing effectiveness. Additional software packages for market segmentation, analysis and forecasting, can make direct marketing communications even more targeted and precise. For example, the geodemographic classification systems of the market analysis companies – Mosaic, Superprofiles, PIN and Acorn – allow business-to-consumer marketers to overlay their own customer databases with additional data to find segments (or clusters) of customers with similar profiles.

As the direct marketing industry gradually matures, its practitioners are becoming increasingly proficient in their understanding of the concepts, and of how to *apply* them. Their effectiveness has thus been enhanced by technological development, although the theory of what direct marketing can do is far ahead of actual practice.

The improved targeting of direct marketing (together with more stringent data protection regulation) is helping to change the industry's public image which has for a long time been tarnished by the association with junk mail and intrusive phone calls. These are not, however, in themselves generic terms, but rather describe poorly targeted output. In the consumer market, figures suggest that direct mail has become a more acceptable way of buying goods. Various surveys have found that a very high percentage (normally over 65 per cent) of direct mail sent to the household is both opened and read. Direct mail from institutions already being dealt with was found to be better received. These findings are supported by the experience of the Royal Bank of Scotland: since introducing direct marketing, the Bank has found that if their *targeting* is right the majority of customers are interested to know about new products and product changes.

Many direct marketing agencies admit that clients have been worried about using direct marketing because of the industry's poor image. Increasingly, however, companies are being reassured by:

1. the improved industry image (although many problems do persist in this area);
2. most importantly, demonstrations of how properly targeted direct marketing can work for them.

Increased proficiency in direct marketing practice has thus been, and continues to be, a significant factor in the growth of direct marketing.

Changes in the market-place

Changing market conditions, both in business-to-consumer and business-to-business markets is the final area which has contributed to the growth of direct marketing. The impact of technological developments combined with general economic trends has produced a set of circumstances favourable to the adoption of dm. However, since 90 per cent of firms now use some form of direct marketing (*Direct Response*, June 1988), it could be said that there does *not* have to be a predisposition towards direct marketing within a company for the discipline to be applied successfully. As one expert has remarked, if a client has a clearly-defined target market, then there are usually good reasons to employ direct marketing: indeed, sometimes even when the target market is not clearly defined, this can be created. According to Andrew Boddington of Limbo, all types of client (whether financial services, consumer goods etc.) can benefit from data-based direct marketing in terms of communication, research and customer servicing. However, in different markets, these benefits will have different emphases.

Business-to-consumer markets

The 'decline of the mass market' is often cited as one of the main factors which is making direct marketing a desirable option for an increasing number of firms. A number of trends, including increased consumer sophistication and individuality and the rise of the single person family and household have resulted in a market-place of unprecedented diversity and choice, necessitating the development of radically new marketing strategies and models.

The *service proposition* is becoming increasingly important to firms. Corporate marketing, often dominated in the past by the concept of the 'unique selling proposition', is now moving towards the *small business philosophy* of staying close to customers, understanding and meeting their needs and treating them well after the sale. The key advantage brought by direct marketing communications to consumers is *personal recognition*; i.e., recognition of an individual's worth as a customer, to the company, now that the company is able to *service* the customer, often remotely (e.g. through direct mail or telephone sales).

Increased competition in many markets has meant that manufacturers must continually create new products in order to maintain and increase their market share. However, the flood of new products tends to *shorten* products' life spans. According to Shaw and Stone (1988), this trend supports the view that: 'in the long run, the only marketing asset a company has is its brand image in customers' minds.' Direct communication can be used as a means of both maintaining customer loyalty and generating revenue.

Finally, the flood of new products and services, together with changing consumer life-style, have made it more difficult and ineffective for distribution to be confined to traditional channels. The use of direct marketing can open up new channel possibilities, as with the Direct Line Insurance example previously given.

The impact of social and economic changes varies from industry sector to industry sector. Because of this, some sectors (such as financial services) have been quicker to exploit direct marketing than others (for example, product marketers and retailers). However, more and more sectors are now becoming service-based. Many of the *utilities* which are purely service businesses, faced with increasing competition, are now understanding their role in providing service to their customers. *Retailers* are also starting to understand that they are in the business of keeping customers – which is a service role. Experts predict that the major areas of new growth for direct marketing are likely to be in areas such as: large retailers, the travel trade, and associations with large memberships, who need to communicate with and provide services for their members.

Business-to-business markets

Changing market conditions have also been noted in business-to-business markets which have encouraged the growth of direct marketing. Depending on their particular industries, marketing managers either have experienced, or are experiencing the following (Schultz and Dewar, 1984):

1. An accelerating shift towards more complex and sophisticated products.
2. Growing purchase decision decentralization which has expanded the number of purchase decision influences almost geometrically, thereby complicating the selling process. Consequently, the length of decision time has increased: the time taken from initial contact to actually signing the order may be months or even years.
3. More sophisticated, computer-literate purchasers aided by desktop computers who are changing the buyer-seller relationship, putting the traditional salesperson at a disadvantage.
4. Increasing trade concentration in almost all categories which creates fewer customers and fewer prospects for more business-to-business sellers.

These factors mean that the modern industrial marketer requires a more *selective* customer communications strategy. Fewer customers mean that the marketer must aim to build *relationships* with those he does possess: this also involves paying more attention to customer needs when developing new products. The reduced effectiveness of the traditional salesman, combined with increased costs (the average call of a single salesman is now around £120), means that alternative methods of cold-calling have had to be found.

Industrial marketers have therefore turned increasingly to direct marketing for a number of reasons (David Kunna, *Direct Response*, November 1989). First, direct marketing is a far more *economical* method of cold-calling: compared with £120 for a single salesman's visit, you can post copies of a business list for around £500 per thousand (i.e., 50p per cold-call)! Secondly, direct marketing is a more *effective* way of cold-calling: it gathers and qualifies leads, establishes who the decision-makers are, and, through the use of a customer database, it builds relationships.

Thirdly, direct marketing enables a company to approach its sales and marketing tasks in a structured way: you can dictate who you speak to when and how often; you can alter your message and its emphasis to suit your audience.

An example of a company using these techniques is British Telecom who over the last five years have developed a sophisticated customer database and sophisticated direct marketing strategies. Direct marketing has been found to have more advantage in the business market, where there are a vast number of products and services to be marketed and one of the major spin-offs of the initiative has been in the *small business market*. Previously, salesmen had not had the time to visit these small businesses; and British Telecom was unwilling to make a massive increase in the field sales force to deal with them. The cost-effective way of reaching the market was using BT's own medium: the telephone. British Telecom set up groups in each of its districts called 'telephone account managers' who now manage groups of small businesses over the telephone, ringing them four times a year. Results, according to Philip Mounsel (Manager of Direct Marketing, Customer Communications) have been 'fantastic' in terms of sales and increased revenue. Attitudes towards BT are around 50 per cent better than average for BT; and 90 per cent of small businesses said that they would *like* to have their accounts managed over the telephone.

A second example is the Royal Mail who are in the process of developing a database which is enabling them to identify and understand their customers. According to Direct Marketing Product Manager Anne McOwat, customers have *told* the Royal Mail that they want to speak to the organization more. McOwat freely admits that, before database work was carried out, the Royal Mail did not know who some of their customers (including large companies) were! Databased direct marketing has enabled the Royal Mail to:

1. gain knowledge of individual customers;
2. take customer needs more into account in product development;
3. provide a better *service* to customers.

As a result of these changes, the Royal Mail predicted that 1990 would see a lot of new products coming from various parts of the marketing department.

INTEGRATING ABOVE- AND BELOW-THE-LINE CAMPAIGNS

'Integration' appears to be the newest buzzword in direct and database marketing. It has been argued here that direct marketing's full potential is only realized when it is given *strategic* consideration, and is used in conjunction with other media. If above-the-line advertising is also considered as a form of contact strategy (although a broadly targeted one), then the database can play a central role in co-ordinating above and below-the-line communications. Certainly, companies now appear to be using more media, with FMCG companies and banks beginning to make moves towards integration. According to Chris Jewell (Head of Marketing, Personal Sector) of the Royal Bank of Scotland, 'integration is a stated aim, and a philosophy we embrace. It is done whenever practical and sensible.' McCann Direct works closely with its above-the-line agency on an increasing number of projects.

However, according to several experts, the implications of integration are not being fully thought through. Integration means not only using the same pictures (or timing) for above and below-the-line work, but rather requires the tone, manner, style, purpose and proposition to be *extended* throughout the communications media. The huge potential of dbm for integration is thus, at present, largely unexplored.

The belief that 'database marketing is direct marketing done properly' is, as already noted, widely held. It is nevertheless a misleading point of view and is perhaps indicative of the general level of understanding of dbm techniques. As Roberts and Berger (1989) point out, marketing programmes designed to capitalize on the information available in the customer database will often involve direct *elements* simply because the database allows for the analysis and identification of individual customers, prospects or distributors. Database marketing involves using the database to solve a much wider range of problems.

Although direct marketing is a fundamental application, it is nevertheless only one of a wide range of applications of dbm. When the Automobile Association (AA) developed its current corporate database, the original objective was to drive direct marketing programmes. Increasingly, however, (according to Peter Mouncey) the database is seen as 'a major source of management information; that information will drive a whole range of applications'. For example, the AA now uses the CCN MOSAIC package to analyse the catchment areas of retail outlets. The AA has also developed a way in which it can help judge the effectiveness of above-the-line campaigns, by looking at net gains and losses of membership through MOSAIC (which holds the IBS boundaries).

Andrew Boddington of BBH Limbo also emphasizes the huge potential for using geodemographic software packages to analyse above-the-line media. Although such media selection is done on gut feeling, demographics can act as a good base: a marketer can equate his or her desired profile, for example, to the readership of the title, or the viewer profile of the television channels or slots that he or she wants to advertise in. As yet, the area remains largely unexplored; its development may be hindered by the vested interests of the media people.

Most importantly, however, database marketing offers extensive benefits when it is seen as a *marketing planning resource*. The database can generate a huge amount of market and customer data, thus reducing the need for market research. Indeed, campaigns (and questionnaires) can be designed to obtain the required information. A good example of such use is provided by the coupons used by some FMCG companies.

At its most sophisticated, then, database marketing has the potential to drive marketing policy.

CONCLUSION

The development and growth of database marketing techniques can be viewed either as an opportunity or a threat by the advertising industry. In any direct marketing campaign there will be three parties; the client, the agency, and the suppliers of a range of ancillary services. Unlike in mainstream advertising a client moving into direct marketing need not choose an agency. It may instead decide to use a small in-house team to co-ordinate the activities of various suppliers, or a large in-house team to manage all the necessary activities.

The potential complexities involved in using direct marketing as part of an overall strategic approach would seem to favour the use of a specialist agency or consultancy. However, this will depend upon the client's perception of its own strengths and, significantly, by the perceived quality of the services offered by the agency. If the American experience is repeated in the UK then both clients and agencies will have to reconsider their traditional promotional methods as techniques move away from mass communication approaches to targeted messages using modern technology to identify and isolate key individuals. This will require a major educational programme for all concerned, both clients and agencies.

ACKNOWLEDGEMENTS

This paper is based upon preliminary research funded by a research grant from the University of Strathclyde, UK. It involved a survey of expert opinion from both suppliers and users of direct and database marketing in the UK. The authors would like to thank the many people who through their time and effort contributed to the paper. The views expressed are however those of the authors.

REFERENCES

Baier, M. (1985) *Elements of Direct Marketing*. New York: McGraw Hill.
Clark, J. (1989) *What is Direct Marketing?* London: IBIS Direct Marketing Exhibition and Conference.
Fletcher, K. (1985) Health education and the new media. In *Health Education and the Media*. Oxford: Pergamon Press.
Gummesson, E. (1987) The new marketing – developing long term interactive relationships. *Long Range Planning*, 20, pp. 10–20.
Keynote (1988) *Direct Marketing* 2nd Edition. London: Keynote Publications.
Ogilvy & Mather Direct (1985) *Direct Marketing: New Opportunities for Business to Business Selling*. London: Ogilvy & Mather.
Roberts, M. & Berger, P. (1989) *Direct Marketing Management*. Englewood Cliffs. NJ: Prentice-Hall.
Rapp, S. & Collins, T. (1987) *Maxi-Marketing*. New York: McGraw Hill.
Shaw, R. & Stone, M. (1988) *Data Base Marketing*. Aldershot: Gower.
Schultz, D. & Dewar, R. (1984) Technological challenge to marketing management. *Business Marketing* (USA), 69, March, pp. 30–41.

Fletcher, K., Wheeler, C. and Wright, J. (1991) 'Database marketing: a channel, a medium or a strategic approach?'. *International Journal of Advertising*, 10(2): 117–127. Reproduced with permission.

Issues in customer information management 4.3

Keith Fletcher and Linda Peters

HOW AND WHY IS THE INFORMATION WORLD CHANGING?

The age old marketing concept – that the customer is king – has been given new life and new corporate relevance by the development of low cost, user-friendly(ier) computerised information systems. These driving forces have led to the birth of the activity known as 'database marketing'. The development of customer database information systems is seen by many as a necessary long-term strategic investment, particularly in sectors where corporate differentiation relies primarily on unique service delivery.

Marketing is concerned with customer relationships and IT is having a major impact in this area by changing both the nature of the relationship and the balance of power between the parties involved (Fletcher 1990). When viewed as a long-term investment for competitive advantage, the use of IT in sales allows a much closer customer relationship. However, as companies try to make use of this new technology, they are frequently hampered by a lack of relevant and comprehensive data on their customers, some lacking very fundamental details.

Increasingly companies using database marketing are building their own customer information files, constantly refining their knowledge of their customers and prospects and enhancing this information by gathering customer information during market transactions. The possible impact of this is a reduction in traditional market research using external agencies, and a clash between the two cultures and codes of conduct of database marketing and market research. Where the relationship between supplier and market moves towards electronic hierarchies – when IT is used, not simply to speed communication but to change business processes and introduce tighter coupling between firms sharing data (Malone *et al.* 1986) – issues of ethical conduct, regulation and legislation arise.

Trends in market research

Market researchers are increasingly concerned by a perceived loss of opportunity to provide desired services to their clients. Fletcher (1990) points out that a number of prominent market researchers have noted that information technology has the potential, not only to change the way in which data are collected, but also to change the structure of the market research industry with the use of external and internal database information gathering of behavioural data leading to a shift in emphasis in many firms away from the use of custom research.

Rose (1994) states that the continuous research sector in the UK has experienced fundamental changes, characterised by a move away from traditional market research approaches to the use of electronic databases and the technology and people which support them. This growth in primary data collection, that is data obtained directly from the source, has been facilitated by the use of computer technology and electronic media and is likely to increase dramatically, particularly with the growth in the channels through which these data can be collected.

Shepard (1990) predicts that the next major source of data, in addition to internal performance and external demographic or psychographic overlay data, will be individual level research data based on internally generated customer surveys. Quick (1994) comments that 'In today's fragmented, segmented markets individuals are behaving as individuals rather than simply as representatives of a household unit . . . Any marketer who believes in consumer-led marketing has the need, the requirement, an obligation to track continuously and rigorously the ultimate consumer or user of their brand.'

The impact of database capabilities upon traditional market research activities has been profound. Roberts (1992) states that 'Some aspects of traditional research are being supplanted by database marketing activities. The ability to collect, purchase, and use data as part of the sales or consumption process, for example, removes the necessity of collecting these data after the fact with all the attendant problems of reliability and validity. While the behavioural data that are the stock in trade of database marketing are extremely valuable, it does not preclude a need for attitudinal data which must still be collected by more traditional means'. There is a danger in this trend of losing the richness and wealth of experience which traditional market research techniques have developed in favour of simpler methods which may be more easily captured and processed by computer databases.

Conflict

A conflict arises between database marketing practices and market research when non-market researchers use traditional market research techniques to collect data on individuals for the purposes of marketing, but without sufficient notification to respondents that the information is not anonymised (known as 'sugging' – selling under the guise of research). This is not as straightforward a case of opportunistic behaviour on the part of database marketers as it might first appear. Many database marketers take great care in attempting to inform respondents of the purpose of their data collection. However, there is still a hot debate between marketers and market researchers on whether the general public sufficiently understands the difference between research and selling approaches, and the Database Marketing Association codes give only general guidance on the need to prevent sales approaches appearing to be research studies.

European and American codes of conduct in relation to each of the industries concerned, market research and database marketing, are broadly similar. It is not the intention of this study to address the similarities and differences of the respective codes, but to examine the conflict which arises between database marketing practices and market research practices when gathering information from respondents.

There have been recent attempts in the UK by The Market Research Society to address the issue of database use in market research. A special seminar was held in 1994 in which feedback and views, especially from client companies using databases, were solicited by members of the MRS Professional Standards Committee. These views were later incorporated into the production of a guideline document stressing the need for clarity and transparency of purpose in data collection.

The European Union Data Protection Directive, due for adoption in December 1995, states its objectives as: (1) the removal of obstacles to the free movement of personal data resulting from divergent national data protection laws and (2) assuring for every individual whose personal data are processed in the Community an equivalent protection of rights, in particular the right to privacy, wherever the processing is carried out (http://www.cec.iu/en/comm/dg15/datapro.html). The current status of market research companies in the UK gives them special exemption (under Method 2 registration) from compliance with the 7th principal of the Data Protection Act when carrying out confidential survey research. They are therefore not required to divulge to respondents the information which is held on them. These exemptions stem from the anonymised nature of market research information. It is therefore in the interest of the market research community to highlight and clarify the distinction between market research and database building activities.

The issues of confidentiality and privacy

One UK market research practitioner, Santry (1994), states that '. . . the emphasis is not on generating leads directly for the company but generating huge databases of personal information – data under the guise of research (*dugging* perhaps?)'. He points out that in the 1990s consumers do the selling, they sell their information. The short-term practices of some companies mean that people will make themselves more secure and less willing to participate, and information fortressing and misleading information will be the result. The issue of privacy is primarily an issue of control.

Our very concept of what constitutes privacy, and the legal safeguards necessary to ensure its protection, can be open to question. 'Private life is not something given in nature from the beginning of time. It is a historical reality, which different societies have construed in different ways. The boundaries of private life are not laid down once and for all; the division of human activity between public and private spheres is subject to change'. (Prost & Vincent 1991). While this highlights the challenge firms face in understanding the boundaries of privacy, it also confirms the notion of privacy as a socially negotiated construct which may, at least in part, be mutually defined by the parties involved.

Bowers (1994) states that 'Communicating these concerns is important both for the public and for the research industry. It is important for the public because the information we gather is used to understand the public's reaction to government policies and social and political events. It is also used to understand the public's preferences for products and services and the rationale for those choices . . . it is important for the research industry because we rely on public co-operation to gather information. We feel that we will get better co-operation when the public understands our interest in protecting both their identities and the information they contribute'.

Bickert (1992) warns marketers thus: 'As a last word of caution, the current data avarice, which is leading marketers to seek out and capture more and more personal information, has a definite downside. The more effective the information gathering, storage, and retrieval process becomes, the greater the tendency will be to encroach on individual privacy . . . At some point, marketers are likely to bump their heads on an effectiveness ceiling, where responsiveness [by consumers to direct marketing offers] increases no further without the addition of personal sensitive data to the analysis process. Maintaining the balance between information and individual privacy will be one of the important challenges in the 1990s'.

METHOD

The following study reports on primary data gathered from 18 in-depth interviews by the authors with senior managers in market research companies, database marketing related companies, and financial services (referred to as 'client') companies in both the USA (San Francisco) and the UK (London) between April and July 1994. The interviews explore a variety of expert opinions from those who, by virtue of their position within a company and the nature of the firm's business, found themselves at the forefront of current developments in both business practice and legislative concerns. The interview structure focused upon three main topics: (1) the impact of database marketing developments and activities upon the market research industry; (2) the perceived relationship between database marketing and market research activities; and (3) the ethical issues faced by practitioners, legislators and regulators, and the general public in the area of customer information management. All interviews were recorded and later transcribed for analysis. To avoid respondent identification or transparency, nationality is indicated only where the geographical context of their statements needs to be understood.

The majority of client companies interviewed had been building and using their databases for 15 to 20 years. However, the use of more sophisticated database marketing techniques was relatively recent, with three of the client companies in the process of establishing what in their view was a strategic database marketing system.

FINDINGS

Changing information collection and usage

The problems encountered by several of the firms interviewed in the development and use of information systems include the inheritance of accounting or product-based systems which were not customer focused, a 'system' as opposed to a 'user' focus in technology development, the collection of data rather than information, and the collection of information which was unrelated to decision needs. Commenting upon the needs which client companies were increasingly seeking database specialist services to fulfil, one respondent commented:

> 'Until recently people who bought our lists and our database clients were very different. Latterly the industries are converging. More companies are seeing data as mainstream to their activities. Very few companies are good at analysing data, and holding them properly . . . very few understand the data in their databases for marketing purposes'. (DBM respondent)

> 'From the other side of the coin, we sometimes ask clients if they can sort on a lifestyle basis, and I am still astounded by how few can. We most of us use the term database most of the time nowadays, but in effect an awful lot are still lists of name and address, and half of them don't even have telephone numbers'. (MR respondent)

In order to remedy this problem, several of the firms interviewed, particularly in the USA, have made extensive use of direct information sources, often redesigning application forms and other initial contact documents, to gather the needed data. In addition, they also turn to external information sources provided by companies such as Donnelley and Dun & Bradstreet. The provision of these data services reflects a growing change in the way information technology impacts upon both inter-firm and corporate/customer contact.

None of the client companies interviewed sold their customer data to outside parties, because of regulatory restrictions, their own industry codes of conduct, and a recognition that the passing of data to outside parties might undermine the relationships which they wished to build with their customers. However, the need was expressed for primary data from external sources, even where respondents recognised the superiority and wealth of data collected directly from customers by the company itself, as they felt them to be particularly useful in supporting marketing to non-customers, where contact has yet to be established.

Traditional marketing and sales communication systems are fast giving way, in many competitive environments, to more direct forms of customer contact. Recognition of poor customer knowledge (often the result of a proliferation of independent, account-based customer databases), the increased power of buyers through access to electronic-based markets, and competitive rivalry have all led to the interest in, and development of, database marketing, particularly within the financial services sector.

> 'It is a more effective communication with our customer and a more effective way to build relationships. We give the impression that we know our customer, we send appropriate communication. I think that they appreciate that because they know the other side of the coin'. (Client respondent)

Recognition of the importance of information management amongst firms is growing, together with the need to focus information collection and management to address corporate needs. Many of those in the survey felt that, while some firms are still collecting everything they can in the way of data on their customers, and trying to come to terms with the task of managing the volume and relevance of the data they collect to their businesses, they are driven by the feeling that they have no choice. In today's' business environment, those who do not reach a successful understanding of their information needs and the most cost-effective ways to fulfil them will find themselves out of business.

> 'As it [database information] gets more and more widely used, it gets more important that it is used properly'. (DBM respondent)

The hidden costs of holding and utilising data are beginning to be appreciated. The identification of, and concentration on, key characteristics about the firms' customers, an understanding of what makes them buy those particular products or services, is the prime aim of marketing decision makers. Many find that for every question asked, ten more are raised. Understanding what customer data can *do* for a company is becoming the key issue.

> 'We are able to do very sophisticated selections for mailings and inserts, but usually the marketing department responsible cannot make a decision as to who they want to include or exclude'. (Client respondent)

The ability to identify local specialist markets may indeed be a growth area for customer information management, working in tandem with centralised marketing communication strategies and new product development. As direct marketing activities increase, there is genuine concern for the quality of the data collected from individuals.

The assertion by Fletcher (1990) that information technology will impact the structure of the market research industry by exerting pressure for market research companies to polarise into large data factories or small specialist agencies was confirmed by the market research respondents in our study, with a shift in emphasis in many firms away from the use of custom research.

> '. . . we see that, where before some of our clients were spending 75% of their budget on custom research and 25% on database panel data, it is now sometimes almost the reverse – 75% of their time on panel data, database information, and 25% on the custom side'. (MR respondent)

Client company respondents, particularly in the USA, noted an increased desire amongst firms to modify market research data to incorporate customer and customer satisfaction data. Additionally they found an increase in the use of database information as a basis for commissioned market research.

One market research respondent in the USA commented that if the quality and relevance of client's company databases were better they could carry out surveys which were more useful to those companies. Most of the client company respondents stated that there were market research companies which took the trouble to understand their business in this way as opposed to simply providing a contracted service. The creation of corporate customer databases has made this an increasingly complex issue for all concerned.

The role of primary data in database development

While primary data collection was often the remit of market research, the collection of behavioural and demographic data has increasingly been carried out through database marketing means (either within firms by their marketing departments or through outside specialist service providers). The client companies interviewed identified a trend towards greater use of customer specific (as opposed to aggregated) research data, and a plan to incorporate customer satisfaction data into their customer information files on an identifiable basis. This of course means that market researchers working with these client companies may find themselves facing conflicts between their code of conduct (which prevents the disclosure of respondent identity) and corporate client needs.

One respondent in the survey commentated that we now live in a society where one must market to the lifestyles. The primary data gathered by market researchers, while valuable for directional guidance, have limitations for database marketing because of their anonymised nature.

One large client company interviewed, while admitting that lifestyle information was useful 'if you do not have anything better', puts a great deal of resources into developing its own internal segmentation model. This is particularly important where key information is not publicly available and must be gathered directly from customers, or inferred through anonymised market research on current customers.

Such proprietary database models can help firms focus their resources both in terms of distribution, advertising and communications, and new product development.

Commenting on the use of lifestyle data, one respondent stated that in relation to awareness of products and services, and customer's attitudes towards them, lifestyle data were not very relevant. Where fast information is needed to provide a fundamental understanding of what is going on then lifestyle data were seen as useful. However, this was understood to be the starting point rather than the end result of their database use.

Database marketing and market research conflicts

The database marketing practitioners interviewed for this study were universal in their desire sufficiently to inform and notify data subjects of intended data use, and in their concern to curb abusers.

While the database marketers interviewed felt in general that most consumers are able to make the distinction between selling approaches and true research the market researchers felt that this was not the case (one respondent stating that consumers were naive about database marketing data collection such as warranty cards). While several attempts at raising public awareness of the differences have taken place on both sides of the Atlantic, the effectiveness of these attempts were questioned by the market research respondents. In both geographic samples it was often seen as a question of cost, with the professional associations concerned lacking the resources to mount an effective campaign. This is compounded by the fact that both database marketing associations' codes themselves only give general guidance, and customers may not be informed at the point of data collection that their data are being collected or the purposes or uses to which they will be put.

Market researchers in the study were concerned by a perceived loss of opportunity to provide desired services to their clients, and had a concern over the standards of the alternative data suppliers.

How might market research and database marketing relate?

How should market research relate to database marketing? Southorn (1994) points out that even with respondent consent to disclose their identity to a third party (rule A.2 of the MRS Code), clause B2 of the Code does not allow market researchers to do this if there is a possibility that the information will be used for non-research purposes. In effect, there is one rule for researchers working within client companies (which may choose to wear their 'marketing' hat for such activities, as long as they do not promote a questionnaire which collects identified data as 'market research') thus allowing them to use their skills in the design, management and analysis of surveys to enhance a marketing database; and another for agency researchers who are unable to link their market research skills with database building. Agency researchers do not have this option since using the name of a market research company normally identified with anonymous research activities to promote a survey where the data will not be anonymous is equivalent to associating (by implication) the two activities. To work around this clause, some market research companies may set up another company alongside the research agency, handling any identified surveys through it. Alternatively, the market research company may provide data collection services for clients through its own staff resources, but indicate to the respondent that it is working on behalf of the client company, and not identify itself as a market research company. It could be argued that this last option may be difficult to implement in a company where staff are expected, at several organisational levels, to wear 'research' and 'marketing' hats alternatively.

When asked about the extent to which traditional market research work may be carried out internally by companies, utilising their own databases and staff research expertise, one respondent replied:

> 'That question is like "what is the future for market research?"; information is too valuable, they certainly can not contract it all out. For information providers, the practicality of it is that you need more analysts or more people who know what they are doing with information to make it valuable'. (DBM respondent)

This is not to say that anonymised market research is on the way out. Many companies felt that there were advantages to having an 'anonymous' face between themselves and their customers when collecting sensitive or personal data. Market research was seen to have other strengths as well:

> '. . . what it [database marketing] is not good at is a truly balanced, truly objective view of the overall market-place that pure market research can offer. Pure market research can help you with the [broader] decisions [i.e. determining overall market share], database marketing can help you, but if you are not very careful it can give you a bum steer. When it comes to [tactical] decisions [i.e. distribution, communications] each can apply, and very often the large samples of database marketing are actually far more robust . . .'. (DBM respondent)

While companies increasingly seek to develop individual level data on their customers, the importance of aggregate data on customer attitudes is recognised, and use is made of anonymised market research to gather such information.

> 'We are doing more and more market research into customer attitudes, and I see that as on-going. We will never pick that up from our product, we get lots of behavioural information but not attitudinal information. That is the biggest thing that we want'. (Client respondent)

When asked about the difficulty of gathering primary information from identified customers to validate, at household level, external overlay data – that is psychographic, demographic, behavioural and/or geographic information gathered through secondary sources – another respondent replied:

> 'It turns off the customers. You can only ask a certain amount . . . they are already queasy about giving information . . . They are pretty good about giving income and age in market research studies'. (Client respondent)

What then is the picture formed by these differing types of data, data collection methods, and data use in relation to confidentiality and privacy issues?

Confidentiality and privacy

The market researchers taking part in the survey were especially concerned about the falling response rates and potential for inaccuracy and unrepresentativeness that might result from the gathering of identifiable personal data, sometimes seen as simply gathered for their own sake.

Both business and legal communities have been unable to establish clear criteria for information collection and use which meaningfully differentiate between that which has the potential to be harmful and a threat to individual privacy and that which does not. As stated previously, the market research industry codes state clearly the need for respondent confidentiality in research surveys. How is this viewed by other related industries, and by customers themselves?

> 'The codes describe what we do, they do not determine what we do'. (MR respondent)

The maintenance of respondent confidentiality in research activities was seen as vital, indeed as a core research axiom, by all those interviewed, regardless of industry. It was recognised that research and selling activities are fundamentally different, and to confuse the public as to the purpose and intended use of data would be damaging to all concerned, limiting access to sensitive and attitudinal information through loss of public confidence and instigating tougher legislative restrictions on information gathering activities.

> 'You are probably going to get more accurate, objective comments when they are assured confidentiality'. (Client respondent)

> 'Market researchers seem to know that you need to be protective of a respondent's confidentiality and that [market research] reports that come with statistical qualifiers [for example limitations due to small response rates] can be interpreted in a number of ways; but they do not seem to work very hard at educating their own clients about these things'. (MR respondent)

Very often the issue of data collection is clouded by the feelings data subjects have regarding the compilation of public data. A great concern, particularly amongst respondents in the USA, is that restrictions on data gathering and use applied to the public sector will be imposed upon the private sector, although some regulation of the passing of information to third parties is seen as necessary by many of the USA respondents in the survey. In the UK, where the majority of restrictions apply to the private sector only, public outcries over privacy impact directly on the legislative environment of firms, even if the privacy concerns centre upon the fear of a 'big brother' like surveillance capacity being developed by public bodies. It is doubtful whether the UK public truly appreciates the extent to which public information consolidation and use goes unregulated.

Regulating methods of data collection

The availability of personal information on consumers is perhaps the most striking area of divergence between Britain and the USA. The US Freedom of Information act allows access to a wealth of data. However, consumer concerns over privacy have put the availability of data under threat, with several states now banning the sale of auto registration data, the core component of many database enhancements.

> '. . . in this type of environment for the most part, marketers and advertisers have not harnessed this type of information in a way that is of benefit to

consumers . . . I would hope that one day I would actually get a solicitation that was relevant to me . . . I worry that with even more regulations that it will impede the ability to allow that to happen'. (Client respondent, USA)

With the development of information superhighways, the flow of information will increasingly become two-way. Information will become available to consumers through new channels, but the use of these electronic channels will also facilitate the flow of information the consumer broadcasts to companies, a fact not yet fully appreciated by the general public. A case in point is the widespread use in the USA of reverse telephone directories, which can identify the name and address of incoming callers.

'First, the whole electronic management of data has become more powerful, it is easier to collect and manipulate data. Secondly, regarding the resistance to intrusion of organisations for data collection and use, we should make it more difficult to collect data without data subject permission, like scanner data [which are collected as part of the transaction without specific permission from the data subject]'. (MR respondent)

The issue of data collection is, understandably, the key area of divergence in both views and practice between market researchers and database marketers.

'I have to speak out of both sides of my mouth; as an individual I want more privacy, as a researcher I want less privacy, because the more we can know about an individual the more effective our marketing programmes can and will be'. (Client respondent)

The extent to which traditional and legitimate opinion collection may be limited by regulation is of concern both in Europe and the USA. Various restrictions on initial contact without prior consent are being explored by both legislative communities, with worrying effects upon the ability of market researchers to obtain representative samples for opinion gathering. Even large respondent panels, collecting and recording large amounts of behavioural and attitudinal data, are still self-selected and therefore not randomly sampled, an important consideration when generalising research results.

'Access to data collection by market research organisations is the key issue . . . it is a matter of deep concern and the issues have become clouded by so many issues brought on by other organisations, that the central issue of being able to collect data for legitimate opinion collection purposes is being limited in a serious way by these other secondary issues that I think are very minor . . . we must make sure that legislators get the message about the importance of being able to collect that kind of information and that they are not trying to sell a product or develop information about the individual'. (DBM respondent)

While the opt-in approach (where express consent is given by the individual for data use) is now being replaced in legislative thinking in Europe by the opt-out approach (where consent to data use is implicitly given unless the individual formally requests to be excluded), this does lead to an 'all or nothing' situation for consumers. A targeted opt-out scheme, giving consumers the opportunity to specify areas of interest where direct marketing would be welcomed, was experimented with in the USA (which has always favoured the opt-out option), but was too costly to maintain.

> 'The last point is that if people know that they can stop something they don't always want to stop it. It is the uncertainty about what is happening that is worrying, not the actual thing that happens'. (DBM respondent)

Regulation of the transfer of data to third parties

There are three approaches to information use in relation to customer privacy issues: (1) the anonymised approach of market researchers where individual identity is not disclosed; (2) identity-specific customer information which is specific to, and only utilised by, a particular company; and (3) identity-specific data which are made available to third (or outside) parties. This third area, usually associated with list-broking activities, is increasingly including customer specific omnibus surveys jointly carried out by two or more companies the identities of which are not always disclosed to respondents. While respondents are told that their name may be passed on to companies interested in marketing to them, and are given the opportunity to opt-out of such use, they are often unaware of which these companies may be. The issue of satisfactory notification was recognised by all those interviewed as a difficult one.

> 'I would like to see one day all letters where a company has rented in a list saying "we have got your name from X" and name them. If you said that then the consumer would feel in control'. (DBM respondent, UK)

While opt-out rates vary from one type of individual to another, and from one type of list to another, many feel that where companies are transparent about intended data use the customer is more receptive to disclosure.

> 'If you feel that you are being intruded upon by a corporation which has access to knowledge that they shouldn't have access to, it will have an impact. Right now, the corporations are hidden behind a curtain, and the curtain is the third party vendor'. (Client respondent)

The curtain has been increasingly raised on the secretive practices of some direct marketers, often much to the relief of those currently in the industry. All interviewed agreed that in order to gain public confidence, and the level of information needed adequately to target direct marketing activities, database marketing practitioners must disclose sufficient information to consumers regarding data use. The impact of legislation and self-regulation upon the direct marketing industry is seen by many practitioners as a necessary step in raising standards and gaining public confidence. Making very sensitive data available to direct marketers can have laudable benefits. One respondent cited the example of a list made available to marketers of children's products of parents who had recently lost a child, which was used as a suppression device to exclude such parents from their mailings. However, the difficulty in such data availability is the problem faced by legislators in determining who might have legitimate use for such data, and the problem of self-regulatory bodies in exercising sufficient control over abuse. Particularly in the USA, the desire to allow freedom of information and the need to control its abuse is being impacted by a reactionary tendency on the part of consumers concerned about privacy.

'. . . in terms of regulation I usually understand it as a consumer before I want it as a business person . . . the right to privacy supersedes the right a business has to obtain that information'. (DBM respondent)

The problems faced by self-regulation

Of concern in the USA is the feeling on the part of client companies that the self-regulatory bodies in the market research and direct marketing industries lack both the will and the means to stem abuse.

'The adherence to good taste and respect for customers is often just driven by the bottom line . . . that is the ultimate conflict because they [market research and database marketing companies] are not going to lose the consumer, they are just compiling information'. (Client respondent, USA)

'Because there is a bad track record for co-operative organisations and their control of the "outlaws", the outlaws will always be outlaws, so I can be a direct marketer and I don't have to pay attention to the DMA and its code of conduct, and I won't. So it is up to the lawyers to say "you cannot do that". And even then the outlaws are going to do things until they get caught, prosecuted and put in jail'. (Client respondent, USA)

The co-operation and standardisation of regulations across the market research and database marketing industries would increase the self-regulatory control of these activities, and signal to all concerned a willingness to address these issues. The self-regulation of the direct marketing industry in the UK is amongst the most effective in Europe. The complexity of the issues however makes legislation difficult, and the ability to regulate the diversity of direct marketing activities requires the concerted efforts of a number of self-regulating bodies.

One potentially important development in database marketing regulation in the UK is the increase in participation of individuals within professional association membership through the Institute of Direct Marketing. This may lead to a greater sense of individual accountability and facilitate the development and training of practitioners in acceptable direct marketing methods. It may also encourage corporate responsibility in addressing issues of conduct, understanding that corporate credibility is contingent upon individual as well as corporate behaviour. The knowledge that personal professional credibility is linked to individual behaviour is a powerful motivator is maintaining industry standards.

Is there an ethical conflict?

It is important to note that respondents in the survey felt, on the whole, that there was no conflict between the two industries when good practice prevailed and the difference between selling and research was made clear and adhered to. It was in the area of defining what constitutes 'good practice' in each industry that conflicting views between respondents arose.

'. . . it really is important for the market research and database marketing industries to get together. If we could get together we could form rules that both of us could live with. Market researchers could then dip their toes into a revenue potential which could transform the prospects of the industry ethically. In response, the market research industry could have a crack at influencing the standards of those of us using questionnaires . . . It is imperative that we get together'. (DBM respondent)

'All these issues are going to cause the consumer to want more information, and want to know more about what is happening. They will want to know the detail and the mechanics behind things that previously they haven't cared about . . . I am sure in general those [companies] which address it positively will benefit; the consumer will understand at the end of the day and will accept it'. (Client respondent)

'I wish I could come up with some brilliant close to all this but . . . my motivation is better to match needs with services so that everybody wins. I do not think that has really been achieved to the extent that it should . . . There are not a lot of people who have figured out how effectively to do this yet'. (Client respondent)

CONCLUSION

Many of the writers on database marketing have predicted a decline in external market research agency use by companies with the growth in their own database marketing capabilities. While this may be valid in the sphere of behavioural data collection, insufficient attention has been paid to the effect of consumer attitudes towards privacy, and the consequent legislation and regulation which results. This paper set out to explore three main areas of concern relating to interactions between database marketing activities and market research activities. First, exploring the impact of database marketing developments and activities upon the market research industry revealed that:

- Increasingly, companies are utilising database marketing techniques and sources to gather purchase behaviour and demographic information on their customers and potential customers. However, their need for attitudinal data (which is increasing) is still primarily fulfilled by market research providers.
- Companies are increasingly able and willing to interrogate their own customer information, and to 'customerise' market research data. This will lead to a greater need for the strategic skills of market researchers, but also highlights the divergent approaches of these two disciplines in relation to customer information management issues.
- Market research is being forced to move from an historical perspective – 'what was' – to a more innovative and future orientated approach – 'what if'. This will open up the possibility of an enhanced role in new product development and strategic decision support for those market research companies able to meet these needs. This also highlights the need for greater business orientation in market research training.

Secondly, exploring the relationship between database markcting and marketing research activities revealed that:

- An understanding has yet to be gained about the true difference between market research and database marketing relationships with customers and respondents. These activities fall at opposite ends of the relationship continuum, with market research tending to focus on discrete respondent 'transactions' and database marketing focusing on long-term relationship building with the individual.
- Market research data are important components in customer information management; they can lead to database marketing activities being less 'sales' and more 'marketing' orientated through the inclusion of attitudinal data.
- Database marketers and client market research users both recognise and appreciate the value of market research skills as a core competency in the strategic use of customer information.
- Market researchers and database marketers see an increased need for cross-discipline training.
- The benefits and competencies of market research – its role in supporting database marketing information and the importance of its underlying basis of anonymised information – needs to be promoted and elucidated to the customer information management community and to the general public as a whole.

Thirdly, in exploring the ethical issues faced by practitioners, legislators and regulators, and the general public in the area of customer information management it was revealed that:

- The database marketing and market research communities were not in conflict where it was felt that the fundamental difference between their aims – selling and research respectively – was made clear. The prime difficulty lay in the establishment of clear guidelines to differentiate these activities in the minds of all concerned, and in particular with the general public.
- It was recognised that information devolution within organisations will make such issues of greater concern, and will require a more focused approach to assigning responsibility for customer relationship development within organisations.
- Concerns over information availability and quality were shared by all those interviewed. The questions of sufficient notification, intent of use, and data subject control over their data collection and use were recognised as complex, and guidance from legislators and regulators was seen as important.
- Respondents all shared a frustration at their powerlessness to curb abusers, and the lack of political will and support in this area.
- Respondents felt that greater co-ordination and co-operation was needed between the legislative and regulatory bodies and practitioners to address these issues.
- These ethical issues were experienced by respondents at a very personal level. Should such issues fail to be addressed by political and business communities, the growth in corporate and public cynicism in this area could well mar its future development.

These findings, together with the future developments outlined for both the database marketing and market research industries, point to an increasingly important role for both activities as companies focus their marketing and strategic efforts upon the development of longer-term relationships and away from more isolated sales approaches. However, if a more co-ordinated and co-operative effort is not made by all parties concerned to address the ethical issues inherent in customer relationship management activities, the future of this effective and interesting area of marketing may well be constrained by ad hoc and reactionary legislative activity. This would indeed be a loss to us all.

REFERENCES

Bickert, J. (1992). *Database marketing: an overview.* In E. L. Nash, *The Direct Marketing Handbook*, (2nd Ed.) McGraw-Hill.

Bowers, Diane (1994). RIC promotes professionalism. *Marketing Research*, 6, 3.

Fletcher, Keith (1990). *Marketing management and information technology.* Hertfordshire: Prentice Hall.

Malone, T., Yates, J. and Benjamin, R. (1986). Electronic markets and electronic hierarchies. Centre for information System Research, MIT, April.

Prost, A. and Vincent, G. (Eds.) (1991). *A history of private life.* Belknap Press, Harvard.

Quick, G. (1994). You know who buys – do you care who uses? *Research Plus*, March.

Roberts, Mary Lou (1992). Expanding the role of the direct marketing database. *Journal of Direct Marketing*, 6, 2.

Rose, James (1994). An info revolution is overtaking MR. *Research Plus*, March.

Santry, Eamonn (1994). *Research*, 337, June.

Shepard, D. (1990). *The new direct marketing.* David Shepard Associates. New York: Irwin Publishing.

Southorn, C. (1994). The anonymity principal. *Research*, 338, July.

Fletcher, K. and Peters, L. (1996) 'Issues in customer information management'. *Journal of the Market Research Society*, 38(2), April: 145–160. Reproduced with permission.

4.4

The role of organizational factors in the adoption and sophistication of database marketing in the UK financial services industry

Keith Fletcher, George Wright and Caroline Desai

INTRODUCTION

Marketing is currently undergoing a transformation. In recent years mass marketing techniques have been shown to be increasingly expensive and less effective as customer markets fragment. Customers' affluence, increased demands, and the greater availability of choice have all contributed to increasing fragmentation of markets and have been influential in transforming marketing. Central to this transformation has been the growing trend to develop a relationship with customers using information technology applications. Webster (28:1) noted that 'customer relationships will be seen as the key strategic resource of the business.' Companies are centering business around the customer, moving as McKenna (18:75) described, from 'monologue to dialogue,' integrating the customer into the company for competitive advantage.

The view that competitive advantage can be gained through the strategic application of information technology is not a new one. Some authors (21, 22) have presented the idea of information technology as a strategic weapon. What is new to marketing is the increasing importance of information technology and, more significantly, the value of information obtained through information technology as an asset to companies in its own right (12).

The financial services sector in the UK is currently at the forefront of those who approach information technology in marketing as a strategic tool. This sector has focused strongly on database marketing as an expansion of direct marketing activities.

Database marketing

As companies increasingly face the challenge of moving from monologue to dialogue with customers, the use of direct marketing has increased. Direct marketing, still strongly linked to direct mail, can be applied to other media such as telephone sales.

Companies aim to communicate more effectively and efficiently by approaching target customers directly. Because it is oriented toward receiving a response, direct marketing has become particularly attractive, as the results of a campaign can be measured directly.

Concurrent developments in computer software and hardware have enhanced the dialogue with customers. For example, a database of customer information files can be used to enhance direct marketing techniques by maintaining an active list of prospects and customers. At its most basic level database marketing (DBM) is a tactical tool. As the sophistication of the database increases, more information is held until a customer information file with detailed, strategic information evolves. This information can be applied to strategic effect with applications beyond direct mail. The core of database marketing is the customer information file. Technology allows the customer information files to be enhanced so that the customer database provides a sophisticated means of communicating efficiently and effectively to a clearly defined target. Replies can be recorded in the database, adding to the value of the information held and again allowing targeting to be adjusted and refined if needed. Fletcher, Wheeler, and Wright (9:133) suggested that DBM is 'a new approach to marketing . . . requiring a redefinition of the relationship between a company and its customers.'

For firms, the attractiveness of using DBM lies in a number of characteristics. First, DBM facilitates communication, a dialogue between customer and company that can be recorded and analyzed over time. This forms the basis of a more effective relationship and efficient targeting. It also leads to the development of a long-term relationship with customers. Second, DBM is the source of critical information on customers and markets, the basis of improved decision making. Third, the information, if maintained, is a major strategic tool providing an opportunity to gain a strategic advantage over competitors by better use of marketing information internally, and greater awareness of the market.

Issues

The use of DBM
Direct marketing is frequently the impetus behind the growth of DBM, and there is evidence that interest in both is growing in the financial services sector of the United Kingdom (9). From 1990–1992, Mayes (16) estimated an eight percent increase in the growth of direct marketing in the financial services sector, and other reports (6) suggest this trend is set to continue. This survey sought to establish the current scale of use and sophistication of DBM in the financial services sector.

The strategic state of DBM
DBM is an application of information technology that has both tactical and strategic uses. Shaw and Stone (26) and Fletcher (7) have argued that DBM can play a strategic role and give competitive advantage only when correctly developed. Without the sustainable competitive advantage that can be gained through using DBM applications to change competitive forces, the initial high cost of DBM cannot be justified.

The capability of firms to enter the strategic phase of DBM use can be said to depend on existing levels of information technology operations (11, 17, 19) and the strategic and organizational context within which decisions are made and implemented.

Organizational context includes organizational culture, decision-making modes, and interactions within the structure and with the outside world. Organizational factors specifically affecting successful implementation of DBM have been suggested by Fletcher *et al.* (9): notably, a marketing and information orientation, investment justification, and the role of organizational barriers.

Despite the major changes currently underway in marketing and the growing interest in the use of strategic information technology to gain competitive advantage, King, Grover, and Hufnagel (14) noted the lack of empirical research into the area of using information technology for competitive advantage. Sabherwal and King (24) later commented that empirical research has focused on information systems related factors, with less attention being paid to organizational and environmental factors. Although insights into the impact of contextual factors have been provided by case approaches such as Knights and Murray's (15), there is a need to support insights with large-scale empirical research, rather than in-depth single-case studies as argued for by King *et al.* (14) and Sabherwal and King (24).

This article empirically tests the relationship of these organizational variables with both adoption and the level of sophistication of a specific information technology innovation, DBM systems, in the UK financial services industry.

ORGANIZATIONAL FACTORS

The focus of this article is to measure organizational variables and relate them to the use and sophistication of strategic information systems in marketing. This survey sought to establish the scale of use and nonuse of DBM in the financial services industry, and to identify the organizational factors influencing use and nonuse of DBM. Of those companies using DBM, organizational factors influencing the degree of sophistication are also explored. Understanding the ways in which organizational variables relate to information systems, we hope to identify those organizational factors crucial in the adoption and subsequent development of sophisticated information technology applications.

The following outlines those organizational factors identified on the basis of an extensive review of the literature as important in the adoption and sophistication of information technology. As such, they present the foundation of the organizational variables examined here. The questions used in measuring variables are listed in the Appendix.

The organizational issues explored are broadly defined in six areas: the size and complexity of the organization, the structure of the organization, the organization's decision-making style, the organizational culture, attitudes toward resources, and the connections held within the company and with the outside world.

Size and complexity

Previous research has found that size is positively related to innovation (23). David (4) and Davies (5) proposed models that put forward organizational size as a critical determinant of adoption of information technology applications. While smaller firms may be more innovative, they do not necessarily have the resources to adopt strategic information technology. This is supported by Nooteboome (20), who argued that earlier innovations requiring higher capital outlays are the domain of larger firms; however, he then stated that later innovations requiring flexibility are more likely to be the domain of smaller firms. As DBM in the financial services sector is a mainframe-based application and expensive, it is likely to be within the financial capacity of only larger firms. Size can be expected to be a factor in adoption.

Organizations vary in the skills they possess and how they are integrated. The complexity of an organization was defined by Rogers (23) as the degree to which the organization's members possess a high level of knowledge and expertise, expressed by professionalism and formal training. Therefore, the presence of formally trained marketing, information technology, and direct marketing staff is likely to aid adoption and sophistication.

Structure

In this article, the term *structure* relates to the hierarchy and power in organizations, which would impact information technology development. We focused on centralization, formalization, and the power of direct marketing.

Centralization reflects the degree to which decision making is concentrated with a few individuals. Rogers (23) found that centralization initially inhibited innovation, but could be helpful once innovation was in place. Adopters have been found to be decentralized relative to latter adopters (2), although these findings have been disputed (10). We anticipated that centralization might inhibit adoption of DBM, but be likely to lead to greater sophistication once adopted, as this would allow for a standardized approach to developing technologies.

Formalization refers to the degree to which rules and procedures are followed in an organization. John and Martin (13) found a positive relationship between formalization and implementation of innovative programs. As creative responses are frequently required in marketing, excessive formalization of rules and procedures may inhibit consideration of innovative responses such as the adoption and sophisticated development of DBM.

As previously noted, direct marketing is seen as a precursor to the development of DBM. Within the structure of an organization the amount of power given to direct marketing was thought to influence the likelihood that DBM would be adopted and its development given a high priority.

Style of decision making

Organizations, particularly those in the financial services industry, currently face difficult choices when confronted with rapid technological change. Organizations can choose whether to make a revolutionary jump to an advanced stage of information technology sophistication, or take smaller, slower, incremental steps. The first approach is riskier but holds first-move advantages. The second, incremental approach allows organizations to consolidate before moving on, but in periods of rapid change they risk being left behind by competitors. Those organizations more incremental in their decision making are expected to be less likely to adopt strategic technologies such as DBM. Less incremental decision makers are expected not only to adopt DBM earlier, but also to display a greater degree of sophistication.

Organizational culture

Culture is a system of values and beliefs operating within the company. The two aspects of culture relevant here are *marketing orientation* and *information orientation*. Fletcher *et al.* (9) identified these two variables as being relevant to the successful implementation of DBM.

If a firm is to make the customer the center of the organization's thinking and activity, then implementation of the marketing concept is required (1). DBM is a specialized form of marketing that focuses on the customer and does so by harnessing information technology, making it easier to make customer-related marketing decisions. The degree to which marketing is accepted as an orientation, therefore, determines whether DBM will be recognized as a significant need within the firm, leading to both adoption and increased sophistication.

The second element, an information orientation, is essential because it provides the backbone of strategic planning and decision making. Information will enhance marketing and can be seen to be a separate but complementary orientation. Companies with high information orientations are expected to be more likely to accept the importance of strategic information technology such as DBM and support its use.

Resources

The availability of money and other resources will have a strong impact on information technology. These were considered along two dimensions, slack and control.

Slack (3) refers to the degree of uncommitted resources available in the organization. As the cost of systems is a heavily constraining factor in the development of information technology (8), slack may be an enabling factor for the adoption of DBM and other information technology applications.

Nolan (19) suggested that the level of *control* placed on information technology developments was an important organizational factor influencing development. A balance between strict control over resources and flexibility is needed to allow focused innovations to develop. It is anticipated that those organizations with less control will be more likely to adopt innovative information technology. The two resource requirements for marketing to develop DBM are access to computing facilities and the gathering and storage of information in a customer information file.

Connections

Rogers (23) commented that the interconnectedness of a system and its openness are associated with innovation. *Internal* and *external networks* allow the exchange of ideas within the company and with the external environment. The boundary-spanning role of information technology can therefore be developed to create new opportunities. The existence of networks is expected to relate positively to DBM adoption and sophistication.

METHODOLOGY

The financial services industry

The financial services industry served as the focus of this study as an industry actively investing in information technology in marketing. Having experienced rapid change since deregulation in 1986 in terms of competition and customer expectations, the financial services industry has shown growing interest in DBM as a means of achieving success. Furthermore, research into the use of DBM in the financial services industry has been limited. Indeed, Thwaites and Lee (27) noted the lack of attention paid to direct marketing activities in the financial services industry in the past decade, despite its growing importance. The same lack of attention can be noted for DBM in the financial services industry.

The survey

The basis of this study was a sample of all major banks, building societies (savings and loan institutions), and insurance companies in the UK financial services market. This included the largest 180 life and general insurance companies (by gross premium income), the largest 44 building societies (selected by total assets), and the largest 28 banks (selected by net income and operating income measures).

A detailed 12-page questionnaire was sent to named information technology and marketing directors. Two mailings resulted in 109 usable responses, covering 86 of the sampled firms (49%). For surveys of this type in this industry, this is considered a good response rate. Questions designed to measure the organizational variables described are outlined in the Appendix.

To measure the extent of DBM use, respondents were first asked if they used direct marketing, defined in the questionnaire as 'an interactive system of marketing based on a mailing list which uses one or more marketing media to effect a measurable response and/or transaction at any location.' Respondents answered yes or no to this question. DBM was then defined as follows: 'Database marketing stores this response and adds other customer information (lifestyles, transaction history, etc.) on an electronic database memory and uses it as basis for longer term customer loyalty programmes, to facilitate future contacts, and to enable planning of all marketing.' Respondents then noted whether they had or did not have such a system.

To measure sophistication of DBM use, respondents provided a subjective assessment of their company DBM sophistication using questions on a seven-point attitude scale. Objective measures of sophistication were achieved by a count of the number of types of results of campaigns measured, a count of the amount of information held in the customer information file, and a measure of the degree to which the 'virtuous circle' of planning, implementation, and control was complete (25). All four measures correlated positively, indicating that the subjective measure of the sophistication of DBM use was valid. From this point it was possible to correlate DBM sophistication with organizational factors.

Responses were analyzed using the SPSS statistical computer package. Users and nonusers were compared using the Mann-Whitney U statistic and t tests. Correlations between variables and sophistication were obtained using the Spearman rank correlation coefficient.

FINDINGS

DBM use

Direct marketing was used by 75 percent of the firms, confirming its importance to the industry. When questioned about having DBM, 54 percent of the firms claimed to have a DBM system. These two findings reflect the continuing investment in below-the-line direct marketing activities, often at the expense of traditional media, commented on by practitioners. There is still substantial room for growth of DBM. Firms that wish to improve their direct marketing capabilities by storing response data on customers and prospects will need to move from purchased mailing lists to more carefully selected and profiled analyses of customers and prospects. This will require a DBM system. As the market continues to change and more firms adopt direct marketing techniques, these trends are likely to continue.

Adoption is not sufficient for strategic use of DBM, as the system may not yet be capable of strategic applications. This was true for many firms because the self-assessed measure of sophistication obtained from those companies with a DBM system was low. A mean sophistication level of 3.4 ($SD = 1.8$) was noted on a seven-point scale. The implication is that in the financial services industry, DBM is mainly being used as a tactical tool.

Organizational factors and users and nonusers of DBM

A number of differences in organizational characteristics between the users and the nonusers of DBM were found to be significant. These are presented in Table 1. As predicted, the findings show that DBM users are more likely to be larger organizations. This would support the view that larger companies are able to finance large information technology investments such as DBM. Users of DBM also employed more people in the marketing and direct marketing functions. The fact firms with larger direct marketing departments were more likely to adopt DBM supports the view that the presence of direct marketing activity is often a precursor to DBM adoption, and its development will help DBM.

In terms of complexity, the measure of the extent of formal qualifications held by marketing, information technology, or direct marketing personnel was not significantly related to DBM adoption. At the adoption stage, it would seem the existence of marketing and direct marketing functions is critical, rather than the qualifications held by these personnel.

Structure, as investigated by formalization, centralization, and direct marketing power, was not found to be significantly related to DBM adoption. It would appear that these issues do not impact on the adoption of DBM as anticipated. However, the style of decision making was significant. Organizations that adopted DBM were less likely to show incremental decision making. The willingness of organizations to make jumps in their information technology investment decisions would seem, therefore, to be a key factor in the adoption of DBM.

Marketing orientation and information orientation differed among adopting organizations. DBM users demonstrated a significantly higher degree of marketing orientation and information orientation. This supports the view that if the organization does not have a basic marketing orientation, DBM is not likely to be understood or pursued as a source of competitive advantage. DBM also represents a valuable source of customer information. Firms without an information orientation are unlikely to realize the value of information as an asset in its own right, and therefore are unlikely to be willing to adopt DBM. It is an important reminder that applications of information technology in marketing, such as DBM, in themselves do not create success but are driven by context. An understanding of the importance of marketing and the value of information reflect the culture of the organization. In the case of DBM adoption, the culture of the organization needs to reflect two key variables: a marketing orientation and an information orientation.

In DBM organizations, compared with non-DBM organizations, the degree of organizational slack was greater. This meant that resources were available to the marketing function for information technology developments such as DBM. Additionally, the level of control placed on marketing in terms of resources needed for DBM (computing and storage) was less in those firms using DBM. Firms that used DBM, therefore, can be said to allow a greater degree of self-control in their marketing functions. This clearly represents a supportive organizational context for strategic IT applications to develop.

The extent of formal and informal networks was not found to be related to the adoption of DBM. Possibly the effects of information technology in the form of networks will only become apparent once DBM is in place. Networks may be an effect of DBM rather than bringing about the adoption of DBM.

Firms wishing to adopt DBM need to consider the role that their organization will play in adoption. Size will be an advantage because of the resources required, as will the existence of a direct marketing department. It is best to make a definite and complete move to DBM, rather than hoping to slowly and incrementally move into DBM. The latter approach will delay the adoption and leave firms at a disadvantage to their more decisive competitors.

Once made, the decision to adopt DBM needs support in the form of resources, particularly access and control over computing resources. DBM adoption is unlikely to occur if computing facilities and any other resources are not freely and openly available. Adopting DBM is not purely a matter of decision making and resources: Organizational culture and context play critical roles. Those firms that adopt DBM are more likely to be oriented to marketing concepts and the value of information.

Organizational factors and sophistication of DBM

Having identified variables influencing the adoption of DBM, we sought to investigate any organizational differences between companies with high levels of sophistication in DBM and those with low levels of sophistication. Self-assessed and objective measures of sophistication indicated that average levels of sophistication were low. Table 2 presents the results of correlations between organizational factors and levels of sophistication of DBM use.

Organizational size as a whole was found to be unrelated to DBM sophistication. Direct marketing size, as reflected in the number of people employed in the function, although significant in the adoption of DBM, was not correlated to sophistication. Whereas direct marketing is often a precursor to DBM development, size in itself is not sufficient to lead to sophistication.

Table 1 Comparison of the organizational differences between users and nonusers of DBM

Organizational variables measured	Question no.[a]	Non-DBM users	DBM users	U or t
Size	1	2,792	5,987	U = 1104*
	2	61	177	U = 912**
	3	154	335	U = 1114
	4	3	43	U = 649***
Complexity	5	3.5	3.3	U = 660
	6	2.4	3.1	U = 311
	7	3.7	4.1	U = 504
Structure				
Centralization	8	5.9	6.1	U = 1237
Formalization	9	4.1	4.0	U = 1390
	10	3.6	3.2	U = 1201
Direct marketing power	11	30.4	33.0	t = 1.16
Style				
Incremental decision making	12	32.3	29.8	t = 1.9*
Culture				
Marketing orientation	13	61.9	66.6	t = −1.892*
Information orientation	14	46.0	66.3	t = −7.09**
Resources				
Slack	15	3.0	3.7	U = 1050**
	16	3.2	4.2	U = 932***
Control	17	5.1	4.7	U = 1144*
	18	5.1	4.4	U = 1022**
Connections				
Internal networks	19	5.0	5.3	U = 1248
	20	5.5	5.4	U = 1390
External networks	21	4.0	4.3	U = 1262
	22	4.5	4.1	U = 1234

[a]See Appendix
*$p < .05$. **$p < .01$. ***$p < .001$.

The complexity of the organization, not significant in adoption, was partly correlated to sophistication. The extent of formal qualifications held by the marketing and DM functions were found to be positively related to sophistication ($\rho = .025$, $p < .05$, $\rho = .024$, $p < .05$, respectively). The qualifications held by information technology personnel were not correlated with sophistication. The sophisticated, strategic use of DBM requires that firms have a fuller understanding of the potential of DBM and how to use it. Formal qualifications in marketing and direct marketing would be likely to contribute to understanding and developing the potential of DBM from a marketing perspective. The fact that understanding at a formal level from a marketing perspective is significant, and not information technology, reiterates the view that the success of DBM depends mainly on understanding its potential as a strategic marketing tool and not as an information technology function.

Of the structural measures, neither the degree of centralization in decision making, nor one of the measures of formalization (the degree to which rules and procedures are followed in decisions), was correlated to sophistication or adoption. Direct marketing power, although not related to adoption, was strongly correlated with sophistication ($\rho = .42, p < .001$).

It may be the case that the centralization and formalization aspects of organizational structure are not important until fairly high levels of sophistication have been achieved. One measure of formalization that emphasized the encouragement of creative responses (Question 10) revealed a negative correlation ($\rho = -.45, p < .001$), suggesting that firms with increasing sophistication were less likely to encourage creative responses. It could be suggested that DBM sophistication requires a standardized approach. This cannot be stated conclusively without further investigation.

The style of decision making in organizations was found to be significant not only when adopting DBM, but also in the degree of sophistication achieved. Those firms that had DBM but used more incremental decision making showed a negative relationship with sophistication ($\rho = -.34, p < .001$). From this it can be inferred that small, incremental steps in approaching decisions inhibit both adoption of DBM and subsequent DBM sophistication. As DBM is a new approach to marketing, a new creative approach to change is required.

Marketing orientation and information orientation were both found to be strongly positively correlated to sophistication of DBM systems ($\rho = .54, p < .001; \rho = .61, p < .001$). These two elements of organizational culture continue to play a strong role in developing sophisticated DBM after adoption. Our finding that a marketing and information orientation is critical to adoption and sophistication of DBM reflects the fact that DBM is customer and information focused.

Organizational slack was positively correlated to degree of sophistication ($\rho = .20, p < .05; \rho = .34, p < .001$). Resources need to be available after DBM has been adopted to encourage further development of the system.

The degree to which the organization controls marketing's use of computing and storage, a consideration in the adoption of DBM, was not found to be related to sophistication. Whereas the extent of resources available is a constraining factor on increasing sophistication, control over resources does not appear as important.

The comparison of DBM users and nonusers showed no significant differences on the extent of internal and external networks. Sophistication in DBM was found to be positively correlated to the extent of internal networks in the firm ($\rho = .018, p < .05$), but not external networks. This would imply that DBM as a sophisticated information technology application does encourage boundary spanning between functions.

At the initial stages of development, DBM is likely to be a tactical tool. The findings show that certain variables are important as DBM develops in facilitating sophistication. In developing sophistication, size is not what matters, but rather the effectiveness with which DBM is used by marketing. A marketing and information orientation needs to provide a nourishing environmental context for DBM sophistication to develop. The potential for the application needs to be understood by marketing and direct marketing. Resources are required, and decisions should be proactive. Waiting to see what others will do will not develop DBM. Firms need to continue to commit to DBM after initial adoption to reach its full strategic potential.

CONCLUSIONS

The financial services industry in the UK is undergoing considerable change. As a result, as an industry it has been investing heavily in information technology

Table 2 Correlation of DBM sophistication with organizational variables

Organizational variable	Question no.[a]	ρ
Size	1	−0.0559
	2	−0.1510
	3	0.0102
	4	0.0363
Complexity	5	0.2493*
	6	0.2422*
	7	0.1144
Structure		
Centralization	8	−0.1415
Formalization	9	0.1469
	10	−0.4454*
Direct marketing power	11	0.4233*
Style		
Incremental decisions	12	−0.3405*
Culture		
Marketing orientation	13	0.5406*
Information orientation	14	0.6079*
Resources		
Slack	15	0.2091*
	16	0.3463*
Control	17	−0.0318
	18	0.0777
Connections		
Internal networks	19	0.1315
	20	0.1811*
External networks	21	0.1457
	22	−0.0065

[a] See Appendix.
* $p < .05$.

applications for competitive advantage, focusing on their development in marketing, in particular, as a source of future success. The low level of sophistication reported places DBM use in the financial services industry in the turnaround stage. DBM can be both tactical and strategic. Its benefits are considerable, but to achieve them requires sophisticated, strategic DBM. The present sophistication of DBM in the UK financial services industry needs to be developed urgently if firms are to realize the potential of their investment. The findings in this study point to a number of organizational variables significant in both adoption of DBM and developing sophistication of use to achieve its strategic potential.

Three key organizational variables were identified as relevant to both the adoption and sophistication of strategic information systems such as DBM. First, a marketing and information orientation is present within the culture of the organization. A culture that emphasizes the centrality of the customer and understands the value of information is critical in the process of learning how to manage strategic information technology such as DBM. Firms focusing on this culture are in a position to facilitate a new approach to marketing and relationships with customers. Second, the style of decision making influences both adoption and sophistication. Adopters showed themselves to be less incremental in their thinking. They opened their organizations to change and took large steps toward focusing on the benefits of DBM. Maintaining open thinking and decision making also facilitated sophistication. Third, resources need to be made available, a practical recognition of the importance given to strategic information technology developments. Hence, organizational slack was found to relate to both adoption of information technology and continued development.

A number of organizational variables differed in their importance between adoption and sophistication. At different stages of strategic DBM development, the importance of certain elements of the organization may vary. To achieve a level of sophistication and greater opportunity for strategic use of DBM, organizational changes need to be reflected in the organization. Given the current low level of sophistication of DBM noted in the financial services industry, firms should consider those organizational factors conducive to increasing sophistication and strategic use of DBM.

As expected, in the adoption phase, larger firms have an advantage in terms of resources available; however, size was not correlated to sophistication. This means that once the initial investment in DBM has been made, size no longer holds an advantage. As firms develop sophistication, the level of complexity in the organization increasingly has an impact. To develop DBM to its full strategic potential, marketing and direct marketing skills need to be developed. That the level of formal qualifications for information technology was not significantly correlated to DBM sophistication reinforces the view that a marketing orientation is central to the strategic use of DBM, rather than the technology itself.

Although the existence of organizational slack was related to both adoption and sophistication, on the issue of control the two stages differed. When adopting technology, firms face difficulties making the decision to change existing resource structures. Debate over control of computing and storage facilities is likely to be a part of this. With increasing sophistication this was not found to be a significant issue. Once in place, DBM sophistication can be facilitated by resolving the issue of control of resources and expanding resources available.

The other area where adoption and sophistication differed related to internal connections. Insignificant in adopters, the existence of internal networks was found to be positively related to sophistication. Internal networks allow the boundary-spanning role of information technology to take shape, opening up the organization. The internal opening up of the organization would facilitate a marketing orientation and exchange of information and ideas between departments.

A number of measures expected to relate to adoption and sophistication did not do so. Measures regarding the structure of the organization, namely, the degree of centralization and formalization, were found to have no bearing on the adoption or sophistication of DBM. The style of decision making and resources available to make decisions may be more important. External networks, which were expected to relate positively to adoption and sophistication, were not found to be significant. It seems reasonable to conclude, given that internal networks showed a correlation to sophistication, that with increasing sophistication and development, this may be found to be significant in the future. Given the current low level of sophistication in the FSI, these may be areas for future study as use of DBM expands.

The purpose of this article was to focus on organizational factors influencing adoption and sophistication of a strategic information technology system, DBM. In itself, information technology is not a source of advantage: It is not going to evolve beyond tactical use in the initial adoption stages as strategic support for the organization without complementary organizational changes. On the basis of the findings presented, the role of organizational factors in strategic DBM development can be understood more fully, and those factors important in adoption and subsequent successful sophistication can be identified.

REFERENCES

1. Baker, M. (1985), *Marketing Strategy and Management*, New York: Macmillan.
2. Bamossy, G., and Eenennaam, F. (1989). *Competitive Influences on the Adoption of High Tech Innovations: An Empirical Study of Early and Late Adopters*. Athens. Greece: European Marketing Academy Congress. pp. 429–440.
3. Cyert, R., and March, J. (1963), *A Behavioral Theory of the Firm*, Englewood Cliffs. NJ: Prentice Hall.
4. David, P. (1983), *Technical Choice, Innovation and Economic Growth*, Cambridge, England: Cambridge University Press.
5. Davies, S. (1979), *The Diffusion of Process Innovations*, Cambridge, England: Cambridge University Press.
6. DunnHumby Associates (1993), *Computers in Marketing: Special Report*, London: Author.
7. Fletcher, K. (1990), *Marketing Management and Information Technology*, Englewood Cliffs, NJ: Prentice Hall.
8. Fletcher, K., and Wright, G. (1995) 'Organisational, Strategic and Technical Barriers to the Successful Implementation of Database Marketing,' *International Journal of Management Information Systems*, 15(2), 115–127.
9. Fletcher, K, Wheeler, C., and Wright, J. (1994), 'The Strategic Implementation of Database Marketing Problems and Pitfalls,' *Long Range Planning*, 27(1), 133–141.
10. Gatigon, H., and Robertson, T. (1985). 'A Propositional Inventory for New Diffussion Research,' *Journal of Consumer Research*, 11 (March), 849–867.
11. Gibson, C. and Nolan, R. (1974), 'Managing the Four Stages of EDP Growth,' *Harvard Business Review*, 52 (January–February), 76–88.
12. Glazer, R. (1991), 'Marketing in an Information-Intensive Environment: Strategic Implications of Knowledge as an Asset,' *Journal of Marketing*, 55(4), 1–19.
13. John, G., and Martin, J. (1984), 'Effects of Organisational Structure of Marketing Planning on Credibility and Utilization of Plan Output,' *Journal of Marketing Research*, 21 (May), 170–183.
14. King, W. R., Grover, V., and Hufnagel, E. (1989), 'Using Information and Information Technology for Sustainable Competitive Advantage: Some Empirical Evidence,' *Information Management*, 17 (2), 87–93.
15. Knights, D., and Murray, F. (1990), *Information Technology and the Marketing Driven Firm: Problems and Prospects* (PICT Policy Research Paper No. 9) London: ESRC.
16. Mayes, R. (1993), 'Euro Spend for DM Climbs to Top £20 Billion,' *Precision Marketing*, August 23, p. 6.
17. McFarlan, F., McKenney, J., and Pyburn, P. (1983), 'The Information Archipelago – Plotting a Course,' *Harvard Business Review*, 61(1) (January–February), 145–156.
18. McKenna, R. (1991), 'Marketing Is Everything,' *Harvard Business Review*, 69(1) (January–February), 65–79.
19. Nolan, R. (1979), 'Managing the Crisis in Data Processing,' *Harvard Business Review*, 57(2) (March–April), 115–126.
20. Nooteboome, B. (1988), 'Diffusion, uncertainty and firm size,' *International Journal of Research in Marketing*, 6, 109–128.
21. Parsons, G. L. (1983), 'Information Technology: A New Competitive Weapon,' *Sloan Management Review*, 25(1), 3–14.
22. Porter, M., and Miller, V. (1985), 'How Information Technology Gives You Competitive Advantage,' *Harvard Business Review*, 64(4) (July–August), 149–160.
23. Rogers, E. (1983), *Diffusion of Innovations*, New York: Free Press.
24. Sabherwal, R., and King, W. (1992), 'The Factors Affecting Strategic Information Systems Applications: An Empirical Assessment,' *Information and Management*, October 23, pp. 217–235.
25. Shaw, R. (1991), *Computer-Aided Marketing and Selling*, Oxford: Butterworth Heinemann.
26. Shaw, R., and Stone, M. (1988), *Database Marketing*, Aldershot: Gower.
27. Thwaites, D., and Lee, S. (1994), 'Direct Marketing in the Financial Services Industry,' *Journal of Marketing Management*, 10, 377–390.
28. Webster, F. (1992), 'The Changing Role of Marketing,' *Corporation Journal of Marketing*, 56 (October), 1–17.

Appendix Details of questions relating to variables measured

Variable[a]	No.	Question	Variable[a]	No.	Question
Size	1	Roughly how many people does your organization employ in total?			My organization prefers to consolidate existing decisions before moving on.
	2	How many employees work primarily in the marketing area?			My organization prefers not to make any major changes without gaining experience in the area.
	3	How many employees work primarily in the IT area?			My organization prefers to make a single purposeful decision rather than small incremental steps.
	4	How many employees work primarily in the direct marketing area?			
Complexity (all . . . none, don't know)	5	How many of the marketing personnel have a formal marketing qualification?			My organization prefers to make decisions as late as possible.
	6	How many of the direct marketing personnel have a formal direct marketing qualification?			My organization prefers to make decisions after watching what our competitors do.
	7	How many of the IT personnel have a formal computing/IT qualification?			My organization prefers to make big IT decisions where the practicality of the technology is certain.
Centralization	8	If you wished to increase the amount and sophistication of your computerized marketing activities, at what level would the authorization have to be made (main board level . . . junior management)?	Information orientation	13	Insufficient space to include all 17 items here.
			Marketing orientation	14	Insufficient space to include all 14 here.
			Slack (easily available . . . available with difficulty)	15	To what extent are resources available if marketing wished to make greater use of computing facilities?
Formalization (true . . . untrue)	9	My organization emphasizes rules and procedures in making decisions that cause change.		16	To what extent are resources available if marketing wished to increase the amount of customer information they gathered?
	10	My organization encourages creative responses to challenging situations.	Control (low control . . . high control)	17	What level of control would be placed on marketing use of computing facilities and resources?
Direct marketing power	11	If your organization has a direct marketing unit/person to what extent does it/he/she control the following (a great deal . . . not at all) direct marketing campaigns marketing campaigns information collection information storage information processing internal data transfer marketing software design marketing software acquisition We do not have a direct marketing person or unit		18	What level of control would be placed on marketing need to gather and store information?
			Connections (never . . . very frequently)	19	How often do you have formal meetings with specialists from other functional areas within your own organization?
				20	How often do you have informal meetings with your specialists from other functional areas within your own organization?
				21	How often do you have meetings with marketing people and marketing organizations external to your own organization?
Incrementalism (true . . . untrue)	12	My organization prefers to build on past experience when making big decisions.		22	How often do you have meetings with IT people and IT organizations external to your own organization?

[a] All use seven-point attitude scales where scales are given.

Section 5
Electronic Media

Some of the most recent and exciting developments in marketing communications are the convergence of various information technologies, the rise of electronic media and the advent of the interactive consumer. Since its commercialization in 1989, the Internet and its related technologies have created a wave of interest from academics and practitioners into what it means for the future of retailing, advertising, communications, service delivery and so on. This section offers some of the papers that are almost certain to become seminal works in the field by the fact that they are some of the first pieces of serious research.

Hoffman and Novak (1996), despite its youth, is rapidly achieving the status of a true classic. The title is highly descriptive of the content and the reader will not be disappointed. As well as offering a new hypermedia communications model, the authors offer a comparison of various traditional and electronic media on a number of criteria such as interactivity, feedback, synchronicity, etc. and a hypermedia network navigation model. As an introduction to both the subject and some of the conceptual issues that arise from the new media, this is an excellent paper.

Kierzkowski, McQuade, Waitman and Zeisser (1996) take a more pragmatic (but no less excellent) view of the problem. They are more concerned with the new media as a new market space and how organizations can actually reach what are rapidly becoming known as digital consumers. Although less than ten years old at the time of the article, it is clear that the digital economy was up and running and that a substantial and rapidly increasing number of purchases were being made via the Internet. These authors suggest and explore three lines of opportunities that companies can engage in – information delivery, relationship building and channel/intermediation. They then adapt the hierarchy of effects model to suggest an attract – engage – retain – learn – relate cycle with practical suggestions of implementation at each stage. Overall, this is a very useful article to introduce the subject of the interactive consumer. The interactive theme is developed further by Alba *et al.* (1997). This paper looks at the implications of shopping from home. The authors explore in some depth the implications for the consumer, the retailer and the manufacturer and investigate why any or all of these might need to or wish to enter the electronic marketplace. They conclude that the two biggest issues from the producer and retailer perspective are disintermediation and brand management (especially price competition).

The final paper in this section, Gatarski and Lundkvist (1998), raises an interesting issue that only exists in the world of electronic media – the existence of artificial consumers. The use of search engine and agent technology in some ways mimics the role of the intermediary but is much more rigorous and literal in its application of searching, sorting and sifting rules. These agents programmed and sent into the Internet to retrieve specific and relevant information, are becoming closer and closer to independent, artificial intelligences, so much so that the authors call them artificial consumers. Gatarski and Lundkvist conclude that there is a need to develop new theories of consumer buying behavior and of communication to account for the human – agent – information – sponsor.

Marketing in hypermedia computer-mediated environments: conceptual foundations

5.1

Donna L. Hoffman and Thomas P. Novak

Firms communicate with their customers through various media. Traditionally, these media follow a passive one-to-many communication model, whereby a firm reaches many current and potential customers, segmented or not, through marketing efforts that allow only limited forms of feedback from the customer. For several years, a revolution has been developing that is dramatically altering this traditional view of advertising and communication media. This revolution is the Internet, the massive global network of interconnected packet-switched computer networks, which as a new marketing medium has the potential to radically change the way firms do business with their customers.

The Internet operationalizes a model of distributed computing that facilitates interactive multimedia many-to-many communication (for a complete history, see Hafner and Lyon, 1996). As such, the Internet supports discussion groups (e.g., USENET news, moderated and unmoderated mailing lists), multiplayer games and communication systems (e.g., MUDs [Multiuser Dungeons], IRC [Internet Relay Chat], chat, MUSEs [Multiuser Shared Environment]), file transfer, electronic mail, and global information access and retrieval systems (e.g., archie, gopher, World Wide Web).[1] The business implications of this model, in which 'the engine of democratization sitting on so many desktops is already out of control, is already creating new players in a new game' (Carroll, 1994, p. 73), will be played out in as yet unknown ways for many years to come.

We focus on the marketing implications of commercializing hypermedia computer-mediated environments (CMEs), of which the World Wide Web (Berners-Lee et al., 1993) on the Internet is the first and current networked global implementation. Although we provide a formal definition of a hypermedia CME subsequently, at this point we informally define it as a distributed computer network used to access and provide hypermedia content (i.e., multimedia content connected across the network with hypertext links). Although other CMEs are relevant to marketers, including private bulletin board systems; conferencing systems such as The WELL (Rheingold, 1992); and commercial on-line services such as America Online, CompuServe, Prodigy, and the Microsoft Network, we restrict our focus to marketing activities in hypermedia CMEs accessible via the Web on the Internet.

From a commercial perspective, the Web consists of locations, or sites, that firms erect on servers and consumers visit. On the Web, consumer-oriented network navigation consists of visiting a series of *Web sites* to search for information and/or advertising about products and services or consumer content (possibly advertiser-supported) or place an order for a product.

Consumers visit a site by directly entering its Web address in the browser or clicking on a hypertext link leading to it from some other site. Once there, consumers navigate through the site using a series of point-and-click motions with a mouse or entering textual information into pop-up windows and 'fill-out-forms' with keyboard strokes. From there, the consumer chooses where to go next in the site. Often, the offerings are presented as a nonlinear graphical menu or map of choices to the consumer. The navigation process continues, terminated only when the consumer jumps to another off-site hypertext link within the Web or exits the Web navigation experience entirely.

The Internet is an important focus for marketers for several reasons. First, consumers and firms are conducting a substantial and rapidly increasing amount of business on the Internet.[2] Although there is some controversy surrounding the estimates of the size of the Internet, surveys performed to date by O'Reilly, FIND/SVP, Times Mirror, and Hoffman, Kalsbeek, and Novak (1996) suggest that there are at least 10 million Internet users in the United States alone. The number of computers (hosts) connected to the Internet topped 9.47 million (Network Wizards, 1996) as of January 1996 and has been doubling every year since 1982. Note that a single host supports anywhere from a single user to, in some cases, thousands of users. As of March 21, 1996, Open Market's (1996) directory of "Commercial Services on the Net" listed 24,347 firms, and there were 54,800 entries in the "Companies" directory of Yahoo's (1996) guide to the Web, with the total number of Web sites doubling approximately every two months.

Second, as Malone (1995) has argued, the market prefers the decentralized, many-to-many Web for electronic commerce to the centralized, closed-access environments provided by the on-line services. Significantly, all the major on-line services now offer Web access to their subscribers and have or are expected to announce plans to allow members to self-publish their own *home pages* on the Web, as well. Additionally, virtually all the major communications conglomerates have Web sites, as they shift their strategic orientations away from so-called interactive televisions applications to Web-based publishing, communication, and multimedia marketing efforts.

Third, and this follows from the first and second points, the World Wide Web represents the broader context within which other hypermedia CMEs exist. Indeed, much of the foundation we develop here is relevant to on-line services, particularly as they begin to function more as full-service Internet access providers and less as closed, proprietary networks. Thus, restricted on-line services are special cases of the open-access World Wide Web. Open access results in lower entry barriers so that virtually anyone can both access and provide content to the Internet. In essence, the Web 'levels the playing field'.

Both the Web and proprietary on-line services are examples of developments in *electronic commerce*, which, as Rangaswamy and Wind (1994) have noted, included such developments as EDI (electronic data interchange), kiosks, electronic classified advertisements, and on-line services such as CompuServe and Minitel, the French videotex system (Cats-Baril and Jelassi, 1994). With the possible exception of EDI, which is moving to the Internet because its 'open architecture' system is more inclusive and offers numerous advantages over private networks, none of these mechanisms for facilitating commerce electronically has the same far-reaching scope and potential for transformation of the business function as does the World Wide Web.

Fourth, the Web provides an efficient channel for advertising, marketing, and even direct distribution of certain goods and information services. For example, Verity and Hof (1994) suggest that it may be nearly one-fourth less costly to perform direct marketing through the Internet than through conventional channels. Neece (1995) reports that SunSolve Online™ has saved Sun Microsystems over $4 million in 'FAQs'[3] alone since Sun 'reengineered information processes around the WWW [Web]'. A recent study by IBM Corporation (1995) suggests that on-line catalogs on the Internet can save firms up to 25% in processing costs and reduce cycle time by up to 62%. Along with the suspected increases in efficiency, the anecdotal evidence mounts that marketing on the net also may be more effective than marketing through traditional media. For example, one vendor estimated that his marketing efforts on the Web resulted in '10 times as many units [sold] with 1/10 the advertising budget' (Potter, 1994).

GOALS AND ORGANIZATION OF THE PAPER

Although there have been recent scholarly efforts detailing the impact of new information technologies on marketing (e.g., Blattberg, Glazer, and Little, 1994; Glazer, 1991), the existing research does not discuss the impact that hypermedia CMEs such as the World Wide Web have on marketing theory and business practice. Despite the massive amount of attention given to the Internet in the popular press (see, e.g., the more than 6000 references to the Internet in *ABI Inform* through November, 1995) and the belief in many business circles that the Web represents a phenomenal marketing opportunity, virtually no scholarly effort has been undertaken by marketing academics to understand hypermedia CMEs, both as media for marketing communications and as markets in and of themselves. We draw from the relevant literatures in psychology, communications, media studies, organizational behavior, and human – computer interaction, and concentrate our efforts on developing a conceptual foundation for understanding consumer behavior in hypermedia CMEs.

Therefore, our goals are to introduce marketers to this revolutionary new medium, propose a preliminary process model of consumer navigation behavior in a hypermedia CME, examine the research issues that correspond to the process model, and derive marketing implications for electronic commerce all to stimulate critical inquiry in this emerging area. To that end, the article is organized as follows: We discuss three models of communication that underlie traditional and new media and develop a media typology that reveals new insight into the distinctions among traditional media and CMEs. Then, using an expanded concept of flow (Csikszentmihalyi, 1977, 1990), we introduce a preliminary process model of network navigation in CMEs. We next present a series of 15 research issues involving the flow construct and process model, while paying attention to the marketing implications that follow from the research issues. Finally, we offer conclusions about the importance of this emerging area of inquiry to both marketing scholars and practitioners interested in electronic commerce.

HYPERMEDIA COMPUTER-MEDIATED ENVIRONMENTS

We begin by outlining a series of three communication models that serve to identify several unique characteristics of hypermedia CMEs such as the Web. We then describe a new media typology that positions the Web in the broader context of new and traditional media and discuss the marketing implications of the communication models and typology.

Communication models

Model 1: Mass media

In Figure 1, we present a simplified model that underlies many models of mass communication (e.g., Katz and Lazarsfeld, 1955; Lasswell, 1948). The primary feature of Figure 1 is a one-to-many communications process, whereby the firm (F) transmits content through a medium to consumers (C). Depending on the medium (i.e., broadcast, print, and billboards), either static (i.e., text, image, and graphics) and/or dynamic (i.e., audio, full-motion video, and animation) content can be incorporated. No interaction between consumers and firms is present in this model. Virtually all contemporary models of mass media effects are based on this traditional model of the communication process (e.g., see Kotler, 1994, Chapter 22).

Model 2: Interpersonal and computer-mediated communications

In Figure 2, we present a simplified model of interpersonal communication that is based on traditional models of communication from sender to receiver. The solid and dashed lines indicate communication flows through a medium for two distinct persons. This model incorporates a feedback view of interactivity, which is consistent with Rafaeli's (1988, p. 111) definition of interaction as 'an expression of the extent that in a given series of communication exchanges, any third (or later) transmission (or message) is related to the degree to which previous exchanges referred to even earlier transmissions'. Although Figure 2 is shown here for one-to-one communication

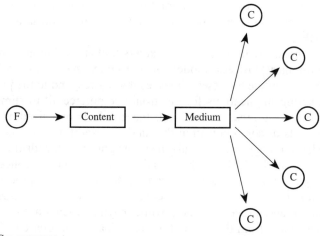

Note: F = firm; C = consumer.

Figure 1 Traditional one-to-many marketing communications model for mass media.

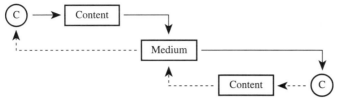

Note: C = consumer.

Figure 2 Model of interpersonal and computer-mediated communication.

between two consumers, the model can easily be extended to represent many-to-many interpersonal communication (i.e., teleconference, face-to-face group meetings, or on-line chat rooms). Note that unmediated face-to-face interpersonal communication is a special case of Figure 2. From a marketing perspective, the model in Figure 2 is implicit in developments of word-of-mouth communication models.

Person-interactivity, the key feature distinguishing Figure 2 from Figure 1, is defined as interactivity between people that occurs through a medium or is unmediated, as in the case of face-to-face communication. In this view of interactivity, media are 'important only as a conduit, as a means of connecting sender and receiver, and are only interesting to the extent that they contribute to or otherwise interfere with the transmission of messages from sender to receiver' (Steuer, 1992, p. 77–78).

Hypermedia CMEs

Nearly 50 years ago, Busch (1945, p. 106) proposed a hypertext-like system called *Memex*, which would consist of 'a device in which an individual stores all his books, records, and communications, and which is mechanized so that it may be consulted with exceeding speed and flexibility'. Nelson (1967) discussed hypertext in terms of a network of paths and associations, with an emphasis on approximating the way the human brain connects information. Bornman and von Solms (1993, p. 260) provide a current definition: '*Hypertext* suggests the concept of non-sequential writing of information that allows the user to connect information together by means of different paths or links'. *Multimedia* uses a computer to integrate and provide interactive access to both static (i.e., text, image, and graphics) and dynamic (i.e., audio, full-motion video, and animation) content, whereas hypermedia combines the node-and-link access of hypertext with multimedia content. Gygi (1990) and Smith and Wilson (1993) provide more extensive discussion of hypertext and hypermedia.

We define a *hypermedia CME* as a dynamic distributed network, potentially global in scope, together with associated hardware and software for accessing the network, which enables consumers and firms to (1) provide and interactively access hypermedia content (i.e., 'machine interactivity') and (2) communicate through the medium (i.e., 'person interactivity'). We further define *network navigation* as the process of self-directed movement through a hypermedia CME. This nonliner search and retrieval process provides essentially unlimited freedom of choice and greater control for the consumer and may be contrasted with the restrictive navigation options available in traditional media such as television or print. Furthermore, network navigation permits much greater freedom of choice than the centrally controlled interactive multimedia systems, such as video-on-demand and home-shopping applications of so-called

Interactive Television; the text-based French Minitel system (Cats-Baril and Jelassi, 1994); the menu-based information-acceleration approach (Hauser, Urban, and Weinberg, 1993); or the experimental systems for monitoring information processing, such as Mouselab (e.g., Payne, Bettman, and Johnson, 1993).

Model 3: A new model for hypermedia CMEs

In Figure 3 we present a many-to-many communication model for hypermedia CMEs. The content in Figure 3 is hypermedia, and the medium is a distributed computer network. Figure 3 differs from Figure 2 in that interactivity can also be *with* the medium (i.e., machine interactivity) in addition to *through* the medium (i.e., person interactivity).

Figure 3 is based on a communication model outlined by Steuer (1992) and shown in Figure 4. The mediated model represented in Figure 4 suggests that the primary relationship is not between the sender and the receiver, but rather with the mediated environment with which they interact. According to this view, information or content is not merely transmitted from a sender to a receiver, instead 'mediated environments are created and then experienced' (Steuer, 1992, p. 78). In Steuer's model of mediated communication, *machine interactivity* is 'the extent to which users can participate in modifying the form and content of a mediated environment in real time' (p. 84). Steuer calls his model a *telepresence view* of mediated communication, where *presence* is defined as 'the natural perception of an environment' and *telepresence* is defined as 'the mediated perception of an environment, (p. 76). Following Steuer, when interacting with a computer-mediated environment, the consumer perceives two

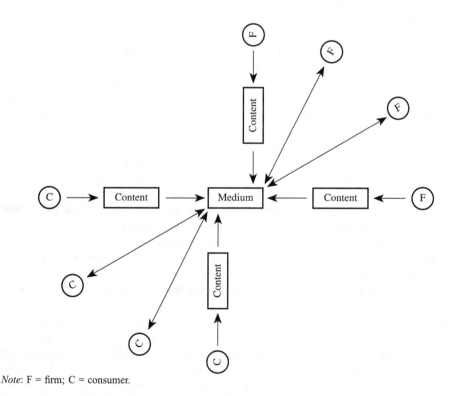

Note: F = firm; C = consumer.

Figure 3 A model of marketing communications in a hypermedia CME.

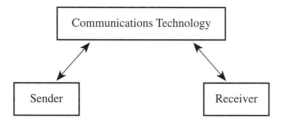

Note: Adapted from Steuer.

Figure 4 Mediated communication.

environments: (1) the physical environment in which he or she is present and (2) the environment defined by the hypermedia CME. The strength of the experience of telepresence is a function of the extent to which a person feels present in the hypermedia CME, rather than in his or her immediate physical environment.

In Figure 3, we show the range of communication relationships possible in a hypermedia CME. Consumers can interact with the medium (e.g., 'surf the Web' using browsing software) as can firms (e.g., business-to-business marketing in Commerce-Net). In addition, firms can provide content to the medium (e.g., a firm establishes a corporate Web server). Finally – in perhaps the most radical departure from traditional marketing environments – consumers can put product-related content in the medium. For example, individual consumers have established Web pages for automobiles (e.g., the Ford Probe, Porsche, car audio equipment, and solar cars), toys (e.g., Legos and Barbie Dolls), and television shows (e.g., Friends, The X-Files, Married with Children, and Rugrats). Furthermore, note that Figures 1 and 2 are contained within Figure 3. Thus, a hypermedia CME also can be used for computer-mediated communication among consumers and/or firms (*through* the medium, or person interactivity), as well as potentially for one-to-many mass communication, though applications of the latter have met with considerable consumer resistance (e.g., Godwin, 1994).

Media characteristics

Studying media characteristics provides a structured context for comparing different media types, including traditional media and new media (Valacich *et al.*, 1993; Williams, Strover, and Grant, 1994). Traditional media include both mass media (e.g., television, radio, newspaper, magazines, direct mail), and personal communications (e.g., word of mouth). New media encompass interactive media, such as videotex, interactive CD-ROM, on-line services, and hypermedia CMEs, as well as emerging so-called interactive multimedia, such as pay-per-view, video-on-demand, and interactive television.

The media typologies referenced in Table 1 reveal that media differ along many different dimensions, for example, channel characteristics (Reardon and Rogers, 1988; Rogers, 1986), social presence (Rice, 1992, 1993), and uses and gratifications (Perse and Courtright, 1993). However, hypermedia CMEs were not in existence at the time these typologies were proposed. Although the typologies cited include the computer as a communications medium, it is defined narrowly in terms of email, bulletin boards, and computer conferencing.

Table 1 Review of media comparisons

Source	Communication media compared	Characteristics of communication media
Dennis and Valacich (1994)	Face-to-face, phone, memo, voice mail, videoconference, email, electronic phone, and group support systems	Feedback, symbol variety, concurrency, persistence, ability to rehearse
Perse and Courtright (1993)	Television, video cassette recorder, movies, conversation, phone, computer, newspapers, magazines, books, and radio	11 communication needs (relaxation, entertainment, forget work, friendship, learning, pass time, excitement, feel less lonely, satisfy habits, acknowledge feelings, get someone to do something for me) and social presence
Reardon and Rogers (1988)	Interpersonal communication, interactive media, and mass media	Message flow, source knowledge of the audience, segmentation, interactivity, feedback, asynchronicity, emotional versus task-related content, control, privacy
Steuer (1992)	44 new and old media including newspapers, fax, interactive television, three-dimensional films, sensorama, and the Star Trek Holodec	Subjective classification according to vividness and interactivity
Stewart and Ward (1994)	Television, radio, magazines, and newspapers	27 characteristics for 'gross media comparisons'
Rice (1992)	Email, voicemail, videoconferencing, and on-line databases	Social presence, information richness
Rice (1993)	Face-to-face, email, meetings, phone, desktop video, text, and voicemail	Social presence, appropriateness for ten communication activities (exchange information, negotiate, get to know someone, ask questions, stay in touch, exchange time-sensitive information, generate ideas, resolve disagreements, make decisions, confidentiality)
Valacich and colleagues (1993)	Distributed verbal, face-to-face verbal, distributed electronic, and face-to-face electronic	Communication concurrency
van Dijk (1993)	Two-way cable, videotex, data networks, email, videophone, and interactive video	Kinds of information, mode of communication

Furthermore, many of the characteristics listed in Table 1 are either subjective in nature or require the application of valid measurement procedures. Therefore, we propose a new media typology based on seven objective characteristics. Although objective characteristics do not allow the media to be compared with respect to such psychological dimensions as communication needs, social presence, or control, they do permit a relatively error-free classification. Thus in Table 2, we characterize 35 traditional and new media with respect to seven objective characteristics. We have already discussed person-interactivity and machine-interactivity and the distinction between one-to-many and one-to-few (Figure 1), one-to-one and few-to-few (Figure 2), and many-to-many (Figure 3) communication models. Content simply identifies whether static or dynamic information can be delivered by the medium. For unmediated interpersonal communication, experiential content includes stimuli affecting additional sensory modalities, such as tactile, proprioceptive, or olfactory senses.

Table 2 Objective characteristics of media

	Person-interactivity	Machine-interactivity	Number of linked sources	Communication model	Content[a]	Media feedback symmetry	Temporal synchronicity
Mass Media							
Billboards	no	no	one	one-to-many	T, I	yes	n/a
Newspapers	no	no	one	one-to-many	T, I	yes	n/a
Magazines	no	no	one	one-to-many	T, I	yes	n/a
Direct mail	no	no	one	one-to-many	T, I	yes	n/a
Radio	no	no	few	one-to-many	A	no	n/a
Broadcast television	no	no	few	one-to-many	A, V, (T)	no	n/a
Cable television	no	no	few	one-to-many	A, V, (T)	no	n/a
Satellite television	no	no	many	one-to-many	A, V, (T)	no	n/a
500 channel cable television	no	no	many	one-to-many	A, V, (T)	no	n/a
Interactive Media							
Local hypertext	no	yes	one	one-to-many	T	yes	yes
Local hypermedia	no	yes	one	one-to-many	T, I, A, V	no	yes
Dial-up bulletin board service (information only)	no	yes	one	one-to-many	T	yes	yes
CD-Interactive	no	yes	one	one-to-many	T, I, A, V	no	yes
Videotex	no	yes	few	one-to-many	T	yes	yes
Pre-Web On-line Services	no	yes	few	one-to-many	T, I	no	yes
Interactive television	no	yes	few	one-to-many	T, I, A, V	no	yes
World Wide Web	no	yes	many	many-to-many	T, I, A, V	no	yes
Interpersonal Communication							
Mail	yes	no	one	one-to-one	T	yes	no
Fax	yes	no	one	one-to-one	T	yes	no
Telephone	yes	no	one	one-to-one	A	yes	yes
Videophone	yes	no	one	one-to-one	A, V	yes	yes
Face-to-face	yes	no	one	one-to-one	A, V, E	yes	yes
Face-to-face (group)	yes	no	few	few-to-few	A, V, E	yes	yes
Town meeting	yes	no	many	many-to-many	A, V, E	yes	yes
Computer-Mediated Communication							
Email	yes	yes	one	one-to-one	T	yes	no
Voice mail	yes	yes	one	one-to-one	A	yes	no
Talk program	yes	yes	one	one-to-one	T	yes	yes
Email (carbon copy: list)	yes	yes	one	one-to-few	T	yes	no
Multiparty chat	yes	yes	few	few-to-few	T	yes	yes
MUDs	yes	yes	few	few-to-few	T	yes	yes
See you see me	yes	yes	few	few-to-few	A, V	yes	yes
Mailing lists	yes	yes	many	many-to-many	T	yes	no
Usenet newsgroups	yes	yes	many	many-to-many	T	yes	no
Web (forms/annotation)	yes	yes	many	many-to-many	T, I	yes	no
Internet Relay Chat	yes	yes	many	many-to-many	T	yes	yes

[a]T = Text; I = image; A = audio; V = video; E = experiential. (T) = there is a minor amount of text content.

The remaining three characteristics may be defined briefly as follows: The *number of linked sources available* specifies how many sources of content are readily accessible or available to the user at any given usage opportunity. *Media feedback symmetry* refers to whether different parties in the communication process employ differing media bandwidths for sending information. For example, in an Interactive CD, feedback is asymmetric, because the Interactive CD sends high bandwidth information but the consumer sends low bandwidth information. From the consumer's perspective, this facilitates interactivity because a few simple cursor, mouse, or joystick movements produce dramatic modifications in the environment. When there is symmetric media feedback, all sources in the communication process employ the same media bandwidth for sending information – for example, telephone, mail, and face-to-face communication. *Temporal synchronicity* is a property of interactive media only, does not apply to mass media, and means interaction occurs in real time.

In Figure 5, we present a perceptual map, produced by plotting object scores for 35 media types resulting from a nonlinear principal components analysis (Gifi, 1990) of the data from Table 2. The nonlinear principal components analysis is equivalent to a multiple correspondence analysis (Hoffman and de Leeuw, 1992), with ordinal restrictions imposed on category quantification of variables assumed to have a known underlying orders of categories.[4] To simplify presentation, only the object scores for the rows of Table 2, and not the category quantifications for the columns of Table 2, are plotted.

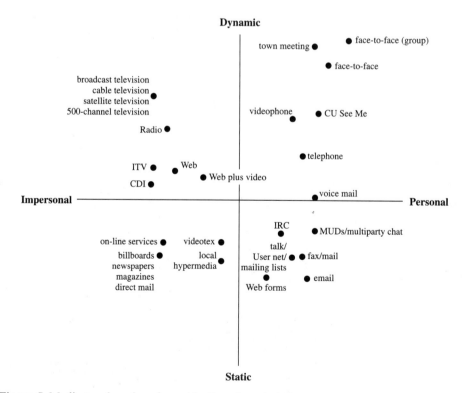

Figure 5 Media typology based on objective characteristics.

Following orthogonal rotation of axes, Figure 5 has a clear interpretation. The horizontal axis differentiates impersonal from personal communication media, and the vertical axis differentiates dynamic from static media. Reardon and Rogers (1988, p. 297) argue that 'new communication technologies are interactive in nature, and thus cannot be easily categorized as either interpersonal or mass media channels'. Indeed, Figure 5 shows that traditional mass media channels occupy positions at the upper left (broadcast media) and lower left (print media), whereas interpersonal media occupy the upper-right position and mail and fax occupy the lower-right position. New media occupy largely intermediate positions, in agreement with Reardon and Rogers (1988), who view new interactive media as combining properties of mass (impersonal) and face-to-face (personal) communications channels.

Figure 5 identifies two points for the Web, one assuming text, image, and audio content (Web alone) and one assuming text, image, audio, and video content (Web plus video). Web plus video content occupies a central position in Figure 5; that is, it is the most 'typical' of all communications, sharing characteristics with a wide variety of other media types. The many-to-many communication model underlying the Web positions the Web closer to the personal side of the horizontal axis than it does traditional mass media.

The central position of the Web in Figure 5 corresponds to an important strategic interpretation of the Web as a marketing medium; namely, the Web combines elements from a variety of traditional media, yet is more than the sum of the parts. For example, broadcast media in the top left quadrant of Figure 5 provide relatively short-term exposure with low information content, whereas the print media in the bottom left quadrant provide relatively long-term exposure with high information content. Advertising strategy on the Web must account for both short-term (decision of which link to select next) and long-term (reading detailed information provided at a commercial site) exposure.

We next discuss a process model of network navigation in hypermedia CMEs such as the Web. There are several unique features of CMEs as media and marketing environments that motivate the process model. As virtual hypermedia environments incorporating interactivity with both people and computers, CMEs are not simulations of real-world environments, but alternatives to them. Within the virtual environment, both experiential (e.g., net-surfing) and goal-directed (e.g., on-line shopping) activities compete for consumers' attention. Consumer skill in functioning in the virtual environment, as well as challenges posed by the environment, introduce a competency issue that does not exist in such a fundamental manner in the physical world. This issue of whether consumers' skills are competent to meet the challenges of the virtual environment plus the telepresence created by immersion in an interactive hypermedia environment bear directly on the construct of flow, which underlies the process model.

A PROCESS MODEL OF NETWORK NAVIGATION IN HYPERMEDIA CMES

The flow construct

Although consumer researchers have explored the role of play in the consumption experience (e.g., Holbrook et al., 1984), we believe the concept of flow in a hypermedia CME holds wider applicability and underlies many crucial components of the consumer's interaction with the firm and its offerings. Simply stated, *flow* is the 'process of optimal *experience*' (Csikszentmihalyi, 1977; Csikszentmihalyi and LeFevre, 1989, p. 816, emphasis added) preceded by a set of antecedent conditions necessary for the experience to be achieved and followed by a set of consequences that occurs as a result of the process.

We define the *flow experience* in a CME as the state occurring during network navigation, which is (1) characterized by a seamless sequence of responses facilitated by machine interactivity, (2) intrinsically enjoyable, (3) accompanied by a loss of self-consciousness, and (4) self-reinforcing. In the flow experience, which formalizes and extends a sense of playfulness (Csikszentmihalyi, 1977; Csikszentmihalyi and LeFevre, 1989), consumers are so acutely involved in the act of network navigation in the hypermedia CME that 'nothing else seems to matter' (Csikszentmihalyi, 1990, p. 4).

Two primary antecedents must be present in sufficiently motivated users of a hypermedia CME for the flow experience to occur. Consumers must focus their attention on the interaction, narrowing their focus of awareness so that irrelevant perceptions and thoughts are filtered out, and they must perceive a balance between their skills and challenges of the interaction.

The key consequences of the flow experience for consumers are increased learning, exploratory and participatory behaviors, positive subjective experiences, and a perceived sense of control over their interactions in the hypermedia CME.

When in the flow state, irrelevant thoughts and perceptions are screened out and the consumer focuses entirely on the interaction. The flow experience involves a merging of actions and awareness, with concentration so intense that there is little attention left to consider anything else. A consumer's action in the flow state is experienced as a 'unified flowing from one moment to the next, in which he is in control of his actions, and in which there is little distinction between self and environment, between stimulus and response, or between past, present and future' (Csikszentmihalyi, 1977, p. 36). Self-consciousness disappears, the consumer's sense of time becomes distorted, and the resulting state of mind is extremely gratifying.

Flow has been previously noted as a useful construct for describing human–computer interactions (Csikszentmihalyi, 1990, Ghani, Supnick, and Rooney, 1991; Trevino and Webster, 1992, Webster, Trevino, and Ryan, 1993). Our conceptualization extends these ideas by explicitly developing the flow construct in the context of network navigation in a hypermedia CME and arguing that flow consists of a process state that requires a set of antecedents to occur and results in a set of consequences.

On first inspection, the flow experience may appear to be similar to attention and involvement, as well as other construct events (Privette and Bundrick, 1987) of peak experience and peak performance. Privette's (1983) and Privette and Bundrick's (1987) distinction between flow, peak experience, and peak performance is helpful for understanding how flow differs from these related construct events, as well as from attention and involvement. Privette considers attention and involvement to be common qualities of flow, peak experience, and peak performance, but attention and involvement do not differentiate between the three. Flow is characterized by fun and occurs in structured activities in which action follows action. Peak performance is characterized by a clear focus, a strong sense of self (rather than loss of self, as in flow), and a sense of fulfillment, whereas peak experience is characterized by a transpersonal and spiritual quality that has much higher levels of experienced joy than flow has.

Flow is a central construct because of the nature of commercial activity in a CME such as the World Wide Web. It is important to understand that commercial activity on the Web consists of much more than purchasing products in on-line storefronts. Hoffman, Novak, and Chatterjee (1995) identify six functional categories of commercial activity on the Web: on-line storefronts, Internet presence sites, content sites, malls, incentive sites, and search agents. To date, Internet presence sites, rather than on-line storefronts, dominate commercial activity. Using the typology proposed by Hoffman, Novak, and Chatterjee, Kaul (1995) found that only 18% of a random sample of 290 Web sites served as on-line storefronts. The remaining 82% were informational or image-based Internet presence sites or directories of other commercial sites.

Internet presence sites either provide detailed information on a firm's offerings (e.g., the Web sites of Federal Express, Sun Microsystems, Volvo) or create an image and attempt to built an ongoing relationship with the consumer (e.g., the Web sites of Zima, Reebok, David Letterman). Internet presence sites are a new form of nonintrusive advertising, in which the customer actively chooses to visit and interact with the firm's marketing communication efforts. Recent efforts involve the merging of information and image in innovative ways (see, e.g., L. L. Bean's sophisticated 'trail metaphor' Web site at www.llbean.com). Measures of duration time spent at an Internet presence site, depth of search through the site, navigation patterns through the site, and repeat visits to the site are crucial outcome measures for evaluating the effectiveness of such sites. Flow affects all of these outcome measures and is an important consideration for understanding consumer behavior in commercial Web sites.

The process model described subsequently has direct implications for understanding experiential behavior. The primary focus of this process model is on network navigation in integrated destination sites (Hoffman, Novak, and Chatterjee, 1995), rather than on mechanisms for search and choice in such environments. Nevertheless, goal-directed processes of prepurchase search and choice in a CME take place against a background of network navigation and involve flow within and across Web sites; we address those issues, as well.

The process model

In Figure 6, we present a preliminary process model of network navigation in a hypermedia CME. For expository purposes, we diagram only the most important links. The model in Figure 6 shows neither the complex set of feedback loops and pathways nor the fully dynamic nature of the process. A consumer enters the hypermedia CME and engages in network navigation. There are several points of exit from the environment, as well as opportunities to continue navigation, with flow in essence serving as the glue holding the consumer in the hypermedia CME.

In the following section, we introduce a series of 15 research issues related to the components of the process model shown in Figure 6. We have mapped the research issues on the boxes and pathways of the Figure to provide an overview of how they relate to the process model. Of the first five research issues the first three deal with flow measurement, whereas the next two deal with consumer heterogeneity and flow in CMEs. In the second five research issues, we discuss experiential and goal-directed behavior in a CME. In the final five research issues, we deal with the consequences of flow.

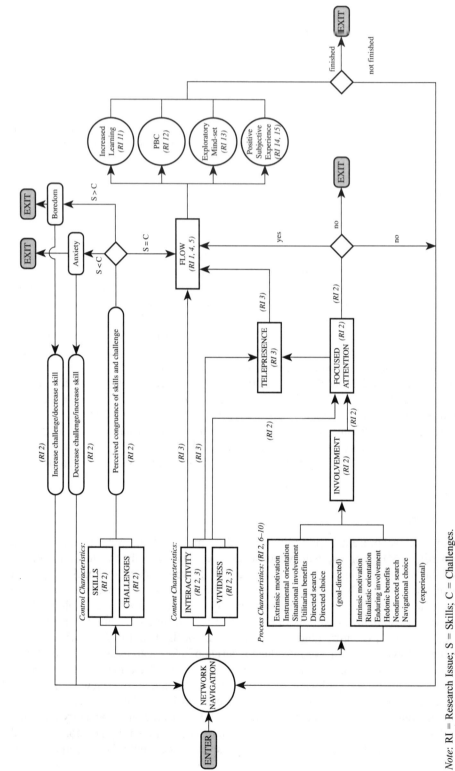

Note: RI = Research Issue; S = Skills; C = Challenges.

Figure 6 A model of network navigation in a hypermedia CME.

RESEARCH ISSUES

Flow measurement

1. Measurement approaches

Reliable and valid measurement of flow is necessary for further development of the preliminary process model in figure 6. We view flow in a CME as measurable along a continuum and note that flow can be inferred from its antecedents and consequences. Likert scales provide one approach to measuring flow. Ghani, Supnick, and Rooney (1991) and Ghani and Deshpande (1994) operationalized flow as a self-report scale containing items measuring enjoyment and concentration. Perceptions of control, skill, and challenge were significantly related to this flow measure. Trevino and Webster (1992) used four items to measure flow. The four items dealt with components of control, attention focus, curiosity, and intrinsic interest. Webster, Trevino, and Ryan (1993) used a 12-item scale expanded from Trevino and Webster's study to measure flow, again measuring the same four components of flow. Although these components correspond more to antecedents of flow than to the flow experience, the scales used were significantly correlated with a variety of consequences of flow, such as enjoyment, positive attitudes, and future usage intentions.

Privette (1983) and Privette and Bundrick (1987) take an alternative approach to measuring flow by asking respondents to describe construct events they have personally experienced involving flow, peak experience, peak performance, average events, misery, and failure. Brief descriptions of these construct events are provided, and respondents provide personal examples of and rate each construct event using Privette's (1984) experience questionnaire. Lutz and Guiry (1994) used a modified version of Privette's experience questionnaire in a study on consumption experiences.

The most widely used approach to measuring flow is the Experience Sampling Method (Csikszentmihalyi and Csikszentmihalyi, 1988; Csikszentmihalyi and LeFevre, 1989; Ellis, Voelkl, and Morris, 1994; Mannell, Zuzanek, and Larson, 1988). With the Experience Sampling Method, respondents are electronically paged at random intervals throughout the day, at which point they immediately complete a self-report experiential sampling form with open-ended items and rating scales. On a typical experiential sampling form, respondents rate the experience in which they are currently engaged on the challenge of the experience, their own skills in the experience, a series of items measuring affect and arousal, and items measuring motivation, concentration, and creativity.

A comprehensive flow measurement procedure for a CME must include measures of the antecedent conditions (see Research Issues 2 and 3), consequences (see Research Issues 11 through 15), and variables related to the psychological experience of flow (e.g., lose track of time, self-awareness, concentration, mood, control). We anticipate that qualitative research (such as verbal protocol statements obtained from consumers as they interact with a CME), process tracing measures of actual behavior during the interaction, and survey research (both traditional and electronic) will all be necessary to develop reliable and valid measures of flow in a CME.

2. Primary antecedents of flow

Two primary antecedent conditions are necessary for the flow state to be experienced: (1) skills and challenges must be perceived as congruent and above a critical threshold and (2) focused attention must be present. *Skills* are defined as the consumer's capacities for action, and *challenges* as the opportunities for action available to the consumer in a CME. Only when consumers perceive that the hypermedia CME contains challenges congruent with their own skills can flow potentially occur. If network navigation in a CME does not provide for congruence of skills and challenges, then consumers either become bored (i.e., their skills exceed the challenges) or anxious (i.e., the challenges exceed their skills) and either exit the CME or select a more (or less) challenging activity within it (see Figure 6).

Csikszentmihalyi's (1977) original model specified that flow occurred when an equal match between skill and challenge was perceived, regardless of whether skill and challenge were equally high or equally low. More recent reformulations (Csikszentmihalyi and Csikszentmihalyi, 1988; Csikszentmihalyi and LeFevre, 1989) specify that 'flow results from experience contexts characterized by a match between challenge and skills only when both challenges and skills exceed the level that is typical for the day to day experiences of the individual' (Ellis, Voelkl, and Morris, 1994, p. 338). Congruent skills and challenges that lie below the person's typical level are said to result in an apathy state (Csikszentmihalyi and Csikszentmihalyi, 1988). Congruent, above-threshold skills and challenges as a prerequisite for flow are also consistent with the theory of an optimal stimulation level (e.g., Holbrook and Gardner, 1993; Raju, 1980; Steenkamp and Baumgartner, 1992).

Considerable disagreement exists over how many channels, or categories, should be used to represent the various patterns of congruence or incongruence of high and low skills and challenges and how these channels should be labeled. Ellis, Voelkl, and Morris (1994) note that 3-channel (Csikszentmihalyi, 1977), 4-channel (Csikszentmihalyi, 1988), 8-channel (Csikszentmihalyi and Nakamura, 1989; Massimini and Carli, 1988), and 16-channel (Massimini and Carli, 1988) models have been developed; recently, Clarke and Haworth (1994) proposed a 9-channel model. The labeling of these channels also can be inconsistent. For example, Csikszentmihalyi and Csikszentmihalyi (1988) define low skill and low challenges as *apathy*, whereas Clarke and Haworth (1994) call this combination *relaxation*.

There is also debate about the best way to determine whether skills or challenges exceed the critical threshold or typical level. Most often, within-subject standardization is used (e.g., Csikszentmihalyi and Csikszentmihalyi, 1988; Csikszentmihalyi and LeFevre, 1989). However, Ellis, Voelkl, and Morris (1994) note that within-subject standardization precludes studying individual differences, which have been found to be an important predictor of flow (see Research Issue 4). Consequently, some researchers (e.g., Clarke and Haworth, 1994) do not employ within-subject standardization.

The presence of focused attention is also necessary to experience flow. *Focused attention* is characterized as 'a centering of attention on a limited stimulus field' (Csikszentmihalyi, 1977, p. 40). Webster, Trevino, and Ryan (1993) note that the computer screen functions as the limited stimulus field and that subjects report being 'mesmerized' during their computer interactions. In Figure 6, we indicate the role of the content characteristics of vividness and interactivity in attracting attention. The performance characteristics of ease of use, mapping (naturalness of how human actions are connected to actions in the hypermedia CME; Steuer, 1992), speed, and range all combine to increase interactivity. *Vividness* is defined as 'the representational richness of a mediated environment as defined by its formal features' (Steuer, 1992, p. 81), such as its breadth and depth. *Breadth* refers to the number of sensory dimensions presented and is closely related to media concurrency (Valacich *et al.*, 1993) and media richness (Daft and Lengel, 1986; Daft, Lengel, and Trevino, 1987). *Depth* is the resolution or the quality of the presentation (Steuer, 1992) and is highly correlated with media bandwidth. In the hypermedia CME, both breadth and depth, in general, are high.

Extrinsic and intrinsic motivation (Csikszentmihalyi, 1977, Chapter 1; Davis, Bagozzi, and Warshaw, 1992; Graef, Csikszentmihalyi, and Gianinno, 1983) are important process characteristics that affect focused attention through involvement (Zaichkowsky, 1986). Davis, Bagozzi, and Warshaw (1992, p. 1112), in summarizing the motivational literature, note that extrinsic motivation applies to activities performed because they are instrumental to achieving a valued outcome, whereas intrinsic motivation applies to activities performed 'for no apparent reinforcement other than the process of performing the activity'. Extrinsic motivation creates situational self-relevance (Bloch and Richins, 1983; Celsi and Olson, 1988), whereas intrinsic motivation, or *autotelic activities* (Csikszentmihalyi, 1977, Chapter 2), create intrinsic self-relevance. We define *involvement* as felt involvement (Celsi and Olson, 1988), which is formed by the presence of situational and/or intrinsic self-relevance. Felt involvement affects attention and comprehension effort (Celsi and Olson, 1988). In the context of human – computer interaction, Webster, Trevino, and Ryan (1993) find significant positive correlations between factors for intrinsic interest and/or curiosity and focused attention.

3. Secondary antecedents of flow

Because of the presence of focused attention and perceived congruence of skills and challenges, two additional antecedents – interactivity and telepresence – enhance flow. These additional antecedents increase the subjective intensity of the consumer's flow state, though they are not sufficient alone to produce a flow state. A strong sense of telepresence (i.e., the mediated perception of an environment) is induced by vividness and interactivity (Sheridan, 1992), as well as focused attention. Although the user of a hypermedia CME always experiences some level of telepresence and interactivity, higher levels can boost flow. Feedback loops, however, also must be considered. When telepresence is too high – for example, when the medium is too 'hot' (McLuhan, 1964, p. 36) – challenges may become greater than skills and flow cannot be achieved (Steuer, 1992).

For marketers, the primary and secondary antecedents of flow suggest that flow is not a constant state. Consumers move in and out of flow – as a function of control, content, and process characteristics. To some extent, all these characteristics may be influenced by marketing activities. The congruence of skills and challenges is something that can be facilitated by interface design. For example, a user-specified difficulty level can be designed to avoid anxiety in novice users and boredom in experienced users. Because lack of congruence may lead the consumer to exit the CME, it is important to provide opportunities for consumers to actively select activities that create congruence. Content characteristics such as interactivity and vividness lead to telepresence and can be affected directly through product design considerations. Process characteristics, specifically the distinction between extrinsically and intrinsically motivated consumers, are an important segmentation basis.

Consumer heterogeneity and flow in CMEs

4. The autotelic personality

Consumers are heterogeneous in their ability to experience flow in a CME. Csikszentmihalyi (1977, pp. 21–22) distinguishes between autotelic experiences, activities, and personalities. Flow is the autotelic experience; autotelic activities are those activities relatively more likely to lead to flow; and the autotelic personality trait characterizes a person 'who is able to enjoy what he is doing regardless of whether he will get external rewards from it' (Csikszentmihalyi, 1977, p. 22) and who thus is more likely to experience flow for a given activity. Csikszentmihalyi (1988) later suggests that the ability to experience flow may be learned in the family, developed through practice, or even have a neurological component. Whatever the underlying explanation for the individual differences, Ellis, Voelkl, and Morris (1994) find that considerable variation in subjective experience was explained by variables that indicated the autotelic nature of the person, over and above the variance explained by the perceived congruence of skills and challenges. For marketers, the crucial implication is that the relative likelihood a person will experience flow is an important segmentation basis in a CME.

5. Optimal stimulation level and flow

People with a higher optimal stimulation level (OSL) are more likely to possess the autotelic personality trait. The fundamental idea of OSL theories (e.g., Zuckerman, 1979) is that an intermediate level of stimulation obtained from the environment corresponds to the most favorable affective reaction. Furthermore, there are individual differences in the OSL – with people having a higher OSL exhibiting increased curiosity-motivated, variety-seeking, risk-taking (Steenkamp and Baumgartner, 1992), and exploratory behavior (Raju, 1980). Holbrook and Gardner (1993) found the duration time of consumption of an experiential good to be related to an optimal arousal level, which has clear implications for experiential consumer behavior in a CME.

As we previously discussed, flow in a CME requires the congruence of above-threshold skills and challenges. Yet, people with low optimal stimulation levels are more likely to experience anxiety in their initial interactions with a CME, as they will be overwhelmed by the wide variety of options available to them and will perceive their skills to be well below the uncomfortably high stimulation level of the CME (i.e., the challenges of the task). Furthermore, people with low OSLs who have mastered the basics of network navigation also are more likely to later become bored with a CME, as they will be relatively less likely to seek out sufficiently high challenges to maintain congruence with their increasing skills. Thus, we anticipate that people with higher OSLs are more likely to possess the autotelic personality trait and experience flow in a CME.

Experiential and goal-directed behavior in a CME

6. Definition of experiential and goal-directed behavior

Two broad categories of behavior in which consumers engage during time spent in a CME are goal-directed and experiential behavior. Goal-directed and experiential behavior are characterized respectively by (1) extrinsic versus intrinsic motivation,

(2) instrumental versus ritualized orientation, (3) situational versus enduring involvement, (4) utilitarian versus hedonic benefits, (5) directed versus nondirected search, and (6) goal-directed versus navigational choice.

For example, the corporate buyer using the Web to close a deal for computer components experiences an extrinsically motivated, instrumental, goal-directed flow state. On the other hand, net surfers exploring the Web in their daily quest for the latest interesting sites experience an intrinsically motivated, ritualized, experiential flow state. It is important to recognize that consumers engage in both goal-directed and experiential behaviors, flow may occur with both types of behaviors, and the optimal design of a CME site differs according to whether the behavior is goal-directed or experiential.

In the communications literature, a distinction is drawn between instrumental and ritualized orientations to media (Rubin, 1984; Rubin and Perse, 1987). Ritualized orientations focus 'more on the medium, rather than on particular content', are 'associated with diffuse motives (e.g., pass time, habit, relaxation)', and are a 'less intentional and non-selective orientation, a time-filling activity' (Rubin and Perse, 1987, p. 59). In contrast, instrumental orientations are 'more intentional and selective', which reflects 'purposive exposure to specific content' (p. 59). The distinction between instrumental and ritualized orientations bears considerable resemblance to the classification of expected benefits in the marketing literature into utilitarian and hedonic or experiential benefits (e.g., Havlena and Holbrook, 1986; Srinivasan, 1987), which as we previously noted are, respectively, extrinsically and intrinsically motivated.

We also can differentiate flow states resulting from goal-directed and experiential behaviors on the basis of involvement and search behavior. Most commercial Web sites currently provide information rather than offer an opportunity to purchase a product. Thus, much of today's consumer search activities are more likely to involve what has been termed *ongoing search* than *prepurchase search* (Bloch, Sherrell, and Ridgway, 1986, p. 121). Similarly, Biehal and Chakravarti (1982, 1983) distinguish between directed and nondirected learning. Bloch, Sherrell, and Ridgway (1986) note that ongoing search is a function of enduring involvement with the product (or with the CME), whereas prepurchase search is a function of situational involvement with the purchase.

For choice, in experiential behavior, 'activities are not guided by goals or outcomes, but by the process itself' (Bloch, Sherrell, and Ridgway, 1986, p. 121). Similarly, Deci and Ryan (1985, p. 155) note that for intrinsically motivated people engaged in flow, choice is 'intuitive and spontaneous' and does not involve conscious, deliberate decisions. Consumer choice in goal-directed behavior is based on a clearly definable goal hierarchy, and movement through this goal hierarchy involves choices among products and services, information sources, and navigational alternatives. Consumer choice in experiential behavior is dominated by choices among navigational alternatives and corresponds to a relatively unstructured and continually changing goal hierarchy.

7. Search motives and involvement for experiential and goal-directed behavior
Goal-directed versus experiential behaviors depend on distinct search motives combined with the object of involvement:

Search motive	Involvement	Behavior
Task completion	Situational involvement with **goal** →	Goal-directed
Prepurchase deliberation	Situational involvement with **product** →	Goal-directed
Build information bank	Enduring involvement with **product** →	Experiential
Opinion leadership	Enduring involvement with **product** →	Experiential
Recreation	Enduring involvement with **process** →	Experiential

Goal-directed behaviors are characterized by situational involvement and directed search. In general, a CME user is involved with a specific task-completion goal. Marketers are particularly concerned with understanding the prepurchase deliberations for product purchase goals. Search motives in experiential behaviors, however, are more varied. When the consumer exhibits enduring involvement with a product or product category, Bloch, Sherrell, and Ridgway (1986), Biehal and Chakravarti (1982, 1983), and Bettman (1979) indicate that consumers may search to build an information bank or knowledge base in their memories for potential future use. In addition, Richins and Root-Shaffer (1988) find that enduring involvement (occurring in experiential flow) led to opinion leadership, whereas situational involvement did not. Thus, an opinion leader may be motivated to search and engage in experiential behaviors to disseminate product news, advice, and personal experience by word of mouth. Moreover, consider that consumers may be involved with the CME itself. Bloch (1995) suggests that there are two likely segments of consumers who navigate a CME: (1) those who exhibit enduring involvement with an interest area and (2) those who are navigating because they exhibit enduring involvement with computers. We propose that the latter segment is engaged in nondirected search for recreational purposes (Bloch, Sherrell, and Ridgway, 1986; Csikszentmihalyi, 1983).

Thus, experiential behavior is relevant for (1) word-of-mouth strategies based on influencing opinion leaders, (2) providing entertainment and recreation, and (3) enhancing consumers' product knowledge, whereas goal-directed behavior is relevant for task-specific use of a CME, such as prepurchase deliberation. This distinction is critical and suggests that marketers should take care to focus not only on goal-directed behaviors in a CME (e.g., product purchase), but also on nondirected experiential behaviors (e.g., net surfing), which are strategically important as well.

8. External memory

A CME can provide devices for external memory: User-generated 'bookmark files' containing custom lists of consumers' favorite Web sites are cases in point, as is comparative information about brands (e.g., product reviews), which is directly retrievable through an on-line storefront. Although information gained from goal-directed search activity is more accessible in memory than that from experiential search activity, CMEs provide services for external memory that negate this advantage. Biehal and Chakravarti (1983) find that information retrieved from directed search (goal-directed) had greater memory accessibility than information retrieved from nondirected search (experiential). Furthermore, the likelihood of choosing a brand for which information was acquired during directed search was not significantly different than the likelihood of choosing a brand for which information was externally available; in both situations, the choice likelihood was greater than when brand information was acquired through nondirected search. However, the external memory devices present in CMEs imply that information retrieved from nondirected search should have a greater impact on subsequent consumer choice behavior than that in traditional environments, because the external memory devices are used by the consumer.

9. Choice behavior and decision making in a CME

We also distinguish goal-directed and experiential behavior on the basis of consumer decision and choice processes. Most research on consumer choice and decision making in marketing, deals with activities directly involving or motivated by product purchase (e.g., Payne, Bettman, and Johnson, 1993). Although theories of problem-solving behavior have been developed for extensive, limited, and routine problem-solving scenarios, all three scenarios are typically motivated by a purchase outcome. In a CME, however, the process of network navigation continually confronts the consumer with an ongoing series of decisions that are potentially but not necessarily related to a purchase outcome or other task completion. Although existing models of adaptive decision making can explain much of goal-directed choice in a CME, they hold relatively lesser applicability to navigational choice in flow occurring from experiential behavior. In addition, CMEs provide devices that augment the individual decision processes with input from communal or machine agents.

Choice in experiential behavior primarily involves an ongoing series of navigational decisions of what to do next. This is a highly unstructured activity and, as was noted previously, corresponds to an intrinsically motivated, ritualized, hedonic use of the CME. Nonetheless, a key assumption of the nature of adaptive decision behavior expected in goal-directed situations – 'that people are motivated to use as little effort as necessary to solve a problem' (Payne, Bettman, and Johnson, 1993, p. 13) – would realistically hold in nondirected experiential situations as well. Thus, in deciding among navigational alternatives, heuristics and noncompensatory decision rules most likely would be applied in experiential activities. Relatively little research, however, deals with choice behavior during experiential activities, so we must be cautious and not overly dependent on goal-directed decision strategies to provide explanations of consumer choice. We liken flow from experiential behaviors to navigating through an amusement park where the visitor is presented with a wide array of ride choices in a nonlinear fashion.

For flow occurring with experiential behaviors, outcome variables other than choice should be investigated. For example, Holbrook and Gardner (1993) argue that duration time is a critical outcome measure of consumption experiences, and Olney, Holbrook, and Batra (1991) use viewing time as a dependent variable in a model of advertising effects. Indeed, duration times are a useful behavioral indicator of experiential versus goal-directed orientations. For example, 43% of all calls to the French Minitel system are for the electronic telephone directory (a goal-directed activity) but account for only 21% of the total connect time. On the other hand, only 6% of all calls to Minitel are for the chat services (an experiential activity), but they account for 15% of the total connect time (Cats-Baril and Jelassi, 1994).

In structured decision environments, such as an on-line storefront offering a variety of goods, the strategies typically applied by consumers in traditional environments (e.g., Payne, Bettman, and Johnson 1993, Chapter 2) are more likely to be used. These strategies, however, will be augmented by powerful decision aids (e.g., Payne, Bettman, and Johnson 1993, Chapter 7) that are feasible only in a CME. At the most basic level, these decision aids involve information displays that increase the consumer's processing capacity, whereas more sophisticated approaches use decision support systems to assist the decision maker. Both of these categories of decision aids are local rather than network-based, because they involve only information presented at a given location in a CME.

Intelligent interface agents (e.g., Maes, 1994) provide a network-based decision aid, which is particularly useful for vastly enhancing the consumers' ability to perform search activities by reducing information overload. An example of an agent present on the World Wide Web is Digital Research Laboratory's Alta Vista search engine (www.altavista.digital.com), a robot program that automatically traverses the World Wide Web in search of hypermedia documents and stores and categorizes them in an extensive and rapidly growing database that can be accessed by an intelligent search interface. As of March 1996, the Alta Vista database can access 11 billion words found in over 22 million Web pages.

Although agents have been portrayed in the popular media as engaging in semiautonomous, high-level, human-like interactions, 'the most successful interface agents are those that do not prohibit the user from taking actions and fulfilling tasks personally' (Maes, 1994, p. 31). Thus, agents can serve as effective decision aids in an information intensive environment. One promising approach in a networked environment such as a CME are collaborative interface agents (Lashkari, Metral, and Maes, 1994), which combine decision aids across a segment of similar consumers, rather than rely on a single consumer's input.

10. Developmental patterns of flow states

We expect that experiential behavior dominates a user's early flow experiences in a CME, but that over time goal-directed behavior also leads to flow experiences. Early interactions in the hypermedia CME that lead to flow are characterized by a nondirected, time-passing, ritualized quality. Over time, ritualized use evolves into instrumental use as consumers accumulate experience navigating within the medium. A greater degree of technical skill is required to successfully perform goal-directed behaviors than experiential behaviors. Experiential behaviors, in which the consumer experiments and becomes familiar with the CME, are accompanied by an increase in skills that the consumer develops to meet the challenges presented by the environment. In other words, learning occurs and consumers begin to seek greater challenges. Thus, an 'instrumental' orientation is likely to dominate a consumer's later interactions in the environment, though both orientations may be present at different points in time, depending on consumer characteristics.

This discussion has important implications for the adoption of CMEs, particularly for those people seeking the 'killer application'. Developmental patterns of flow states suggest that goal-directed behaviors such as home shopping and home banking do not necessarily lead to flow for new users of a CME. On the other hand, experiential behaviors, such as browsing on-line magazines, participating in interactive chat rooms, and exploring a Web corporate home page for a topic with which the consumer exhibits enduring involvement, would be more likely to lead to flow and thus stimulate adoption in new users.

The consequences of flow

In the final set of research issues, we address consequences of flow. Based on the existing literature, consumers who experience flow in a hypermedia CME achieve increased learning, increased perceived behavioral control (PBC), increased exploratory and participatory behavior, and positive subjective experiences. In addition, we briefly consider potentially negative consequences of flow. Research Issues 11 through 15, seen in the context of the network navigation model in Figure 6, contrast consumers who experience the flow state versus those who do not. These research issues apply to both heterogeneity *across* consumers according to their ability to experience flow (Research Issue 4) and heterogeneity *within* consumers according to whether flow is experienced (Research Issues 2 and 3). Thus, flow is viewed as both a trait and a state, much as Webster and Martocchio (1992) view playfulness as both a trait and a state. Note that other researchers have viewed positive mood as both a trait and a state (e.g., George, 1991).

11. Consumer learning

Consumers who experience the flow state are more likely to retain more of what they perceive than consumers who do not. Playfulness (Webster and Martocchio, 1992) and flow (Webster, Trevino, and Ryan, 1993) have been found to relate to learning. Early ritualized use of a CME (i.e., scanning, exploring, and wandering; see Canter, Rivers, and Storrs, 1985) facilitates the learning needed to progress to instrumental usage involving browsing and searching (i.e., purposive search behavior to identify on-line vendors selling products or services desired by the consumer). Webster, Trevino, and Ryan (1993) suggest that because consumers develop and apply their abilities through exploratory behaviors that characterize flow interactions, learning is a reasonable outcome of the flow state.

The distinction between directed and nondirected learning (Bettman, 1979; Biehal and Chakravarti, 1982, 1983) further differentiates flow occurring in goal-directed and experiential behaviors. In experiential behavior, ongoing, nondirected search produces latent learning (Hilgard and Bower, 1966, pp. 199–200), in which the consumer learns about the environment, 'even if the specific knowledge gained has no direct relevance to current purchases' (Bettman, 1979, p. 88). In goal-directed behavior, a produce choice decision or specific task completion is the primary goal for learning. Consumer learning suggests that flow resulting from goal-directed behaviors leads to more informed decisions, whereas flow resulting from experiential behaviors leads to greater recall and word-of-mouth activities.

12. Perceived behavioral control

Consumers who experience the flow state in a hypermedia CME are expected to have greater PBC than those who do not. *Perceived behavioral control* is defined as 'the perceived ease or difficulty of performing the behavior and ... is assumed to reflect past experience as well as anticipated impediments and obstacles' (Azjen, 1988, p. 132). Perceived behavioral control is a component of Azjen's (1988, 1991) theory of planned behavior, extends the well-known theory of reasoned action (Azjen and Fishbein,

1980), and is useful for predicting behaviors that are not under complete volitional control. Similar to the original expectancy-value model, the theory of a planned behavior posits that conceptually independent determinants of attitudes toward the behavior, subjective norms with respect to the behavior, and a new component – *perceived control over the behavior* – affect behavioral intentions. In addition, PBC directly affects behavior. Thus, usage of a hypermedia CME (for those people with the prerequisite technology) depends jointly on motivation (intentions) and ability (behavioral control).

Perceived behavioral control (cf. Bandura's [1977, 1982] earlier notion of *perceived self-efficacy*) also can be interpreted as a confidence construct and is an important determinant of CME usage, because behavior in a CME is strongly influenced by consumers' confidence in their ability to engage in network navigation. A consumer's perception of behavioral control over CME use and its impact on intentions and actions is more important that real control (Azjen, 1988).

Flow significantly correlates with perceived control (Ghani, Supnick, and Rooney, 1991). Webster, Trevino, and Ryan (1993) define control as one of four dimensions of flow and find that it significantly correlated with two of the other three dimensions (curiosity and intrinsic interest, but not attention focus). Webster and Martocchio (1992) find a significant correlation between microcomputer playfulness and self-rated computer competence. Because the hypermedia CME is, first and foremost, an interactive environment, it affords the foundation for consumer control that is impossible in traditional, passive media. Control comes from both consumers' perception of their ability to adjust the CME and their perception of how the CME responds to their input, with consumer adjustment taking the form of network navigation.

We here imply that flow resulting from experiential behavior results in increased PBC over network navigation, whereas flow resulting from goal-directed behavior results in increased PBC over task completion. Because the former is a prerequisite for the latter, experiential behavior flow facilitates the learning necessary to 'move up' to goal-directed activities.

13. Exploratory behavior

We expect that consumers who experience the flow state in a hypermedia CME exhibit more exploratory behaviors than those who do not. Webster, Trevino, and Ryan (1993) found that flow correlated positively with experimentation and perceptions of software flexibility and modifiability. Other researchers have found that higher levels of playfulness or flow in human-computer interactions correlate with higher experimentation (Ghani and Deshpande, 1994; Ghani, Supnick, and Rooney, 1991; Katz, 1987). This argues for a flexible hypermedia environment that encourages exploratory behavior on the part of consumers. Implications of increased exploratory behaviors are increased risk taking in goal-directed behaviors (Raju, 1980; Steenkamp and Baumgartner, 1992) and broader exposure to content in experiential behaviors. Furthermore, increased exploratory use has been found to lead to greater extent of use (Ghani and Deshpande, 1994).

14. Positive subjective experiences

We expect that consumers who experience the flow state in a hypermedia CME exhibit more positive subjective experiences than those who do not. Webster, Trevino, and Ryan (1993, p. 412) note that 'higher playfulness results in immediate subjective experiences such as positive mood and satisfaction' (Csikszentmihalyi, 1977; Levy, 1983; McGrath and Kelly, 1986). Previous research on human-computer interactions (Sandelands and Buckner, 1989; Starbuck and Webster, 1991; Webster and Martocchio, 1992) has shown that higher degrees of pleasure and involvement during computer interactions lead to concurrent subjective perceptions of positive affect and mood. A study conducted by Gardner, Dukes and Discenza (1993) shows that the more people use computers, the more their self-confidence with respect to computers increases. This in turn causes more favorable attitudes toward computers. Csikszentmihalyi (1977, p. 36) notes that 'people seek flow primarily for itself', thus, flow itself serves as a positive reinforcer, which increases the probability of further use of a hypermedia CME.

Together, positive subjective experiences and the increased PBC resulting from flow feed back into the planned behavior model discussed previously and increase the probability that the CME will be used in the future. Webster, Trevino, and Ryan (1993) find flow to be positively correlated with expectations of future voluntary computer interactions. Thus, we anticipate that the positive affect generated by flow translates into longer duration time spent visiting a CME and increased repeat visits.

15. Distortion in time perception

The positive subjective experience of flow also has been linked to a distortion in time perception (Csikszentmihalyi, 1977), whereby the consumer is unaware of the passage of time. Hauser, Urban, and Weinberg (1993) provide a model of how, in the presence of time pressure, the allocation of search time to negative information sources increases, whereas in the absence of time pressure, the allocation of search time to positive information sources increases. Thus, to the extent that the flow state reduces time pressure and increases time spent at the site, it contributes to a relatively greater amount of time being allocated to searching for positive information sources. Because of the tendency of computer-mediated environments to encourage negative word-of-mouth communications, actions that marketers can take to facilitate positive search behavior become particularly important.

Negative consequences of flow

There are some potentially negative consequences of flow that must be considered. Because flow can be its own reward, consumers may explore a CME for its own sake, rather than purposely search for specific information. Thus, too much flow may distract the consumer from purchase-related activities. As Webster, Trevino, and Ryan (1993, p. 422) note, playfulness may produce longer time to task completion; at an extreme, 'playful computer systems may be so enjoyable that employees neglect other tasks'. However, if one marketing objective of a hypermedia CME is to encourage the consumer to spend time at the site examining product-related information, for example, then this is not necessarily a problem. Flow has also been linked to over involvement (Csikszentmihalyi, 1977), which leads to mental and physical fatigue. A related source of cognitive fatigue stems from the overwhelming complexity inherent in global hypermedia content (Gygi, 1990).

DISCUSSION AND CONCLUSION

The hypermedia CME represents a fundamentally different environment for marketing activities than do traditional media and so-called interactive multimedia.

The many-to-many communication model turns traditional principles of mass media advertising (based on the one-to-many model of Figure 1) inside out, rendering impossible the blind application of marketing and advertising approaches that assume a passive, captive consumer. Thus, marketers must carefully consider the ways in which advertising and communication models can be adapted and reconstructed (e.g., see Hoffman and Novak, 1996) for the interactive, many-to-many medium depicted in Figure 3. In that new communication model, consumers can actively choose whether to approach firms through their Web sites and exercise unprecedented control over the management of the content with which they interact.

The opportunity for customer interaction in the hypermedia CME also is unprecedented. This can be utilized in numerous ways, including (1) the design of new products, (2) the development of product and marketing strategy, and (3) the innovation of content. The evolution of content in a hypermedia CME depends on not only the evolution of existing metaphors and communication codes from traditional media, but also new techniques and conventions inherent in the possibilities of the medium itself (Biocca, 1992). One implication of this is that the content that makes hypermedia CMEs commercially successful likely has not been invented yet and may require more than a simple continuous innovation of existing content (Grossman, 1994).

Because consumers vary in their ability to achieve flow, new bases for market segmentation are needed for marketing in hypermedia CMEs. Scholars must determine the variables that relate to a consumer's propensity to enter the flow state. Such information can be used to develop marketing efforts designed to maximize the chances of the consumer entering the flow state. Because we believe that repeat consumption behavior, that is, repeat visits to a hypermedia CME, are increased if the environment facilitates the flow state, the marketing objective at trial must provide for these flow opportunities.

In summary, the new medium-as-market represented by the hypermedia CME – of which the World Wide Web on the Internet currently stands as the preeminent prototype – offers a working example of a many-to-many communication model in which the consumer is an active participant in an interactive exercise of multiple feedback loops and highly immediate communication. As such, it offers dynamic potential for growth and development, as well as a virtual revolution in both the way marketing academics and practitioners alike approach the problem of effective, consumer-oriented marketing in emerging media environments.

REFERENCES

Ajzen, Icek (1988), *Attitudes, Personality, and Behavior*. Chicago: Dorsey Press.

___ (1991), 'The Theory of Planned Behavior', *Organizational Behavior and Human Decision Processes*, Special Issue: Theories of Cognitive Self-Regulation, 50 (2), 179–211.

___ and Fishbein, M. (1980), *Understanding Attitudes and Predicting Social Behavior*. Englewood-Cliffs, NJ: Prentice-Hall.

Bandura, A. (1977), 'Self-Efficacy: Toward a Unifying Theory of Behavioral Change', *Psychological Review*, 84, 191–215.

___ (1982), 'Self-Efficacy Mechanism in Human Agency', *American Psychologist*, 37, 122–47.

Berners-Lee, T, R. Cailliau, N. Pellow, and A. Secret (1993), 'The World-Wide Web Initiative', in *Proceedings 1993 International Networking Conference*. [http://info.isoc.org/ftp/isoc/inet/inet93/papers/DBC.Berners-Lee]

Bettman, James (1979), *An Information Processing Theory of Consumer Choice*. Reading, MA: Addison-Wesley Publishing Company.

Biehal, Gabriel and Dipankar Chakravarti (1982), 'Information Presentation Format and Learning Goals as Determinants of Consumers' Memory-Retrieval and Choice Processes', *Journal of Consumer Research*, 8 (March), 431–41.

___ and ___ (1983), 'Information Accessibility as a Moderator of Consumer Choice', *Journal of Consumer Research*, 10 (June), 1–14.

Biocca, Frank (1992), 'Communication Within Virtual Reality: Creating a Space for Research', *Journal of Communication*, 42 (2), 5–22.

Blattberg, Robert C., Rashi Glazer, and John D. C. Little, eds. (1994), *The Marketing Information Revolution*. Boston: Harvard Business School Press.

Bloch, Peter H. (1995), personal email communication, University of Missouri, (April 12).

___ and Marsha L. Richins (1983), 'A Theoretical Model of the Study of Product Importance Perceptions', *Journal of Marketing*, 47 (Summer), 69–81.

___, Daniel L. Sherrell, and Nancy M. Ridgway (1986), 'Consumer Search: An Extended Framework', *Journal of Consumer Research*, 13 (June), 119–26.

Bornman, H., and S. H. Von Solms (1993), 'Hypermedia, Multimedia and Hypertext – Definitions and Overview', *Electronic Library*, 11 (4/5), 259–68.

Bush, V. (1945), 'As We May Think', *Atlantic Monthly*, 176 (1), 101–108.

Canter, David, Rod Rivers, and Graham Storrs (1985). 'Characterizing User Navigation Through Complex Data Structures', *Behaviour and Information Technology*, 4 (2), 93–102.

Carroll, Jon (1994), 'Guerrillas in the Myst', *Wired*, 2 (August), 69–73.

Cats-Baril, William L. And Tawfik Jelassi (1994), 'The French Videotex System Minitel: A Successful Implementation of a National Information Technology Structure', *MIS Quarterly*, 18 (March), 1–20.

Celsi, Richard L., and Jerry C. Olson (1988), 'The Role of Involvement in Attention and Comprehension Processes', *Journal of Consumer Research*, 15 (September), 210–24.

Clark, Tim (1995), 'Net Savings', *Inter@ctive Week*, (October 23), 66.

Clarke, Sharon G., and John T. Haworth (1994), "Flow' Experience in the Daily Lives of Sixth-Form College Students', *British Journal of Psychology*, 85 (4), 511–23.

Csikszentmihalyi, Mihaly (1977), *Beyond Boredom and Anxiety*, San Francisco: Jossey-Bass.

___ (1983), 'Measuring Intrinsic Motivation in Everyday Life', *Leisure Studies*, 2 (May), 155-168.

___ (1988), 'The Future of Flow', in *Optimal Experience: Psychological Studies of Flow in Consciousness*, Mihaly Csikszentmihalyi and Isabella Selega Csikszentmihalyi, eds. Cambridge: Cambridge University Press.

___ (1990), Flow: *The Psychology of Optimal Experience*. New York: Harper and Row.

___ and Isabella Selega Csikszentmihalyi (1988), *Optimal Experience: Psychological Studies of Flow in Consciousness*. Cambridge: Cambridge University Press.

___ and Judith LeFevre (1989), 'Optimal Experience in Work and Leisure', *Journal of Personality and Social Psychology*, 56 (5), 815–22.

___ and J. Nakamura (1989), 'The Dynamics of Intrinsic Motivation: A Study of Adolescents', in *Handbook of Motivation Theory and Research*, Vol. 3, R. Ames and C. Ames, eds. New York: Academic Press, 45–71.

Draft, Richard L. and R. H. Lengel (1986) 'Organizational Information Requirements, Media Richness and Structural Design', *Management Science*, 32(5), 554–71.

___, ___, and L. K. Trevino (1987), 'Message Equivocality, Media Selection and Manager Performance: Implications for Information Systems', *MIS Quarterly*, 11, 355-66.

Davis, Fred D., Richard P. Bagozzi, and Paul R. Warshaw (1992), 'Extrinsic and Intrinsic Motivation to Use Computers in the Workplace', *Journal of Applied Social Psychology*, 22 (14), 1111–32.

December, John and Neil Randall (1995), *The World Wide Web Unleashed*, 2d ed. Indianapolis, IN: Sams.net Publishing.

Deci, Edward L., and Richard M. Ryan (1985), *Intrinsic Motivation and Self-Determination in Human Behavior*. New York: Plenum Press.

Dennis, Everett E., and Joseph S. Valacich (1994), 'Rethinking Media Richness: Towards a Theory of Media Synchronicity', working paper, Terry College of Management, University of Georgia (May 3).

Ellis, Gary D., Judith E. Voelkl, and Catherine Morris (1994), 'Measurement and Analysis Issues With Explanation of Variance in Daily Experience Using the Flow Model', *Journal of Leisure Research*, 26 (4), 337–56.

Gardner, Donald G., Richard L. Dukes, and Richard Discenza (1993), 'Computer Use, Self-Confidence, and Attitudes: A Causal Analysis', *Computers in Human Behavior*, 9 (4), 427–40.

George, J. M. (1991), 'State or Trait: Effects of Positive Mood on Prosocial Behaviors at Work', *Journal of Applied Psychology*, 76 (April), 299–307.

Ghani, Jawaid A., and Satish P. Deshpande (1994), 'Task Characteristics and the Experience of Optimal Flow in Human-Computer Interaction,' *Journal of Psychology*, 128(4), 381–91.

___, Roberta Supnick, and Pamela Rooney (1991), The Experience of flow in Computer-Mediated and in Face-to-Face Groups', in *Proceedings of the Twelfth International Conference on Information Systems*, Janice I. DeGross, Izak Benbasat, Gerardine DeSanctis, and Cynthia Mathis Beath, eds. New York: The Society for Information Management, 229–37.

Gifi, Alert (1990), *Nonlinear Multivariate Analysis*. Chichester, England: John Wiley & Sons.

Glazer, Rashi (1991), 'Marketing in an Information-Intensive Environment: Strategic Implications of Knowledge as an Asset', *Journal of Marketing*, 55 (October) 1–19.

Godwin, Mike (1994), 'Electronic Frontier Justice and the 'Green Card' Ads', *Internet World*, 5 (6), 93–95.

Graef, Ronald, Mihalyi Csikszentmihalyi and Susan McManama Gianinno (1983), 'Measuring Intrinsic Motivation in Everyday Life', *Leisure Studies*, 2, 155–68.

Grossman, Lawrence K. (1994), 'Reflections on Life Along the Electronic Superhighway', *Media Studies Journal*, 8 (1), 27–39.

Gygi, Kathleen (1990), 'Recognizing the Symptoms of Hypertext ... and What to Do About It', in *The Art of Human-Computer Interface Design*, Brenda Laurel, ed. Reading, MA: AddisonWesley, 279–87.

Hafner Katie and Matthew Lyon (1996) *When Wizards Stay Up Late: The Origins of the Internet*. New York: Simon and Schuster. [http://www.hambrecht.com/]

Havlena, William J., and Morris B. Holbrook (1986), 'The Varieties of Consumption Experience: Comparing Two Typologies of Emotion in Consumer Behavior', *Journal of Consumer Research*, 13 (December), 394–404.

Hauser, John R., Glen L. Urban, and Bruce D. Weinberg (1993), 'How Consumers Allocate Their Time When Searching for Information', *Journal of Marketing Research*, 30 (November) 452–66.

Hilgard, Ernest R., and Gordon H. Bauer (1966), *Theories of Learning*, 3rd ed. New York: Appleton-Century-Crofts.

Hoffman, Donna L. And Jan De Leeuw (1992), 'Interpreting Multiple Correspondence Analysis as a Multidimensional Scaling Method', *Marketing Letters*, 3 (3), 259–72

___, William D. Kalsbeek, and Thomas P. Novak (1996), 'Internet Use in the United States: 1995 Baseline Estimates and Preliminary Market Segments', working paper, Owen Graduate School of Management, Vanderbilt University (April). [http://www2000.ogsm.vanderbilt.edu/baseline/1995.Internet.estimates.html]

___, Thomas P. Novak, and Patrali Chatterjee (1995), 'Commercial Scenarios for the Web: Opportunities and Challenges', *Journal of Computer-Mediated Communication*, Special Issue on Electronic Commerce, 1 (December). [http://shum.huji.ac.iljcmc/vol1/issue3/vol1no3.html]

___ and ___ (1996), 'A New Marketing Paradigm for Electronic Commerce', working paper, Owen Graduate School of Management, Vanderbilt University (January).

Holbrook, Morris B., Robert W. Chestnut, Terence A. Oliva, and Eric A. Greenleaf (1984), 'Play as a Consumption Experience: The Roles of Emotions, Performance, and Personality in the Enjoyment of Games', *Journal of Consumer Research*, 11 (September), 728–39.

___ and Meryl P. Gardner (1993), 'An Approach to Investigating the Emotional Determinants of Consumption Durations: Why Do People Consume What They Consume for as Long as They Consume It?', *Journal of Consumer Psychology*, 2 (2), 123–42.

IBM Corporation (1995), 'Electronic Purchasing', IBM Electronic Commerce Services (February 8). [http://wwwl.ibmlink.ibm.com]

Katz, E., and P. F. Lazarfeld (1955), *Personal Influence*, Glencoe, IL: The Free Press.

Katz, J. A. (1987), 'Playing at Innovation in the Computer Revolution', in *Psychological Issues of Human Computer Interaction in the Work Place*, M. Frese, E. Ulich, and W. Dzida, eds. Amsterdam: North-Holland, 97-112.

Kaul, Aditya (1995), personal email communication, University of Tasmania (April 27).

Kotler, P. (1994), *Marketing Management: Analysis, Planning, Implementation and Control*, 8th ed. Englewood Cliffs, NJ: Prentice-Hall.

Lashkari, Yezdi, Max Metral, and Pattie Maes (1994), 'Collaborative Interface Agents', working paper, MIT Media Lab. [http://agents.www.media.mit.edu/groups/agents/abstracts.html]

Lasswell, H. D. (1948), 'The Structure and Function of Communication in Society', in *The Communication of Ideas*, Lyman Bryson, ed. New York: Harper and Brothers.

Levy, J. (1983), *Play Behavior*. Malabar, FL: Robert E. Krieger.

Lutz, Richard J. And Michael Guiry (1994), 'Intense Consumption Experiences: Peaks, Performances, and Flows', presented at the AMA's Winter Marketing Educators' Conference, St. Petersburg, FL (February).

Maes, Pattie (1994), 'Agents That Reduce Work and Information Overload', *Communications of the ACM,* 37 (July), 31–40.

Malone, Thomas W. (1995), 'Inventing the Organizations of the 21st Century: Control, Empowerment, and Information Technology', presentation for the Harvard Business School Colloquium, Multimedia and the Boundaryless World (November 16–17).

Mannell, Roger C., Jiri Zuzanek, and Reed Larson (1988), 'Leisure States and 'Flow' Experiences: Testing Perceived Freedom and Intrinsic Motivation Hypotheses', *Journal of Leisure Research*, 20 (4), 289–304.

Massimini, Fausto and Massimo Carli (1988), 'The Systematic Assessment of Flow in Daily Experience', in *Optimal Experience: Psychological Studies of Flow in Consciousness,* M. Csikszentmihalyi and I. Csikszentmihalyi, eds. New York: Cambridge University Press, 288–306.

McGrath, J. E., and J. R. Kelly (1986), *Time and Human Interaction*, New York: Guilford.

McLuhan, M. (1964), *Understanding Media: The Extensions of Man*. New York: Penguin Press.

Modahl, Mary (1995), 'Forecasts of the Core Economy', in *Forrester Research Report*. Cambridge, MA: Forrester Research (September 11). [http://www.forrester.com/]

Neece, Jerry (1995), personal communication, Senior Product Manager, Sun Microsystems.

Nelson, T. (1967), 'Getting it Out of Our System', in *Information Retrieval: A Critical Review*, G. Schechter, ed. Washington, DC: Thompson Books.

Network Wizards (1996), *Internet Domain Survey*. Menlo Park, CA: Network Wizards. [http://www.nw.com/zone/WWW/top.html]

Oliver, Richard W. (1995), personal communication (November 9).

Olney, Thomas J., Morris B. Holbrook, and Rajeev Batra (1991), 'Consumer Response to Advertising: The Effects of Ad Content, Emotions, and Attitude towards the Ad on Viewing Time', *Journal of Consumer Research,* 17 (March), 440–53.

Open Market (1996), *Commercial Sites Index*. Menlo Park, CA: Open Market. [http://www.directory.net/]

Payne, John W., James R. Bettman, and Eric J. Johnson (1993), *The Adaptive Decision Maker*. Cambridge: Cambridge University Press.

Perse, Elizabeth and John A. Courtright (1993), 'Normative Images of Communication Media: Mass and Interpersonal Channels in the New Media Environment', *Human Communication Research,* 19 (4), 485–503.

Potter, Edward (1994), 'Commercialization of the World Wide Web' Internet conference on The WELL, (November 16).

Privette, Gayle (1983), 'Peak Experience, Peak Performance, and Flow: A Comparative Analysis of Positive Human Experience', *Journal of Personality and Social Psychology*, 45 (6), 1361–68.

___ (1984), *Experience Questionnaire*, Pensacola, FL: The University of West Florida.

___ and Charles M. Bundrick (1987), 'Measurement of Experience: Construct and Content Validity of the Experience Questionnaire', *Perceptual and Motor Skills*, 65, 315–32.

Rafaeli, S. (1988), 'Interactivity: From New Media To Communication', in *Advancing Communication Science: Merging Mass and Interpersonal Processes*, R. P. Hawkins, J. M. Wieman, and S. Pingree, eds. Newbury Park, CA: Sage Publications, 110-34.

Raju, P. S. (1980), 'Optimum Stimulation Level: Its Relationship to Personality, Demographics, and Exploratory Behavior', *Journal of Consumer Research*, 7 (December), 272–82.

Rangaswamy, Arvind and Yoram Wind (1994), 'Don't Walk In, Just Log In! Electronic Markets and What They Mean for Marketing', working paper, Pennsylvania State University (December).

Reardon, Kathleen K. And Everitt M. Rogers (1988), 'Interpersonal Versus Mass Communication: A False Dichotomy', *Human Communication Research*, 15 (2) 284–303.

Rheingold, Howard L. (1992), 'A Slice of Life in My Virtual Community'. [gopher://nkosi.well.sf.ca.us/00/Community/virtual_communities92]

Rice, Ronald E. (1992), 'Task Analysability, Use of New Media, and Effectiveness: A Multi-Site Exploration of Media Richness', *Organizational Science*, 3 (4), 475–500.

___ (1993), 'Media Appropriateness: Using Social Presence Theory to Compare Traditional and New Organizational Media', *Human Communication Research*, 19 (4), 451–85.

Richins, Marsha L., and Terri Root-Schaffer (1988). 'The Role of Involvement and Opinion Leadership in Consumer Word-of-Mouth: An Implicit Model Made Explicit', in *Advances in Consumer Research*, Vol. 15, Michael J. Houston, ed. Provo, UT: Association for Consumer Research, 32–36.

Rogers, Everett M. (1986), *Communication Technology: The New Media in Society*. New York: The Free Press.

Rubin, Alan M. (1984), 'Ritualized and Instrumental Television Viewing', *Journal of Communication*, 34 (3), 67–77.

___ and Elizabeth M. Perse (1987), 'Audience Activity and Television News Gratifications', *Communication Research*, 14 (1), 58–84.

Sandelands, L. E., and G. C. Buckner (1989), 'Of Art and Work: Aesthetic Experience and the Psychology of Work Feelings', in *Research in Organizational Behavior*, L. L. Cummings and B. M. Staw, eds. Greenwich, CT: JAI Press.

Sheridan, Thomas B. (1992), 'Musings on Telepresence and Virtual Presence', *Presence: Teleoperators and Virtual Environments*, 1 (1), 120–26.

Smith, Pauline A., and John R. Wilson (1993), 'Navigation in Hypertext Through Virtual Environments', *Applied Ergonomics*, 24 (4), 271–78.

Srinivasan, T. J. (1987), 'An Integrative Approach to Consumer Choice', in *Advances in Consumer Research*, Vol. 14, Melanie Wallendorf and Paul Anderson, eds. Provo, UT: Association for Consumer Research, 96–101.

Starbuck, W. J., and J. Webster (1991), 'When Is Play Productive?', *Accounting, Management, and Information Technology*, 1, 71–90.

Steenkamp, Jan-Benedict and Hans Baumgartner (1992), 'The Role of Optimum Stimulation Level in Exploratory Consumer Behavior', *Journal of Consumer Research*, 19 (December), 434–48.

Steuer, Jonathan (1992), 'Defining Virtual Reality: Dimensions Determining Telepresence', *Journal of Communication*, 42 (4), 73–93.

Stewart, David W., and Scott Ward (1994), 'Media Effects on Advertising', in *Media Effects, Advances in Theory and Research*, Jennings Bryand and Dolf Zillman, eds. Hillsdale, NJ: Lawrence Erlbaum Associates.

Trevino, Linda Klebe and Jane Webster (1992), 'Flow in Computer-Mediated Communication', *Communication Research*, 19 (5), 539–73.

Valacich, Joseph S., David Paranka, Joey F. George, and J. F. Nunamaker (1993), 'Communication Concurrency and the New Media: A New Dimension for Media Richness', *Communication Research*, 20 (2) 249–76.

Van Dijk, Jan A. G. M. (1993), 'The Mental Challenge of the New Media', *Medienpsychologie: Zeitschrift fur Individual & Massenkommunikation*, 5 (1), 20–45.

Verity, John W., and Robert D. Hof (1994), 'The Internet: How It Will Change the Way You Do Business', *Business Week*, (November 14), 80–86, 88.

Webster, Jane and Joseph J. Martocchio (1992), 'Microcomputer Playfulness: Development of a Measure With Workplace Implications', *MIS Quarterly*, 16 (June), 201–26.

Webster, J., L. K. Trevino, and L. Ryan (1993), 'The Dimensionality and Correlates of Flow in Human Computer Interactions', *Computers in Human Behavior*, 9 (4), Winter, 411–26.

Williams, Frederick, Sharon Strover, and August E. Grant (1994), 'Social Aspects of New Media Technologies', in *Media Effects, Advances in Theory and Research,* Jennings Bryand and Dolf Zillman, eds. Hillsdale, NJ: Lawrence Erlbaum Associates.

Yahoo (1996). [http://www.yahoo.com/]

Zaichkowsky, Judith L. (1986), 'Conceptualizing Involvement', *Journal of Advertising*, 15 (2), 4–14.

Zuckerman, Marvin (1979), *Sensation Seeking: Beyond the Optimal Level of Arousal.* Hillsdale, NJ: Lawrence Erlbaum Associates.

NOTES

1   For a discussion of the technical terms used in this paper, consult one of the many reference books on the Internet (e.g., December and Randall, 1995). A comprehensive listing of books about the Internet can be found at http://www.switch.ch/switch/Internet-Books.txt. The http address is a Uniform Resource Locator (URL) that specifies the exact location of a document on the Internet. Note that URLs are used in the Reference list to indicate where on-line versions of documents can be identified. Although these URLs were accurate at the time this article was written, it is possible that over time, some of these URLs may have changed or no longer exist.

2   The most recent figures decision makers are using for business planning and research purposes are that the total core economy for electronic commerce on the Internet will approach $45.8 billion by the year 2000 (Modahl, 1995), including $14.2 billion for infrastructure, $2.8 billion for consumer content, $6.9 billion for business content, and $21.9 billion in on-line trade (made up of $6.9 billion in retail and $15 billion in EDI). Additionally, Modahl (1995) forecasts that $46.2 billion in consumer assets will be managed over the Internet by the year 2000, broken down as $29.9 billion in mutual funds and $16.3 billion in deposits. However, analysts at Hambrecht and Quist (1995, www.hambrecht.com) estimate a much larger Internet economy of $73 billion by the year 2000, comprised of $13 billion in infrastructure, $10 billion in content, and $50 billion in transactions. On the other hand, Alex, Brown and Sons (Clark, 1995) forecast a much smaller Internet economy, reaching somewhere between $13.5 billion and $16 billion by 1998, composed of a $6 billion infrastructure, $5 billion to $7 billion in communication access, and $2.5 billion in content. Currently, the total Internet economy is estimated at $2 billion (Modahl, 1995). Additionally, the market for the largely digital electronic convergence of content systems, publishing, and so on is already estimated at over $1 trillion (Oliver, 1995). None of these forecasts include efficiency savings from moving processes and transactions on-line.

3   A FAQ is a frequently asked question to which standardized replies are both readily available and desirable.

4   In this case, ordinal restrictions were imposed on the number of linked sources (one, few, many) and the three-category variable specifying presence of text content. The communication model also was treated as two separate ordinal variables – the number of senders (one, few, many) and the number of receivers (one, few, many). Because all other variables were either binary (person-interactivity, machine-interactivity, audio, video, image, experiential, and media feedback symmetry) or nominal (temporal synchronicity), no other ordinal restrictions were imposed.

Hoffman, D. and Novak, T. P. (1996) 'Marketing in hypermedia computer-mediated environments: conceptual foundations'. *Journal of Marketing*, 60, July: 50–68. Reproduced with permission from *Journal of Marketing*, published by the American Marketing Association.

Marketing to the digital consumer

5.2

**Alexa Kierzkowski, Shayne McQuade, Robert Waitman
and Michael Zeisser**

The rapid development of interactive media such as online services and the World Wide Web has taken many consumer marketers by surprise. While some marketers are still wondering what to do and how to do it, others are moving forward – but often with mixed success.

Our recent analysis of 95 *Fortune 500* consumer marketing companies with product or service-related Web sites reveals that consumer marketers fall far short of leveraging the full capabilities of interactive media. While over 90 percent of all the digital marketing applications examined provided product or service information and featured basic e-mail capabilities, only about half offered links to other sites and non-product-related content, and fewer than half provided any sort of interactive content, such as a game or a diagnostic requiring some user input. Most revealingly, only a handful of the examined sites made an effort to seriously collect information about their users, and fewer than 5 per cent provided an opportunity to allow user-to-user communications, a unique – and one of the most popular – characteristics of interactive media.

Most consumer marketers therefore still approach interactive media through the static, one-way, mass-market broadcast model of traditional media. The results of such an approach are uninspiring applications that fall far short of the new media's potential. Shrewd marketers will instead learn to create entirely new forms of interactions and transactions with consumers. To do so they'll need a new marketing model more appropriate to the new consumer marketspace[1] and new approaches to integrating interactive media into their business system and marketing programs.

We believe that digital marketing is an attractive proposition for more consumer product or service categories than is typically assumed. In fact most consumer marketers – be they in financial services, travel music, and books, even food and beverages – should be exploring how to capture the digital world's business opportunities.

EVOLUTION'S GRIP

For marketers of consumer goods or services, the emergence of a new consumer marketspace is no longer a matter of speculation or hype. In the consumer world, users of many popular branded products subscribe today to interactive media at rates two to three times the national average (Exhibit 1). By 2000, there will be between 30 and 40 million of such 'digital' consumers.

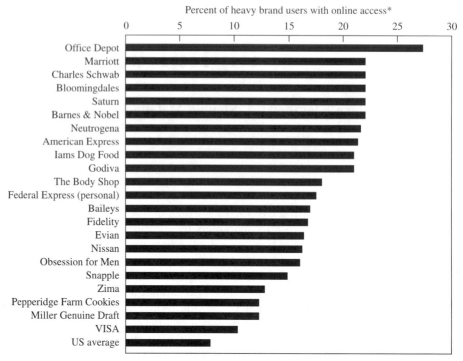

*includes access to online services and the internet

Exhibit 1 Online access by heavy users of brands.
Source: Yankelovich, 1995 data

Digital consumers are, generally speaking, attractive for marketers (Exhibit 2). Digital consumers are more likely than their non-wired counterparts to spend more to get the best and to make an effort to use new devices and methods. Household income levels among current subscribers to online services and Internet users are considerably higher than average, as are education levels. Meanwhile, key technological barriers are falling – particularly the speed of content delivery. By the year 2000, more than 50 per cent of these digital consumers are expected to access interactive media at speeds five to 500 times faster than they can today.

A back-of-the-envelope calculation, based on published estimates[2], suggests that a substantial Internet economy is emerging. Potential revenues across infrastructure, content, and trade businesses suggest an estimated $40 to $50 billion Internet economy in place by the year 2000.

The rise of this consumer marketspace is clearly aligned with the evolutionary progress of the marketing function from a mass-market model to more interactive personalization of goods, services, and interactions. With interactive media, marketers can dynamically deliver personalized services and content, in real time, one consumer at a time. This is due to the unique and powerful characteristics of interactive media: it is addressable, meaning that each user can be identified and targeted separately; it allows for two-way interaction; services can be tailored for each individual customer; and purchases can be made and influenced online

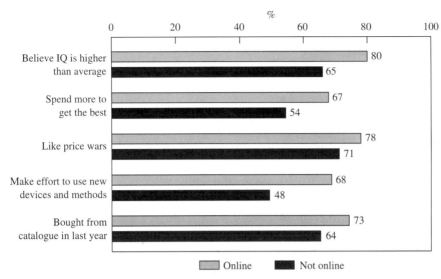

Exhibit 2 Appeal of online consumers.
Source: Yankelovich

(Exhibit 3). Capturing the business opportunities associated with these unique characteristics is the essence of digital marketing.

WHERE TO START?

Several broad types of attractive digital marketing opportunities already exist. In fact, aggressive players are already starting to make money with them. We believe there are three main opportunities today:

1. **The information-delivery opportunity**. Marketers can use interactive media to provide higher service and lower cost by delivering information about products or services. Examples of marketers pursuing this opportunity include Federal Express, UPS, and Sun Computers.
2. **The relationship-building opportunity**. Marketers can leverage interactive media to identify attractive self-selected users/prospects, enhance loyalty by providing value-added services, and use what they learn about their customers to customize existing or cross-sell new products and services. Examples include Volvo, Zima, Hyatt, Fidelity, Citibank Direct, HotHotHot, and many others.
3. **The channel/(dis)intermediation opportunity**. Marketers can use interactive media as a new channel and either go direct to eliminate traditional intermediaries or establish an entirely new role as a value-added intermediary. Examples include United Airlines, Amazon.com, Quicken, and Shoppers Advantage.

But these opportunities are unlikely to offer any meaningful opportunity to those companies that fail to make digital marketing an integrated part of their business system and marketing programs. In each of the following examples, marketers are succeeding by closely tying digital marketing to their core business systems.

```
┌─────────────────────────────────────────┐
│  On-demand availability                   │
│  24-hour access                           │
│  24-hour service                          │
│  ─────────────────────────────────────   │
│  Addressable                              │
│  Direct communication to an               │
│  individual user                          │
│  ─────────────────────────────────────   │
│  Two-way interactive                      │
│  Learn from direct feedback               │
│  Enable user-to-user interaction          │
│  ─────────────────────────────────────   │
│  Effective information delivery           │
│  More content than any other media        │
│  Easy to search large databases           │
│  ─────────────────────────────────────   │
│  Customized                               │
│  Easily tailor communication and          │
│  products/services                        │
│  ─────────────────────────────────────   │
│  Seamless transactions                    │
│  Influence consumers when closest         │
│  to the transaction                       │
│  Enable purchase online                   │
└─────────────────────────────────────────┘
```

Exhibit 3 Attractive characteristics of interactive media.

The information-delivery opportunity

UPS provides a compelling example of how information and customer service can be efficiently provided on the Internet. Since package delivery services are as much about providing information and customer service as they are about delivering packages, providing timely and easy-to-use package tracking and other related information (e.g., pricing, delivery times) is a key basis of competitive differentiation.

UPS has found that their site on the World Wide Web allows them to improve quality and response time in dealing with customer information requests; it is also more cost-effective.

This can be seen in Exhibit 4. We estimate the cost of dealing with package tracking requests via telephone to be about 90 cents per package, whereas the marginal cost of answering these requests on the Internet is zero. The total costs of maintaining a Web site to answer their current volume of package tracking requests is estimated at about $900,000 per annum. If only 75 per cent of online package tracking requests would otherwise have been done through calls to the 1-800 number, the costs would have been about $2.6 million. Therefore on this function alone UPS is saving in the order of $1.7 million per annum. As the volume of requests continues to grow, so too will this cost saving.

The same benefits realized in answering package tracking queries are also captured for other information needs in various ways. These include an automated cost calculation tool, online package pickup requests, and personalized maps to display the time to delivery from specific locations.

Example: UPS Package Tracking   *http://www.ups.com*

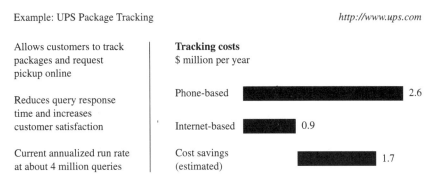

Allows customers to track packages and request pickup online	**Tracking costs** $ million per year
Reduces query response time and increases customer satisfaction	Phone-based — 2.6
	Internet-based — 0.9
Current annualized run rate at about 4 million queries	Cost savings (estimated) — 1.7

Exhibit 4 Digital delivery of information.

Beyond these advantages, UPS's Web site affords them a valuable marketing and relationship-building opportunity. UPS can use their site to learn more about customers and on that basis tailor their services through targeted price incentives and volume incentives, among other things.

The relationship-building opportunity

This is well-illustrated by a single-store retailer in Pasadena, California, called HotHotHot which sells hot sauces, chili mixes, and other spicy food. Ordinarily, the company would be limited in its distribution reach to customers within physical proximity to their store, or to those to whom it might reach through catalogue sales. But in creating one of the Web's first commercial storefronts, owners Monica and Perry Lopez succeeded in establishing an effective direct purchasing channel that gives chiliheads all over the globe access to HotHotHot's selection of over 100 different hot sauces.

The Lopezes opened their store in November 1993, and the following summer began to plan the Web site with a design company which has subsequently gone on to design the Web sites of Pacific Bell and Columbia Tristar, among others. In late 1993 only 5,000 Web sites existed. The compelling design of the site and HotHotHot's unique product offering – sauces carry such attention-grabbing names as Nuclear Hell and Endorphin Rush – soon commanded considerable publicity in the online world. Listing in Yahoo!'s 'What's Cool' and being linked from America Online's and Intel's sites have further contributed to the site's popularity. By promoting the site in the chilihead newsgroup, HotHotHot has brought itself to the attention of chiliheads everywhere. Since the day the site became operational, HotHotHot has received daily orders, creating a steady revenue stream representing 20 per cent of total sales. (Catalogue orders account for 10 per cent, and the retail store for the remaining 70 per cent). What is more, the site drives store traffic, with online customers from all over the United States and Europe stopping by the store when they are in Pasadena.

The economics of marketing online work for HotHotHot – and demonstrate online's advantages over traditional direct marketing. The store doesn't purchase mailing lists for its catalogue effort, but rather sends catalogues only when requested. Even with the self-selected customer base of their catalogue channel helping to lower costs, marketing costs still represent 22 per cent of catalogue revenue. Marketing costs on the Web site amount to only 5 per cent of online revenue (Exhibit 5).

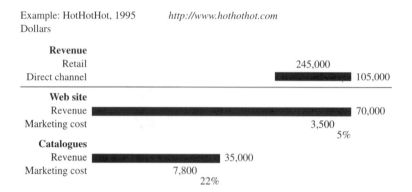

Example: HotHotHot, 1995   *http://www.hothothot.com*
Dollars

Exhibit 5 New channel opportunity.

The Web site has also proven to be a good way for HotHotHot to learn about its customers. Information collected from users reveals that they are mostly male, and like their hot sauce especially fiery – at least that's what they say in their communications. Feedback via email is substantial. It requires an hour and a half daily to read and respond to it, but Monica Lopez appropriately values this customer input and regularly implements suggestions. While the HotHotHot Web site is a successful digital marketing effort by any standards, Lopez recognizes that the medium is still new and quite rough around the edges. But with plans to continue to refine the site and develop it into a true community of interest, the Web site looks like it will be an increasingly integral part of HotHotHot's business.

The channel/(dis)intermediation opportunity

United Connection provides an intriguing example of how digital marketing allows companies to capture the third opportunity of digital marketing – bypassing traditional intermediaries. United Connection is software that allows travelers to book their flights directly without a travel agent. Developed by United Airlines, it is available free of charge to frequent travelers in United's Mileage Plus rewards program. Once a traveler loads the software onto a PC, she or he not only has access to flight information on all major airlines, but can also make a reservation or a booking. At the moment tickets are sent by mail, although with the growing emphasis on paperless ticketing, this will increasingly no longer be necessary.

The economics of such a service are compelling for the airline (Exhibit 6). Typically, travel agent commissions can amount to 10 per cent of the price of a trip. If a typical $500 round-trip fare is purchased through the service, the airline saves $50, and sometimes more if it can avoid other typical travel agent discounts or bonuses such as overrides. Assuming a yearly transaction volume of about 0.8 to 1.0 million tickets, United Airlines would save between $36 and $45 million in distribution costs with its direct-booking services. Eaasy Sabre, a similar service offered by a subsidiary of American Airlines, could be saving the airline about $50 million annually. No wonder then that most airlines have begun or are reported to be about to launch similar services.

Example: Travel industry

Airline distribution costs: $500 round-trip fare

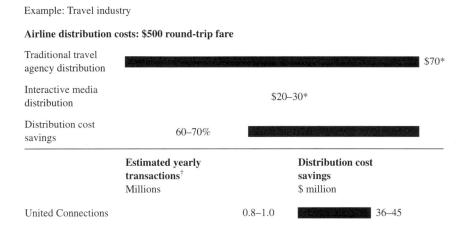

	Estimated yearly transactions[†] Millions	Distribution cost savings $ million
United Connections	0.8–1.0	36–45
Eaasy Sabre	1.0–1.2	45–54

*Approximate figures
[†]As of first quarter 1996

Exhibit 6 Disintermediation opportunity.
Source: Literature search, McKinsey estimates

United Airlines has marketed its direct-booking service aggressively. It advertised the availability of United Connection in many general interest business magazines and in its in-flight magazines, creating broad awareness among potential heavy users. Further, to incent usage, travelers earn 500 frequent flyer points for every ticket purchased through the service. This is well worth it, given the savings achieved for the airline. From a consumer relationship-building perspective, a service such as United Connection presents significant benefits for the airline. By establishing a direct relationship with travelers, the airline can build greater loyalty, and sell more seats. The direct-booking software memorizes trips frequently made, making it easy for the traveler to book the same itinerary again at a later date. Seating and meal preferences can be set, providing added convenience and making the service truly tailored to individual travelers.

In summary, we believe that digital marketing is an attractive proposition for many more consumer product or service categories. Some categories of products or services, such as software or travel, are 'natural fits' with interactive media (i.e., they are information intensive; transactions can be made online; current interactive media users are heavy users). Other categories such as automotive are well suited for digital marketing because they are attractive for relationship – as opposed to mass – marketing. The combination of both these factors, a category's fit with interactive media and its attractiveness for marketing-oriented relationship building, suggests a significant breadth of opportunity for digital marketing (Exhibit 7).

HOW TO DO IT?

Our survey results show that many consumer marketers approach interactive media in the same way they might approach traditional media like television, magazines, or even

High

News Software Selected groceries Interactive games	Insurance Financial Music services Books Real estate Travel brokerage services
Sporting goods Convenience stores Gasoline	Toys White Autos Medical goods services High-end Consumer apparel electronics Fine Baby jewelry products

Fit with
interactive media

Low

Low   High

Potential for relationship building

Exhibit 7 Categories suitable for digital marketing.

direct marketing channels. Yet there are fundamental differences between the two. For example, traditional media involves one-way communication from the marketer to the customer, while interactive media allows marketers to establish a dialogue. Further, marketing through traditional media takes place in a mass-market environment, while interactive media allows marketers to reach (and interact) with individual consumers.

What this means for consumer marketers is that they must build a new model for marketing in new media environments, one that is built around five elements which we believe to be essential factors for success in digital marketing (Exhibit 8):

1. Attract users.
2. Engage users' interest and participation.
3. Retain users and ensure they return to an application.
4. Learn about their preferences.
5. Relate back to them to provide the sort of customized interactions that represent the true 'value bubble' of digital marketing.

Each of the five success factors suggests a number of issues that marketers must address. While the answers to many of these issues will be specific to a given marketer, we are beginning to identify best practices that may guide companies in getting more from their digital marketing efforts.

Attract

Unlike direct and traditional mass marketing, where the interaction is essentially imposed on the consumer, digital marketing requires consumers to voluntarily visit an interactive application, such as a World Wide Web site, or to choose to use a dial-up airline reservation service such as United Connection. Since the current clutter on the Internet virtually ensures that the 'build it and they will come' model is insufficient to draw consumers, marketers need to actively attract users in the first place. Typically, this is achieved by 'billboard' advertisements and links from other sites, listings on the 'what's cool' services, and leveraging existing marketing communications such as advertising or product packaging.

What: **Customize interaction and value delivery**

How: Personalized/customized communications and products/services

Real-time interactions

Linkages to core business

What: **Attract customers to the application**

How: Audience creation

Mnemonic branding

"Piggyback" advertising

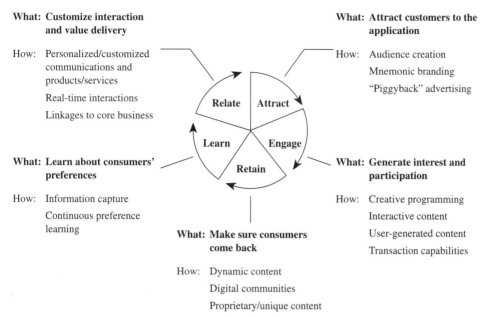

What: **Learn about consumers' preferences**

How: Information capture

Continuous preference learning

What: **Generate interest and participation**

How: Creative programming

Interactive content

User-generated content

Transaction capabilities

What: **Make sure consumers come back**

How: Dynamic content

Digital communities

Proprietary/unique content

Exhibit 8 Digital marketing framework and levers.

Two issues merit particular consideration; first, the issue of branding, or what to call the application. Based on the precedent of telephone services where the success of services such as 1-800-MATTRESS or 1-800-FLOWERS is partially due to their names – it may be essential to have a mnemonic 'address' for a digital marketing application which is easy and intuitive for consumers to find and remember, such as *www.zima.com* or *www.hyatt.com*. This becomes even more important due to the need to build digital marketing applications into the marketing mix, which means using the same name for the interactive application as for the product or service that is being promoted. Since problems with name availability and copyright are already beginning to surface, all emerging and aspiring digital marketers should take steps now to ensure the availability of their brand name on the Internet.

The second issue relates to the economics of attracting users. Simply put, attracting users can quickly become unjustifiably expensive relative to the economic value that the digital marketing application is likely to generate in the short term. Marketers must be careful no matter what vehicle they choose to attract users, whether that vehicle involves offering incentives (e.g., certain banks' no-fee bill pay services), using traditional media advertising for digital marketing applications (e.g., United Airlines' magazine ads for United Connection), or making new media promotions (e.g., links to other sites). In all cases, marketers should validate the economics of their promotional activities against their effectiveness, challenging, for example, whether the right types of users are attracted to the digital marketing application, and whether there are more optimal marketing vehicles that the marketer should experiment with. For example, 'piggyback' marketing, which involves leveraging existing marketing efforts to draw traffic to a site, is becoming increasingly prevalent. UPS now features its Internet address at the end of television advertisements and many advertisers list theirs on traditional print advertisements.

Engage

Having attracted users to a digital marketing application, it is imperative that marketers engage users' interest and participation to achieve an interaction or a transaction – that is, after all, a major point of creating the application in the first place. This engagement stage is where too many digital marketing applications fall short. For some applications, the exhibited content is uninspiring, trivial, or poorly presented, while for other applications it is so sophisticated or graphic that it is simply too time-consuming to browse given the unfortunate constraints on bandwidth of most present Internet connections.

The key to engaging users is twofold: mastering creative programming for interactive media (the form) and providing content that is valuable to consumers (the substance).

Very few – if any – marketers have fully cracked the creative programming challenge. Directories such as Yahoo!, Internet-related technology sites such as Netscape, or broad publishing sites such as Pathfinder clearly engage thousands of users every day. However, for each of these seemingly successful applications, there are dozens of others – many developed by world-class marketing companies – that fail to engage users, often because of the questionable quality of their creative programming. A clear lesson learned to date is that simply transferring content from traditional media such as catalogues or co-opting direct marketing copy usually does not work because it often fails to create interaction. In fact, developing content for interactive applications is becoming an expert skill, as evidenced by the emergence of specialized agencies such as Organic Online, CKS, Poppe Tyson, Modem Media, and many others. Marketers who do not have such specialized in-house expertise should not hesitate to outsource their content creation.

In the matter of substance, where marketers are struggling to create content that the consumer will find valuable, the seat auctions held by Cathay Pacific and American Airlines on the World Wide Web may prove to be an interesting example. Arguably, the auctions leverage many of the unique capabilities of the Internet while meeting the objectives not only of consumers but also of the airlines. Other examples include Saturn, the car company, which attempts to engage users by allowing Saturn car owners to find and to communicate with one another, or Bristol-Myers-Squibb, which allows women to exchange opinions and advice at *www.womenslink.com*. Both of these digital marketing applications attempt to engage users by creating virtual 'communities of interest'. Finally, American Express and Charles Schwab attempt to engage users by providing them with convenience-oriented content, including electronic access to their financial records, or one-stop-shop information that consumers might find helpful for making financial decisions.

It is too early to say whether these particular forms of digital marketing truly engage users or whether there is a better way to create or manage content to generate interest and participation. New technology developments such as the Java programming language will further enhance what digital marketers can do on interactive media. The key for digital marketers will be the continued willingness to experiment while maintaining a clear focus on what delivers value to the consumer.

How to organize for digital marketing

Many marketers have found that digital marketing initiatives sometimes require significant and profound changes to their marketing organization. Many of the organizational challenges of digital marketing are not new. Marketers have faced them as they integrated other marketing vehicles (such as direct response marketing, direct mail, and 1-800 services) that triggered organizational or channel conflicts. Digital marketing compounds these issues because of its more profound potential impact on the relationship between marketers and consumers, and therefore on the business systems of marketing companies.

While the world of digital marketing is still too young to have yielded definite answers on what works and what does not in terms of organization, some patterns are beginning to emerge. Based on research with 12 *Fortune 500* consumer goods/services companies with a presence in interactive media, we have identified four key stages for the development of the digital marketing organization (see exhibit on following page).

1. The 'ad hoc activity' stage. In this first stage, companies establish a basic online presence. However, there is no formal organization dedicated to the effort, which is often led by self-selected individuals. There are no dedicated skills in place.

2. The 'focusing the effort' stage. The organization recognizes the effort as a learning experiment. Typically a cross-functional steering committee led by a senior executive develops a set of policies/principles for how the company will 'go digital'. A small number of resources (five to ten people) are dedicated to the digital marketing effort, although its reporting structure is still considered temporary.

3. The 'formalization' stage. At this stage, the digital marketing organization has found a long-term 'home' within the business. It focuses now on improving its digital marketing efforts. The organization grows from 10 to 50 people and begins to develop its own structure, typically separating the technology-related from the marketing-related digital marketing activities.

4. The 'institutionalizing capability' stage. This stage is characterized by the development within the digital marketing organization of dedicated experts and skills, often around technology platforms like the World Wide Web, online services, and dial-up services, and the emergence of 'general managers' for the various initiatives that ensure the linkage with the core business.

Development stages of digital marketing organization

	Ad hoc stage	Focus stage	Formalization stage	Institutionalizing stage
Activities of digital marketing organization	Establish a basic online presence Rally internal interest and skills	Create policies to limit and unify effort Track what works and what doesn't	Build the business of/for a digital presence Develop/gather appropriate skills	Manage delivery against value proposition Manage organizational interdependencies
Structure and reporting	No formal structure in place Low visibility	Steering committee established Temporary reporting relationship	Organizational structure emerges Formal 'home' established for digital marketing group	Distinct business unit/department in place Linkages to core business
People involved	A few, often self-selected Part-time	Fewer than 5–10 Full-time	10–30 full-time Heavy support from 1–2 sources (e.g., agency)	More than 50 full-time 'Web' of external support sources
Skills in place	No institutional expertise or specialization	Few experts with little specialization	Experts emerging	Dedicated experts and skills in place
Funding source	Little or none	Corporate or ad hoc	Business or functional units	Business units

Retain

Once you've drawn consumers to your site in the first place, and then have engaged them with suitably interactive and valued content, you must make sure that they keep returning to your site. Maintaining ongoing contact is essential to developing relationships with consumers. Retaining users emphasizes the need for marketers to recognize that digital marketing is not a one-time project, but requires continued resource commitments over time.

Arguably, digital marketers who are capable of truly engaging users may be well on their way to retaining them. However, there are some subtle differences between engaging and retaining.

Emerging evidence suggests that while consumers may visit a site once out of curiosity, they will not return there without a reason. At a minimum, this implies that marketers must keep their sites 'fresh' by continuously renewing content and/or providing content that is inherently changeable on an ongoing basis, such as stock quotes or weather reports. For many marketers, particularly those with content-intensive digital marketing applications such as Levi Strauss or Toyota, this requirement raises the issue of the skills needed and costs required to maintain fresh content. Many marketers treat online marketing like traditional advertising by developing an application, launching it, and then stepping back from it. However, the efforts required to maintain a vibrant digital marketing application do not stop at launch. As a result, some marketers have significantly underestimated ongoing content maintenance resource requirements. An emerging trend to control the cost and complexity associated with content management is to shift the burden of creating content onto the user. For example, an athletic shoe company could allow sporting associations to use its site to publicize upcoming sporting events. Assuming interest on the part of the associations, this solution may both lower the marketer's cost of creating content, which is now effectively borne by the users, leverage a unique capability of interactive media by acting as a central distribution point for perishable information, and provide value to consumers through one-stop shopping for hard-to-get information.

The second difference between engaging and retaining has to do with a unique – yet often overlooked – opportunity for marketers: the creation of switching costs for users as a means to retain them. This occurs as users invest their own time and energy in the interaction with a digital marketing application, therefore creating an important disincentive to repeat that investment with another application. With Quicken, the financial management software, the more consumers input their own financial information into the software, the more they actually raise their own switching costs. Another example is user-to-user relationships: the more consumers invest time and develop familiarity in interacting with others, the less likely they are to start building these virtual relationships again elsewhere. This explains the growing emphasis among digital marketing application developers on communities of interest. New comparative agent technologies such as those pioneered by companies like Agents, Inc. present another example of switching costs: in an existing application, users spend time revealing their preferences in music or movies, and are then offered suggestions for other things they may enjoy based on the information gained by the software from other users.

The lesson is that digital marketers must explicitly think about how to build switching costs as they define their strategy to retain users of their digital marketing application.

Learn

Due to their very nature, interactive media open up unprecedented opportunities for marketers to learn about consumer demographics, attitudes, and behaviors. Demographic and attitudinal information may come in the form of e-mail communications to marketers, opinions volunteered on bulletin boards or information gathered in surveys, questionnaires, or registration processes. Behavioral information may be gleaned from transactional records or 'click-streams', which track how users behave in a site.

Currently, of course, the potential to leverage the learning opportunity of interactive media is limited. There may not yet be enough of the 'right' digital consumers to treat interactive media as a representative learning tool; further, many of these consumers are reluctant to provide information about who they are and what they want, for lack of interest or for fear of privacy invasion. Similarly, the technologies needed to capture actionable information are only slowly becoming available. There also remains considerable uncertainty around whether it will be the marketer, the access provider, or some other party such as a payment aggregator who will capture and own the most valuable information about consumers.

While significant, these issues do not reduce the importance for marketers of explicitly considering consumer learning objectives when they develop digital marketing applications. This will require defining what type of information may be most valuable to them, what that information is worth, and how to best leverage their digital marketing application to obtain it. Marketing research, for example, holds immediate digital marketing learning potential. A packaged goods company is beginning to use its digital marketing application to hold virtual focus groups, to test new product concepts, and to get feedback on ideas for promotional programs. Another opportunity exists to enhance what is already known about consumers. A hotel company, for example, is beginning to use its digital marketing application to complement its existing customer profile database by collecting information about the accommodation preferences of its rewards program members. A third opportunity will be for marketers to gather information that they do not yet hold about consumers. The potential value of that information could someday be tremendous for marketers to expand into and cross-sell new products or services, and create entirely new forms of consumer relationship and loyalty programs.

Relate

Relating is one of digital marketing's most important value creation opportunities. In essence, it represents the opportunity to customize the interaction and tailor either the product or the marketing effort to one consumer at a time; interactive media provides unprecedented opportunities for a marketer to 'relate' to a consumer. As a two-way, addressable communication and distribution channel, interactive media gives the marketer two important opportunities; to learn about an individual consumer in the course of continued interaction, and to deliver either a personalized service or product, or a communication about the availability of such a personalized service or product. An example is online publications such as the one developed by the *Wall Street Journal* which delivers a personalized online newspaper compiled on the basis of a users' specified interests, 'published for a circulation of one'. Another example is provided by Amazon.com, a virtual bookstore on the World Wide Web. While selling books, Amazon.com also leverages agent technology to learn about consumers' literary tastes, uses that information to recommend titles and then e-mails users when titles become available. From a consumers' perspective, the service provided by Amazon.com is truly personalized and potentially highly valued for that very reason.

Relating, of course, presents many challenges for marketers. This may explain why there are only very few truly personalized digital marketing examples. One reason is that relating requires marketers to 'push' their thinking about the full potential of interactive media in their specific service or product category and to consider how to make the digital marketing initiative an integral part of the existing business system, as it fundamentally affects the nature of the product or service provided by the marketer to consumers. Particularly for large, established marketers, how to integrate digital marketing initiatives with existing marketing programs or information systems presents a challenge.

However, the economics of 'relating' are potentially attractive. The efficiency and effectiveness of customizing interactions and gathering information on interactive media should make relationship marketing to a large audience more attractive on a network than it currently is in the physical world.

THE CHALLENGES AHEAD

Digital marketing is still at an early stage. As with most technological innovations, the full marketing potential of interactive media will reveal itself only when consumers and marketers identify – or fortuitously stumble upon – truly 'new things to do'. It is critical therefore for marketers to look ahead and to prepare for the challenges that digital marketing will inevitably bring about. The three most important challenges and their implications for marketers are:

Constantly enhance the consumer value proposition

While much of the digital 'revolution' is over-hyped, it will nevertheless fundamentally change the traditional marketing balance of power by giving the consumer more control over their relationship with marketers. In an interactive, two-way, addressable world, it is the consumer – and not the marketer – who decides with whom to interact, what to interact about, and how to interact at all. Marketers have to earn the right to the digital relationship, and they have to do so by continuously enhancing the value they offer consumers. As the early experimenters have learned, the heart of that challenge is the difficulty of identifying the 'hooks' for developing relationships with digital consumers. A food manufacturer, for example, thought that digital consumers would be most interested in finding out about nutrition; consumers, however, tended to ask about how they could buy regional products that were not distributed where they currently live.

Build relationships and skills to prepare for continuous change

Digital marketing will continue to evolve extremely rapidly for the foreseeable future. From a marketer's perspective, most of these developments will come from outside the organization. As John Hagel points out, the Internet economy is evolving around a number of 'webs', each with its own direction and dynamics.[3] Digital marketers need to keep tabs on these webs to identify early on the developments that might affect their digital marketing efforts. Resources should be directed toward following external developments such as the emergence of new technologies, new players, or insights about consumer behavior. In addition, marketers will need to build – internally or through relationships – some of the more specialized skills that are emerging in digital marketing. For example, new companies are emerging in the field of audience creation (attracting users to digital marketing services), such as Cybernautics, and in intelligent agent development (creating value-added services based on a user's preferences), such as Agents, Inc. Looking ahead, digital marketers will need to keep abreast of these developments, and to continuously embrace those that will allow them to improve their services.

Manage the interdependencies – both internally and with intermediaries

A third, and perhaps the most significant, challenge for digital marketers will be to manage the interdependences between their digital marketing efforts and both the rest of the organization and existing outside partners, such as distributors and retailers. To have meaningful impact on the bottom line, digital marketing will have to become an integral part of doing business for many marketers. In many organizations the potential for significant conflict has already become apparent. Internally, for example, marketers are finding it difficult to integrate their digital marketing efforts with existing functional areas (e.g., marketing or customer service) and business units, not to mention information systems. For example, there is much debate in several companies about whether the digital marketing group should be set up as an independent entity or as a support unit. The answer, of course, depends on factors such as the size of the potential commercial opportunity of digital marketing, the existing culture within the organization, and the need for cross-functional integration.

Externally, the challenge of managing relationships with existing intermediaries is just as important. Salesforces, distributors, and retailers often perceive digital marketing as a major potential threat to their 'ownership' of consumers. In automotive, for example, the challenge is to make a manufacturer's digital marketing initiatives a 'win-win-win' proposition for dealers and car buyers; in travel, airlines have to manage relationships with the travel agency community very carefully when they offer direct booking digital marketing services to their frequent travelers. As the potential impact of digital marketing on the core business grows, managing these interdependencies will likely emerge as one of the most important challenges for marketers.

IMPLICATIONS FOR MARKETERS

Over the next three to five years, interactive marketing is likely to become an increasingly significant part of the consumer marketing landscape, at least in the US. This development will challenge many large marketers. For many of them, however, digital marketing could yield good outcomes as long as they are aware of three major factors – company, competition, and category (Exhibit 9). It is imperative for marketers to consider what interactive media should – or should not – mean to them.

Company factors
Company consumers use interactive media
Company willing to build capabilities
Competitive factors
Competitors using interactive media to gain share of spending with core customers
Opportunity to use interactive media to displace incumbent marketer
Category factors
Product/service well suited
Relationship marketing makes sense

Exhibit 9 Commitment factors

NOTES

1 For a discussion of this term, *see* Jeffrey F. Rayport and John J. Sviokla, 'Exploring the virtual value chain', *Harvard Business Review*, November – December 1995 and also reprinted in *The McKinsey Quarterly*, 1996 Number 1, pp. 20–36.
2 Forrester Research Inc., *The Internet Economy*, September 1995.
3 'Spider versus Spider', *The McKinsey Quarterly*, 1996 Number 1, pp. 4–18.

Kierzkowski, A., McQuade, S., Waitman, R. and Zeisser, M. (1996) 'Marketing to the digital consumer'. *The McKinsey Quarterly*, 3: 5–21. Reproduced with permission.

Interactive home shopping: consumer, retailer, and manufacturer incentives to participate in electronic marketplaces

5.3

**Joseph Alba, John Lynch, Barton Weitz, Chris Janiszewski,
Richard Lutz, Alan Sawyer, and Stacy Wood**

A confluence of technological, economic, and cultural forces has made possible a new and revolutionary distribution channel known generically as interactive home shopping (IHS). Although only in its infancy, IHS has the potential to change fundamentally the manner in which people shop as well as the structure of the consumer goods and retail industries. Projections about the diffusion of IHS are sometimes breathtaking: Forecasts of IHS sales range from $5 billion to $300 billion by the year 2000 (Reda, 1995; Wilensky, 1995). In contrast to such projections, current sales are barely perceptible. Internet sales in 1996 were estimated at $500 million – less than 1% of all nonstore shopping (Schiesel, 1997). Combining Internet, other online services, television home shopping, CD-ROM catalogs, and conventional catalogs, all nonstore retailing combined accounts for only 5% to 10% of all retail sales, with little growth in recent years. Therefore, IHS will need to offer benefits superior to current nonstore channels in order to realize the more ambitious sales forecasts that have been set for it.

Our goal is to examine the effects of consumer, retailer, and manufacturer behavior on the diffusion of IHS and the impact this new retail format could have on the retail industry. In the first half we analyze the demand-side issues, examining what IHS offers consumers that could motivate them to alter their present shopping behavior. In the second half we examine the impact of this new channel on industry structure and the competitive positioning of individual firms.

Interactive Home Shopping Defined

In defining IHS, we conceptualize *interactivity* as a continuous construct capturing the quality of two-way communication between two parties. (For an elaborated treatment of interactivity in the context of electronic media, see Hoffman and Novak, 1996). In the case of IHS, the parties are the buyer and seller. The two dimensions of interactivity are response time and response contingency. Because IHS involves electronic communication, the response can be immediate – similar to the response time in face-to-face communications. Response contingency is the degree to which the response by one party is a function of the response made by the other party. We use the term *home* merely to indicate that the customer can engage in this interaction in a location other than a store. Figure 1 illustrates a somewhat futuristic form of IHS.

The scenario portrayed in Figure 1 is highly interactive. Judy, the consumer, using an electronic shopper, BOB, can specify the type of merchandise sought and then screen the located alternatives to develop a smaller set of options that she can view in detail. The interaction requires the parties to query each other's databases. In contrast, this level of interactivity and selection is not available from current Internet retail sites, which function as an unwieldy collection of electronic catalogs (Rigdon, 1996). Consumers cannot search quickly and easily for specific items of merchandise, nor can they screen and compare merchandise on the basis of their idiosyncratic desires. Individual retailers provide road maps to facilitate search within their sites but avoid formats that would satisfy consumers' comprehensive needs. However, capabilities such as those described in Figure 1 – along with the design and production of customized clothing – soon could become available to consumers (Cortese, 1996; Hill, 1995; Maes, 1995; Negroponte, 1995).

Judy Jamison sits in front of her home electronic center reviewing her engagement calendar displayed on her television screen. She sees that she has accepted an invitation to a formal cocktail party on Friday night and she decides to buy a new dress for the occasion. She switches to her personal electronic shopper, BOB, and initiates the following exchange:

BOB: Do you wish to browse, go to a specific store, or buy a specific item?
Judy: Specific item
BOB: Type of item?
Judy: Black dress
BOB: Occasion? (menu appears on screen)
Judy: Formal cocktail party
BOB: Price range? (menu appears)
Judy: $300–$500
BOB: 497 items have been identified. How many do you want to view?
Judy: Just 5

[Five pictures of Judy in each dress appear on the screen with the price, brand name, and the IHS retailer selling it listed beneath each one. Judy clicks on one of the dresses and it is enlarged on the screen. Another click and Judy views the dress from different angles. Another click and specifications such as fabric and laundering instructions appear. Judy repeats this routine with each dress. She selects the one she finds most appealing. BOB knows her measurements and picks the size that fits her best.]

BOB: How would you like to pay for this? (menu appears)
Judy: American Express
BOB: Nieman Marcus [the firm selling the dress Judy selected] suggests a Xie scarf and Koslow belt to complement this dress

[Judy clicks on the items and they appear on the screen. Judy inspects these items as she inspected the dresses. She decides to purchase both accessories. BOB then asks Judy about delivery. Judy selects two-day delivery at a cost of $5.00.]

BOB: Just a reminder. You have not purchased hosiery in 30 days. Do you wish to reorder at this time?
Judy: Yes
BOB: Same shades?
Judy: Yes

Figure 1 Illustration of IHS

The scenario illustrates the following critical attributes affecting the adoption of IHS:

- faithful reproduction of descriptive and experiential product information,
- a greatly expanded universe of offerings relative to what can be accessed now through local or catalog shopping,
- an efficient means of screening the offerings to find the most appealing options for more detailed consideration,
- unimpeded search across stores and brands, and
- memory for past selections, which simplifies information search and purchase decisions.

Our scenario implies that the consumer owns the intelligent search agent BOB, which might be a software package bought by Judy and parameterized to fit her needs on the basis of data she provides. However, other search engines also might be owned and controlled by the retailer (e.g., http://www.landsend.com) or an independent third party, as in Continuum Software's 'Fido the Shopping Doggie' (http://www.shopfido.com) or Andersen Consulting's Bargain-Finder (http://bf.cstar.ac.com/bf). The consumer might enter a site to be interrogated by the retailer's search engine. Finally, the search engine might be operated by a third-party expert in a product category, as in *Business Week*'s Maven agent for finding personal computers (http://www.maven.businessweek.com). The consumer might pay a service charge to use the site, or retailers might pay to have their information available at the site.

We assume that all of these types of search agents will exist but will have different mixes of information desired by the other parties. However, consumers must have access to vendors' databases if the scenario portrayed in Figure 1 is to become reality. In the current transitional period, product search often is dictated by the vendor. Moreover, global search across vendors can be thwarted by actions taken by individual vendors. In the end, technological and market forces will determine the extent to which consumers can gain access to the information they desire. In the latter half of this article we consider vendors' incentives to inhibit information exchange and their likelihood of success. First, however, we consider the critical attributes affecting consumers' incentives to adopt IHS.

THE DEMAND SIDE: CONSUMERS AND IHS

Consumer trade-offs

Similar to any innovation, IHS will need to match or exceed the utility provided by traditional formats to succeed. In Table 1 we compare six retail formats in terms of benefits and costs to the consumer. The three in-store formats are a prototypical convenience-goods store (supermarket), a specialty-goods store (department store), and a shopping-goods store (category specialist) (cf. Copeland, 1923); the nonstore formats are the traditional catalog, the present Internet offering, and the IHS format described in Figure 1. Although the scenario in Figure 1 is intriguing, department and specialty stores afford buyers the opportunity to touch and feel merchandise and obtain information from sales associates. 'Category killers' such as Best Buy and Office Depot offer comparisons across a wide array of alternatives in a specific merchandise category. Also, all in-store formats allow immediate delivery.

Table 1 Dimensions affecting relative attractiveness to consumers of alternative retail formats

Dimension	Supermarket	Department store	Category specialist	Catalog	Current Internet retailer	IHS format
Providing alternatives for consideration						
Number of categories	Medium	Medium	Low	Low	Low	Low or High
Alternatives per category	Medium	Low	Medium	Medium	Low	High
Screening alternatives to form consideration set						
Selecting consideration set	Medium	High	Medium	Low	Low	High
Providing information for selecting from consideration set						
Quantity	Medium	Medium	Medium	Medium	Medium	High
Quality	High	High	High	Medium	Low	Low or High
Comparing Alternatives	Medium	Medium	High	Low	Low	Depends on Supplier
Ordering and fulfillment: transaction costs						
Delivery Time	Immediate	Immediate	Immediate	Days	Days	Days
Supplier Delivery Cost	Low	Low	Low	High	High	High
Customer Transaction Cost	High	High	High	Low	High	Low
Supplier Facility Costs	High	High	High	Low	Low	Low
Locations for Placing Orders	Few	Few	Few	Everywhere	Many	Many
Other benefits						
Entertainment	Low	High	Medium	Low	Low	Medium
Social Interaction	Medium	High	Medium	Low	Low	Low
Personal Security	Low	Low	Low	High	High	High

It is important to clarify our orientation and assumptions before discussing the relative merits of these retail formats in detail. First, our analysis assumes that technology has developed to the point in which a highly evolved IHS system is readily available to a significant number of households. Therefore, as characterized in Table 1, IHS enables consumers to access merchandise unavailable in their local markets, gather veridical information about merchandise at a low cost, efficiently screen the offering of a broad cross-section of suppliers by avoiding unwanted alternatives and unimportant features, and easily locate the lowest prices at which a specific item is offered. As we discuss in the following sections, IHS retailers currently enjoy considerable latitude in designing their offerings to exploit or subvert such activities.

Second, the values used to describe a format are illustrative. It is not our intention to argue the specifics, which can vary across retailers within a given format (e.g., across those selling products that can rather than cannot be digitized, those emphasizing depth rather than breadth of selection). Our assessment of performance of the six retail formats is based on the well-developed retail industry structure in the urban and suburban United States. In less developed retail environments, nonstore formats could be much more attractive (Quelch and Klein, 1996).

Table 1 illustrates three main points:

- For a given product category, a comparison of traditional retail formats (e.g., department stores, category specialists, catalogs selling clothing or consumer electronics) makes apparent the basis for competition. The benefits provided by different formats influence the types of merchandise that can be sold successfully; product, situation, and consumer characteristics affect the relative weights of these benefits when consumers select a format (Day, Shocker, and Srivastava, 1979; Dickson, 1982). For example, most apparel is sold in department and specialty stores because these outlets offer the service and accessories sought by customers buying clothing. In contrast, apparel sales make up a smaller percentage of total sales at discounters. Catalog apparel sales skew toward unfitted clothing items. Catalogs are especially attractive for occasions where the purchaser cannot achieve a superior fit by visiting a store (as when buying a gift for a relative in a distant city).

- Catalogs dominate current Internet retailers. It is therefore unsurprising that there are so few examples to date of businesses making significant revenues by selling merchandise on the Internet.
- The IHS format differs from current Internet retailers primarily by providing more alternatives for consideration, the ability to screen alternatives to form consideration sets, and information to facilitate selection from the consideration set.

We expect changes in the benefits relating to consumer information acquisition to drive any change from the current, nearly nonexistent penetration of Internet retailing to the more optimistic sales projections for IHS. Consequently, we focus our analysis on the dimensions in the first three sections of Table 1, which bear on the cost of information search, rather than on those in the bottom half of the table.

Retailers and retail formats compete in the types of information they convey effectively to customers. Just as in Erlich and Fisher's (1982) analysis of 'derived demand for advertising', we analyze 'derived demand for retailer information about products'. Erlich and Fisher note that information reduces the wedge between the market price received by the seller and the 'full price' paid by the buyer. The wedge between market price and full price includes the costs of obtaining information about products and of dissatisfaction from disappointing purchases. Consumers demand information that reduces this wedge. Such information alternatively can be derived from their own prior knowledge, advertising, or 'other selling efforts' – notably information from retailers.

Although we focus on retail competition through information, we recognize that retail formats differ on many factors, such as entertainment and personal safety, that contribute to the utility consumers obtain from the 'total shopping experience' (cf. Tauber, 1972) and that transaction costs related to ordering and fulfillment are an important basis for competitive advantage. For example, Verity and Hof (1994) suggest that it could be 25% less costly to engage in direct marketing with electronic channels. Although consultants and the popular press widely draw similar conclusions, we regard this as an open question. On the one hand, the IHS retailer is not burdened with the cost of locally convenient stores. On the other hand, the IHS retailer faces the cost of delivering merchandise in small quantities to individual consumers. It is premature to assess the relative efficiencies. Using catalogs and electronic grocery shopping (e.g., Peapod [Donegan, 1996]) as guides, however, it is not clear that consumers will enjoy large monetary cost savings by using IHS.

However, here, we focus on the informational effects of electronic commerce as they pertain to retailer-consumer interaction. Excellent discussions of enhanced consumer-to-consumer interaction and the implications for marketing are available elsewhere (Armstrong and Hagel, 1996; Hoffman and Novak, 1996).

Providing alternatives for consideration

A significant benefit of IHS compared with other retail formats is the vast number of alternatives that become available to consumers. Through IHS, a person living in Florida can shop at Harrod's in London in less time than it takes to visit the local Burdines department store.

Economic search theory implies that if there are N alternative brands or sellers available in a market, and the consumer considers only a subset n < N, the utility of the chosen (best) alternative from the subset increases with n (Hauser and Wernerfelt, 1990; Ratchford, 1980; Stigler, 1961). However, in terms of the benefits of search, there are strong diminishing returns. As additional alternatives are examined, the potential increase in benefits offered by the next alternative is small. Inasmuch as the cost of searching for and evaluating new alternatives continues to increase, a point is reached at which the expected cost of considering additional alternatives is greater than the potential increase in benefits. At this point, the consumer terminates search for additional alternatives. Research also indicates that consumers reach this point quickly: Consumers rarely visit more than one or two outlets when they are buying expensive consumer durables (e.g., Newman and Staelin, 1972; Wilkie and Dickson, 1985).

Because IHS search costs are low and decline with experience using the interface, simply providing consumers an opportunity to consider a thousand alternatives versus ten alternatives could be enough to switch some of them from in-store shopping to IHS. However, other consumers could find it too tedious and stressful to look through information on hundreds of products identified for consideration, unless there is reason to expect that the added alternatives are systematically different from the first ones considered, with a different distribution of utilities. Consequently, the mere capability of IHS to increase the universe of potential options is not a major reason for its adoption.

Screening alternatives to form consideration sets

The attractiveness of the opportunity to inspect an expanded number of alternatives is dependent in part of the consumer's ability to sort efficiently through a potentially daunting amount of information. A particular advantage of IHS over alternative formats is that consumers can screen information so that they can focus on alternatives that match their preferences.

In most product categories, consumers have prior beliefs and preferences about alternatives (Hauser and Wernerfielt, 1990; Ratchford, 1982; Roberts and Lattin, 1991; Simonson, Huber, and Payne, 1988). Consumers use this information to make purchase decisions more efficiently by forming a small consideration set and then evaluating alternatives within this subset in more detail. The savings in search costs involved in using this two-step process often overwhelms the potential opportunity cost of overlooking the 'best' alternative that would have been uncovered by carefully inspecting the entire universe of alternatives.

Interactive home shopping enables the formation of consideration sets that include only those few alternatives best suited to a consumer's personal tastes. This screening can be done almost instantaneously using electronic agents that use information about an individual consumer's specific preferences and the alternatives available (Maes, 1994). In Figure 1, for example, BOB located 497 'suitable' black dresses from a potentially much larger universe and rank-ordered these dresses on the basis of criteria (black/formal/$300-$500) supplied by Judy. An additional screening phase that is based on criteria derived from prior interactions and stored in the agent's memory (such as the style she prefers and her trade-offs between price and quality) might reduce the set dramatically. The remaining alternatives then could be searched in more detail to choose the 'best' of this reduced set. If the screening criteria are highly correlated with Judy's full utility function, Judy can be reasonably confident that the alternative chosen after screening has utility close to that associated with the choice she would have made if she had inspected all 497 alternatives exhaustively (Feinberg and Huber, 1996).

Others have noted that consumers often rely on memory for the generation of alternatives for consideration (Alba and Chattopadhyay, 1985; Hutchinson, Raman, and Mantrala, 1994; Kardes, *et al.*, 1993; Nedungadi, 1990). In such cases, memory plays a screening function that is often only imperfectly correlated with the consumer's utilities. An efficient and dispassionate search agent should produce appropriate brands that otherwise would not have been considered, implicitly replacing memory with explicit product criteria for screening the universe of available options to a manageable consideration set.

Note that both BOB and retail store buyers have access to the same universe of merchandise and screen that universe to offer a subset intended to appeal to end consumers. However, the assortments offered by store-based retailers are developed for market segments with significant within-segment heterogeneity. Store customers are required to expend resources to form smaller consideration sets tailored to their needs. Consumers could find that the set provided by the retailer is insufficient and opt to visit another store.

Interactive home shopping has the potential to tailor consideration sets from a much broader set of alternatives for specific individual consumers. The usefulness of these customized approaches will depend on the consumer effort necessary to calibrate the screening mechanism and the accuracy with which the mechanism correlates with the consumer's full utility function for meaningful alternatives. The lower bound on effort to calibrate screening criteria comes from the use of past purchase history – as in the Peapod grocery shopping service, which keeps lists of regularly purchased items for automatic rebuy. At the other extreme, the screening criteria in many current Internet retailing sites are cumbersome in requiring the consumer to enter many responses to calibrate the function (e.g., *Money Magazine*'s Best Places to Live site on Pathfinder.com, Firefly at http://www.agents-inc.com for music and films).

Some search agents require less data input from the consumer but at a cost of including only a few criteria that collectively explain a relatively small percentage of variance in a consumer's overall preferences. A good example is the use of a standard Internet search engine like Alta Vista to shop for Advanced Photo System cameras. Others strike a better balance in asking for a compact set of preferences highly related to a person's tastes but only allow search of a limited set of alternatives (e.g., Dell's computer site http://dell.com for computers, RackesDirect women's clothing site at http://www.rackes.com/rackes.html, Fido the Shopping Doggie service for shopping in a broad cross-section of categories). Therefore, screening criteria can be established in different ways. In the BOB example, Judy explicitly stated her criteria when initiating the search. In the Internet sites mentioned previously, screening criteria are limited to a small set specified by the retailer.

Providing information to evaluate alternatives in the consideration set

One of the primary benefits offered by traditional retailers is information that enables consumers to predict how satisfied they would be if they purchased various offerings. The degree to which this information is useful to consumers depends on the nature of the information provided and its reliability. Consumers should seek out formats that enable them to make selections that maximize consumption utility net of price and search costs (Ehrlich and Fisher, 1982), even if competing retail formats offer identical merchandise (Hauser, Urban, and Weinberg, 1993).

Quantity of information
Retail formats differ in the sheer amount of information provided about the merchandise they offer. For example, Lands' End not only provides faithful visual information but often gives great detail about the construction process, stitching, and materials. Other catalogs provide only a few specifications per item, such as price, weight, and brand or model. More information could increase ability to predict consumption utility but add to processing costs.

Store-based retailers also differ in the information they make available to consumers. Specialty and department stores often provide trained and knowledgeable sales associates, whereas discounters do not. Consequently, the effective 'database' of attributes available to consumers is much greater at specialty and department stores than it is at discounters and catalogers. Store-based retailers have an additional characteristic that radically increases the usefulness of the information available to consumers, that is, interactivity. Interaction between a customer and sales associate enables store-based retailers to provide information about the attributes that matter to the customer. Such selectivity gives consumers all the advantages of a large database without the large information processing costs. Perhaps for this reason, post-purchase reports from buyers of major durables indicate that the salesperson was the most useful information source consulted, outstripping *Consumer Reports*, advertising, and friends (Wilkie and Dickson, 1985).

Conversely, catalogers, discounters, and present Internet retailers are forced to make decisions about which attributes to promote on the basis of what is most desired by the market as a whole or by relatively crude segments of the market. However, consumers differ in their needs and therefore in the information that will be of interest to them. Consequently, the information provided by catalogers and discounters will be less valuable because it is not tailored to idiosyncratic desires.

Interactive home shopping should prove superior even to specialty and department store retailers in terms of the sheer quantity of attribute information it can provide about each stock-keeping unit. As a result of the interactivity of IHS, retailers need not fear that the provision of information about an attribute that matters only to a few will impose search costs on the majority. In this respect, IHS resembles department and specialty stores. However, because attribute information is available consistently from a central database, IHS effectively becomes a 'super sales associate' (i.e., one that never gets sick, is not moody, learns quickly, and never forgets). In contrast, store-based retailers have a difficult time retaining knowledgeable sales associates, and in many cases it is not cost-effective for them to do so. It should cost far less to add information to an IHS database than to attempt to disseminate the same information to sales associates through conventional training.

Quality of attribute information

Information economists often distinguish among search, experience, and credence goods (Darby and Karni, 1973), typically in terms of consumers' ability to know quality before and after buying. In economic parlance, search goods are those whose quality and value to the consumer can be assessed easily prior to purchase. The quality of experience goods is difficult to assess prior to purchase and usage; however, because quality can be assessed accurately after one use, the consumer knows quality when an opportunity arises to repurchase the same brand. For credence goods, quality cannot be known even after repeated purchase and use.

A tempting conclusion that is based on this trichotomy is that merchandise now selected in store environments primarily on the basis of search and credence attributes is most amenable to electronic retailing (because direct experience is not required), whereas merchandise purchased on the basis of experience attributes will be purchased in stores. By similar reasoning, IHS and catalogs should be more successful with merchandise dominated by visual attributes and should fare less well when touch, taste, and smell are important for evaluating quality. The latter senses require direct experience consuming or sampling the product (Anderson, 1995).

However, these conclusions fail to consider the key issue regarding the quality of information. The quality or usefulness of information is determined by the degree to which consumers (or their agents) can use the information obtained prior to purchase to predict their satisfaction from subsequent consumption, which in turn depends intimately on consumers' inference rules (Alba and Hutchinson, 1987; Broniarczyk and Alba, 1994) and consumers' confidence in the reliability of these rules (Wright and Lynch, 1995). In the analysis that follows, we adopt Wright and Lynch's (1995) reinterpretation of the search/experience/credence distinction in terms of consumer inferences. Specifically, for experience and credence (but not search) goods, there is at first a low subjective correlation between product attributes observable prior to purchase and benefits at the time of consumption. For experience goods, brand names enable highly reliable inferences about consumption benefits after one purchase and use. This is not true for credence goods, presumably because feedback from the first use takes a long time to materialize and is not predictive of consumption utility if the same brand were to be repurchased.

In addition, though information economists initially spoke of search, experience, and credence 'goods', it is now clear that all goods have some combination of search, experience, and credence attributes. A search good is simply one for which the consumption benefits most important to consumers are predicted reliably by attribute information available to them before buying. This reasoning implies that the same product can be a search, experience, or credence good, depending on the benefits that are important to consumers and the inferences consumers make about how well those benefits are predicted by information available prior to purchase.

These observations have important implications in the present context because retail formats differ greatly in their capability to provide information about attributes linked to consumption benefits. Consequently, attributes that are search attributes in one format might be experience attributes in another – and this dictates patterns of competition among retailers over time. For example, if the key attributes of ice cream relate to experienced flavor, Ben & Jerry's Cherry Garcia might be a search good at a Ben & Jerry's store, which allows a consumer to taste the ice cream prior to purchase. It would be an experience good at first if a person were buying at a supermarket that sells ice cream only in cartons and does not allow tasting prior to purchase. Consequently, the Ben & Jerry's store initially would have an informational advantage over the supermarket. However, when the consumer learns that Cherry Garcia on the carton label reliably predicts experienced flavor, the supermarket no longer would be at a disadvantage. Similar dynamics explain why mail order computer giants Dell and Gateway have a customer mix dominated by experienced users (Templin, 1996).

Similar principles govern the relative advantage or disadvantage of store-based retailers relative to nonstore retailers that sell through catalogs or IHS. For example, critical information in the purchase of apparel might include search attributes such as color and style – which ostensibly can be assessed accurately in a department store or catalog – as well as experiential attributes such as fit, which can be searched readily before purchase only in the department store. However, when buying the item through nonstore outlets, the ability to assess color depends on consumers' inferences about the faithfulness of photographic reproduction and piece-to-piece variation in dyeing. Also, fit might seem unpredictable unless the nonstore retailer has consistent sizing and the consumer has learned over time to infer what fit is implied by a particular brand and size.

These examples illustrate three important points: First, consumers make inferences about product attractiveness on the basis of information provided by retailers, and retail formats compete on the information they provide as cues for these inferences; second, different consumers possess different rules, and this affects the extent to which the information provided by any particular format leads to competitive advantage; and third, the cues that are deemed to provide a reliable basis for inference are likely to change with experience with the brand. The following issues further emphasize the need to consider predictability of satisfaction rather than a simple classification of suitability of 'goods' to IHS that is based on the traditional search/ experience/credence distinction:

1. *The (in)adequacy of searchable experiential information.* In certain purchase situations, information for some products with important experiential attributes cannot be gathered prior to consumption. In such cases, in-store shopping offers little advantage over IHS. For example, flowers and wine are consummate sensory products. However, consumers who send flower arrangements via FTD must base their decisions on pictures in the florist's shops, and purchasers of wine frequently must rely on labels or advice from a retail sales associate. Therefore, some products possessing important experience attributes could be no less amenable to IHS than to traditional shopping. In yet other cases, experiential attribute information could be conveyed *more* effectively electronically than in-store. For example, the electronic bookseller Amazon (http://www.amazon.com) has space for customers to post their own reviews of books, with positive word of mouth clearly influencing sales.

2. *Consistency and predictability.* The ability to product satisfaction from observable attributes is not inherent in the specific consumption benefits driving satisfaction, nor is in inherent in the retail format. Actions by retailers and manufacturers can increase consumers' ability to predict post-purchase satisfaction from attributes observable before purchase. Consider the case of running shoes purchased by a consumer who cares about comfort and protection from injury. We might expect that these features could be assessed better when buying from a store, such as Athletic Attic, than from a cataloger. Road Runner Sports, however, provides information for each shoe in its catalog, making it easy to assess suitability for underpronators and overpronators, and customers can submit their old shoes for a custom analysis and suggestions for suitable replacements.

   Manufacturers' actions also influence the customer's ability to predict consumption satisfaction from pre-purchase information. If manufacturers become more consistent in the characteristics they build into differing models in their product lines, consumers' ability to predict satisfaction will rise accordingly. Comfort and sizing are important attributes of running shoes that require direct experience with the product. However, when a particular brand is consistent in the height of its arch support and the roominess of its toe box, the predictability of comfort and size is enhanced. In essence, brand name converts experience attributes to search attributes that can be effectively communicated verbally or visually (see Agins, 1994).

3. *Other determinants of satisfaction.* Satisfaction is determined by more than the consumption experience with the product; it also is affected by the belief that one has exhaustively searched the set of acceptable alternatives such that there is no regret regarding a missed opportunity (Gillovich and Medvec, 1995). Interactive home shopping provides the potential for a more extensive search than that which consumers could accomplish in a store.

   These considerations imply that consumer adoption depends on more than the (retail format-independent) importance of search, experience, and credence attributes to the consumer.

Comparison of alternatives

Retail formats differ in the extent to which they facilitate the comparison of alternatives in the consideration set. For example, most in-store retailers stock alternative colors, styles, and brands in each product category. An appealing characteristic of category specialists such as Circuit City and Office Depot is the breadth of selection and customers' ability to make side-by-side comparisons of brands. Similarly, consumers shopping for apparel can compare the fit of different alternatives. Current Internet retailers to not offer this opportunity. In addition, current IHS retailers are selective in the information presented, whereas in-store retailers allow the consumer to control the basis for comparison of alternatives.

Research shows that consumers acquire and process information in ways made easiest by the constraints of the information format (Bettman and Kakkar, 1977). However, consumers prefer formats that promote maximum flexibility to engage in either attribute- or alternative-based processing (Bettman and Zins, 1979). This preference for flexibility to engage in attribute-based processing should be stronger for novices in a product class than for experts (Bettman and Park, 1980); experts know what levels of an attribute are attractive without having to rely on relative information to make that assessment (Mitchell and Dacin, 1996).

It is argued that effort looms large when decision makers consider the effort-accuracy trade-off required in any given decision task – so much so that decision makers could focus more on effort reduction than on accuracy maximization (for a discussion, see Todd and Benbasat, 1994). In this context, the advantages of IHS are apparent. The initial (and effortful) decision phase involving attribute-based, side-by-side comparisons will be compressed if an efficient screening mechanism is available. This should inspire consumers to learn and use more information in the course of decision making (cf. Kardes and Kalyanaraman, 1992; Russo, 1977). In addition, the transformation of the decision from a memory-based to a stimulus-based choice should enhance the precision of the decision process and therefore the optimality of the ultimate decision (see Alba, Marmorstein, and Chattapadhyay, 1992; Biehal and Chakravarti, 1983; Lynch, Marmorstein, and Weigold, 1988).

The combination of IHS search, screen, and comparison features also should prompt consumers to make their decisions more rapidly (cf. Greenleaf and Lehmann, 1995). Research shows that the addition of attractive alternatives to a choice set could prompt consumers to delay their choice (Tversky and Shafir, 1992), perhaps because of the perceived possibility that even more attractive options have yet to be inspected (Karmi and Schwarz, 1977). Insofar as search and comparison minimize the possibility of regret over choosing a suboptimal product, both decision speed and satisfaction with the decision process should increase.

A caveat is appropriate at this point. Most aspects of an efficient search engine point to improved decision quality. However, it has been noted recently that though some decision aids could improve decision making, abuse is possible (Todd and Benbasat, 1994). In particular, Widing and Talarzyk (1993) show that the decision aid most likely to be a part of an electronic search agent (i.e., a cutoff rule that enables formation of a consideration set containing only those alternatives that pass consumer-specified attribute cut-offs) can lead to suboptimal decisions in efficient choice sets. In addition, a separate stream of research shows that a second likely characteristic of IHS – visually rich presentation – can distort the decision process by diverting attention to peripheral cues and away from information that is most important for the task at hand (Jarvenpaa, 1989, 1990; cf. Edell and Staelin, 1983).

Summary of key consumer factors affecting use of the IHS format

Many factors will influence a consumer's decision to shop electronically versus in-store. We focus on the benefits pertaining to the consumer's information acquisition and processing that enable consumers to locate and select merchandise that satisfies their needs, because the fundamental benefit of IHS is to lower the cost of information search (Bakos, 1991). In summary, then, the growth of IHS is dependent on the following factors:

- *Vast selection* If the format does not allow for quick and comprehensive inspection of an expanded set of options, electronic commerce will mimic the shopping experience now available through catalogs and achieve a relatively low level of penetration.

- *Screening*: If consumers cannot screen the large number of options made available, the advantages of vast selection will be outweighed by the costs of search.
- *Reliability*: If consumption benefits are predicted more reliably from experiential information searchable in stores than from surrogate information searchable through IHS and consumers are unwilling to bear the risk, in-store shopping will continue to prosper.
- *Product comparisons*: To be successful, IHS must allow the consumers to tailor the basis for comparison of alternatives in order to make the system compatible with the process by which consumers prefer to make decisions. Interactive home shopping has the potential to provide superior information presentation formats for making these comparisons.

Without these benefits, IHS will not develop beyond the relatively unattractive collection of electronic catalogs representing the present Internet offering. In the next section we review the incentives and disincentives for retailers and manufacturers to stimulate the development of the IHS channel and provide the appropriate information to attract consumers.

THE SUPPLY SIDE: RETAILERS, MANUFACTURERS, AND IHS

For many retailers the most significant threat posed by IHS is that profits will be eroded drastically by intensified price competition that will ensue as consumers' search costs are lowered. Consequently, many retailers are making limited, experimental investments in electronic commerce that, ironically, have none of the characteristics we describe previously as necessary for IHS to be preferred to existing formats. Many firms participate through stand-alone sites (such as World Wide Web home pages) that increase the costs of conducting cross-store comparisons. When third-party electronic search agents such as Bargain Finder (http://bf.cstar.ac.com/bf/) are created to compare prices charged by different vendors for the same compact disc, some retailers deny access. When participating in interactive malls, some firms require exclusivity agreements that protect them from the kinds of cross-store comparisons that would make IHS truly useful to the consumer.

It is reasonable to assume that firms that have made substantial commitments to an existing business format or technology will adopt defensive responses to radical change (Leonard-Barton, 1995). In the case of IHS and other radical changes, we argue that these defensive approaches are likely to fail in the long run, because the ultimate nature of the IHS channel and its appeal to consumers is beyond the control of individual firms. Firms might attempt to build walls around their offerings that make comparison across retailers and manufacturers difficult. However, consumers will prefer retailers that freely provide such information and make cross shopping easy; therefore, isolationist vendors could be bypassed in the search process. Eventually, intelligent agents will allow consumers to search across vendors to find offerings that possess the set of attributes desired. Attempts to limit information will be met with new formats that disseminate information (Bakos, 1991). Therefore, an electronic version of *Consumer Reports* could emerge that makes recommendations and informs consumers of where to find the best deal.

In the remaining portion of this article, we discuss that nature of competition in an IHS environment, approaches that firms can take to build competitive advantage in this environment, and some important issues confronting IHS retailers and manufacturers.

The role of price and quality

To complete a sale, a vendor must be considered by a consumer and the consumer must fail to consider a superior alternative (Nedungadi, 1990). Retailers believe that an IHS presence can increase the probability of being considered, but conditional on the achievement of that goal, IHS can have only a negative effect on profits by intensifying price competition with other IHS alternatives. Inasmuch as established retailers have less to gain in terms of increasing consideration probability, it is perhaps unsurprising that few of the most aggressive entrants into IHS have a large store-based presence. But the conclusion that IHS must lower profits through higher price competition does not necessarily follow. Generally speaking, information that is easy to obtain or that can discriminate unambiguously among options tends to receive higher weight in the consumer's decision process. Price information possesses both properties, which suggests that the concerns of retail firms are well founded. However, just as in the debate on economic affects of advertising (Mitra and Lynch, 1996; Rosen, 1978), IHS also can reduce the cost and increase the discriminating power of information regarding merchandise quality.

A strong parallel can be drawn between the introduction of IHS into the present retail environment and the development of discount stores 40 years ago (Sheffet and Scammon, 1985). Discount stores offered consumers an opportunity to forgo personalized service in return for lower prices. The result was an increase in price competition followed by attempts to avoid such competition through fair trade laws. Proponents of fair trade laws argued that, without some protection for department and specialty stores, discounters would drive them out of business; this, it was argued, would leave a shopping environment in which price could be discerned easily but nuances of quality could not. Consequently, consumers would become more price sensitive, sellers would adjust over time to compete more on price and less on quality, and consumers would suffer through the lack of interest in providing superior merchandise and service quality. Although the advent of discount stores did increase price competition in some merchandise categories, many consumers shop at retailers, such as Nordstrom, that provide superior information and services even though they charge a higher price. Such inherent consumer heterogeneity suggests that no one retail format can dominate all segments.

The potential impact of IHS on the nature of competition in the retail industry should be considered in this context. Although consumers shopping through an IHS channel will be able to collect price information with little effort, they also will be able to review at a low cost quality-related information about most search attributes and some experience attributes. For example, an electronic merchant of custom oriental rugs can convey clearly real differences in patterns and materials used for construction. An electronic grocery service such as Peapod can enable customers to sort cereals by nutritional content, thus making it easier to use that attribute in decision making. Insofar as (1) quality-related information is important to consumers and (2) brands within a category are differentiated, IHS can lead to less price sensitivity at the brand level and more sensitivity to search attributes associated with quality than does traditional shopping (cf. Mitra and Lynch, 1995).

This is a critical point for manufacturers that offer differentiated merchandise with superior performance attributes. Similarly, retailers that carry unique merchandise and/or provide superior information about merchandise could face less rather than more price competition. Perhaps this is why vendors cooperating with multiple-category search agents such as Fido the Shopping Doggie (http://www.shopfido.com/Vendors.html) are predominantly manufacturers and retailers selling highly unique merchandise such as arts and crafts, alternative music, hot sauces and spices, and gourmet foods and wines. Conversely, manufacturers of 'me-too' brands competing on cost can expect more intense price competition with the diffusion of IHS, and retailers carrying nationally branded merchandise with limited service also will face increased price competition.

Therefore, the introduction of the IHS channel will intensify the competitive environment, but this need not shift the emphasis from quality to price. By providing more information to consumers with minimal search cost, manufacturers and retailers with differentiated offerings will have a greater opportunity to educate consumers about the unique benefits they offer, and consumers will find it easier to access and compare the offerings of firms competing on price.

Developing competitive advantage in IHS

'Location, location, location' is the classic response to the question about the three most important factors in retailing. The development of IHS certainly reduces the importance of location. The successful IHS retailer will need to adopt a strategy that seeks competitive advantage in one or more of the following areas: (1) distribution efficiency, (2) assortments of complementary merchandise, (3) collection and utilization of customer information, (4) presentation of information through electronic formats, and (5) unique merchandise.

Distribution efficiency

Consumers perform a major portion of the distribution function when purchasing from stores. They transport merchandise from stores to their homes and bring unsatisfactory merchandise back to the store. In an IHS system, these substantial costs of home delivery and returns will be fully borne by the seller and must be factored into the price. Because these costs are substantial, IHS players that can select and package multiple items for delivery to individual households will have a competitive advantage over IHS competitors that lack such skills. The importance of this advantage naturally is greater when the preparation for shipping constitutes a large fraction of the overall price of the product.

Assortments of complementary merchandise

The opportunity to make multiple-item sales is important for two reasons. First, by making multiple-item purchases from an IHS supplier, customers reduce the shipping costs, which thereby reduces the net price. Second, the IHS retailer is in an ideal position to tailor a secondary offering to a customer on the basis of the customer's primary purchase objective. We might suggest that electronic agents will put together complementary bundles of products from multiple suppliers. However, to accomplish this task, the agents would need to possess an extremely broad knowledge base, such as information on what ties and shirts go together and what ingredients are needed to make a good Brunswick stew. Even without the presence of electronic agents, IHS offers retailers an opportunity to merchandise their wares in ways not previously possible. Traditional merchandising is limited by physical constraints. Floor space and shelf space limit the number of complements that can be placed in close proximity to any given product. However, even the Internet allows nearly unlimited cross-referencing through hypertext. Interactive home shopping faces no such problems, and the efficient IHS merchandiser should realize superior gains in customer retention and cross-selling – goals that are increasingly important regardless of distribution channel (e.g., Reicheld, 1993). The opportunity to cross-sell extends well beyond shirts and ties. Diversified vendors that own subunits that are only modestly related to each other in terms of the consumer goal they serve could realize synergies not possible with conventional channels (cf. Benjamin and Wigand, 1995 on 'virtual value chains').

Collection and utilization of customer information

Database marketing is an important capability for IHS retailing (cf. Blattberg and Deighton, 1991; Peppers and Rodgers, 1993). Interactive home shopping will increase the importance and accelerate the development of database marketing because more comprehensive customer-specific data can be captured. All consumers who shop electronically can be identified at the individual level. Moreover, unlike other formats, consumer browsing can be tracked. That is, records can be constructed not only of what consumers bought, but also what they inspected and for how long.

Interactive home shopping retailers can use these data to provide information-based value to the customer by (1) using technology to identify and display consideration sets most suited to individual consumer tastes and (2) providing information about those options that enables consumers to predict their satisfaction after purchase. Consumers, in turn, are likely to become loyal to an IHS retailer offering this service. This loyalty advantage could be sustainable for two reasons: First, consumers who experience high satisfaction may not defect to competing IHS retailers: and second, as consumers patronize a particular IHS retailer more frequently, more information can be collected. Thus, a cycle is created wherein consumer satisfaction provides the opportunity to learn how to provide greater satisfaction. Consumers would incur switching costs and an initial decrease in customer service if they took their business to a competing IHS retailer. Insofar as information about the consumer is proprietary, sustainability ensues.

Presentation of information

Traditionally, some stores have sought differentiation on the basis of atmospherics and service. Both still could play a role in IHS, and each will require a new technical skill set, as evidenced by the recent acquisition of software company Davidson and Associates and interactive entertainment company Sierra On-Line by CUC International, a leading direct marketer and interactive retailer.

Unique merchandise

From the retailer's perspective, the most straightforward method for increasing differentiation and reducing price competition is to sell merchandise that cannot be offered elsewhere. Uniqueness traditionally has been achieved in several ways:

- *Private labels*: IHS retailers can develop their own private-label merchandise that they offer exclusively.
- *Branded variants*: Alternatively, retailers can work with manufacturers to provide 'branded variants' sold exclusively through that retailer (Bergen, Dutta, and Shugan, 1996). The intent is to provide incentives for retailers to provide better service when inter-store (but not inter-brand) competition is reduced. (As noted subsequently, however, this method of achieving uniqueness could lose some effectiveness in the context of IHS.)
- *Offering assortments of complements tailored to customer needs*: One way for retailers to make their merchandise 'unique' is by creating bundles of complements that are available only separately elsewhere. For example, with each bottle of wine offered by Virtual Vineyards (http://www.virtualvin.com), customers can get complementary recipes from noted Bay-area chefs. Although some of the wines are available elsewhere, Virtual Vineyards allows its customers to anticipate satisfaction, when serving the wine with a particular meal. In essence, the wine-recipe bundle rather than the bottle of wine becomes the unit of analysis. Interactive home shopping retailers can use customer information skills noted previously to suggest bundles that lead to multiple sales and increased customer satisfaction – with the side benefit of reducing shipping costs.

IMPLICATIONS FOR FIRMS IN THE RETAIL INDUSTRY

The success of consumer product manufacturers and retailers in the IHS environment will be determined by the degree to which their strengths and weaknesses match the capabilities required to build competitive advantage (Aaker, 1989). In Table 2 we provide such a comparison. In this table, we assess each type of firm in terms of the skills previously identified as bases for competitive advantage in the IHS channel. We consider the likely impact of IHS on their businesses and how their businesses are likely to adapt. Afterward, we examine the impact of IHS on manufacturers.

Entry into IHS by retailers

Table 2 leads to some interesting insights when contrasted with Table 1. Table 1 suggests that catalog retailers are more vulnerable to IHS than are other retail formats. Interactive home shopping retailers and catalogers share the same limitations in terms of delivery timing and providing information about experience attributes; interactive home shopping dominates catalogs in terms of the information provided.

Table 2 IHS success capabilities possessed by firms

Skills for developing advantage	Catalog retailers	Traditional stores	Category specialists	Merchandise manufacturers
Distribution efficiency to homes	High	Medium to High	Medium	Low
Provision of complementary assortments	High	High	Low	Medium
Collection and use of customer information	High	Medium to High	Low	Low
Presentation of merchandise information	High	Medium to High	Low	Medium
Ability to offer unique merchandise	Medium	Medium	Low	High

However, Table 2 indicates that catalog retailers are best prepared to exploit IHS, inasmuch as they possess order fulfillment systems and database management skills that match the requirements of IHS. As an example, Lands' End (http://www.landsend.com) has a 'Specialty Shopper Service' that coordinates outfits for a whole wardrobe, helps the customer find his or her correct size, and keeps a file on sizes, tastes, past purchases, and address and credit card numbers. Also, the skills necessary for effective visual presentation of information in IHS follow closely the visual presentation of information in IHS follow closely the visual merchandising skills necessary for catalogs. Catalogers can reap efficiencies by listing their products electronically rather than in a more expensive print format when penetration of IHS justifies the production of electronic assets by savings of significant paper and postage costs.

However, the ability of currently successful catalogers to adapt to IHS can be expected to vary sharply, depending on the strategy the catalog retailer has used to establish competitive advantage. For example, Spiegel sells primarily branded merchandise, which is susceptible to price comparisons. Catalog retailers that emphasize branded merchandise will be particularly vulnerable compared with a retailer such as Lands' End, which has developed high-quality, private-brand merchandise.

Interactive home shopping is ideal for retailers, such as Nieman-Marcus, Harrod's, Gumps, and Saks, that enjoy strong national reputations for high-quality, unique merchandise, but that have only spotty or regional penetration. Such retailers are well positioned to take advantage of the market-expanding feature of IHS by attaining an international presence without making significant investments in store locations, visual merchandising, and leases (Rennie, 1993). Most of these stores currently possess an effective mail-order catalog operation. Interactive home shopping also is ideal for niche retailers that appeal to a far-flung customer base (cf. Quelch and Klein, 1996; Wernerfelt, 1994). For example, HotHotHot (http://www.hothothot.com) is a specialty store that carries more than 450 brands of hot sauce. The Internet gives this firm international exposure without significant advertising and only 300 square feet of store space (Carlton, 1996).

Conversely, national chains such as Sears have far less incentive to participate. These chains possess high levels of penetration through their ubiquitous stores. Even among national department store chains, there are clear differences in incentives to enter IHS. Both Sears and JCPenney have saturated the domestic market with stores, but JCPenney is also the largest catalog retailer in the United States. This catalog operations provides the infrastructure for fulfillment and visual merchandising that is well suited to IHS. Sears exited the 'Big Book' catalog business largely because its catalog fulfillment operations and technology were antiquated and because the cost of rebuilding these systems was prohibitive. This absence of efficient fulfillment systems for individual orders creates a further disincentive for Sears to engage in IHS.

Adaptation of in-store retailers to IHS

The DEFENDER model (Hauser and Shugan, 1983) suggests that in-store retailers should react to emerging IHS retailers by emphasizing attributes of their offering for which they have a comparative advantage. Therefore, store-based retailers should (1) focus on merchandise that has important experiential attributes that are search attributes in a store but experience attributes in IHS, (2) capitalize on their relative advantage in providing information tailored to the needs of specific customers, (3) emphasize the noninformational benefits of shopping, (4) complement IHS with their in-store business, and (5) place more emphasis on unique merchandise.

Because it is more difficult to provide some experience information through IHS, in-store retailers must focus on merchandise that possesses characteristics consumers can assess veridically only through contact with the merchandise. For example, bedding and linens come in standard sizes and are amenable to IHS; consequently, department stores might need to decrease space allocated to this merchandise and increase floor space devoted to tailored clothing. They also might need to increase resources devoted to personalized service associated with those items (e.g., alterations). Similarly, department stores should shift their merchandise mix to emphasize items for which immediate, low-cost access to the merchandise is important.

To offset the ability of IHS retailers to provide personalized information at home, in-store retailers should improve the personalized information they offer using their sales associates or in-store kiosks. For example, Best Buy uses kiosks extensively to alleviate physical store constraints and provide detailed product information. Media Play uses in-store listening stations to enable acoustic sampling of compact discs prior to purchase. Used-car superstore CarMax provides kiosks that allow flexible screening criteria, side-by-side viewing of screened options, and the printing of car lot location maps for candidate cars – all of which greatly reduce search costs inherent in navigating a huge and heterogeneous on-site inventory.

Because IHS retailers can provide greater informational benefits, in-store retailers must emphasize ancillary benefits such as entertainment and opportunities to socialize. For many consumers, shopping is an experience that transcends product purchase. One method of differentiating a retail outlet is to provide benefits that enhance the experience. Traditionally, this has involved improvements in ambiance. Increasingly, the entertainment value of shopping is being emphasized. Incredible Universe, Niketown, and the Mall of America are possible harbingers of the future. (For a discussion of how IHS retailers might respond to these efforts by in-store retailers and improve the social experience benefits for IHS customers, see Armstrong and Hagel, 1996).

In-store retailers with an IHS presence can use IHS as a source of advertising to presell merchandise and to check its availability in local stores. This would enable the customer to pick it up or have it delivered from the local store.

In-store retailers and IHS retailers will need to reduce their reliance on nationally branded merchandise to lure people into their sites and will need to redouble their efforts to develop private label brands. Therefore, the trend seen in store-based retailers such as JCPenney – which increasingly promotes private label brands such as Arizona jeans – could accelerate.

Impact on category specialists and discounters

In light of the consumer analysis in Table 1, category specialists appear particularly vulnerable to IHS retailing. Aside from the immediacy of delivery, this shopping format offers few informational and noninformational benefits. In addition, these formats emphasize branded merchandise for which price competition will increase with the advent of IHS. However, the nature of these outlets varies greatly in terms of their operation, merchandise, and relationships with suppliers.

Toys 'R' Us enjoys national (and increasingly international) penetration. If Toys 'R' Us were to sell electronically, it might experience significant cannibalization of its in-store sales, making IHS less attractive to it than to an entrepreneur entering the toy business through IHS or even to an F. A. O. Schwartz, which is smaller and more specialized.

Circuit City appears to be as vulnerable as Toys 'R' Us is to competition from IHS retailers. However, the structure of the consumer electronics industry is considerably different from the toy industry. The consumer electronics industry is dominated by a few suppliers that make most of their profits from sophisticated, high-technology products. The benefits of these products can be credibly demonstrated only in a store environment. To motivate electronics retailers to provide this information to consumers, manufacturers employ several mechanisms designed to protect specialty retailers from price competition from mass merchandisers that sell only the low-end and mid-range models that dominate the market. (For example, co-op advertising offers to mass merchandisers can be made contingent on pricing cooperation.) Moreover, distribution of high-end products to IHS retailers would encourage free riding and reduce in-store retailers' incentive to provide product-differentiating information.

Home Depot is similar to Toys 'R' Us in terms of distribution intensity but is less vulnerable because many of its goods demand immediacy, highly tailored advice from expert associates, or direct (non-video) inspection of size, specifications, or colors. Home Depot also offers a level of hand-holding from expert sales associates that cannot be duplicated electronically. Moreover, bulky do-it-yourself merchandise can be expensive to ship directly to homes.

Implications for manufacturers and retailers

Disintermediation

The most important structural change that could be brought about by IHS is disintermediation, wherein manufacturers bypass the retailer and sell directly to consumers. Although the IHS channel does offer manufacturers an opportunity to deal directly with consumers (cf. Benjamin and Wigand, 1995; Pine, Peppers, and Rogers, 1995), Table 2 illustrates the limited capabilities of most manufacturers to succeed as IHS retailers – which suggests that the degree of disintermediation will not be significant.

Manufacturers cannot easily and efficiently duplicate a variety of services that retailers perform for both manufacturers and consumers (see Sarkar, Butler, and Steinfield, 1996). The classic functions undertaken by retailers and other firms in a distribution channel include breaking bulk (converting caseload shipments into individual items); providing assortments that permit one-stop shopping; holding inventory to make merchandise available when customers want it; and providing a variety of transaction features and services that include credit, alteration and assembly of merchandise, attractive display, dressing rooms, personal assistance in selecting merchandise, repair services, return services, and warranties (Levy and Weitz, 1995). Although these functions *can* be provided by manufacturers selling directly through IHS, present retailers might be more efficient at performing these functions. Manufacturers are not highly skilled at selling directly to customers. They lack the efficient systems to fulfill orders at a household level and have limited capability to offer the complementary products that increase customer satisfaction and reduce shipping costs. Similarly, manufacturers may not be able to deal with high return rates encountered in nonstore retailing formats.

We noted previously that JCPenney's catalog operation is the largest in the United States. It is undergirded by an extremely efficient and capital-intensive system for accepting orders, packing them together, and shipping them to customers to be picked up at local stores and catalog distribution centers. The difficulty and expense of duplicating such a system drove Sears from the catalog business; the scale economies are high. It seems unlikely that many manufacturers would find it worthwhile to build such a fulfillment operation from scratch or to replace retailers in the supply chain with outsourcers to handle the functions now performed for them by retailers.

These fulfillment-based disincentives to disintermediate will be lower among products for which fulfillment costs contribute only a small fraction of the sales price to consumers. Products such as computer software, branded jewelry, and high-end perfumes fit this description.

Finally, although manufacturers might be tempted to generate incremental sales by adding a direct IHS channel to their store-based channels, entry into IHS could alienate the stores that now carry their lines. Unless the manufacturer believes it would be more profitable to sell directly than through stores, it will hesitate to disintermediate for fear of alienating those stores that currently carry its lines.

These considerations implicitly identify those manufacturers that might have an incentive to disintermediate. Manufacturers possessing extremely strong brand names and the ability to produce a complementary merchandise might consider disintermediation. Consider Levi Strauss. Its brand names are among the strongest in the apparel industry. Network externalities are weak for the markets it faces, either because it produces complements demanded by consumers (e.g., Dockers slacks and shirts) or because, for core products such as Levi's 501 Blue Jeans, consumers can be assured of a match without buying the complementary items from the same seller. In contrast, a maker of dress slacks such as Savane would have less incentive to consider disintermediation because its brand name has less pull and because demand for Savane slacks benefits from significant network externalities when sold in department and specialty stores carrying other manufacturers' lines.

The foregoing discussion applies to manufacturers of nationally branded merchandise that distribute through store-based retailers. Small manufacturers and entrepreneurs, conversely, are more prone to disintermediate because their alternatives to IHS are less attractive. Small or new firms – even those with superior new products – find it difficult to obtain shelf space or awareness. For these producers, IHS could reduce barriers to entry by making it possible for consumers to locate them. In this sense, IHS functions just like advertising in helping heterogeneous consumer segments find products that match their tastes (Rosen, 1978).

Brands and branding

A brand is a search attribute that assures consumers of a consistent level of product quality. It might be the only attribute available to assess some credence goods. Because a brand offered by different outlets can be easily compared by IHS shoppers, manufacturers of branded merchandise are particularly vulnerable to price competition at the retail level; consequently, IHS retailers will find it unattractive to sell their merchandise. It is ironic that strong brands increase the attractiveness of IHS to consumers by providing sufficient information to predict satisfaction without experiencing the merchandise, but that this same mechanism makes these brands less attractive for retailers to carry in the face of IHS.

In the present retail environment, branded-goods manufacturers employ restricted distribution in a territory, relying on location to reduce price competition among retailers and ensure retailer cooperation. This mechanism is not feasible in the low search cost environment of IHS retailing. Therefore, manufacturers of branded merchandise must focus on other methods for insulating IHS retailers from price competition. One method is the production of private-label brands for each retailer. Alternatively, the manufacturer can produce 'branded variants' of nationally branded products. These branded variants might be retailer-specific manufacturer model numbers (e.g., Sony Model MA 3150, which is sold only by Service Merchandise).

Neither of these alternatives will be relished by manufacturers that have developed strong national and international brands. It is obvious why such manufacturers would be loathe to find themselves mainly as suppliers of private-label merchandise. The prospect of employing an expanded branded-variant strategy also is perilous, albeit in more subtle ways. Increasing the number of branded variants could have the effect of lowering the average attractiveness of the manufacturer's offerings. The easy search-and-compare aspects of IHS could render transparent the existence of trivial differences between models, forcing manufacturers to create larger differences in their variants to satisfy retailer demands of noncomparability across retailers. However, if a significant amount of purchasing still occurs in store, the manufacturer risks losing sales because the variant carried by the store is not the variant desired by the consumer. It seems that manufacturers will be driven to produce variants that are exclusive to each retailer with which they do business (e.g., 'Liz Claiborne for Macy's').

The preferred solution for manufacturers is to create a level of brand power that ensures cooperation from retailers in terms of resale price maintenance and other tactical mandates. Manufacturers that hold such power could threaten defectors subtly (Barrett, 1991). Few brands hold such sway, however, and it is likely that even fewer will be able to maintain such power with distribution through IHS. Nonetheless, 'brand building' is another option for manufacturers that fear the leveling effects of IHS. On the surface this could seem counter-intuitive: The threat of IHS to vendors is that its information features will speed commoditization and expose parity where it exists; parity should decrease the value of the brand.

Nonetheless, in product classes in which technology cannot provide advantage and for firms that cannot win technological battles, image building becomes an option. For example, in the case of fashion goods, brands can attain cachet through a carefully crafted marketing strategy. Plainly, brands will have least influence in non-image, parity product classes. However, parity is not a limiting factor when credence attributes are important – and nearly all products possess credence attributes (Levitt, 1981). For example, when quality is difficult to assess, brand name serves as a surrogate (see our previous discussion). And, as marketers long have known, brands can signal quality or other dimensions of differentiation falsely through long-term positioning tactics or explicit attempts to frame consumer decisions (cf. Gardner, 1983; Hoch and Deighton, 1989). Therefore, another irony of IHS could be that the technology that enables consumers to make more intelligent comparisons in some cases can induce manufacturers to take actions intended to produce an opposite outcome in other cases. As with other determinants of IHS success, the importance of the brand and the viability of brand-building strategy will vary as a function of the product class and firms' individual competencies.

RESEARCH OPPORTUNITIES

The advent of IHS raises significant questions pertaining to consumer behavior and industry structure. Previous research focuses on heuristics used by consumers to make choices when search and comparison are relatively difficult and costly. Such a focus has been appropriate because the environment, often aided by the retailer, tends to discourage consumer search (see Hoch and Deighton, 1989). In contrast, the potential IHS search environment is highly interactive, information intensive, and low in cost. In this alternative environment, research questions in need of attention include the following:

- What fundamental changes occur in information processing as a function of the availability of electronic search agents? With few exceptions (e.g., Widing and Talarzyk, 1993), consumer research fails to examine the heuristics and resulting decision quality that are enabled by the search and screening operations that constitute the most attractive features of IHS. A related question involves the influence of search agents on consumer learning. Traditional shopping affords consumers the opportunity to learn the distribution of attribute values across alternatives; search agents merely produce a set of alternatives that satisfy particular criteria. Thus, on some dimensions of product knowledge, search agents can produce undesirable outcomes.

- How does the balance of memory-based versus stimulus-based processing shift as the search environment changes? Some researchers criticize research on consumer choice for focusing on stimulus-based paradigms and ignoring important memory-based aspects present in nearly all consumer decisions (Alba, Hutchinson, and Lynch, 1991). Our assumptions regarding an effective IHS system, conversely argue in favor of greater attention to stimulus-based processing inasmuch as electronic search agents will reduce memory constraints significantly. An especially large effect should be observed when the optimal choice set includes items from different produce categories (Ratneshwar and Shocker, 1991). Although human memory might be bounded by temporarily salient options, electronic agents can retrieve all alternatives tagged with the consumer's goal or desired benefit (e.g., 'gift').

- Important questions also exist regarding short-term memory and perceptual issues. Just as the cognitive implications of hypertext are virtually unexplored (Rouet *et al.*, 1996), consumer researchers must understand how memory constraints affect decision making as consumers move from brand listings to brand attributes to third-party evaluations to complementary product information, and so on. From a vendor's perspective, there is an information vacuum regarding optimal display format. Insofar as search agents efficiently retrieve requested alternatives, impulse purchasing will occur less frequently (cf. Park, Iyer, and Smith, 1989). Vendors must understand the cognitive and perceptual rules that can prompt consumers to make electronic detours in their search for goods and services.

- How do the content and presentation of product information affect consumers' willingness to make choices without directly experiencing the product? Are there ways to create 'consumption vocabularies' (West, Brown, and Hoch, 1996) that increase consumers' willingness to infer experiential benefits from descriptive, electronically provided information?

- How are consumer confidence and satisfaction affected by search processes that enable efficient screening? The ability to screen products by attribute creates a much more manageable information environment but simultaneously allows some attractive options to go unnoticed. Do consumers experience a greater but illusory sense of confidence in choices made from effortfully but incompletely constructed consideration sets?

- How will consumers react to the collection of detailed information about their needs and purchase behavior by IHS retailers? The utilization of this information to tailor merchandise presentations provides a benefit to consumers, but will consumers be willing to make this personal data available? What can IHS retailers do to assure consumers that personal information will not be misused?

- What are the true dynamics of price sensitivity in this environment? Although greater amounts of information should increase sensitivity among comparable goods and reduce sensitivity for differentiated goods, empirical research is required to understand how this general conclusion is moderated by type of good, branding, and the manner in which vendors present information.

- How will the nature of the relationships among manufacturers, retailers, and consumers evolve as a function of technology-based reductions in search costs (cf. Zettelmeyer, 1996)?

- To what extent will vendors be able to control the search environment? In part, technological developments can determine the ability of vendors to inhibit search and comparison. At present, Internet vendors can prevent entry by search agents. However, irrespective of technology, to what extent will market forces determine not only control of entry but also search procedures allowed by vendors?

- We argue that disintermediation will not blossom in the present environment because of the critical functions now performed by retailers. Looking to the future, how will IHS interact with developments in distribution and flexible manufacturing to enable manufacturers to mass customize their offerings and deliver them efficiently to customers?

- Many traditional retailers will find themselves in multiple channels – maintaining their bricks-and-mortar operations while also creating an electronic presence. What are the economics of such dual systems and how sustainable are existing stores if electronic sales grow to significant levels? In other words, if total sales do not increase, at what point does cannibalization reduce the viability of stores?

These questions are a mere sample of a much larger set both within and beyond the scope of our analysis. Clearly, predictions about the ultimate fate and form of IHS are risky. However, it is equally clear that this emerging channel provides marketing researchers and practitioners with much opportunity to test their theories and apply their tools.

REFERENCES

Aaker, David (1989), 'Managing Assets and Skills: the Key to a Sustainable Advantage', *California Management Review*, 31 (Winter), 91–106.

Agins, Terry (1994), 'Go Figure: Same Shopper Wears Size 6, 8, 10, 12', *The Wall Street Journal*, (November 11), B1.

Alba, Joseph W. and Amitava Chattopadhyay (1985), 'Effects of Context and Part-Category Cues on Recall of Competing Brands', *Journal of Marketing Research*, 22 (August), 340–49.

___ and J. Wesley Hutchinson (1987), 'Dimensions of Consumer Expertise', *Journal of Consumer Research*, 13 (March), 411–54.

___, ___, and John G. Lynch (1991), 'Memory and Decision Making', in *Handbook of Consumer Theory and Research*, Harold H. Kassarjian and Thomas S. Robertson, eds. Englewood Cliffs, NJ: Prentice Hall, 1–49.

___, Howard Marmorstein, and Amitava Chattopadhyay (1992), 'Transitions in Preference Over Time: The Effects of Memory on Message Persuasiveness', *Journal of Marketing Research,* 29 (November), 406–16.

Armstrong, Arthur and John Hagel III (1996), 'The Real Value of On-Line Communities', *Harvard Business Review,* 74 (May/June), 134–41.

Anderson, Christopher (1995), 'The Accidental Superhighway: A Survey of the Internet', *The Economist*, (July 1), 50–68.

Bakos, J. Yannis (1991), 'A Strategic Analysis of Electronic Marketplaces', *MIS Quarterly*, 15 (September), 295–310.

Barrett, Paul M. (1991), 'Anti-Discount Policies of Manufacturers Are Penalizing Certain Cut-Price Stores', *The Wall Street Journal*, (February 27), B1–B5.

Benjamin, Robert and Rold Wigand (1995), 'Electronic Markets and Virtual Value Chains on the Information Superhighway', *Sloan Management Review*, 37 (Winter), 62–72.

Bergen, Mark, Shantanu Dutta, and Steven M. Shugan (1996), 'Branded Variants: A Retail Perspective', *Journal of Marketing Research*, 33 (February), 9–19.

Bettman, James R. And Pradeep Kakkar (1977), 'Effects of Information Presentation Format on Consumer Information Acquisition Strategies', *Journal of Consumer Research*, 3 (March), 233–40.

___ and C. Whan Park (1980), 'Effects of Prior Knowledge, Exposure, and Phase of the Choice Process on Consumer Decision Process: A Protocol Analysis', *Journal of Consumer Research*, 7 (December), 234–48.

___ and Michel A. Zins (1979), 'Information Format and Choice Task Effects in Decision Making', *Journal of Consumer Research*, 6 (September), 141–53.

Biehal, Gabriel and Dipankar Chakravarti (1983), 'Information Accessibility as a Moderator of Consumer Choice', *Journal of Consumer Research*, 10 (June), 1–14.

Blattberg, Robert C. and John Deighton (1991), 'Interactive Marketing: Exploiting the Age of Addressability', *Sloan Management Review*, 33 (Fall), 5–15.

Broniarczyk, Susan and Joseph W. Alba (1994) 'The Role of Consumers' Intuitions in Inference Making', *Journal of Consumer Research*, 21 (December), 393–407.

Carlton, Jim (1996), 'Think Big', *The Wall Street Journal*, (June 17), R27.

Copeland, Melvin T. (1923), 'Relation of Consumer's Buying Habits to Marketing Methods', *Harvard Business Review*, 1 (April), 282–89.

Cortese, Amy (1996), 'Software's Holy Grail', *Business Week*, (June 24), 83–92.

Darby, Michael R. And Edi Karni (1973), 'Free Competition and the Optimal Amount of Fraud', *Journal of Law and Economics*. 16 (April), 66–86.

Day, George S., Allan D. Shocker, and Rajendra K. Srivastava (1979), 'Customer-Oriented Approaches to Identifying Product Markets', *Journal of Marketing*, 43 (Fall), 8–19.

Dickson, Peter R. (1982), 'Personal-Situation: Segmentation's Missing Link', *Journal of Marketing*, 46 (Fall), 56–64.

Donegan, Priscilla (1996), 'The High Tech in a High Touch Way', *Progressive Grocer*, (December), 133.

Edell, Julie A. and Richard Staelin (1983), 'The Information Processing of Pictures in Print Advertisements', *Journal of Consumer Research*, 10 (June), 45–61.

Ehrlich, Isaac and Lawrence Fisher (1982), 'The Derived Demand for Advertising: A Theoretical and Empirical Investigation', *American Economic Review,* 72 (June), 366-88.

Feinberg, Fred M. and Joel Huber (1996), 'A Theory of Cutoff Formation Under Imperfect Information', *Management Science*, 42 (January), 65–84.

Gardner, Meryl Paula (1983), 'Advertising Effects on Attributes Recalled and Criteria Used for Brand Evaluations', *Journal of Consumer Research*, 10 (December), 310–19.

Greenleaf, Eric A. and Donald R. Lehmann (1995), 'Reasons for Substantial Delay in Consumer Decision Making', *Journal of Consumer Research*, 22 (September), 186–99.

Gilovich, Thomas and Victoria Husted Medvec (1995), 'The Experience of Regret: What, When, and Why', *Psychological Review*, 102 (April), 379–95.

Hauser, John R. and Steven Shugan (1983), 'Defensive Marketing Strategies', *Management Science*, 3 (Fall), 327–51.

___, Glen L. Urban, and Bruce D. Weinberg (1993), 'How Consumers Allocate Their Time when Searching for Information', *Journal of Marketing Research*, 30 (November), 452–66.

___ Birger Wernerfelt (1990), 'An Evaluation Cost Model of Consideration Sets', *Journal of Consumer Research*, 16 (March), 393–408.

Hill, G. Christian (1996), 'Cyberslaves', *The Wall Street Journal*, (June 17), R20.

Hoch, Stephen J. and John Deighton (1989) 'Managing What Consumers Learn from Experience', *Journal of Marketing*, 53 (April), 1–20.

Hoffman, Donna L. and Thomas P. Novak (1996), 'Marketing in Hypermedia Computer-Mediated Environments: Conceptual Foundations, *Journal of Marketing*, 60 (Winter), 50–68.

Hutchinson, J. Wesley, Kalyan Raman, and Murali K. Mantrala (1994), 'Finding Choice Alternatives in Memory: Probability Models of Brand Name Recall', *Journal of Marketing Research*, 31 (November), 441–61.

Jarvepaa, Sirkka L. (1989), 'The Effect of Task Demands and Graphical Format on Information Processing Strategies', *Management Science*, 35 (March), 285–303.

___ (1990), 'Graphical Displays in Decision Making – The Visual Salience Effect', *Journal of Behavioral Decision Making*, 3 (3), 247–62.

Kardes, Frank R. and Gurumurthy Kalyanaraman, (1992), 'Order-of-Entry Effects on Consumer Memory and Judgment: An Information Integration Perspective', *Journal of Marketing Research,* 29 (August), 343–57.

___, Gurumurthy Kalyanaraman, Murali Chandrashekaran, and Ronald J. Dornoff (1993), 'Brand Retrieval, Consideration Set Composition, Consumer Choice, and the Pioneering Advantage', *Journal of Consumer Research*, 20 (June), 62–75.

Karni, E. And A. Schwarz (1977), 'Search Theory: The Case of Search with Uncertain Recall', *Journal of Economic Theory*, 16 (October), 38–52.

Leonard-Barton, D. (1995) *Wellsprings of Knowledge.* Cambridge, MA: Harvard Business School Press.

Levitt, Theodore (1981), 'Marketing Intangible Products and Product Intangibles', *Harvard Business Review*, 59 (May/June), 94–102.

Levy, Michael and Barton Weitz (1995), *Retailing Management*, 2d ed. Burr Ridge, IL: Richard D. Irwin, Inc.

Lynch, John G., Jr., Howard Marmorstein, and Michael F. Weigold (1988), 'Choices from Sets Including Remembered Brands: use of Recalled Attributes and Overall Evaluations', *Journal of Consumer Research*, 15 (September), 169–84.

Maes, Patricia (1994), 'Agents that Reduce Work and Information Overload', *Communications of the ACM*, 37 (July), 31–40.

___ (1995), 'Intelligent Software', *Scientific American*, (September), 84–86.

Mitchell, Andrew A. and Peter A. Dacin (1996), 'The Assessment of Alternative Measures of Consumer Expertise', *Journal of Consumer Research*, 23 (December), 219–39.

Mitra, Anusree and John G. Lynch, Jr. (1995), 'Toward a Reconciliation of Market Power and Information Theories of Advertising Effects on Price Elasticity', *Journal of Consumer Research*, 21 (March), 644–59.

___ and ___ (1996), 'Advertising Effects on Consumer Welfare: Prices Paid and Liking for Brands Selected', *Marketing Letters*, 7 (March), 644–59.

Nedungadi, Prakash (1990), 'Recall and Consumer Consideration Sets: Influencing Choice without Altering Brand Evaluations', *Journal of Consumer Research*, 17 (December), 263–76.

Negroponte, Nicholas (1995), *Being Digital*, New York: Alfred A. Knopf.

Newman, Joseph W. and Richard Staelin (1972), 'Prepurchase Information Seeking for New Cars and Major Household Appliances', *Journal of Marketing Research*, 9 (August), 249–57.

Park, C. Whan, Easwar S. Iyer, and Daniel C. Smith (1989), 'The Effects of Situational Factors on In-Store Grocery Shopping Behavior: The Role of Store Environment and Time Available for Shopping', *Journal of Consumer Research*, 15 (March), 422–33.

Peppers, Don and Martha Rodgers (1993). *The One to One Future*. New York: Currency Doubleday.

Pine, B. Joseph II, Don Peppers, and Martha Rogers (1995), 'Do You Want to Keep Your Customers Forever?', *Harvard Business Review*, 73 (March/April), 103–114.

Quelch, John and Lisa Klein (1996), 'The Internet and International Marketing', *Sloan Management Review*, 38 (Spring), 60–75.

Ratchford, Brian T. (1980), 'The Value of Information for Selected Appliances', *Journal of Marketing Research*, 17 (February), 14–25.

___ (1982), 'Cost-Benefit Models for Explaining Consumer Choice and Information Seeking Behavior', *Management Science*, 28 (February), 197–212.

Ratneshwar, S. and Allan D. Shocker (1991), 'Substitution in Use and the Role of Usage Context in Product Category Structures', *Journal of Marketing Research*, 28 (August), 281–95.

Reda, Susan (1995), 'Interactive Home Shopping: Will Consumers Catch Up with Technology?' *Stores* (March), 20–24.

Reicheld, Frederick F. (1993), 'Loyalty-Based Management', *Harvard Business Review*, 71 (March/April), 64–73.

Rennie, W. R. (1993), 'Global Competitiveness: Born Global', *McKinsey Quarterly*, (September 22), 45–52.

Rigdon, Joan (1996), 'Caught in the Web', *The Wall Street Journal* (June 17), R14.

Roberts, John H. and James M. Lattin (1991), 'Development and Testing of a Model of Consideration Set Composition', *Journal of Marketing Research*, 28 (November), 429–40.

Rosen, Sherwin (1978), 'Advertising, Information, and Product Differentiation', in *Issues in Advertising*, David Tuerck, ed. Washington, DC: American Enterprise Institute, 161–91.

Rouet, Jean-Francois, Jarmo J. Levonen, Andrew Dillon, and Rand J. Spiro (1996), *Hypertext and Cognition*. Mahwah, NJ: Lawrence Erlbaum Associates.

Russo, J. Edward (1977), 'The Value of Unit Price Information', *Journal of Marketing Research*, 14 (May), 193–201.

Sarkar, Mira, Brian Butler, and Charles Steinfield (1996), 'Intermediaries and Cyberintermediaries: A Continuing role for Mediating Players in the Electronic Marketplace', *Journal of Computer-Mediated Communications*, 1 (3) (http://jcmc.huji.ac.il/vol1/issue3/).

Schiesel, Seth (1997), 'Payoff Still Elusive on Internet Gold Rush', *The New York Times*, (January 2), C17.

Sheffet, Mary Jane and Debra L. Scammon (1985), 'Resale Price Maintenance: Is it Safe to Suggest Retail Prices?', *Journal of Marketing*, 49 (Fall), 82–91.

Simonson, Itamar, Joel Huber, and John Payne (1988), 'The Relationship between Prior Brand Knowledge and Information Acquisition Order', *Journal of Consumer Research*, 14 (March), 566–78.

Stigler, George (1961), 'The Economics of Information', *Journal of Political Economy*, 69 (January/February), 213–25.

Tauber, Edward (1972), 'Why Do People Shop?', *Journal of Marketing*, 36 (October), 42–49.

Templin, Neal (1996), 'Veteran PC Customers Spur Mail-Order Boom', *The Wall Street Journal*, (July 17), B1.

Todd, Peter and Izak Benbasat (1994), 'The Influence of Decision Aids on Choice Strategies: An Experimental Analysis of the Role of Cognitive Effort', *Organizational Behavior and Human Decision Processes*, 60, 36–74.

Tversky, Amos and Eldar Shafir (1992), 'Decision Under Conflict: An Analysis of Choice Aversion', *Psychological Science*, 6 (November), 358–361.

Verity, John and Robert Hof (1994), 'The Internet: How Will It Change the Way You Do Business', *Business Week*, (November 14), 80–86, 88.

Wernerfelt, Birger (1994), 'An Efficiency Criterion for Marketing Design', *Journal of Marketing Research*, 31 (November), 462–70.

West, Patricia M., Christina L. Brown, and Stephen J. Hoch (1996), 'Consumption Vocabulary and Preference Formation', *Journal of Consumer Research*, 23 (September), 120–35.

Widing, Robert E. II and W. Wayne Talarzyk (1993), 'Electronic Information Systems for Consumers: An Evaluation of Computer-Assisted Formats in Multiple Decision Environments', *Journal of Marketing Research*, 30 (May), 125–41.

Wilensky, Dawn (1995), 'The Internet, The Next Retailing Frontier', *Discount Store News*, (December 4), 6–7.

Wilkie, William, L. and Peter R. Dickson (1985), 'Consumer Information Search and Shopping Behavior', Management Science Institute paper series, Cambridge, MA.

Wright, Alice and John G. Lynch Jr. (1995), 'Communication Effects of Advertising Versus Direct Experience When Both Search and Experience Attributes are Present', *Journal of Consumer Research*, 21 (March), 708–18.

Zettelmeyer, Florian (1996), 'The Strategic Use of Consumer Search Cost', working paper, Massachusetts Institute of Technology.

Alba, J., Lynch, J., Weitz, B., Janiszewski, C., Lutz, R., Sawyer, A. and Wood S. (1997) 'Interactive home shopping: consumer, retailer, and manufacturer incentives to participate in electronic marketplaces'. *Journal of Marketing*, 61(3), July: 38–53. Reproduced with permission from *Journal of Marketing*, published by the American Marketing Association.

5.4 Interactive media face artificial consumers and marketing theory must re-think

Richard Gatarski and Anders Lundkvist

INTRODUCTION

Marketers and marketing theory have evolved in the real and physical world. In that world humans produce, communicate and behave bounded by physical constraints. One such constraint is media access. We cannot distribute a specific printed magazine to all the people in the global market. But things are changing. Magazines and an increasing number of other content-based products are now handled in a digital, non-physical form. The original concept of the market as a physical meeting point is further challenged by business in cyberspace. Here the real world is extended into virtual worlds. One example of such a space is the World Wide Web, where media access is almost global and the cost for content reproduction is close to zero. Consequently Rayport and Svikola (1995) use the label *marketspace* to distinguish the new information world from the physical world.

> Marketspace – a virtual realm where products and services exist as digital information and can be delivered through information-based channels.

Another constraint in the physical world is human capacity. Restrictions in our cognitive abilities made consumer behaviour researchers interested in scientific studies of the brain. As John A. Howard (1994) wrote in his textbook:

> Several years ago, H. A. Simon proposed that human beings have a limited capacity to process information. As a consequence consumers can have difficulty in making the buying decision.

We have studied electronic commerce in marketspaces where artificial actors, so called agents, have started to supplement human actors. One example where agents acted as consumers was Ringo, which was presented at a computer technology conference (Shardanand and Maes, 1995):

> a technique for making personalized recommendations from any type of database to a user based on similarities between the interest profile of that user and those of other users. In particular, we discuss the implementation of a networked system called Ringo, which makes personalized recommendations for music albums and artists.

Simultaneously a number of economic, artistic and philosophical ideas are realized. Marketing consultants Peppers and Rogers (1993) discuss new possibilities enabled by electronic technology. With the concept 'One-to-One marketing' they question the need for mass communication. Brenda Laurel's (1993) artistic idea of 'Computers as Theatres' seems to be the underlying concept in Microsoft Network (MSN). Former theater director Bob Bejan has turned MSN into one of the growing onLine services. Maybe because Bejan and his staff created an action-filled stage show rather than an electronic market. And the psychologist Sherry Turkle (1995) brings forward philosophical ideas about human identity. She makes it evident that new electronic technology has created people with multiple selves.

All this must be a challenge to marketers who at physical places used to find real consumers with a single and fairly stable identity. Marketing theory can no longer suppose that setting. The virtual world offers new possibilities, such as agents with an information processing capacity that differs from that of the human brain. For instance, what is known to a human being, e.g., what pleasure stands for, might not be obvious to an agent.

Motivation and domain

Our aim is to make evident that many fundamentals of comtemporary marketing theory do not hold for many of the new possibilities offered by digital technology.

The article provides an overview of *interactive media* and *artificial consumers*, the latter in the form of agents. We attempt to clarify these two concepts and outline their meeting with existing theories about marketing communication and consumer behaviour.

Important notions from the evolution of marketing theory

One important point is that marketing theories were developed in response to environmental changes, as when radio and later television brought forward new problems in the first half of the 20th century. GRP and day-after-recall became two of the new tools that are essential to users of broadcast media. Another important point to note is an interest in the consumers' role that many contemporary marketing scholars bring forward.

The transition of marketing management can be described as shifting focus from the market as an object to the consumers as individuals. Philip Kotler's well-known product 'Marketing Management' is in itself a good example of this development. Earlier editions, e.g., Kotler (1984), focus heavily on the process of bringing tangibles to the market. Later editions, e.g. Kotler (1994), include chapters about intangibles and services. The main focus has always been on finding ways for companies to hand over the outcomes of the production process to their less informed consumers.

Kotler's view on marketing has been criticized. Other researchers focus on services, relationships, co-production and consumer experience. Evert Gummesson (1994), one of the pioneers in service management studies, suggests grounds for a new marketing paradigm. He argues that *Relationship Marketing* (networks and interactions) are the core of marketing practices.

Porter and Millar (1985) integrated production in marketing. They brought forward a theory about production value chains. Normann and Ramirez (1994) remarked that Porter more or less ignored the consumers. They add that value is constantly created in interaction with many different players, including consumers, suppliers, employees and managers. Thus consumers are *co-producers*. Another important aspect in marketing is experiential consumption, Holbrook and Hirschman (1982). Here researchers argue that consumption produces a series of human experiences, generated all the way from purchase through product use ending with post-purchase. Normann and Ramirez (1994) explicitly support this view by stating that producers must enable consumers to produce their own experiences.

Many scholars present results from research that indicates consumers preference for products that are individually tailored. Pine (1993) outlines a number of important management strategies under the label *Mass Customization*. By adding the notion communications flexibility, Peppers and Rogers (1997) developed that idea into *One-To-One Marketing*. Gilmore and Pine (1997) propose four basic approaches to how customization can be accomplished. In an insert they recognize that every customer is more than his or her own market:

> a widespread recognition that multiple markets reside within individual consumers, will turn the entire notion on markets and customers completely inside out.

In summary we see a focused research interest in consumers and the processes where their experiental consumption is created. Researchers point out that the value of those experiences increases when marketing relations become customized. According to our view consumption can no longer be seen as something separate from communication, buying, post-purchase, etc.

PROBLEM DESCRIPTION

We foresee a number of problems that arise when marketing theory faces the possibilities offered by electronic media. And their solutions seem to require more than simply applying existing theory, such as how to advertise in electronic marketspaces. No single situation can illustrate all the emergent patterns we must bring forward here. Therefore this section describes a number of situations where existing marketing theory is challenged.

The model introduced in Figure 1 will help us to illustrate how information is exchanged in the different cases we present. P stands for Producers and C for Consumers. Later we add A for Agents, or Artificial consumers to the model.

We start our description with a well-known situation that helps us isolate five marketing presuppositions.

When producers communicate with consumers

Marketing communication normally implies that the producer determines what information is to be shared with the consumer, as illustrated in Figure 2. Consider the

Figure 1 Model for information exchange (Source: Gatarski and Lundkvist).

Figure 2 Producers communicate to consumers (Source: Gatarski and Lundkvist).

case when publishers offer a new book to the market. As marketers know, names are important. So one step is to create a title for the book. This is carefully accomplished in a dialogue with the author(s). One example is when Donald A. Norman's *Psychology of Everyday Things* was re-titled to *The Design of Everyday Things*. The old title suggested to consumers that the book dealt with psychology. A misunderstanding since the author really wrote about design. The book must also be made known to and physically available on the market. Traditional advertising, PR activities, and other strategies are used to inform consumers about the book. Publishers utilize different means in order to push the books to the market. One of those is cover design. As one publisher says 'There are so many books in the stores, that the book has to shout to its buyer'. Be it a reseller or an end consumer. Impulse buying behaviours allow the book only a few seconds of consumer attention. Such fast processes favour well-known authors, since the consumer has limited resources to evaluate the author.

The activities illustrated above have to be managed in an efficient manner. So marketers have developed concepts such as brand and product name, reach/frequency/impact, package design, position, attitude and distribution (which has been separated from communication, although these activities are coordinated). Underlying all these concepts are presuppositions that:

1. producers produce and communicate, consumers receive and consume;
2. consumers are human;
3. production, communication and consumption are separate processes;
4. producers have to reach, and stay in the mind of consumers;
5. marketplaces are geographically separated entities.

When consumers converse with producers

Let us continue with a 'new' element in the marketing environment: *onLine media*. In order of appearance to the world a few of these are: CompuServe Interactive (CSi), Prodigy, America Online (AOL), and the World Wide Web (WWW). OnLine media offers *interactivity, conversation* and *extended information search*, three concepts that need explanation.

Interactivity
Gene Youngblood, referred to in Eerikäinen (1992) identifies three levels of interaction: 1 – interrupt, 2 – selection and 3 – responsiveness (conversation). Thus interactivity is more than a simple choice, like click or no-click. Sheizaf Rafaeili (1988, pp. 111) defines interactivity as:

an expression of the extent that in a given series of communication exchanges, any third (or later) transmission (or message) is related to the degree to which previous exchanges referred to even earlier transmissions.

Banners illustrate how interactivity could be implemented. People who browse onLine media are exposed to advertisements in the form of so-called banners. Products advertised in banners are sometimes only minutes away. Consumers may click the banner, enter their credit card number and have the product shipped the next minute. Banners were initially implemented in the same way as traditional newspaper ads, billboards, etc. That is, everyone was exposed to the same advertising message all the time. Lately we have seen many different banner styles. For example banners that are:

- *dynamic*, replaced at every new visit;
- *animated*, contain animated elements and/or loops through a number of messages;
- *interactive*, automatically customized for each individual user.

Consider the case when a consumer is exposed to a banner advertising a book. If that banner is interactive, it will not only allow the consumer to purchase the book, but will also remember that it created interest or even made a sale. So, the next time it should try to advertise something else. A new offering that might go well with the book. Banners like this are becoming frequent in onLine media.

Now we start to see what happens when communication, in the meaning of sharing information, meets interactivity. A rendezvous that results in something beyond communication. This extended process includes the creation of new messages. This is what Gene Youngblood calls *conversation*. Our next step is to investigate what happens when conversation meets production.

Conversation

Our first example describes how a producer of physical goods invites consumers to a conversation, as illustrated in Figure 3. MySki Inc. uses the Internet to enable consumers to interactively design their own products. Customers visiting www.myski.com enter information about their height, skill level, and skiing style, and are immediately recommended a ski model and length. Using more customization tools, they can then choose the colours, logos and personalized text that they want to appear on the top surface of their skis and then view them in three-dimensional VRML. Once ordered, the Evolution Ski Company, Inc., handcrafts the skis. Since MySki converse in a global medium, they provide in-country customer support in the native language of 25 countries. The conversation does also build an ever-growing consumer database. What this may result in is still unknown to us, as MySki started in December 1996.

Figure 3 Consumers converse with producers (Source: Gatarski and Lundkvist).

In our next example Chris Macrae, a brand manager consultant and author of several books, is in control of a conversation process. Macrae is running the worldwide e-mail summit 'Chartering marketing's future in (brand) learning organizations'. The summit engages more than 100 practitioners, consultants and researchers all over the world. All members are encouraged to e-mail postings to Macrae, who categorizes the inputs and distributes them to the other members. When asked about how he finds members, Macrae replies 'I occasionally do an Alta Vista search on my own name to see if anyone apart from myself (I mean the web I edit www.brad.ac.uk/branding/) is referring to me'. One of his strategies with the summit is to communicate (share) his ideas and books. But a far more interesting point is his conscious attempt to converse with the market as one part in the production of his next book. That conversation might very well include the titling process.

Now we see that Macrae's consumers are co-producers. And that MySki use onLine media to enable their customers to design their own products. This is far away from the old producer-communicates-with-the-consumer scene.

So far we have discussed the information exchange between consumers and producers. But there are also important relations between different consumers. The next three cases describe consumers-to-consumers conversations and how these can be related to producers.

When consumers converse with consumers

We start with a case when consumers converse under the producers' management (see Figure 4). In the automobile industry the marketing of Saturn from General Motors has brought worldwide attention. Saturn brand managers enable the customers to play an important part in the market communication. They encourage their customers to really keep in touch with other customers by supporting local Car-clubs. Many customer clubs keep information about its members as a company secret, but this is not the case with Saturn Car-clubs. Anyone may join and access information about other members. To increase accessibility, Saturn has recently taken advantage of onLine media, and has envisioned a searchable Extended Family Database on the Internet.

Other areas where customers strengthen their relation with another are found in the computer and software industries. Computer user groups have been flourishing for over thirty years. Benefits from these groups are found in both product development and customer support. Thus customer-generated knowledge has relieved the producer of many functions. In other words, consumers have been supporting themselves, with guidance from the producer. User groups did not depend on electronic media, but electronic Bulletin Board Systems (BBS) quickly emerged as an efficient solution. Consumers sharing the same interest are able to create their own electronic forum, making it accessible from all over the world at any time. Existing onLine media host a

Figure 4 Producers manage consumer conversation (Source: Gatarski and Lundkvist).

vast number of forums. Many are constituted from a shared interest, as in computers, cars and games or in personal health such as cancer and diabetes. All these forums pose new challenges to the practice of market communication.

The next case, illustrated in Figure 5, shows how consumers manage the conversation and actually tell the producer what to do. Among the 1000+ forums at CompuServe, there is one where computer modems from Megahertz are discussed. In November 1995 a person offered his Megahertz modem for sale in that forum. The next day a representative from the Megahertz Forum asked why he wanted to sell. The answer was elaborate, but could be summarized as that some malfunctions made the customer dissatisfied. During the next week thirteen other persons from different countries joined the discussion, sharing similar problems. Yet other ones wrote that they had intended to buy a Megahertz modem, but what they read had convinced them not to buy. The discussion heated up, but no representative from the producer participated. On the eighth day one of the participants posed a direct question to the representative. He asked what could be done about the problem and added 'if you ignore it, it will go away – will not work here'. Two days later the representative replied that he had been observing the discussion, but he had nothing to contribute. This turned the conversation into comments about placing trust in the producer. Participants also made recommendations to Megahertz on what to expect from them when it comes to market conversation and behaviour in electronic media.

Saturn is a case where the producer guided consumer's conversation. Megahertz is a case where consumers tell the producer how conversation should be done.

Our next step is to introduce consumer communities with little or no producer insight, see Figure 6. The Diabetes Forum at CompuServe was started in 1989 by a diabetic who wanted to discuss his disease with other people sharing his disease. Note, not with doctors or any other medical staff. During the first year 2000 members joined the forum. Today it is one of the largest forums in the world with more than 55000 members. Among them are consumers of different pharmaceutical products as well as consumers of public or private health care services. The basic idea of the Diabetes Forum is to share information and solutions provided by consumers. The method is simple, forum members are encouraged to share experiences. Members

Figure 5 Consumers manage producers through conversation (Source: Gatarski and Lundkvist).

Figure 6 Consumers converse without producers (Source: Gatarski and Lundkvist).

participate in several hundreds of discussions, ask questions and share solutions, in such different areas as mixing drugs, advanced research and training. Discussions are saved in different libraries. Members are also able to search extensive archives of medical articles on diabetes. External researchers and speakers are occasionally invited to electronic conferences, which add interest and depth to the forum. The Diabetes Forum differs from the Saturn Car-club and the Megahertz Forum in an important way. Though all these activities should be of interest to pharmaceutical companies, only on rare occasions are producers invited to share the discussions.

The case of Megahertz showed the example of consumers conversing with consumers as a setting of the producer, built to enhance relations with consumers. From the consumers' view the conversation constitutes a shared community where the producer undoubtedly plays an important role. In the case of the Diabetes Forum the roles have changed, consumers converse with consumers to find alternatives to a relation with the producer.

When artificial actors, or agents, supplement current marketing actors

The situations we have illustrated show that a lot of data is generated and stored in the onLine systems. The sheer size of that data volume might actually create new problems. Herbert Simon (1971) and Daniel Bell (1976) were among the pioneers to explore this situation. Richard Saul Wurman (1989) uses the concept of Information Architecture as one way to help us turn data into knowledge. Information architects take complex information and convey it to a target audience as simply as possible. While their designs use physical objects; ranging from product packaging to printed books, electronic means such as Internet sites or virtual worlds will play an increasingly larger role. Furthermore Database Mining, an advanced form of computer-aided marketing research, is increasingly used to manage vast data volumes (Berild, 1996).

Extended information search
The search for and processing of information, are important ingredients in consumer behaviour models (Engel *et al.*, 1986; Howard, 1994; Evans *et al.*, 1996). We have made an attempt to supplement those models with sources based on onLine media. The classification scheme below is based on our research, in this case from the WWW. The concepts presented in Table 1 are in chronological order, i.e., when they arrived on the scene.

Information agents

Agent technology which is based on artificial intelligence science, offers a more automated information management. Nicholas Negroponte (1995), founder of the MIT Media Lab, envisions a future where agents can read every newspaper and catch every broadcast on the planet, and from it construct a personalized summary. The following quote from the conference proceedings of *Autonomous Agents 1997* offers an introduction to our new assistants:

> Agents are computational systems that inhabit dynamic, unpredictable environments. They interpret sensor data that reflect events in the environment

Table 1 Extended information search in onLine media (Source: Gatarski and Lundkvist)

1. Human conversation
   Conversation over electronic media, e.g., e-mail, newsgroups, etc.

2. Information brokers
   Professional outsourcing, sometimes referred to as information brokers. In this case humans manage the search on your behalf. In Scandinavia Observer Pressurklipp (www.observer.se) offers such services.

3. Hotlist
   Hotlists are indexes put up by humans with different interests and purposes. Like the one offered by the library at the University d'Aix-Marseilles (www.univ.aix.fr/bibli/bibadres.htm).

4. Indexes and directories
   This class of sources includes tools for search and index management. Users are often invited to register and maintain their own information in the database. Examples of such indexes are Sunet (www.sunet.se/sweden/main.tml) and Yahoo! (www.yahoo.com).

5. Search engines
   Autonomous sources like these are based on computer software programs that continuously scan the Internet. Every search engine has its own set of rules on how to index. An extensive selection of search engines can be found at Netscape (www.netscape.com) or C-net (http://www.cnet.com/Content/Reviews/Compare/Search/).

6. Meta search engines
   Users are able to pose a question simultaneously to a number of search engines. Users gain in range, but lose in depth. One example in Metacrawler (www.metacrawler.com).

7. Custom-made search engines/agents
   This class is used both for scanning the whole Internet and for scanning and indexing the user's local site only. Excite (www.excite.com) is one supplier of tools and applications.

8. Push technology
   Push providers monitor a number of content sources and match that with specifications from the subscribing users. Examples are Pointcast (www.pointcast.com) and Newshound (http://www.newshound.com/). The Angle, from BroadVision Inc., even allows the user to design their own interface.

and execute motor commands that produce effects in the environment. An agent is 'autonomous' to the degree that it decides for itself how to relate sensor data to motor commands in its efforts to achieve goals, satisfy motivations, etc.

Scientists have already considered how agents might help human consumers to find goods and services in the marketplace. The professor, in both Cognitive Science and Psychology, Donald Norman (1994) exemplified: 'Thus, agents might set up schedules, reserve hotels and meeting rooms, arrange transportation and even outline meeting topics, all without human intervention'. And Mitchel *et al.* (1994) envisaged agents performing tasks such as 'providing services for work and home, such as paying bills, making travel arrangements, submitting purchase orders and locating information in electronic libraries'. An example of the latter is Video-On-Demand systems. Ramanathan and Rangan (1994), engaged in their design, wrote 'Personal service agents, as their name implies, play a central role in tailoring the fabric of multimedia services to fit the needs and preferences of clients'. In this case the media is dependent on agent technology!

Artificial consumers
Agent researchers, such as Maes and Sycara (1977), state that agents have been built for a wide range of applications, including agents for buying/shopping, agents as

reminders, agents as eager assistants, agents as filters/critics, agents as matchmakers, and agents as guides. We would like to regard these consumer representations as *artificial consumers*. Figure 7 illustrates the information flow between consumers and the agents representing them. As we noted above, consumption is an emotion-filled experience that goes beyond buying. Barbara Hayes-Roth (1977) describes synthetic agents that 'operate in simulated environments' such as virtual worlds, MUDS, or video games. They emphasize qualities such as believability and personality, rather than deep intelligence or expertise, and may play roles in interactive systems for entertainment, art, and education'. We have not found any research where synthetic agents are used as market actors. Instead we bring forward two shopping agents (whose main difference is their intellectual capacity) that exemplify how artificial consumers might behave.

BargainFinder

Here consumers use artificial representations as their conversing shopping partners, see Figure 8. BargainFinder does comparison shopping for rock or pop CDs on the Internet. The agent is not very smart. It knows nothing about its user and it knows only the ten stores defined by its programmer. It was presented in June 1995 by Andersen Consulting as part of the SMART STORE(R) Virtual initiative investigating electronic commerce. Any user can enter an artist and album name, click the shop button and BargainFinder will immediately browse ten Internet sites that sell music CDs. Within seconds the user is presented with information about the shopping results. This includes whether the album was found or not, price and shipping information and links to the actual sites.

Andersen Consulting's goal in presenting BargainFinder was not only to raise questions, but to present ideas about ways technology can make the Internet a better environment for commerce. We have no access to the results from the survey that users are invited to participate in. Instead we have seen that some stores block access from agents and the only information communicated is availability, price, shipping and costs.

Figure 7 The Introduction of artificial consumers (Source: Gatarski and Lundkvist).

Figure 8 Consumers converse with agents (Source: Gatarski and Lundkvist).

ShopBot

In more advanced cases many consumers converse with a shared artificial consumer as illustrated in Figure 9. ShopBot was developed at the Department of Computer Science and Engineering, University of Washington. The agent originally shopping for computer software titles in a similar way that BargainFinder looked for music CDs. ShopBot is no longer available on the Internet, because ShopBot's creator has left the university for commercial tasks. During its short life it was able to demonstrate a capability to find new vendors and automatically learn how to shop at those vendors (Doorenbos *et al.*, 1997). In other words, ShopBot was intelligent enough to extend its knowledge about shopping sites.

It learned how to shop by assuming three regularities on shopping sites. These were navigation schemes (e.g., a searchable index), uniformity (e.g., stocked items are described in a consistent format) and vertical separation (e.g., product descriptions start on a new fresh line). By doing dummy queries with known products, ShopBot was able to compare the data received with expected data. This comparison thus told ShopBot how the site structured its shopping forms.

Some of the limitations of ShopBot were that it could not distinguish between upgrades to a product and a product itself. It also assumed that product descriptions reside on a single line. The research team also pointed out some architecture problems. ShopBot was dependent on searchable indexes, while many smaller sites do not have such indexes. Its linear performance would have given it a difficult task when more merchants populate the web. And ShopBot relied heavily on HTML (one Internet coding format), while Java (another format) is increasingly used when shopping sites are built.

When agents converse with agents

As we see, agents learn. Accordingly Genesereth and Ketchpel (1994) remark that the knowledge one agent gathers could be of value to other agents, organizations or humans. The Knowledge Query and Manipulation Language (KQML) is one of the languages used for agent-to-agent communication. KQML is implemented in numerous agent systems, such as the Media on Demand service presented by Nygren *et al.* (1996). Another way to enable agent communication, or rather conversation, is through a proprietary system. This is the method the design team behind the Firefly tools decided to use.

Firefly Inc. launched Firefly Online, a conversation space devoted to music and film, in January 1996. This product is now split into Bignote and Filmfinder. Recently Firefly have developed their technology into a tool-kit, offered to anyone who organizes production in onLine environments. Firefly's Automated Collaborative

Figure 9 Consumers and Producers converse with a shared Artificial Consumer (Source: Gatarski and Lundkvist).

Filtering and an enhancement, Feature-Guided Automated Collaborative Filtering[TM] (FGACF) [TM], help end-users navigate electronic information in a highly personalized way. According to them the technology in effect automates the word-of-mouth process by which people often navigate information, using people who share their experiences to guide them, Figure 10 illustrates such a multi-agent system.

Users enter their profiles, i.e., name, age, sex, interests and other voluntary information in Firefly Passports. These passports could be regarded as an interface to the consumers' artificial representation. Then the site sorts the users to recommend new selections based on the likes and dislikes of one's nearest psychographic neighbours. Any site can exchange Passport profiles with other sites through the Firefly Central. According to Firefly Inc., over one million passports are already issued by Firefly-enabled sites on the Web.

We have found that many users, including ourselves, issue multiple passports. This is what Ingela did. She used Firefly Online to help her select a CD for a friend's birthday. Ingela constructed a passport that represented her friend. Then she let the system recommend something other users with similar interests as her friend seemed to like. Who knows, maybe these other users were constructed representations as well?

The bookseller Barnes & Noble, Inc. has announced that they will use the Firefly tools. Steve Riggio, chief operating officer at Barnes & Noble, Inc. said in a press release (March 10, 1997):

> Firefly's leading technology complements Barnes & Noble's commitment to customer service, selection, technology and accessibility. This innovative functionality will offer our online customers a different but equally rich experience as can be found in any of our retail stores.

Other proprietary systems use agent technology to construct marketspaces with artificial consumers that, in addition to conversing, actually negotiate, buy and sell valuables. Guttman *et al.* (1997) report on such an experimental system involving about 200 (real) persons trading goods, services and currency. Among the results was that available technology in agent intelligence is sufficient. What is lacking is human trust in their agent.

DISCUSSION

Separation of production, communication and consumption may well function in a world producing tangibles. But we show many examples where production and consumption becomes an integrated process. MySki, Macrae's e-mail summit and the

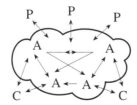

Figure 10 Consumers, artificial and human, converse with producers in a multi-agent system.

Diabetes Forum exemplify this. Thus we must ask if the existing dichotomy of producers and consumers is relevant in onLine marketspaces.

At the communication arena we find similar patterns. A single actor no longer directs communication. There is an increased complexity which goes beyond sending and receiving when onLine media is introduced. Marketing actors in onLine systems create, store and reuse information in a way that challenges existing theories about marketing communication. We have brought forward the concept of conversation that might offer marketing researchers new insight. Media that supports conversation depends on a built-in memory. Hotlists, search engines and interactive banners have such memories. But what do marketers know about them?

We described agents, marketing actors that are non-human. We have chosen to call them artificial consumers, with as yet unknown capacities. We know that ShopBot was dependent on certain characteristics in shopping sites. But we do not know how many sites ShopBot could learn and remember. Marketers have emphasized experience and emotions as important factors in consumers' decision making. What importance do they have in onLine marketspaces? How does Firefly's Automated Collaborative Filtering technology handle consumer emotions?

It is also important to note that one human may be represented by one or more artificial consumers. At the same time, many humans may choose to let one single artificial consumer do their shopping. Marketers have to consider not only human consumers but also artificial consumers acting in new electronic marketspaces. Maybe it is time for marketers to study agent behaviour.

Even supposedly up-to-date marketing textbooks about marketing communication and consumer behaviour do not discuss electronic agents or investigate how interactivity is changing our view on marketing (Howard, 1994; McQuail, 1994; Mowen, 1993; and Windahl et al., 1992). McQuail (1994) developed his older findings (1984) without taking into consideration what interactive media already had accomplished at that time. Evans et al. (1996) do not even mention electronic agents.

Scientific journals offer no more insight than the textbooks. In the last two years' issues of *Journal of Business Research* we found only one article (Good and Stone, 1995) that covers the problems we discuss. Out of 66 listed ongoing marketing research projects all over the world, only two projects focus on the use of agents (Hoffman, 1997).

In addition our interpretation is that contemporary marketing conferences have few contributions that reflect agents and electronic conversation. But some papers offer hope, such as Bruce et al. (1996) who discuss such implications. They combine concepts of custom-oriented management with part-time marketers and IT, and write:

> Hence, the nature and substance of marketing is undergoing change and clearly IT has an active part to play in the reshaping of marketing, both currently and in the longer term.

CONCLUSIONS

All the problems we have highlighted need solutions. Thus new marketing tasks must be managed. At this moment we do not know the models that will help managers and researchers. Contemporary marketing theory evidently fails to deal with the problems we describe.

Our conclusion is that while some existing theory guide us, other theory will hinder us. Finally we propose a search for new theories, rather than ways to fit new problems into old solutions.

REFERENCES

Bell, D. (1976) *The Coming of Post-Industrial Society.* Basic Books

Berild, S. (1996) Report and notes from Data Warehouse World 96, SISU Publications, Stockholm.

Bruce, M., Leverick, F. F., Littler, D., and Wilson, D. (1996) The changing scope and substance of marketing: The impact of I. T. *Proceedings of the 25th EMAC Conference*, Budapest University.

Doorenbos, R. B., Etzioni, O., and Weld, D. S. (1997) A scalable comparison-shopping agent for the world-wide web, in *Proceedings of the First International Conference on Autonomous Agents.* New York: ACM Press.

Eerikäinen, H. (1992) The transformation of media technology and postmodern culture: A new aesthetic environment, in T. Varis (ed.) *The New Media.* Helsinki: The University of Industrial Arts.

Engel, J. F., Blackwell, R. D., and Miniard, P. W. (1986) *Consumer Behavior,* 5th edn. New York: CBS College Publishing.

Evans, M. J., Moutinho, L., and Van Raaij, W. F. (1996) *Applied Consumer Behaviour.* London: Addison-Wesley.

Genesereth, M. R., and Ketchpel, S. P. (1994) Software agents, *Communications of the ACM,* July, 48–53, 147.

Gilmore, H., and Pine, B. J. (1997) The four faces of mass customization, *Harvard Business Review,* January, 91–101.

Good, D. J., and Stone, R. W., (1995) Computer technology and the marketing organization. An empirical investigation, *Journal of Business Research,* November, 197–209.

Gummesson, E. (1994) Making relationship marketing operational, *The International Journey of Service Industry Management* 5 (5) 5–20.

Guttman, R., Maes, P., Chavez, A., and Dreilinger, D. (1997) Results from a multi-agent electronic marketplace experiment. Submitted to *Modeling Autonomous Agents in a Multi-Agent World (MAAMAW'97),* Ronneby, Sweden.

Hayes-Roth, B. (1997) Introduction, in *Proceedings of the First International Conference on Autonomous Agents.* New York: ACM Press.

Hoffman, D. (1997) Commerce in cyberspace: research opportunities for marketing scholars. Newsletter downloaded from http://www2000.ogsm.vanderbilt.edu/wake/commerce.html.

Holbrook, M. B., and Hirschman, E. C. (1982) The experiental aspects of consumption: Consumer, fantasies, feelings and fun, *Journal of Consumer Research,* September, 132–40.

Howard, J. A. (1994) *Buyer Behavior in Marketing Strategy,* 2nd edn. Englewood Cliffs, NJ: Prentice Hall, p. 61.

Kotler, P. (1984) *Marketing Management: Analysis, Planning Control* (3rd edn.). Englewood Cliffs, NJ: Prentice Hall.

Kotler, P. (1984) *Marketing Management: Analysis, Planning, Implementation and Control,* 8th edn. Englewood Cliffs, NJ: Prentice Hall.

Laurel, B. (1993) *Computers as Theatre.* London: Addison-Wesley.

Maes, P., and Sycara, K. (1997) Software agents, Tutorial presented at *the First International Conference on Autonomous Agents,* Marina Del Rey, Ca., February.

Maes, P. (1997) Agents that reduce work and information overload, *Communications of the ACM,* July.

McQuail, D. (1984) *Communication,* 3rd edn. London: Longman.

McQuail, D. (1994) *Mass Communication Theory: An Introduction,* 2nd edn. Sage.

Mitchel, Tom *et al.* (1994) Experience with a learning personal assistant, *Communications of the ACM,* July, 81–91.

Mowen, J. C. (1993) *Consumer Behavior,* 3rd edn. New York: McMillan.

Negroponte, N. (1994) Less is more: interface agents as digital butlers, *Wired,* June.

Negroponte, N. (1995), *Being Digital.* New York: Alfred A. Knopf.

Norman, D. A. (1994) How might people interact with agents, *Communication of the ACM,* July.

Normann, R. and Ramirez, R. (1994) *Designing Interactive Strategy: From Value Chain to Value Constellation,* John Wiley & Sons.

Nygren, K., Jonsson, I.-M., and Carlvik, O. (1996) An agent system for media on demand services. Paper presented at *PAAM'96,* London.

Peppers, D., and Rogers, M. (1993) *The One to One Future: Building Relationships One Customer at a Time.* New York: Doubleday.

Peppers, D., and Rogers, M. (1997) *Enterprise One to One.* Doubleday Currency.

Pine, B. J. II (1993) *Mass Customization.* Harvard Business Press.

Porter, M., and Millar, V. (1985) How information gives you competitive advantage, *Harvard Business Review,* July–August, 2–13.

Rafaeili, S. (1988) Interactivity: from new media to communication, In R. P. Hawkins *et al.* (Eds.) *Advancing Communication Science: Merging Mass and Interpersonal Processes.* Sage.

Ramanathan, S., and Rangan, P. V. (1994) Architectures for personalized multimedia, *Proceedings of IEEE Multimedia*, Spring 1994, IEEE Computer Society, Los Alamitos, CA.

Rayport, J. F., and Svikola, J. J. (1995) Exploiting the virtual value chain, *Harvard Business Review*, November-December, 75–85.

Shardanand, U. And Maes, P. (1995) Social information filtering: algorithms for automating 'word of mouth', *CHI '95 Proceedings: Conference on Human Factors in Computing Systems: Mosaic of Creativity*.

Simon, H. A. (1971) Designing organizations for an information-rich world. In M. Greenberger (ed.) *Computers, Communications, and the Public Interest*. Baltimore: John Hopkins Press, 37–52.

Turkle, S. (1995) *Life in the Screen: Identity in the Internet*. New York: Simon and Schuster.

Windahl, S., Signitzer, B. H., and Olson, J. T. (1992) *Using Communication Theory: An Introduction to Planned Communication*, Sage.

Wurman, R. S. (1989) *Information Anxiety*. New York: Doubleday.

Gatarski, R. and Lundkvist, A. (1998) 'Interactive media face artificial consumers and marketing theory must re-think'. *Journal of Marketing Communications*, 4(1), March: 45–59. Reproduced with permission.

Section 6

Public Relations, Publicity and Crisis Management

This section brings together different aspects of the public relations function, from its origins to strategic and functional development, and introduces the reader to the developing area of crisis management. The aim of the collection is to provide a range of quality discussion and empirical research in key areas of this important aspect of the marketing communications mix.

Appropriately, the section opens with the classic work from Kotler and Mindak (1978) which explores the evolution of corporate public relations and marketing public relations as two discrete functions, identifying overlapping activities and suggesting a methodology for integrating the two. This discussion is continued by Kitchen (1993) who reports empirical research which identifies the growing importance of public relations in diverse firms in FMCG markets, and particularly the growing integration between corporate and marketing public relations.

The dynamic nature of the international business environment is revealed by Dibb, Simkin and Vancini (1996), who identify three key strategies used by PR consultancies to cope with an increasingly aggressive marketplace, together with an increasing willingness to harness new media and technology to the PR function. The degree of attention paid to stakeholder groups is investigated by Greenley and Foxall (1996), who identify the importance firms give to consumers as stakeholders. They also reveal associations between stakeholder groups, including the influence of consumer orientation as a predictor of competitor and employee orientation.

Much of the public relations and publicity literature is found to be occupied with strategies and techniques for normal PR and marketing events and situations. Little of the literature, however, is devoted to strategies and techniques for assisting firms when a public relations crisis occurs and the excellent paper from Jorgenson (1994) is included to address this shortfall. It investigates how a company's response to a crisis can impact audience reactions positively or negatively.

The final paper in this section, from Meenaghan (1991), examines the role of sponsorship as a public relations activity, identifying the increasingly legitimate role it plays in the marketing communications mix.

Marketing and public relations – Should they be partners or rivals?

6.1

Philip Kotler and William Mindak

One can sense growing confusion as to the future roles of marketing and public relations in the modern organization:

- **Marketing people** are increasingly interested in incorporating publicity as a tool within the marketing mix, although this tool has normally been controlled by public relations.
- **Public relations** people are growing increasingly concerned with their company's marketing practices, questioning whether they 'square' with the company's social responsibility. They seek more influence over marketing and more of a counseling and policy-making role.
- At the same time, a new corporate function called **public affairs** has split off from public relations, causing some confusion as to the scope of public relations.

In nonprofit organizations particularly (e.g. hospitals, colleges, and museums), where public relations is a well-established function, marketing is emerging as a 'hot' topic. Public relations people are beginning to worry that they won't be able to control this new function or, what is worse, will end up working for marketing.

Where does marking end and public relations begin? Where does public relations end and public affairs begin? The increasingly fuzzy boundaries have led to conflict among these departments. Usually they choose either to operate independently with little teamwork or to bicker over resources and strategies.

Yet marketing and public relations *are the major external functions of the firm*. Both functions start their analysis and planning from the point of view of satisfying outside groups. Both are relative newcomers on the corporate scene. Both normally operate separately, at some loss in overall effectiveness.

RELATIVE LEVELS OF USE

Enterprises fall into four classes with respect to their use of marketing and public relations (Exhibit 1):

Class One enterprises barely use either function in a formal sense. An example would be small nonprofit organizations such as social service agencies. Their administrators do not recognize having marketing problems or tasks as such. Nor do they feel they have the budgets to support a formal public relations staff.

Class Two enterprises have a well-established public relations function but no marketing function. Almost every hospital and college has a public relations officer

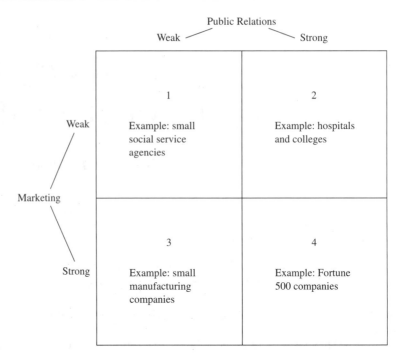

Exhibit 1 Four levels of use of marketing and public relations in enterprises.

who takes responsibility for designing publications, attracting favorable press coverage, and counseling the president on the institution's image. On the other hand, hardly any hospitals and colleges have created a marketing position, although interest in the marketing function is growing rapidly.

Class Three enterprises operate a strong marketing or sales organization but a weak or nonexistent public relations function. For example, small manufacturing concerns are heavily involved in finding and serving customers, but they do little to cultivate other publics. They may not have any stockholders to please; they may have no community groups to appease. Public relations is run minimally in these enterprises.

Class Four enterprises operate strong marketing and public relations departments. Typical are the large Fortune-500 corporations, whose marketing activities have impact on a large number of publics in a way that warrants sizeable public relations activities. In these organizations the marketing and public relations departments normally operate independently under separate officers, both of whom report to top management. In a few cases, public relations is under marketing, but this is an exception to the rule. Marketing may have responsibility, however, for the part of public relations dealing with product publicity.

New emphases

Some enterprises are currently moving to strengthen either marketing or public relations relative to the other. In the following two cases, marketing is being given increased influence relative to public relations:

Financial institutions discovered public relations before they discovered marketing. Their thinking ran primarily along lines of publics, community relations, consumer education, and 'imagery.' Now banks and savings and loan associations are rapidly moving toward marketing thinking. They refer more to 'markets,' 'profit centers,' and 'positioning.' Their associations sponsor annual marketing conferences with rapidly growing attendance. The top marketing person is likely to have more power than the top public relations officer.

Hospitals have long depended on public relations for communicating with their publics. But they gave little thought to marketing until recent years, when they began to experience low bed occupancy, loss of patients to newer hospitals, changing levels of demand for different services, and low utilization of hospital facilities during weekends. These problems have sparked a strong interest in marketing. The Evanston Hospital, Evanston, Illinois, appointed a full-time marketing vice president, probably the world's first. Other hospitals are seeking to bring in marketing through establishing a marketing job position. Some hospitals have thought of adding marketing to the job responsibilities of the public relations director but are facing doubts about whether their public relations director has the skills and attitudes for effective marketing planning.

Other institutions, in contrast, are strengthening their public relations relative to marketing:

'A major food company has set up a product review board. This group reviews the nutritional contribution of planned new products before they are brought to market and must be convinced of their nutritional validity before project approval is given. This procedure grew out of policy conceived by the public relations director. He is also head of the review board which has absolute authority in this area.'[1]

'Exxon has announced the formation of a Public Affairs Department whose function is to identify issues and develop plans with full consideration for the audiences to be reached and the communication vehicles or means for reaching these audiences. The advertising emphasis has moved from marketing to corporate issues.'[2]

These developments pose a number of interesting questions for the management of any company:

- Are the company's marketing managers sufficiently sensitized to public issues when they develop their plans?
- Are the company's public relations people sufficiently trained to apply market-oriented reasoning to their own activities?
- Is the company allocating the proper budgets to marketing and public relations?
- Are the organizational arrangements optimal for taking advantage of the interdependence of marketing and public relations?

To deal with these issues, we will have to first analyze how these functions evolved.

THE EVOLUTION OF MARKETING

A widespread misconception prevails that marketing is a very old subject. The truth is that marketing is a relatively new subject. Modern marketing, as we know it today, evolved over many years through the five stages shown in Exhibit 2(A).

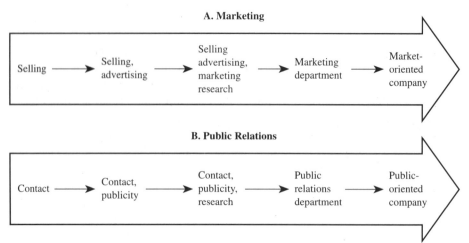

Exhibit 2 Evolution of the fields of marketing and public relations.

Early functions

Marketing's origins trace back to the ancient function known as *selling*, with which it is often confused. As soon as early man produced surpluses of certain goods, he began to look for trading opportunities, first on a barter basis, and later on a monetized basis. The fine art of finding buyers, displaying goods attractively, and negotiating effectively developed early in the history of civilization and continues to undergo refinements to this day.

In the late nineteenth century, with the development of national markets and mass communication, manufacturers began to recognize the value of regular *advertising* as a supplement to their sales force activities. Advertising expenditures could produce customer leads, generate customer awareness and interest, and reinforce loyalty. Companies hired their own advertising specialists and/or advertising agencies to perform this function.

The rapid growth of national markets in the twentieth century increased the need for *marketing information* on which company marketing management could base their planning. Sellers recognized that they could reduce their risk by spending money to find out what customers really wanted, how customers perceived the company and its products, and so on. The first marketing department was formally established by the Curtis Publishing Company in 1911, and the example was soon followed by U.S. Rubber (1916) and Swift & Co. (1917).

Coordination and orientation

These three functions – sales, advertising, and marketing research – operated fairly independently of each other, although nominally they were supposed to be coordinated by the vice president of sales. But his heart lay in the sales force, and he tended to neglect the other two functions. This led to the fourth stage, when these functions – and others such as customer service, pricing, marketing planning – were finally combined into a *marketing department*. The purpose of a marketing department was to develop a balanced marketing program which coordinated all the marketing mix instruments and forces impinging on the customer. To head this department, a vice president of marketing was appointed.

The establishment of a marketing vice presidency did not automatically insure that the company as a whole was *market oriented*. This stage only came about when the various departments of the company (purchasing, R & D, engineering, finance, manufacturing) all adopted and practiced a customer philosophy (i.e., they recognize that in the words of Peter Drucker, 'the purpose of the company is to create a customer.'[3]).

To some observers, even a market orientation is not enough. They call upon the firm to become public-oriented, to exhibit a greater concern over its impact on the environment, consumer's health and safety, and consumer pocketbooks. In short, they would place marketing under increased public relations control.

To complicate the matter further, the concept of marketing recently has been 'broadened' to cover the problem of marketing any entity to any public, whether a product, service, place, person or idea.[4] Generic marketers argue that communicating with the public is not enough. Often the objective is to influence a public, and this is best done by considering the problem in terms of *exchange theory* and not simply *communication theory*.

Marketers may be in a better position to plan for achieving desired responses from target publics than public relations people. Extension of this argument to the limit suggests that marketers should take over the public relations function.

EVOLUTION OF PUBLIC RELATIONS

Public relations is also a relatively new corporate function although it, too, has its roots in ancient human activities.

Edward L. Bernays, one of the fathers of modern public relations, posited that the three main elements of public relations are as old as society: a) informing people, b) persuading people, and c) integrating people with people.[5] And he traced public relations from primitive society (in which leaders controlled by force, intimidation, and persuasion) to Babylonia (where kings commissioned historians to paint favorable images of them).

Historical milestones

The Renaissance and Reformation freed men's minds from established dogmas, leading institutions to develop more subtle means to influence people. In America, historical milestones for 'public relations' include:

- Samuel Adams' use of the press to unite the colonists against the British.
- The abolitionist movement's use of public relations as a political tool to rally support for blacks in the North, including the publication of *Uncle Tom's Cabin*.
- P. T. Barnum's use of public relations to generate newsworthiness about an event – the arrival of his circus – by placing articles in newspapers.

Corporate public relations evolved more recently and passed through the five stages shown in Exhibit 2(D). In the first stage, corporations established a *contact* function to influence legislators and newspapers to support positions favorable to business.

The legislative contact function became known as *lobbying*, and the newspaper contact function became know as *press relations*. George Westinghouse is credited with the formal establishment of public relations when he hired two men in 1889 to fight the advocates of direct current electricity and to promote instead alternating current.[6]

The next stage occurred when companies began to recognize the positive value of planned *publicity* to create customer interest in the company and its products. Publicity entailed finding or creating events, preparing company or product-slanted news stories, and trying to interest the press in using them. Companies recognized that special skills are needed to develop publicity and began to add publicists to their ranks.

Somewhat later, public relations practitioners began to recognize the value of conducting *research* into public opinion prior to developing and launching public relations campaigns. The emerging sciences of public opinion measurement and mass communication theory permitted more sophistication in the conduct of public relations. Forward looking firms added specialists who could research public opinion.

P. R. Department

These functions – contact, publicity, and research – were typically ill-coordinated. For example, those doing government work had little to do with those arranging publicity; those developing publicity made little use of research. This finally led to the concept of a *public relations department* integrating all the work going on to cultivate the goodwill of different publics of the company. Over time, the public relations department developed further subspecialties dealing with each public (stockholders, neighbors, employees, customers, government agencies) and each tool (conferences, publicity, graphics, etc.)

The presence of a modern public relations department did not insure that the company as a whole acted like a *public company*. The vice president of public relations had limited influence over other departments and needed the backing of top management to press for public-oriented actions by all the departments. Companies were facing formidable new challenges in the form of consumerism, environmentalism, energy conservation, inflation, shortages, employment discrimination, and safety. The public relations people wanted a more active role in counseling the company and its departments on how to act as public citizens.

ALTERNATIVE MODELS OF RELATIONSHIP

Marketing and public relations are both reaching maturity and seeking more policy making roles within the corporation. They deal with the external environment as their starting point for planning. One hopes to make the company more market-oriented while the other hopes to make the company more public-oriented – objectives which are not necessarily compatible. What relation should the two functions have to each other?

We can conceive of five different models for viewing the relationship between marketing and public relations (Exhibit 3):

Separate but equal functions (A)

The traditional view of the two functions is that they are quite different in their perspectives and capacities. Marketing exists to sense, serve, and satisfy customer

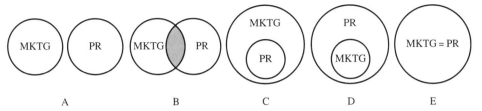

Exhibit 3 Models of the possible relationship between marketing and public relations.

needs at a profit. Public relations exists to produce goodwill in the company's various publics so that these publics do not interfere in the firm's profit-making ability.

The educational backgrounds of marketing and public relations practitioners differ considerably, producing almost two separate 'cultures':

- **Marketers**, for the most part, are trained in business schools where they gain skills in economic, quantitative, and behavioral analysis. Trained to be profit-oriented in their planning activities, they normally get little exposure to the subject of communications and mass media.
- **Public relations practitioners**, on the other hand, come out of journalism schools where they are expected first to learn media skills, be good spellers and grammarians, and learn how to write summary leads. Many journalists who do not find opportunities in journalism enter public relations as a second choice. They normally come with little training in political, economic or social analysis and some of them grew up with anti-business attitudes.

No wonder the two groups carry around denigrating stereotypes of each other. Marketing people often view public relations people as press agents, flacks, sponsors of pseudo-events (e.g. Miss 'Pickle-Queen of 1977'). Public relations people view marketers as hucksters, 'numbercrunchers,' deodorant salesmen. Often each views the other's function in its narrowest perspective. Marketing really *is* sales; public relations really *is* publicity.

A public relations scholar recently articulated the traditional view when he said:

> 'The extension of the marketing concept to nonprofit agencies appears to me to be describing public relations under a new garb. I hold strongly that marketing men should confine themselves to the marketing field and use advertising and product publicity as part of the marketing mix. I don't think that most marketing oriented persons have the experience, aptitude or approach for sound public relations.'[7]

Equal but overlapping functions (B)

Another school of thought says that while marketing and public relations are important and separate functions, they share some common terrain. The most obvious common group is product publicity. Carefully planned publicity can create great visibility and interest in a product or brand. How should publicity skill be supplied to, say, a product manager? The company can either locate product publicity in the marketing department or 'borrow' it as needed from the public relations department.

The more important product publicity is to product success, the better it is to locate it within the marketing department.

Another common ground is customer relations. Marketing is adept at selling to customers and less adept at responding to customer complaints after the product is sold. Customer complaints tend to reach the public relations department. Public relations personnel try to salve the customer's wounds and get the marketing department to avoid practices that will lead to similar grievances in the future. A latent function of the public relations department is to 'watchdog' the marketing department.

Marketing as the dominant function (C)

Some marketers advance the view that corporate public relations should be placed under the control of the corporate marketing department. They argue that public relations exists essentially to make it easier for the firm to market its goods. Public relations is not in the corporate picture simply to do good deeds. One of the most articulate spokesmen for this view is Howard Geltzer of Ries and Geltzer:

> 'I grew up in the General Electric "school," which views public relations as a fundamental marketing tool. In every client situation, our public relations tactics are closely tied to the strategic marketing objectives. I view the role of public relations to support and further the overall marketing objectives. This occurs most successfully when public relations reinforces the impact of other marketing communication techniques, like promotion and advertising, by adding another voice to the overall position. In my opinion, public relations as a separate entity from marketing is outdated and no longer feasible in today's economic environment.'[8]

Public relations does a poor job of measuring its contribution to profits, some criticize. Public relations practitioners measure impact in communicating terms: specifically, how many clippings or mentions they could count. A new measurement approach is needed that measures how well public relations contributes to moving the marketing objectives forward.

The 'broadening of marketing' movement views public relations as a subset of marketing. The generic task of marketing is:

> 'The analysis, planning, implementation, and control of carefully formulated programs designed to bring about voluntary exchanges of values with target markets for the purpose of achieving organizational objectives.'[9]

Thus marketers can view any public as a 'target market' if the problem is formulated as one of how to incentivize the voluntary exchange of valued resources between two parties. The valued resources include time, energy, attention, and goodwill, as well as money. Levy and Zaltman advanced the view 'that all interactions may be interpreted from a marketing point of view.'[10]

Public relations as the dominant function (D)

It is also conceivable that in some quarters marketing will be viewed as a subfunction of public relations rather than the reverse. The argument would be made that the firm's future depends critically on how it is viewed by key publics, including stockholders, financial institutions, unions, employees, community leaders, as well as customers.

The task of the firm is to satisfy these publics as much as possible. Satisfying the customers is one part of the task, the part called *marketing*. Satisfying the customers must be kept in balance with satisfying other groups. Marketing cannot be allowed to go its own way regardless of the consequences. Marketing should be put under public relations control to make sure that the goodwill of all key publics is maintained.

In for-profit firms, this view is implemented by transferring some power to approve or disapprove of certain practices of the marketing department to the public relations people. We saw earlier examples of a food company and an oil company creating greater public relations control over marketing.

Nonprofit organizations express this view in another way. The nonprofit organization normally has a public relations director before it ever recognizes a need for marketing. When marketing problems emerge, the administration may choose to expand the job responsibilities of the public relations officer to include some marketing work, rather than establish a separate job position for marketing. Or a marketing person might be hired and asked to report to the public relations director. The public relations director will go through the motions of learning about marketing concepts and tools. This is not always successful, and often marketing remains a stepchild of the public relations program.

Marketing and public relations as the same function (E)

Another way of viewing the two functions is as rapidly converging in concepts and methodologies. They both talk in terms of publics and markets; they both recognize the need for market segmentation; they both acknowledge the importance of market attitudes, perceptions, and images in formulating programs; and the primacy of a management process consisting of analysis, planning, implementation, and control. In some organizations, the two functions might be feasibly merged under a vice president of marketing and public relations. This person is in charge of planning and managing the external affairs of the company.

Exhibit 4 shows the planning methodology such as a department would follow. The first step calls for auditing the present position of the firm and its major products in the eyes of target markets and publics. The audit would answer such questions as:

- How visible is the firm to different publics?
- How favorably is the firm seen by different key publics? What negatives exist in the current image?
- What factors cause the negative impressions?
- What threat power do these various publics have on the firm?

The second step calls for defining a desired position for the firm and its products vis-à-vis its competition:

- Does this position make marketing sense?
- Does it make public relations sense?
- Can it be achieved given the firm's resources?

The third step calls for the developing a portfolio of products and services that is well-balanced cyclically, seasonally, and in terms of risks to reversals in public opinion. The firm should not rely too heavily on products that are vulnerable to public criticism and legislative action.

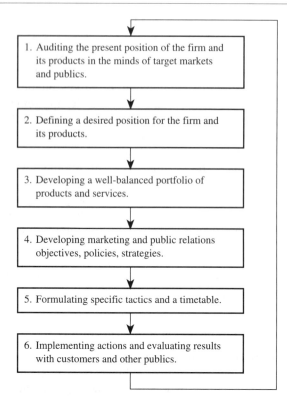

Exhibit 4 Joint methodology of marketing and public relations.

The fourth step calls for setting specific marketing and public relations objectives, policies, and strategies to guide conduct and performance in the market place and public arena. Strict marketing objectives and strategies should be tempered by such considerations as:

- Is the product healthful and safe?
- Is the pricing defensible?
- Is the environmental harm minimal?

The fifth step calls for developing specific tactics and a timetable to implement marketing and public relations strategies. The implications of specific tactics should be reviewed for their potential in creating public relations backlash.

The sixth step calls for implementing planned actions and monitoring their impacts on customers and other key publics:

- Are plans being achieved?
- Are the publics responding in the expected way?
- Should strategies or tactics be changed?

What about this model? In principle, it synthesizes the two functions so as to reduce interdepartmental conflict and lack of coordination. It would hopefully avoid the difficulties recently experienced by two giant corporations when they failed to take a joint marketing/public relations programming of their marketing activities:

'It has not been clearly established that General Motors deliberately misled many purchasers of Buicks, Oldsmobiles, and Pontiacs by delivering their cars with motors also used in Chevrolets or that New York Telephone intended to conceal existence of less expensive services from certain subscribers. However, because such customers of both companies have felt they were deceived, there have been scores of unfavorable media reports and further damage to the public reputation of business as a whole and additional anti-business regulation may result.'[11]

LOOKING AHEAD

The neat and tidy divisions separating marketing and public relations are breaking down. It may be that the best way to solve a marketing problem would be through public relations activities. It also is possible that the best way to solve a public relations problem might be through the disciplined orientation that marketing provides.

Both marketing and public relations people want more of a voice in corporate policy making. To the extent that marketers incorporate sound public relations in their thinking, this will obviate the need for an expanded corporate public relations department. To the extent that they fail to do this, public relations people are going to press for more influence over marketing decisions.

Not all managements, however, are responsive to using corporate public relations for high level counseling. Many prefer to treat public relations practitioners as simply communication specialists. The president of a Fortune 500 food corporation told one of the authors:

> 'I don't expect counsel from my public relations department about public issues or the stand my company should take about these issues. I consult issues "experts" in product safety, government, and other areas. I then go to public relations to help effectively communicate our position to mass and selective audiences. I don't think public relations people have had the training or knowledge to give advice on "issue positions"'.[12]

This company set up a separate public affairs department in which the real expertise on public issues is expected to lie. The growth of public affairs departments in recent time has removed some of the argument from public relations directors that they should provide a counseling as well as a communications function to top management.

On the other hand, viewing public relations as simply a communications function will lead a lot of chief executive officers to miss some of this function's potential value. It could even be counter-productive, according to Harry Dreiser, an experienced public relations practitioner:

> 'Assuming the public relations director is a thoroughgoing professional, seasoned and skilled, this process wastes his talents and may give rise to real public relations problems. He ought to be in on the decision process early, and have a chance to affect it. He contributes his knowledge of the media and how they are likely to treat a corporate action, and his perception of the public and its attitudes. If he is to be fully effective he cannot be simply handed a decision and told to go out and sell it. He must know the bits and pieces of fact and opinion

that went into the making of the decision, and if it is a decision with profound public relations implications he should have a chance to influence it as well.'[13]

Educational gap

The counseling potential of the public relations director depends on his being 'a thoroughgoing professional, seasoned and skilled.' This begs the question of what training a fully effective public relations director should have. The present arrangements for training public relations people leave a great deal to be desired. Public relations people receive their training for the most part in schools of journalism, which equip them to spell but hardly to understand economics and take a management point of view. Business schools still refuse to offer majors or even courses in public relations. Thus there is a serious educational gap.

Against great odds the professional public relations societies are trying to raise the quality of practitioners. One of the authors recently spoke to a chapter of the Public Relations Society of America arguing that the profession's future depended on its ability to provide counsel to top management on policy issues. The audience listened politely, but the question and answer session that followed became animated only when the failure of public relations neophytes to *spell correctly* was brought up as an issue.

Public relations and marketing have managed to establish themselves as essential corporate functions. As corporations undergo increased regulation and pressure from interest groups and government agencies, new patterns of operation and interrelation can be expected to appear in these functions. No one model will be appropriate for all enterprises. The environmental pressures facing the individual enterprise, as well as its own history, will dictate whether to strengthen its marketing function or public relations function or even whether to start a new pattern of meeting and coping with external opportunities and threats.

NOTES

1 Private correspondence from a public relations specialist.
2 Don E. Lee, Public Affairs Director, Carter Oil Company, Houston in an address to the American Academy of Advertising, reproduced in their *Proceedings* of 1976 edited by C. Dennis Schick, 1977, 17–19.
3 Peter F. Drucker, *The Practice of Management* (New York: Harper & Row, 1954), 37.
4 See Philip Kotler and Sidney J. Levy, 'Broadening the Concept of Marketing,' *Journal of Marketing*, (January 1969), 10–15. Also see Philip Kotler, *Marketing for Nonprofit Organizations* (Englewood Cliffs, N.J.: Prentice-Hall Inc., 1975).
5 Edward L. Bernays, *Public Relations* (Norman, Oklahoma: University of Oklahoma Press, 1952).
6 Scott M. Cutlip, 'The Beginning of PR Counseling,' *Editor and Publisher*, (Nov. 26, 1960), 16.
7 Private note from an eminent professor of public relations at a leading university.
8 Private correspondence to the authors.
9 Philip Kotler, 'A Generic Concept of Marketing,' *Journal of Marketing*, (April 1972), 46–54.
10 Sidney J. Levy and Gerald Zaltman, *Marketing, Society and Conflict* (Englewood Cliffs, N.J.: Prentice-Hall, Inc., 1975), 6.
11 Denny Griswold (ed.), *Public Relations News*, 32 (May 2, 1977), 1.
12 Private interview.
13 Private interview.

Kotler, P. and Mindak, W. (1978) 'Marketing and public relations – Should they be partners or rivals?'. *Journal of Marketing*, 42, October: 13–20. Reproduced with permission from *Journal of Marketing*, published by the American Marketing Association.

Public relations: a rationale for its development and usage within UK fast-moving consumer goods firms

6.2

Philip J. Kitchen

INTRODUCTION

This article is concerned with exploring the ways in which public relations may be developing within fast-moving consumer goods (FMCG) firms in the United Kingdom. Traditionally these firms have been associated with advertising, sales, promotion, and personal selling with the use of publicity (as opposed to public relations) in support of marketing and corporate communications objectives. In a previous article[1] Kitchen and Proctor noted that public relations was changing and appeared to be developing and extending its influence in a variety of firms. However, the material on which this comment was grounded appeared in American, as opposed to UK, literature.[2-5] The question of whether public relations is increasing in emphasis and expenditure in UK firms, which, of course, has relevance for UK marketers, is one worthy of further exploration. In particular answers to specific questions are desirable:

- To what extent has there been a shift in emphasis and expenditure towards the use of public relations by FMCG firms?
- If such a shift has taken place, what are the underlying factors occasioning such a change?
- Are FMCG firms placing increased emphasis and expenditure on public relations?
- If firms are moving towards public relations to what extent is such movement occasioned by environmental considerations?
- Is there any evidence to support the viewpoint that a degree of integration and interaction is taking place between corporate and marketing public relations?

This article seeks to explore these questions.

BACKGROUND

In relation to modern business organizations the seeming essentiality and functionality of public relations can hardly be disputed.[6] Notwithstanding its current topicality the development of public relations has evolved significantly since its early inception as 'press agentry' at the start of the twentieth century.[7] From its somewhat shady background as press agentry, public relations now appears on the management scene as a multifaceted and essential management discipline.[8] Its multifaceted nature could be explored in terms of the evolution of management thought;[9] from the perspective of its diverse literature;[5,10] from the diversity of courses available in the United Kingdom in further and higher education;[11] or could be illustrated by the development of public relations as a marketing tool.[12,13]

While it may be difficult to show that the principles of public relations are consistent and enduring, its practice has been extensively influenced by social forces, scientific developments, and a continually changing environment. Companies now need to communicate with a number of differentiated publics, extending beyond *quid pro quo* relations. According to the British Institute of Public Relations[7] 'public relations is the planned and sustained effort to establish and maintain goodwill and mutual understanding between an organization and its publics'. Such a definition entails diversity of publics and such diversity inevitably requires message differentiation and design. While public relations may have significant value in terms of corporate communication activities, it may also be significant in terms of marketing.

Various authors have pointed to the use of public relations for marketing purposes,[2,12,14,15] or its relevance to marketing communication.[4,13,16,17] While marketing and public relations have mulled over the parameters of their respective disciplines (i.e. marketing and PR), many organizations are moving towards a greater integration and connection between the two disciplines. One recent example of this integration was British Petroleum's corporate advertising (1991) showing their involvement in bringing electricity and educational opportunities to Third World countries. This may seem to have little to do with the marketing of petroleum and oil until the purpose of such advertising is considered – this being to create the image of BP as a 'warm caring company whose concerns extend beyond marketing'. The friendly warm imagery was further extended by promotional advertising of a more traditional nature depicting the ambience, goods obtainable, and benefits associated with BP petrol stations. Further examples of sponsorship comprising both corporate and marketing elements were illustrated in the recent (1992) Olympics and in the move towards television programme sponsorships. Sponsorships and other forms of communication may represent an approach to communication which penetrates consumer perceptual filters in an indirect way. Moreover problems with advertising inflation literally mean that marketing communication budgets are driven 'down the line' to public relations activities, among others. However whether these comments are applicable or have relevance to FMCG firms remains to be seen.

RESEARCH METHOD

The objective of this article is to explore the questions noted in the introductory section. FMCG firms manufacturing branded goods were contacted to provide a sample for an exploratory study. Other firms producing own-label and generic goods were excluded given their propensity not to be involved in marketing communication activities.[18-20] FMCG firms were chosen primarily because of their traditional reliance on advertising and below-the-line communications. Choosing such firms presented some difficulties in terms of research access. A mechanism for circumventing these difficulties, described in a previous paper by Kitchen and Proctor,[1] where PR agencies dealing with the FMCG sector were surveyed was considered as an initial first step to accessing firms in the FMCG sector. In the latter case, in-depth interviews were carried out, where possible at corporate and marketing levels, with appropriate executives. General communications are those concerned with corporate activities while marketing communications are those concerned with the marketing function. While recognizing that firms are drawn from different manufacturing sectors the qualitative findings indicate that PR is in greater usage within such firms.

Initially 34 firms, using *The Times* 1000[21] as a sampling frame, were contacted by letter addressed to a named individual. From this point of contact only two firms expressed a willingness to participate in the research. Further contact was then made by telephone and ten companies were subsequently identified as willing to participate in the research. The ten firms were either corporate holding companies or divisions/strategic business units. Interviewees responded to an interview schedule spanning both corporate and marketing communications in relation to public relations. Perhaps some comment on what is meant by an 'interview schedule' is in order. Some confusion may arise in the distinction between 'survey research' and the research method actually utilized. Survey research is defined by Tull and Hawkins[22] as:

> ... the systematic gathering of information from respondents for the purpose of understanding and/or predicting some aspect of the behaviour of the population of interest ... As the term is typically used, it implies the information has been gathered with some version of a questionnaire.

Survey research would, at this stage, be inappropriate given the exploratory nature of the research. While the aim was indeed to gather information, an understanding of the development of PR in FMCG firms was required. Exploratory research is concerned with discovering the general nature of the problem and the variables which relate to it. The primarily inductive research approach is necessitated because of the need to probe a new, probably substantive, methodological area. Such an approach is justified where there is a need to gain insights and ideas. Although such an approach may serve to harvest a wealth of information, significant caution is required in interpreting the results. For example, while the research method was advantageous in terms of flexibility – enabling the researcher to adapt and extend the programme in response to emergent findings and, further, providing a mechanism for interviewees to identify public relations issues of key concern to themselves – it was disadvantageous because of the inherent limitations associated with the research method. For example it was necessary to avoid attributing too much importance to particular comments in isolation. Generally anecdotes which vastly enrich the findings are used only where a statement is reflective of a general trend. Responses may have been influenced by interviewer intervention or skewed by subjective interpretation. For these reasons the research method deployed cannot guarantee clear and unambiguous interpretation of the results. The results cannot be projected across an entire population and over-generalization needs to be avoided. This ties into a straightforward exposition of the characteristics of exploratory research.

> Exploratory research is characterized by a high degree of flexibility, and it tends to rely on convenience or judgement samples, small scale surveys or simple experiments, case analyses, and subjective evaluation of the results.[22]

In this case an interview schedule was developed based on initial interviews conducted with two firms. Although the interview schedule contains specific categories of response, questions were not necessarily asked in a sequential order. Instead the interview schedule allowed freedom to create questions, add additional questions, probe responses which appeared to be relevant, and generally develop the best set of data in any practical way. In the findings, specific companies cannot be named because the nature of the findings corresponds with competitive intelligence. However the ten companies are:

- Either market leaders or significant market share holders in their respective segments.
- Commonly found among the top 50 advertisers in the United Kingdom.[23]

Interviews took place between December 1989 and June 1990; all were recorded on cassette tape, and transcriptions made. The transcriptions (covering some 200 plus pages) form the essential material from which the empirical findings in this article are derived.

The purpose of the interview schedule was to provide a mechanism in order to explore and research questions specified in the introduction. Thus the article is organized around them.

Areas of marketing communication explored included a discussion of five broad areas of the communication mix (advertising, personal selling, sales promotion, marketing PR/product publicity and sponsorship) – whether these areas were increasing or decreasing in emphasis and expenditure and the perceived reasons. PR in support of marketing and general communication was also explored; areas of PR included publicity, advertising, public affairs, issues management, and lobbying; whether they were in greater use, and the reasons why. Third, three questions were asked about PR expenditure in relation to the previous decade. Other issues were explored as the interview(s) unfolded. To ensure that interviewer and interviewees were 'speaking the same language' basic 'textbook' definitions of each area of communication were utilized.

RESEARCH FINDINGS

As stated above this article explores the stipulated research questions. One method of exploration which could be adopted would be to describe each firm individually; this however would be somewhat laborious. The method of exploration adopted will draw on the findings from each phase of the interview schedule. Thus a commencement will be made to explore the empirical findings in terms of changes perceived by executives in marketing communications and their underlying reasons for such changes, this corresponding to a discussion of any changes in marketing communication variables in terms of emphasis and expenditure. An exploration of aggregate perceptions of corporate communications then takes place by analysing changes and the perceived underlying reasons, this corresponding to changes in corporate communication variables in terms of emphasis and expenditure. Changes in PR expenditure over the past decade will be considered. Finally the argument will then be summarized in the context of the research questions. Opportunity will be taken to include anecdotal statements by FMCG executives where these are reflective of a general trend. The tables are each derived by ascertaining a specific sense of direction towards usage of a particular communication tool by individual respondents together with a descriptive outline of their rationale for this movement. This can be seen as inherently descriptive rather than analytic, but nonetheless serves to lay a foundation on which further research can be grounded.

MARKETING COMMUNICATIONS

This section draws on the qualitative findings from the ten firms to establish whether there has been a general trend towards the use of PR in marketing communications. This is established by considering subdivisions of marketing communications and whether interviewees perceived any increase or decrease in emphasis and expenditure in these areas. Table 1 records perceptions of change within the marketing communications area. The five main elements of marketing communications are: advertising, sales promotion, personal selling, marketing PR/product publicity and sponsorship. Four of these elements are defined by Korlet[12] as:

1. *Advertising* – any paid form of non-personal presentation and promotion of ideas, goods, and services by an identified sponsor.
2. *Sales promotion* – short-term incentives to encourage purchase of a good or service.
3. *Personal selling* – oral presentation in a conversational form with one or more prospective purchasers to encourage purchase of a good or service.
4. *Marketing PR/product publicity* – the latter indicates non-personal stimulation of demand for a product or business unit by planting commercially significant news about it in a published medium or media that is not paid for by the sponsor. Marketing PR is a wider area which includes sponsorships, and PR tags to sales promotion devices.
5. *Sponsorship* (this latter area is not defined in the marketing literature) – all companies interviewed, however, were heavily involved in this area, and saw it as overlapping between general/corporate and marketing communications. A survey published by Linstead and Turner[24] found sponsorship resourced from different sources for arts and sports. Their findings are included as a guideline to sources of sponsorship monies. Budget sources are indicated in Table 1.

It would be inappropriate to view the elements of marketing communications as mutually exclusive. A more correct approach is to view them as mutually interactive and synergistic, as with the more straightforward marketing mix which considers product, price, promotion and place. Like the marketing mix, each area of the communication mix should be planned and co-ordinated with other communication mix areas to achieve communication objectives. This ties in with standard 'how communication works' models and response hierarchy approaches, for example AIDA[25,26]. It would be extremely rare for a company to use one type of promotion; a mix of communication types would be used. For example manufacturers of branded baked beans would have salespersons who visit buyers where their goods are stocked,

Table 1

	Arts (%)	Sports (%)
Part of PR budget	65.4	33.3
Part of the advertising/promotional budget	13.7	47.9
Taken from another budget	9.9	6.8
Other	11.1	12.0

advertise nationally in mass media, distribute sales promotion devices (i.e. pence-off coupons or competitions), publicize in mass media or trade publications, and presumably may sponsor sports, arts and other activities likely to enhance brand or corporate image. The functions performed by different communication mix areas are dissimilar. Advertising appeals to large audiences and creates awareness and interest in product categories or brands, personal selling offers key account servicing and one-to-one contact, flexibility, and closure. Without selling, much advertising would be wasted. PR and sponsorships would perhaps provide credible information and create favourable imagery, while sales promotions should stimulate short-run sales and supplement other communication mix types. Each of the communication mix areas will now be explored. This exploration is prefaced by Table 2 which records aggregate FMCG executives' perceptions of communication mix change in terms of emphasis and expenditure over the past decade.

Advertising

Table 2 shows that six of the ten companies perceived a decline in advertising in terms of emphasis and expenditure, three showing an increase, and one the same as a decade ago. Reasons given for the companies which showed a movement away from advertising are that media costs and clutter are causing marketers to re-evaluate communications tactics; and where benefits of coverage can be spread across brands then this tactic is utilized. Table 3 summarizes findings from each company.

The major rationale for changes in Company 1 was increased advertising cost and perceptions of audience fragmentation. Company 2 also observed inflationary pressures in their (food) business. Food inflation was perceived to be less than general

Table 2 Perceptions of Change in Marketing Communications in Terms of Emphasis and Expenditure (1980–89)

	Area of marketing communications				
	Advertising	*Sales promotion*	*Personal selling*	*Marketing PR/ product publicity*	*Sponsorship*
Company					
1	—	+	—	+	+
2	—	+	—	+	+
3	+	+	—	#	+
4	#	#	—	+	+
5	—	+	+	+	+
6	+	+	—	+	+
7	+	—	—	+	+
8	—	+	—	+	+
9	—	+	NC	+	+
10	—	—	—	+	NC
Student 2./test	− 0.5	0.8	− 1.5	1.5	1.5

Test: if greater than +1 or -1 = significant at the 0.5 level
Code: − = Decrease; + = Increase; # = Same; NC = no comment
A decrease (-), increase (+) or no change (#) in emphasis and expenditure in each communication mix area, or a movement towards other communication mix areas was specifically stated by the interviewee(s). This then provided a basis for the perceived reason for any changes in emphasis and expenditure relative to the past decade.

Table 3 Perceptions of Changes in Advertising in Terms of Emphasis and Expenditure

Company	Increase/ decrease	Reason
1	Decrease	Increase cost, audience fragmentation
2	Decrease	Increased cost, advertising inflation
3	Increase	No change, increase in line with inflation
4	Same	No change in emphasis or expenditure; recognition of PR's complementarity
5	Decrease	Increased expense, need to spread media benefits across brands
6	Increase	Noted PR's complementarity to advertising
7	Increase	Noted some scepticism towards advertising among younger age groups, development of marketing PR
8	Decrease	Audience fragmentation
9	Decrease	Advertising now prohibitively expensive
10	Decrease	Increased cost, audience fragmentation

inflation, averaging 4–5 per cent per year through the 1980s, so was 2–3 per cent less than general inflation. Simultaneously advertising inflation had averaged at 15 per cent per year, sometimes 20 per cent. Another advertising decline factor was oversubscription in the television media with new entrants adding to media clutter. Company 2 mentioned that VCRs and remote control, coupled with multi-set households, were further fragmenting and diminishing mass market audiences because of interference to commercial breaks.[27,28] Company 3 increased advertising expenditures in line with inflation.

Company 4 stated that advertising emphasis and expenditure had not diminished in the 1980s but added that PR operated in a complementary way. Company 5 stated that advertising was becoming much more expensive and therefore adopted an 'umbrella strategy for their major brands'. Advertising formed the major proportion of expenditure in marketing communications for Companies 6 and 7 but related expenditure on marketing PR was growing rapidly. Company 7 said that some of their products were now being targeted towards younger age groups and that they would now use PR rather than advertising because 'these age groups are sceptical toward advertising' (Marketing Manager). Company 8's decline in advertising expenditure was associated with changing consumer habits (audience fragmentation) and a perceived need to create and maintain two-way dialogue between company and consumers; this was done via sales promotion either in-store or on-pack. Such sales promotions provided an opportunity to gather marketing intelligence. Company 9 noted a siphoning off or diversion of funds towards PR or the achievement of PR objectives and stated that advertising on 'prime-time television' was now prohibitively expensive and that company values could be communicated in a variety of ways (source: PR Manager). Movement away from advertising within Company 9 had been coupled with a far greater scrutiny on how marketing communication budgets were allocated. Company 10 also noted a shift away from TV advertising (because of expense) into radio, press and outdoor. To quote the interviewee:

> The television media has become very cluttered; over the past three decades the net supply has hardly changed; this creates significant pressure on prices. If you

cannot spend marketing money via classic advertising it has to go down the line, and one way to do this effectively is via product PR, but the reasons for utilizing this tool are based on physical economics.

(Public Relations Director)

The main reasons within those companies which perceived a decline in advertising emphasis and expenditure over the past decade can be summarized as advertising inflation, media clutter, audience fragmentation, audience receptivity, physical economics, attractiveness of available alternatives, and a move towards marketing PR/product publicity.

Sales promotion

Following on from the first table – where seven of the ten firms indicated increased emphasis and expenditure – Table 4 summarizes findings from each company in relation to sales promotion as part of the communications mix.

Companies 7 and 10 stipulated reduced interest and expenditure on sales promotion. The former had decreased emphasis and expenditure overall, largely because of EPoS (electronic point of sale)[29] and retailer requests for less price-off and banded pack promotions. The latter noted that their sales promotional tactics were now more sophisticated and linked to consumer and brand values. Likewise Company 10 noted reduced activity largely because of retailers seeking reduced prices as they moved in the direction of own-label and generic manufactures.[30] Company 4, while emphasis and expenditure remained unchanged, noted that sales promotion had changed its form and made the point that 'high-quality premium products do not use couponing or price-off promotions ... but serve to enhance product quality' (Public Affairs Director). Trade promotions in this firm were offered in the form of marketing financial inducements and merchandising. Companies 2 and 4 stated that companies marketing high-quality premium products needed to make products more aspirational and this was linked to consumer behaviour via the trading-up phenomenon which is the perceived tendency, resulting from greater affluence in Western markets for

Table 4 Perceptions of Changes in Sales Promotion in Terms of Emphasis and Expenditure

Company	Increase/ decrease	Reason
1	Increase	Demand for tailormades from trade
2	Increase	Aligned with marketing PR, linked to brand values
3	Increase	Move from many small to few large promotions linked to brand values, need to create product publicity
4	Same	More sophisticated, made aspirational and linked to brand values and marketing PR
5	Increase	No comment
6	Increase	PR tags now attached
7	Decrease	EPoS (electronic point of sale), greater sales promotion sophistication, retailer interaction
8	Increase	Linked to marketing PR
9	Increase	PR tags now attached
10	Decrease	Retailer request for reduced prices

consumers to trade up to higher-quality, more exciting, more expensive products. This often runs in parallel with concerns about diet and fitness. This has led to the need to provide products with a quality image, and also to packaging developments, for example foil bags, which keep products fresher while looking more attractive on retailers' shelves. This trend, in conjunction with the move towards convenience eating and healthier diets, has created significant marketing and general communication challenges (*source*: internal document provided by an interviewee). Despite a similar or reduced expenditure and emphasis on sales promotion, Companies 4 and 7 indicated that usage of this tool was now closely linked to marketing PR.

In Company 1 sales promotion usage had increased significantly through the 1980s both for trade and consumers. With trade, significant emphasis was placed on the development of 'tailormades', that is promotions developed in conjunction with specific major customers. Company 2 indicated that sales promotion, while playing a greater role in the communications mix, was also targeted to create consumer value while simultaneously geared to create PR opportunities. In Company 3 the emphasis had changed to a small number of large promotions (from a large number of small promotions) which were targeted to consumer needs, linking into a requirement to generate favourable publicity. Company 5 supported this viewpoint indicating that sales promotions were now more focused, reinforcing brand values and benefits. Trade emphasis was on 'tailormades', and their main reason for the tactical thrust in sales promotion was divergence of funds away from advertising as a result of pressure on media space and media costs (Marketing Manager).

Companies 6, 8, and 9 stated increased sales promotional activity. In Company 8 this was owing to its perceived cost-effectiveness and the desirability of maintaining 'top-of-mind' recognition of brands. They stipulated also a growing link between sales promotion and marketing PR. In Company 9, sales promotion had enjoyed significant growth in the 1980s and latterly with PR tags. The aim behind such sales promotions was to generate excitement, support the trade, and reward brand-loyal customers (*source*: PR Manager).

In summary, for those companies which were supportive of increased emphasis and expenditure on sales promotion the main reasons were: reinforcement of brand values, linked to consumer needs, generation of marketing PR/product publicity, resulting from redirection of marketing budgets, and perceived cost-effectiveness. Companies perceived increased emphasis and expenditure in sales promotion but perhaps in a changed form. Emphasis is being placed on promotions which reinforce brand values and benefits or tie into consumer needs; several companies stated specific examples. Promotions are geared to links with marketing PR and to generate positive newsworthy stories about companies and their brands. Sales promotion expenditures have been enhanced by re-direction of marketing budgets away from advertising and recognition of the perceived cost-effectiveness of sales promotion. In the past decade sales promotion seems to have grown in importance becoming an essential tool in the arsenal of communications weaponry in FMCG firms. Notably absent from this euphoria is Company 10. While the stipulated reason for reduced activity in sales promotion was retailer needs for lower prices, recent American research by Jones[31] quoted executives describing sales promotions as 'a vicious circle of promotion, commotion, and demotion'. It may be some time before other UK companies encounter such findings.

Personal selling

Table 2 showed that nine out of the ten firms indicated decreased emphasis and expenditure on personal selling. Company 9 noted a greater move towards retail grocery concentration. Unanimity was evident with eight of the other nine companies; decline in emphasis and expenditure in personal selling was as a result of two major factors: first was concentration of the grocery trade leading to centralization of buying activity by multiples; second was an internal change – the development of key account salesmanship or, in other words, senior sales executives, and the growth of support teams in relation to centralized buying functions. In addition to key account selling, Company 3 had also started to utilize telesales rather than personal contact. Company 5 was supportive of the point made about retail concentration stated in conjunction with Company 10, that the number of outlets on which salesmen could call had halved in the past decade. Company 8 mentioned that small retailers now shopped via cash and carrys. Company 7's salesforce had declined only marginally. Company 6 spoke of growth in the wholesale sector and an increased merchandizing function for salesforce personnel. In summary, the major reasons for a perceived decline in emphasis and expenditure on personal selling are: concentration in the grocery trade, centralization of buying function by multiples, development of key account sales, experimentation with telesales, increased merchandizing, and some growth of the wholesale function.

Marketing PR/product publicity and sponsorship

Sponsorship has been included under the heading of marketing PR primarily because this is where many companies placed it in terms of describing the communication mix. It is evident that sponsorship is not necessarily the sole preserve of marketing communications. Nine companies (Table 2) stated that increased emphasis and expenditure had taken place in marketing PR/product publicity and sponsorship. These companies (exception was Company 10) saw sponsorship as part of the public relations function which came under the heading of marketing communications. Two exceptions to this scenario of growth were Company 3 (marketing PR/product publicity) and Company 10 (sponsorship – no comment). The discussion will commence with these two apparent exceptions. Company 3 perceived little increase in activity in terms of marketing PR/product publicity, although there was a movement away from high visibility one-off events towards ongoing educational programmes, primarily sponsorship. The rationale for participation in sponsorships was given as follows:

> We feel we have to emphasize the product, the lifestyle and imagery, so in sport we have been working with governing bodies in ... [various sporting associations] ... Sponsorship equates to a large number of children growing up with brand imagery top-of-the-mind because it's always been there when they're playing the sport; it's all part of the image build (PR Manager).

Sponsorships were seen as very important and an area of growth for Company 3. This was seen as part of public relations but less emphasis had been placed on product publicity. Company 10 indicated no change in emphasis and expenditure on sponsorship but gave the view that a significant increase had taken place in product publicity, an increase led by consumer attitudinal change:

> Women want to know a lot more about a product before they buy it; its
> nutritional content and toxicology ... You cannot put across a sophisticated
> nutrition story through advertising, it is necessary to use other forms of
> communication (Corporate PR Manager).

Within Company 10 a significant proportion of expenditure was now utilized to provide
consumers with support literature. These factors relative to growth in sponsorship for
Company 3 and marketing PR/product publicity for Company 10 were endorsed by the
eight other companies who indicated increased emphasis and expenditure in these
areas. Figure 1 shows the rationale supporting growth for these companies.

Table 1 indicates that marketing PR/product publicity, sponsorship and sales
promotion are undergoing increased emphasis and expenditure, while notably
advertising and personal selling is declining. Sponsorship, an area virtually ignored in
the marketing literature[12,26,32,33] is enjoying increasing emphasis and expenditure.
Sponsorship is an area which creates PR opportunities for marketing and
general/corporate communications and is also mutually beneficial. Each area listed
under the heading of sponsorship, marketing public relations, and product publicity is
enjoying increased emphasis and expenditure in the majority of firms interviewed.

In the light of the findings thus far, changes in emphasis and expenditure within the
promotional mix can plainly be linked with environmental factors underpinning
development and growth in public relations at the marketing level. These findings
support the establishment of support for an increased shift towards the use of PR at a
marketing level which is, of course, one of the questions with which this article is
concerned. What may be of greatest interest is not so much the emergence of
marketing PR or an increased emphasis and expenditure on it, but the movement
towards complementarity and integration of marketing public relations with the other
elements of the communication mix. All ten firms reported that use of marketing PR
helps to achieve marketing objectives, although there is ambiguity concerning
effective measurement. Only one firm (Company 9) had linked marketing PR into
market research via tracking studies and (to this company at least) proved its viability
as a marketing tool.

GENERAL CORPORATE COMMUNICATIONS

This section draws on qualitative findings to establish whether there has been a
general trend towards the use of PR in general/corporate communications. This is
done by considering major areas of such communications and increase or decrease in
emphasis and expenditure over the past decade (1980–89). Table 5 records
perceptions of change within this area. Six main areas of general/corporate
communications are explored including publicity, issues management, public affairs,
lobbying, financial PR, and corporate advertising. Definitions of each of these areas
were taken from Cutlip et al.[34] In addition a further category was explored concerning
links between general/corporate and marketing communications.

Publicity

Table 5 shows that nine of the ten companies interviewed stipulated increased
expenditure and emphasis on publicity (Company 4 excepted). Company 1 (PR

Company	Main marketing PR	Development	Cause
1	• Media sponsorships • Combine with sales promotion and advertising • Press release	Significant	Cost of advertising; effectiveness of PR; need to reach target audiences
Quote: 'Sponsorships are related primarily to [our] market and are concerned with going back to basic principles of brand strategy and in identifying a sponsorship format that will link into what the brand is all about' (PR Manager – accountable to Marketing)			
2	• Sports sponsorships • Media relations • Link with sales promotion	Significant	Cost of advertising; flexibility of press media; TV potential coverage; focus on particular markets
Quote: 'Sponsorship fits in with product targeting in family products – i.e. family sports; and further creates opportunity for TV coverage, i.e. gets our name on the box cheaply' (Marketing Manager).			
3	• Sports sponsorships • Link to sales promotion • Media relations	Some	Consumer needs; enhance visibility; increase consumption
4	• Sports sponsorships • Link with sales promotion • Brand support	Massive	Growth of differentiated media; complimentary to advertising
5	• Sports • Free magazines • Event days • Educational support	Some	Advertising expense; need to maintain image; educational needs
Quote: 'We need to communicate the house and brand names in the most effective ways, but so far it has been difficult to measure results from sponsorships and marketing PR. We take every opportunity we can to create positive brand and corporate publicity ... We need to get the ... name in front of people; youth and children especially as they are going to be in the market longer; and in front of mothers' (PR Manager)			
6	• Publicity • Major emphasis at corporate level • Sponsorship (major emergent element)	Some	Audience fragmentation; media clutter
7	• Publicity • Link to SP • Competitions	Significant	Audience receptivity
Quote: 'The ... was a highly successful campaign because we spoke to our target market indirectly, not from us, but from people they would regard highly, have respect for, want to listen to, and value their opinions' (Marketing Manager)			
8	• Marketing PR • Link to sales promotion • Product publicity	Minor	Competitive usage
9	• Link to sales promotion • Largely led by corporate policy • Environment sponsorships • Media relations • Educational	Significant	Consumer attitudinal change; market research; support brand and corporate image; consumer needs
10	• Product publicity	Some	Consumer educational and special interest needs

Figure 1 Rationale for Increased Emphasis and Expenditure in Marketing PR/Product Publicity/Sponsorship

Table 5 Perceptions of Change in General/Corporate Communications in Terms of Emphasis and Expenditure (1980–89)

Company	Publicity	Issues management	Public affairs	Lobbying	Financial PR	Links between general and marketing PR	Corporate advertising
						Area of general corporate communications	
1	+	+	+	+	+	Yes	#
2	+	+	+	#	+	Yes	−
3	+	+	+	+	N/A	Yes	−
4	#	+	+	+	+	Yes	+
5	+	+	+	#	N/A	Yes	−
6	+	+	+	#	N/A	Yes	+
7	+	+	#	#	N/A	Yes	−
8	+	+	+	#	N/A	Yes	−
9	+	+	+	#	N/A	Yes	−
10	+	+	+	+	+	Yes	−
Student 2./Test	1.5	1.5	1.5	0	0	1.5	−0.83

Test: if greater than +1 or -1 = significant at the 0.5 level
(Code: − = Decrease; + = Increase; # = Same; N/A = not applicable)
A decrease (-), increase (+) or no change (#) in emphasis and expenditure in each corporate communications area, or a movement towards other elements of corporate communication areas was specifically stated by the interviewee(s). This then provided a basis for the perceived reason for any changes in emphasis and expenditure relative to the past decade.

Manager) stated that significant effort goes into planning, setting objectives, and implementation of publicity. This could mean interaction with various publics – government, business, media, academic, special groups, distribution, consumers, consumer groups, or internal relations. Ten years ago the publicity function in Company 1 was about getting stories in one major magazine, today it has expanded enormously.

In Company 2 publicity had diversified into new releases, feature articles, pictorial releases in the form of video tapes and films, background editorial, speeches, and news conferences. Company 3 reported increased emphasis on publicity, especially in terms of liaison with trade customers. Company 4 stated that media relations, although not in greater use, had become more focused on segmented media sectors to reach specific target audiences. The public affairs director stipulated that media relations had to be done far more crisply, cleanly 'the company had to be portrayed in a far more sophisticated, almost simpler way. A decade ago company images were obscured and cluttered by the messages they were giving'. Company 5 had only recently started to build and seek publicity opportunities. The whole general/corporate communications area was linked to corporate image by Company 6's PR manager who stated that:

> ... in today's highly competitive and geographically expanding marketplace, a company's image and corporate identity are vital elements in the communication process. How a company is perceived and how it presents itself can have a marked effect on its business success.

Publicity was seen as an opportunity for Company 6 to spread media benefits across a variety of brands, given a strong house name. In Company 7 publicity had increased in emphasis and expenditure because of the need to present the company in the best possible light to a variety of audiences. A similar perception was evident in Company 8. In Company 9 media relations had undergone significant growth primarily because of running proactive, public relations programmes – and such programmes were perceived as unimportant if they did not gain media coverage. Involvement with the media was once seen as a hot potato within Company 9 but it is seen now as an opportunity. According to the PR manager: 'We seek to develop the relationships we enjoy with our publics, and in so doing enhance the reputation we have earned over the years'. Finally Company 10 stipulated publicity had increased in emphasis and expenditure at all levels of the firm. Their reasons for this were: a more informed public, acceptability about media messages concerning business activity, and a perceived relationship to a variety of publics with whom the firm interacts. The major reason for increased emphasis and expenditure on publicity are: the recognition of a more sophisticated informed public, the need to create and maintain an environment in which marketing can perform its function, to act as a major vehicle of corporate communication, to provide an interface for communication with various publics, and the perceived acceptability to media of business messages.

Issues management

All ten firms in Table 5 perceived issues management as of increased emphasis and expenditure over the past decade. Companies indicated very significant increase in terms of issues, staffing, and allocated budgets. Issues management within Companies 1 and 2 had developed significantly over the past decade and was concerned with preventive and reactive PR. An awareness of issues and of how to deal with them is largely planned in advance. (Preventive PR can also be termed proactive PR and deals with a company's strengths; it is traditionally employed in dealing with company goals and achievements. Reactive PR is concerned with a company's weaknesses and tries to restore the company to the status quo by repairing its reputation, preventing market erosion, and regaining lost sales. Another common form of terminology for reactive PR is 'vulnerability relations').[35]

In Company 3 issues management was entitled 'damage limitation' and this was a notable area of increased activity over the past decade. Within Company 5 greater use of issues management was based on perceptions of increased consumer sophistication, and greater receptivity to issues such as product tampering. Green issues were also coming to the fore. This company perceived a necessity to be proactive, and a close interaction with marketing management was necessary. Company 6 involvement with this area took place, in the main, through trade associations, though they also promoted their own position. Within Company 7, a similar trade association interaction was in evidence, but also the area of issues management was of developing interest, emphasis, and expenditure owing to consumerist organizations becoming more vociferous and radical. Company 8 perceived issues management growth stemming from environmental activity and their perceived need to be proactive.

Issues management in Company 9 had undergone growth through the 1980s, stimulated by environmental turbulence occasioned by the health food lobby. They were now proactive in this area, especially since there is public interest and concern over what constitutes safe food. Finally Company 10 said that issues management had developed against a backcloth of environmental turbulence, the need to manage the area well, and their need to be seen to be proactive rather than reactive. The major reasons for increased emphasis and expenditure in issues management were: environmental turbulence, proliferation of issues and crisis management scenarios, informed and sophisticated consumers, need for better developed media relations, growth in radicalized and vociferous consumer groups, development of proactive and reactive PR, and the strengthening of internal management teams and budgets.

Public affairs

Public affairs had increased in terms of emphasis and expenditure in nine of ten firms, as shown in Table 5 (the exception was Company 7). In many of these companies a charitable arm was seen as separate from, but complementary to, public affairs, serving to create a 'halo effect' of advantage to specific companies, although few would seek to take advantage of it. The 'halo effect' refers to benefits derived from charitable or community involvement supporting a favourable corporate image. The exception to not seeking to take advantage of this was Company 1 which, in addition to being seen to be a good corporate citizen cognizant of 'green' issues, found that charitable issues were a concern in the sense of linking into overall strategy. They took the view that 'the difficulty is finding a charity that links into strategy and helps sell more boxes and cans ... That's what it's all about!' (PR Manager). In Company 2 public affairs was titled 'Corporate Affairs' and a new director had recently been appointed. They are a member of the 'Per Cent Club' and devote 0.75 per cent of net profits annually to worthy causes. This served to help to create the aforementioned halo effect. Company 3 was heavily involved with several corporate charitable sponsorships. The point was made that many educational sports sponsorships are done for marketing purposes but it was perceived as difficult to draw the line in terms of effects springing from general/corporate and marketing PR. Over the past decade there has been a very significant increase in emphasis and expenditure on public affairs.

Public affairs was also a major growth area in Company 4. The major role of public affairs was to create 'a level playing field' in which marketing could perform its function. Public affairs was considered to be a growth area, not within, but alongside, PR! According to the public affairs director major questions which need to be answered by public affairs are:

1. What are the limitations to growth?
2. What are the limitations on selling the product(s)?
3. How to overcome consumer resistance?

In Company 5 public affairs had also increased in terms of emphasis and expenditure via the mechanism of social responsibility – seen as community involvement. Company 6 stipulated that significant development had taken place in public affairs, occasioned by Business in the Community involvement and charitable interaction. In addition to corporate activity in public affairs, a budget is also set aside at SBU (strategic business unit) level for local charitable interaction as the company seeks to be seen as a responsible local community member. Company 7 was the one exception to growth in this area.

The interviewee from Company 8 stated that public affairs had enjoyed increased emphasis and expenditure. Growth of public affairs was also evident in Company 9, in order to build and sustain close connections with various ministries and trade associations. They were also heavily involved in social responsibility via community relations, and had a significant charitable interaction. Public affairs had been an area of concern for Company 10, and was interpreted as 'being the need to build a positive frame of reference in the community, either nationally or at factory locations'. To further quote from the interview:

> We spend a lot of time and money, making contacts with public authorities because we know there are going to be times when we need their understanding, sympathy, and support.

Publicity cannot fulfil these requirements, managers had to become involved in the community, building corporate citizenship, and exhibiting social responsibility. According to the PR manager: 'We carry out these activities because they are necessary and they are good for the firm'. Charitable interaction was evident in all the firms, often not done for marketing purposes. The gap between corporate and marketing sponsorships was difficult to define in terms of the effects flowing from them and the need to link charitable donations or sponsorships into marketing strategy was evident in some of the firms interviewed. Major reasons for the growth in public affairs were: the need to focus on corporate social responsibility and community involvement, to be seen as good corporate citizens, to distinguish between public affairs and charitable interaction (the latter creating a 'halo effect'), to take on board 'green issues', and finally to create and maintain an environment in which marketing can perform its function more effectively.

Financial PR

Financial PR had increased in four companies. Notably these are corporate companies or semi-autonomous divisions of such companies. The other six companies, which could be regarded as SBUs, while agreeing the importance of financial PR, saw it as the preserve of corporate headquarters. They indicated that levels of activity in this function had certainly not decreased over the past decade. The four firms stipulating increased emphasis and expenditure did so for differing reasons. Company 1 had a great deal of interaction with financial analysts which was not the case a decade ago. The PR manager reported in relation to financial analysts that:

> We sort out what messages we want them to receive, then we determine how we organize this ... A lot more effort is given to the sorts of messages required, and consequently how to get those messages across in more effective ways ... And in making sure it's indelibly left with them.

A similar point was made by Company 2 but with a focus on identifying key financial target audiences and developing financial PR concerning messages not only about business performance, but also how well managed the firm was. Such PR would utilize major trade journals or the *Financial Times*, but would also be juxtaposed by a series of annual activities held to influence key business opinion formers in order to elevate company status and reputation. Similar points to these were also made by Companies 4 and 10. With the latter financial PR was entitled 'investor relations' and was not only regarded as an extremely important area but also was rapidly becoming more so. Financial PR was seen as informing the City how well the company was performing and how well managed it was. An important subdivision of financial PR is investor relations. Both areas are of vital importance to companies in the 1990s.

Lobbying

Lobbying enjoyed increased emphasis and expenditure in four companies as shown in Table 5. This was necessitated by the legislative flow from the UK and European Community, and a necessary increased involvement with appropriate ministries and trade associations.

Corporate advertising

Corporate advertising had an increased emphasis and expenditure within Companies 4 and 5. Company 1 stated that no change had taken place in this area over the previous decade. The other seven firms stated that corporate advertising had declined in emphasis and expenditure. Some firms saw the function of corporate advertising as fundamental to create and sustain corporate identity and this was the case with the two firms which had increased activity. One firm saw the necessity, previously unrecognized, to create a house identity via advertising nationally or on-pack. For those firms stipulating a decrease in emphasis and expenditure the rationale was basically that corporate image could be established and maintained by other forms of communication.

Links between general and marketing PR

All ten companies saw considerable interaction between corporate and marketing public relations in terms of identification of core values which could be spread across brands, products, and represent the company also. Notably many of the areas of general/corporate communication can also carry information about brands, and in the case of sponsorships the dividing line between the two areas of communications is unclear.

Many areas of general/corporate public relations have enjoyed greater emphasis and expenditure through the 1980s. The greatest growth area in declining ascendancy are issues management, public affairs, publicity, and lobbying, closely followed by financial PR.

CHANGES IN PR EXPENDITURE

The question of expenditure needs to be raised at this time. Companies were not willing to divulge details of expenditure on public relations in terms of either marketing or general/corporate communications. Firms allocated communication expenditures from different budgets as would be expected. An interesting point was made by Company 10 that a degree of relative autonomy was afforded to brand managers to allocate their marketing communication budgets in order to achieve objectives; but what was spent this year was not necessarily a predictor of what would occur in the future. Tracking expenditure on PR, according to their PR manager, was not a good idea because:

> Changes of emphasis and expenditure for its own sake are of interest to an academic but not to us; it's all history, it's all over; what we spend next year has got no relationship to what we did last year; and what determines what's going

to happen next year is what we think we can do with products, and what we think the opposition's going to do.

Despite this comment, which is founded in the task-based method of determining budgets, answers were sought, as given in each firm's case, to the following three questions:

Question 1: Has your company spent more, or is your company spending more, in real terms, on PR-related activities over the past five to ten years?

Question 2: Using 100 as an index of expenditure on PR-related activities in 1980, what changes have there been in expenditure incurred over the last ten years?

Question 3: In real terms are you spending more on PR now than in the past?

In Table 6, the indexes yielded by answers to Question 2 are developed for each company for 1985 and 1989 from a starting point index of 100 in 1980. Given an average annual inflation rate of 8 per cent, and using the *Economic Trends* Index of Retail Prices (Food),[36] the 1980 index of 100 would be expected to increase to 146.6 by 1985 and to 215.42 by 1989. However, Table 6 shows that PR expenditures were well *above* the rate of inflation, doubling between 1980 and 1985 and quadrupling between 1980 and 1989. Some of the interviewees predicted an average annual inflation rate of 20 percent for advertising, so the 1980 index of 100 would increase to 248.83 by 1985 and to 619.16 by 1989. In other words, if a firm had maintained its advertising expenditure in proportion to the time and space accessed, it would have had to spend 2.5 times as much by 1985 and 6.2 times as much by 1989. It is not unremarkable, therefore, to see a movement away from advertising to other areas of the communication list. With regard to advertising inflation, attempts made to track down data via the Advertising Association and by personal contact with the publishers of *MEAL*[37] revealed that no such data are available. The answers to 1 and 3 are also shown in Table 6.

Table 6 Changes in Expenditure on PR

Company	Question 1	Question 2 1980	Question 2 1985	Question 2 1989	Question 3
1	Yes	100	300	550	Yes
2	Yes	100	...	400	Yes
3	Yes	100	...	...	Yes
4	Yes	100	400	800	Yes
5	Yes	100	139	284	Yes
6	Yes	100	175	400	Yes
7	Yes	100	90	195	Yes
8	No[a]	100	200	100*	No[a]
9	Yes	100	400	900	Yes
10	Yes	100	120	143	Yes
Totals	90%	Mean = 100	228	419	90%
Student 2./n test	1.5	n/a	+128%	+191%	1.5

Test: if greater than +1 or −1 = significant at the 0.5 level
[a] This is a qualified response, the company was progressing until taken over by another

As shown in Table 6, nine firms, the exception being Company 8, responded positively to Questions 1 and 3; this response is in the nature of a general trend to increased PR expenditure. Question 2 in Table 6 indicates that growth was about 128 per cent between 1980 and 1985, and 191 per cent between 1985 and 1989. The main increase, therefore, has taken place between 1985 and 1989 for the majority of these companies. While Table 6 does not differentiate between marketing and general/corporate PR it is evident from earlier comments that increased expenditure has taken place in both for the majority of companies.

DISCUSSION IN THE LIGHT OF THE RESEARCH QUESTIONS

This article has sought answers to several interesting questions as stated in the introduction. The ten FMCG firms operate in a diversity of product sectors and it was anticipated that views concerning public relations would vary from firm to firm in accordance with historical precedent, organizational culture, and environmental trends in the specific sectors in which the firms compete. But overall, in exploration of the research questions, there is correspondence in the qualitative responses to a shift towards usage of public relations at both marketing and general/corporate levels; and this shift is contingent primarily on environmental considerations.

Major finding from the interview process are:

- PR is enjoying increased emphasis and expenditure in corporate and marketing communications.
- At the marketing level this is occasioned by changes in the environment in which the traditional marketing communications mix is deployed.
- Underpinning these communication mix changes are distribution, audience, and cost characteristics.
- At corporate level a far wider diversity of communication tools is being utilized, again environmental turbulence is underpinning developments.
- A four-fold increase in expenditure on PR, on average, has taken place between 1980 and 1989.
- Interaction between corporate and marketing PR is perceived as taking place.

CONCLUSION

As explored in the body of this article it is argued that public relations is of increasing emphasis and expenditure to FMCG firms occasioned by environmental considerations. While this could be viewed against the background of a general increase in public relations across all sectors of industry the findings in relation to these types of firm may suggest the need to understand the nature and deployment of promotion and corporate communications more clearly. The research questions were explored by in-depth interviews with executives in public relations and marketing in ten firms. Public relations was perceived to be enjoying increased emphasis and expenditure in the firms interviewed, occasioned by rapid ongoing environmental activity and change specifically in relation to advertising, personal selling, sales promotion, sponsorship, and marketing PR/product publicity and with a far wider diversity of tools at the general/corporate level under the PR banner.

The framework within which the article is set is one which is gaining increased attention, both in marketing and public relations. While there is strong descriptive evidence in this article of increased public relations activity both in marketing and corporate communications – and, further, some evidence of interaction between the two types of communications – such evidence needs placing on a more robust footing by further research in the area. One of the major problems encountered in the research is the lack of a sound theoretical base on which deductive hypotheses could be grounded. Thus while the approach adopted is exploratory and descriptive the argument propounded is largely inductive in character. The conclusions are drawn from a small subgroup within the FMCG sector. Such a subgroup is certainly important based on their strong propensity for above-the-line communications. The research reported nonetheless could be regarded as probing a new, probably substantive, methodological area[38] which is presently, owing to its state of development, resting on still unformalized and unintegrated, hypothetical and methodological arguments.

Thus this article could be seen as an introduction to the subject under consideration. While interviews are one way of obtaining information in an exploratory sense the general approach adopted needs tightening. Specifically public relations in relation to marketing and corporate communications requires greater analysis before firm conclusions can be reached. The question of whether an increase in PR emphasis and expenditure is taking place in FMCG firms requires further analysis with a larger sample of firms. However, based on the qualitative interviews, an analysis has been put forward in relation to the research questions – it has been tentatively established that there has been increased emphasis and expenditure on public relations based on environmental factors, together with a perceived degree of integration between corporate and marketing public relations. The evidence points to a growing development of usage of and correspondence between general/corporate and marketing public relations – a correspondence affecting the propensity of fast-moving consumer goods firms to market their products and, indeed, themselves.

NOTES AND REFERENCES

1 Kitchen, P. J. and Proctor, R. A., 'The Increasing Importance of Public Relations in Fast Moving Consumer Goods Firms', *Journal of Marketing Management*, Vol. 7 No. 4, October 1991, pp. 357–70.
2 Bernstein, J., 'PR in Top Communication Role', *Advertising Age*, Vol. 59, November 1988, p. 28.
3 Dilenschneider, R. and Edelman, D., 'PR on the Offensive', *Advertising Age*, Vol. 60, 13 March 1990, p. 20.
4 Novelli, W. D., 'Stir Some PR into Your Communication Mix', *Marketing News*, Vol. 22, 5 December 1988, p. 19.
5 Walker, A., 'The Public Relations Literature', *Public Relations Quarterly*, Summer 1988, pp. 27–31.
6 Moore, H. F. and Kalupa, F. B., *Public Relations, Principles, Cases and Problems*, 9th ed., Richard D. Irwin, Homewood, IL, 1985.
7 Institute of Public Relations, United Kingdom, 1991.
8 Rice, M., 'Press Agents that Became Part of a Management Team', *Campaign*, August 1980.
9 Cutlip, S. M., Center, A. H. and Broom, G. M., *Effective Public Relations*, Prentice-Hall International, Englewood Cliffs, NJ, and Hemel Hempstead, 1985.
10 Lesly, P. (Ed.), *Lesly's Public Relations Handbook*, Prentice-Hall, Englewood Cliffs, NJ, 1983.
11 Kitchen, P. J., 'Developing Use of PR in a Fragmented Demassified Market', *Marketing Intelligence & Planning*, Vol. 9 No. 2, 1991.
12 Kotler, P., *Marketing Management, Analysis, Planning Implementation and Control*, Prentice-Hall International, Englewood Cliffs, NJ, and Hemel Hempstead, 1991.
13 White, J., *How to Understand and Manage Public Relations*, Business Books, London, 1991.
14 Gage, T. J., 'PR Ripens Role in Marketing', *Advertising Age*, Vol. 52, 5 January 1981.
15 Kreitzman, L., 'Balancing Brand Building Blocks', *Marketing*, 13 November 1986.

16 Goldman, T., 'Big Spenders Develop Newspaper Strategies', *Marketing Communications*, Vol. 13 No. 1, January 1988.

17 Merims, A. M. 'Marketing's Stepchild: Product Publicity', *Harvard Business Review*, Vol. 36 No. 5, November – December 1972.

18 Livesey, F. and Lennon, P., 'Factors Affecting Consumers Choice between Manufacturer Brands and Retailer Own Labels', *European Journal of Marketing*, Vol. 12 No. 2, Summer 1978.

19 Murphy, P. and Laczniak, G., 'Generic Supermarket Items: A Product and Consumer Analysis', *Journal of Retailing*, Vol. 55 No. 2, Summer 1979.

20 Sheath, K. and McGoldrick, P., 'Generics – Their Development in Grocery Retailing and the Reaction of Consumers', UMIST Working Paper, August 1981.

21 *Times 1000*, Financial Times Publications, 1989.

22 Tull, D. S. and Hawkins, D. I., *Marketing Research: Measurement and Method*, 5th ed., Macmillan, London, 1990.

23 *Marketing Week*, 1990, 1991.

24 Linstead, S. and Turner, K., 'Business Sponsorship of the Arts; Corporate Image and Business Policy', *Management Research News*, Vol. 9 No. 3, pp. 11–13.

25 Strong, E. K., *The Psychology of Selling*, McGraw-Hill, New York, NY, 1925.

26 Evans, J. R. and Berman, B., *Marketing*, 4th ed., Maxwell Macmillan International, New York and London, 1990.

27 Kirkham, M., 'The Need for VCR Research', *ADMAP*, July 1982.

28 Lind, H., 'Probing the Big Turn-off', *Marketing*, 24 February 1983.

29 Bloom, D., 'Point of Sale Scanners and Their Implications for Market Research', *Journal of the Market Research Society*, Vol. 22 No. 4, 1980.

30 Swan, J., 'Price-Product Performance Competition between Retailer and Manufacturer Brands', *Journal of Marketing*, Vol. 38 No. 3, July 1974.

31 Jones, J. P., 'The Double Jeopardy of Sales Promotions', *Harvard Business Review*, Vol. 68 No. 5, September/October 1990.

32 Zikmund, W. and D'Amico, M., *Marketing*, 3rd ed., John Wiley & Sons, London, 1989.

33 Cohen, W. A., *The Practice of Marketing Management*, Macmillan, London, 1988.

34 Cutlip, S. C., Center, A. H. and Broom, G. H. *Effective Public Relations*, 6th ed. Prentice-Hall International, Englewood Cliffs, NJ, and Hemel Hempstead, 1985.

35 Goldman, J., *Public Relations in the Marketing Mix: Introducing Vulnerability Relations*, NTC business Books, Lincolnwood, IL, 1984.

36 *Economic Trends* (1981–1991), Central Statistical Office, HMSO, London.

37 Further information on *MEAL* data can be obtained directly from Register House, 4 Holdford Yard, Cruikshank Street, London WC1X 9HD. Tel: 0171 833 1212.

38 Mills, C. W., *The Sociological Imagination*, Oxford University Press, New York, NY, 1959, pp. 31–72.

Kitchen, P. J. (1993), 'Public relations: A rationale for its development and usage within UK fast-moving consumer goods firms'. *European Journal of Marketing*, Vol. 27, Issue 7, pp. 53–75. Reproduced with permission.

6.3 Competition, strategy, technology and people: the challenges facing PR

Sally Dibb, Lyndon Simkin and Adam Vancini

INTRODUCTION

Public relations is widely defined. There are generally two core elements, however: communication and management. According to Hunt and Grunig (1994), public relations is the formal way in which organisations communicate with their publics. Public relations, though, is planned or managed, so public relations is the management of communication between an organisation and its publics. In many businesses, PR activity occurred only when an organisation faced a crisis of confidence in its publics (Jefkins, 1988). However, over the last decade, the public relations (PR) industry has grown in size and importance as more organisations have recognised the need to maintain consistent and on-going communications with their publics and target audiences – and not only in times of crisis (Dibb *et al.* 1994a). Having established its credentials and a significant portion of the promotional mix budget, the turbulent business environment, harmonisation of Europe, opportunities in the ever more accessible Eastern bloc, dramatic changes in media technology, the evolving debate about corporate brand management and competitive pressures of a maturing industry (Hiebert, 1992; Shell, 1992) are forcing many leading PR consultancies to now face up to the growing challenges in the industry.

Among these trends are management changes which should present an impressive opportunity for the public relations function (Kitchen and White, 1992). There is increasingly diverse involvement, in most sectors of industry and commerce, of stakeholders: simple shareholder ownership-dividend concern is now only one issue. Stakeholders, too, are more broadly defined: interest groups such as suppliers, customers, the community, environmental groups and employees are all seen to have stakes in the actions of businesses (anon, 1993; Lindenburg *et al.*, 1994). It is no longer possible for companies to simply operate within the limits of the law and assume that they have met their responsibilities. As these outside stakeholders become a more significant influence on a company's ability to successfully operate, the organisation must take an active role in informing its publics of company actions and policies to increase their levels of involvement and knowledge. For most companies it is in their own best interest to maintain good relationships with the various interest groups which exist: an important role for public relations.

There are various current trends highlighted in the literature (e.g.: Horner, 1992; Jarboe, 1994; Kitchen and White, 1992; Mazur, 1994), including the maintenance of employee relations, the importance of corporate branding, environmental concerns, trading bloc changes, technology within the media, plus the blurring divide between certain PR and advertising activities. These are creating opportunities and, potentially, threats for organisations operating in the PR industry:

- The maintenance of good employee relations is dependent on effective communication between management and labour (Lindenburg *et al.*, 1994, Mazur, 1994). The need for effective employee communications is especially recognised during periods of corporate change. The implementation of IT programs, the need for corporate downsizing which often necessitates redundancies, and the actions taken during business re-process engineering – all currently live issues in many businesses – present unstable conditions for labour and raise the potential for management/labour tension. Executives are now realising the importance of good internal and external communications during these periods of stress in maintaining good relations with the workforce.
- Increasing importance is being placed on both corporate branding and product branding. PR is seen as a means to increase this brand awareness, building favourable attitudes among customers and in turn increasing sales. It is no longer sufficient for a company to simply brand its products. At present, the decisions of the customer can be as often a result of company familiarity as product familiarity (Wilcox *et al.*, 1995).
- The recent Brent Spar incident is a case in which the actions of an environmental special interest group 'succeeded in turning (an isolated incident) into a symbol of man's misuse of the oceans' (Wybrew, 1995), dominating the policy of a major multinational corporation. The facts of this incident were not as important as the image of the firm and the interpretation of its actions. The effects of the Brent Spar case on the bottom line of Shell will never be known but 'the incident will probably dominate the firm's actions for years to come'. PR was used effectively by the environmental pressure groups, but also by beleaguered Shell. This is unlikely to be the last of such high profile cases, with the growing consumer awareness of 'green' issues.
- Changes involving trading blocs such as the EU and NAFTA are creating political and regulatory impacts: these policies have wide-ranging effects on most industries (Hiebert, 1992). As changes to regulatory systems and international organisations occur, there is an increasing need for businesses to lobby for legislation and regulations which promote their respective industries, drawing on the skills of the PR practitioner.
- The opening of Eastern Europe and the former Soviet Union has caused dramatic changes in the world business environment (Shell, 1992; Dibb *et al.*, 1994a). This includes the creation of a huge new market for western goods and the massive switch from government-controlled enterprise to private industry. Western companies and brands are utilising the full range of marketing communications tools to enter these markets, specifically to lay careful foundations with regulators and trade bodies.

Each of these factors serves to create the need for good communications. In addition, there are changes in the functions of the media which are affecting the way in which PR operates (Brody, 1992, Dibb *et al.*, 1994b): such as the grey areas which have come to exist between advertising and PR – infomercials and advertorials (Wilcox *et al.*, 1995) – and changing technology (Angela Heylin of Charles Barker). However, no matter the driver or specific changing force, the common link is that the changes which are occurring are providing the PR function with several opportunities including offering the function the opportunity to become more than just a tactical tool in the promotional mix. There is no doubt that this is a time of significant growth for the function of public relations (BDO SH, 1994; Dibb *et al.*, 1994a). Equally, there are important trends developing which will have significant impact on the shape of the industry and the working practices of the consultancies. The industry needs to take stock of these issues and understand their implications.

This paper reviews these issues based on the opinions of leading exponents and practitioners as surveyed during the summer of 1995. The sentiments of these practitioners expanded significantly on recent papers in the literature, describing a series of underlying trends which must be formally addressed by PR practitioners if market opportunities are to be taken.

A SURVEY OF CURRENT TRENDS

This paper presents (a) an overview of the analysis of the most important trends in the PR sector, and (b) an evaluation of the way in which PR consultancies are dealing or facing up to these significant issues. The primary source of information for this study was provided through extensive interviews with leading UK PR consultancies, supported by a review of the literature and the views of trade associations/interested parties. Some of the consultancies interviewed included Burson-Marsteller, Charles Barker, Countrywide, Hill-Knowlton, PRA, Scope Communications and Shandwick. A core list of key themes came out very strongly, including the competitive situation and increasing specialisation; internationalism; recruitment, training, motivation of personnel; involvement in clients' strategy formulation; establishing the value of PR activity; the significant ripples caused by the information highway and changing technology in the media; and an increasing overlap with the world of advertising. Each of these issues is discussed, along with some immediate concerns in terms of their likely impact.

Competition and specialisation

Of the practitioners who were interviewed for this study, all indicated important changes occurring in the nature of competition in the PR industry. In particular, concern was expressed regarding the changing nature of the competitive groups as well as the strategies which are currently being pursued by the most successful firms. It was felt by all respondents that the most important of these strategies appears to be the nature of specialisation of the various firms.

Specialisation has been mentioned consistently as one of the most important drivers of the PR industry (Public Relations Consultants' Association, 1994; Shimp, 1993). The ability for firms to specialise has been one of the main reasons that smaller, more focused firms are apparently able to provide effective competition for the large consultancies. The need for specialisation has caused large consultancies to concentrate in specific sectors. For example, some of the most innovative and fastest growing PR firms have built their businesses by specialising on specific areas of PR, such as *Text 100* in high-tech areas and *Medical Actions Communications* in the health-care field.

The concept of specialisation – niching – is an accepted warfare strategy and one well deployed in the marketing domain (Saunders, 1991). Specialisation in PR is manifesting itself in a curious mix of guises. First, small firms have the ability to compete with the larger PR consultancies by focusing on a particular specialisation. Second, large firms are creating an internal structure which focuses on specialisation. By creating what are in effect many small, specialist firms acting under one roof, the large PR consultancy can achieve the same level of specialisation as the smaller firm, whilst enjoying the benefits of being a large agency. In addition, multi-dimensional teams can be created by combining various specialisations, which allows the consultancy to provide the most appropriate product to the customer. Third, there are several non-industry firms such as law firms and management consultancies which, due to their existing capabilities, can provide competition in certain specialist areas of PR. Examples of this can be seen in competition from law firms in areas such as public affairs and lobbying, and management consultants moving into internal PR (Dibb *et al.*, 1995).

For the large PR consultancy the increase in specialisation requires a different strategic outlook than has historically existed. While in the past, PR firms have tried to become one-stop shops for PR and all the related functions, now these firms must become highly focused specialists. The combination of small, internal divisions based on specialisation, with large firm's capabilities which allow for cross-functional inter-specialist support, means the big PR consultancies seem to be in a good position to compete with these other groups.

Internationalisation

Comments from all respondents suggest that the credibility to effectively implement an international campaign is increasingly deemed necessary by clients selecting a PR consultancy. This involves combining in-house language and culture skills and knowledge of global marketing environment issues, suitable branch networks or strategic alliances with PR firms in key international business centres. This research has found that the variety of ways chosen by PR practitioners to develop an international presence and capability has involved every conceivable combination of these approaches. It would seem that in the PR industry, the jury is still out as to the best means of developing an international capability. The requirement, though, to be seen as an international player is unanimously acknowledged as a leading strategic focus.

The concept of internationalisation is a widely debated issue in the PR industry. While some firms see internationalisation as the key to future strategies, others wonder whether the truly international campaign is necessary or even achievable, given cultural, brand and language differences (Doyle, 1994). Nevertheless, internationalisation is seen to be a crucial aspect of the business environment, and one the large PR consultancies must address.

The discrepancy of opinions regarding the relative importance of internationalisation could be caused by several factors. While some of the executives who were interviewed saw internationalisation as the key to future strategies, others were of the opinion that this feature is simply 'window dressing'. Those executives who played down the importance of internationalisation generally – and perhaps not surprisingly – came from smaller and more domestically focused companies. However, even those who emphasised internationalisation agreed that the means of becoming 'international' are extremely expensive and may not be cost-effective in terms of revenue gains. This raises further questions about whether these moves towards internationalisation will become profitable and if so, over what time frame. A rather more fundamental question concerns whether an international PR campaign is really what the customer wants. On this subject again the interviewees were not in agreement, yet none could support their assertions with client feedback or market research findings. This lack of evidence indicates a need for consultancies, especially those which have internationally driven strategies, to perform a customer audit to develop a better understanding of key customer needs and perceptions in relation to internationalisation. It is only by finding out how important this factor is to their customers that these firms will be able to understand the full importance of internationalisation.

Despite the confusion and disagreement about internationalism generally, large PR consultancies demonstrated surprisingly consistent opinions about the need for campaigns to be locally focused to be successful. While the international campaign does exist, each of the firms surveyed maintained that the strength of any campaign came from the ability to perform in a focused and locally orientated fashion, reflecting local customer values, the perceptions of those target publics, brand values, local media activity, culture and language. Here, there is significant overlap with the thoughts of the leading advertising agencies (Dibb *et al.*, 1994b), who also believe they must offer pan-European and global capability in order to maintain client loyalty and commitment, but through locally customised media applications.

Personnel, strategy and evaluation

While the importance of good PR is becoming more widely recognised by marketing professionals and corporate boards, the image of the PR industry does not seem to be making considerable gains (Kitchen and White, 1992). This is attributable to several factors. The first of these is the history of the image of publicity and PR in the UK. While PR no longer can be considered as canvassing and journalist-baiting based on 'champagne lunches', there is still a negative perception of the depth, expertise and professionalism of PR in the minds of many media personnel and corporate managers. While the importance of relationship building in the media is still recognised as a core requirement in PR to facilitate its application (Mazur, 1994), there are several other aspects of PR which are of far greater importance (Brody, 1992). While the historic image of PR cannot be quickly changed, there are several issues which must be addressed in helping to enhance the image of PR, including the training and recruitment of practitioners, the use of PR in strategy, the justification of the tool's worth, and the overall professionalism of the industry.

While the need to up-grade the industry's own image is a perfect application for a PR campaign, there are in fact several management areas in which the PR industry lags behind other industries. To enhance the reputation of PR and further establish its credentials, these must be addressed. Of the executives interviewed, most agreed that the three primary areas are:

1 The investment in personnel including recruitment and training necessary to recruit and retain good people. The importance of people as the most valuable resource in the industry further emphasises this point (Kinnick and Cameron, 1994). In addition, there is an accepted need for PR to develop better management skills and processes.
2 The limited use of PR as a strategic tool as opposed to simply a tactical promotional tool.

3 The need for PR to establish and provide a means for evaluating its results which it can in turn effectively communicate to its clientele.

Personnel

As in any services business, an important part of establishing PR as a legitimate professional service comes from the hiring and retention of quality people (Dibb *et al.*, 1994a). Since personnel is also the greatest cost to PR firms, it is especially important that the value of this essential asset is not overlooked. As with most marketing services, the recession forced PR firms to look carefully at their cost structure, resulting in many redundancies and budget cuts. However, despite industry concern regarding the reduction in personnel, most executives agree that the redundancies helped weed out those who were 'less essential', and in the long-term, strengthened the industry. While the recession may indeed have helped to slim down operations and identify essential and non-essential personnel, there still seems to be a low investment in human resources and training throughout the industry. Although human resources represent over 50% of costs, employee training accounts for less than 1% of employee costs. This lack of training investment is acknowledged by the executives interviewed who almost all expressed disappointment in the amount of training provided for their personnel. Disappointment was also expressed regarding the industry's approach to graduate recruitment. These views concur with the recent survey by Kinnick and Cameron (1994) into the teaching of public relations management, poor structuring of programmes and erratic emphasis on PR tools versus process skills in courses. Their study found that few graduates or trainees were given adequate grounding in either the tactical or process skills of public relations.

In general, most firms do have formal recruitment programmes, but the total amount of graduate recruitment is felt to be minimal relative to the industry size. It also appears that the poor general image of the PR industry has contributed to a vicious circle in which the best and the brightest marketing personnel and graduates tend to avoid PR due to its lack of respectability and relative immaturity as an accepted profession within marketing communications (anon, 1993: Kinnick and Cameron, 1994).

Developing effective recruitment and training programmes is especially important given the PR industry's stated and apparently widespread desire to play an increasing role in strategy formulation (Horner, 1992; Mazur, 1994). While PR is seemingly increasingly available as a strategy tool and to assist in the strategy formulation of clients (anon, 1993), it is difficult to imagine PR firms contributing to their clients' strategy without the knowledge of, and/or training in, management processes and strategic planning skills. Once again the issue of legitimising the industry emerges, with the inevitable conclusion that if the industry wishes to be seen as truly 'professional' (along the lines of advertising or marketing research), it must make the attempt to professionalise. Where better to start than with its most vital resource, its people: recruitment, training, skill-base, motivation and nurturing.

Strategy

One of the most important short-term and long-term goals for the PR industry is to establish itself as a contributor to strategy formulation and not just as a marketing tool (Horner, 1992; Mazur, 1994). This is seen as leverage for growth; a means for boosting the image of PR and its practitioners; and a way of building on the boardroom links developed by the PR consultant anyway as part of establishing a well-structured PR mechanism for clients (Kitchen and White, 1992). The leading practitioners interviewed believe that as consultancies move more into the role of strategic advisors, PR will become more respected and seen more as an integral function within a client organisation.

For the PR industry to successfully move into a strategic function, firms must begin training personnel in strategic management. In the short term, strategic skills can be enhanced by recruiting managers from blue chip companies' management programmes. A potential barrier which emerges is the restraining factor which comes from management skills in a creative industry and the likelihood that managerial processes could stifle creativity or cause inordinate delays. However, it is believed that the friction between creativity and management does not seem to be significant in the PR industry; executives hope the two aspects are not mutually exclusive. It should be emphasised that while respondents generally want to work at a more strategic level, a few pragmatic senior figures recognise that many PR firms have a credibility gap to overcome in achieving this goal. There is the added risk that PR firms begin to antagonise management consultancies, who currently often act as the strategy advisors.

If PR is to contribute to the task of strategy formulation, changes are needed both internally and externally. Internally, PR firms must develop a more strategic focus, as opposed to being strictly creative. Externally, PR firms must show they have the ability to be more than just a tactical promotional function, turned to in moments of crisis to help overcome adverse publicity or maximise a product breakthrough. Firms must then communicate with their clients regarding the role of PR as a strategic aspect rather than as a simple tactical promotional tool. One leading practitioner went as far as stating, 'in order to be permitted to fulfil our remit as PR experts, we increasingly have to demonstrate we understand a client's business strategy. We are still unusual. We have a few directors who can do this. Once there, why not use our experiences and awareness of the client's diverse mix of publics to help in his strategy formulation? Indeed, to survive in the ever-evolving communications business, with radically changing technologies, we will need to do more of this work!' The skill-base in most PR consultancies is still far from adequate to fulfil this desire, as is the credibility of PR to occupy the role of strategic advisor.

Evaluation

As in all areas of marketing communications (Flandin et al., 1992), there is a growing need to prove the value and worth of PR budgets. Marketing budgets are not infinite and in times of slump, promotional budgets are generally severely trimmed back. The perhaps dated image of the PR industry as lobbyists used to wining and dining journalist contacts has created a negative perception which must be overcome by the ever more professional PR practitioners. Given the PR profession's goal of becoming a recognised and legitimate strategic function (Brody, 1992), this is particularly important if credentials are to be established. Most management functions must be monitored as part of the strategic process, and assessment is only possible with some sort of concrete evaluation (Flandin et al., 1992). Most promotional industries are trying to establish performance measures and benchmarking of successful applications. PR is not any different and PR firms increasingly must be able to justify their expense with observable results (Jarboe, 1994). In most businesses, any function which does not directly add value will be subject to intense scrutiny by senior management (Dibb *et al.*, 1994a). It is therefore necessary for the PR industry to further establish itself by definitive evaluation processes (Wiesendanger, 1994): whether by greater use of qualitative tracking and perception studies, clippings counts, attempts to develop more objective mathematical assessment models, or ideally, some combination of these approaches.

Technology

Technological advances are impacting on all business functions in all industries. PR is certainly not unaffected (Kitchen and White, 1992; Wiesendanger, 1994). While this subject was outside the scope of this study explicitly, the practitioners surveyed raised important concerns about the information technology explosion and some obvious impacts on the world of PR. The Internet, business television, smart telephony and the increased use of video were raised specifically. Segmentation of the media, including cable television, interactive software and the growing use of direct mail, clearly has implications in terms of the application of PR and the greater range of skills required by PR practitioners. Increases in the speed of information transfer have greatly affected the ways in which PR consultancies do business, and potentially offer a means for PR consultancies to differentiate themselves. In addition, while historically PR practitioners have been wordsmiths, visual application software and changing technology have opened up a range of new possibilities for PR consultants. There is widespread agreement that technology is going to change the face of PR and the daily working practices of PR practitioners. To what extent is very much an unknown!

Views on the Internet vary from consultancy to consultancy. While some see the information highway as the wave of the future, others still have to be convinced that the majority of communications receivers will have or want access to this tool. As the information highway is becoming more of a reality there are ever-increasing channels for communication. Since the marketer's dream is to segment the market as much as possible and create brand differentiation (Doyle, 1994), the best case scenario for PR is one which still allows personal selling, with its persuasive and communication benefits. The intriguing mix of the info-highway and PC/TVs can create this, with the operator choosing the required path to follow. In effect this allows marketers to cater to any individual's particular needs by giving the targeted customer/media personnel the ability to ignore any unwanted information. This approach, respondents believe, should be applied to PR. As more people have access to the broadening forms of IT-based communication, there are ever-increasing possibilities for PR practitioners to reach their audiences.

If the most effective use is to be made of the new technologies, it is important to consider how different forms of communication affect the message delivered: for example, how do individuals perceive messages when they are delivered in different fashions, particularly through IT systems/networks? Some PR executives believe that it is only a matter of time before use of printed media is virtually eliminated! Others anticipate a negative reaction to certain IT-based communications applications in specific markets or for certain brands. As 'high-tech' communications become more common, it is going to be necessary for any organisation in which communications plays an important role to be able to deliver messages in the most appropriate means, including by the latest information-highway.

The increasing uses for technology not only apply to the PR consultancy's ability to deliver its product but also relate to strategy work and particularly to the desire for internationalisation. In particular, the problems which arise in internationalising often occur because companies are unable to portray a common set of values or company culture throughout the organisation (Keegan, 1989). The quick and easy means for delivering information through such routes as e-mail, faxes, and televised conferences can help international companies to maintain internal coherence as well as delivering a more consistent message in other countries. By making the transfer of information easy, a multinational leverages the ideas of its staff and spreads organisational values (Quelch and Hoff, 1986).

The effects of changing technology are of great concern to the PR industry. Not only does technology affect the type of PR being undertaken, it also affects the means for communicating messages, and in fact, constantly creates new areas of emphasis for marketing communications in general. Since the primary purpose of PR is to communicate, the changes in technology have a particularly significant role in this industry. Through this research, it has become apparent that new technology affects almost every area of PR. For the future prospects of PR, it is necessary for most firms to take advantage of the benefits which these technologies offer. This entails not only using new means to deliver messages, but creating new areas of the PR function such as infomercials and advertorials which broaden the scope of the industry, resulting in industry growth and a quickly changing, ever more complex operating environment.

One last area which most respondents mentioned is the grey region which exists between PR and advertising. This area includes such new communications tools as infomercials and advertorials: there appears to be a war building over which function will control these features (Burnett, 1993; Wilcox *et al.*, 1995). Several of the interviewees mentioned these areas as points of potential conflict and it will be interesting to see which profession, advertising, PR or other, will take up these roles.

CONCLUSIONS

The PR industry appears to be facing a period of significant change. While the changes which are occurring in the world's business environment are confronting most industries with new challenges as well as new opportunities, these changes are having particular effect on the PR industry. As with most areas of marketing services, PR is being forced to respond to these changes, affecting the outlook of every PR consultancy.

The management trends which have developed in the 1990s present many opportunities for the public relations function. These trends include the growing concern of stakeholders other than for the traditional issue of ownership/dividends. There are many other individuals and groups which businesses must consider while making strategic and tactical decisions. Groups such as suppliers, customers, the community, environmental groups and employees all have stakes in the actions of businesses and it is now necessary for most companies to consider these players and influences. As these outside stakeholders become a factor in a company's ability to successfully operate, it is in the business's best interest to take a proactive role in informing these groups as to corporate strategy, actions and policy.

In the course of this study, it has become apparent that the majority of PR consultancies in the UK are forming strategies which take into account the key trends. The primary strategies which have come to light include the move to specialisation as a means to compete in an increasingly aggressive environment; internationalisation as a lever for growth and as a competitive tool against rivals; and, to enhance the image and professionalism of the PR industry, an increase or improvement in training, recruitment, evaluation, and in the role of strategy forming for clients. An important development is the awareness of the increasing use of different media and new technology to become more competitive and to create new vistas in which PR can function.

The various trends which are occurring in the PR industry provide an interesting environment in which PR consultancies must operate. While PR has often been viewed as a 'Cinderella' industry, to quote one leading practitioner, the current direction of the industry seems to be very much in the hands of the practitioners. If the leaders in the PR industry can seize the opportunities with which they are presently faced, PR might very well be able to make the jump from tactical marketing tool to a strategic necessity for clients. While the majority of the participants in this study are aware of these opportunities, seemingly PR is not fulfilling its potential. The primary findings of this study are that PR consultants must continue to focus on the strategies which will increase their business capabilities (internationalisation, technology and specialisation) as well as those which will enhance the industry's image as a whole (training and evaluation). If these goals can be met, the PR industry may finally gain the recognition it seeks, and take advantage of the core underlying trends.

REFERENCES

Anon, (1993), 'Public Affairs Matures as Strategic Management Tool', *Public Relations Journal*, 49 (2), p. 8.

BDO Stoy Hayward Management Consultants, (1994), *The Public Relations Sector*, London: Department of Trade and Industry.

Brody, E. W., (1992), 'Long-Term Results – and Penalties', *Public Relations Quarterly*, 37 (2), pp. 22–28.

Burnett, J. J., (1992), *Promotion Management*, Boston: Houghton Mifflin.

Dibb, S., Kojima, R. and Simkin, L., (1995), 'Marketing Practice in Management Consultancies', *Journal of Management Consulting*, 11 (4), forthcoming.

Dibb, S., Simkin, L., Pride, W. and Ferrell, O. C., (1994), *Marketing: Concepts & Strategies*, Boston: Houghton Mifflin.

Dibb, S., Simkin, L. and Yuen, R., (1994), 'Pan-European Advertising: Think Europe – Act Local', *International Journal of Advertising*, 13 (2), pp. 125–136.

Doyle, P., (1994), *Marketing Management and Strategy*, London: Prentice-Hall.

Flandin, M. P., Martin, E. and Simkin, L., (1992), 'Advertising Effectiveness Research: a Survey of Agencies, Clients and Conflicts', *International Journal of Advertising*, 11 (3), pp. 203–214.

Hiebert, R. E., (1992), 'Public Relations and Mass Communications in Eastern Europe', *Public Relations Review*, 18 (2), pp. 177–187.

Horner, T. F., (1992), 'Superficial PR Doesn't Do The Job', *National Underwriter*, 96 (22), pp. 45–46.

Hunt, T. and Grunig, J. E., (1994), *Public Relations Techniques*, Fort Worth: Holt, Rinehart and Winston.

Jarboe, G., (1994), 'Count Your Clippings', *Marketing Computer*, 14 (5), p. 22.

Jefkins, F., (1988), *Public Relations Techniques*, London: Heinemann.

Keegan, W. J., (1989), *Global Marketing Management*, Englewood Cliffs, NJ: Prentice-Hall.

Kinnick, K. N. and Cameron, G. T., (1994), 'Teaching Public Relations Management: The Current State-of-the-Art', *Public Relations Review*, 20 (1), pp. 73–88.

Kitchen, P. J. and White, J., (1992), 'Public Relations – Developments', *Marketing Intelligence & Planning*, 10 (2), pp. 14–17.

Lindenburg, J. G., Schlachtmeyer, A. and Jones, M. B., (1994), 'Trends in Benefits Design', *Journal of Compensation & Benefits*, 9 (6), pp. 60–62.

Mazur, L., (1994), 'The Bigger Picture', *Marketing*, Feb. 14, p. 111.

Public Relations Consultants' Association, (1994), *So You Want To Work In PR*, London: Public Relations Consultants' Association.

Quelch, J. and Hoff, E. (1986), 'Customising Global Marketing', *Harvard Business Review*, May/June, 64 (3), pp. 59–68.

Saunders, J. (1991), 'Marketing and Competitive Success', in *The Marketing Book* (Ed, Baker, M.), London: Butterworth Heinemann.

Shell, A., (1992), 'As Iron Curtain Falls, Public Relations Rises', *Public Relations Journal,* 48 (1), p. 14.

Shimp, T., (1993), *Promotion Management and Marketing Communications,* Fort Worth: Dryden.

Wiesendanger, B., (1994), 'Plug Into a World of Information', *Public Relations Journal,* 50 (2), pp. 20–23.

Wilcox, D., Ault, P. and Agee, W., (1995), *Public Relations Strategies and Tactics*, New York: Harper Collins.

Wybrew, J., (1995), 'Brent Spar – Far More Than a PR War', *The Institute of Public Relations Journal*, 14 (2).

Dibb, S. Simkin, L. and Vancini, A. (1996) 'Competition, strategy, technology and people: the challenges facing PR'. *International Journal of Advertising*, 15(2): 116–127. Reproduced with permission.

Consumer and non-consumer stakeholder orientation in U.K. companies

6.4

Gordon E. Greenley and Gordon R. Foxall

The interests of stakeholder groups constitute diverse sets of expectations, needs and values (Harrison and St. John, 1994; King and Cleland, 1978). Failure on the part of companies to satisfy the interests of particular stakeholder groups may be detrimental to company performance (Freeman, 1984, MacMillan and Jones, 1986), although it may not be possible to satisfy the interests of all groups simultaneously owing to the scarcity of resources and managerial capabilities (Barney, 1991; Grant, 1991; Mahoney and Pandian, 1992). Moreover, as companies become part of networks of strategic alliances, the implementation of their strategies will depend on the control of these alliances, which may also have implications for their treatment of the competing interests of stakeholders (Webster, 1992). Despite these problems, there is no empirical evidence concerning the relative attention that companies give to stakeholder groups.

This article addresses this deficiency by reporting an empirical study concerning the attention given by a sample of U.K. companies to five stakeholder groups: competitors, consumers, employees, shareholders, and unions. The article first discusses the current literature on stakeholders, from which the research hypotheses were derived. Second, it describes the methodology used, including the multivariate measures used to assess company orientation to each stakeholder group. Finally, the article presents and discusses the results and their implications for understanding stakeholder orientation.

LITERATURE ON STAKEHOLDERS

A stakeholder is any group or individual who can affect, or is affected by, the achievement of an organization's purpose (Rhenman, 1968; Freeman, 1984). The strategic importance of stakeholders is emphasized by MacMillan and Jones (1986), who argue that 'stakeholder support is essential, or their opposition must be negated, if a major strategic change is to be successfully implemented.' The range of stakeholder interests encountered by most companies is illustrated by Freeman's (1984) 'stakeholder map,' which describes the range of groups as: government, political groups, shareholders, financial community, activist groups, consumers, consumer advocate groups, unions, employees, trade associations, competitors, and suppliers.

This stakeholder map represents a wide and diverse range of interests (Harrison and St. John, 1994), given that each stakeholder group has its own set of expectations, needs, and values (King and Cleland, 1978). This diversity of interests provides a potential problem for companies: failure to satisfy particular groups may be detrimental to the achievement of an organization's purpose (Harrison and St. John, 1994; Freeman, 1984; Rhenman, 1968), as defined by the organization's executives in its mission and objectives, and may result in opposition to major strategic change (MacMillan and Jones, 1986), as planned by its executives in its strategies. However, attempting to satisfy the interests of all groups may not be possible, depending on the scarcity of current resources and managerial capabilities (Barney, 1991; Grant, 1991; Mahoney and Pandian, 1992), and may require difficult decisions about the allocation of scarce current resources among stakeholders. Attempting to satisfy all stakeholder groups may also include difficult decisions about the acquisition of additional future resources and managerial capabilities, the accumulation of slack resources, and their allocation to stakeholder groups.

The search of the literature has identified four key issues: stakeholder orientation, associations among stakeholder orientations, the importance of consumers, and market environment alignment. These issues are discusses later, and are depicted in Figure 1.

Addressing stakeholder interests

The marketing and strategic management literatures differ with respect to whether or not companies should attempt to address the interests of all stakeholder groups. In the

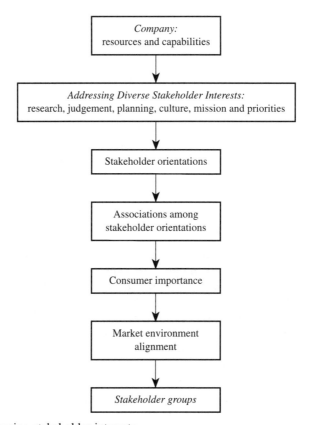

Figure 1 Addressing stakeholder interests.

marketing literature, consumers constitute the central group. The emphasis is on not only orientating corporate decision-making in general to the consumer, but also on giving specific priority to satisfying consumers' needs in preference to those of other stakeholder groups (Anderson, 1982; Kotler, 1991; Piercy, 1992). In the trend towards relationship marketing, Webster (1992) goes so far as to claim that, owing to the development of new organizational forms that have prompted attention toward relationships, the key strategic resource is consumer relationships. Much of the strategic management literature, by contrast, generally assumes that companies should, in order to be successful, satisfy the interests of all their stakeholder groups (Freeman, 1984; Hill and Jones, 1992; Pearce and Robinson, 1994). Kimberly *et al.* (1983) and Kotter (1990) have argued that it is critical for companies to address these diverse stakeholder interests, whereas Chakravarthy (1986) maintains that a necessary condition for 'excellence' in the continued cooperation of all groups.

In spite of these entrenched positions, and the prescriptive principles to which they give rise, little empirical evidence has been published to show what attention companies actually given to potentially conflicting stakeholder interests. What evidence there is comes from two broadly based organizational studies, in which stakeholders were only part of the overall investigations (Aupperle *et al., 1995; Posner and Schmidt, 1984; these studies are reviewed later). Consequently, this evidence cannot contribute to understanding the relative attention that companies give to stakeholder groups, when addressing their diverse interests.*

Although there is negligible empirical evidence, there are two broad conceptual approaches that theorize about the way that companies should attempt to address the diverse interests of stakeholders. The first has been developed by Miller and Lewis (1991) as a value exchange model (see also Miller *et al.*, 1985 and Kotter, 1990). The principle of this model is that the company is faced with planning a balance between its own set of values and needs, and the set of values and needs of each stakeholder group. In this conceptualization, a balance should be pursued by developing exchange relationships with each stakeholder group. The authors recommend that the company should plan to optimize the satisfaction of each set of values and needs, and that the model will be in balance when none of the sets dominates those of the other groups. If an imbalance arises between groups, then resources should be reallocated between groups in order to restore and maintain a balance. In the second approach, Mintzberg (1983) proposes that a balance between internal and external stakeholder groups will result from the different sources of power that they can exert over the company, which he presents as a range of power configurations (see also Pfeffer, 1981). Companies will not seek to optimize the satisfaction of each stakeholder group, but will react to those groups that wield the most power. Campbell and Yeung (1991) also address the problem that firms must make policy decisions about which groups they should attempt to satisfy. In the marketing literature considerable power is assumed to lie with consumers (Anderson, 1982). In addressing this external power, the marketing function is likely to develop internal power, in that it is the function which obviously has most to do with satisfying consumers. This power base means that the objectives of the marketing function are the most likely, of all the business functions, to become the objectives of the whole organization (Hickson *et al.*, 1971; Pfeffer and Salancik, 1977).

These considerations suggest that empirical investigation should first seek to elucidate the relative attention that companies give to stakeholder groups. The prescriptive literature identifies the following elements of managerial and corporate behavior that impinge on the level, style, and content of a company's orientation to each stakeholder group.

Research

As mentioned earlier, Harrison and St. John (1994) and Pearce and Robinson (1994) emphasize the difficulty of analyzing and understanding the diverse interests of stakeholders. However, Harrison and St. John (1994) advocate that a comprehensive understanding of all stakeholder interests is essential to an effective strategic management process, which should be an ongoing and interactive process. Indeed, information inputs are obviously essential to all decision-making throughout strategic management (Grant, 1991; Hill and Jones, 1992; Pearce and Robinson, 1994; Pettigrew and Whipp, 1993). Unfortunately empirical studies of how companies achieve an understanding of their stakeholders are not available, although conceptual models for understanding stakeholders have been proposed (Freeman and Reed, 1983; Harrison and St. John, 1994). However, before such models can be used by firms, information obviously needs to be acquired and judgments made to provide inputs for using these models to achieve an understanding. Therefore, research is needed to understand the interests of each stakeholder group.

Planning

Planning is clearly part of strategic management (Hill and Jones, 1992; Hunger and Wheelen, 1993; Pearce and Robinson, 1994). Several researchers have identified and explained the importance of planning, both as a process for effective management and as a means for improving performance (Dutton and Duncan, 1987; Dyson and Foster, 1982; Greenley, 1983; Ramanujam and Venkatraman, 1987; Sinha, 1990). As mentioned previously, Miller and Lewis (1991) see the core problem of addressing stakeholder interests as one of planning a balance between satisfying the firm's own needs and values, and addressing the diverse range of stakeholder interests. Harrison and St. John (1994) go further and advocate that indeed the whole scope of strategic planning should encompass plans for addressing stakeholder interests. Part of this process includes the relative extent of planning for addressing each stakeholder group, given the availability of resources and managerial capabilities (Barney, 1991; Grant, 1991; Mahoney and Pandian, 1992), which may need to be rationed among stakeholders. Therefore, the relative extent of planning for each stakeholder group reflects attention given to stakeholders.

Corporate mission

An effective mission statement is of central importance for developing strategies that address stakeholder interests (Campbell *et al*., 1990; Campbell and Tawadey, 1990; Campbell and Yeung, 1991; Harrison and St. John, 1994; Pearce and David, 1987). Pearce (1982) argues that stakeholders' interests should be the first inputs in developing a mission, and hence should be the starting point of strategic planning (Hill and Jones, 1993). However, the claims of some stakeholder groups may not be legitimate, and illegitimate claims may impinge on resource allocation to legitimate stakeholder claims (Campbell and Tawadey, 1990; Freeman, 1984). Conversely, Harrison and St. John (1994) claim that the mission statement should also be a vehicle for communicating the firm's overall direction and purpose to its stakeholders.

Indeed, the empirical study by Hooley *et al*. (1991) concluded that, although the mission is meant to have its major impact internally, the external influence should be to improve consumer satisfaction. Therefore, the relative importance of each stakeholder group in the mission reflects the attention given to stakeholders.

Corporate culture

Despite the various focuses on corporate culture in the literature (for example, see Alvesson, 1989; Schein, 1985), the central theme is that it is a set of values, beliefs, and assumptions that guide the decisions and actions of managers (Cleland and King, 1974; Guth and MacMillan, 1986; Schein, 1985). Corporate culture also guides decision-making in strategic planning (Harrison and St. John, 1994; Hassard and Sharifi, 1989), and indeed McDonald and Leppard (1991) found that certain beliefs and values within corporate culture can be a barrier to effective strategic planning. As corporate culture guides the scope of strategic planning, it is also pertinent to planning strategies for addressing stakeholders (Harrison and St. John, 1994). Kotter and Heskett (1992) claim that successful firms particularly value the interests of customers, shareholders, and employees in their cultures, whereas Harrison and St. John (1994) suggest that, for success, firms should particularly value the interests of customers, competitors, and employees. Similarly, Deshpande *et al*. (1993) concluded that companies with a market culture perform better than companies without this focus. In companies where the personal values, beliefs and assumptions of managers are openly discussed, within the context of corporate culture, there will be an opportunity to compare the diverse interests of stakeholder groups with the response of 230 fully completed questionnaires. The sample has similar proportions of service and manufacturing companies, and all companies were represented by their CEOs. To test for nonrespondent bias the results from the later respondents were compared to those of the early respondents. No significant differences were identified between the two sets with respect to the majority of variables.

Reliability and validity

Reliability

The reliability of each of the stakeholder orientation scales was tested using Cronbach's coefficient alpha, as shown in Table 1 (Churchill, 1979; Nunnally, 1967). Given that this is initial and exploratory research, the range of coefficients from 0.81 to 0.62 is acceptable (Churchill, 1979; Nunnally, 1967). These values are also consistent with scales that are made up of a small number of items, as the value of alpha is dependent on the number of scale items (Norusis, 1990). Reliability is also reflected in the value that alpha would have if each item were deleted from each respective scale.

Validity

Content, convergent, and discriminant validity were assessed.

Content validity

As mentioned earlier the questionnaire was piloted, during which the respondents were asked to explain their understanding of the questions. Adjustments to the wording were accordingly made.

Table 1 Reliability of measures of stakeholder orientation

Scale and Item	Item to total correlation	Alpha if item deleted
Competitor orientation; alpha 0.72		
($F = 93.3\ p = .000$)		
Planning	0.58	0.61
Research	0.46	0.68
Corporate culture	0.43	0.70
Corporate mission	0.58	0.62
Consumer orientation; alpha 0.62		
($F = 30.0\ p = .000$)		
Planning	0.48	0.48
Research	0.39	0.66
Corporate culture	0.43	0.53
Corporate mission	0.48	0.53
Shareholder orientation; alpha 0.66		
($F = 126.4\ p = .000$)		
Planning	0.57	0.49
Research	0.51	0.55
Corporate culture	0.36	0.64
Corporate mission	0.44	0.63
Employee orientation; alpha 0.66		
($F = 54.8\ p = .000$)		
Planning	0.49	0.56
Research	0.39	0.62
Corporate culture	0.39	0.64
Corporate mission	0.51	0.54
Union orientation; alpha 0.81		
($F = 126.0\ p = .000$)		
Planning	0.70	0.72
Research	0.65	0.77
Corporate culture	0.66	0.75
Corporate mission	0.60	0.79

Convergent validity

For each of the stakeholder orientation scales (as shown in Table 1), all pairwise correlations were examined. All these coefficients are significant at the $p < 0.05$ level, whereas 85% are significant at the $p < 0.01$ level. Also, as Table 1 shows, all the item to total correlations are high. Therefore, there is evidence of convergent validity.

Discriminant validity

Two assessments of discrimination were made. First, a single-factor test was performed (Podsakoff and Organ, 1986). The stakeholder orientation and market environment variables were factor-analyzed together, using principle components analysis. If the variables load onto a single factor that accounts for substantial variance, then little discrimination on the part of the respondents is evident, and common method variance is a likely problem. The analysis produced four factors with eigenvalues greater than one, which account for 60% of the variance, as shown in Table 2. As the stakeholder orientation variables and the market environment variables loaded onto different factors, and as all exhibit high unique factor loadings,

Table 2 Results of single-factor test for discriminant validity

Variable	Factor 1	Factor 2	Factor 3	Factor 4
Consumer orientation	0.79			
Competitor orientation	0.71			
Employee orientation	0.70			
Competitive hostility		0.78		
Market turbulence		0.75		
Union orientation			0.78	
Shareholder orientation			0.74	
Market growth				0.86
Ease of market entry				0.53
Technological change				0.44
Eigenvalue	2.1	1.5	1.3	1.1
Percentage of variance	21.1	14.7	12.7	11.0

the results provide evidence for discriminant validity. The second assessment was based on the results of testing the first hypothesis, as exhibited in Table 3. As this table shows, there are statistically significant differences between the relative levels of attention that the respondents give to the interests of each stakeholder group. This suggests discrimination between the variables used to measure orientation to each of the stakeholder groups, rather than responses to a common organizational construct, such as 'good management' (Churchill, 1979). Again, there is evidence of discriminant validity.

RESULTS

H1: Relative extent of stakeholder orientation

The results that are pertinent to testing hypothesis 1 are presented in Table 3, which are made up of the mean scores of each measure of stakeholder orientation with respect to each stakeholder group. For each measure the significance of the differences between each pair of stakeholder group means was tested using t-tests. As

Table 3 Relative attention to stakeholder groups

	Consumer (mean)	Competitor (mean)	Shareholder (mean)	Employee (mean)	Union (mean)	Significance of pairwise mean differences[a]
Research	5.2	4.4	2.7	3.7	1.7	All at $p < 0.0001$
Judgment	6.2	5.6	5.0	5.8	3.9	All at $p \leqslant 0.005$
Planning	6.1	4.7	4.8	5.1	2.7	All at $p \leqslant 0.005$, except[b]
Culture	6.4	6.2	6.3	4.5	2.2	All at $p \leqslant 0.004$, except[c]
Mission	6.7	5.7	6.4	5.3	1.7	All at $p < 0.0001$
Priority	6.3	5.0	5.0	5.3	3.0	All at $p \leqslant 0.01$, except[d]

[a] Two-tailed test.
[b] Competitors/shareholders not significant.
[c] Competitors/shareholders, and consumers/shareholders not significant.
[d] Competitors/shareholders not significant.

the table shows, the majority of respective pairs of means are significantly different. Therefore, H1 is rejected, as significantly different levels of orientation are given to these stakeholder groups. The most attention is given to consumers, followed by competitors and shareholders, then employees, and finally unions.

Research is seemingly only of high importance in understanding consumers, although in some companies it also seems to be important for understanding competitors. However, it is of low importance for understanding the other groups. Management judgment appears to be more important than formal research for all stakeholder groups, although again understanding consumers received the highest mean score. Consumers are seemingly the subject of most planning, followed by that given to employees, whereas similar attention is given to shareholders and competitors. The results suggest that competitors, consumers, and shareholders have similar levels of importance in corporate cultures, and that these cultures are not dominated by a particular stakeholder group. However, employees seem to get much less attention, whereas unions are again unimportant. Consumers are given the most attention in mission statements, with the mean score being almost at the top of the scale, whereas shareholders are also given a very high level of attention, followed by competitors and employees. In the assignment of priorities, the consumer is again the most important group; competitors and shareholders have a similar level of priority, followed by employees, whereas unions were again given the lowest priority.

H2: Associations among stakeholder orientations

To test the second hypothesis, zero-order and partial correlation coefficients were determined between each of the stakeholder orientations, and their significance was tested with two-tailed tests. The results are given in Table 4. Each of the pairs of zero-order and partial coefficients is similar, as are the levels of significance indicating that each significant association is little influenced by the other variables. Of the 10 possible associations, six are significant; five at the 0.001 level and one at the 0.01 level, and all the coefficients are positive. This suggests a reasonable amount of

Table 4 Zero-order and partial correlation coefficients between stakeholder orientations

	Competitor	Shareholder	Employee	Union
Consumer				
Zero-order	0.41[a]	0.10	0.42[a]	0.03
Partial	0.40[a]	0.06	0.45[a]	0.04
Competitor				
Zero-order		0.33[a]	0.25[a]	0.09
Partial		0.28[a]	0.20[a]	0.00
Shareholder				
Zero-order			0.19[b]	0.26[a]
Partial			0.18[b]	0.24[a]
Employee				
Zero-order				0.13
Partial				0.16

[a] $p < .001$, two-tailed test.
[b] $p < 0.01$.

association between the stakeholder orientations. Competitor, employee, and shareholder orientation are each significantly associated with three of the four other respective stakeholder groups. Although consumer orientation is only significantly associated with competitor and employee orientation, these coefficients are the highest of the set, indicating the strongest associations between the orientations. Therefore, given the range of identified associations between the stakeholder orientations, the second hypothesis is supported.

H3: Dependency of nonconsumer stakeholder orientation on consumer orientation

Multiple regression analysis was found to test the third hypothesis. Four equations were planned – one each for competitor, employee, shareholder, and union orientation as the dependent variable. The independent variables for all equations were consumer orientation as the predictor variable and the market environment variables as control variables (as Table 6 shows, multicollinearity is not a problem). As this is a new type of investigation, the independent variables were entered into each equation using combined forward and backward stepwise entry, and zero-order and partial correlation coefficients were calculated. The maximum probability of the F statistic for each of the variables to enter each of the equations was set at 0.05, and at 0.10 to be removed. The acceptable level of tolerance for each variable was set at 0.0001. For competitor and employee orientation equations were formed and the results are given in Table 5. However, for shareholder and union orientation, equations were not formed. The results suggest that consumer orientation is a predictor of both competitor and employee orientation. In both cases the zero-order and partial correlation coefficients have similar values, suggesting that consumer orientation has a main effect on competitor and employee orientation, after allowing for any effects from the other independent variables. For competitor orientation the results suggest that technological change and competitor hostility are also predictor variables, having significant betas and partial correlations. However, the change in R^2 is quite small for both variables, raising multiple R from 0.41 to 0.48. For employee orientation market turbulence is a significant variable, although the rise in multiple R is small; from 0.42 to only 0.46. These results support the third hypothesis, because they show that competitor and employee orientation are dependent on consumer orientation.

Table 5 Results of multiple regression analysis

	Multiple R	R^2	ΔR^2	ΔF	$p \leqslant$	Beta	Zero-order r	Partial r	F	p
Competitor orientation										
Step 1. Consumer orientation	0.41	0.17	—	—	—	0.39	0.41	0.40	42.6	0.000
Step 2. Technological change	0.45	0.21	0.04	9.8	0.002	0.17	0.25	0.18	7.6	0.006
Step 3. Competitor hostility	0.48	0.23	0.02	5.5	0.021	0.14	0.17	0.16	5.5	0.020
Employee orientation										
Step 1. Consumer orientation	0.42	0.17	—	—	—	0.45	0.42	0.45	55.2	0.000
Step 2. Market turbulence	0.46	0.21	0.04	11.2	0.001	−0.21	−0.13	−0.22	11.2	0.001

H4: Consumer orientation and the market environment

To test the fourth hypothesis zero-order and partial correlation coefficients were determined between consumer orientation and each of the market environment variables, and their significance was tested using a two-tailed test. The results are given in Table 6. As will be seen, none of the coefficients are significant at the 0.01 and 0.001 levels. Therefore, despite the prediction of the fourth hypothesis, the results suggest that consumer orientation is not associated with these measures of the market environment.

DISCUSSION

This empirical study has generated evidence about the relative attention companies give to various stakeholder groups. It has provided initial evidence for understanding how they tackle the problem of addressing the diverse interests of stakeholders, given the potential consequences of resources and capabilities for addressing all stakeholder interests.

Relative extent of stakeholder orientation

Most CEOs in the sample claim that top priority is given to satisfying consumers. This result supports the overall premise of the marketing literature and the empirical results of Posner and Schmidt (1984). They also support the theory that companies prioritize the various groups when addressing the diverse interests of their stakeholders (Mintzberg, 1983; Campbell and Yeung, 1991). The order of priority seems to be consumers, competitors and shareholders, employees, and unions.

This consumer priority is reflected in the use of formal research for understanding stakeholder needs, which is seemingly only of high importance for understanding consumers. For the other stakeholders, management judgment is the major approach. This suggests that a comprehensive understanding of all stakeholders is not pursued, as suggested by Harrison and St. John (1994). However, some CEOs may perceive that, of all the stakeholder group interests, those of consumers are subject to the most change, are more difficult to understand, and therefore require formal research. In comparison, the interests of other stakeholders may be perceived as being relatively stable over time, and therefore judgments can be made about how they should be satisfied. It could also be perceived that satisfying consumers will lead to satisfying other stakeholders, which is discussed later. The implication is, therefore, that significant resources are only allocated to understanding consumers.

Table 6 Zero-order and partial correlation coefficients between consumer orientation and market environment variables

	Market growth	Market turbulence	Competitor hostility	Ease of market entry	Technological change
Consumer orientation					
Zero-order	0.15	0.16	0.02	−0.01	0.15
Partial	0.10	0.13	0.03	0.01	0.08

Two-tailed test: none of the coefficients are significant at $p < 0.01$ or $p < 0.001$ levels.

The responses given to the extent of planning to satisfy stakeholder interests is not consistent with the model of Miller and Lewis (1991). Clearly more planning goes into satisfying consumers, whereas Miller and Lewis (1991) suggest that the model should be in balance, with similar attention being given to all stakeholders. This result suggests that different power bases may lead to variation in attention to stakeholder interests (Mintzberg, 1983), where external needs associated with consumption are balanced with internal needs associated with production. It could also be that, for some firms there is indeed a shortage of resources and capabilities, and therefore certain stakeholders are prioritized.

Despite the previous results, the responses suggest that the importance of consumers in corporate culture is similar to that of competitors and shareholders. This result is more reflective of the Miller and Lewis (1991) model, with some balancing of stakeholder interests. It differs slightly to the claims of Harrison and St. John (1994) and Kotter and Heskett (1992) – the former suggest that consumers, competitors, and employees are the key stakeholders, whereas the latter suggest consumers, shareholders and employees. The results support those of Deshpande *et al.* (1993), reflecting a market focus culture. Despite the overall prominence of consumers, it seems that the interests of a single group are not dominant in the set of values, beliefs, and assumptions that guide decisions in strategic planning.

However, the results for relative importance in the mission again reflect the prominence of consumers. This suggests that the interests of consumers are at the forefront of the starting point of strategic planning (Campbell and Yeung, 1991; Hill and Jones, 1993; Pearce, 1982). However, the claims of several stakeholders are seemingly legitimate in the mission (Campbell and Tawadey, 1990; Freeman, 1984), and there is a balance between internal and external stakeholders, as advocated by Hooley *et al.* (1991).

Associations among stakeholder orientations

Given that there is much association between the orientations and that all the correlation coefficients are positive, the implication is that attention given to a particular stakeholder group is not in isolation to the attention given to other groups. This result reinforces the earlier results about corporate culture, where three key stakeholders seem to be in balance within the culture, giving further support to the Miller and Lewis (1991) model. It also supports the Freeman (1984) proposition of a 'map' of stakeholders, as opposed to disparate groups. This result is also consistent with key predictions in the relationship marketing literature. It illustrates the relative strength of certain central associations within marketing systems, reflecting the integrations of stakeholders within networks (Christopher *et al.*, 1991; Webster, 1992).

However, this result is not consistent with the U.S. study by Aupperle *et al.* (1985), which suggested that as attention to consumers increases, attention to some of the other stakeholders declines. Indeed, the implication from the current study is that increased attention to a particular group of stakeholders will be accompanied by further attention to other groups. Therefore, of the groups studied, it suggests that particular stakeholders will not be neglected in favor of others, even though higher priority is attached to consumers. Again this is supportive of the theory of relationship marketing.

Stakeholder orientation dependency on consumer orientation

Consumer orientation was identified as a predictor of competitor and employee orientation, but not of shareholder and union orientation. The former association is consistent with the argument that gaining control over consumers will contribute to gaining control over competitors, by ensuring that product offerings are more attractive and effective than those of competitors. This result is consistent with the proposition of Day and Wensley (1988), that consumer and competitor orientations should be in balance, and indeed goes further by suggesting that the former predicts the latter.

As consumer orientation is also a predictor of employee orientation it suggests some indirect control over employees, and that the interests of consumers can be balanced with those of employees. In other words, satisfying consumers leads to demands on the company, which result in employment opportunities. It suggests that the balance between consumer and competitor orientation proposed by Day and Wensley (1988) can be extended by adding employees to the model, and that the claim of Harrison and St. John (1994), of consumers, competitors, and employees, can be supported. These results are also supported by the results of the exploratory factor analysis (see Table 2). Here the first factor is composed of consumers, competitors, and employees orientations, accounting for over 20% of the variance. This result is also consistent with key predictions in the relationship marketing literature. As companies increasingly become part of networks of strategic alliances, the implementation of strategies will depend on control of these alliances (Christopher et al., 1991; Webster, 1992). Therefore, the results empirically support the importance of consumer orientation in gaining control within alliances, and support the claim that consumers are a key resource within strategic alliances (Webster, 1992).

Consumer orientation is seemingly not a predictor of shareholder orientation, although earlier in the article it was theoretically predicted that control over consumers could lead to higher returns for shareholders. However, such increases in turnover may not be passed on to shareholders as higher returns. For example, decisions on dividend payments may also be subject to political influences. Therefore, consumer orientation may not necessarily be associated with attention to shareholders. Although consumer orientation is not a predictor of union orientation, this can be explained by the universally low importance attached to unions.

These results also suggest that, within these companies, there is little perceived conflict in addressing the needs of consumers, competitors, and employees. This result supports the Miller and Lewis (1991) prediction of a balance, although in the results on relative attention consumers were given priority. Here the interpretation could be that indeed addressing the interests of some stakeholders is in balance, but as consumer orientation allows for some control of other stakeholders the companies perceive of a causal effect, from consumer orientation to competitor orientation and to employee orientation. Therefore consumer orientation is about addressing this perceived causal effect, as opposed to a view that consumer interests per se are more important that those of the other stakeholders. Again this implication is consistent with the theory of relationship marketing. It suggests the perception of synergies when addressing the various sets of interests within networks, and a perception of the impact of causal effects within strategic alliances (Christopher et al., 1991; Conner, 1991 Gummesson, 1987; Webster, 1992).

Consumer orientation and the marketing environment

As consumer orientation is not associated with measures of the market environment it suggests that, in this sample, consumer orientation is not important for alignment to the environment (Chakravarthy, 1982; Hooley and Saunders, 1993; Powell, 1992). However, as reported earlier, environment variables may not necessarily impact on marketing operations (Hooley *et al.*, 1990; Jaworski and Kohli, 1992). This result suggests two alternative scenarios. The first is based on the assumption that consumer orientation should be associated with market environment variables. This includes market turbulence (as changes of customer needs), with which an association should be obviously identified. Similarly, consumer orientation should be associated with market growth, as it provides a basis for understanding the purchasing behavior of consumers, which determines market growth. As competitor hostility increases there should be greater attention to consumers in order to tackle this hostility. Similarly, as barriers to market entry fall, greater attention to consumers should allow for the further creation of barriers. Finally, as technology changes there should be greater attention to consumers, in order to allow for the conversion of technological advances into consumer benefits and competitive advantage. Despite the claims of the respondents about the importance of their consumers, the lack of association between consumer orientation and these measures suggests that the companies have not achieved a high level of consumer orientation. Although they may believe that they are indeed oriented to their consumers, these key market variables that were measured are not reflected in this orientation.

The second scenario is that consumer orientation should not be associated with the market environment. Here the argument is that companies should attain and sustain a high level of consumer orientation, despite prevailing and changing market conditions. The expectations, needs, and values of consumers should be continuously monitored and addressed, regardless of changes in the market environment. Indeed, companies should seek to satisfy their consumers regardless of any changes in consumer interests, regardless of market growth, regardless of changes in competitive rivalry, and regardless of new technological benefits. Therefore, consumer orientation is based on the company-specific attitudes, which are incorporated into the corporate culture, and is independent of market change.

Limitations, research directions, and managerial implications

Although this study has provided initial empirical evidence, it features two limitations, which are consistent with this type of study. As the data were collected from a single country, there may be problems in generalizing the results to other countries. Also, as the study collected cross-sectional data, a limitation is that the identified associations may not be continuous in a longitudinal setting. As a consequence of these results there are several directions for further research. First, based on the limitations, further insights could be gained from a country-comparative study and from a longitudinal study. Second, a broader investigation is needed into the role of stakeholders in strategic alliances, and the relative power that they are able to exert in these networks in the pursuance of their interests. A third direction would be a more detailed investigation of the approaches that companies take in order to understand the respective interests of their stakeholder groups, the planning that they do in order to address these interests, and how they implement and control the achievement of these plans. Fourth, further research might take the form of an exploration of managerial perceptions of causal relationships between consumer orientation and orientations to other stakeholder groups and, where these relationships are perceived to exist, the ways in which they are used to control stakeholders. A fifth direction would be to seek further detailed understanding of associations between the various stakeholder orientations, the reasons why these associations are seen to be important, and the advantages that are to be gained from strengthening these associations. Finally, further work might take the form of an exploration of the opposing scenarios about the relationship of consumer orientation with the market environment, and whether stakeholder orientations are contingent upon environment variables.

There is also a range of key managerial implications – all of which require consideration of the allocation of resources and managerial capabilities:

1. More formal research may be needed to achieve a comprehensive understanding of the diverse interests of stakeholders.
2. Achieving a balance in addressing the interests of key stakeholders should be incorporated in all aspects of strategic planning.
3. Key stakeholder groups that should be in balance are consumers, competitors, and employees, which also represent a diverse set of interests.
4. Achieving control of consumers, through a consumer orientation, also implies control over competitors and employees, and possibly other stakeholder groups.
5. Consideration should be given to the true level of consumer orientation achieved, which may be different to that perceived by some managers, despite changes in the market environment.

REFERENCES

Alvesson, M., Concepts of Organizational Culture and Presumed Links to Efficiency. *Omega* 17 (4) (1989): 323–333.

Anderson, P. F., Marketing, Strategic Planning, and the Theory of the Firm. *Journal of Marketing* 46 (Spring 1982): 15–26.

Aupperle, K. E., Carroll, A. B., and Hatfield, J. D., An Empirical Examination of the Relationship between Corporate Social Responsibility and Profitability. *Academy of Management Journal* 28 (2) (1985): 446–463.

Barney, J. B., Firm Resources and Sustained Competitive Advantage. *Journal of Management* 17 (1991): 99–120.

Bennett, R., and Cooper, R., Beyond the Marketing Concept. *Business Horizons* 22 (June 1981): 76–83.

Chakravarthy, B. S., Adaptation: A Promising Metaphor for Strategic Management. *Academy of Management Journal* 7 (1982): 35–44.

Chakravarthy, B. S., Measuring Strategic Performance. *Strategic Management Journal* 7 (1986): 437–458.

Campbell, A., and Tawadey, K., *Mission and Business Philosophy: Winning Employee Commitment*, Heinemann, Oxford. 1990.

Campbell, A., and Young. S., Creating a Sense of Mission. *Long Range Planning* 24 (4) (1991): 10–20.

Campbell, A., Devine, M., and Young, D., *A Sense of Mission*, Hutchinson, London. 1990.

Christopher, M., Payne, A., and Ballantyne, D., *Relationship Marketing*, Heinemann, London. 1991.

Churchill, G. A., A Paradigm for Developing Better Measures of Marketing Constructs. *Journal of Marketing Research* 16 (February 1979): 64–73.

Cleland, D. I., and King, W. R., Developing a Planning Culture for More Effective Strategic Planning. *Long Range Planning* 7 (3) (1979): 70–74.

Connor, K. R., A Historical Comparison of Resource-Based Theory and Five Schools of Thought Within Industrial Organizational Economics: Do We Have a New Theory of the Firm? *Journal of Management* 17 (1) (1991): 121–154.

Davis, D., Morris, M., and Allen, J., Perceived Environmental Turbulence and Its Effect on Selected Entrepreneurship, Marketing, and Organizational Characteristics in Industrial Firms. *Journal of the Academy of Marketing Science* 19 (1) (1991): 43–51.

Day, G. S., and Wensley, R., Assessing Advantage: A Framework for Diagnosing Competitive Superiority. *Journal of Marketing* 52 (April 1988): 1–20.

Deshpande, R., Farley, J. U., and Webster, F. E., Corporate Culture, Customer Orientation, and Innovativeness in Japanese Firms: A Quadrad Analysis. *Journal of Marketing* 57 (January 1993): 23–37.

Dutton, J. E., and Duncan, R. B., The Influence of the Strategic Planning Process on Strategic Change. *Strategic Management Journal* 8 (1987): 103–116.

Dyson, R. G., and Foster, M. J., The Relationship of Participation and Effectiveness in Strategic Planning. *Strategic Management Journal* 3 (1982): 77–88.

Freeman, R. E., and Reed, D., Stockholders and Stakeholders: A New Perspective on Corporate Governance, in *Corporate Governance: A Definitive Exploration of the Issues,* C. Huizinga, ed., University of California Press, Los Angeles. 1983.

Freeman, R. E., *Strategic Management: A Stakeholder Approach,* Pitman, Boston. 1984.

Grant, R. M., *Contemporary Strategy Analysis*, Blackwell, Oxford. 1991.

Greenley, G. E., Effectiveness in Marketing Planning. *Strategic Management Journal* 4 (1983): 1–10.

Greenley, G. E., Market Orientation and Company Performance: Empirical Evidence from U.K. Companies. *British Journal of Management* 6 (1) (1995): 1–13.

Gummesson, E., The New Marketing – Developing Long-term Interactive Relationships. *Long Range Planning* 20 (4) (1987): 10–20.

Guth, W. D., and MacMillan, I. C., Strategy Implementation Versus Middle Management Self Interests. *Strategic Management Journal* 7 (1986): 313–327.

Harrison, J. S., and St. John, C. H., *Strategic Management of Organizations and Stakeholders*, West, St. Paul, MN. 1994.

Hassard, J., and Sharifi, S., Corporate Culture and Strategic Change. *Journal of General Management* 15 (2) (1989): 4–19.

Hickson, D. J., Hinnings, C. R., Lee, C. A., Schneck, R. E., and Pennings, J. M., Strategic Contingencies: Theory of Intra-Organizational Power. *Administrative Science Quarterly* 16 (2) (1971): 216–229.

Hill, C. W. L., and Jones, G. R., *Strategic Management: An Integrated Approach*, 2nd ed., Houghton Mifflin, Boston. 1992.

Hooley, G. J., Cox, A. J., and Adams, A., Our Five-Year Mission – To Boldly Go Where No Man Has Been Before. *Proceedings of the 1991 MEG Annual Conference*, Cardiff Business School, (1991): 559–577.

Hooley, G. J., Lynch, J., and Jobber, D., Market Environment, Competitive Strategy, and Performance, in *Advanced Research in Marketing,* H. Muhlbacher and C. Jochum, eds., Proceedings of the 19th Annual Conference of the European Marketing Academy, Innsbruck, Austria, (1990): 1725–1741.

Hooley, G. J., and Saunders, J., *Competitive Positioning,* Prentice-Hall, London. 1993.

Hunger, J. D., and Wheelen, T. L., *Strategic Management*, 4th ed., Addison-Wesley, Reading, MA. 1993.

Jaworski, B. J., and Kohli, A. K. Market Orientation: Antecedents and Consequences. Working paper, Marketing Science Institute, Cambridge, MA. 1992.

Kimberley, J., Norling, R., and Weiss, J. A., Pondering the Performance Puzzle: Effectiveness in Interorganizational Settings, In *Organization and Public Policy*, R. H. Hall and R. E. Quinn, eds., Sage, Beverly Hill, CA. 1983.

King, W. R., and Cleland, D. I., *Strategic Planning*, Van Norstrand Reinhold, New York. 1979.

Kohli, A. K., and Jaworski, B. J., Market Orientation: The Construct, Research Propositions and Managerial Implications. *Journal of Marketing* 54 (April 1990): 1–18.

Kotler, P., *Marketing Management: Analysis, Planning and Control,* Prentice-Hall, Englewood-Cliffs, NJ. 1991.

Kotter, J. P., *A Force for Change: How Leadership Differs from Management*, Free Press, New York. 1990.

Kotter, J. P., and Heskett, J. L., *Corporate Culture and Performance*, Free Press, New York. 1992.

MacMillan, I. C., and Jones, P. E., *Strategy Formulation: Power and Politics*, 2nd ed., West, St. Paul, MN. 1986.

Mahoney, J., and Pandian, J. R., The Resource-based View within the Conversation of Strategic Management. *Strategic Management Journal* 13 (1992): 363–380.

McDonald, M., and Leppard, J. W., Marketing Planning and Corporate Culture: A Conceptual Framework Which Examines Management Attitudes in the Context of Marketing Planning. *Journal of Marketing Management* 7 (3) (1991): 209–212.

Miller, R. L., and Lewis, W. F., A Stakeholder Approach to Marketing Management Using the Value Exchange Models. *European Journal of Marketing* 25 (8) (1991): 55–68.

Miller, R. L. Lewis, W. F., and Merenski, J. P., A Value Exchange Model for the Channel of Distribution: Implications for Management and Research. *Journal of the Academy of Management* (Fall 1985).

Miller, D., The Structural and Environmental Correlates of Business Strategy. *Strategic Management Journal* 8 (1) (1987): 55–76.

Mintzberg, H., *Power in and around Organizations,* Prentice-Hall, Englewood-Cliffs, NJ. 1983.

Narver, J. C., and Slater, S. F., The Effect of Market Orientation on Business Profitability. *Journal of Marketing* 54 (October 1990): 20–35.

Norusis, M. J., *SPSS Statistics Guide*, SPSS, Chicago. 1990.

Nunnally, J., *Psychometric Theory*, McGraw-Hill, New York. 1967.

Pearce, J. A., and David, F. Corporate Mission Statements: The Bottom Line. *Academy of Management Executive* 1 (2) (1987): 109–115.

Pearce, J. A., and Robinson, R. B., *Strategic Management*, 5th ed., Irwin, Homewood, IL. 1994.

Pearce, J. A., The Company Mission as a Strategic Tool. *Sloan Management Review* (Spring 1982): 15–24.

Pettigrew, A., and Whipp, R. *Management Change for Competitive Success*, Blackwell: Oxford. 1991.

Pfeffer, J., *Power in Organizations*, Pitman, Marshfield. 1981.

Pfeffer, J., and Salancik, G. R., The External Control of Organizations: A Resource Dependency Perspective. Harper and Row, New York. 1978.

Piercy, N., *Market-Led Strategic Change*, Butterworth-Heinemann, Oxford. 1992.

Podsakoff, P. M., and Organ, D. W., Self-Reports in Organizational Research: Problems and Prospects. *Journal of Management* 12 (1986): 531–544.

Posner, B. Z., and Schmidt, W. H., Values and the American Manager: An Update *California Management Review*, 26 (3) (1984): 202–216.

Powell, T. C., Organizational Alignment as Competitive Advantage. *Strategic Management Journal* 13 (1994): 119–134.

Ramanujam, V., and Venkatraman, N., Planning System Characteristics and Planning Effectiveness. *Strategic Management Journal* 8 (1987): 453–468.

Rhenman, E. *Industrial Democracy and Industrial Management,* Tavistock, London. 1968.

Schein, E., *Organizational Culture and Leadership,* Jossey Bass, San Francisco. 1985.

Scherer, F. M., *Industrial Market Structure and Economic Performance*, Rand McNally, Chicago. 1980.

Sinha, D. K., The Contribution of Formal Planning to Decisions, *Strategic Management Journal*, 11 (1990): 479–492.

Slater, S. F., and Narver, J. C., Does Competitive Environment Moderate the Market Orientation-Performance Relationship. *Journal of Marketing* 58 (1994): 46–55.

Walker, O. C., Boyd, H. W., and Larreche, J. C., Marketing Strategy: Planning and Implementation. Irwin, Homewood, IL. 1992.

Webster, F. E., The Changing Role of Marketing in the Corporation. *Journal of Marketing* 56 (1992): 1–17.

Greenley, G. E. and Foxall, G. R. (1996) 'Consumer and non-consumer stakeholder orientation in U.K. companies'. *Journal of Business Research*, 35(2), February: 105–116. Reproduced with permission from Elsevier Science.

Consumer reaction to company-related disasters: the effect of multiple versus single explanations

6.5

Brian K. Jorgensen

INTRODUCTION

On December 21, 1988, Pan Am flight 103 crashed into the town of Lockerbie, Scotland, killing all 258 passengers and crew members aboard, as well as a number of people on the ground. All who heard about the disaster wondered how it could have occurred. Was it weather conditions, terrorism, poor security? Who was to blame? Would or could it happen again? As company, government, and media representatives searched for answers, the public tried to make sense of the wide array of causal speculations, explanations, and excuses that filtered through to it.

When large-scale negative company-related incidents occur they can be very important because they have the potential of directly and indirectly affecting large numbers of people. Recent incidents involving bad meat from Jack in the Box Restaurant and syringes in Pepsi cans attest to the high level of publicity that these kinds of incidents can generate. From a marketing perspective, company-related disasters and crises can be particularly damaging when a company's products bear the company name. Brand equity and customer loyalty may drop rapidly if a company is blamed for a serious negative incident.

Consumer behavior scholars have studied consumer attributions following relatively small-scale company-related annoyances, such as defective merchandise (Folkes 1984) and delayed airline flights (Folkes, Koletsky, and Graham 1987). However, consumer reactions to major company-related disasters, such as jet crashes, oil spills, or drug-related scares, have been largely neglected. Further, the tendency of attribution theorists to focus their study on single, as opposed to multiple, causal explanations (Leddo, Abelson, and Gross 1984) seems to be carried over into the consumer behavior literature.

This paper investigates consumer reaction to multiple versus single explanations for image-threatening company-related disasters within a framework of attributional theory and conjunctive explanations. Following a review of the literature, the results of a preliminary experiment in this area are presented. Opportunities for future research are then addressed.

ATTRIBUTIONAL THEORY AND COMPANY-RELATED DISASTERS

Because company-related disasters are highly negative and unexpected, consumers are likely to try to understand the cause of these types of incidents (Bucher 1957; Veltfort and Lee 1943; Weiner 1986). However, members of the general public usually do not have first hand information regarding company-related incidents from which to develop their own causal attributions. Rather, in these situations third party sources, such as the media or company representatives, must generally supply possible or probable causes. The important question then becomes how consumers react to the explanation or explanations that have been offered. Of the various available approaches to the study of attributions, Weiner's (1986) attributional theory is particularly well-suited to the study of consumer reactions to company-related events because Weiner's theory focuses on the consequences of attributions, rather than on the process by which the attributions are made.

According to Weiner's theory, once a person has made a causal attribution, he is expected to experience particular affects or be motivated to perform particular behaviors based on where he determines that the cause falls along three distinct dimensional continua. These three dimensions are locus, controllability, and stability. The locus dimension addresses the degree to which the cause is internal to or external to the target of the attribution. Thus, for example, an airline accident that is attributed to an improper instruction by an air traffic controller may be considered external to the company, while an accident due to pilot error would probably be considered internal. Controllability concerns the extent to which a cause is within the control of the target entity. Therefore, using the previous example, the air traffic controller problem would probably be considered uncontrollable by the company, while the pilot error problem might be seen as more controllable. Stability reflects the degree to which a cause is something unchanging as opposed to fluctuating or changing over time. Given the infrequency with which they occur, most company-related disasters should tend to be caused by relatively unstable causes, and, therefore, stability is not further considered here.

Weiner's causal dimensions are theorized as influencing various emotional reactions and, ultimately, behavior (Weiner 1986). With particular reference to the company disaster situation, the controllability and locus dimensions, which are somewhat overlapping in most cases, are expected to influence the emotions of anger and pity (Folkes 1984). Behavior is thought to be indirectly affected through the attributionally-induced affective states and resulting attitudes.

EXPLANATIONS OF COMPANY-RELATED DISASTERS

Impression management

The way in which consumers react to a company-related disaster situation may depend not only on the attributional circumstances underlying the incident but also on the way in which management responds. 'Impression management' describes the process by which people, or in this case companies, control others' impressions of them (Leary and Kowalski 1990; Russ 1991). Impression management can be particularly important in response to serious negative events (Schlenker 1980).

One of many approaches that management might take to manage impressions following a company-related disaster is referred to in the crisis management literature as 'telling one's own story' (Meyers and Holusha 1986). In other words, management is advised to give its own explanation for what caused the incident. Often, more than one factor may be potentially responsible for a particular incident. For instance, the deaths linked to Jack in the Box hamburgers were eventually traced to both bad meat (an external cause) and improper cooking temperatures (an internal cause). In other cases, until the actual cause or causes are isolated, a number of potential explanations may be available, some of which may be better for the company than others.

The conjunctive fallacy and conjunctive explanations

Little, if any, of the research stemming from Weiner's (1986) attributional theory has addressed the consequences of multiple attributions. However, in the judgment and inference literature, Tversky and Kahneman (1983) and others have investigated the different effects of multiple or 'conjunctive' versus single statements and explanations on people's judgments and predictions. These investigations have centered around what has become known as the 'conjunctive fallacy'.

The conjunctive fallacy

The conjunctive fallacy, or conjunctive error, describes people's tendency to estimate the joint probability of 'A and B' to be greater than the probability of 'A' or 'B' individually, where A and B are descriptions of a person or thing or explanations for an event or action (Tversky and Kahneman 1983). Thus, for example, when asked to judge the likelihood of possible causes of an airline accident, people might consider the conjunction of 'sunspot activity and pilot error,' to be more likely than 'sunspot activity.' This tendency is regarded as a fallacy or error because it is statistically impossible for a conjunction of two items to be more likely than either of the items that make up the conjunction.

The robustness of findings of conjunctive errors in various contexts has led to a number of investigations into why people make these types of errors (e.g., Leddo, Abelson, and Gross 1984; Locksley and Stangor 1983; Tversky and Kahneman 1983; Wells 1985; Zuckerman, Eghrari, and Lambrecht 1986). Initially, the conjunctive fallacy was linked to the 'representativeness' of the component items (Tversky and Kahneman 1983; Wells 1985). Thus, for example, if pilot error is considered to be a more representative cause of airline accidents than is sunspot activity, then the combination of the two explanations may appear more representative, and thus more probable, than the sunspot cause. Wells (1985) found some support for a representative explanation by showing that the combination of representative and unrepresentative statements produced strong conjunctive error effects, while the combination of two unrepresentative or two representative statements produced lower error rates.

Another possible explanation for the conjunctive fallacy is that subjects are misinterpreting the single statements as though they were meant to exclude the conjunctive statements. So, for example, subjects might be interpreting the 'pilot error' explanation for an airline accident as 'pilot error without sunspot activity.' Leddo, Abelson, and Gross (1984) have discounted this explanation, noting that the errors have been found in a between-subjects study, where subjects saw only the single or the conjunctive explanation (Pennington 1984), and that in other studies the statement 'A' was replaced with 'A, whether or not B,' without a weakening of conjunction effects (Locksley and Stangor 1984; Tversky and Kahneman 1983). On the other hand, Morier and Borgida (1984) have found that certain task features in conjunctive problems, such as ranking versus rating the probability of simple and conjunctive statements, can reduce, but not eliminate, conjunctive errors. They have also found that some conjunction problems can be debiased by clarifying wording.

The conjunctive fallacy has also been attributed to improper combination procedures on the part of subjects. Abelson, Leddo, and Gross (1987), have shown that the likelihood of a conjunction can often be approximated by a geometric mean of each of the conjunction's components. Also, Yates and Carlson (1986) have shown that a procedure for summing the likelihoods of conjunction components can predict incidence of errors in some instances.

Conjunctive explanations

In comparing conjunctive effects across a wide array of studies, Ableson, Leddo, and Gross (1987) find much stronger conjunctive effects in explanation tasks then in other tasks. Further, Locksley and Stangor (1984) find that rare events or outcomes are much more likely to bring about conjunctive errors than common events or outcomes. Presumably, more common events can be more easily explained by single causes.

Since company-related disasters are generally accompanied by explanations, and since these are relatively uncommon events, the conjunctive explanations literature seems highly relevant to the company disaster situation. However, this connection should still be made with some caution. First, the array of possible causes for company-related disasters is much more complex than for the outcomes described in the conjunctive explanation studies. For example, some causes may be insufficient in and of themselves to cause a disaster but may be able to contribute to a disaster in conjunction with another cause. This possibility is not addressed in the conjunctive explanations literature.

Further, the conjunctive explanations literature addresses the effects of conjunctive versus single explanations on judgments of the likelihoods of the explanations. Effects of multiple versus single explanations on affective responses, attitudes, and behaviors are not addressed. Although a more likely explanation may be presumed to be a better explanation, and may, therefore, be expected to lead to stronger reactions, this line of reasoning is not yet supported in the literature.

STUDY AND HYPOTHESES

As a preliminary study of single versus multiple explanations, an experiment was designed to study consumer reactions to a company-related disaster, where the disaster is attributed to either an internal/controllable factor, an external/uncontrollable factor, or both an internal/controllable factor and an external/uncontrollable factor (hereafter referred to as 'mixed' or 'mixed/ambiguous'). Given the robustness of the conjunctive explanation findings, the conjunctive error effect was expected to be observed:

H1: A multiple cause for a negative company-related incident that includes both internal/controllable and external/uncontrollable factors will be judged as more likely than at least one of the single factor causes making up the multiple cause.

Weiner's (1986) attributional theory proposes that when a negative outcome is controlled by the attributional target, greater blame and anger and less sympathy should be expressed toward the target than if the outcome is uncontrollable. Anger and sympathy should, in turn, influence general attitudes toward the attributional target, such that consumers should express more negative attitudes and purchase intentions toward companies connected with negative events where the cause appears to be internal/controllable, as opposed to external/uncontrollable. Therefore:

> *H2*: Consumers will express greater anger, less sympathy, poorer attitudes and purchase intentions, and higher levels of blame toward a company involved in a negative incident to the extent that the cause of the incident is perceived as more internal to and more controllable by company management.

Although mixed/ambiguous causal attributions, have began to be used in attributional studies (e.g., Weiner, Graham, Peter, and Zmuidinas 1991), systematic theoretical or empirical analyses of their properties and effects have not yet been carried out. However, Weiner, *et al.* (1991) suggest that affective and behavioral reactions to mixed attributions should fall within the range between the reactions to each single cause that makes up the mixed cause. How closely the reactions to the mixed attribution mirror those of one or the other of the single attributions may depend to a large degree on the circumstances of the situation. In the present study, the mixed attribution presents a situation where the company that is connected with the negative event is the only volitional entity that can be blamed for the incident. Since blame is generally accorded only to volitional entities (Anderson 1991), the level of blame, as well as the levels of other affective and behavioral responses, should, in this case, be more similar between mixed and internal/controllable attributions than between mixed and external/uncontrollable attributions.

> *H3*: Where the external cause of a company-related disaster is not controlled by a person or entity, the reported levels of affects, attitudes, and blame for a mixed set of explanations should be more comparable to levels for the internal/controllable attribution than to levels for the external/uncontrollable attribution.

Methodology

An experiment was conducted with 36 subjects consisting of 18 adult undergraduate students and 18 adult members of a church group. The subjects were run in two groups on the same day. A vignette approach was chosen because this approach has been widely used in attribution studies of this type and also because company disaster information generally reaches the consumer in the form of a story, such as a news story or a conversation. Following the description of a fatal airliner crash, one of three alternatives was suggested as the possible cause of the crash: (1) bad weather (external/uncontrollable), (2) poor aircraft maintenance (internal/controllable), or (3) bad weather and poor maintenance (ambiguous/mixed). The study design was completely between-subject, with 12 subjects viewing each distinct vignette.

On the experimental cover sheet, subjects were instructed to read the company-related vignette and imagine that they were reading a current news story. They were further instructed not to turn back to the story after they had finished reading it. On the page following the cover sheet, subjects were presented with the vignette. The vignette was followed by a questionnaire, which included a number of dependent measures and manipulation checks. The first question measured subjects' overall reaction to the airline referenced in the vignette on four seven-point semantic differential scales anchored by very unfavorable – very favorable, bad – good, negative – positive, dislike very much – like very much. These scales were averaged for the attitude measure. Next, three questions measured, on seven-point scales, how much anger and sympathy subjects felt toward the airline, if any, and the extent to which subjects felt that the airline was to blame, if at all. A measure of purchase intention was then presented, in which subjects were asked to rate the likelihood that they would choose to fly with this particular airline as opposed to other comparable airlines. This measure was taken on a seven-point scale anchored by very unlikely – very likely.

Finally, subjects responded to manipulation checks designed to test whether the causal dimension manipulations had successfully presented causes that were perceived as either internal/controllable or external/uncontrollable. A six item set of scales was modified from Russell (1982). Two each of the six seven-point items measured the extent to which the subject found the cause to be controllable/uncontrollable, internal/external, and stable/unstable, respectively. Each pair of scales was averaged to arrive at a single scale score for each dimension. The stability measures were taken to assure that the manipulations did not differentially affect stability.

RESULTS AND DISCUSSION

The data were analyzed by one-way ANOVA for each of the manipulation checks and dependent variables. Cell means for each dependent variable are presented in the Table. The results of specific statistical analyses are presented in the Table.

Manipulation checks

As expected, the causal attribution given had a significant effect on controllability ($F(2,33) = 12.25$, $p < .0001$) and locus ($F(2,33) = 14.76$, $p < .0001$). Paired tests using the .05 level indicated that for both of these manipulation check variables the

Table 1

Variable	Causal Attribution(s)		
	Internal/Controllable *n = 12*	*Both* *n = 12*	*External/Uncontrollable* *n = 12*
Controllability	5.42	5.13	3.33
Locus	5.00	3.92	2.46
Stability	2.92	3.04	3.29
Likelihood	0.75	0.67	1.33
Anger	4.67	5.00	3.17
Sympathy	2.50	2.83	3.50
Blameworthiness	5.08	5.08	2.83
Attitude toward Company	− 1.52	− 1.44	− 0.54
Purchase Intention	− 2.00	− 1.83	− 0.17

external/uncontrollable attribution differed from the internal/controllable and mixed/ambiguous attributions, which did not differ from one another. However, in directional terms, the mixed attribution was situated substantially more midway between internal and external with regard to locus than with regard to controllability. Also as expected, the judged stability of a cause was not significantly affected by causal attribution.

Hypothesis 1

Contrary to expectations, whether the airline crash seemed due to an internal/controllable, an external/uncontrollable, or a mixed cause had no effect on the judged likelihood that the cause given was indeed the actual cause. Thus, a conjunctive error was not demonstrated in this case. A number of possible reasons for this result can be suggested.

First, unlike nearly all conjunctive explanation and conjunctive error studies, this study was a completely between-subjects study. Thus, while subjects in traditional conjunctive error studies are exposed to both the individual causes and the conjunctive cause, the subjects in this study saw only one or the other. Those studies showing that conjunctive errors are attributable to the way tests are constructed and worded (e.g., Morier and Borgida 1984) support the idea that through debiasing, which can be effected through a between-subjects study, the conjunctive error may be greatly reduced or eliminated.

The results here may also be partly attributable to the fact that the causes making up the conjunctive explanation were judged to be fairly equally likely. Conjunctive errors have usually been found to be more pronounced in situations where one component cause is considered much more likely than the other. Further, studies that trace conjunctive errors to statistically incorrect averaging processes (e.g., Abelson, Leddo, and Gross 1987; Yates and Carlson 1986) also suggest that the errors should be more likely in cases of unequal component causes.

The failure to observe conjunctive error effects may also stem from the complexity of company crisis situations. Consumers may feel ill-equipped to judge for themselves and may, instead, defer to the trustworthiness of the source of the information to determine the likelihood that what is reported is true. If this is the case, future studies should show that both common and unusual causes reported by the same source should be considered equally likely candidates for the true cause.

Hypotheses 2 and 3

Affective measures and blame

According to Weiner's (1986) attributional theory, a negative event that is due to controllable causes should lead to greater anger and blame and to less sympathy than an event that is due to uncontrollable causes. The effect of attribution on anger was significant ($F(2,33) = 3.62$, $p < .05$). However, pairwise tests at the .05 level found a difference only between the external/uncontrollable attribution and the mixed attribution. Still, directional results supported both hypotheses 2 and 3 in that both internal/controllable and mixed attributions led to greater anger than did the external/uncontrollable attribution. Although not significant, the results for sympathy were also in the predicted direction.

As expected, the effect of attribution on blame was significant ($F_{(2,33)} = 10.52$, $p < .001$). In addition, pairwise tests at the .05 level supported hypothesis 3 in that the higher levels of blame for internal/controllable and mixed attributions were significantly different from the level of blame for external/uncontrollable attributions, although not significantly different from one another.

Attitude and purchase intentions

The effect of attribution on attitude approached significance ($F_{(2,33)} = 2.73$, $p < .10$), with a directional indication that attitudes were poorer towards companies connected with negative incidents when the causal attribution was internal/controllable or mixed than when the attribution was external/uncontrollable. The effect of attribution on purchase intention was significant in the expected direction ($F_{(2,33)} = 6.23$, $p < .01$). Pairwise tests indicated that external/uncontrollable attributions led to higher purchase intentions than did internal/controllable or mixed attributions.

With regard to purchase intentions, the scenario in the vignettes used here may have resulted in stronger results than would a scenario in which the company-related disaster does not have an effect on the product itself. Whereas an oil spill or chemical leak will not affect the product that is sold at the gas pump or the drug store, an airline crash may signal that the airline is offering an inferior product.

Summary and general discussion

The results of this study do not lend support to the hypothesis that conjunctive errors play a role in consumer reaction to company disasters, although the study does not rule out the possibility that in other disaster settings conjunctive errors could play a role. The study does, however, support the expectation that consumers' affects, attitudes, and, perhaps, behaviors following a negative company-related incident may be influenced by their understanding of the cause or causes underlying the incident. Also, under the particular circumstances of the vignette presented in this study, consumers' reactions to a mixture of internal/controllable and external/uncontrollable causes were similar to their reactions to a sole internal/uncontrollable cause. However, this result may not necessarily generalize to every case. If, for example, the external cause had been an attribution to a volitional entity, such as a terrorist, the result may have been different, since more blame may have been focussed externally. Also, a greater difference between the likelihoods of the two component explanations may have affected the relative likelihood of the conjunctive explanation, and perhaps other variables as well.

FUTURE DIRECTIONS AND CONCLUSIONS

Consumer reaction to various explanations for company-related disasters is an important area of research that has received little attention. This preliminary research into the area of conjunctive explanations suggests that differences in a company's approach to a disaster situation can have important consequences. The number and types of explanations for a particular incident that reach the consumer may influence emotions, attitudes, and behaviors towards the company.

The research presented here suggests the need for further investigation into a number of different questions regarding single versus multiple explanations for company-related disaster situations. One important research direction would entail an examination of mixed attributions situations where the external cause is controllable by a person or group outside of the company. Another interesting question concerns disaster situations where there is no effect on the company's product, such as in the case of the Exxon Valdez oil spill or the Union Carbide Bhopal incident. A third direction would be the examination of incidents where multiple explanations consist of two internal/controllable or two external/uncontrollable explanations, rather than a mixture of one of each type.

REFERENCES

Abelson, Robert P., John Leddo, and Paget H. Gross (1987), 'The Strength of Conjunctive Explanations,' *Personality and Social Psychology Bulletin*, 13 (June), 141–155.

Anderson, Norman H. (1991), 'Psychodynamics of Everyday Life: Blaming and Avoiding Blame,' in *Contributions to Information Integration Theory, Volume II: Social*, ed. Norman H. Anderson, Hillsdale, NJ: Erlbaum, 243–275.

Bucher, Rue (1957), 'Blame and Hostility in Disaster,' *American Journal of Sociology*, 62 (March) 467–475.

Folkes, Valerie S. (1984), 'Consumer Reactions to Product Failure: An Attributional Approach,' *Journal of Consumer Research*, 10 (March), 398–409.

_____, Susan Koletsky, and John L. Graham (1987), 'A Field Study of Causal Inferences and Consumer Reaction: The View from the Airport,' *Journal of Consumer Research*, 13 (March), 534–539.

Leary, Mark R. and Robin M. Kowalski (1990), 'Impression Management: A Literature Review and Two-Component Model,' *Psychological Bulletin*, 107 (1) 34–47.

Leddo, John, Robert P. Abelson, and Paget H. Gross (1984), 'Conjunctive Explanations: When Two Reasons are Better than One,' *Journal of Personality and Social Psychology*, 47 (November), 933–947.

Locksley, Anne and Charles Stangor (1984), 'Why Versus How Often: Causal Reasoning and the Incidence of Judgmental Bias,' *Journal of Experimental Social Psychology*, 20, 470–483.

Meyers, Gerald C. and John Holusha (1986), *When It Hits the Fan: Managing the Nine Crises of Business*, New York: Mentor.

Morier, Dean M. and Eugene Borgida (1984), 'The Conjunction Fallacy: A Task Specific Phenomenon,' *Personality and Social Psychology Bulletin*, 10 (June), 243–252.

Pennington, N. (1984), *Technical Note on Conjunctive Explanations*, Unpublished manuscript, Center for Decision Research, University of Chicago.

Russell, Dan (1982), 'The Causal Dimension Scale: A Measure of How Individuals Perceive Causes,' *Journal of Personality and Social Psychology*, 42 (June), 1137–1145.

Schlenker, Barry R. (1980), *Impression Management,* Belmont, CA: Wadsworth, Inc.

Tversky, Amos and Daniel Kahneman (1983). 'Extensional Versus Intuitive Reasoning: The Conjunction Fallacy in Probability Judgment,' *Psychological Review*, 90 (October), 293–315.

Veltfort, Helene Rank and George E. Lee (1943), 'The Coconut Grove Fire: A Study in Scapegoating,' *Journal of Abnormal and Social Psychology*, 38 (April) 138–154. (Clinical Supplement)

Weiner, Bernard (1986), *An Attributional Theory of Motivation and Emotion*, New York: Springer-Verlag.

——, Sandra Graham, Orli Peter, and Mary Zmuidinas (1991), 'Public Confession and Forgiveness,' *Journal of Personality*, 59 (2), 281–312.

Wells, Gary L. (1985), 'The Conjunction Error and the Representativeness Heuristic,' *Social Cognition*, 3 (Fall), 266-279.

Yates, J. Frank and Bruce W. Carlson (1986), 'Conjunction Errors: Evidence for Multiple Judgment Procedures, Including "Signed Summation,"' *Organizational Behavior and Human Decision Processes*, 37 (April), 230–253.

Zuckerman, Miron, Haleh Eghrari, and Mark R. Lambrecht (1986), 'Attributions as Inferences and Explanations: Conjunction Effects,' *Journal of Personality and Social Psychology*, 51 (6), 1144–1153.

Jorgensen, B. K. (1994) 'Consumer reaction to company-related disasters: the effect of multiple versus single explanations', in C. T. Allen and D. Roedder Johns (editors), *Advances in Consumer Research*, 21: 348–352. Reproduced with permission.

6.6 The role of sponsorship in the marketing communications mix

Tony Meenaghan

INTRODUCTION

The purpose of this paper is to examine the development of commercial sponsorship and its role in the marketing communications mix. It seeks to do so by focusing on two main areas.

The development of sponsorship

The following questions are examined:

1. What is sponsorship?
2. What factors are behind its past development?
3. What is happening now in the sponsorship market?
4. What developments are likely in the future?

Sponsorship in a management context

The following questions are examined:

1. What is its role in marketing communications?
2. Who are its audiences and what can sponsorship achieve with these audiences?
3. How is the correct sponsorship programme selected?
4. How must it be implemented and subsequently evaluated?

DEFINING COMMERCIAL SPONSORSHIP

Sponsorship is a relatively recent development and can truly be described as an area of marketing in which basic principles are still being laid down. The following definition is appropriate at the present stage of sponsorship's development.

> Commercial sponsorship is an investment, in cash or in kind, in an activity, in return for access to the exploitable commercial potential associated with that activity.

What this definition is saying is that from the sponsor's point of view the price paid is his investment in return for permission to exploit a particular activity. Essentially the sponsor is buying two things:

1. the exposure potential which the activity has in terms of audience, and
2. the image associated with that activity in terms of how it is perceived.

It is important to regard sponsorship as similar to advertising in that money is invested for commercial purposes. It must not be confused with other forms of corporate giving such as patronage or charity where the motives are altruistic, with the returns expected to be to society and not to the company itself.

THE SIZE OF THE SPONSORSHIP MARKET

Recent decades have seen the very rapid development of commercial sponsorship. An analysis of the UK sponsorship market provides a graphic illustration of this development with UK sponsorship expenditure showing a 10-fold increase between 1974 and 1986. In 1974 expenditure on sponsorship in the UK was estimated at £18 million (Table 1). In 1990 it was estimated that £288 million was spent on sponsorship in the UK (Mintel, 1990).

On a world-wide basis commercial sponsorship is increasingly recognized as a legitimate communications option for marketing management. In 1986 direct sponsorship expenditure world-wide was valued at 3.6 billion dollars, a figure which represents between 2.5 per cent and 3.5 per cent of all advertising expenditure world-wide. In 1987, world-wide expenditure was estimated at 4.1 billion dollars (ISL Marketing, 1988) (Table 2).

The development of sponsorship however is not equally distributed across all markets. In 1984 comparative figures for sponsorship as a percentage of total advertising spend showed considerable variation even among the more developed economies. As can be seen from Table 3, sponsorship in Italy was estimated at 9 per cent of total advertising expenditure compared with only 1.4 per cent in the US market (AGB, 1986). These estimates of sponsorship spending do not include the expenditure which is necessary to ensure the proper exploitation of the chosen sponsorship. The acknowledged industry norm is that expenditure at least equal to the direct sponsorship costs is necessary for adequate exploitation.

Table 1 UK expenditure on sponsorship 1980–1990 (£ million)

Year	Total expenditure
1980	35
1981	72
1982	105
1983	128
1984	145
1985	167
1986	191
1987	220
1988	250
1989	258
1990 (forecast)	288

Source: Mintel

Table 2 World-wide sponsorship expenditure in 1987

	Expenditure (Millions of US dollars)	Percentage of world expenditure
USA	1850	45.1
Western Europe	1329	32.2
Japan	420	10.2
Africa	22	0.5
Americas (excl. USA)	220	5.4
Asia (excl. Japan)	128	3.1
Australasia	80	2.0
Middle East	60	1.5
World-wide total	4100	100.0

Source: *Sponsorship – Has the new medium come of age?* ISL Marketing Ltd., Lucerne, 1988.

Table 3 Sponsorship expenditure as a percentage of advertising expenditure in 1984 (in $ millions)

Country	Advertising expenditure	Sponsorship expenditure	%
Italy	2,580	226	8.8
USA	73,380	1,000	1.4
UK	5,670	157	2.8
West Germany	5,192	98	1.9
Netherlands	2,003	55	2.8

Source: *Advertising Associations*

Driving forces behind sponsorship's development

The dramatic growth of commercial sponsorship as a marketing activity is probably due to the following reasons:

1. *Government policies on tobacco and alcohol*: Changing government policies on advertising for alcohol and cigarettes caused manufacturers of such products to seek alternative promotion media.
2. *Escalating cost of advertising media:* Part of the attraction of commercial sponsorship is the belief that it provides a highly cost-effective marketing communications tool compared with traditional advertising.
3. *The proven ability of sponsorship*: The proven ability of commercial sponsorship to achieve marketing objectives has been responsible for its increased usage.
4. *New opportunities due to increased leisure activity*: Increasingly our leisure-conscious society provides opportunities for sponsorship involvement. This is clear from the wide range of activities currently being pursued in both sports and arts compared with earlier decades.
5. *Greater media coverage of sponsored events*: Increasingly, media coverage, particularly on television, is being directed towards sports and cultural activities, thereby creating opportunities for broadcast sponsorship.
6. *Inefficiencies in traditional media*: A large part of the attraction of sponsorship for sponsors has been its potential as a way to overcome the inefficiencies of traditional advertising media. One such inefficiency is zapping, which decreases the actual audience for television advertising. A further attraction of sponsorship

Table 4 UK expenditure on sponsorship 1980–1988 (£ million)

Year	Sports	Arts	Other	Total
1980	30	3	2	35
1981	60	7	5	72
1982	85	11	9	105
1983	100	15	13	128
1984	110	19	26	145
1985	125	22	20	167
1986	140	26	25	191
1987	160	28	32	220
1988	180	30	40	250

Source: Mintel, 1988

has been the opportunity to escape from the 'clutter' associated with traditional media (although it must now be admitted that certain sports activities are themselves becoming increasingly cluttered).

CURRENT DEVELOPMENTS IN SPONSORSHIP

As a relatively youthful and dynamic industry, commercial sponsorship is undergoing several fundamental changes.

Patterns of expenditure

There is evidence of a trend towards sponsorships that are more diverse than the traditional areas of arts and sport. For example, in the UK, expenditure on sponsorship of non-sports, non-arts activities showed a 20-fold increase over the period 1980–1988 (Table 4) compared with a six-fold increase in sports expenditures (Mintel, 1988). While sport remains the largest sector for sponsorship expenditures, new opportunities are opening up in emerging areas such as popular music, broadcast sponsorship and cause-related marketing activities.

New breed of sponsor

While tobacco and alcohol companies may have initially been drawn to sponsorship for the reasons outlined above, the very success of their involvements has encouraged other entrants. Initially commercial banking institutions entered the sponsorship fray. They were subsequently followed by other financial institutions such as merchant banks and building societies. More recently sponsorship has been taken up by high-tech companies such as computer firms and Japanese electronic firms. Coincident with these changes has been a greater level of sophistication and commercial-mindedness in choice of sponsorship programme.

Increasingly sophisticated support services

A further development has been the improvement in support services available to the sponsor. Sponsorship consultants have become increasingly more specialized and professional while advertising agencies which were initially sceptical have become more involved on behalf of clients. Research agencies have begun to respond to the needs of sponsors for information; several of them now provide profiles of audiences, images of sports and arts activities as well as various methods of measurement.

Future prospects for sponsorship

A continuation of the trends indicated earlier, coupled with the increased commercialization of sports and the arts, the growth of new media, such as cable and satellite television, and the increasing sophistication of corporate sponsors, will ensure the continued growth of commercial sponsorship.

COMMERCIAL SPONSORSHIP IN THE MARKETING COMMUNICATIONS CONTEXT

Given the functions which commercial sponsorship is called upon to perform, it is clear that sponsorship must be viewed as an element of marketing communications within the broader context of the marketing mix of product, price, distribution and marketing communications, i.e., the traditional '4Ps' framework. Commercial sponsorship fits quite naturally alongside advertising, public relations, personal selling and sales promotion in that its basic function lies in achieving marketing communications objectives.

Each method of marketing communication assists in achieving the overall marketing communications objective on behalf of the organization. The task facing management is to evaluate the strengths and weaknesses of each method and to determine the ability of each method to assist in the achievement of objectives.

The various methods of communication must then be combined to complement one another in the most cost-effective manner. The situation is analogous to the different sections of an orchestra being integrated to ensure the best possible overall performance.

SPONSORSHIP OBJECTIVES AND TARGET AUDIENCES

Businesses have a wide variety of audiences with whom they wish to communicate. These are indicated in Figure 1.

The internal public

Increasingly organizations are recognizing the importance of the internal staff public and the necessity to synchronize both the external strategy and the internal back-up systems and staff. With this in mind model organizations such as IBM, Digital, Marks & Spencer are developing 'corporate culture' programmes. Within these programmes sponsorship has a major role to play in fostering staff pride, rewarding effort and in articulating the values of the organization to its staff. The results in terms of staff morale and improved industrial relations are the major benefits of such programmes.

Key decision-makers

Sponsorship allows us to build goodwill among opinion-formers and decision-makers. These can be business associates, government and trade union officials as

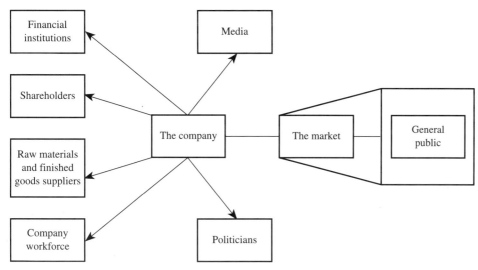

Figure 1 Corporate publics.

well as opinion-formers in the media. Furthermore, as sponsorship is normally built around a particular event, it allows us to offer corporate hospitality to these key decision-makers as our guests. In this way sponsorship is more subtle in its effects than other methods of marketing communication.

The company's target markets

For the purpose of simplicity, objectives in relation to target markets can be subdivided into (i) corporate objectives and (ii) brand objectives.

(i) Corporate objectives
Sponsorship is highly regarded for its ability to achieve certain objectives on behalf of a company. It can:

(a) Increase public awareness of the company.
   There are numerous examples of companies achieving awareness objectives via the medium of sponsorship. Cornhill Insurance via its cricket sponsorship increased awareness in the UK market from 2 per cent to 16 per cent (Dinmore, 1980). Similarly Canon increased its awareness level from 18.5 per cent to 79 per cent over the three-year period of its sponsorship of the English Football League. This result was achieved with considerable support expenditure in other media (Barrie, 1990).
(b) Change the corporate image.
   Changing the corporate image is often a key objective for sponsorship involvement. By its association with Formula One Motor Racing, Yardley managed to dilute the feminine connotations of its name, enabling the introduction of male cosmetics as a result of this newer more macho image. Other corporate image objectives may require sponsorship to act as a medium of community involvement or to counter adverse publicity.

(ii) Brand objectives

Sponsorship is highly regarded for its ability to achieve both brand awareness and brand image objectives. Recently Budweiser and Foster's have used sponsorship as a key element in gaining awareness for their products in European markets. Similarly, it can be used to position a brand on the market or to alter its image within that market. In the Irish market 7-Up have used an innovative popular music sponsorship programme to support nationwide tours by up-and-coming Irish rock bands who later featured in a series of television programmes entitled '7 Bands on the Up'. This sponsorship had the effect of providing access to and repositioning the brand with the youth market (Byrne, 1990).

Within the marketing communications mix, commercial sponsorship can be regarded as a highly cost-effective medium to achieve awareness and image-related objectives at both the corporate and brand level.

SELECTING THE CORRECT SPONSORSHIP

Having identified the role sponsorship is expected to play, the next logical aspect of sponsorship management is the selection process. Potential sponsoring companies are inundated with requests for sponsorship funding. In 1984, Philips reported that they had received 10,000 such requests (Kohl and Otker, 1985). The existence of an agreed sponsorship policy provides an effective method of weeding out inappropriate proposals.

A sponsorship policy must of its nature be company-specific and reflect that company's vision of itself and its products. Generally a sponsorship policy will clearly identify both acceptable and unacceptable areas of activity. For example, a company may decide not to sponsor individuals, blood sports, or a politically sensitive activity such as a rugby tour of South Africa. Similarly a policy may indicate acceptable areas of opportunity, e.g., the Arts, at the upper, rather than the mass level. All potential sponsorships which have successfully passed the policy-screening stage must then be evaluated against selection criteria which have been determined in advance.

A classification of sponsorship criteria

While individual companies must specify the selection criteria which they deem appropriate for their company overall or for particular audiences, the following criteria will generally be part of the selection decision.

The ability to fulfil objectives

A key criterion in the evaluation of any sponsorship proposal is its ability to fulfil stated objectives. These objectives, as indicated earlier, can be stated in both awareness and image terms at both the corporate and brand level. In the case of awareness objectives, success stories can be found at the corporate level (e.g., Cornhill and Canon) and at the brand level (e.g., Fosters and Budweiser).

A second major objective for sponsorship involvement lies in the area of image development. The very fact that a particular sponsorship has its own personality and perception in the public mind is a key criterion in sponsorship choice. This 'image by association' effect is well established in marketing theory. Just as different magazines display qualities of prestige, mood creation, credibility, authority, and other characteristics, similarly there is obviously a 'rub-off' or 'halo-effect' from associating with a particular sponsorship. This image through association or 'rub-off' effect is a central criterion in sponsorship selection.

At the corporate level, Gillette, a very American company, through its involvement with cricket, a traditionally British sport, effectively erased its American image. Similarly at the brand level Pepsi have sponsored concert tours by both Michael Jackson and Tina Turner, to suggest a more youthful image.

Coverage of the defined target audience

As stated, businesses can have a variety of audiences for their sponsorship activity and the ability of a sponsorship programme to match the defined target audience is a critical factor in selecting the particular sponsorship.

This matching process can take place at a number of levels.

A. Demographic
    To gain coverage of their particular markets Rolex sponsor polo while Lee Cooper sponsor rock music. In the past sponsorship selection has been bedevilled by poor profiling of audiences for sports, arts and other activities. However, the efforts of enlightened sports and arts bodies and certain research companies have improved the quality of information considerably and sponsors are now able to evaluate potential sponsorships against their ability to reach their defined target audiences. One such research company, RSL Ltd., publish a leisure monitor which indicates the profile of audiences for major sports and arts activities in the UK (RSL, 1990).

B. Geographic
    The ability of the proposed sponsorship to cover the geographically defined market is also critical in selection. For a multinational company, the ability of the sponsorship to cover its various markets is important. For this reason Coca-Cola sponsor the Olympic Games while a domestically focused company such as Barclays Bank sponsor the Football League in the UK.

C. Life-style
    The ability of the sponsorship to reflect the life-style of the target audience is another important selection criterion. For this reason Volvo select both tennis and golf, while brewing and cigarette companies are more likely to sponsor darts and snooker.

The level of coverage of the target audience

The amount of likely exposure and the audience size likely to be exposed to the company's message is an important selection determinant. Depending on the activity being proposed the potentially exposed audience can be measured in terms of:

(a) Participants – e.g., New York Marathon.
(b) On-site fans.
(c) Media coverage, e.g., the 1986 World Cup was seen in 166 different countries with a gross cumulative audience of 13,506,689,000 viewers (ISL Marketing, 1988).

Potential media coverage is often a key determinant in the selection process. For companies seeking corporate hospitality it may represent a useful bonus; for major branded goods companies it may be the basis of their involvement.

The costs associated with the sponsorship programme

Affordability may be a key criterion. In costing any sponsorship the cost of 'leveraging' the programme with support activity must be included. (Leveraging refers to the additional effort, largely promotional, which must be invested by the sponsor in order to properly exploit the opportunity provided as a result of securing particular sponsorship rights.)

Depending on the sponsor's rationale for involvement, various other criteria such as the opportunities for guest hospitality, staff knowledge of the proposed sponsorship, the organization of the sponsored activity and the distraction factor involved may be employed to evaluate the various opportunities available.

The process of sponsorship selection can be rendered more systematic if the following approach is used. Each proposal, once short-listed following satisfaction of policy guidelines, is evaluated against the criteria deemed appropriate for the particular programme. To do this each selection criterion should be ranked in terms of priority of preferred attainment and each proposal scored in terms of its ability to fulfil the stated criteria. A total score can thus be computed for each sponsorship proposal, enabling a more objective evaluation.

Implementing the sponsorship programme

The success of the sponsorship programme will be dependent to a large extent on how it is implemented. A critical factor is that the sponsorship be implemented as part of a marketing campaign and thus integrated with other elements of marketing communications. The sponsor must also support the sponsorship by additional advertising and promotions. It is commonly agreed that a figure of at least equal value to the direct fee payment must be used in leveraging the original sponsorship investment.

MEASURING SPONSORSHIP RESULTS

Having chosen the most appropriate sponsorship and ensured its proper implementation, it is then necessary to evaluate the sponsorship programme against the objectives stated at the outset. As is the case with all forms of marketing communication whether it is advertising or commercial sponsorship, the evaluation process is greatly facilitated if measurement is undertaken at several key stages.

(a) At the outset measurement is required to determine the company's present position in terms of awareness and image with the target audience.
(b) Interim Tracking may be necessary if the sponsorship is longer term in order to detect movement on the chosen dimensions of awareness, image and market attitude.
(c) Final evaluation must take place when the sponsorship is completed to determine performance levels against the stated objectives.

Bases for measuring sponsorship effectiveness

There are five main methods of measuring sponsorship effectiveness.

1. Measuring the level of media coverage/exposure gained

The level of media coverage gained as a result of sponsorship involvement is frequently used by sponsors as an indicator of performance. Such evaluation consists of measuring:

(a) the duration of television coverage;
(b) monitored radio coverage; and
(c) the extent of press coverage in terms of single column inches.

The monitoring of media coverage as a proxy measure of sponsorship effectiveness is widely used, essentially because it is practicable. However, it is important to recognize that the level of media coverage merely indicates the extent of the publicity resulting from the sponsorship and as such, is basically similar to indicating the level of advertising time or space bought. As such, this measure on its own does not evaluate the effectiveness of the exposure gained.

2 Measuring the communications effectiveness of sponsorship involvement

As sponsorship is used to achieve basic communication objectives such as awareness and image, there is a tendency to evaluate sponsorship results in communications rather than sales terms. Levels of awareness achieved, attitudes created, perceptions changed or associations suggested are measured against stated objectives. One such example is provided by Cornhill Insurance in the UK, who decided to measure the effectiveness of their sponsorship using a research study every six months to establish the following:

1. unprompted name awareness;
2. prompted name awareness;
3. unprompted awareness of Cornhill as a sports sponsor;
4. prompted awareness of Cornhill as a sports sponsor;
5. attitudes towards sponsorship.

The results of four six monthly research studies indicated that unprompted awareness increased from 2 per cent to 8 per cent to 13 per cent to 16 per cent with evidence of a fall-off in cricket's off-season. Its investment of £2 million returned an estimated £15–20 million worth of new business over a short period (Dinmore, 1980).

Sponsoring companies also attempt to evaluate sponsorship results by focusing on the degree to which respondents associate the company or the product with the sponsored activity. An example of this type of research in terms of levels of awareness and degree of association is provided in Table 5 (Mintel, 1980, 1986, 1988, 1990).

It is particularly notable from Table 5 that there is a dramatic increase in the awareness level for Marlboro as a motor racing sponsor from 6 per cent to 42 per cent over a six-year period from 1974 to 1980.

The degree to which a sponsoring company is associated with a particular sponsorship activity can be correlated with classification variables such as sex, age and social class, thereby enabling the sponsor to determine the level of awareness he has achieved with his identified target market.

Similar types of studies of corporate involvement in art sponsorship generally show low awareness and association levels. However, it must be recognized that arts sponsorship tends to offer high awareness levels within select minority populations, and thus the results of any awareness/association studies must be seen in this light.

Table 5 Motor racing sponsorship awareness

	Percentage of respondents mentioning each sponsor			
	1974	*1977*	*1980*	*1988*
Texaco	18	45	47	60
John Player	22	43	44	66
Marlboro	6	25	42	55
Rothmans	11	13	13	50
None/don't know	35	20	19	n/a

Source: Mintel

As well as creating corporate or brand awareness, one of the particular capabilities of commercial sponsorship is in altering corporate or brand image. One such example is the case of IVECO trucks in the US market. IVECO established through research that the reason their trucks were not selling particularly well on the US market was because they were perceived as weak European vehicles compared to their more macho American competitors. The sponsorship of heavyweight boxing enabled IVECO to associate with a macho activity and reach key decision-makers. Subsequent research showed that this particular campaign was highly successful.

3. Measuring the sales effectiveness of sponsorship
In commercial sponsorship, as is the case with advertising and marketing communications generally, the matter of keying sales results to given expenditures is highly problematic for a variety of reasons.

(i) The simultaneous usage of other marketing inputs.
(ii) The carry-over effect of previous marketing communications effort.
(iii) Uncontrollable variables in the business environment such as competitor activity or changing economic conditions.

While these factors make the keying of sales results to sponsorship investment somewhat more difficult, many sponsors point to sales results as evidence of sponsorship effects even if providing conclusive proof of this effect is difficult. American Express found that card usage rose by nearly 30 per cent during the period it ran the Statue of Liberty campaign in the USA (Gottlier, 1986).

4. Monitoring guest feedback
Where the objective of sponsorship involvement is the provision of guest hospitality, the monitoring of guest opinions can provide a measure of sponsorship impact. Similarly, where company staff or the local community are being targeted the monitoring of feedback can also provide a useful measure of effectiveness. Other sources of feedback can be the participants, spectators and activity organizers as well as the company's own sales force.

5. Cost – benefit analysis
Where the motivation for sponsorship involvement is more philanthropic than commercially rational, it is necessary to go beyond conventional marketing measures

to evaluate the effects achieved. In such instances, it may be necessary to utilize the collective opinion of senior management as the basis for evaluation.

CONCLUSION

Commercial sponsorship, while initially used in a rather cavalier manner by many sponsoring companies is today regarded as a highly cost-effective method of marketing communication. The increased sophistication of present day sponsors, the increasing range and standard of support services and the substitution by sponsorship recipients of a hard-nosed commercialization for a previously held commercial naivety have all ensured much more sophistication in terms of sponsorship usage. Such changes allied to accumulated learning experience have led to the current recognition of commercial sponsorship as a legitimate option within the marketing communications mix.

REFERENCES

Byrne, M. (1990) The public relations and marketing opportunities of music sponsorship. *Case Study: Seven-Up. Arts Council Seminar, Sponsorship and the Irish Music Industry.* (National Concert Hall, Dublin 22.5.90).
Dinmore, F. (1980) Cricket Sponsorship. *The Business Graduate (UK)*, Autumn, pp. 68–72.
Gill, B. London: CSS International Holdings Ltd. (Personal interview 1990).
Gottlier, M. (1986) Cashing in on a higher cause. *The New York Times*, July 6th.
ISL Marketing Ltd. (December 1988) *Sponsorship: has the new medium come of age?* Lucerne: ISL.
Kohl, F. and Otker, T. (1985) Sponsorship – some practical experiences in Philips consumer electronics. ESOMAR Seminar. Paper delivered at Below-the-line and Sponsoring Seminar, 6–8 November 1985, Milan: Esomar.
Mintel Special Report on Sponsorship (1988) London: Mintel.
Mintel Special Report on Sponsorship (1990) London: Mintel.
RSL. Leisure Monitor (1990) Harrow, Middlesex UK: Research Services Ltd.
Sport on Television and Sports Sponsorship (1986) New Media Dept., AGB Intomart, p. 42.
Various special reports on Sponsorship (1980, 1986, 1988, 1990) Mintel, London.

Meenaghan, T. (1991) 'The role of sponsorship in the marketing communications mix'. *International Journal of Advertising*, 10(1): 35–47. Reproduced with permission.

Section 7
Sales Promotion

The aim of this section is to provide a theoretically well-founded discussion of sales promotion activities. This is achieved by the inclusion of articles which detail activities classed as sales promotion, together with exploration of the merits and demerits of such activities, and strategies for effective management of commonly used promotional activities. Appropriately, three articles in this section – from Jones (1990), Boddewyn and Leardi (1989) and Peattie and Peattie (1993) – provide the reader with a detailed history of sales promotion, with each article then exploring a different aspect of the technique.

Jones (1990) also examines and evaluates the effectiveness of sales promotion in the short and long term, and explores its symbiotic role in marketing communications in achieving marketing efficiency, whereas the different types and functions of sales promotion activities used throughout the world are described by Boddewyn and Leardi (1989), together with useful observations on effective control and maximization of promotion campaigns. The emphasis on effective management is continued in the following three articles which explore two particular sales promotion activities from the promotional toolkit – the competition and the coupon respectively. Peattie and Peattie (1993) provide depth insights into the relationship between customers, competitions, and marketing outcomes, together with useful consideration of the benefits and risks of the technique.

On a slightly different tack, Bawa and Shoemaker (1987) examine the effects of direct mail coupons on brand choice behaviour, identifying positive short-term outcomes for mature brands.

The double jeopardy of sales promotions

7.1

John Philip Jones

For more than a decade, sales promotions have grown in importance, becoming the most popular tool in the marketer's kit. A brief look back helps to explain how tougher market conditions and shrinking profits pushed marketers to use promotions to fight for share. But a hard look at the numbers and a careful consideration of the logic of promotions reveals their disastrous short- and long-term costs – the double jeopardy of sales promotions.

Since World War II, consumer goods markets in the United States have been inexorably maturing – and gradually stagnating. They have been slowing in aggregate growth and eventually, in one market after another, stabilizing in total volume, except for annual increases of 1% or 2% caused mainly by population growth.

During the 1970s, an important change took place: the number of stabilized markets overtook the number of still growing markets (see Figure 1). Now, more than a decade later, stable markets are much the rule and growing ones the exception. An examination of consumer usage data collected by Mediamark Research shows that only 13 out of 150 large consumer goods markets grew by more than 10% in 1989.

This lack of market vitality appears irreversible since it represents a seemingly permanent ceiling on consumers' purchase levels in all except a few areas – mainly financial and other services and high-tech, not the traditional categories of packaged goods and consumer durables. A number of important markets, including cigarettes, coffee, dairy products, and hard liquour, are actually declining.

This stagnation of markets has affected manufacturers in two ways. First, manufacturers find it harder to grow, in particular to improve their profits. With effortless earnings growth gone, manufacturers have been forced to adopt tougher (albeit reasonably successful) policies. All of the following strategies were plentifully evident during the 1980s:

- Fighting with fury for market share, using promotions (generally a high-cost activity) as the main tactical weapon.
- Seeking and exploiting small but growing segments of static markets, often through range extensions of existing brand names. This has led to a fragmentation of markets and a splintering of consumer franchises. There were 31 major brands of toothpaste in 1989, for example, versus 7 in 1979; 52 big brands of coffee, against 33 a decade earlier; and 28 models of Ford cars, compared with 7 in 1960.
- Exploring untraditional product categories. Sometimes, however, this strategy backfired, as manufacturers applied their expertise less successfully than in their

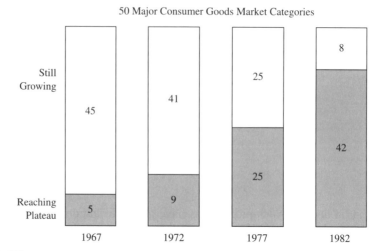

Figure 1 When consumer markets flattened.

Source: U.S. Department of Commerce, Bureau of the Census, Census of Manufacturers, 1986.

original fields of endeavor. For example, Procter & Gamble burned its fingers with ventures in orange juice (Citrus Hill) and potato chips (Pringle's).

- Searching for more business overseas, such as McDonald's extensive overseas ventures.
- Pruning costs, for instance, through reduced 'theme' advertising and R&D expenditures. The danger with cutting R&D investments is, of course, the risk of eating the seed corn.
- Finally and most significant, embarking on mergers and acquisitions, despite their steeply rising cost, in a search for scale economies and diversification.

The second effect on manufacturers stems partly from the growing market stagnation and partly from the inflationary conditions of the 1970s. Business became accustomed to declining income (measured in real terms). During the nine years of high inflation, 1974 to 1982, aggregate corporate profits were static in real terms in 1979 and declined in 1974, 1975, 1980, 1981, and 1982.

Even profit itself came to be regarded, at least for a while, as a less than adequate measure of corporate performance. '"Profit," it cannot be said often enough, is an accounting illusion,' wrote Peter Drucker at the time. 'The announcement of "record profits" is being greeted with skepticism by the Stock Exchange and with hostility by the public at large.'[1]

During the 1970s, managers got into the habit of simultaneously boosting the list prices of their goods and making deep promotional price cuts. Producers therefore sliced profit away before they could benefit from it. The habit of mind associated with this procedure has not totally disappeared. Indeed, it offers the most plausible explanation for a tacit and possibly unconscious shift of goals on the part of many businesspeople. Despite a good deal of talk about the importance of profit, the actual pursuit of profit appears to have given way de facto to a search for growth in naked sales volume.

These two factors have led to much puzzlement and frustration. But they have certainly not led to any slackening of the competitive impulse. Competition – in particular competitive response – has become increasingly aggressive as manufacturers react in frustration to what they see as the inertia of markets. Their yardstick of success is market share. The initial competitive drive and the reaction it generates can cancel one another out, but the drive continues unabated because manufacturers have an atavistic fear of relaxation.

Manufacturers regard sales volume and market share as the keys to the future. This view is not entirely fallacious insofar as volume can represent a source of repeat business and of manufacturing and marketing scale economies. But producers' concentration on sales volume has caused them to neglect the price they pay and the earnings they are obliged to sacrifice as a result of the marketing plans they embark on so optimistically.

But there is an even more worrisome set of problems for manufacturers than massive, and often concealed, costs created by these attempts to boost short-term volume at their competitors' expense – ill effects that come to life in the long term. These short- and long-term outcomes represent a double jeopardy that managers of consumer goods companies unthinkingly and unwittingly encounter as a routine part of their marketing operations.

PROMOTIONS IN THE SHORT TERM

The saturation of markets and the urge to drive up market shares have been major underlying causes of a significant change of emphasis between theme advertising (in advertising accounting parlance, 'above the line,' because it represents actual outlays) and promotions ('below the line,' because they sacrifice income). During the past decade and more, manufacturers have increased promotional expenditures more than their advertising budgets until promotions accounted for an estimated 66% of total expenditures above and below the line in 1986, compared with 58% in 1976.[2]

Manufacturers have pumped increasing quantities of money into promotions, believing that promotions have a greater and more immediate proportionate effect on sales than theme advertising has. Historically, the responsiveness of sales to promotional activity is not very much in dispute, but there are enormous concealed problems in the proper measurement of such effects.

A promotion enables a manufacturer to buy tonnage sales on a once-and-for-all basis. It rarely stimulates repeat purchases. And although a promotion normally has a measurable short-term effect on sales, the downside is that in most cases manufacturers pay an exorbitant price. The only explanation for this is their failure to calculate rigorously enough what they are really paying for the tonnage.

In most circumstances, promotions mean price reductions. Even manufacturers' own terminology disguises this fact, calling them 'investments.' They are in reality income sacrificed; they should appear on the income side of the ledger (as a reduction, a negative item), not on the expenditure side (as money paid out). Trade promotions, accounting for 37 percentage points of the 66% of the total advertising dollars spent on promotions,[3] are virtually always rebates, even when described as 'slotting allowances' and 'display incentives.' Of consumer promotions, which account for the remaining 29 percentage points, the most important are coupons and various types of temporary price reductions (TPRs) – price rebates printed on the labels, banded packs, free samples, and so on. These devices, both those directed at the trade and those at the consumer, are mostly variations of price cutting.

Given enough historical data to calculate a coefficient of price elasticity, the sales effect of price cutting can be quantified, though with a good deal of trouble. This number is simply the percentage by which sales of a brand will increase immediately as a result of a 1% reduction in price. It is preceded by a minus sign, demonstrating that lower prices cause sales to go up and vice versa.

The elasticity can of course be calculated for sales into the retail trade as well as for sales to the consumer, and there are some interesting differences between the two. The focus here, however, is on the consumer. But trade and consumer promotions can be connected. In particular, the retailer does not always retain the profit from a trade promotion but sometimes passes it to the customer, for example, by doubling the value of manufacturers' coupons.

Price elasticity is essentially a measure of how easily the consumer will accept a competitive brand as a substitute for the brand being examined. Low elasticity means that substitution is difficult and a change in price will not affect demand for the brand very greatly. The opposite also holds: high elasticity means that a price change greatly affects demand. As the number of competitors grows – which tends to happen despite slow growth in markets – we would logically expect price elasticities in general to rise. A survey by Gerard Tellis, a professor at the University of Southern California, provides some evidence to support this hypothesis.[4]

Calculations of price elasticity are not simple, but they have often been made. They are almost always based on a narrow range of price variations, which means that they should not be extrapolated too far outside this range. They are nevertheless useful for sales optimization and profit maximization, a process in which I participated in the early 1960s.

A number of estimates of the average price elasticity of groups of brands have been published. The most recent major study, reported in Tellis's article, reviews data on 367 brands that appeared in the academic literature from 1961 to 1985. Certainly, the most striking feature of Tellis's survey is the high level of the average price elasticity, – 1.76. This means that for an average brand, a 1% price reduction would boost sales by 1.76%. Of course, manufacturers do not vary their prices in 1% increments; a more realistic 10% price reduction would lift sales by 17.6%, an impressive figure. But this increase alone provides an extremely incomplete picture of the effect of the price reduction, as I will demonstrate later.

Table 1 displays the effect of a 10% price reduction based on price elasticities of – 1.6, – 1.8, – 2.0, and – 2.2. Tellis argues that typical marketplace elasticities may be much higher than the – 1.76 average he worked out from the 367 cases. The empirical support for this claim is more tenuous, however, than that for his – 1.76 average. Estimates based on European experience suggest that even this figure may be too high.[5] I have therefore limited the calculations to the range of four coefficients, which covers not only Tellis's average but also elasticities on both sides of it.

The sales projections in the table give ample support to the view that promotions can shift merchandise. The attraction they hold for brand managers is therefore understandable, particularly if managers find themselves in the uncomfortable situation of running brands whose shipments during the year have been unexpectedly slow and whose sales targets have to be met by December 31. The pressure is especially great if a brand manager's career is on the line.

Table 1 Sales and profit outcomes of a 10% price reduction

Variable cost (as a percent of NSV)	Price elasticity level	Effect on sales	Effect on net profit (if 5% of NSV)	Effect on net profit (if 10% of NSV)
40%	−2.2	+22%	+20%	+10%
50	−2.2	+22	−24	−12
60	−2.2	+22	−67	−34
40	−2.0	+20	No change	No change
50	−2.0	+20	−40	−20
60	−2.0	+20	−80	−40
40	−1.8	+18	−20	−10
50	−1.8	+18	−56	−28
60	−1.8	+18	−92	−46
40	−1.6	+16	−40	−20
50	−1.6	+16	−72	−36
60	−1.6	+16	−104	−52

But the attractive volume figures are not the whole story; the brand managers must look at the effect on costs. To do this, they have to make assumptions about cost structures. In table 1, I have worked out alternatives on the basis of ratios that are reasonably typical for real brands: a variable cost representing 40%, 50%, and 60% of net sales value (NSV),[6] and net profit representing 5% and 10% of NSV.

The obvious feature of the profit calculations is that most of the sales increases provided by the price reductions yield a lower profit than before the sales rise. Indeed, some of the resulting profit reductions are disastrously large. The reasons for this unappealing outcome are an increase in variable costs (including raw materials, packaging, and labor) required by the extra sales volume, in conjunction with a reduction in NSV that applies to all sales resulting from the lower price.

Manufacturers undertake a certain amount of promotion for defensive reasons – for instance, to maintain high distribution and display for brands in an increasingly concentrated retail trade, especially the supermarket trade. This is understandable, although manufacturers should not neglect the countervailing force to retailers' strength, which is using consumer advertising to pull the merchandise through the retail pipeline and, perhaps equally important, making sure that retail buyers are aware of this activity.

Although it is difficult to distinguish offensive from defensive motives in promotional activity, I believe that the former are generally more important. Indeed, it seems clear that in most circumstances, manufacturers that promote heavily are deliberately exchanging profit for volume; in other words, making less profit on more sales or, to make the point more crudely, slicing into their own margins in dumping their merchandise.

PROMOTIONS IN THE LONG TERM

Looking beyond the distressing short-term effects, the manufacturer may be able to spot the even more worrying long-term legacy of promotions. There are three related points to consider about the long range:

1. There is overwhelming marketplace evidence that 'the consumer sales effect is limited to the time period of the promotion itself.'[7] A price-off promotion causes sales to rise, but once the promotion stops, they return to their original level. The 'blip' on the A.C. Nielsen consumer purchases graph looks like the silhouette of a top hat. The reason is simply that the strategy for such a promotion aims to move merchandise by bribing the retailer and the consumer. When the bribe stops, the extra sales also stop. (In an exceptional circumstance, when a brand is on a strongly rising sales trend, a promotion admittedly can put sales more or less permanently a notch higher than at the beginning.)

Some commentators have argued that a portion of promotional money has a long-term, franchise-building effect.[8] There is a little truth in this argument when it relates to promotions that encourage repeat purchase. But TPRs and coupons – which together account for the lion's share of promotion budgets – have just about the weakest long-term effect of any below-the-line activity. TPRs in particular lack the customary stress on building a consumer franchise that features the brand's competitive benefits or builds warm, nonrational associations with it. These are factors that might encourage the public to buy the goods on a more continual basis. As a consequence, promotions bring volatile demand while franchise building leads to stable demand.

A promotion often also produces what Nielsen calls a 'mortgaging' effect by bringing forward sales from a later period. Thus full-price sales following the promotion period may be even slower than they would otherwise have been. This prolongs the period when the manufacturer is paying a heavy promotional subsidy to the consumer.

All this leads to a significant weakening of the brand. A parallel point, for which there is patchy evidence, is that brands supported more by advertising than by promotions often carry a higher-than-average list price without much trouble and tend therefore to be more profitable. The consumer will pay the premium price because the advertised brands have offered more psychological added values than heavily promoted brands.

2. Promotions fuel the flames of competitive retaliation far more than other marketing activities. As a result, they bring diminishing returns with frightening rapidity. When the competition gets drawn into the promotion war, the effect can be a significant muting of the sharp sales increases predicted by the original price elasticity coefficients – with an even more disastrous effect on the profit outturn of the promotions.

The long-term result of such retaliation is sometimes the elimination of all profit from total market categories. There is no shortage of examples of this self-destructive effect. Two dramatic instances I remember are the market for laundry detergents in Denmark during the 1960s and the once-large market in Britain for fruit concentrates, which were mixed with water to make soft drinks. In both markets, heavy promotions eventually caused strong brands to degenerate into virtually unbranded and unprofitable commodities.

3. Promotions are said to devalue the image of the promoted brand in the consumer's eyes. This agrees with common sense, although there is little evidence to support it. Indeed, the argument may not be quite as powerful as it appears because an established consumer franchise takes a long time to decay as people's familiarity with and usage of the brand do more to maintain the image than external marketing stimuli

do. On occasion, promotions undoubtedly have had an unfavorable influence on consumers' brand perceptions. This evidently happened to Burger King in the late 1970s and early 1980s, when the chain became locked in a promotion war with McDonald's.

As a rule, promotions can never improve a brand image or help the stability of the consumer franchise. At Unilever, a saying describes the vicious circle as promotion, commotion, demotion.

Consumer advertising, on the other hand, can strengthen the image. This represents a long-term effect in addition to short-term sales generation, and it leads to a growing perceived differentiation of the advertised brand from rival brands. Differentiation reduces a rival's ability to substitute for the advertised brand, thus leading to greater stability (that is, less elasticity) of consumer demand. (I should note that certain informed observers doubt whether the low creative quality of present-day campaigns actually leads to as much image building as past advertising was capable of doing.)

THE RETURN ON ADVERTISING

But if promotions exact massive short-term costs and bring about worrisome long-term problems, can advertising investments promise anything better in either the short or long term?

The strictly short-term effect of advertising can, on occasion, be quantified through a calculation of the advertising elasticity of a brand. This number measures the percentage increase in sales to be expected from a 1% increase in advertising weight. Preceding the coefficient is a plus sign, since (it is hoped!) an increase in advertising will produce growth in sales.

Calculating an advertising elasticity involves complex regression calculations, but (as for price elasticity) the computation has been carried out in hundreds of cases. The spread of research based on single-source scanner data will make it easier to make such calculations in the future.[9]

The most recently published examination of advertising elasticity, based on 128 cases, yielded an average short-term advertising elasticity of +0.22.[10] This figure jibes well with earlier studies. The difference between this coefficient of +0.22 and the average price elasticity of -1.76 is certainly large. But it would be extremely dangerous and costly to conclude that promotions are therefore more effective. The major difference between promotions and advertising is that promotional price reductions cost the manufacturer much more money than advertising increases do, so that it is misleading to evaluate their relative effectiveness by their sales effects alone.[11]

In Table 2, I am concerned solely with the operational changes that a manufacturer is accustomed to making in the marketing variables. Business does not operate with 1% advertising variations any more than it does with 1% price changes. From my experience of advertising pressure testing and the difficulties of measuring its effects, 50% is the minimum uplift in the advertising appropriation that will get the needle to swing.

It is strikingly obvious from the table that, despite the small sales effects of the extra advertising, this volume produced good profit increases in most cases. This is quite different from the effect of the price reductions analyzed in Table 1 when serious earnings erosion undercut the substantial sales growth.

Table 2 Sales and profit outcomes of a 50% advertising increase

Variable cost (as a percent of NSV)	Advertising to sales ratio	Advertising elasticity level	Effect on sales	Effect on net profit (if 5% of NSV)	Effect on net profit (if 10% of NSV)
40%	4%	+0.1	+5%	+20%	+10%
50	4	+0.1	+5	+10	+5
60	4	+0.1	+5	No change	No change
40	4	+0.2	+10	+80%	+40%
50	4	+0.2	+10	+60	+30
60	4	+0.2	+10	+40	+20
40	4	+0.3	+15	+140	+70
50	4	+0.3	+15	+110	+55
60	4	+0.3	+15	+80	+40
40	6	+0.1	+5	No change	No change
50	6	+0.1	+5	−10%	−5%
60	6	+0.1	+5	−20	−10
40	6	+0.2	+10	+60	+30
50	6	+0.2	+10	+40	+20
60	6	+0.2	+10	+20	+10
40	6	+0.3	+15	+120	+60
50	6	+0.3	+15	+90	+45
60	6	+0.3	+15	+60	+30
40	8	+0.1	+5	−20	−10
50	8	+0.1	+5	−30	−15
60	8	+0.1	+5	−40	−20
40	8	+0.2	+10	+40	+20
50	8	+0.2	+10	+20	+10
60	8	+0.2	+10	No change	No change
40	8	+0.3	+15	+100%	+50%
50	8	+0.3	+15	+70	+35
60	8	+0.3	+15	+40	+20

But before we rush headlong out of promotions and into advertising, thereby making the advertising agencies our friends for life, let me remind readers that the world is a confusing place and that there are some additional complications to be examined.

FROM THEORY TO PRACTICE

By helping project the sales volume and profit that are likely to follow marketing actions, mathematical techniques are meant to sharpen the efficiency of corporate practice. This discipline is rarely applied in the United States and in other sophisticated marketing environments, however, because few manufacturers will take the considerable trouble to develop the tools – that is, to estimate the price elasticity and advertising elasticity of their brands. This is more than a once-and-for-all process because the actual outturn of promotional and advertising activities may differ slightly from predictions, so producers must monitor price and advertising elasticities continuously and adjust them as necessary.

Obviously, the first task is to do a good deal of homework to produce the elasticity coefficients. In addition, I make three operational recommendations:

Price elasticity and list price

The first possibility a manufacturer should consider is a permanent price increase for the particular brand. At the lower levels of price elasticity, the loss of sales from a 5% or 10% price increase would be so small, and the added revenue from the higher price so significant, that the price reduction would probably lead to a net increase in the income earned by the brand. This is a realistic possibility for brands with price elasticities of -1.0 and less. If the elasticity is less than -0.5, the chance of a major profit increase is very good indeed.

Price elasticity and promotion planning

Promotions must be carried out in a planned and well-disciplined fashion. To test the soundness of the planning for each brand's promotional program, manufacturers should estimate how much promotion is necessary for defensive purposes – that is, to maintain competitive levels of display in supermarkets (or whatever the arena is) and to counter aggressive promotional action of the largest and most direct competition.

This is of course a judgment call. But the projections of sales and profit from particular price reductions provide the best available data on which evaluation of the probable results of the manufacturer's own moves can be based. Moreover, the producer, with a good deal of trouble but little additional expense, can provide itself with something extra by way of background data. This will come from close analysis of the marketplace effectiveness of every promotion staged, which should include an objective evaluation of performance against initial targets.

This recommendation may appear rather trite and unnecessary, but I am aware of only a handful of manufacturers that make any effort to do this. An old adage, too easily forgotten, says that manufacturers should always strive to achieve a double benefit from their marketing programs: first, additional profit, and second, increased knowledge and expertise.

Advertising elasticity and advertising planning

A common problem in computing the advertising elasticity of a brand is that the mathematics, no matter how skillfully executed, may show a complete absence of sales effect attributable to the advertising. There can be two reasons for this, mathematical insensitivity and inadequacy or (against the manufacturer's own judgment) an absence of any sales effect to be discovered.

There is no fundamental reason to be disheartened by the discovery that a well-loved campaign has no effect on sales. The fact may be disappointing, but the accurate intelligence itself should be welcomed.

It does, however, put the manufacturer in a difficult position. If management is obliged to conclude that the emperor in fact has few clothes, the most pressing task is to find out how to achieve a measurable effect that can be evaluated for its financial implications. This means embarking on an energetic program of experimentation, covering alternative advertising campaigns, budgets, media, and phasing, and this should go on until the manufacturer and the advertising agency manage to throw up some perceptible results (or are forced to give up in despair). The research costs will be heavy because the manufacturer must evaluate extensive market testing not only for short-term sales-generating effects but also for any long-term job it may be doing.

This work may involve something that can be monitored reasonably directly (for example, the advertising may be slowly modifying consumers' perceptions of brand attributes). But its effects could very possibly be well below the surface. For instance, the advertising may be doing a protective job for the brand in a competitive environment, and this may be measurable only when a cutback causes an erosion in market share – a very serious outcome that could take a long time to surface. This possibility means that experimentation, particularly if it involves downweighting, must be carefully evaluated over a long period of time.

But what should be done if, after giving advertising every chance, there is no perceptible short- or long-term effect? Quite frankly, the manufacturer should cut its losses. A brand can be maintained in effective distribution by a minimal level of promotional support and with only enough theme advertising to keep the brand name intermittently in front of the salesforce and the retail trade. And sometimes there is no theme advertising at all. Growth from brands that are modestly supported in this way is too much to expect, but they can maintain a low level of profitable sales, in some cases for decades. I was associated with such a brand, Lux toilet soap. Lux is sold extremely widely and is the market leader in a number of countries around the world. While it has received no theme advertising support in the United States since 1967, to this day it maintains a measurable and profitable market share.

In regard to advertising that does have a demonstrable marketplace effect, it probably influences the consumer by strengthening the image attributes of the brand and hence its perceived difference from the competition. The process, which is stimulated by image-building advertising and nourished by repeat purchases, gives competitors difficulty in substituting for the brand (thus reducing the price elasticity of demand for it). With this protection, demand for the brand will be less responsive to promotional price cutting. This is the reason why larger and stronger brands have the balance of their marketing efforts tipped more toward theme advertising than smaller and weaker brands have.

Whatever a manufacturer decides to emphasize in a campaign, the goal is marketing efficiency. The mathematical technique I have described has demonstrated uses in furthering such efficiency. It can lift the veil that the frantic search for sales volume and market share throws over actual results. It can show manufacturers the nature of the double jeopardy they face when embarking on promotion programs without analyzing the short- and long-term consequences in costs and foregone profits.

Author's note: For their counsel and suggestions, I thank Simon Broadbent of Leo Burnett, William Weilbacher of the Bismark Corporation, and Boris Wilenkin of Unilever.

NOTES

1 Peter F. Drucker, *Managing in Turbulent Times* (New York: Harper & Row, 1980), pp. 29, 11.

2 Estimates by Donnelly Marketing. More recent, unpublished figures from Batten, Barton, Durstine & Osborn, New York, jibe with these estimates. The most recent estimate of below-the-line expenditure is 69%.

3 Simon Broadbent, *The Advertiser's Handbook for Budget Determination* (Lexington, Mass.: Lexington Books, 1988), p. 28.

4 Gerard J. Tellis, 'The Price Elasticity of Selective Demand: A Meta-Analysis of Econometric Models of Sales,' *Journal of Marketing Research*, November 1988, p. 331.

5 One analysis produced an average price elasticity of −1.32, according to Simon Broadbent in 'Price and Advertising: Volume and Profit,' *Admap*, November 1980, p. 536. Andrew Roberts calculated −1.67 in 'The Decision Between Above- and Below-the-Line,' *Admap*, December 1980, p. 590.

6 Taking published estimates of advertising-to-sales ratios for the main U.S. industries, *Advertising Age* has analyzed them according to advertising's percentage of sales and its percentage of margin (indirect cost). From these data, it is possible to extrapolate the average ratios of variable cost by industry. 'Advertising-to-Sales Ratios, 1989,' *Advertising Age*, November 13, 1989, p. 32.

7 James O. Peckham, Sr., *The Wheel of Marketing* (privately published but available through A.C. Nielsen, second edition, 1981), p. 69.

8 See, for example, Robert M. Prentice, 'How to Split Your Marketing Funds Between Advertising and Promotion,' *Advertising Age*, January 10, 1977, p. 41.

9 For an examination of this innovation, see Magid M. Abraham and Leonard M. Lodish, 'Getting the Most Out of Advertising and Promotion,' HBR May–June 1990, p. 50.

10 Gert Assmus, John U. Farlet, and Donald R. Lehmann, 'How Advertising Affects Sales: Meta-Analysis of Econometric Results,' *Journal of Marketing Research*, February 1984, p. 65.

11 This point is trenchantly argued in Simon Broadbent, 'Point of View: What Is a "Small" Advertising Elasticity?' *Journal of Advertising Research*, August–September 1989, p. 37.

7.2 Sales promotions: practice, regulation and self-regulation around the world

Jean J. Boddewyn and Monica Leardi

To stimulate distributors to carry their products and entice consumers to try them out and re-purchase them, many firms give away free samples, distribute coupons and trading stamps, run contests and games of chance, offer price rebates, link the purchase of one good to another, and use other forms of sales promotion (SP) – often in concert with advertising programmes.

The appeal of sales promotions is related to several factors: the increasing cost and clutter of television commercials; the difficulty of effectively differentiating a growing number of comparable products and services by means of 'straight' advertising; the simpler targeting of distributors and consumers through sales promotions; and the easier tracking down of SP performance, compared to measuring the effects of regular advertising. While advertising focuses more on reasons *why* consumers should buy a product, sales promotions emphasize why they should buy it *now*. Still, doubts have been expressed about the ability of sales promotions to generate long-lasting customer loyalty.

PRACTICE

The variety, volume and relative importance of sales promotions are increasing in many countries. In the United States, annual expenditure on sales promotion – both to the trade and to consumers – have surpassed advertising expenditures every year since 1974, and they are growing faster than advertising expenditures.

Yet estimating promotion expenditures and their trends is a notoriously difficult task because of unstandardized nomenclatures, incomplete statistics, varying rates of inflation, and fluctuating exchange rates which distort the comparison of figures expressed in US dollars (Starch INRA Hooper, 1987). Besides, the various subsectors – traditional mass media, direct mail, sales promotion, etc. – are prone to exaggerating their size and growth.

Thus, quoting Saatchi & Saatchi numbers, Perriss (1988) and Wentz (1988) estimate US expenditures on 'sales promotion, point-of-sale and others' at $22 billion (see Table 1), while COMART Associates (the US subsidiary of the London-based KLP Group), in their recent promotion brochure, talk of a $100+ 'promotion market' in the United States. COMART Associates also mention that 64 per cent of all US marketing expenditures in 1986 were invested in sales promotions, compared to 58 per cent 10 years earlier, but lower proportions have been quoted by other observers.

Some additional KLP estimates for 1987 are given in Table 2.

Table 1 Estimated worldwide promotion spending, 1987–1990

	1987	1988	1989	1990	1990–1987 Increase (percentage)
	(Billions of US Dollars)				
Television, print, radio and outdoor	150	164	177	191	+27
Direct mail (*North American and Europe only*)	28	32	37	43	+54
Sales promotion, point-of-sale, and others (*United States only*)	22	24	27	30	+36
	199	220	241	265	+33

Source: Saatchi & Saatchi Co., as reported in Wentz (1988) and Periss (1988).

Further breakdowns of SP expenditures are rarely available. Dun and Bradstreet (1988) reported that more than 2,000 US companies currently use money-off coupons; 7.15 billion manufacturers' coupons were redeemed by US consumers in 1987, out of the 215.2 billion coupons distributed. The distribution figure represented a 51 per cent increase since 1983, but the growth is likely to level off in coming years.

THE IAA SURVEY

The use and effectiveness of sales promotions worldwide are affected by many factors such as the degree of literacy, the quantity and quality of the available channels of distribution and media (including the postal service), and the controls applying to their use. Many SP techniques are controlled through government regulations, industry codes and guidelines (self-regulation), and media acceptance rules.

In 1987, the International Advertising Association (IAA) conducted an international survey of these controls. Thirty-six countries answered – about half of them developed nations:

Argentina	India	Peru
Australia	Ireland	Philippines
Austria	Italy	Singapore
Belgium	Japan	South Africa
Brazil	Korea	Spain
Canada	Malaysia	Sweden
Chile	Mexico	Switzerland
Denmark	Netherlands	Thailand
Finland	New Zealand	United Kingdom
France	Nigeria	United States
F.R. Germany	Norway	Venezuela
Hong Kong	Paraguay	Zimbabwe

Before analysing the IAA survey findings, it is necessary to understand the various forms of sales promotions as well as their advantages and disadvantages.

KEY DEFINITIONS

Cooke (1985) said that *sales promotion* refers to those promotional activities which enhance and support mass selling and personal selling, and which help complete

Table 2 Estimated sales promotion spending for 1987

Country	Estimated spending in US dollars
United Kingdom	5.00 billion
F.R. Germany	2.75–3.80 billion
Italy	2.20 billion
Netherlands	0.85–1.50 billion
Sweden	240 million
Spain	3.4 million
France	3.15–3.40 million

Source: private communication from the KLP group.

and/or coordinate the entire promotional mix (advertising, personal selling, publicity, sales promotion) and make the marketing mix (product, price, product, channels of distribution) more effective.[1]

The International Chamber of Commerce (ICC) defines *sales promotion* as marketing devices and techniques which are used to make goods and services more attractive by providing some additional benefit, whether in cash or in kind, or the expectation of such a benefit. The ICC's International Code of Sales Promotion Practices (1986) covers the following promotional items: premium offers of all kinds; reduced prices and free offers; the distribution of trading stamps, vouchers and samples; charity-linked promotions; and prize promotions of all types, including incentive programmes. This paper relies mainly on the ICC definition and covers most of the above promotional practices as directed at *consumers* (trade incentives were not covered in the IAA survey).

Before turning to more specific definitions borrowed from the AAAA (1978), one can generalize about SP practices in terms of the following characteristics:

> Techniques and devices commonly used on a *temporary basis*,
> to make goods and services *more attractive* to distributors or final consumers,
> by providing them with some additional *benefit or inducement* (incentive) or the expectations of such a benefit,
> whether in *cash*, in *kind* (nature) and/or *services*,
> whether *immediately* or *at a later time*,
> whether *freely* or *conditionally*.

A *premium* is an additional benefit which is conditioned upon (depending upon) the purchase of a product or service. ('If you buy this, you will also get that'.) Premiums may be offered free or at a price lower than their usual retail value. Premiums may be in or on the package, near the package (a tear-off coupon placed on the shelf or near the product being promoted, free-in-the-mail and/or self-liquidating (that is, requiring some cash and a proof of purchase to acquire the premium offer).[2]

A *gift* is a product or service which is given freely and is not conditional on the purchase of a product or service. ('It is yours, whether you buy anything or not'.) Free samples are gifts.

A *competition* is a prize in the form of a premium offered or a gift given only to *some* distributors or consumers ('Not all can win'), following some contest or game based on skill, chance or some combination of the two. What distinguishes a contest from a game of chance is the action the consumer is required to perform. A *contest* is characterized by three factors: skill (ability, sagacity, etc.), a prize and a consideration (for instance, some proof of purchase). Contests may involve submitting photographs, writing essays, answering difficult questions, which are to be judged by a jury. A *game of chance* (e.g., a sweepstake) is characterized by chance, a prize and no consideration – that is, participation must be free. An example of a sweepstake is sending in a freely available certificate which entitles the consumer to the chance of winning a prize in cash, goods or services (e.g., a television set or a vacation). Another type of competition is a 'match-and-win' pre-drawn sweepstake where the consumer has a card with different boxes on it and must scratch off several boxes to try to match the offered prizes. (Some legal experts consider such pre-drawn sweepstakes as 'chance events' rather than as true 'games of chance' where the winners are not predetermined.) This definition of competitions excludes pure *lotteries* which always involve some consideration (e.g., buying a ticket), in addition to prize and chance.

A *coupon* is a certificate given to consumers, which entitles them to an immediate price reduction when they purchase the stated item. Coupons may be distributed through the mail, in public places, door-to-door, in newspapers and magazines, and in, on or near packages.

Free sampling refers to small quantities of the product provided for free to demonstrate its features and benefits. Samples may be distributed through the mail, in public places, door-to-door, in or on packages, through store demonstrations, etc.

Price reductions offer the consumer an immediate amount off the usual retail price, or offer a larger pack at no increase in the retail price. Examples of price reductions are 'cents-off' label-price packs (e.g., special 99c price instead of $1.29), bonus packs (e.g., four for the price of three), and larger units offered at the price of the regular-sized unit (e.g., a 1.5 litre bottle for the price of a 1.0 litre one).

Refund offers allow the consumer to recover a certain amount from the disbursed retail price – either in cash or in coupon value – when proof of purchase of a designated product is presented. There are single-brand and multi-brand refund offers. Multi-brand offers require the consumer to collect proofs of purchase from several related brands (e.g., of cereals or detergents) before the refund can be obtained.

Continuity offers unlike the above sales-promotion techniques, are designed for long-term action by encouraging consumers to purchase the product at more frequent intervals. They include stamp plans (collecting a certain number of stamps that may later be traded for cash, merchandise or a combination of the two) and in/on pack continuity premiums encouraging the consumer to complete a set of merchandise (e.g., a set of towels or dishes) by purchasing the promoted brand repeatedly in order to acquire additional/complementary units of the product offered as a premium.

Tie-in or group promotions (combined offers) involve two or more brands simultaneously; the consumer is offered an incentive to purchase all of the participating brands. This technique is usually linked to a common theme, and often uses other forms of sales promotion (e.g., refunds, coupons and contests). An example of a group promotion would be to offer two different household products (e.g., soap and toothpaste) tied together as a refund promotion which entitles the consumer to receive a rebate if he or she bought the two products.

THE CONTROL OF SALES PROMOTIONS

The use of premiums, gifts and competitions (PGCs) and other forms of sales promotion has long been debated – not only in terms of their promotional effectiveness (see above), but also in the light of their impact on: (1) trade competition; (2) consumer protection and (3) the general public interest.

Trade competition is affected when the use of PGCs makes various products and services available outside their usual channels of distribution, often at a lower price or even for free. Both large and small companies do use PGCs instead of more costly media-advertising campaigns. However, it is felt in some countries (e.g., the Federal Republic of Germany) that large firms can more readily use some types of PGCs than smaller ones although even small firms use them.

Consumer protection is involved when PGC offers are false, misleading or unfair (e.g., when addressed to young children whose ability to comprehend the offer may be limited). Late deliveries of premiums and prizes, and the occasional cancellation of games are also controversial in this respect.

The *public interest* is particularly at stake in games of chance to the extent that they encourage gambling, generate false hopes (particularly among the poor) and/or exert undue psychological pressure on consumers to buy goods. These moral arguments, however, have been weakened by the proliferation of lotteries run by various governments and by their tolerance or even sponsorship of casino gambling.

Consequently, a number of governments have enacted various regulations designed to prohibit, curtail or supervise the use of sales-promotion techniques. Industry itself has often developed general guidelines and/or detailed codes to promote standards of good behavior and as a basis for the handling of complaints. In addition, various media have specific rules of acceptance for PGCs in some countries. A few general comments about these controls are in order before the rest of this paper presents more specific information about national practices.

Unconditional gifts are least regulated. They are usually considered as a legitimate way of encouraging people to try a new product – provided the sample is relatively small compared to the value of the normal sized product.

The use of the word 'free' is allowed under several mandatory regulations and voluntary codes even when the benefit is conditional upon a purchase or some other action although, in this case, it really represents a premium (that is, a 'free offer') rather than a 'free gift'. Some national or state/provincial regulations, however, ordain that the words 'free' and 'gratis' are misleading whenever consumers have to pay for the main item in order to obtain the premium (e.g., in Norway and Canada's British Columbia). Other governments allow such words as long as the price of the main item is not increased when the premium is offered (e.g., the United States and United Kingdom). In a recent decision by a US self-regulatory body, the use of the word 'free' was rejected when used to promote packs of 25 cigarettes at the same price as a pack of 20 cigarettes – with the wording 'available without extra charge' being recommended instead of 'free'.[3]

Competitions (games of chance, contests, lotteries, match-and-win games and sweepstakes) have frequently been restricted, but rather inconsistently. Some countries (e.g., Norway) permit games of skill, but not of chance; others allow games of chance, provided they are taxed (e.g., Italy); some nations object to competitions being linked to proof of purchase (e.g., France, the United States and Sweden); while a fourth group sets limits on the value of the prizes (e.g., Australia and Japan). Pure lotteries run by a government or in the name of a recognized charity are commonly authorized under strict controls, but they were not covered in the IAA study. If skill contests are too simple and most people are able to win, they can be considered to amount to premiums (e.g., in France where 'everybody wins' promotions are not allowed under self-regulation).

Premiums present a more confused picture. The following sections summarize the major arguments for and against premiums although they sometimes apply equally to gifts and competitions.[4]

PROS AND CONS OF PREMIUMS

Favourable arguments

- *Premiums may stimulate competition and thus benefit consumers* by inducing them to try new brands, thereby enabling new competitors to enter markets previously dominated by established firms and widening the choices available to consumers.
- *Premium offers may force established competitors to lower their prices* and thus benefit consumers, assuming a market economy free of monopolies, cartels and resale-price maintenance obligations. Competition also ensures that consumers can choose to buy products without premiums, if they so prefer.
- *Premiums may save consumers money* since they do not have to purchase separately the goods and services represented by the premium. In competitive situations, a company may not be able to increase its prices to fully cover the costs of premiums; it hopes, instead, for a future increase in profits from the growth in sales generated by the goodwill and consumer acceptance engendered by the premium offer.
- *Consumers may benefit directly from premiums.* If premiums are forbidden, firms may have to use other promotional techniques (e.g., advertising) that do not offer such direct benefits as a lower price or an additional product or service given for free or offered under advantageous circumstances. Besides, some product attributes are better conveyed through sales promotions (e.g., free samples) than through advertisements.
- *Premium offers may constitute a new and efficient channel of distribution* for people who would not usually go to an established retailer that normally sells the products or services offered as premiums. This new channel is often cheaper than the traditional ones since the premium offerers buy the premium items at low cost in large quantities, and absorb all or some of their distribution expenses.
- *Premiums may increase awareness among consumers of the 'added value' being offered* as a result of the substantial advertising devoted to sales-promotion campaigns. When consumers receive more of a product for the same retail price as the normal-sized product, they may feel that they are obtaining more value for their money.

Unfavourable arguments

- *Goods and services should be sold on their own merits as to price, quality, availability of service, etc.* In this context, premiums could confuse consumers who may experience some difficulty in comparing 'combined offers' of a main item and a premium with 'single offers' without a premium, and in evaluating different combined offers – in other words, they hamper 'market transparency'.
- *Premium offers may divert the interest of the consumers from the main item* and thus entice them to buy the product or service out of interest for the premium itself. Other marketing practices such as advertising may also induce consumers to

purchase a product on emotional grounds, but advertisements usually serve an informative function, while some premium offers may give no information about the main product. The situation of some consumers not returning the main product even if they can keep the premium – out of a feeling of gratitude or because of the bother involved – is linked to this argument. Sales-promotion practitioners counter that premiums are usually connected to an advertising campaign or to packages and labels that give adequate production information.

- *Consumers may tend to overestimate the value of premiums.* Even if the value of the premium can be accurately estimated (some countries require that their value be stated), there is a risk that the combined offer has an overpersuasive effect on consumers, and makes the value of the premium appear to be greater than it really is (this may be particularly true when the consumers are children). Businesses counter that this criticism is largely based on conjecture, and that excesses would be subject to misleading advertising laws.
- *Premiums may restrict the consumers' freedom of choice.* In some cases, the consumer may only be interested in either the main item or the premium, yet have no opportunity of acquiring either separately. Some countries do require that the main item and the premium be available separately.
- *Premiums may represent a waste of economic resources and be a possible cause of inflation.* It could be preferable for consumers to be able to obtain a price reduction or a rebate. These assertions have been challenged by businesses on economic and freedom-of-choice grounds.
- *Premiums may divert some trade from established outlets whose main business is to offer such products or services.* This may go against public policies such as the protection of small or traditional businesses, and it may be considered as a form of unfair competition in countries such as the Federal Republic of Germany and Italy which are keen on protecting such businesses.
- *The language used to explain the premium may mislead the consumer.* In some cases, the words used have become debased, whether through accidental misuse or deliberate misinterpretation (e.g., '$1,000,000 will be awarded to *you*' – when it is really a reference to the total value of a prize-draw scheme rather than to the actual value of the award to the winner of the top prize).
- Some premiums – particularly, those linked to competitions – may be considered to be *unfair to consumers* to the extent that they generate some 'psychological compulsion to buy' and/or play on people's credulity, instinct to gamble, etc. Such views often reflect an élitist bias on the part of some regulators who assume that people are generally incapable of fending for themselves.

THREE FINAL OBSERVATIONS ABOUT CONTROLS

Firstly, as is true of all forms of marketing regulations, there is an unresolved conflict in most countries between the protection of business firms (e.g., traditional stores against premium offerers) and the protection of consumers.

Secondly, one can distinguish between: (1) those countries (e.g., the United States and United Kingdom) where the emphasis is on consumer *information* (that is, making sure that sales-promotion offers are truthful and not misleading), and (2) those which stress consumer *protection* – often, a matter of protecting consumers *against themselves* by force of law and by limiting their choice, rather than one of protecting them against unfair or misleading practices.

Thirdly, while national controls are stressed in this paper, they raise some *international* questions in terms of trade restrictions. Thus, the US government has been concerned about Japanese restrictions on premiums, gifts and competitions which US firms would like to use in Japan. There have been similar problems in the European Economic Community where national regulations bearing on premiums were argued to restrict intra-Community trade (Krämer 1986, pp. 17ff.).

MAJOR SURVEY FINDINGS

In one way or another, all 36 countries forbid the false or misleading presentation of sales promotions as well as their unfair use. In fact, self-regulatory codes and guidelines often limit themselves to stressing their truthful and honest handling, without going into many details. Regulation, on the other hand, goes as far as prohibiting or severely restricting some forms of sales promotion.

The United States and the United Kingdom are the countries which are most favourable to sales promotions. They control them the least because of the favourable arguments presented above, and self-regulation is well developed in these nations. A similar lack of regulation is found in many less-developed countries, but this situation is more a reflection of their overall state of underdevelopment than of a positive view toward sales promotions. On the other hand, Scandinavian countries, Belgium and the Federal Republic of Germany are very negative toward premiums because they consider that such offers *per se* tend to distract consumers from the merits of the principal product or service or are 'overattractive'. At the limit, premiums are considered a form of misleading promotion because of the intrinsic complexity of 'combined offers'. Most other developed countries acknowledge the common use and popularity of sales promotions, but strictly regulate them in order to prevent abuses.

The International Chamber of Commerce's International Code of Sales Promotion Practice has been officially adopted by about a quarter of the countries surveyed, but this code is at least informally accepted in most nations. There are few specific national bodies and codes dealing exclusively with sales promotions. However, to the extent that they are advertised, sales promotions come under the control of national advertising self-regulatory bodies and of advertising-agency associations.

Very few countries anticipate major changes in national regulation and self-regulation in 1988–1989.

A greater number of major restrictions and even prohibitions apply to *competitions* (contests, sweepstakes, games of chance, etc.) than to *premiums* (e.g., coupons and trading stamps) and to *gifts* (free samples, etc.) – in that order. One important regulatory concern is about allowing consumers to participate in competitions without having to purchase a product or service, that is, to participate without a 'consideration'.

Among various types of sales promotions, *price reductions* were the most popular by far (29 out of 32 countries), but coupons, gifts, skill contests, games of chance, rebates and free samples were 'significantly used' in about two-thirds of the responding countries. On the other hand, two-thirds indicated 'little or no use' of trading stamps.

The use of sales promotions is growing faster than the use of 'straight' advertising in 14 countries, and at about the same rate in 13 other nations. Only respondents from

Brazil, France and Peru replied that advertising is still growing at a faster pace than sales promotion.

Both related and unrelated products can be used as *premiums* practically everywhere although various restrictions apply to their value, to the duration of the offer, and to what products can be used in sales promotions.

Price rebates are conditionally allowed in most countries, but *trading stamps* are forbidden in at least five countries (New Zealand, Norway, the Philippines, Sweden and Venezuela) and not used in five more (Argentina, India, Korea, Nigeria and Paraguay).

Skill contests are conditionally permitted everywhere, but prior government authorization is required in 10 countries; a maximum value applies to prizes in seven; the names of the winners must be published in 15, and they cannot be used in connection with various products. Similar requirements apply to *games of chance* where the drawing of winners must be supervised by an independent organization.

Multiple-unit offers (such as 'three for the price of two') are allowed everywhere, except in Norway and Sweden, but certain conditions apply in various countries. There are restrictions on the use of the word *free* in many countries. *Free samples* are allowed everywhere although some countries impose limits on their size and on the types of product that can be given away as samples.

Liquor, tobacco and pharmaceutical products are often restricted: no sales promotions can be conducted for them, and/or they cannot be used as premiums or prizes.

Twenty-four countries allow the use of premiums, gifts and games of skill in connection with *children*, but games of chance directed at them are forbidden in nine countries. Most self-regulatory systems stress that special care must be taken in advertising to children in view of their special vulnerability.

CONCLUSIONS

Sales promotions have become an important part of the marketing mix used by domestic and multinational companies – at least, where over-regulation and other institutional problems such as a poor postal service and underdeveloped media have not hampered their growth. For that matter, the growth of global markets and of international marketing campaigns as well as the greater availability of cross-border media and of expert sales-promotion agencies in many countries suggests that the use of sales promotions will keep growing as an alternative or complement to traditional media advertising. In this context, several European conferences have already been scheduled for 1988–1989 in order to capitalize on the European Economic Community's goal of creating a true common market of some 320 million Europeans by 1992 through the lowering of trade barriers, including incompatible or prohibitive restrictions.

Such opportunities, however, will require that unwarranted or excessive regulatory barriers to the use of premiums, gifts, competitions and other forms of sales promotions be eliminated nationally, within free-trade areas, and internationally. Thus, as Perriss (1988, p. 13) has noted, the deregulation of the television medium has resulted in a major expansion of advertising expenditures in countries like Italy, while very restricted markets, such as the Federal Republic of Germany, have grown very slowly. However, there are still unanswered questions as to whether sales promotions will lend themselves to regional and/or global standardization in the light of varying consumer habits, regulatory restrictions, media availability and other factors (Petersen, 1988; p. 6).

REFERENCES AND SUPPLEMENTARY BIBLIOGRAPHY[5]

Advertising Standards Authority (UK) (1985) Focus on sales promotions. *Case Report 122*. London: Advertising Standards Authority.

Advertising Standards Council [Canada] (1980) *Combination Offers*. Toronto, Canada: Advertising Standards Council.

American Association of Advertising Agencies (1978) *Sales Promotion Techniques: A Basic Guidebook*. New York: Prepared by the Sales Promotion.

Bloch, C. (1976) *Study of Premium Promotions in the EEC (Translation)*. Strasbourg, France: Centre of Analysis and Political Economy of the Louis Pasteur University.

Boddewyn, J. J. (1988) *Premiums, Gifts, Competitions and Other Sales Promotions: Regulation and Self-regulation in 42 Countries*. New York: International Advertising Association.

Code of Advertising Practice [CAP] Committee (1984) *The British Code of Sales Promotion Practice* (fourth edition). London: Advertising Standards Authority.

Cooke, E. F. (1985) Defining sales promotion difficult, important. [AMA] *Marketing News*, p. 38.

Council of Better Business Bureaus. *Do's and Don'ts in Advertising Copy*. Arlington, VA: various dates. (This handbook includes sections on free offers, premiums, contests and games of chance.)

Dun & Bradstreet Corporation (1988) Study finds slight rise in 1987 coupon redemption. *News*, 12 July.

Feinman, J. P., Blashek, R. D. and McCabe, R. J. (1986) *Sweepstakes, Prize Promotions, Games and Contests*. Homewood, Illinois: Dow Jones-Irwin.

International Chamber of Commerce (1973 and 1986) *International Code of Sales Promotion Practice*. Paris: International Chamber of Commerce.

Krämer, L. (1986) *EEC Consumer Law*. Brussels: E. Story-Scientia.

Organization for Economic Cooperation and Development (1977) *Premium Offers and Similar Marketing Practices*. Paris: OECD.

Perriss, J. (1988) Is the global village a myth? The effect of worldwide media trends in advertising. *International Advertiser*, I, 12–14, 35.

Petersen, L. (1988) Global promotion: is it the answer to a non-existent need? *Promotion [Adweek]*, 6–7, 21.

Starch INRA Hooper, Inc. (1987) *Twenty-first Survey of World Advertising Expenditure [1986]*. New York: International Advertising Association.

Seipel, C.-M. (1987) Premiums – Forgotten by theory. *Journal of Marketing*, pp. 26ff.

Ulanoff, Stanley, M. (ed.) (1985) *Handbook of Sales Promotions*. New York: McGraw-Hill Book Company.

Wentz, L. (1988) Europe opens wallet: Saatchi. *Advertising Age*, 4 July, 26.

NOTES

1   Cooke (1985) defines the related concepts as follows:
    Promotion: that part of the marketing mix whose function is to inform and persuade. Promotional media are mass selling, personal selling and sales promotion.
    Advertising: any paid form of non-personal presentation of ideas, goods or services by an identified sponsor. It includes both mass-selling and sales-promotion media.
    Mass Selling: advertising (and some publicity) in the mass media. It is usually the major method of promoting ideas, goods or services that involve simple messages to large markets.
    Personal Selling: oral presentation to prospective buyers for the purpose of making sales. It is usually the major promotion method for ideas, goods or services that involve complex messages to small markets.
    Publicity: any unpaid form of non-personal presentation of ideas, goods or services. It is primarily a sales-promotion medium.

2   An example of a self-liquidating premium offer is to send in a specified amount of cash and a proof of purchase (e.g., part of the package or label) in order to receive an extra product or service.

3   'Brown and Williamson Tobacco Corporation, Richland Lights 25 and King Size Cigarettes.' *NAD Case Report 2379* (21 April 1986) and *NARB Panel Report* 42 (5 February 1987).

4   This section borrows from the literature (see references) including the Bloch and OECD studies which were rather prejudiced against premiums. The unfavourable arguments listed here have often been challenged by business practitioners.

5   A full copy of the IAA report (*Premiums, Gifts, Competitions and Other Sales Promotions: Regulation and Self-regulation in 42 Countries*) can be ordered from the International Advertising Association, 342 Madison Avenue, Suite 2000, New York 10017, USA (Telephone 212/557-113). In this article, only 36 countries are covered, except when answers were not provided by the responding countries.

Boddewyn, J. J. and Leardi, M. (1989) 'Sales promotions: practice, regulation and self-regulation around the world'. *International Journal of Advertising*, 8: 363–374. Reproduced with permission.

7.3 Sales promotion – playing to win?

Ken Peattie and Sue Peattie

INTRODUCTION

The 1980s were the competitive decade, when values of competitiveness and competition were espoused in business and society as never before. Within marketing, competitions as a sales promotion tool gained an increasingly high profile and appeared in markets where below-the-line promotions were supposed to be beyond-the-pale. As sales promotions boomed in practice, they became an increasing focus of academic interest and research, but sales promotion competitions have remained something of a mystery. To date they have usually been lumped together with other below-the-line techniques with which they have relatively little in common.

The authors have developed their personal interest in sales promotion competitions (unfortunately connected with entering rather than winning) into researching their use in marketing. The research project has evolved in three stages. It began with a literature search and a three year survey of over 2,600 competitions. This article is the first of two resulting from this initial stage. It examines the growth in competition use, and attempts to develop a framework to analyse their nature and their potential to influence consumer behaviour. The follow-up article presents the detailed survey results to analyse the use of competitions in practice, and to develop some guidelines suggesting how competitions can be designed and managed effectively.

Stage two (currently underway) follows up companies identified as competition users in the survey, to find out why and how they chose, developed and evaluated their competitions. The final stage will study the response of customers to competitions, to see if their response matches the marketers' expectations.

Although 'push' competitions aimed at salesforces or channels are common in many industries, the focus of the research are those aimed at 'pulling' demand from consumers. The survey only included national or regional (not just local) competitions, which were associated with a product or service (and not part or all of the product or service itself, as is the case with the football pools, or regular magazine competitions).

THE GROWTH OF SALES PROMOTIONS

Below-the-line growth during the 1980s was startling. For much of the decade promotional expenditure grew almost twice as fast as advertising expenditure

(Shultz 1987; Keon and Bayer 1986); and in 1984 it accounted for $80 billion in the US alone, compared to $48 billion spent on advertising (Rhea and Massey 1986). Sales promotions began to swallow up to 70% of the marketing communications budgets of many large companies (Shultz 1987); and by the end of the decade global expenditure on promotions had equalled media ad spend, accounting for 39% of total marketing expenditure, according to the WPP Group (FT 1989). Several factors have encouraged marketers to make greater use of sales promotions (Shultz 1987; Strang 1976; Dickson and Sawyer 1990; Quelch 1983; Addison 1988).

1. *Rising prices and advertising 'clutter'* – eroding advertising's cost effectiveness as consumers become increasingly desensitized to mass media advertising.
2. *Sales promotions becoming 'respectable'* – through increasing use by market leaders and increasing professionalism among sales promotion agencies.
3. *Increased impulse purchasing* – retailers are responding to greater impulse buying and value seeking among consumers by pushing manufacturers into more, and more effective, sales promotions.
4. *Shortening time horizons* – increasing rivalry and accelerating product life cycles make the fast sales boost that promotions are perceived to offer, attractive.
5. *Micro-marketing approaches* – as a response to fragmenting markets, where sales promotions can provide more tailored and targeted communication than mass media.
6. *A 'snowball' effect in some markets* – Lal (1990) suggests that practitioners in markets where promotions are commonplace are virtually obliged to follow suit, or risk losing market share and competitive position. The work of Fader and McAlister (quoted in Lattin and Bucklin 1989) suggests that the proliferating promotions in many markets train consumers to buy promoted goods.
7. *'Manageability'* – the other mix elements can appear relatively unwieldy as competitive weapons. Developing new products is lengthy, costly and risky. The stakes are often too high to permit experimentation, and success depends heavily on the input of other functions. Changing pricing structures can be costly in administrative and systems management terms (and can drag marketers into awkward political territory with financial management). Channel changes can be difficult to achieve frequently or quickly.
8. *Measurability* – assessing the impact of sales promotion can be problematic, but authors such as Doyle and Saunders (1985) and Moriarty (1985) have proved that, with care, it can be done with some precision. The problems of measurement are fewer than for advertising (Shultz 1987), and the use of POS scanner information provides greater scope for future assessment.

THE GREAT SALES PROMOTION DEBATE

Despite their importance in practice, sales promotions have not received the level of academic interest inspired by advertising (Keon and Bayer 1986). Although there has been a recent upsurge in academic interest, the results have been inconclusive. Most researchers agree about promotions' effectiveness in boosting short term sales, but a debate rages about their long term effects. It has been observed that repeat purchase probabilities for a brand after a promotional purchase are lower than after a non-promotional purchase (Shoemaker and Shoaf 1977; Guadagni and Little 1983; Jones and Zufryden 1981). Reasons suggested for this include the following.

1. A promotion is an 'external stimulus which, once removed, won't create repeat purchases (Dodson *et al.* 1978; Bawa and Shoemaker 1987).
2. Consumers' price expectations (or reference price) will be lowered by promotional pricing and they will resent paying post-promotional 'normal' prices (Monroe 1973; Winer 1986; Kalwani *et al.* 1990).
3. Promotions 'use up' the low probability purchasers, whose failure to repurchase after the promotion will depress the observed repeat purchase rate (Neslin and Shoemaker 1989).
4. Promotional pricing will lower a brand's evaluation because people use price as a surrogate measure of quality (Dodson *et al.* 1978). Doob *et al.* (1969) suggest that consumers reason that 'I paid a lot for this brand, therefore I must really like it'; so lowering the price may devalue the brand in consumers' eyes.
5. Regular purchasers stockpile during promotions and then buy less afterwards (Frank and Massey 1971).

Other researchers conclude that if consumers are satisfied by a promoted brand, then they will be more likely to repurchase in future (Cotton and Babb 1978; Rothschild and Gaidis 1981). There is also evidence that price promotions don't lower consumer perception of brand quality (Davis *et al.* 1992) and that they don't alter the long term sales trends for established brands (Peckham 1973; Brown 1974).

Another debate concerns whether promotions encourage consumers to switch between brands, or simply to change their purchase timing decisions. Moriarty (1985) found promotions to have little effect between competitor brands, and Doyle and Saunders (1985) found that sometimes consumers simply retime purchase decisions when pre-warned of future promotions.

The lack of consensus among researchers into the effect of promotions is not the only problem which the practitioner, academic or student faces when trying to learn from the established literature. There are further complicating factors in trying to apply the lessons learnt.

1. *An over-reliance on price.* The research conducted so far is heavily biased towards price-based promotions. Such promotions assume that consumers are price averse or value seeking (Tellis and Gaeth 1990) and are price aware. In fact customers can often be to some extent price seeking, because of the use of price as a surrogate measure for quality (Tellis and Gaeth 1990). Dickson and Sawyer (1990) found that consumers are often surprisingly hazy about the price details of their purchases.
2. *Product variations.* Most promotions research relates to only one or two types of product. The response to promotions has been shown to vary according to the product's stage in its life cycle (Peckham 1973) and its familiarity (Cotton and Babb 1978). So the effectiveness of a promotion for one product type will not guarantee its success for others.
3. *Consumer variations.* The response to promotions varies according to the consumer's level of product information (Tellis and Gaeth 1990), and their

expectations of promotion frequency and attractiveness (Lattin and Bucklin 1989; Krishna *et al.* 1991). Numerous reports from marketing agencies suggest that responses to different types of promotion also vary according to consumers' age and ethnic origin.

4. *Side effects*. Promotion may bring about changes other than the conventional aims of encouraging consumer trial, brand switching or stockpiling. Promotions may raise product awareness among consumers regardless of short-term purchasing patterns (Lattin and Bucklin 1989); they may lead to store substitutions as well as brand or product substitutions (Kumar and Leone 1988; Walters 1991); and they may stimulate sales of complementary products (Berman and Evans 1989; Walters 1991).

5. *Cross promotional effects*. A promotion may be affected by complementary trade promotions; by linkages with advertising and by the presence of simultaneous competitor promotions.

'UNBUNDLING' THE SALES PROMOTIONS TOOLKIT

Historically the marketing literature has bundled sales promotions together in a balanced 'above-and-below-the-line' equation. This approach bundles together promotional tools which are very different in their nature, uses and benefits. The debate over the effectiveness of sales promotions may partly result form the fact that researchers are analysing subtly different forms of promotion. In particular, the literature, which has mostly focused on price-based, value-increasing promotions, may not be applicable to value-adding promotions such as competitions or giveaways. Diamond and Campbell (1990) found that consumers in different market segments vary in terms of preferring price or non-price based promotions (particularly in relation to social class).

The growing importance of promotions has reached a point where each tool in the below-the-line toolkit must surely deserve its own distinct literature. This article aims to consolidate and contribute to the embryonic body of knowledge on competitions, whose development to date has been somewhat fragmented and biased towards US practitioner-orientated publications.

SALES PROMOTION COMPETITIONS

Competitions are becoming an increasingly important and sophisticated weapon in the marketer's armoury. In the UK they are the second favourite promotional tool after price promotions (Skuce 1990). In the US, Donnelley Marketing's 1991 Survey of Promotional Practise showed that although coupons were still the favourite promotion (with 95% of marketers planning to use them in the next year), sweepstakes (planned by 68%) and other competitions (31%) were also popular (media advertising had reached a new low, accounting for only 30.6% of promotional spend).

Our three year sample of 2,646 competitions included over 750,000 prizes, worth some £47.7 million. This represents an enormous investment simply in terms of prizes, and doesn't include the costs of designing, delivering and administering the competitions themselves. The increasing visibility of competitions in the marketplace partly relates to their proliferation; partly to the size of prizes now being offered (British Airways 'World's Greatest Offer' featured £6m worth of free flights); and partly to their use in high-profile battles between market leaders, such as Pepsi and Coca-Cola slugging it out with heavily advertised instant win contests.

THE CONSUMER AS A COMPETITOR

Price based promotions deliver perceived increased value for the customer by manipulating the price/quantity equation. The popularity of such promotions has encouraged an over-emphasis on the rational economic dimensions of consumer response to promotions, and an oversimplification of the concept of consumers' 'value consciousness'.

Competitions promote a product without tampering with the price/quantity value equation, and instead add value by making purchase or awareness of a product a 'ticket' to entering a competition. This has several advantages.

1. *Price stability* – avoiding some of the headaches associated with administering temporary price changes, and the havoc they can wreak on budgets and forecasts.
2. *Process stability* – adding value without changing the core product's quantity or quality, sidesteps potential problems with packaging and processing.
3. *Reference price stability* – important if Dodson *et al.* (1978) are correct in their assertion that 'media distributed coupons and money-off deals will result in significantly reduced loyalty once these deals are retracted'.
4. *Quality image maintenance* – allowing market-leading brands to be promoted without the risk of promotional pricing being interpreted as a move down-market.
5. *Appropriateness* – in channels, markets or cultures where price promotions may not be acceptable. In Japan redeeming coupons at the point of sale is thought to be embarrassing. Competitions have become the top promotional tool in this major market. Charities are frequent users of competitions since price promotions are inappropriate.

In the research conducted on consumers who respond to special prices and coupons, there are two bases of response, 'value consciousness' (defined by Monroe (1973) as the ratio of quality to price, but perhaps better considered as a ratio of price to utility) or 'deal or coupon proneness' (Lichtenstein *et al.* 1990). If 'coupon-prone' consumers exist, the existence of 'competition prone' or competitive consumers seems logical enough; and this logic was proven by the findings of Diamond and Campbell (1990).

A 1986 Harris/Marketing Week poll revealed that 70% of the UK population had entered a competition linked to a product or service, with over a third entering within the previous month (Cummins 1989). American consumers appear to be even more competition crazy. A survey of 500 US households by Premium Incentive Business and Better Homes and Gardens (PIBBHG 1989) found that 81% of consumers were inclined to participate in competitions and that 21% had entered 10 or more in the past year. A similar study in 1988 by Frankel and Co. found that 37% of consumers had entered some form of competition in the last 30 days (compared to 8% who had taken advantage of a reduced price promotion).

COMPETITIVE CONSUMER BEHAVIOUR

Defining consumers as either competition prone or not rather misses the subtleties of the appeal of competitions. It is possible to define six types of consumer which appear to make intuitive sense in relation to competitions.

1. *Non-Competitors* – who consider competitions a waste of time, stamps or telephone units. They would deliberately not enter a competition to which they were entitled through their habitual purchases.
2. *Passive Competitors* – who would enter a competition which they qualified for through their habitual purchases, but who wouldn't change their purchasing patterns to enter.
3. *Brand-Switchers* – who would buy a particular brand (perhaps abandoning usual brand loyalty) to enter an attractive competition. Brand switching is a proven and significant phenomenon in many consumer markets (Kuehn 1962; Morrison 1966; Bass 1974; Vicassim and Jain 1991).
4. *Product Switchers* – who, for example, in order to enter a competition might buy and consume a type of food or drink which was not on their shopping list in place of one that was. Such 'category switching' in response to promotions has been observed (Cotton and Babb 1978; Moriarty 1985) but has received less attention from practitioners and academics than brand-switching. This may reflect a tendency to concentrate on direct rather than indirect competitors.
5. *Hoarders* – who will alter their buying behaviour between brands and product types, and will also alter the timing of their purchases to increase their chances of winning a given competition. The effect of promotions on interpurchase times has been the subject of some academic study (Neslin *et al*. 1985; Gupta 1988). However, these tend to assume that usage rates of a product, and therefore purchase intervals, are demand driven. There is an argument that usage may be partly supply driven, and that a consumer may tend to use more of a product of which they have plenty (e.g. the more milk there is in fridge, the more one of the authors will drink).
6. *Dog Fooders* – who will buy almost anything to enter a competition (regardless of the core product's utility). Purchases are made on the basis that they will 'come in useful onc day' or 'will make a nice present for . . .'. Low value purchases may even be written off as part of the cost of entry. Such behaviour may sound unlikely, but it certainly exists among the small but growing number of hobbyist competitors. Many of these buy any product plastered with the word 'Win' (including bags of Winalot – hence their name). At a more mundane level, the authors have met numerous quite normal people who purchased The Daily Mail, simply to enter British Airways' 'World's Greatest Offer'.

This classification covers a range of attitudes towards competitions from indifference to near obsession. Some observations can be made about such a segmentation.

1. The categorization applies to consumers in relation to a specific competition. Individual consumers will move between these categories according to how attractive they find any competition. An avid competitor faced with a competition which they perceive as difficult, costly and for a prize they already own, may behave as a non-competitor. A staunch non-competitor might break a lifetime's

habit if they saw a competition offering their heart's desire as a prize. So although individuals may tend towards one classification, they may change in relation to different competitions.

2. The classification (and its use in Figure 2) implies that increasing the amount that consumers buy is a more profound change than persuading them to switch products or brands. Academically there is evidence for and against this proposition. In practice it isn't easy to generalize because the opportunity to alter brand choice and purchase timing decisions will depend on brand loyalty, shelf life, cost and bulk of a given product. For a product where retiming purchases is easy and brand loyalty is high it would be more sensible to add an 'Active Competitor' who will remain brand loyal but would buy more of a product to enter a competition.

3. Moving down the typology there is an increasing amount of self-persuasion being applied by the competitor to overcome barriers to changing their consumption behaviour, such as brand loyalty or economic rationality. As well as economic and psychological barriers to entering competitions, there can be physical barriers. To enter all phases of the recent 'Hovis – Slice of Life' competition would require the purchase of at least 12 loaves of bread in a short space of time. Any competitor without a large freezer or a rugby team to feed might have found this difficult.

4. Although the categories imply substitutions from a written shopping list, this won't necessarily be so. Many competitions are clearly aimed at generating impulse purchases. So, although the term 'shopping list' is used for simplicity, 'the set of the consumer's habitual, occasional or planned purchases' would be more accurate.

CHANGING CUSTOMER BEHAVIOUR THROUGH COMPETITIONS

Having defined consumers in terms of their attitude to a competition, we can also define them in relation to their involvement with a given brand.

1. *Non-users* – who do not use the product or its direct or indirect competitors. These are often the principal target of promotions (Keon and Bayer 1986).
2. *Potential users* – who do not use the product or any directly competing brands, but who use indirect competitors and who could be persuaded to buy (perhaps on impulse) through manipulation of the marketing mix.
3. *Rival loyals* – McAllister and Totten (1985) and Grover and Srinivasan (1992) show that successful promotions can attract substantial numbers of a rival's otherwise loyal customers.
4. *Brand switchers* – Grover and Srinivasan (1992) found evidence of distinct 'switcher' market segments whose consumers hop between the various competing brands.
5. *Own loyals* – within own loyal and rival loyal segments, we can distinguish between long-term, brand loyal consumers and those who are 'last purchase loyal' (Kahn and Louie 1990). These tend to be repeat purchasers until something encourages them to realign their loyalties.

Cross referencing the consumer's competitiveness against their brand involvement produces a picture of the opportunities presented by sales promotion competitions (Figure 1). The model presented in Figure 2 shows the possibilities for converting a consumer's brand involvement through a competition.

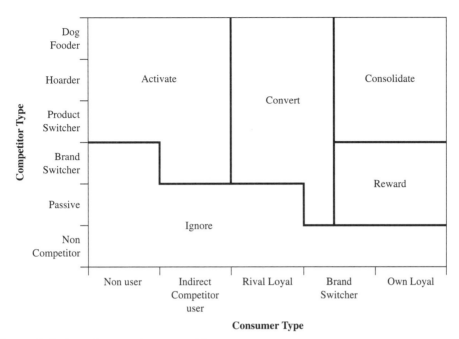

Figure 1 Options for targeting competitions.

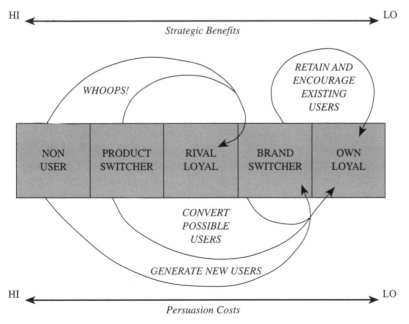

Figure 2 The roles of promotion in converting consumers.

These models imply that there are two key targets for a competition. A competition can generate new users, and (providing that some can be converted into loyal customers) this will provide long term benefits of increased turnover and an expanded market. Such opportunities exist because the tendency to repurchase a promoted brand which proves satisfactory, is particularly strong among those who were previously non-users (Cotton and Babb 1978; Rothschild and Gaidis 1981). The other target is increased usage among loyal or occasional (brand switching) purchasers. This will produce more of the short-term tactical sales uplift traditionally associated with promotions. There may be greater consumer resistance to the promotional message from non-users, and so the persuasiveness of the competition (and probably the cost) will need to be greater than for boosting sales among loyal or occasional purchasers.

The potential of competitions to create such changes in consumer behaviour can be shown by the results of a Neilsen Promotion Service survey in Canada. This found that 55% of competition entrants choose brands specifically to enter a competition, of which 95% bought the brand again after the competition; while 27% had switched product types specifically to enter a competition.

THE ATTRACTION OF COMPETITIONS

Why do competitions attract consumers? The glib answer is that the chance of getting something for nothing is always attractive. Selby and Beranek (1981) consider their attractiveness as a function of the entry cost (including stationery and time); the value of prizes; the number of prizes and the perceived probability of winning. They conclude that economic rationality should dictate that risk averse or risk neutral consumers (see Friedman and Savage 1952) will avoid competitions, keeping entry levels low. They conclude that the large number of entrants suggests that in practise people don't approach competitions in a spirit of economic rationality, and that their utility is related to the pleasures of gambling and the occupation of leisure time. This is further backed up by another Premium Incentive Business survey which showed that 60% of competitors entered 'just for the fun of it' and 61% of entrants into competitions were found to be 'unsure of what the prizes offered were' (PIB 1986).

Selby and Beranek's ideas can be extended in four key ways.

1. *Replacing the monetary value of prizes* – with the less convenient but more meaningful concept of their utility to the entrant. Some prizes are desirable because they are 'priceless' (a date with a 'Star' has become an increasingly popular prize in the US, increasing threefold in use over the last five years); or they are exactly not what the competitor would purchase if they had the money. The PIBBHG survey found that consumers preferred travel rather than cash as a prize. Wining a luxurious 'waste of money' has the attraction of indulgence without any associated guilt or dilemmas of choice.

2. *Adding a skill factor* – Selby and Beranek concentrate on skill-free sweepstakes where a competitor's perceived chance of winning reflects their assumptions concerning the likely number of correct entries, and their own chance of being correct. Some competitors welcome the 'fair' nature of sweepstakes, whereas more confident competitors might prefer skill based competitions believing that their chances of winning are increased.

3. *Adding the satisfaction of the urge to compete* – to the list of attractions. Competitiveness is a natural instinct which varies in its strength between individuals. Cassidy and Lynn (1988) see the desire to compete against others or 'against the clock' as forming two of the six key components in our motivation to achieve.

4. *Considering credibility.* The odds of getting a consumer to respond to a competition is directly related to their view of its credibility (PIB 1986). Sponsors now often try and boost a competition's credibility by announcing that the winners will be chosen by a Justice of the Peace.

BENEFITS OF COMPETITIONS AS A SALES PROMOTION TOOL

Competitions offer a wide range of potential benefits and opportunities for their sponsors.

1. *Temporary sales uplifts* – can be generated by getting Brand-switchers, Product-switchers and Dog-fooders to purchase. The contribution of already brand-loyal Hoarders will be negated by a later loss of business. Some of those switching brands to enter a competition may stay loyal once the competition has ended (or at least until a competitor runs a competition). Competitions can be especially useful in terms of generating trial of new products.

2. *Demand smoothing* – particularly useful for products where promotional offers of the '15% extra free' type aren't feasible (such as pints of draught lager during winter).

3. *Market research/mailing list opportunities.* There is an inherent logic that suggests that if customers want to win your product, they may also be willing to buy it. Offering your product as a prize can help to generate product awareness and to track down potential customers. This is common among products which are large, infrequent, glamorous purchases such as cars and holidays. British Airways' 'World's Greatest Offer' ticket draw was used to create a database of entrants for future promotions. Questions within competitions can be used to research consumer attitudes and tastes. However, there is always the danger that the answers provided will reflect what the competitor thinks the sponsor wants to hear, not what the consumer really thinks.

4. *Idea generation.* Cadburys recently ran a competition requiring the submission of a recipe using cocoa. Their next promotion was, not surprisingly, a giveaway booklet of cocoa recipes. The widespread use of slogans in competitions might suggest that they would be a valuable source of 'hooklines' for advertising campaigns. However, the rigid format used and the poor quality of published winning slogans suggests that they pose little in the way of a threat to the jobs of advertising agency copywriters.

5. *Packaging revamps.* Eye-catching competition packs can add sparkle to the image of brands whose familiarity may be a strength, but may allow them to be taken for granted. Rowntree's ran a series of competitions for Kit-Kat allowing a familiar product to have a new high-impact wrapper while retaining the original distinctive brand strength. During one twelve month period there was only two months in which it was possible to buy a non-competition flashed Kit-Kat.

6. *Advertising campaigns link-ups*. Promotions such as the Golden Wonder Win and Island or the Kit-Kat Tjaerborg Holiday competitions both featured spin-off national ad campaigns using TV, newspapers and posters.

7. *Point-of-sale opportunities*. In an age where a supermarket may carry over 35,000 different product lines, catching the consumer's eye with POS displays is increasingly vital. In-store competitions can be a basis for differentiation between retailers. Tesco has led the way, at one point sponsoring some 26 concurrent in-store promotional competitions. Gateway, Asda and Bejam have also used competitions as a key element of their promotional magazines. These help to encourage consumers to collect and read the magazines allowing them to fulfil their promotional task of communicating and influencing.

8. *Public relations opportunities*. PR can be generated from prizegiving or from links to charitable donations, where a certain amount is being donated per entry, as with the Andrex Elefriends Appeal Competition.

9. *Reduce the effectiveness of a rival's sales promotion*. 'Me too' competitions may fail to be effective if the competitive consumers are already stocked up with the brand first off the mark.

10. *Message reinforcement*. This can be done by making the content focus on the benefits of the product by ranking them or matching them to the advertising theme. Quaker's Crunchy Bars linked into the squirrel motif of their advertising and packaging by running a spot-the-ball type competition, reworked as 'Spot the Squirrels'. Alternatively, the Post Office developed competitions aimed to stimulate awareness about postcodes which required correct use of a postcode to qualify for entry.

These characteristics paint a picture of competitions as a marketing tool able to perform a wide variety of tasks, and able to act as an integrating mechanism for an entire marketing campaign. A good example of a well designed competition which achieved such integration came from Vauxhall. It involved a direct mailshot to consumers combining product information and advertising copy with the competition details. Consumers were given the specifications of each Vauxhall car model, along with a lifestyle description of six different couples. Entering the competition forced entrants to consider what the attributes of each car were, and which would best fit their sort of lifestyle. The slogan to complete was 'I'm smitten by Vauxhall cars because . . .' . This reinforced the advertising campaign, while prompting consumers to consider the appeal of Vauxhall cars generally. Submitting the entry involved visiting the nearest dealer, providing opportunities for potential customers to meet the products and the salespeople. This shows the way that competitions can form a key element of a sophisticated and interactive marketing campaign, which informs and persuades customers by 'involving' them with the product and the promotional message.

THE RISKS OF COMPETITIONS

Before this article becomes too euphoric about competitions, its worth considering what can go wrong. Practitioner-orientated journals are littered with horror stories of mismanaged competitions. Pitfalls include the following.

1. *Poor response*. Time Life's 'Library of Nations' competition received two entries, one late and one incorrect. Here the cost of entry in terms of buying a book, finding the answer to six questions and completing a tiebreak overcame the attractions of potentially winning a weekend in Amsterdam.
2. *Timescale mismatches*. Some competitions have a long gap between competition launch and closing date, but a relatively short window of opportunity to purchase special promotional packs. Only having the chance to buy three special packs when four are needed (as happened to the authors in the Windmill Bread Holiday Break Competition) causes frustration and does nothing for a brand's image.
3. *Entrapment*. Competitions which try and dupe unsuspecting competitive consumers into further purchases will risk disaffecting non-hoarding consumers. The 'Further purchases required' smallprint on many grocery competitions is becoming infamous within the 'comping' fraternity.
4. *Big prize/long odds competitions*. Some competitions feature big prizes but odds so long that any numerate consumer is unlikely to be attracted. A good example was Duracell's 'Win a Million Pounds' competition which featured odds against winning of 1.3 million billion to 1. This prompts the question of whether it contravenes the ISP code of conduct on sales promotions which states that promotions should be 'so designed and conducted as not to cause avoidable disappointment'.
5. *Mechanical errors*. The printing and security of instant win cards must be carefully managed to avoid the experience of Esso whose 'Noughts and Crosses' game produced twenty claims for the first prize of £100,000 when only a couple should have existed. Such risks have led to a specialist sales promotions insurance industry, pioneered by Promise (a division of Brokers Jewit Duchesne) who cover the risk of coupon redemptions or prize distribution above expectations.
6. *Associating the product with losing*. Most competitions have more losers than winners, and there is always the risk of the product being associated with a failure to win on the part of the consumer. Rowntree Mackintosh's 'Spell and Win' competition required consumers to collect letters to spell and win various prizes. Each prize name obviously had one letter equivalent to a Penny Black, and the avid chocolate bar eater would soon find each unwrapping of a bar was associated with disappointment as yet another duplicate letter turns up. Many companies appear to be trying to avoid disappointment by awarding a money-off-next-purchase voucher to all entrants.

CONCLUSIONS

With market leaders like Heinz relying increasingly on promotions, and competitions in particular, traditional prejudices such as 'Advertising is for winners, sales promotion is for losers' and 'Promotions are only good for tactical sales uplifts' look increasingly weak. Promotions worth £3 million played a key role in Heinz's centenary celebrations (Gerrie 1986). The company has run a competition giving away six figures in prizes for the last five years. These were backed up by a sophisticated monitoring system using feedback-scratch cards, to analyse the effects of behaviour and buying patterns among participants. With 60% of a sample of 30,000 participants to three competitions returning cards, Heinz have built up an accurate picture of the effect that sales promotion competitions can have, and their effectiveness when used through different grocery chains. Such a sophisticated approach to competitions is something that most other companies can only aspire to. Hopefully further research into the effectiveness of competitions will provide practitioners with a firmer base of knowledge on which to base their plans for future promotional competitions.

REFERENCES

Addison, J. (1988), 'Promotional Rescue', *Director*, November, pp. 139–143.

Bass, F. M. (1974), 'The Theory of Stochastic Preference and Brand Switching', *Journal of Marketing Research*, 11, No. 1, pp. 1–20.

Bawa, K. and Shoemaker, R. W. (1987), 'The Effects of a Direct Mail Coupon on Brand Choice Behaviour', *Journal of Marketing Research*, 14, pp. 370–376.

Berman, B. and Evans, J. (1989), *Retail Management*, New York, Macmillan.

Brown, R. G. (1974), 'Sales Response to Promotions and Advertising', *Journal of Advertising Research*, 14, No. 4, pp. 33–39.

Cassidy, T. and Lynn, R. (1988), 'A Multifactoral Approach to Achievement Motivation: the Development of a Comprehensive Measure', *Journal of Occupational Psychology*, No. 62, pp. 301–312.

Cotton, B. C. and Babb, E. M. (1978), 'Consumer Response to Promotional Deals', *Journal of Marketing*, 42, July, pp. 109–113.

Cummins, J. (1989), *Sales Promotion: How To Create and Implement Campaigns That Really Work*, London, Kogan Page.

Davis, S., Inman, J. J. and McAlister, L. (1992), 'Promotion Has a Negative Effect on Brand Evaluations – Or Does It? Additional Disconfirming Evidence', *Journal of Marketing Research*, 29, No. 1, pp. 143–148.

Diamond, W. D. and Campbell, L. (1990), 'Going Beyond "Coupon Proneness": Social Class and Preference For Different Types of Grocery Sales Promotions'. In: *Enhancing Knowledge Development in Marketing*, (Eds) Parasuraman *et al.* AMA Educators' Proceedings 1990, pp. 20–24.

Dickson, P. R. and Sawyer, A. G. (1990), 'The Price Knowledge and Search of Supermarket Shoppers', *Journal of Marketing*, 54, July, pp. 42–53.

Dodson, J. A., Tybout, A. M. and Sternthal, B. (1978), 'Impact of Deals and Deal Retractions on Brand Switching', *Journal of Marketing Research*, 15, No. 1, pp. 72–81.

Donnelley Marketing (1991), 'Couponing Still Top Promo Tool', *DM News*, 13, No. 13, p. 7.

Doob, A. N., Carlsmith, J. M., Freedman, J. L., Landauer, T. K. and Solong, T. (1969), 'Effect of Initial Selling Price on Subsequent Sales', *Journal of Personality and Social Psychology*, 2, No. 4, pp. 345–350.

Doyle, P. and Saunders, J. (1985), 'The Lead Effect of Marketing Decisions', *Journal of Marketing Research*, 22, No. 1, pp. 54–65.

Financial Times (1989), 'Worldwide Marketing Expenditure 1989', 30 November, p. 13.

Frank, R. E. and Massey, W. F. (1971), *An Econometric Approach to Marketing Decision Models*, Cambridge, MA., MIT Press.

Friedman, M. and Savage, L. J. (1952), 'The Utility Analysis of Choices Involving Risk'. In: *Readings in Price Theory*, Chicago.

Gerrie, A. (1986), 'Sale of the Century', *Marketing*, 2 October, pp. 28–32.

Grover, R. and Srinivasan, V. (1992), 'Evaluating the Multiple Effects of Retail Promotions on Brand Loyal and Brand Switching Segments', *Journal of Marketing Research*, 29, No. 1, pp. 76–89.

Guadagni, P. M. and Little, J. D. (1983), 'A Logit Model of Brand Choice Calibrated on Scanner Data', *Marketing Science*, 2, Summer, pp. 203–238.

Gupta, S. (1988), 'Impact of Sales Promotion on When, What and How Much to Buy', *Journal of Marketing Research*, 25, No. 4, pp. 342–355.

Jones, M. J. and Zufryden, F. S. (1981), 'Relating Deal Purchases and Consumer Characteristics to Repeat Purchase Probability', *Journal of the Market Research Society*, 23, pp. 84–89.

Kahn, B. E. and Louie, T. A. (1990), 'Effects of Retraction of Price Promotions on Brand Choice Behaviour for Variety-Seeking and Last-Purchase-Loyal Consumers', *Journal of Marketing Research*, 27, No. 4, pp. 279–289.

Kalwani, M. U., Yim, C. K., Rinne, H. K. and Sugita, Y. (1990), 'A Price Expectations Model of Customer Brand Choice', *Journal of Marketing Research*, 27, August, pp. 251–262.

Keon, J. W. and Bayer, J. (1986), 'An Expert Approach to Sales Promotion Management', *Journal of Advertising Research*, June/July, pp. 19–26.

Krishna, A., Currim, I.S. and Shoemaker, R. W. (1991), 'Consumer Perceptions of Promotional Activity', *Journal of Marketing*, 55, April, pp. 4–16.

Kuehn, A. A. (1962), 'Consumer Brand Choice – A Learning Process', *Journal of Advertising Research*, 2, December, pp. 10–17.

Kumar, V. and Leone, R. P. (1988), 'Measuring the Effect of Retail Store Promotions on Brand and Store Substitution', *Journal of Marketing Research*, 25, No. 2, pp. 178–85.

Lal, R. (1990), 'Manufacturer Trade Deals and Retail Price Promotions', *Journal of Marketing Research*, 27, No. 6, pp. 428–444.

Lattin, J. M. and Bucklin, R. E. (1989), 'Reference Effects of Price and Promotion on Brand Choice Behaviour', *Journal of Marketing Research*, 26, No. 4, pp. 299–310.

Lichtenstein, D. R., Netemeyer, R. G. and Burton, S. (1990), 'Distinguishing Coupon Proneness From Value Consciousness: An Acquisition-Transaction Utility Theory Perspective', *Journal of Marketing*, 54, No. 3, pp. 54–67.

McAllister, L. and Totten, J. (1985), 'Decomposing the Promotional Bump: Switching, Stockpiling and Consumption Increase', paper presented at ORSA/TIMS 1985 Joint Meeting.

Monroe, K. B. (1973), 'Buyers' Subjective Perceptions of Price', *Journal of Marketing Research*, 8, No. 1, pp. 70–80.

Moriarty, M. M. (1985), 'Retail Promotional Effects on Intra- and Interbrand Sales Performance', *Journal of Retailing*, 61, Fall, pp. 27–48.

Morrison, D. G. (1966), 'Testing Brand Switching Models', *Journal of Marketing Research*, 3, November, pp. 401–409.

Neslin, S. A., Henderson, C. and Quelch, J. (1985), 'Consumer Promotions and the Acceleration of Product Purchases', *Marketing Science*, 4, Spring, pp. 147–165.

Neslin, S. A. and Shoemaker, R. W. (1989), 'An Alternative Explanation for Lower Repeat Rates After Promotion Purchases', *Journal of Marketing Research*, 26, No. 3, pp. 205–213.

Peckham, J. O. (1973), *The Wheel of Marketing*, Northbrook, IL., A. C. Nielsen Company.

PIB (1986), 'Prize Offering: Believability Affects Entrants' Response to Sweepstakes', *Premium Incentive Business*, 45, no. 3, p. 25.

PIBBHG (1989), 'Accounting For Consumer Behaviour: Why They Enter One Promo Over Another', *Premium Incentive Business*, 48, No. 2, pp. 8–10.

Quelch, J. A. (1983), 'It's Time To Make Trade Promotion More Productive', *Harvard Business Review*, 61, No. 3, pp. 130–136.

Rhea, M. J. and Massey, F. (1986), 'Sales Promotion Ripe for Research', *Marketing News*, 20, pp. 26–27.

Rothschild, M. L. and Gaidis, W. C. (1981), 'Behavioural Learning Theory: Its Relevance to Marketing and Promotions', *Journal of Marketing*, 45, Spring, pp. 70–78.

Selby, E. B. and Beranek, W. (1981), 'Sweepstakes Contests: Analysis, Strategies, and Survey', *The American Economic Review*, 17, No. 1, pp. 189–195.

Shoemaker, R. W. and Shoaf, F. R. (1977), 'Repeat Rates of Deal Purchases', *Journal of Advertising Research*, 17, April, pp. 47–53.

Schultz, D. E. (1987), 'Above or Below the Line? Growth of Sales Promotion in the United States', *International Journal of Advertising*, 6, pp. 17–27.

Skuce, S. (1990), 'Don't Neglect the Flexible Competition', *Promotions and Incentives*, August, pp. 36–38.

Strang, R. A. (1976), 'Sales Promotion: Fast Growth, Faulty Management', *Harvard Business Review*, 54, July/August, pp. 115–124.

Tellis, G. J. and Gaeth, G. J. (1990), 'Best Value, Price-Seeking and Price Aversion: The Impact of Information and Learning on Consumer Choices', *Journal of Marketing*, 54, April, pp. 34–45.

Vicassim, N. J. and Jain, D. C. (1991), 'Modelling Purchase-Timing and Brand-Switching Behaviour Incorporating Explanatory Variables and Unobserved Hetrogeneity', *Journal of Marketing Research*, 28, No. 1, pp. 29–41.

Walters, R. G. (1991), 'Assessing the Impact of Retail Price Promotions on Product Substitution, Complementary Purchase, and Interstore Sales Displacement', *Journal of Marketing*, 55, April, pp. 17–28.

Winer, R. S. (1986), 'A Reference Price Mode of Brand Choice for Frequently Purchased Products', *Journal of Consumer Research*, 13, September, pp. 250–256.

Peattie, K. and Peattie, S. (1993) 'Sales promotion – playing to win?'. *Journal of Marketing Management*, 9: 225–269. Reproduced with permission from *Journal of Marketing Management*. © Westburn Publishers Ltd 1993.

7.4 The effects of a direct mail coupon on brand choice behavior

Kapil Bawa and Robert W. Shoemaker

The number of coupons distributed has grown dramatically from 81.2 billion in 1979 to 163.2 billion in 1984 (Peckham, 1985). Though coupons are becoming an increasingly important element of the promotional budget, some major questions about the effects of coupons on consumer brand choice behavior remain unanswered. First, how does the likelihood of coupon redemption vary by the degree of preference for the promoted brand and by coupon face value? Second, do consumers alter their purchase patterns for the promoted brand after redeeming the coupon? Examination of these issues would be useful in answering several managerial questions. In particular, the answers could help determine whether the coupon promotion should be targeted to current users of the brand or to nonusers and what face values should be used.

Considerable research has been done on consumer response to promotions or deals, but many of the findings relate to deals in general and not to coupons specifically. Further, the nature of the data used makes it difficult to establish the 'true' effect of coupons on brand choice behavior because many factors such as coupon availability and face value are not controlled for.

We address the questions mentioned by using data from a field experiment on coupon effectiveness. The analysis begins with the development of a general model of the coupon redemption decision for a specific brand. The model provides a basis for predicting how consumers with different degrees of preference for the promoted brand would react to the coupon and whether they would alter their brand choice behavior after redeeming the coupon. The hypotheses are tested with data from a scanner panel of 5192 households, each of which had received a direct mail coupon for a consumer product.

PRIOR RESEARCH: PROMOTION EFFECTS ON BRAND CHOICE BEHAVIOR

Few prior studies have addressed the specific question of how households with different degrees of preference for the promoted brand react to coupons. However, several prior studies on deals can be used to predict the likely response to coupons. In the following literature review, we discuss the findings relating to two separate aspects of promotions: (1) how promotional purchases affect subsequent brand choices and (2) how response to the promotion varies by prior probability of purchasing the promoted brand.

Prior studies on brand choices subsequent to a promotional purchase

Aaker (1973, p. 597) tested the hypothesis that 'aggregate long-run purchase patterns of families familiar with a given brand (non-new triers) are not affected by interim promotion purchases of the same brand'. His findings, though not specific to coupons, suggest that repeat buying for those who had consistently bought the promoted brand is unlikely to be affected by the coupon redemption.

A similar analysis on the effects of a deal purchase on subsequent repeat purchasing was conducted by Kuehn and Rohloff (1967, p. 75). Their analysis suggests some conversion to a promoted brand after a deal purchase, at least for some segments of the market. That is, the estimated probability of buying the brand after a household has bought the brand on deal is greater on average than the estimated probability before the deal purchase.

Klein (1981) conducted a number of coupon experiments and contrasted sales of the control group with sales of the experimental (couponed) group. He showed that the cumulative difference in sales between the two groups generally became stable within several weeks after the coupon drop. This finding suggests that coupon redemptions have at least no long-term effects on repeat purchasing.

Two of these studies are not specific to coupon promotions. That is, they are based on price promotions or a general definition of 'deals'. However, the three studies taken together suggest the possibility that a coupon promotion could produce a short-term increase in repeat buying for some segments of buyers. If such an increase does occur, Aaker's (1973) results suggest it is not likely to be observed for buyers who are familiar with the promoted brand. Klein's findings (1981) indicate that if there is an effect, it will not be long term.

Response to promotions by prior probability of purchasing the promoted brand

Kuehn and Rohloff (1967, p. 71) examined the association between a household's prepurchase probability (the probability of purchasing a specific brand before it is offered on deal) and its likelihood of making deal purchases. Their results (see Mean I, Table 3, p. 71) imply that buyers with a high prepurchase probability for a given brand are much more likely to purchase that brand on deal than those with a low prepurchase probability.

Neslin, Henderson, and Quelch (1985) studied the effect of coupons and other promotions on purchase acceleration. They found a positive association between use of coupons and larger purchase quantities. This association was stronger for loyal buyers of the coffee brands than for nonloyal coffee buyers. Though this finding is on purchase quantity rather than brand choice, it does suggest that consumers with a higher prior probability of purchasing the promoted brand are more responsive to the coupon promotion than those with a lower prior probability.

Shoemaker and Tibrewala (1985) conducted a survey to determine which food-shoppers intended to redeem coupons with different face values. They found stated intentions to redeem to be much higher for those who were loyal to the promoted brand. They also found (p. 45, Table 5) that an increase in face value had only a small effect on the stated redemption rates of loyal brand buyers, but produced a substantial percentage increase in stated redemption among the infrequent or nonbuyers of the brand.

These findings on coupon promotions and other consumer promotions suggest that coupons for a specific brand are more likely to be redeemed to the extent that the consumer has a higher 'prior' probability of purchasing the brand.

MODELING THE EFFECT OF A DIRECT MAIL COUPON ON A HOUSEHOLD'S CHOICE OF THE PROMOTED BRAND

A household's reaction to a direct mail coupon offer for some specific brand (brand A) can be predicted from a cost – benefit model. The model is used to predict the probability of coupon redemption as a function of prior purchases of the promoted brand, prior purchases of the household's favorite competing brand, the household's handling costs, and coupon face value.

Households obtain benefit from coupon usage and also incur costs in using coupons. The benefits take the form of monetary savings resulting from the redemption. For any given household, the benefits can be assumed to vary directly with the face value of the coupon.

At the same time, a number of costs may be associated with coupon usage. Shimp and Kavas (1984) conducted a survey among coupon users and found that the need to purchase nonpreferred brands in order to take advantage of coupon offers was perceived as a salient consequence of coupon usage (p. 799). This might be described as a negative consequence, or cost, of coupon usage. In addition, researchers such as Blattberg *et al.* (1978) and Narasimhan (1984) have suggested that households incur opportunity costs of time when they use deals or coupons.

These studies indicate that the costs of coupon usage fit into two broad categories. One is a 'handling' cost associated with the resources required to clip the coupon, store it, carry it to the store, and redeem it. This cost can be measured in monetary terms as the time required multiplied by the value of the redeemer's time. A second type of cost can be termed the 'substitution' cost. It is the cost of switching to the couponed brand (brand A) if brand A is less preferred than the household's regular or favorite brand(s). The substitution cost is the opportunity cost of having to purchase a nonpreferred brand in order to use the coupon. Brand A could be less preferred than other brands for a wide variety of reasons such as poor quality, unappealing taste, high price, unattractive packaging, or limited retail distribution. The substitution cost for each brand can be measured in monetary terms as the price reduction that would be required to make the buyer indifferent between the buyer's preferred brand and the 'substitute' brand.[1]

Let us define $P_c^i(A)$ as the prior probability that household i would buy brand A on the current purchase occasion c. $P_c^i(A)$ is assumed to be a function of the substitution costs $(SC_c^i(j))$ for all brands j ($j = A, \ldots, N$). It is assumed to increase as the substitution cost for brand A decreases and as the substitution costs for other brands increase.

The probability $R_c^i(A)$ that household i would redeem the brand A coupon on choice occasion c is modeled as a function of the coupon face value (FV), the handling cost for household i (HC_i), the household's prior probability of buying brand A, $P_c^i(A)$, and the household's probability of buying its favorite competitive brand (other than brand A), $P_c^i(C)$. That is,

$$(1) \qquad R_c^i(A) = g[FV, HC_i, P_c^i(A), P_c^i(C)].$$

On the basis of the literature review and the discussion of the costs and benefits of coupon usage, we propose the following hypotheses about equation 1.

H_1: The higher a household's prior probability of purchasing brand A, the greater the likelihood that the household will redeem a coupon for brand A. That is, $\partial R_c^i(A)/\partial P_c^i(A) > 0$.

H_2: Among households whose favorite brand is not brand A, the larger the proportion of purchases devoted to their favorite competitive brand (brand C), the lower the likelihood of coupon redemption. That is, $\partial R_c^i(A)/\partial P_c^i(C) < 0$.

H_3: Redemption rates will be higher for coupons with higher face values. That is, $\partial R_c^i(A)/\partial FV > 0$.

Effect of coupons on postredemption brand choice behavior

From the preceding discussion it follows that if the substitution cost for brand A changes as a result of redeeming the brand A coupon and using brand A, the purchase probability for brand A after the redemption will differ from the preredemption probability, $P_c^i(A)$. The potential for change in the substitution cost for brand A is likely to be a function of the extent to which the household is familiar with the brand. The redemption purchase can be viewed as providing information about brand A, which may change the household's substitution cost if the household has limited familiarity with the brand. Hence households that are nonusers or infrequent users of brand A are likely to have the greatest potential for change, because they have less current information about the promoted brand. Similarly, households that are regular users of the promoted brand and have little or no substitution cost are least likely to change after the redemption purchase. This suggests the following hypothesis.

H_4: The largest increase in the probability of purchasing the couponed brand subsequent to the coupon redemption will occur among households that are infrequent users or nonusers of brand A.

METHOD

The hypotheses are tested with data collected in a field experiment. The original objective of the experiment was to determine the effect of different coupon face values on the sales of an established brand. However, the data also can be used to test hypotheses about the effects of coupons on brand choice.[2] A scanner panel of 5192 households was used for the face value experiment; 4887 of these households were purchasers of the product class. Prior to the mailing of the coupons, three groups of panel households were selected and matched on total consumption and usage of the product class and total consumption and usage of the test brand. After a base period of 24 weeks, a low, medium, or high valued coupon was mailed to the three groups, respectively. The test brand is part of a frequently purchased product class. The average purchase cycle is less than three weeks.

The data from this experiment appear to be somewhat unique and particularly suitable for our study, because they satisfy the following conditions. First, as the brand A coupon is known to have been mailed to each household in the sample on the same day, the effects on purchase behavior can be clearly identified. Second, the coupon was delivered to all households, not just those subscribing to a particular newspaper or receiving a particular set of magazines. Therefore any observed differences in redemption between market segments can be attributed to differential response and not to differences in exposure to the coupon promotion. Third, as purchase records are available for a 24-week period prior to the mailing and 12 subsequent weeks, purchasing patterns before and after the coupon distribution can be compared. Finally, the data on coupon redemptions were collected at the household level. As a result, prior probabilities can be estimated for redeemers and nonredeemers.

The effect of promotions by competitive brands was evaluated by computing the number of promotional purchases made (excluding purchases made with the direct mail coupon used in the test) each week for the entire 36-week period. The total level of purchasing associated with competitive promotions was stable over the 36 weeks. In particular, no abrupt changes in the level of competitive dealing coincided with the delivery of the test coupons.

FINDINGS

H_1 states that the coupon redemption rate will be higher for households with a higher prior probability of purchasing the brand. In the initial analyses, the prior probability, $P_c^i(A)$, for each household is estimated as the brand A share of purchases for that household in weeks 1 through 24. The analysis is based on all 3808 households that made at least five purchases of the product class during the 24-week period before coupon delivery. Households that made less than five purchases of the product class are not included in this analysis because there is an inadequate basis for estimating their prior probability. The households included account for more than 95% of the volume purchased by the total panel.

H_1 is tested in two ways. First, the average value of the prior probability is computed separately for the redeemers and the nonredeemers. Among households that redeemed the coupon, the average prior probability is .114 ($n = 332$), whereas for nonredeemers the average is .045 ($n = 3476$). The difference is significant at the .001 level. The redeemer group has a higher prior probability, thereby providing support for the hypothesis. This finding also holds for each of the three face value groups. These findings provide firm support for the hypothesis that households with a higher prior probability of buying the promoted brand are more likely to redeem the coupon.

H_1 also can be tested by observing the levels of redemption in Table 1. The redemption rate is shown as a function of coupon face value and prior purchase probability. As can be seen in the last column, the average redemption rate is .045 for households with the lowest prior probability, .151 for those in the medium group, and .240 for those with the highest prior probability (.20 to 1.0). This same monotonic relationship holds within each face value group. Again, the results are highly consistent with H_1.

H_2 applies to the 3622 households (of 3808) whose favorite brand is not brand A. The favorite brand for each household is defined as the brand most frequently purchased in the 24-week period before coupon delivery. The hypothesis is that the redemption rate for brand A coupons will be lower for households that devote a larger proportion of their purchases to their favorite brand. H_2 is tested by determining the favorite brand during the 24-week predelivery period for each of the 3622 households. The share of purchases accounted for by the household's favorite brand

Table 1 Redemption rates by coupon face value and estimated prior probability of purchasing brand A[a]

Prior probability	Coupon face value			
	Low	Medium	High	Average
0	.037	.042	.058	.045
	(843)	(843)	(830)	(2516)
.01 – .20	.106	.178	.167	.151
	(339)	(348)	(342)	(1029)
.20 – 1.0	.207	.313	.205	.240
	(92)	(83)	(88)	(263)
Average	.068	.097	.098	.087

[a]Based on 3808 households that made five or more purchases of the product class prior to the coupon delivery date. Prior probability is estimated for each household as the brand A share of purchases in the 24-week base period. Sample sizes are in parentheses.

prior to the coupon delivery then is computed for each household. The average share is computed separately for redeemers and nonredeemers of the brand A coupons. For redeemers the average share is 25.6% ($n = 288$) and for nonredeemers it is 32.6% ($n = 3334$). As the two shares are significantly different at the .001 level, H_2 is supported. This result also holds for each of the three face value groups. In addition, among these 3622 households, the redemption rate is only .013 for those who devoted 60% or more of their purchases to their favorite brand. In contrast, the redemption rate is much higher (.075) for those who were less likely to buy their favorite brand.

Combining the findings from the tests of H_1 and H_2 leads to the following conclusions. The group most likely to redeem the brand A coupon is the group most likely to buy brand A. The second most likely group of redeemers consist of households that are not strongly inclined to purchase any specific brand. The group least likely to redeem the brand A coupon comprises households that are highly likely to buy their favorite competitive brand.

H_3 states that the redemption rate will increase with the coupon face value. As can be seen in Table 1, the hypothesis is partially supported. The average redemption rates are .068, .097, and .098 for the low, medium, and high face value groups, respectively. The null hypothesis of equal redemption rates for all three face values is rejected at the .001 level. The low prior probability segment (row 1 of Table 1) shows a similar pattern with redemption rates of .037, .042, and .058. Though these results support H_3, the findings for the remaining prior probability groups (rows 2 and 3 of Table 1) are less clear. Initially redemption rates might appear to be highest for the medium face value among households with higher prior probability levels. However, the sample sizes are smaller for these two segments and the null hypothesis of equal redemption rates for medium and high face values cannot be rejected at the .10 level of significance. In summary, the data suggest redemption does increase as the face value goes from low to medium, but does not differ between medium and high face value groups except among low prior probability households. The finding of greater sensitivity to face value among the low prior probability group is consistent with the survey findings of Shoemaker and Tibrewala (1985).

In the next section we examine brand choice behavior after a coupon redemption. The question addressed is whether a household's share of brand A purchases changes after the coupon redemption. Two procedures are used. One is to examine the aggregate share of brand choices before and after the coupon distribution date or redemption purchase date. The second procedure is based on preredemption and postredemption estimates of purchase probability for individual households.

Brand choice behavior after the coupon promotion

To study the dynamics of brand choice behavior over time, we consider the sequence of consecutive purchase occasions for each household before and after the coupon delivery date as shown in Table 2 (in Table 2, the first occasion prior to the coupon delivery is labeled '1st before' and the first occasion after the coupon delivery is labeled '1st after' and so on). We then record whether the promoted brand was purchased on each of these occasions. Finally, we compute the total number of brand A purchases, as well as brand A's 'purchase share', across households for each occasion.

Table 2 shows the purchase share index (see note 2) for brand A on up to five purchase occasions prior to the coupon delivery date and up to seven purchase occasions after the delivery date. The table is based on all 4887 product class purchasers in the panel. Some households make many purchases of the product class in a 24-week period and some make just a few. As a result, the number of households making five or more purchases prior to the delivery date (3808) is less than the number making one or more purchases (4887) in the same time period (see Table 2).

Several interesting facts can be observed in Table 2. First, as expected, brand A accounts for a relatively stable share of product class purchases on the five purchase occasions prior to the coupon delivery. The average is 10.0 with a range from 8.8 to 10.8. Second, the brand A purchase share index jumps to 15.8 on the first purchase

Table 2 Index of brand A purchase share by purchase occasion before and after coupon delivery date[a]

Purchase occasions	Purchase share index (%)	Sample size (no. of product class purchases)
5th before	10.8	3808
4th before	10.7	4066
3rd before	10.2	4310
2nd before	9.6	4611
1st before	8.8	4887
Average	10.0	
1st after	15.8	4338
2nd after	14.9	3872
3rd after	13.8	3374
4th after	11.3	2953
5th after	12.4	2581
6th after	11.9	2264
7th after	14.4	1953
Average	13.7	

[a]Based on all 4887 product class purchasers in the panel. Purchase share is shown as an index in which 10.0 is the average market share of brand A on the five purchase occasions before the coupon delivery. '1st before' refers to the household's purchase occasion just prior to the coupon delivery date.

occasion after the delivery. The coupon promotion clearly produces a short-term increase in sales. Third, the brand A share of purchases declines gradually to 14.9, 13.8, and 11.3 on the second, third, and fourth purchase occasions after the delivery. Finally, the average share of purchases is 13.7 on purchase occasions one through seven after the delivery date.

The pattern of gradual decline in Table 2 suggests an interesting question. Are the share values of 14.9, 13.8, 11.3, and so on after the first postdelivery purchase occasion due to a temporary increase in repeat buying by the early redeemers or are they a result of delayed coupon redemption by certain households? This question is addressed in two additional analyses relating to purchases by coupon redeemers.

The first analysis examines the number of coupon redemptions by purchase occasion after the coupon delivery date. The results, shown in Table 3, are based on the 4887 product class purchasers in the panel. As the table indicates, only 30% of all brand A coupon redemptions were made on the first purchase occasion after the delivery date; 60% of the redemptions were made by the third product class purchase occasion and 90% by the ninth purchase occasion. Clearly, the effects of the coupon redemptions on sales are observed over many purchase occasions after the coupon delivery date. Hence at least part of the increased purchase share on postdelivery occasions two through seven in Table 2 is due to delayed redemptions.

A second method of disaggregating the Table 2 results is to examine the purchase share of brand A among the brand A coupon redeemers on each purchase occasion before and after the particular household redeemed the coupon. This analysis differs from that shown in Table 2 in that the sequence is relative to the household's redemption purchase, not the coupon delivery date (for example, '1st before' refers here to the household's first purchase occasion prior to the coupon redemption purchase). The results are reported in Table 4. The average brand A share of purchases for these households is 11.2% on the six prior purchase occasions and 11.9% on the succeeding occasions. Though these findings suggest the possibility of a slight increase in repeat purchasing among the segment of 371 redeemers, this

Table 3 Pattern of brand A coupon redemptions by purchase occasion after coupon delivery date

Purchase occasion after coupon delivery date	Brand A coupon redemptions			
	Frequency	Percentage	Cumulative frequency	Cumulative percentage
1st	110[a]	29.6	110	29.6
2nd	61	16.4	171	46.0
3rd	53	14.3	224	60.3
4th	33	8.9	257	69.2
5th	18	4.9	275	74.1
6th	16	4.3	291	78.4
7th	19	5.1	310	83.5
8th	11	3.0	321	86.5
9th	11	3.0	332	89.5
10th or more	39	10.5	371	100.0
Total	371	100.0		

[a]To be read as: '110 households redeemed the brand A coupon on the first purchase occasion after the coupon delivery date'.

Table 4 Brand A share of purchases by purchase occasions prior to and subsequent to the coupon redemption[a]

Purchase occasion	Brand A purchases	Total purchases	Brand A share (%)
6th before	33	241	13.6
5th before	33	326	10.1
4th before	47	338	13.9
3rd before	41	340	12.0
2nd before	34	344	9.8
1st before	30	353	8.5
Average			11.2
1st after	29	314	9.2
2nd after	30	279	10.8
3rd after	27	246	11.0
4th after	31	212	14.6
5th after	25	189	13.2
6th after	25	159	15.7
Average			11.9

[a]Based on all households that redeemed a direct mail coupon for brand A after the coupon delivery date.

segment is less than 30% of the 1376 households that bought brand A at least once before the coupon promotion. Consequently, incremental repeat purchasing appears to have very little effect on aggregate sales of brand A. The pattern of brand A purchasing by these redeemers after their redemption purchase is generally similar to their pattern of purchases prior to the redemption. In particular, the brand A share of purchases did not increase sharply after the redemption (see Table 4) as it did after the coupon delivery date (see Table 2).

From the combined results of Tables 2, 3, and 4, it appears that the gradual return to the precoupon market share shown in Table 2 (15.8, 14.9, 13.8, . . .) is due to the fact that 70% of the redeeming households did not redeem the coupon on the first purchase opportunity. When household brand choices are examined in the aggregate in relation to the redemption date (Table 4), brand choice behavior does not appear to be affected in any clear pattern by the redemption purchase. However, this finding does not preclude the possibility that for certain consumer segments coupon redemption does affect subsequent brand choices. We now examine this issue and test H_4.

H_4 states that the largest increase in the probability of purchasing the couponed brand subsequent to the coupon redemption will occur among households that are nonusers or infrequent users of brand A. This hypothesis is tested by a procedure similar to that used by Aakar (1973, p. 597). That is, a Bernoulli purchase model is assumed for each household and an estimate of the Bernoulli parameter (p) is obtained both before and after the coupon redemption purchase.

To analyze the changes in repeat purchasing by market segment, the 36 weeks were divided into three time periods. Period I covers weeks 1 through 12. Period II ranges from week 13 until the household's last purchase prior to the coupon redemption. Period III ranges from the first purchase after the redemption until week 36. The data from period I are used to classify households as users or nonusers of brand A. Brand A users are defined as households that purchase brand A at least once during the 12 weeks of period I.[3] The analysis is based on all redeeming households that made at least three purchases of the product class in period I and at least one in each of the other two periods. A total of 291 households (of the 371 households that redeemed the coupon) satisfy these criteria. These households made an average of 13.6, 17.0, and 8.8 product class purchases in periods I, II, and III, respectively.

Periods II and III are used to estimate the preredemption and postredemption purchase probabilities, respectively. Preredemption probability (P_{II}) for each household is estimated as the brand A share of all purchases made by the household in period II. Similarly, the postredemption probability (P_{III}) is estimated as the brand A share of purchases made in period III. The change in probability then is calculated for each household as $P_{III} - P_{II}$. The findings are reported in Table 5.

As hypothesized, the change in purchase probability is much greater for the nonuser segment. As shown in Table 5, the average probability for this segment increased from .054 to .091 between periods II and III, resulting in an average increase of .37 for these 129 households (significant at the .05 level). In contrast, a much smaller change is observed for the 162 users. Their average probabilities are .155 and .139 for periods II and III. The average change in the probability (.017) is not significant even at the .10 level. In addition, the two groups differ significantly ($p < .001$) in terms of the changes in their purchase probabilities.

These findings indicate a significant increase in purchase probability for the small segment of the population that consisted of nonusers of brand A who redeemed the coupon. However, because this segment of 129 households is only a small proportion of the total number of brand A buyers (1376) before the coupon promotion, this increase would not have much effect on aggregate sales of brand A.

CONCLUSIONS AND MANAGERIAL IMPLICATIONS

Our analysis of coupon effects for a mature brand in a frequently purchased product class provides support for the model and hypotheses developed in our study. Our results indicate that coupons do produce a short-term increase in the brand's purchase share that is due mostly to redemption purchases. There also appears to be a significant increase in purchase probability among the few nonusers who redeem the coupon. However, this effect is difficult to observe at the aggregate level because the number of nonusers who redeem the coupon is small in relation to the total number of brand A buyers.

Though the tests should be repeated for other established brands as well as for new brands, the initial results suggest it may not be possible to justify a coupon promotion

Table 5 Average change in brand A purchase probability among brand A coupon redeemers by user segment[a]

Segment	n	$\overline{P_{II}}$	$\overline{P_{III}}$	Average ($P_{III} - P_{II}$)
Users of brand A in period I	162	.155	.139	− .017[b]
Nonusers of brand A in period I	129	.054	.091	.037[c]
Total redeemers	291	.111	.117	.006[b]

[a]Based on households that made at least three product class purchases in period I and at least one purchase in each of the two subsequent periods. $\overline{P_k}$ is the average estimated probability in period k.
[b]Not significantly different from zero at the .10 level.
[c]Significant at the .05 level.

with the argument that a substantial number of new buyers will be 'converted' to the promoted brand after the promotion. The added contribution due to increased repeat purchasing appears to be very small. This finding suggests that if a coupon promotion for an established brand is to be profitable, most of the profit must be made on the coupon redemption purchase.

The findings relating to coupon redemption indicate redemption rates are lowest for households that do not purchase the promoted brand prior to the coupon promotion and that are consistent buyers of their favorite competitive brand. Finally, redemption rates are found to increase with coupon face value, but, for our study, medium and high face values appear to have the same effect on redemption.

REFERENCES

Aaker, David A. (1973), 'Toward a Normative Model of Promotional Decision Making', *Management Science*, 19 (April), B435–B450.

Blattberg, Robert C., Thomas Buesing, Peter Peacock, and Subrata K. Sen (1978), 'Identifying the Deal Prone Segment', *Journal of Marketing Research*, 15 (August), 369–77.

___, Gary D. Eppen, and Joshua Lieberman (1981), 'A Theoretical and Empirical Evaluation of Price Deals for Consumer Nondurables', *Journal of Marketing*, 45 (Winter), 116–29.

Freedman, David, Robert Pisani, and Roger Purves (1978), *Statistics*. New York: W. W. Norton and Co.

Klein, Robert L. (1981), 'Using Supermarket Scanner Panels to Measure the Effectiveness of Coupon Promotions', in *Proceedings: Third ORSA/TIMS Special Interest Conference on Market Measurement and Analysis*, John W. Keon, ed. Providence, RI: The Institute of Management Sciences, 118–24.

Kuehn, Alfred A. and Albert C. Rohloff (1967), 'Consumer Response to Promotions', in *Promotional Decisions Using Mathematical Models*, Patrick J. Robinson, ed. Boston: Allyn and Bacon, Inc., 45–148.

Narasimhan, Chakravarthi (1984), 'A Price Discrimination Theory of Coupons', *Marketing Science*, 3 (Spring), 128–47.

Neslin, Scott A., Caroline Henderson, and John Quelch (1985), 'Consumer Promotions and the Acceleration of Product Purchases', *Marketing Science*, 4 (Spring), 147–65.

Peckham, James O., Jr. (1985), 'Using Scanning Data to Analyze the Effects of Manufacturer's Coupons', *Nielsen Researcher*, A. C. Nielsen Company, no. 1, 6–11.

Shimp, Terence A. and Alican Kavas (1984), 'The Theory of Reasoned Action Applied to Coupon Usage', *Journal of Consumer Research*, 11 (December), 795–809.

Shoemaker, Robert W. and Vikas Tibrewala (1985), 'Relating Coupon Redemption Rates to Past Purchasing of the Brand', *Journal of Advertising Research*, 25 (October/November), 40–7.

NOTES

1 Blattberg, Eppen, and Lieberman (1981) propose that when households make deal purchases, they also incur inventory costs in storing the goods purchased. In the specific case of coupon promotions, the general lack of short-term expiration dates implies that most consumers do not need to increase their inventory to above-average levels to use the coupon. Consequently, inventory costs are not included in our model.

2 The experiment was conducted by Information Resources Inc. for a firm that requests anonymity. At the firm's request, the brand name and product class are not identified. The share of purchases in Table 2 is shown as an index in which the average share in the base period is set equal to 10.0. The index is directly proportional to the purchase share.

3 It is important to use the period I data to classify households and the period II data to estimate the preredemption probability. If the period I data were used both for classifying households and estimating the preredemption probability, one would be likely to observe a 'regression to the mean' effect (i.e., the regression fallacy; see Freedman, Pisani, and Purves, 1978, p. 158).

Bawa, K. and Shoemaker, R. W. (1987) 'The effects of a direct mail coupon on brand choice behavior'. *Journal of Marketing Research*, 24(3): 370–376. Reproduced with permission from *Journal of Marketing Research*, published by the American Marketing Association.

Section 8
Personal Selling

The aim of this section is to bring together a collection of articles to provide well-founded theoretical discussion and empirical research in key areas of personal selling.

The first article from Cardozo and Shipp (1987) begins appropriately with a review of traditional selling approaches in the context of the dynamic sales environment and changing customer requirements. They identify adaptational changes in the structure and process of firms and consequential effects on the role of sales management, making recommendations to enable sales managers to adapt effectively to the changed environment. The theme of salesforce management is continued in the second paper from Ingram, Schwepker and Hutson (1992), who use empirical research to identify the reasons why salespeople fail in their work. Investigating a wide variety of possible factors, the authors identify support of sales staff by their management to be a key factor in preventing failure by individual members of the sales force.

Plank and Dempsey (1980) also review traditional theories and models for selling a product or service, noting these are limited to simple persuasion approaches. The authors argue that the industrial buying process is more complex than that allowed for by more traditional models and identify a personal selling framework more suitable for the complex environments which characterise industrial selling.

The last paper, from Powers (1989) is also the last in this collection of Marketing Communications Classics and provides an appropriate link with the first section. One of the most perennial and complex issues marketers must face revolves around the allocation of resources to one communications tool or another – for example, whether more sales force or more advertising might be best. By offering a model to evaluate marketing spend versus expected returns, Powers provides an enabling model to achieve the more effective integration of marketing communications activities recommended to be essential by the eminent authors in Section One.

New selling methods are changing industrial sales management

8.1

Richard Cardozo and Shannon Shipp

The world of industrial sales management is changing, radically and permanently. New selling methods have altered the role of traditional face-to-face selling. These new methods have led to new structures in which the position of the traditional industrial sales manager has less authority and requires a somewhat different set of skills. These new structures have also increased the number of senior sales management positions.

To understand the changing nature of industrial sales management, we studied new selling methods and their effects on managers' jobs in more than 40 industrial firms. These firms, all located in the Midwestern heartland, ranged across industry type and included graphic arts, footwear materials, fluid handling, liquid conditioning, and process control industries. All business units had 100 or more employees, and all respondents were promised anonymity.

This study showed that industrial sales managers face a choice between seeing their jobs shrink around them or moving to new positions. Standing still is not an option. Understanding relationships among environmental forces that lead to new selling methods, and the structural consequences of these methods, can help chief executives and sales managers plan for effective change.

TRADITIONAL INDUSTRIAL SELLING

Using Arthur Miller's fictional creation as a prototype, Willy Loman's industrial counterpart made his rounds on a schedule, calling on established accounts and seeing new customers within a specified geographic area. When he received an order, he wrote it in his order book and mailed or telephoned it to the office. He handled service problems when he came around again to solicit reorders.

In Willy Loman's day, the sales manager's primary responsibilities involved:

- Recruiting sales personnel;
- Deploying them;
- Motivating them; and
- Directing their activities.

The sales manager specified, directly or through subordinate managers, on whom the salespeople were to call and what products or services they were to emphasize. The sales manager supported the salespeople when they had to negotiate with the factory for a better delivery date, with the engineering department for a modification of product specifications, or with the accounting department for credit extension. The manager or subordinate managers worked with salespeople to plan strategy for particular accounts, but the manager's principal role was to lead the sales force into the field to fight competitors and capture sales from customers.

The sales manager carried out this mission through a military-like chain of command. Typically, the basic unit was an individual salesperson assigned to a specific geographic area or to specific accounts within a geographic area. This salesperson reported to a regional supervisor, who, in turn, reported to the general sales manager.

THE RISE OF TELEMARKETING AND NATIONAL ACCOUNT MANAGEMENT

But industrial marketers have reshaped their traditional selling methods because of increasing costs and changing customer requirements.

Increasing costs

Industrial sales calls now cost between $200 and $225 each. With 4 to 4.5 calls needed to close an average industrial sale, costs of obtaining an order may reach four figures.[1] Statistics like these have pushed selling costs as a percentage of sales higher and higher, to the point that for smaller customers face-to-face (FTF) selling has become unprofitable.

Many industrial manufacturers and distributors have switched to telemarketing (TM) to reach smaller customers. These TM programs involve systematic outbound calling by specially selected and trained personnel to solicit new orders and reorders on supplies and equipment. TM programs also offer inbound '800' numbers to receive customer orders and to provide service and information on order status. Most TM programs are linked with automated order entry systems and supported by extensive catalogs and mailings. Firms adopting TM programs have leapfrogged over their less sophisticated competitors, whose 'inside sales' desks performed only a portion of these functions.

To exploit the cost-saving potential of TM, industrial marketers use it not only to supplant FTF selling but also to support and supplement FTF selling. For example, a large manufacturer of control systems used a headquarters TM operation to qualify leads generated by trade shows. Information on promising leads was forwarded to regional field sales offices, where TM groups ascertained customers' specific needs and gave that information to a field salesperson. After a salesperson called on the prospective customer, the regional TM group provided whatever follow-up information was requested. If a sale was made, the regional TM group called back for reorders, while a separate TM group handled service for which on-site repair was not needed.

TM programs have been surprisingly effective in maintaining or increasing market share and improving service levels to small customers. According to our research, they have cut selling costs dramatically – from more than 25 percent of sales to less than five percent in some companies.

TM also has the potential to sell expensive equipment (some individual transactions exceeded $25,000) and sophisticated materials and supplies. Distributors as well as manufacturers have developed successful TM programs.

Changing customer requirements

Instead of maintaining multiple suppliers to assure competitive bids, many industrial purchasers are slashing their vendor lists and developing closer relationships with a much smaller number of vendors.

A major manufacturer of construction equipment, for example, cut its supplier list in one product category from more than 300 vendors to fewer than a dozen. This category accounted for purchases of up to $10 million. In another product category, a construction equipment maker and a major component supplier formed a joint venture to set up a plant to make components and sited it adjacent to the customer's main manufacturing complex. Design teams from both companies worked together to develop lower cost, standardized components for the venture.

In another example, an automobile manufacturer asked for access to a supplier's internal computer so that the auto manufacturer could track the progress of its orders. In response, the supplier arranged a 24-hour 'hot line' that the auto manufacturer could use to obtain up-to-the-minute order status reports, without investment in new software or risk to proprietary data in the supplier's system.

Industrial suppliers increasingly are called upon to provide service and consistent pricing at customer locations that may be scattered throughout the world. For example, a manufacturer of laboratory equipment required its suppliers to support its own service program, which was designed to reach customer sites anywhere outside the Eastern bloc within 48 hours. A large, international buyer of production materials shifted from plant-based to centralized purchasing and pressed its suppliers to quote standard delivery prices (including equalized freight) for any of its locations.

Worldwide consolidation of companies in many industries is accelerating this trend toward centralization and global standardization.

National account management

To meet the changing demands of a small number of important customers, many industrial marketers have adopted national account management (NAM). NAM involves teams of sales, service, and, frequently, technical personnel who interact with purchasing, manufacturing, marketing, engineering, and financial personnel in customer organizations.[2]

NAM teams are typically headed by a senior salesperson who has demonstrated success not only in selling but also in managing. NAM appears to be most effective for businesses that receive a significant proportion of their income from a small number of accounts who require high service levels.

In sum, Willy Loman's world is obsolete for most industrial companies. His largest customers are served by a national account team, whose members meet on a flexible schedule with their counterparts in customers' organizations. His smaller customers are handled by a sophisticated TM staff. The customers he sees have been screened by a TM group.

Willy's modern counterparts are no longer just making a sale. They are establishing a relationship between their company and the customer. As that relationship grows, routine orders will flow from the customer's computer directly to the supplier's computer. Routine service and questions about order status will be handled by telephone or electronic mail.

STRATEGY, STRUCTURE, AND THE SALES MANAGER'S ROLE

In the companies we observed, the manager of the traditional FTF sales force has lost responsibility for the largest and smallest accounts (see Figure 1). The national accounts manager and NAM teams plan account strategy for the largest customers. The responsibilities of the traditional sales manager for those accounts consist primarily in maintaining a sales force to carry out the plans of other managers.

Many of the traditional sales manager's best people have been taken for NAM teams. In addition, the national accounts manager, who is responsible for the business's most important customers, often attains informal status surpassing that of the traditional sales manager, who previously enjoyed the top sales management position.

The traditional sales manager's authority has been further eroded as TM groups have taken over prospecting and qualifying customers, and providing much of the service and reorder solicitation that used to be performed by the sales force of the traditional sales manager. Because TM has also displaced FTF selling to small customers, fewer salespersons are needed. The traditional sales manager thus has reduced authority over a smaller staff.

While the number of sales personnel has fallen, the total number of managers needed to direct the selling effort has increased. In addition to the manager of the traditional FTF sales force, national account managers and TM managers have appeared.

Accompanying this increase in managers is an unprecedented need for coordination. The traditional sales manager has to coordinate selling efforts with the national accounts manager and the TM manager, who share the same customers.

Of course the national accounts manager and the TM manager need to coordinate their activities with those of the traditional sales manager. Each of these positions emphasizes skills different from those required of the traditional sales manager.

	Traditional Stage in Selling Process				New Stage in Selling Process		
Account Size	Prospect/ Qualify	Present/ Close	Service/ Reorder	Account Size	Prospect/ Qualify	Present/ Close	Service/ Reorder
Large	Face-to Face Selling (FTF)	FTF	FTF	Large	National Account Management (NAM)	NAM	NAM
Medium	FTF	FTF	FTF	Medium	Telemarketing (TM)	FTF	FTF & TM
Small	FTF	FTF	FTF	Small	TM	TM	TM

Figure 1 Evolution of selling methods by stage of selling process and size of account.

The national accounts manager

National account managers operate in many ways like product managers – they have significant responsibilities but limited authority. Consequently, national account managers, like product managers, have to rely on their abilities to persuade others to work toward a common objective. Typically, they mobilize the resources of the field sales force, the service function, engineering, and sometimes finance and accounting to execute programs for individual accounts. National account personnel are often called upon to get customer personnel from different departments and widespread sites to cooperate in such programs. Developing account strategy forms a much more important part of a national account manager's activity than of a traditional sales manager's function.

In sum, the national account manager is much more a planner and coordinator, and much less a hierarchical line manager, than is the traditional sales manager.

The TM manager

In contrast, the TM manager is responsible for a defined group of individuals who perform tightly specified tasks. If TM is used to support and supplement the activities of the FTF sales force, the TM manager is often evaluated on the number of customer contacts made and the costs per contact. If a TM program solicits reorders, the TM manager is also judged on sales produced.

If TM is used instead of FTF selling to reach a specified set of customers (typically small and often geographically dispersed), the TM manager functions like a traditional sales manager. In these cases the TM manager is ordinarily evaluated regularly on sales to an assigned market segment and, in some businesses, on new accounts solicited.

Although this job description sounds like that for a traditional sales manager, there are three important differences:

1. Recruiting and selection are easier because the pool of suitable TM personnel is ordinarily larger than that of industrial sales personnel.
2. Training can be more focused and efficient in many TM operations because operators work from a carefully prepared script.
3. Supervision can be far more rigorous because operators typically work in a single location and supervisors can use telemonitoring devices.

These differences mean that the position of TM manager can be filled adequately by a less powerful, less experienced, and less well paid person than a traditional sales manager.

A more subtle difference between the positions of the TM manager and the traditional sales manager is that the TM manager has opportunities to form a new division. For example, suppose the TM manager of a communication equipment manufacturer discovers that customer orders for service parts fall into systematic patterns. The TM manager recommends that a set of parts-and-service kits be made up for sale at a substantially higher margin than individual parts. Despite the cost difference, customers welcome the new kits, which simplify ordering and inventory control. The manager subsequently discovers opportunities for other special parts and assemblies and builds sales to the point that the former TM operation is now a full-fledged operating division, with the TM manager now the division general manager. Other businesses are finding that entrepreneurial flair may be an important qualification for TM management where growth opportunities exist.

The general sales manager

Some businesses which include NAM and TM in addition to FTF selling methods have created a new position of general sales manager. That position has responsibility for overseeing and coordinating activities of the traditional sales manager, the national accounts manager, and the TM manager.

The general sales manager's job is to balance multiple selling methods to achieve several objectives, which may range from cultivating major new national or global accounts to maintaining market share among small customers in New England. The scope of this position is considerably greater than that of the traditional sales manager, who uses one method (FTF selling) to attain a more limited set of objectives. In one business that recently overhauled its selling methods, restructured its sales organization, and appointed a general sales manager, the CEO commented:

> The general sales manager is like a general officer or a theater commander, planning grand strategy and moving ground, sea, and air resources against multiple objectives.

In this analogy, the traditional sales manager resembles a company or battalion commander whose responsibilities are primarily tactical in nature.

ADAPTING TO NEW STRUCTURES

Changes in selling methods have led to a proliferation of sales management positions. The traditional sales manager has several options:

- Move up to the general sales manager slot, expanding responsibilities for sales strategy and coordination;
- Move laterally (and perhaps upwards in status) to become national accounts manager, emphasizing strategic account planning and de-emphasizing sales force administration;
- Move laterally (and typically downwards in status and pay) to become TM manager;
- Remain the traditional sales manager, with diminished responsibility and, often, lower pay; or
- Leave the organization.

Traditional sales managers whose interests, abilities, and growth potential enable them to take advantage of either of the first two choices may welcome the changes in structure brought about by the new selling methods. But traditional sales managers who think themselves unlikely to become national account managers or general sales managers typically resist reorganization and fight against new selling methods. This reaction may force the general manager of the business to make some difficult choices about individuals who have been colleagues for many years.

WHAT SHOULD GENERAL MANAGERS DO?

General managers can take four steps to maximize the benefits of the new selling methods while managing the reorganization necessary to put those new methods into place.

1. **Survival requires change**. Recognize that environmental pressures of increasing costs and changing customer service requirements affect all industrial marketers. Survival and competitive positioning will likely mandate new selling methods. The question for most businesses is not *whether* to adopt new selling methods but *what* new selling method to adopt.
2. **Just as methods affect structures, structures affect methods**. Realize that the relationship between selling methods and structure works two ways: changes in methods lead to changes in structure, but an existing structure may be a formidable obstacle to a new selling method.

   Personnel in the present organization may argue against new selling methods because they fear for their jobs or simply because they do not recognize the same compelling reasons for change that managers do. One business whose personnel effectively blocked adoption of a new method for three years estimated its annual opportunity losses at eight percent of sales, a figure that would have increased pre-tax profits by 50 percent.
3. **Change requires adjustment.** Look ahead to see how a new selling method will affect the organization structure to manage industrial selling. Identify new positions and forecast likely changes in responsibilities and functions of existing positions. Recognize that changing an entrenched structure can be difficult and time-consuming, necessitating plans for transitional organizational structures.
4. **The demands of the job determine personnel.** Compare the demands of the new jobs with capabilities – potential and demonstrated – of available personnel. Begin training and education for those whose responsibilities will be expanded in the new organization. For others, seek transfers within the firm or provide outplacement counseling. Be prepared to be candid with subordinates who inquire about their roles in the new structure.

   Recognize that hiring a sales manager is a much more complex task than it once was. Be prepared to hire more than one person to complete the sales management team. New selling methods imply a different mix of positions, each requiring different sets of skills. Hiring and promotion decisions, therefore, involve selecting a set of individuals with different but complementary talents.

WHAT SHOULD INDIVIDUAL SALES MANAGERS DO?

There is an important corollary here for subordinates. Rather than waiting and fearing what might happen, look beyond the present sales activities and organization to the future. Determine what mix of selling methods you would pursue if you were in charge. Then outline the organization according to these new methods.

If you see a role for yourself in the new structure, sell the plan to the person in charge. This approach benefits the organization and everyone involved by enabling more individuals to participate in planning on a professional basis.

On the other hand, if you think you would not be comfortable in a changed organization, begin looking for alternative opportunities before you're under pressure to do so.

Changes in the business environment require changes in selling methods, which, in turn, lead to changes in organization structure. General managers, sales managers, and their subordinates who recognize these relationships can plan for change and gain a competitive advantage for their businesses and themselves.

NOTES

1 *LAP Report* (New York: McGraw-Hill, 1984).
2 See Merrill Tutton, 'Segmenting a National Account,' *Business Horizons* 30 (January–February 1987): 61–68.

Cardozo, R. and Shipp, S. (1987) 'New selling methods are changing industrial sales management'. *Business Horizons*, 30(5), September/October: 23–38. Reproduced with permission.

Why salespeople fail

Thomas N. Ingram, Charles H. Schwepker, Jr. and Don Hutson

8.2

INTRODUCTION

In today's competitive marketplace, personal selling is the key to success for many industrial firms. As industrial customers become more demanding and attempt to streamline their own operations, it is not uncommon to observe sales organizations being put under intense pressure to meet elevated customer expectations. For example, Xerox recently cut its list of approved vendors from 5,000 to only 450 [1]. Undoubtedly, the sales organizations of the surviving vendors must be able to address Xerox's expectations with highly competent salesforces.

As personal selling becomes more crucial in determining overall success for many organizations, it is important to recognize some of the stark realities which challenge the sales executives charged with developing and sustaining competitive salesforces. First, the costs of recruiting, developing, and deploying a professional sales force are at an all-time high [2]. Second, the chronic problem of salesforce turnover continues to plague many sales organizations. According to one major survey, the average turnover rate in U.S. and Canadian firms is 27% [3]. Furthermore, 20% of the respondents in this survey feel the turnover situation is worsening, and few see any sign for short-term reduction of turnover rates. Finally, sales managers are expected to face a shortage of qualified applicants from which to draw tomorrow's recruits. This is due in part to demographic changes and an identifiable lack of skilled workers who could be trained to succeed in complex sales jobs [4].

As the realities of developing and sustaining a competent sales organization are fully realized, it is clear that the costs of salesforce failure are on the rise. The direct costs of recruiting, training, and, all too often, replacing salespeople provide incentives to gain a better understanding of factors related to salesforce failure. These costs, coupled with losses of revenue associated with sales territory vacancies, can lead sales managers to the logical conclusion that it is far better to improve salesperson performance than to dismiss poor performers [5].

Purpose

The purpose of this study is to examine sales executives' perceptions of salesperson failure in an attempt to better understand why it occurs. Understanding gained in this area may help to prevent salesperson failure, and thus improve overall salesforce performance. First, the relevant literature will be reviewed. This will be followed by discussions of the research methods, results, and management implications.

RELEVANT LITERATURE

A review of the literature uncovered only one empirical article on the topic of salesperson failure. Johnston, Hair, and Boles [6] examined the views of sales managers, salespeople, and students asked to identify factors associated with salesperson failure. These factors were then associated with recommended recruiting and selection practices. Sales managers identified several reasons why salespeople fail, including (1) lack of initiative; (2) poor planning and organization; (3) lack of enthusiasm; (4) lack of customer orientation; and (5) lack of personal goals. In conclusion, they stress the importance of hiring 'trainable' candidates, as well as those with strong personal goals and a realistic view of the sales job. Moreover, they suggest that experienced salespeople should be incorporated into the selection process, and good candidates should not be eliminated because of a lack of sales understanding.

Johnston, Hair, and Boles also queried salespeople and students on their views of what contributes to salesperson failure. Not surprisingly, they found that students 'have numerous misperceptions about which factors contribute significantly to failure in a sales career' ([6], p. 54). Salespeople, being directly involved in the selling function, may have difficulty objectively assessing factors contributing to their failure because of the tendency to place the blame elsewhere, rather than on oneself, for deficiencies. This is partially supported by an attributional bias, known as the self-serving [7] or ego defensive bias [8], in which one tends to accept more causal responsibility for positive than for negative outcomes.

Johnston, Hair, and Boles provide valuable insight into the selection process by which organizations recruit and hire new salespeople [6]. However, they did not consider factors contributing to failure of salespeople who have been on the job for some time.

In contrast to the paucity of research on salesperson failure, there have been numerous attempts to identify those characteristics considered important for good sales performance. In an extensive review of the sales performance literature, Churchill et al. [9] indicate that the determinants of sales performance can be ordered in the following way in terms of their importance in explaining the variance in sales performance: (1) role variables, e.g., role conflict and role ambiguity; (2) salesperson skill levels; (3) motivation; (4) personal factors, e.g., personality characteristics; (5) job-related aptitude; and (6) organizational and environmental factors such as the method of compensation and the degree of competitiveness. However, these variables have had limited success in predicting sales performance. The average correlation coefficient between predictors and performance in 1,653 cases was only 0.19, thus explaining less than four percent of the variation in salesperson performance. Although the typical study looks at the impact of multiple predictors of salesperson performance, study results have been inconsistent and much remains unknown about the variables that may systematically affect salesperson performance [9].

Given the limited research in the area of salesperson failure coupled with the difficulty in identifying factors substantially accounting for success, an empirical exploratory investigation was undertaken to examine what sales executives believe to be the most significant factors contributing to salesperson failure.

RESEARCH DESIGN AND METHODS

Sample

A national mailing list of 410 sales executives was developed from a master list provided by Sales and Marketing Executives International, Cleveland, Ohio. Respondents received a cover letter on university letterhead requesting their cooperation in completing an enclosed questionnaire. A total of 126 completed responses were returned for a response rate of 30.7%. Of those responding, approximately 34% said their company marketed primarily products, 32% services, and 34% both products and services. Firms surveyed employed anywhere from 1 to 7,000 salespeople. More than half (56.9%) of the companies responding compensate their salespeople by a combination of salary and commission, slightly over one fourth (28.4%) by commission only, and the remaining (14.7%) by salary only. Average annual sales per salesperson is $772,223, and average annual pay per salesperson is $41,172.

Measures

A comprehensive battery of failure factors was compiled from a review of the sales literature and discussions with various sales managers. These were used to construct a 29-item questionnaire capturing several antecedents of job performance (aptitude, skills, role perceptions, motivation, and personal, organizational, and environmental variables) as proposed by Walker, Churchill, and Ford [10]. Moreover, these factors are comparable to those employed by Johnston, Hair, and Boles [6], who drew from Moss [11] and Anderson and Hair [12].

   Respondents were asked to rate on a five-point scale (1 = very significant, 5 = not significant) the significance of each factor in determining salesperson failure in their respective industry. Failure was defined as the inability of the salesperson to consistently meet minimum job standards. Furthermore, a set of open-ended questions asked sales executives to indicate which of three factor categories they felt was most significant in causing salespeople to fail: (1) factors that are beyond the control of the salesperson and the employer; (2) factors beyond the control of the salesperson but not beyond the employer; and (3) factors which can be controlled by the salesperson. Finally, to assess how respondents viewed salesperson success, they were asked to indicate what they believed to be the single most important factor for ensuring a salesperson's success in today's marketplace.

RESULTS

Table 1 lists sales executives' mean rankings for the six most and six least significant factors believed to contribute to salesperson failure. Overall, even the least significant of all 29 factors listed received a mean rating just slightly over the theoretical neutral midpoint of 3, indicating that sales executives consider deficiencies in any of the areas to contribute somewhat to salesperson failure. In addition, the mean values of the top six failure factors were extremely close, suggesting from a practical point of view that they are equally important to the survey respondents.

   Additional analysis was conducted to determine whether responses differed based on the following factors: (1) number of salespeople; (2) male-to-female ratio; (3)

Table 1 Most and least significant factors contributing to salesperson failure

Factor	Mean	Rank
Most Significant		
Poor listening skills	1.80*	1
Failure to concentrate on top priorities	1.83	2
A lack of sufficient effort	1.84	3
Inability to determine customer needs	1.84	4
Lack of planning for sales presentation	1.86	5
Inadequate product/service knowledge	1.87	6
Least Significant		
Marital problems	3.41	29
Poor administrative skills	3.19	28
Substance abuse (drugs and/or alcohol)	2.95	27
Emotional immaturity	2.74	26
Pre-call negative assessment of prospects	2.65	25
Deficient job-related aptitude	2.64	24

* 1 = very significant, 5 = not very significant.

product or service sold; (4) method of compensation (salary, commission, or combination); (5) average annual sales per salesperson: and (6) average annual pay. This follows the suggestion of Churchill et al. [9], who point out that situational differences may explain some of the variance in sales performance.

T-test results (Table 2) reveal significant differences on three of the factors based on the ratio of men to women comprising the salesforce. Companies with more than half of the sales force comprised of women identified not concentrating on top priorities, inability to determine customer needs, and poor listening skills as more important in predicting salesperson failure.

In addition, based on a median split, companies with average annual sales per salesperson of $500,000 or less believe a lack of sufficient effort is more significant in contributing to failure than did those with higher average annual sales per salesperson. No significant differences were found for number of salespeople, type of product sold, method of compensation, or salesperson's salary.

When respondents were asked to rank from 1 (most significant) to 3 (least significant) those factors they felt were most significant in causing salespeople to fail,

Table 2 Differences on most significant factors based on characteristics of the firm

Factor	Male	Female	G1	G2	T-Value	Probability
Male Female						
Poor listening skills	2.04	1.36			−3.47	0.001
Failure to concentrate on top priorities	1.93	1.34			−2.30	0.023
Inability to determine customer needs	2.04	1.46			−2.85	0.005
Average Annual Sales Per Salesperson						
Lack of sufficient effort			1.69*	2.19	−2.69	0.009

Only significant findings shown. Pooled variance estimate, two-tail probability $p < 0.05$.
*GI $\leqslant$ $500,000; G2 > $500,000.

90.9% (mean, 1.10) of the sales executives felt that factors which can be controlled primarily by the salesperson are most significant in causing salespeople to fail. Conversely, 89.7% (mean, 2.88) felt factors that are beyond the control of the salesperson and the employer (for example, the state of the economy) were least significant. Factors that are beyond the control of the salesperson but not the employer were ranked in the middle (mean, 1.93).

Finally, when asked to indicate the single most important factor for insuring a salesperson's success in today's marketplace, the respondents' number one answer was a good/positive attitude (Table 3). This was followed by proper training and good work habits or hard work. Interestingly, neither good listening skills nor concentrating on top priorities was ranked as one of the 10 single most important factors for ensuring success, while planning came in tied for ninth. However, deficiencies in these areas were considered to be significant in contributing to salesperson failure.

DISCUSSION

Closer examination of the failure factors yields some interesting findings. Those factors considered to be most significant in contributing to failure can all be influenced by sales management through training and motivation; the salesperson can be taught to become a better listener, how to set and concentrate on top priorities, determine customer needs, and plan and execute an effective sales presentation.

Likewise, training can enhance salespeople's knowledge of the product or service, rather than sending them into the field unprepared. A salesperson's lack of effort might be reversed by better pay, promotion, or recognition. The point is, if these deficiencies are recognized, they can be corrected through proper training, motivation, and supervision.

Those factors deemed less significant in contributing to salesperson failure could be considered personal characteristics, i.e., marital problems, substance abuse, emotional immaturity, and job-related aptitude. Not only are these characteristics often more difficult to detect, but they are much less subject to managerial influence. Other than exercising caution during recruiting and selection, the sales manager can do little to directly alleviate these uncontrollable factors.

These findings support those of Churchill et al. [9], who found that '"enduring" personal characteristics such as aptitude variables and personal/physical traits do have some relationship to performance, but not as much as those characteristics which are "influenceable" through increased training and experience or more effective company

Table 3 Single most important factor for ensuring a salesperson's success

Factor	Percent mentioning
1. Good/positive attitude	12.61
2. Proper training	10.08
3. Good work habits/hard work	7.56
4. Motivation/self-motivation	6.72
5. Knowledge (customer, market, competition, product)	5.88
6. Dedication/desire to succeed	5.04
7. Identifying customer needs	5.04
8. Customer oriented sales approach	5.04

policies and procedures (e.g., skill levels, role perceptions, and motivation).' Deficiencies in influenceable factors were found to be more significant in contributing to salesperson failure than the personal characteristics.

This implies that managers can take an active part in preventing salesperson failure through the use of training and motivational techniques to improve those areas considered most significant in salesperson failure. Deficiency in these areas is likely to thwart the establishment of long-term relationships with clients, and lead to the salesperson's eventual demise.

The findings also suggest that sales managers should pay greater attention to the most significant failure factors because deficiencies in these areas may negatively affect relationship selling efforts. Personal selling involving long-term commitments to customers typically involves establishment of a relationship between two parties [13]. By establishing long-term relationships, the salesperson is establishing the opportunity to satisfy future needs. Consequently, satisfaction of such needs means future sales and profits for the company.

Evidence suggests relationship quality (satisfaction with and trust in a salesperson) is enhanced through perceived salesperson competence [14]. Product/market knowledge is considered to be one of the most important criteria in determining customer satisfaction with salespeople [15]. This study shows that inadequate product/service knowledge is considered one of the most significant factors contributing to salesperson failure.

Moreover, inability to determine customer needs is considered a very significant failure factor. A competent salesperson should, through probing, be able to identify customer needs. Deficiencies in both these areas point to a lack of salesperson competence. Note that competence is considered important for establishing long-term relationships with customers [16].

In addition, relational exchange (selling) involves much effort and planning by both parties [13]. Furthermore, relationships are based on communication between parties. Failure to plan adequately for the sales presentation, as well as failure to concentrate on top priorities, point to inadequacies in the ability to plan. Sales executives rated these deficiencies, coupled with a lack of sufficient effort and poor listening skills, significant in contributing to salesperson failure. Perhaps these are considered very significant because of their importance in establishing relationship selling. Putting forth effort, particularly in terms of planning and communicating (which involves listening as well as speaking), is necessary for establishing long-term relationships with buyers.

Additional findings indicate that sales executives believe factors that can be controlled by the salesperson are most significant in causing salespeople to fail. However, as pointed out, deficiencies indicated by sales executives as the most significant failure factors are within the control of the employer. Attribution theory suggests that supervisors are more likely to look to subordinates for performance explanations, particularly in the case of poor performance [17, 18]. Apparently, sales executives believe salespeople can control their own destiny. While the salesperson does have control over these factors to some extent, proper execution stems from adequate employer inputs in training and motivation. It appears that sales executives are quick to blame the salesperson for failure rather than company-initiated training or motivation techniques.

Finally, while executives considered personal variables to be the least significant factors contributing to failure, they indicated a personal variable (good/positive attitude) to be the single most significant factor for insuring salesperson success. However, a poor or negative attitude was not mentioned as one of the leading causes of salesperson failure. Hence, inadequacy in what is necessary for 'success,' from the sales executives' viewpoint, may not necessarily lead to failure.

Limitations

Sales executives did not indicate the frequency of occurrence of the failure factors investigated. Hence, it is possible that items judged to be least significant in contributing to failure may be rated as such because of their infrequent occurrence. Should one of the less significant factors occur, or occur with more regularity, it is likely that it might be considered more significant. For instance, substance abuse was rated as one of the least significant factors in contributing to failure. However, such activity may be concealed from the sales executive, causing him or her to give this factor a low rating. Moreover, it may not occur with as much regularity as some other factors, thus causing it to be viewed as less significant. Should behavior such as substance abuse be apparent to the sales executive, it probably would be considered a significant factor in contributing to salesperson failure.

CONCLUSION

As competition intensifies and the costs of maintaining a salesforce escalate, companies cannot afford excessive failure in the salesforce. We have attempted to identify factors considered to be most significant in contributing to salesperson failure. It appears costly failure can be avoided through the application of training and motivational techniques designed to address the areas found to be most significant in contributing to salesperson failure. If these areas are adequately addressed before sending salespeople into the field, they will be better equipped to perform, and subsequently less likely to fail.

REFERENCES

1. Ingram, T. N., Improving Sales Force Productivity: A Critical Examination of the Personal Selling Process, *Review of Business*, 12, 7–12, 40 (1990).
2. Hey, Where's My Survey of Selling Costs? *Sales and Marketing Management* 143, 42–45 (1991).
3. Salespeople and Sales Managers Disagree on How to Boost Sales, *Marketing Times*, 16, (July–August, 1990).
4. Bernstein, A., Where the Jobs Are is Where the Skills Aren't, *Business Week*, 3070, 104–108 (September 19, 1988).
5. Darmon, R. Y., Identifying Sources of Turnover Costs: A Segmental Approach, *Journal of Marketing* 54, 46–56 (1990).
6. Johnston, M. W., Hair, J. F., Jr., and Boles, J., Why Do Salespeople Fail? *Journal of Personal Selling & Sales Management* 9, 53–58 (1989).
7. Miller, D. T., and Ross, M., Self-Serving Biases in the Attribution of Causality: Fact or Fiction? *Psychological Bulletin* 82, 213–225 (1975).
8. Stevens, L., and Jones, E. E., Defensive Attribution and the Kelley Cube, *Journal of Personality and Social Psychology* 34, 809–820 (1976).
9. Churchill, G. A., Jr., Ford, N. M., Hartley, S. W., and Walker, O. C., Jr., The Determinants of Salesperson Performance: A Meta-Analysis, *Journal of Marketing Research* 22, 103–118 (1985).
10. Walker, O. C., Jr., Churchill, G. A., Jr., and Ford, N. M., Motivation and Performance in Industrial Selling: Present Knowledge and Needed Research, *Journal of Marketing Research* 14, 156–168 (1977).
11. Moss, S., What Sales Executives Look for in New Sales People, *Sales and Marketing Management* 120, 46–48 (1978).

12. Anderson, R. E., and Hair, J. F., Jr., *Sales Management: Text and Cases*, Random House, New York, 1983.

13. Dwyer, F. R., Schurr, P. H., and Oh, S., Developing Buyer-Seller relationships, *Journal of Marketing* 51, 11–27 (1987).

14. Crosby, L., Evans, K. R., and Cowles, D. Relationship Quality in Services Selling: An Interpersonal Influence Perspective, *Journal of Marketing* 54, 68–81 (1990).

15. Complete Salesmanship: That's What Buyers Appreciate, *Purchasing* 97, 59–66 (1984).

16. Hawes, J. M., Mast, K. E., and Swan, J. E., Trust Earning Perceptions of Sellers and Buyers, *Journal of Personal Selling & Sales Management* 9, 1–8 (1989).

17. Kanouse, D. E., and Hanson, L. R., Negativity in Evaluations, in *Attribution: Perceiving the Causes of Behavior*, E. E. Jones, D. E. Kanouse, H. H. Kelley, R. E. Nisbett, S. Valins, B. Weiner eds., General Learning Press, Morristown, New Jersey, 1972, pp. 47–62.

18. Mitchell, T. R., and Wood, R. E., Supervisors' Responses to Subordinate Poor Performance: A Test of an Attributional Model, *Organizational Behavior and Human Performance* 25, 123–138 (1980).

Ingram, T. N., Schwepker, C. H. Jr. and Hutson, D. (1992) 'Why salespeople fail'. *Industrial Marketing Management*, 21: 225–230. Reproduced with permission from Elsevier Science.

A framework for personal selling to organizations 8.3

Richard E. Plank and William A. Dempsey

INTRODUCTION

Firms that market to organizations usually rely on personal selling for most of their promotional effort. Therefore, it is imperative for these firms that the selling function be performed well. In order to discharge the selling function best, a salesperson must understand the nature of personal selling and how it relates to organizational buying behavior. There is a large literature available concerning the personal selling function. The organizational buying behavior literature, also referred to as industrial buying behavior, has been developing at a rapid pace in the last ten years [15]. However, there has been little work done in bridging these two areas. There is no available model that specifically connects the task of personal selling with multiparticipant organizational buying processes. The purpose of this article is to propose a practical model for selling to organizations. The existing models of selling and organizational buying behavior will be reviewed and then a comprehensive model for selling to organizations will be presented.

FIVE MODELS OF SELLING

There are a number of theories or models that attempt to explain how to sell a product or service. Some of the more common approaches include simple stimulus response, formula selling, needs-satisfaction, grid approach, and the depth approach. These models are briefly reviewed and the advantages and limitations as applied to personal selling to organizations are discussed.

Simple stimulus response

Simple stimulus response is based on buyers responding to a stimulus in a similar manner. The 'canned' sales talk is an example of a pure stimulus response approach to selling. A typical example in practice is the selling of a newspaper subscription over the phone. A salesperson will either memorize or read a sales presentation over the phone. It is assumed that the attributes mentioned in the presentation will be received in a positive manner by the prospect. However, not all prospective customers perceive attributes in the same manner, and this constitutes the major weakness of the 'canned' approach. Nonetheless, a good case can be made for the use of this approach in certain situations [9].

Formulated selling – AIDA

Formulated selling is usually referred to as the AIDA technique. This theory is based on the writings of William James [18] and is said to have been in actual practice since 1898. In its pure form, the theory suggests that a buyer's mind must go through four mental states during a successful sales presentation. The salesperson is instrumental in securing these states. The first mental state is that of Attention (A). The salesperson must obtain the attention of the buyer in order to continue. Next, the buyer must develop an interest (I) in the product or service (D) on the part of the buyer. Once this is achieved, the salesperson can get action (A) by asking for and receiving an order. Formulated selling is perhaps the most often used technique taught in sales training. Its usefulness as a theory for organizational selling is limited by its concentration on the presentation aspects of selling.

Needs-satisfaction

The needs-satisfaction theory dates from the writings of Strong, an early business psychologist [19]. The theory concludes that the buyer must recognize a need in order to buy, and that the salesperson must supply the solution to the need. Thus, the salesperson must identify needs in the mind of the buyer and then provide an attractive solution to the buyer's problem or react to the stated needs of the buyer and fulfill them. Its usefulness as a model for organizational selling is limited, again, by a focus on one buyer (vs. a group of participants in buying). The concept espoused is, however, an important component of any complete model.

Grid system

The grid system is an adaptation of the managerial grid to the selling function [2]. The grid has two axes. One axis involves ego drive and is labeled concern for the sale. The other axis involves empathy and is labeled concern for the customer. The grid concept is directed toward developing high levels of both qualities in a salesperson as the means for ensuring high-level sales performances. A 1–9 scale is used on both axes. A 9,9 rated salesperson is ideal because the highest levels of both qualities have been achieved. The 9,9 rated salesperson is solution oriented in terms of striving to find a fit between the needs of the buyer and the products or services marketed by the selling organization. Again, its usefulness as an organizational model of selling is limited by a lack of explicit recognition that more than one participant may be involved in the organizational buying decision process.

Depth approach

Thompson has developed the depth approach which emphasized the positive elements of several of the previously mentioned models [21]. The theory is psychologically oriented with an emphasis on the elements of communication. Buyer/seller interaction is encouraged, and a balance between presentation structure and creativity is sought. The sales presentation is not viewed as a series of separate and distinct steps, but rather a continuous flow of thoughts and ideas which are structured as necessary. Listening is considered as important as speaking. The usefulness of the depth approach as a theory of organizational selling is limited by its concentration on the presentational aspects of selling.

All of the theories mentioned thus far have been used successfully in practice. Nevertheless, these theories are not fully adequate for an organizational buying situation. A brief review of organization buying theory will be useful in identifying inadequacies in the selling models.

ORGANIZATIONAL BUYING THEORY REVIEW

There are several models of the organizational buying process. The Webster and Wind and Sheth models are the most widely recognized models of the organizational buying process [16, 22]. Webster and Wind have formulated a model in which buying behavior is a function of individual , social, organizational, and environmental factors. These four basic categories contain variables, some of which are related to the buying task and some of which are not related to the buying task. Also central to the decision process is the concept of a buying group or buying center. The purchasing agent is not always the only person in buying processes and, in fact, may not have very much to do with certain buying decisions. Webster and Wind also discuss the various roles of the participants including users, influencers, buyers, deciders, and gatekeepers.

The Sheth model is an information processing model similar to the Howard-Sheth model of consumer behavior [8]. Sheth identifies the industrial buying process as having two types of decisions, autonomous and joint. Recent research has noted the existence of substantial joint decision-making in organizational purchasing decisions. When joint decision-making occurs, potential conflict is possible and interpersonal or interdepartmental influences are an important part of the conflict resolution process. Sheth uses the March and Simon paradigm of four types of conflict resolution, problem solving, persuasion, bargaining, and politicking [12]. O'Shaughnessy has noted that this leaves out another mode of conflict resolution, namely adjudication [14]. Other models have also been offered [5, 17] and recent review articles [7, 15] cite numerous studies of certain facts of organizational buying behavior.

Models of organizational buying process and buying behavior provide the basis for a better understanding of the task environment and problems encountered by salespersons. The major problems center on the concept of the buying center (which may include a number of different participants) and conflict resolution in joint decision situations. A salesperson must determine whether a buying decision will be a joint decision or an autonomous decision. The salesperson must answer a number of key questions. If it is a joint decision, then who are the members in the group decision process and what mode of conflict resolution occurs? None of the selling models mentioned earlier in this article directly address these questions. The selling models are mainly communication-presentation oriented, and it is presumed that the buying decision-maker has been located and that the decision-maker then becomes a part of buyer-seller (salesperson) dyad. A model of organizational selling which overcomes these shortcomings will now be presented.

AN ORGANIZATIONAL SELLING MODEL

A salesperson must deal with two task areas or dimensions when planning, executing, and controlling selling efforts. One basic task area involves sales presentations made by salespersons to prospective customers. The other task or dimension involves determining who the members of the buying group are and what influences their behavior. The dual dimensionality of selling to organizations is illustrated in Fig. 1.

The dimensions shown in Fig. 1 are not mutually exclusive, i.e., they overlap. Dimension 1, which involves a sales presentation, occurs in all personal selling situations. Dimension 2 is also present in all situations, since the salesperson must determine to whom the presentations will be made. It is this second dimension which has not as yet received adequate attention in selling models.

DIMENSION 1

The sales presentation and those events leading up to it usually comprise the area of most concern for the salesperson. The selling models, discussed previously, deal with this aspect of selling. The model developed in this article consists of four phases, and it is assumed that the standard type of prospecting, as discussed in most sales textbooks, has been done.

First stage of organizational selling

The first step in the model involves the salesperson in developing an environment conducive to selling. Initially, this means creating an atmosphere of professionalism.

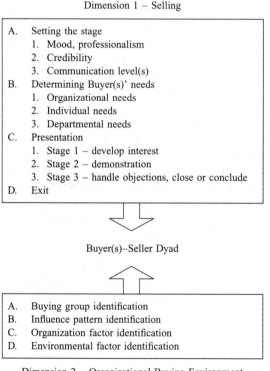

Dimension 1 – Selling

A. Setting the stage
    1. Mood, professionalism
    2. Credibility
    3. Communication level(s)
B. Determining Buyer(s)' needs
    1. Organizational needs
    2. Individual needs
    3. Departmental needs
C. Presentation
    1. Stage 1 – develop interest
    2. Stage 2 – demonstration
    3. Stage 3 – handle objections, close or conclude
D. Exit

Buyer(s)–Seller Dyad

A. Buying group identification
B. Influence pattern identification
C. Organization factor identification
D. Environmental factor identification

Dimension 2 – Organizational Buying Environment

Figure 1 An organizational selling model.

However, what might be considered professional by a purchasing agent may differ from what other members of the buying group such as engineers and production personnel think is professional. Therefore, the salesperson may have to develop different initial communications approaches for each member of the buying group. Credibility as related to the salespeople, their company, and its products and services as perceived by the buyer is an important prerequisite to a sale. Levitt has shown the effect of the selling company's name on the buyer-seller dyad [11]. Establishing credibility is a dynamic process, and it is influenced by some factors outside of the control of the selling organization and its salespersons. Salespeople must establish and/or further develop various credibilities associated with themselves, their company, and the company's product line. This process begins at first contact and continues throughout salespeople's interaction with the people within the customer organization.

Establishing communication levels is an important and sometimes little understood aspect in selling. According to Carl Jung, an individual's personality primarily develops in one of four ways [10]. People may be viewed as having one of four basic styles of behavior, which can be defined as intuitive, thinking, feeling, and sensing. People largely process communications in one of these four styles. Hence, it is advantageous to the salesperson to be able to determine which style is the primary mode of communication processing for each member of a particular buying group. The salesperson can then communicate to the buying group member in the appropriate mode. This ability to communicate in different modes has been referred to as style-flexing [3]. The ability to style-flex helps to create a mood of professionalism and to establish credibility. In addition it increases the likelihood that a sales communication will be interpreted properly and favorably. Overall this process is similar to the concept of rapport building often mentioned in sales textbooks. It is well known that dyadic interactions require that these concepts be utilized to the fullest extent [6, 13, 23].

Determining buyer's needs

The next aspect of Dimension 1 is to determine the needs of the buying organization. A salesperson must recognize that there are not only organizational needs to satisfy in marketing to organizations but also departmental and individual/personal needs. The experienced salesperson may have to take all three sets of needs into account when making sales presentations. To put this into perspective, we can use the Sheth model [16]. The expectations of various buying center members come from a variety of influences. The key to understanding various needs and the attributes associated with filling needs lies in the concept of organization orientation. If a company is technology oriented all members of the firm are likely to have similar backgrounds, educations, and experiences. Individual goals, departmental goals, and organizational goals are more likely to be highly integrated and differences between groups and individuals therefore minimized. On the other hand, companies that are not oriented to a high degree would be more likely to have goal conflicts. In companies with a high degree of organizational orientation we would expect that attributes of a product or service would be ranked very similarly regardless of whether an engineering, quality control, production, or purchasing group member evaluated them. In companies with a low degree of organizational orientation the distinct possibility exists that the attributes could vary not only in degree, but also in order of ranking. Thus, it is possible that a purchasing agent may be interested in price and delivery and an engineer in quality and design. Thus, the salesperson must determine if differences in attributes exist. If so, the sales presentation emphasis may have to be changed when dealing with different members of the buying group.

Organizational sales presentations

The sales presentation component of Dimension 1 contains three interrelated stages. Using AIDA terminology, the salesperson must first gain the attention and interest of the buyer. Then the salesperson moves the buyer toward the purchase by developing the desire for the product through demonstrations and discussions keyed to the buyer's needs. Finally, the sale is consummated after the salesperson has handled the buyer's request for clarification and overcome any doubts the buyer may have had. It should be emphasized that the presentation is not a distinct series of steps but is a fluid process in which two-way communications will normally be utilized.

The sales presentation as described above is valid in a conceptual sense for those instances where the purchase decisions are made autonomously. However, the description of the sales presentation must be modified to accommodate joint decision-making. A major point to recognize is that a close of the sale in a traditional sense is not made with each individual in the buying group. There is no point in asking for an order from an individual in a buying group who cannot make an autonomous decision. When the buying decision is a group or joint decision, then the objective of the sales presentation to group members is to improve each person's relative evaluation of the salesperson's overall offering.

Exit

The last part of Dimension 1 is for the salesperson to make a well-timed and graceful exit. Salespersons should not overstay their welcome, and they should thank the buying participant(s) for their time and any orders made.

The steps presented in Dimension 1 of the model (Fig. 1) are generalizable to most selling situations. A key factor concerning effective sales presentations is making them to the right people. Dimension 2 deals with this factor and other factors that affect organization buying decisions.

DIMENSION 2

The second dimension has four distinct but related tasks which must be accomplished by the successful salesperson. Dimension 2 can be considered an extension of the prospecting work that the salesperson does prior to the first encounter with a firm.

Identifying buying group members

The first task is to identify members of the buying group, if a group exists at all. If an autonomous buying decision situation clearly exists, then the salesperson need go no further in this task area. Many times the knowledge necessary to identify joint decision-making situations is based on the salesperson's experience. An experienced salesperson generally knows by the nature of the product or services and/or the nature of the buying organization the probability of the purchase decision being autonomous or joint. As an example, a salesperson with a technical item used in the customer's product will almost always have to deal with buying participants from production, engineering, and purchasing. Many times, however, it is not this clear cut. If not, the salesperson will usually start with the purchasing department and through questioning and observation identify other buying group members. Since the purchasing agent is often a gatekeeper, the importance of this contact cannot be minimized. The importance of this task should be obvious. If a salesperson misses one of the decision makers, it reduces his or her chances for success.

Identifying influence patterns

The second task involves an attempt by the salesperson to ascertain the influence patterns involved in the purchase decision. Again, if an autonomous buying decision exists the salesperson need go no further in this task area. In joint decision-making situations the influence and decision-making patterns will vary. This variance is determined by a number of forces as indicated in the Sheth model [16]. From a practical standpoint, the salesperson can use experience to predict influence patterns to some extent. In virtually all cases, however, some degree of observation and questioning will have to be utilized. Influence patterns are likely to be routinized across an individual firm's purchasing decisions but not across multiple firms, even in the same industry. Very little research has been done in this area. One approach to understanding influence patterns is through the study of conflict resolution. Sheth [16] has utilized the March and Simon [12] conflict resolution paradigm in the industrial buying behavior area. While there has been no actual research in this area, some preliminary research has been conducted by organizational behaviorists studying decision-making in a large organization [20]. This preliminary research attempted to predict whether bargaining or problem solving types of conflict resolutions would occur in organizations with certain antecedent conditions inherent in the decision process. Results indicated it might be possible for salespeople to predict conflict resolution patterns based on their observance of specific conditions. These specific conditions included communication obstacles, the degree of dependence of group members on one another, and knowledge of another party's needs and problems.

Identifying organizational factors

A third task is attempting to identify organizational factors which may effect the buying function. Often a company will develop policies which have an effect on their purchaser. In some cases a company may strive to develop and maintain a particular image to the general public. A salesperson can usually pick up one of these constraints by observation. Often office furnishings, typewriters, or the type of building will provide inferences. Better yet, is a knowledge of a firm's products and/or services and its marketing philosophy.

Environmental factors

The fourth and final task is that of identifying environmental constraints facing the firm. Most basic marketing texts include such factors as cultural and social forces, political and legal forces, and economic conditions. Again, these factors could have a profound effect on the purchasing function of the firm. A company having to expend large sums of money for pollution control may not have money for new capital equipment. A company experiencing a slackening of demand for its products or services will probably tighten its buying policies. Identifying these constraints involves developing a rudimentary knowledge of the firm and its industry. Often the salesperson can use questions during the rapport building stage of a presentation to obtain knowledge of these constraints.

Dimension 2 operates, at least in parts, simultaneously with Dimension 1. Both sets of tasks are equally important to the salesperson. It must be reemphasized that successfully completing Dimension 2 is important for several reasons. First of all, in it the members of the buying group are identified. Second, the degree of influence of each buying participant is recognized. This can be especially important in situations where multiple calls on members of the buying group are necessary. The salesperson can concentrate on those buyers who have the greatest impact on the decision. Third, conflict resolution patterns may be able to be identified to allow the salesperson to adjust the sales presentations to the method of conflict resolution. Finally, other factors pertinent to the buying function can be identified and handled.

IMPLICATIONS FOR SALES AND MARKETING MANAGEMENT

The model presented in this article differs from other selling models in that it is directly geared to the problem of selling to organizations, while other models are usually lacking in this respect. As Ames has suggested, it is necessary to define and articulate the activities necessary to do a successful selling job [1]. The model presented identifies the various activities that are required in selling to organizations and thus can be used by sales and marketing managers, specifically in developing sales training programs.

The model presented in this article covers the complexity of exchange relationships and it identifies various presentation skills and conditional determinants important in successful selling. As such, the model presents the basic structural elements necessary for a fairly complete sales training program. As an example, one aspect of the sales training program would involve the concept of style-flexing. There are several consulting firms who are involved in utilizing this concept. Salespeople could be trained to identify communication modes and to shift to the appropriate mode as needed. Another aspect of a sales training program would involve teaching salespeople how to identify organizational and environmental constraints and then how to deal with them. Of course, product knowledge and prospecting would be covered in any well-designed sales training program. There are, of course, numerous other topics suggested by the model.

CONCLUSION

A model has been developed which utilizes what is generally known about how organizations buy and what is known about how salespeople should sell to describe in a normative manner how a salesperson should go about selling to an organization. As such, it is intended as a framework for action on the part of the salesperson. Even though it is essentially a communication-oriented model, it may still form the basic framework for developing a sales training program. In addition, the model has suggested numerous areas that require further research in order to further understand the organizational exchange process as a whole [4].

REFERENCES

1. Ames, B. Charles, Build Marketing Strength into Industrial Selling, *Harvard Business Review.* 50, 48–60 (Jan./Feb., 1972).
2. Blake, Robert and Mouton, Jane, *The Grid for Sales Excellence.* McGraw-Hill, New York, 1969.
3. Bledsoe, John L., Your Four Communicating Styles, *Training.* 18–21 (March, 1976).
4. Bonoma, Thomas V. and Johnston, Wesley J., The Social Psychology of Industrial Buying and Selling, *Industrial Marketing Management.* 7, 213–224 (1978).
5. Brand, G. T., *The Industrial Buying Decision.* Cassell/Associated Business Programmers, London, 1972.
6. Evans, F. B., Selling as a Dyadic Relationship – A New Approach, *The American Behavioral Scientist.* 6, 76–79 (May, 1963).
7. Ferguson, Wade, A Critical Review of Recent Organization Buying Research, *Industrial Marketing Management.* 7, 225–230 (1978).
8. Howard, John A. and Sheth, Jagdish, *The Theory of Buyer Behavior.* John Wiley and Sons, New York, 1969.
9. Jolson, Marvin A., The Underestimated Potential of the Canned Sales Presentation, *Journal of Marketing.* 39, 75–78 (January, 1975).
10. Jung, Carl, *Psycholische Typen Raschen.* Verlag, Zurich, 1921.
11. Levitt, Theodore, *Industrial Purchasing Behavior: A Study of Communication Effects.* Division of Research, Graduate School of Business Administration, Harvard University, Boston, 1965.
12. March, J. G. and Simon, H. A., *Organizations.* John Wiley and Sons, New York, 1958.
13. O'Shaughnessy, John, Selling as an Interpersonal Influence Process, *Journal of Retailing.* 32–46 (Winter, 1971–72).
14. O'Shaughnessy, John, Aspects of Industrial Buying Behavior Relevant to Supplier Account Strategies, *Industrial Marketing Management.* 6, 15–22 (1977).
15. Sheth, Jagdish, Recent Developments in Organizational Buying Behavior, in *Consumer and Industrial Buying Behavior.* Arch Woodside, Jagdish Sheth, and Peter Bennett, Eds. Elsevier, New York, 1977.
16. Sheth, Jagdish, 'A Model of Industrial Buyer Behavior,' *Journal of Marketing* 37, 50–56 (Oct., 1973).
17. Stiles, G. W., An Information Processing Model of Industrial Buyer Behavior, Ph.D. dissertation, University of Minnesota, (1972).
18. Still, Richard and Cundiff, Edward, *Sales Management*, 2nd ed. Prentice-Hall, Englewood Cliffs, 1973, p. 47.
19. Strong, Edward K., *The Psychology of Selling and Advertising.* McGraw-Hill, New York, 1925.
20. Thomas, Kenneth, Walton, R., and Dutton, J., Determinants of Interdepartmental Conflict, in *Interorganizational Decision Making*, M. Tuite, R. Chisholm, and M. Radnor, Eds. Aldine, Chicago, 1972.
21. Thompson, Joseph W., *Selling a Managerial and Behavioral Analysis.* McGraw-Hill, New York, 1973.
22. Webster, Frederick E. and Wind, Yoram, *Organizational Buying Behavior.* Prentice-Hall, Englewood Cliffs, 1972.
23. Wilson, D. T., Dyadic Interactions, in *Consumer and Industrial Buying Behavior*, Arch Woodside, Jagdish Sheth, and Peter Bennett, Eds. Elsevier, New York, 1977, pp. 355–66.

Plank, R. E. and Dempsey, W. A. (1980) 'A framework for personal selling to organizations'. *Industrial Marketing Management*, 9: 143–149. Reproduced with permission from Elsevier Science.

8.4 Should you increase sales promotion or add salespeople?

Thomas L. Powers

INTRODUCTION

Industrial marketers face many decisions that impact their potential business success. Perhaps one of the most difficult decision areas involves the choice between adding salespeople or increasing advertising and promotional expenditures. There are normally many trade-offs involved which include both easily measured aspects and those that are difficult to quantify. This paper examines this issue by comparing the relative benefit of each type of activity and presenting a decision model that can aid industrial marketers in making choices of this type.

DEFINING THE ISSUES

Industrial marketers as a matter of course are interested in increasing sales and market share. In order to accomplish this objective, several options are available that involve adjusting one or more aspects of the marketing mix. These include changes to price, promotion, place, or product activities. Of these four primary marketing mix factors that can be dealt with, promotion and price normally offer the quickest market response, and at the same time are the easiest to implement changes to. Typical response functions for each of the marketing mix variables are seen in Figure 1.

Price has an almost immediate sales response to changes made to this factor, although there are several problems associated with it. Adjusting the marketing mix on the element of price usually involves some form of price reduction, whether it be permanent or temporary and through a distributor or direct to-the-customer incentive. If the market is price elastic, there can be an immediate market response. If, however, the market is price inelastic this strategy will not increase sales to the extent that total revenue is lowered by the price decrease and therefore should be avoided.

Price and price-promotional activities under elastic demand conditions still create difficulty, and as seen in Figure 1 normally create an increase in sales on a temporary basis only. The demand for industrial products is usually considered derived demand, which is based on demand for final products that the industrial product is related to. Price decreases therefore can only increase sales in the context of the customer buying ahead, or increasing market share at the expense of competitors.

Buying ahead clearly is a temporary form of sales increase, which must be paid back later in decreasing sales. If, on the other hand, the firm is able to gain market share it must be remembered that competing firms may retaliate. If they feel

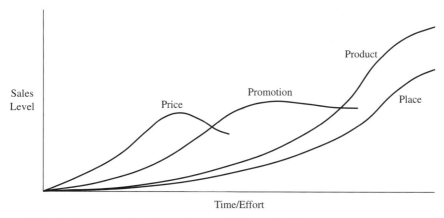

Figure 1 Typical response functions of the marketing mix elements.

threatened by the price move they may respond by decreasing their price by a similar amount, which causes sales for the firm initiating the pricing move to return to a prior level of business or perhaps below it. For these reasons, many industrial marketers are reluctant to lower price, despite the fact that at least conceptually it offers a fast and predictable positive response.

If the industrial marketer chooses to invest in the product aspect of the marketing mix, the sales response occurs at a much slower rate, again as seen in Figure 1. In many cases product development investment may take years before any sales increases are seen. When the impact is felt, however, it may be profound. Product investment can result in great sales increases and a resulting distinct competitive advantage, but the investment and return is very long-term in nature. This increases the relative risk of market and competitive moves during the interim period that may make the future return subject to change. Product investment is therefore usually seen as a necessary part of an ongoing industrial marketing strategy, but not one designed to produce a quick response.

Investment in place, or distribution-related activities, can take even longer to develop a positive return. Development of transportation infrastructures, warehouse facilities, and dealer recruiting are extremely long-term in nature and typically produce sales increases only after a long sustained effort. Because of the nature of this portion of the marketing mix, it also is rarely looked at to create a short-term sales increase.

Promotion, the remaining part of the marketing mix, offers a relatively quick response that unlike pricing actions may not have only a short-term effect. Promotional activity can be independent of price elasticity and can be adopted to many situations and strategies. There are problems that can develop, however. Increased promotional expenditures, whether in advertising or personal sales efforts, can result in an increased competitive response that can eliminate any competitive advantage. In addition, advertising or sales efforts may be improperly conceived or implemented and prove ineffective. The primary characteristics relating to each part of the marketing mix are seen in Table 1.

Since promotion in the form of advertising or personal selling can offer the benefits of a short-term response without the many limitations of pricing action, many

Table 1 Marketing mix characteristics

	Sales response	*Competitive action*	*Measurability*
Price	Immediate, then declining	Immediate	Easily done
Promotion	Quick, however limited over long term	Immediate	Moderately difficult
Place	Slow, high, long-term potential	Difficult to copy	Difficult
Product	Slow, high, long-term potential	Difficult to copy	Difficult

industrial marketers spend considerable time and effort on this activity. A key issue, however, is to allocate resources between advertising and personal selling. This choice can be simplified through a careful examination of the relative advantages and disadvantages of each, and the development of a decision model that aids in the selection process.

PERSONAL SELLING–ADVANTAGES AND DISADVANTAGES

Personal selling offers several advantages to the industrial marketer. These include direct access to customers on a planned basis, control over presentations and approaches, and an increase in the number of employees that, if the situation warrants, can be rotated into other assignments. There is also a degree of accountability of the funds that are spent on this activity. Salespeople can report directly back on the success or failure of their efforts. There are several disadvantages to personal selling, however. These include a lengthy process to recruit and train individuals, and a possibility of loss of control of some aspects of the marketing mix. This includes managing price and presenting product benefits which can deviate from the firm's policies. Another major disadvantage is that if there is a need to lower the marketing effort, reducing the sales force is a painful process that normally requires terminating employees and changing territories and assignments. These personnel changes can be expensive and trying on the manager and salespeople involved.

ADVERTISING–ADVANTAGES AND DISADVANTAGES

Advertising has several advantages that can make it desirable to use. It offers a means of reaching a mass audience with a defined message. Advertising is relatively easy to implement and if there is no longer a need for this type of program, it can be ended quickly and at little or no cost. Advertising programs can be designed to reach a broad cross-section of customers, or based on the message and media chosen, it can zero in on a smaller, well-defined target market. Advertising can be very flexible, where several different types of programs can be used over the course of a year.

Despite these advantages, advertising has several limitations. It cannot be used to focus specifically on individual customers as can be done with personal selling. Also, the thrust of an advertising program cannot be adjusted quickly, once a program has started. It does not have good cost-measurability of its impact in the marketplace, as advertising effectiveness is usually very difficult to measure. The merits of each of these two types of promotional activities are seen in Table 2.

Table 2 Advantages and disadvantages of advertising and personal selling

	Advertising	*Personal selling*

Advantages:	Can be quickly implemented
	Widespread market coverage
	Control of message content
	Easily terminated
		Directability to specific customers
		Development of marketing mix
		  elements to individual accounts
		Employees can reinforce overall
		  personnel efforts
		Accountability of results

Disadvantages:	Cannot target individual customers
	Difficult to change message thrust
	  quickly
	Difficult to determine cost
	  effectiveness
		High cost and time to recruit and train
		  personnel
		Control of message content
		Difficult to reduce personnel

UTILIZING A DECISION MODEL

In order to structure a decision process for an industrial marketer choosing between advertising and personal selling efforts, a model can be developed that uses information inputs in a trade-off approach. Most firms have a base of experience that can be used to help determine the relative effectiveness of these two areas and this expertise is incorporated into the model. Firms typically have information on costs of implementing these activities, including the approximate costs of recruiting and training salespeople. They also may have estimates of the results of programs of this type, although it must be kept in mind that their information may be better for past personal selling efforts than for advertising.

By utilizing a decision model that incorporates these variables, industrial marketing managers can make more informed and better decisions. A model that assists with this choice can be seen as:

$$B = S(L)(M) - [UF + OF + V(S)(L) + T(P)]$$

where:
B = Expected benefit
UF = Up front costs
OF = Ongoing fixed costs
V = Variable costs
P = Termination expense
S = Sales increase
T = Termination probability
M = Product margin
L = Base level of sales

The expected benefit is a function of the anticipated sales increase times the gross margin on sales. Subtracted from this amount are the costs associated with a program of this type which include up front, ongoing fixed and variable costs, and the cost involved to terminate a program early. These variables are described in Table 3. This basic relationship can be utilized on an annual basis or for the duration of a program. An example of this type of trade-off is as follows: If a manager was attempting to choose between an advertising or personal selling program, the following situation might be encountered. For the purpose of illustration this will be done on a one-year

Table 3 Expenses/Revenues associated with marketing activity

Code	Definition	Example – advertising	Example – personal selling
B	Expected	Gross margin increased due to marketing activity	
UF	Up front costs	Print set-up changes: Production costs	Training expense: Recruiting expense
OF	Ongoing fixed costs	Advertising expense	Salary expense: vehicle/travel expenses
V	Variable costs		Salesperson commissions
P	Termination expense	Early cancellation fee	Cost to terminate personnel
		Example – Applicable to both	
S	Sales increase	Amount of sales increase attributable to activity	
T	Termination probability	Probability of terminating program early	
M	Product margin	Margin on product sale	
L	Base sales level	Base level of sales prior to new program	

basis. Two alternatives are available that are designed to increase the sales of a line of products that is currently selling at $1.2 million per year and has a margin on sales of 27%. Personal selling offers the usual benefits associated with this activity, and it is estimated that the sales increase will be 20% if one individual is hired. The costs involved are as follows:

Up front costs (recruiting and training)	= $16,000
Fixed costs per year (base salary and benefits)	= $22,000
Variable costs (salesperson commission)	= 5%
Termination expenses (employee benefit package extended 90 days, assistance with job search)	= $2,000
Termination probability	= 20%

The expected benefit of this program over a one-year period would be:

$$B = S(L)(M) - [UF + OF + V(S)(L) + T(P)]$$

or:

$$B = (0.20)(1,200,000)(0.27) - [16,000 + 22,000 + 0.05(0.20)(1,200,000) + (0.20)(2,000)]$$

$$B = \$64,800 - 50,400$$

$$B = \$14,400$$

In this case the expected benefit is $14,400, which is far less than the anticipated increase in sales and margin. In this example the up front expense of recruiting and training and the fixed salary and benefit expense have greatly diminished the benefit of this program.

The advertising alternative is:

Up front costs (production and development)	=	$6,000
Fixed costs per year (cost of running advertising program)	=	$30,000
Variable costs	=	None
Termination expenses (cost of terminating program with 90 day notice)	=	$5,000
Termination probability	=	10%
Expected sales increase	=	12%

The expected benefit of this program again over a one-year period is:

$$B = S(L)(M) - [UF + OF + V(S)(L) + T(P)]$$

or:

$$B = (0.12)(1,200,000)(0.27) - [6,000 + 30,000 + 0 + (0.10)(5,000)]$$
$$B = \$38,880 - 36,500$$
$$B = \$2,380$$

In this case the expected benefit is $2,380, which, under the assumptions made for the purpose of illustration, makes the personal selling program more advantageous. It must be kept in mind that this estimation is very sensitive to the input information, and the period of the program analysis in particular has a major effect. In this example, even though personal selling was seen to be advantageous, it was penalized by the high up-front expenses that were paid back over only a one-year period. Obviously, the longer a program runs that has high up-front expense the more relatively advantageous it will be.

Most of the information needed to implement this model is available to the industrial marketer. Anticipated costs are relatively easy to obtain and can be based on cost information required to launch a program. The information on anticipated sales increases is more difficult to obtain and must be based on a managerial interpretation of past events as they apply to the current situation. Another information input that is difficult to estimate is the probability of a program having to be terminated early. This must be based on an estimate by management of the possible failure of the program or other eventualities such as resource constraints that must be accounted for. In determining the expected benefit, the comparison between the two types of marketing activities must be done within a similar time period. This article has illustrated this concept showing a one-year period. Additional periods can be utilized, and the process can be expanded to include present value analysis to make the trade-off between up front investment and future returns.

SUMMARY AND CONCLUSION

This article has examined the advantages and disadvantages of various components of the marketing mix as they relate to increasing sales for the industrial marketer. In particular, personal selling efforts and advertising have been discussed within the promotion portion of the marketing mix. A model has been developed and illustrated that can assist industrial marketers in this difficult decision area. By utilizing a decision process of this type, industrial marketers can make better informed and more accurate decisions.

Powers, T. L. (1989) 'Should you increase sales promotion or add more salespeople?'. *Industrial Marketing Management*, 18(4): 259–263. Reproduced with permission from Elsevier Science.

Index

Page numbers in **bold** refer to figures, those in *italic* refer to tables.